DICTIONARY OF INSURANCE

INFORMATION AT YOUR FINGERTIPS

*Up-to-date and comprehensive, Pitman
Dictionaries are indispensable reference
books, providing clear, crisp explanations
of specialist terminologies in an
easy-to-use format.*

*Accounting Terms Dictionary
A Dictionary of Economics and Commerce
Dictionary of Advertising
Dictionary of Business Studies
Dictionary of Banking
Dictionary of Banking and Finance
Dictionary of Law
Dictionary of Purchasing Supply Management*

DICTIONARY OF INSURANCE

C BENNETT

Pitman Publishing
128 Long Acre, London WC2E 9AN

A Division of Longman Group UK Limited

First published in 1992

© Longman Group UK Limited

British Library Cataloguing in Publication Data
A catalogue record for this book can be obtained from the British Library

ISBN 0 273 03327 1

Typeset, printed and bound in Great Britain

CONTENTS

CONTENTS

PREFACE

The *Dictionary of Insurance* is a new volume that forms part of a well-established series of similar books published by Pitman in their series of dictionaries for management and professional studies. The book covers most areas of insurance and includes a number of non-insurance terms that are in some way related to insurance. The book is intended to be a general one and should prove a valuable addition to any business library. It should be particularly helpful to students or any one in insurance who is seeking a quick introduction to, or revision of, a topic. Business advisers and other non-specialists may find it useful as a starting point when their work includes an insurance-related problem.

Insurance is a vast topic and no single volume could be complete in the range of topics covered. It is also difficult to choose the extent to which each topic should be covered. Most topics have been covered by brief summaries but on occasions I have succumbed to the temptation to go into more detail while in some cases terms can be disposed of in a few words.

The book contains Appendices consisting of: abbreviations; special terms; useful addresses; and specimen policy forms. The policy forms are reproduced by kind permission of the insurance companies concerned and will provide an additional point of reference for the reader who wishes to see a term or definition in the context of a policy form. However, the text of the book does not represent an attempt to attribute to any of the companies concerned an interpretation of their own words, clauses or phrases.

The world of insurance never stands still. New forms of cover are constantly being devised and existing terms being revised. The book is not presented as the final authority on any given term and I accept that some items may have been overlooked rather than consciously omitted. Consequently I welcome constructive criticism about items in the dictionary as well as suggestions about items that should have been included. I will gather in any information provided in order that it may be considered for inclusion in any future editions.

Finally, I have to thank my wife, Maureen, for her patience and encouragement throughout the preparation of the book. Along with our friend, Angela Lerwill, to whom I am also grateful, she read the work in its draft form. I also have reason to thank my former colleagues, Mark Dacey and John Moss, insurance lecturers at the Cheltenham & Gloucester College of Higher Education, and Paul Sherriff, solicitor, who gave me advice and assistance, particularly with regard to sources of information during this vast undertaking. I must also record my thanks to the staff at Pitman for their patience and professionalism in all matters relating to the book.

C S C Bennett, Cheltenham
1991

A

A1. The highest classification for seaworthiness of a vessel accorded by *Lloyd's Register of Shipping* (qv). 'A' means that the vessel's hull is strong and seaworthy and the designation 1 means that her rigging and gear are in perfect order.

abandonment. The relinquishment of ownership of damaged or lost property by an insured in favour of the insurer. According to the Marine Insurance Act 1906, s. 61, where there is a constructive total loss (qv) the assured may abandon the subject-matter insured to the insurer as if it were an actual total loss. The assured must give notice of abandonment (qv) to the insurer otherwise his claim, unless an actual total loss (qv), will be treated as a partial loss (s. 62). Unless there is a mistake of fact, the insurer's acceptance of the abandonment will be irrevocable. If the insurers pay full value of damaged property they are entitled to the salvage and if that realises more than the amount paid to the insured, the insurers are entitled to retain the full proceeds. No right of abandonment exists in non-marine insurance but in motor insurance it is common practice for the insurer to take over the remains of a damaged vehicle when making a total loss payment. *See also* ADEMPTION OF LOSS.

abandonment of events. A contingency insurance (qv) which enables the promoters of events (eg plays, exhibitions, fetes) to insure against financial loss if the event is cancelled through circumstances (strikes, fires, storms) beyond their control. Breach of contract, i.e. refusal of key person to appear or perform, is not generally insurable.

ab initio. From the beginning. Insurance policies are void or voidable '*ab initio*' if there is a breach precedent to the policy. *See* UTMOST GOOD FAITH.

abnormal risk. A risk not acceptable to

the insurer on normal terms and conditions because of the presence of unfavourable features.

abortive insurance. A term used in respect of lapsed industrial life policies. Alternatively the term applies only to policies 'not taken up', ie policy entered in the books on the understanding that payment is to begin on delivery of the policy, but before then the policyholder changes his mind, does not pay and so 'aborts' the policy.

absolute assignment. The complete sale of a life assurance policy by the policyholder to the assignee who then becomes the owner and is an assignee for value. Usually the consideration is the surrender value or other agreed price but it may be nominal or for 'natural love and affection' in which case it is called a voluntary assignment. The statutory form of the assignment is given in the Policies of Assurance Act 1867 (qv). There may be certain covenants in the deed or contract of sale, eg the assignee undertakes to pay future premiums. The assignee can give a good discharge for the policy proceeds which he is entitled to receive.

absolute liability. A liability that attaches regardless of fault on the part of the defendant in certain high risk situations. The term has been superseded by strict liability (qv) in view of the admitted exceptions to the rule.

absolute net rate. A rate quoted by an insurer to a broker or other intermediary which makes no allowance for commission. The broker is left to make his own negotiations over price with his own client. Absolute net rates are often quoted in extended warranty insurance (qv).

abstainers insurance. An insurance or terms which are exclusive to total abstainers from the consumption of alcohol. Insurance is on preferential terms and is most commonly available in insurances related to life, health and motor vehicle risks. There are specialist insurers who cater exclusively for total abstainers.

accelerated accrual. The provision by a pension scheme of an accrual rate (qv) greater than one-sixtieth of pensionable earnings for each year of pensionable service. The term is an alternative for uplifted sixtieths.

acceptance. 1. The act of assenting to an offer with the result that a contract is created. It occurs, for example, when an underwriter initials a slip (qv) or the proposer for a life policy pays the premium after receiving an offer, ie the acceptance letter (qv). 2. Acceptance of goods within the Sale of Goods Act 1979, s. 35 is (a) where the buyer intimates to the seller that he has accepted them; or (b) where the goods have been delivered and the buyer does any act with them that is inconsistent with the ownership of the seller; or (c) when, after a reasonable lapse of time, he retains them without intimating to the seller his rejection of them.

acceptance letter. A formal letter issued by the life insurer who wishes to 'offer' cover after considering the information regarding the proposed risk. It intimates acceptance (at ordinary rates or otherwise) and states that the risk will commence on payment of the premium which must be within a stated period, normally 30 days. Until acceptance by the proposer the offer can be withdrawn and the proposer must notify any changes in the facts notified before making payment. The risk covered, the premium charged and the type of assurance are all quoted in the acceptance letter.

accepted value. A value on property which the insurer has accepted and will not dispute in the future unless there is proof of fraud.

accepting office. A term to describe an insurance company that accepts a reinsurance.

access control. The control of access to premises; theft insurers who check it out when premises are surveyed. Insurers may advise in certain types of premises, eg workshops, that entry points should be kept to a minimum

and the movements and activities of visitors controlled. In multi-tenanted premises access control is a key consideration for the insurer.

accessory. *See* MOTOR ACCESSORIES.

Access to Medical Reports Act 1988. An Act giving life insurance proposers the right to see medical reports. Where a proposer permits his doctor to disclose his medical record he has the right to see any report before its submission or within six months. The doctor can wholly or partly withhold the report if, in the doctor's opinion, reading it, or the relevant part, is likely to harm the proposer. The proposer can ask the doctor to change any part he considers to be misleading or inaccurate. If the doctor refuses to make any changes, the proposer can add his own comments. The proposer can, of course, refuse his doctor the necessary permission to disclose his health record.

access to premises. 1. The area through which entry or exit to premises or particular parts of premises is made. Theft insurers will enquire into this aspect of the risk during a survey. Ease of access for potential intruders from the road, footpaths, open spaces, staircase, flat roofs, adjoining premises can be critical. The theft of large amounts of goods is made easier when vehicles can be driven right up to or into the premises, especially if screened from view. 2. The Factories Act 1961 (qv), s. 29 (1) requires, so far as reasonably practicable (qv), that safe means of access must be provided to every place of work, and such places must be made and kept safe for the persons working there. A passage leading to a canteen was held not to be a means of access to a place of work (*Davies* v *De Havilland Aircraft Co Ltd* (1950). Safe floors, passages, gangways, stairs, steps, and ladders are covered under s. 28.

accident/accidental. Accident means an unlooked for mishap or an untoward event which is not expected or designed from the standpoint of its victim. The word is used in different kinds of insurance policies. The main purpose of the word appears to be the desire to safeguard the insurer from losses lacking a fortuitous element. Losses deliberately engineered by the insured are clearly not covered while those where both the means *and* the consequences are fortuitous will be covered. Between these extremes the meaning is not always clear, particularly in personal accident insurance and liability insurance. Policies may refer, *inter alia*, to injury etc caused by an accident or accidental injury.

1. *Personal accident.* It is necessary to consider both the act causing the injury and the outcome to decide if there has been an accident. The act may be intentional, eg stooping to pick up a marble, but the outcome, a torn knee ligament, may be unexpected. The victim with no previous history of knee trouble would feel that he had suffered an accident as although the cause was natural the result was fortuitous and unexpected. This was the view taken in *Hamlyn* v *Crown Accidental Insurance Co* (1893). Insurers able to prove that such injuries had their origin in a pre-existing physical defect would be able to avoid liability. In *Winspear* v *Accident Insurance Co*, the insured was seized with a fit while crossing a stream and drowned; the cause was natural but the outcome was unexpected as drowning is not the probable outcome of a fit, so it was death by accident. An injury is caused by accident when it is the natural outcome of a fortuitous and unexpected cause, eg injury from being run over by a car or injury from drinking poison by mistake (*Cole* v *Accident Insurance Co* (1889)). There is no accident when a person with heart disease collapses and dies while exerting himself. It is the natural outcome of an intended act. The injury is by accident when a person in the agony of the moment (qv) takes an intentional course of action that not unnaturally leads to injury, eg jumping from a fast moving vehicle when otherwise serious injury appears imminent. Also a person is injured by accident when, in the face of danger, he attempts to rescue an endangered person. The moral pressure removes the rescuer's freedom of choice. The person who sustains injury by the negligence or deliberate act of another is injured by accident unless he has consented to the risk, as in a boxing match or by provoking an

attack on his person. The elements also have to be considered. A person who suffers a cold because of inadequate clothing during a very cold spell may be presumed to know the risks involved and cannot claim for an accident. A suitably clad roundsman, whose heated van breaks down in severe weather conditions and leaves him isolated for some time to die from the exposure, meets his death by accident (*North West Commercial Travellers Association* v *London Guarantee and Accident Co* (1895)). Personal accident insurers have found it expedient to draft a policy definition which moves away from the term accident to a more precise statement as to their intention, which typically reads 'bodily injury caused by violent, accidental, external and visible means which injury shall solely and independently of any other cause result in death or disablement as defined . . .'. This definition calls for close scrutiny. *See* BODILY INJURY, VIOLENT MEANS, ACCIDENTAL MEANS, EXTERNAL and VISIBLE and solely and independently of any other cause (qv).

2. *Liability insurance.* A liability policy may indemnify the insured for legal liability for . . . injury or damage caused by accident, or for accidental injury or damage. It is not enough that the injury should be accidental from the victim's point of view. The act or omission causing the damage must be accidental from the insured's point of view so that intended acts producing the expected results will not be covered. Insurers do not intend to cover inevitable damage. They do not usually define accident or accidental so the court will therefore be the final arbiter. However, it seems that the insurer is insuring something that may happen or something that could be prevented by reasonable care. If a contractor is digging a trench and accidentally severs an underground cable the insurer will accept liability or defend any claim against the contractor because the damage is fortuitous though caused by an intended act. A risky situation entered into knowingly by the insured might produce an expected if unintended result. It is hard

to bring this within the term accidental but this happened in the Canadian case of *Canadian Indemnity Co v Walkem Machinery & Equipment Ltd* (1975). W. Ltd negligently sold a poorly repaired crane in a dangerous condition and when it collapsed they were liable in damages and the insurers were held liable to provide an indemnity. On the other hand in *Gray v Barr* (1967) the Court of Appeal held that there was no accident within the terms of the policy when Barr visited Gray in search of his wife with whom Gray had been associating. He took a loaded shotgun to frighten Gray but did not intend to fire it or inflict any injury but during a struggle the gun went off and killed Gray. Barr was acquitted of murder and manslaughter but his claim for indemnity was refused as, *inter alia*, there had been no accident. Gray's death was held to be a foreseeable risk of Barr's intentional act. The court's failure to view this as an accident has been criticised. The insured's degree of foresight appears crucial in these cases. The word accident is intended to narrow the cover and could remove from its scope the special high risk cases where the insured's intended act or omission virtually invites disaster or damage even though such an outcome is not intended but *W Ltd's* case has to be borne in mind. A manufacturer always runs the risk that his quality control system may break down and a defective product emerges on to the market to cause injury but he does not intend or expect this to happen so the outcome is accidental. The key seems to be that the event should be unexpected *and* unintended from the insured's standpoint.

When a market gardener sought compensation for damage to crops by the emission of fluoride from the defendant's chimney the defendant's right to an indemnity turned on whether there had been accidental damage as far as the insured was concerned. While the result was not intended it was not unexpected and could not therefore be accidental damage. The defendant's managing director knew of the danger (the Aus-

tralian case of *Robinson v Evans* (1969)). In a second incident the insured had increased the height of his chimney to overcome the problem but this failed as further damage was caused. This was regarded as accidental as the result was both unintended and unexpected. In the case of pollution risks borderline cases are not uncommon. Claims may arise following the discharge of effluent into a river where there is no defect in the effluent plant and the insured may have received proper advice as to the correct type of plant, or, had no reason to suppose the effluent treated by the plant would cause contamination. Some insurers might accept these incidents as falling within the term accident or accidental as long as third party injury or damage is caused. Others may take a different view. It is always open to the insurer to use additional words, as many do, to limit 'pollution cover' to those cases where the injury/damage has been caused by immediate discharge consequent upon an accident so that even the unexpected results of a normally operating effluent plant will be outside the policy. The general intention of the insurer is to avoid pollution damage caused gradually over time by a normally operating system. Some insurers exclude pollution unless due to a sudden and accidental occurrence (*see* SUDDEN AND ACCIDENTAL POLLUTION).

Some insurers have opted to omit the words accident or accidental from their operative clauses and instead excluded the results of deliberate or inevitable damage. In such cases once the insured has proved that there is third party injury or damage, it is for the insurer to prove that the exception applies (*see* ONUS OF PROOF). The argument, which may not be very different, then centres on whether the injury was deliberate or inevitable. Finally the word accident has to be considered in the context of natural causes. The case of *Mills v Smith* (1964) 1 Q.B. 30I dealt with the effect of natural causes. The court had to decide whether damage, caused to a neighbours property by tree roots, was covered by the public liability section of a householder's policy covering 'damage to property caused by accident'. The insured was liable in nuisance for settlement damage caused by the root action of a tree in his garden taking water from his neighbour's soil. The judge held that this was an accident. Certainly nothing was intended or expected by the insured and this may explain the decision. Although natural causes were involved there had been a moment in time when something unexpected occurred, namely the settlement which was more than the natural movement of the foundations and this had been caused by the tree roots. However, if the policy had referred to 'damage by accidental means' the outcome might have been different although the courts appear reluctant to distinguish between the results and the means (*Robinson* v *Evans* (1970)).

In conclusion it seems that in personal accident policies the injury is accidental if the insured did not intend or expect it, because either way there is a fortuitous element. In liability policies the outcome has to be unintended and unexpected from the insured's standpoint and a certain degree of foresight (eg Barr's case) may make certain results so likely that they cannot be regarded as accidental.

accident book. The Social Security Act 1975 obliges an employer, who normally employs 10 or more people at the same time, to keep an accident book in respect of the premises at which they are employed. The book should be kept in a place where it is readily accessible to all employees. Particulars of an accident can be entered in it by the injured employee or someone on his behalf. The entry counts as formal notification to the employer who may make his own entry if he considers there is a discrepancy between the employee's entry and his own view of what happened. The entries provide some evidence of the views taken and may be relevant if a claim for damages is made against the employer whose employers' liability insurer will want to investigate the entry. Also an insurance surveyor may inspect the book in the course of a survey of the risk.

accident frequency. A measure of the in-

cidence of accidents over a period of time. It is one method of measuring the effectiveness of loss prevention measures.

accident insurance. A term used, traditionally, to describe insurances of: (a) property against accidental loss/damage (other than from fire and related perils (*see* ADDITIONAL PERILS dealt with by fire insurers); (b) persons against accidental injury or sickness; (c) liabilities to third parties and employees from negligence, breach of duty etc. (d) rights or pecuniary interests (eg fidelity guarantee, credit). Covers may overlap wholly or partly with those underwritten by fire, marine or life insurers. Traditionally, insurances are classified as being accident; fire; life; and marine. For statistical and control purposes insurances are classified in accordance with the Insurance Companies Act 1982. *See* ACCOUNTING CLASSES.

Accident Investigation Branch. The part of the Department of Trade responsible for investigating aviation accidents.

Accident Offices Association. An association whose membership was open to all motor and liability insurers and other agreed classes of business. The basic activity for many years was the operation of accident tariffs. It was also concerned with matters of mutual interest, research and making representations to the Government. It also liaised with other organisations (eg the Association of Risk Managers in Industry and Commerce). It was a constituent part of the Association of British Insurers. Membership was voluntary. Originally it operated a tariff in respect of both motor insurance and employers liability insurance by setting minimum premiums and standard covers based on the collective experience of the members. The association no longer exists but many of its functions continue within the Association of British Insurers.

accident report form. A form designed to enable motorists to report incidents and accidents to the insurer. The term is often preferred to 'claim form' as the incident may not lead to a claim and the resultant loss or damage may not be insured under the policy.

accident severity. A measure of the severity or seriousness of losses rather than the number of losses. It measures the amounts of losses and lost time etc and like accident frequency (qv) is a check on the loss prevention and minimisation measures.

accident year. The calendar or accounting year in which an accident or loss occurred.

accidental bodily injury. An insured event under a liability policy when liability for such injury is alleged against the insured. *See* ACCIDENT 2. for an account of the meaning of the term as intended by the insurer.

accidental. *See* ACCIDENT.

accidental damage cover (household policies). Accidental means something that was not deliberate on the part of the insured or something that was not bound to happen. As the term is used in connection with a first party insurance (qv) the damage has to be accidental from the point of view of the insured. *See* ACCIDENT. Accidental damage is insured under household policies as follows: 1. *Cover on buildings and contents.* The cover is usually granted under an optional section headed 'Accidental damage' or 'Any accident or misfortune'. This brings within the policy accidental breakage or other damage (eg spilling paint on to walls and carpets). The premium is normally about 20 per cent extra and there is an excess of £10 to £25. There are exclusions, eg damage caused by: tenants, faulty workmanship, defective design, the use of defective materials, settlement (qv), shrinkage or expansion, wet or dry rot. Damage occurring while the dwelling is unoccupied/unfurnished, let, sublet or lent is not covered. Some general exceptions (qv) also apply (wear and tear; gradual deterioration; electrical, electronic or mechanical breakdown; depreciation; damage caused by vermin, insects, fungus, condensation). 2. *Cover on cables or underground pipes supplying the property.* Accidental damage in respect of pipes and cables for which the insured is responsible is insured. 3. *Cover on fixed glass and sanitary fittings.* Sanitary fittings may be listed as washbasins, splashbacks etc. The cover does not apply if the dwelling is unoccupied or unfurnished. Other exclusions are breakage as a result of a sonic boom, breakage of something that is already cracked and, sometimes, the cost of removing or replacing frames. 4. *During removals.* Some insurers cover accidental damage to contents during permanent removal to another home or can extend the policy to cover accidental damage during such removal.

accidental damage cover. The insurance of accidental damage as a named peril, ie not deliberate or inevitable damage, which is covered, subject to exceptions, under a policy. It is possible to insure both household property and business property against this risk. Accidental damage is covered without being named as a peril in 'all risk' insurances.

accidental damage excess. An alternative term to own damage excess (qv). It refers to the excess (qv) written into the loss or damage section of comprehensive motor policies and applies only in respect of claims involving loss or damage to the insured vehicle. The excess is overridden where the claim is caused by fire or theft, claims for which are paid in full. Most policies contain an accidental damage excess which applies to young and inexperienced drivers as defined.

accidental damage to property. An insured event under a liability policy if liability for the damage is alleged against the insured. *See* ACCIDENT 2. for a fuller account of accidental damage. The property concerned is sometimes defined in the liability policy as meaning 'material property'. There is no intention, unless stated, on the part of the insurer to cover property or rights that may exist in respect of intellectual property (qv).

accidental death. This is an insured event under a personal accident insurance (or other policy incorporating personal accident benefits) provided the cause and timing of the death are within the policy definition. This means the death must be caused by 'violent, accidental, external and visible means which shall solely and independently of any other cause result in death . . . . provided always that death occurs within 12 months.' The time limit is an arbitrary one fixed because the longer the period between sustaining the injury and subsequent death the greater will be the likelihood of an intervening cause. For the purpose of the policy it will not be an accidental death if caused by an excepted risk. *See* ACCIDENT/ACCIDENTAL for a fuller account of that term in regard to personal accident insurance.

'Accidental fire'. The Fire Prevention (Metropolis) Act 1774 (qv), s. 86 enacts that no action can be brought against any person in whose premises a fire begins accidentally. In *Filliter* v *Phippard* (1847) accidental fire was defined as 'fire produced by mere chance or incapable of being traced to any particular cause'. Thus, when fire is traced to negligence, nuisance, or a *Rylands v Fletcher* (qv) object the fire is not 'accidental' and the defence under s. 86 will not apply. Presumably it was intended that any liability for fire should be fault-based.

accidental injury. *See* ACCIDENTAL BODILY INJURY.

accidental means. Personal accident insurers restrict cover to bodily injury caused by accidental means. The term is used in an attempt to draw a distinction between accidental injury and injury by accidental means. A man may intend to do certain acts in a certain way but these acts may have unforeseen consequences. In such a case the result is accidental but the means may not be accidental. If a result follows from the means intended, such means not being used in an ordinary or unexpected way, it is not caused by accidental means, but if in the course of doing an act something unforeseen, unexpected or unusual occurs which causes the injury, the injury is by accidental means. When in the ordinary course an act would not cause an injury and injury in fact occurs, the inference may be drawn that something unexpected, unforeseen or unusual took place in the course of the act and that the injury was therefore by accidental means. Where a tennis ball is thrown by a normally healthy games player and he thereby sprains his shoulder, the injury is not caused by accidental means if it appears from the medical evidence that such a strain is the likely result of throwing a tennis ball and

there is no evidence of anything unusual in the manner of throwing it. The following cases have been cited as being injury by accidental means: a man injuring himself by stumbling when walking; a workman lifting a heavy weight he is accustomed to lifting without any mishap and straining himself in doing so; a man injured in jumping off a train, his two companions having jumped off safely; in all cases the inference is drawn that something unexpected occurred so the injury must have been by accidental means (*Colonial Mutual Life Insurance Society* v *Long* (1931) NZLR). The attempt to draw a line between accidental injury and accidental means is therefore very difficult. In the case of *Hamlyn* v *Crown Accidental Insurance Co Ltd* (1893) the insured injured his knee while stooping to pick up a marble. The court rejected the suggestion that they should distinguish between accidental injury and accidental means. Policy definitions are a matter for interpretation by the courts and there will be reluctance to make the distinction save in those cases where the medical evidence is against the insured so that his pre-existing medical condition may be considered the decisive factor. Personal accident insurers therefore extend their definition in order to confine their liability to bodily injury accidentally caused etc which is the 'sole cause' of the disablement so protecting them where the insured's medical condition is a contributory factor.

accidents only policy. A personal accidents policy under which cover is restricted to death or disablement (as defined) caused by accidental bodily injury. No sickness cover is provided.

accommodation business (or line). Business which is unattractive to the insurer but is accepted to 'accommodate' an existing connection (broker or insured) to preserve the goodwill of that connection.

accommodation line. *See* ACCOMMODATION BUSINESS.

accord and satisfaction. If a claim has been settled and a binding discharge obtained, it cannot be re-opened. The liability insurer who has obtained a suitable discharge in the name of their policyholder will have provided a good defence against future claims based on the same cause of action (qv).

accountants' clause. A clause in a business interruption policy which indemnifies the insured in respect of the cost of an accountant's fee in respect of preparing and submitting the claim. Unless this item is specifically included in the cover the cost will fall upon the insured.

accounting classes. *See* DTI CLASSES.

account sales. A document required in connection with a cargo claim. It will show the proceeds if the goods have been sold.

accrual rate. The rate at which pension benefit increases as pensionable service is completed in a defined benefit pension scheme (qv).

accruals concept. A pensions term referring to the accounting practice whereby revenues and costs are recognised as they are earned or incurred, rather than when money is received or paid out.

accrued rights premium. A type of state scheme premium payable in respect of a member below a stated pensionable age when a defined benefit pension scheme (qv) ceases to be contracted out. In return the state scheme takes over the obligation to provide the member's guaranteed minimum pension *(qv)*.

accumulation factor. A life insurance term referring to the accumulation of a single premium of 1 over a period of time taking account of the interest the premium will earn and the probability of the insured surviving.

accumulation in risk. A build up in the hazardous factors affecting an insured risk or when the number of risks or the size of the area affected by an insured peril is increased. For example, a fire insurer may face the growth of danger of fire and/or an increase in the conflagration hazard by the extension of the area likely to be affected by a fire. When an accumulation in risk does occur, the fire insurer normally charges a higher rate commensurate with the increase in risk but in practice this is not always easy to achieve.

accumulation units. Units issued by a unit trust (qv) where net income is automatically used to buy more units in the same fund. As a result the unitholder benefits from not having to pay an initial charge on his reinvested income.

acquisition costs. Expenses incurred by an insurer in obtaining new business and issuing policies. Commission to intermediaries accounts for the largest portion of acquisition costs.

Act of God. An accident or event which occurs independently of human intervention. It is due to natural causes (storm, earthquake etc) which no amount of human foresight could have guarded against and of which human prudence is not bound to recognise the possibility. It is a defence against strict liability (qv) in tort, eg *Rylands* v *Fletcher* (qv). In *Nichols* v *Marsland* (CA 1876) the defendant was not liable when exceptionally violent storms caused his artificial lakes to flood his neighbour's land but the defence is of very restricted application.

act only policy. A third party motor insurance policy issued by an authorised insurer under which the cover is exactly equal to the minimum cover required to comply with the terms of the Road Traffic Act 1988, s. 145.

actio personalis moritur cum persona. Means 'a personal action dies with the person'. At common law a right of action in tort (qv) ceases on death of the plaintiff or defendant. Following the Law Reform (Miscellaneous Provisions) Act 1934 causes of action survive death and keep claims alive on both sides. Consequently liability insurers grant an indemnity to a deceased insured's legal personal representatives.

active breaches of utmost good faith. Any actual statement which conveys false or misleading information relating to a material fact (qv). Innocent misrepresentation is the unintentional misrepresentation of a material fact. Fraudulent misrepresentation is the deliberate misrepresentation of a material fact. *See* UTMOST GOOD FAITH.

active underwriter. The term was described as ambiguous in the Fisher Report (qv) but the report went on to give the following definition: 'any individual who has actual authority from the Managing Agent to underwrite on behalf of the Names (qv) in a Syndicate (qv) and who takes the underwriting decisions. This may include persons other than the individual named as Underwriter in the published Syndicates Book who signs the Audit Certificate as Active Underwriter'. It is the skill of the active underwriter that determines whether Names make profits or losses. The Managing Agent may carry on the task of active underwriter. Each underwriter operates from a box in the Room (qv) with a staff not usually exceeding 10 and each specialises in a narrow band of risks. The active underwriter has three tasks: (a) accepting risks; (b) settling claims; (c) reinsuring his portfolio of risks. The fourth function, management of the premium fund, falls to the Managing Agent.

actual carrier. *See* GUADALAJARA CONVENTION 1961.

actual total loss. This can occur in one of three ways: (a) Destruction of the subject-matter, (b) Subject-matter so damaged that it ceases to be a thing of the kind insured ('loss of specie'), (c) the insured is irretrievably deprived of the subject-matter (Marine Insurance Act 1906, s. 57).

actuarial reports. Insurance companies carrying on life business must have their accounts inspected by an actuary (qv) who may be an independent consultant or one of the companies own actuaries. The investigation includes an annual valuation of the liabilities of the business the format for which is given in the Insurance Companies (Accounts and Statements) Regulations 1983. The main report covers: a description of the benefits of the life insurance contracts; a list, with details, of each of the internal linked and authorised unit trusts to which benefits are linked; the general principles and methods adopted in the valuation; the rates of interest and tables of mortality and disability used in valuing liabilities; details of reinsurance ceded and reinsurers; particulars of profit distribution to policyholders and bonuses. In addition, every fifth year the actuary must prepare a statement of long-term business in accordance with the 1983 Regulations in the prescribed format. The statement must include details of the methods and bases used in calculating any minimum surrender

values and guaranteed paid up amounts.

actuarial valuation. *See* ACTUARIAL REPORTS.

actuary. A specialist statistician engaged in the application of probability and other statistical theory to insurance. The work of the actuary covers premiums, investment, reserve, dividend and other financial calculations. In life assurance demography and mortality rates are key issues for the actuary.

addendum. A document which notes alterations agreed between the parties to a reinsurance contract.

addition to age. A method used by life underwriters when charging an extra premium to under average lives. The underwriter adds a number of years to the actual age of the proposer in order to determine the actual premium that will be charged.

additional cost clauses. These appear in fire policies. They allow, subject to the adequacy of the sum insured, for certain additional costs to be payable by the insurer in the event of loss. *See* PUBLIC AUTHORITIES CLAUSE and REMOVAL OF DEBRIS.

additional expenses clauses (Cargo – War risks) 1/7/85. Clauses to indemnify the insured for the extra expenses that he is unable to recover under the standard marine or war clauses incurred as a result of the interruption or frustration of the adventure by arrests, restraints, detainment or acts of kings, princes and peoples in prosecution of hostilities, or by blockades or other warlike operations. They also extend to cover the exercise by the carrier of any liberty granted by any war risk clause in the contract of affreightment. Where the goods are landed other than at the port of destination the insurer will pay the landing and warehouse charges and transshipment to the original destination. Alternatively they may pay for the goods to be returned to the port of origin or the cost of sending them to a substituted destination.

additional insurances. As personal accident policies are not contracts of indemnity (they are benefit policies (qv)) the insurer seeks protection against over-insurance. This protection is gained (i) by asking in the proposal form if other similar insurances exist, and (ii) by a condition requiring notification of any other subsisting insurances, whether in force at the time of the proposal or effected subsequently. Unless the insurer agrees to the additional insurance the policy will be voidable from the date of the breach.

additional perils. 1. *Fire insurance.* Perils, also called special perils, added to the cover of a standard fire policy. They may be classified as: (a) *Dry perils.* aircraft (qv); explosion (qv); riot and civil commotion (qv); malicious damage (qv); earthquake (qv). (b) *Wet perils.* storm or tempest (qv); burst pipes; (qv) flood; (qv); sprinkler leakage (qv). (c) *Miscellaneous perils.* impact (qv); subsidence (qv); subterranean fire (qv); spontaneous combustion (qv). 2. *Marine insurance.* The following additional perils can be added to cargo policies at a suitable extra rate: (a) Theft or pilferage. (b) Fresh water damage where there is a danger of exposure to or damage by rain in lighters or on the quay. (c) Non-delivery or excess shipowners' liability. The normal bill of lading does not relieve the shipowner from the whole of his liability as the goods carrier. He remains liable for non-delivery unless able to prove that his failure is occasioned by a peril excluded by the bill of lading. Cargo owners sometimes prefer to insure this form of loss rather than attempt full recovery from the shipowner. (d) Hook and/or oil damage in connection with woollen and other bailed goods. (e) Leakage of liquids and breakage of fragiles can sometimes be covered. However, the usual approach is for the cargo owner who wants wide-ranging cover to seek 'all risks' cover under the Institute Cargo Clauses (A) which have replaced the previous 'All Risk' clauses.

additional premium (AP). An extra charge made by the insurer for an improvement in the cover, change in the risk, extension of the period of insurance, or under an adjustable policy where the record shows that the actual activity exceeded the initial estimate.

additional security. A proportion of the reinsurance premium is retained by a ceding office (qv) as security for due performance of the reinsurer's obliga-

tion under the treaty. The unexpired reserve is associated with the system of premium reserve deposits, under which the ceding office retains a proportion of the premiums ceded to the reinsurer.

additional voluntary contributions (AVCs). Individuals participating in pension schemes can boost their eventual pension by making extra payments which will attract full tax relief in the process. An AVC Plan can be purchased from a pension provider of the individual's choice. *See* FREE STANDING AVCs and IN-SCHEME AVCs.

additions and deletions clause. A clause applicable to certain aviation hull insurances under which the cover is automatically extended to include further aircraft owned or operated by the insured of the same type and value as the aircraft already insured.

ademption of loss. A marine insurance rule to the effect that if, after notice of abandonment (qv) has been given but before legal proceedings have been commenced, circumstances have changed to reduce the loss from total to partial, the insured can claim only for a partial loss. To allow a total loss recovery in the changed circumstances would be contrary to the principle of indemnity (qv). The rule is now mainly of academic interest only as when the notice of abandonment is sent the insurer is asked to accept the notice in order to put the insured in the same position as if legal proceedings had been commenced by the issue of a writ.

adequate plant, machinery, and equipment. An employer must take reasonable care to provide adequate plant and machinery and see that it is properly maintained. This includes the provision of protective devices and clothing, and, in appropriate cases, a warning or exhortation to use such equipment. The employer may also have to take into account any special disabilities of the workman; in *Paris* v *Stepney B.C.* (1951) a one-eyed workman lost the sight of his remaining eye as a result of not wearing goggles—the employer was held liable although there might have been no duty to provide goggles for a normal-sighted man. If an employee is injured by a defect in a tool supplied by the employer and the fault is that of a third party, such as the manufacturer, the employer will be strictly liable for the injury even though guilty of no negligence. *See* EMPLOYERS' LIABILITY (DEFECTIVE EQUIPMENT) ACT 1969. The Act defines equipment as including 'any plant and machinery, vehicle, aircraft or clothing'. In *Coltman* v *Bibby Tankers Ltd* (1988, HL) 'equipment' for the purposes of the Act was defined to include a ship. The definition is conspicuously wide.

adjustment clause. A business interruption policy clause. The gross profit is the main item insured and is estimated. The actual gross profit is calculated at the end of each year and if the initial estimate is too high the clause permits a return of up to 50 per cent of the original premium. If there has been under-insurance average (qv) will apply.

adjustable policies. Insurance and reinsurance policies under which a provisional premium is paid at the inception and adjusted at the end of the year in the light of information declared by the insured. *See* ADJUSTABLE PREMIUMS.

adjustable premium policy scheme. A scheme used by fire insurers as a means of dealing with the problems posed by inflation. It can be applied to buildings worth over £1m insured on a reinstatement basis (qv). The sum insured provides a base value but provision is made for inflation. The premium is adjusted retrospectively at each renewal to reflect actual rates of inflation. If the built-in inflation factor exceeds the actual rate then a return premium is allowed subject to a maximum of 50 per cent. Base values must be certified by qualified surveyors as being adequate. Full average applies.

adjustable premiums. Premiums that are adjusted at the end of the policy term so that the final premium paid reflects the risk actually run and not the risk as estimated. Insurers cannot always determine in advance the magnitude of the risk. It may vary according to turnover, number employed, hire charges etc. The insurer therefore bases the initial premium on the insured's estimate of a relevant variable

(eg wage roll in employers' liability insurance) but adjusts at the end of the year following receipt of a declaration by the insured of the actual figure. If the declared figure exceeds the estimate the insured pays an additional premium. If it is less the insured receives a return premium (qv) subject only to the insurer's minimum premium (qv) requirement. A policy condition (legally a stipulation) obliges the insured to keep records and make declarations. Insurers are precluded by law from relying on breach of condition for failing to keep records for the purpose of claims in respect of liability that has to be insured under the Employers' Liability (Compulsory Insurance) Act 1969.

adjuster. *See* LOSS ADJUSTER.

adjustment. 1. The process of dealing with a claim starting with its investigation and concluding with its settlement or disposal. The work can be carried out by an insurer's own claims staff or by a loss adjuster (qv). 2. The process of adjusting the premium payable by the insured. *See* ADJUSTABLE POLICIES.

adjustment premium. An additional premium payable under the terms of the contract as a result of claims experienced under a policy or insurance or reinsurance.

administration bond. A bond (qv) issued to the Principal Probate Registrar against defaults by the person (i.e. the administrator (qv)) appointed to administer the estate of another.

Administration of Justice Act 1982. An Act of particular interest to liability insurers which came into effect on 1 January 1983. Section 1 abolishes the right to damages for loss of expectation of life (qv) while s. 3 replaces it with an action for bereavement by a spouse or certain close relatives by amending certain provisions in the Fatal Accidents Act 1976 (qv). The new claim was for a fixed amount, £3500 based on half of the average earnings at that time and made variable from time to time. There can no longer be a claim by the estate for the deceased's 'lost years' (qv) meaning that no claim can be made for loss of income by the deceased after the date of death (s. 4(2)). (Suitable amendments have been made to the Law Reform (Miscellaneous Provisions) Act 1934.) Section 2 abolishes actions for loss of services. Section 5 lays down that maintenance provided at public expense is to be taken into account in the assessment of damages for personal injury. Section 6 allows, where there is a possibility that the plaintiff's condition may later deteriorate, for the later re-opening of the case if the deterioration comes about, and making of a further award of damages at that time. The Rules of the Supreme Court (Amendment No 2) 1985 added four new rules relating to provisional damages: claims for such damages must be expressly pleaded; the disease or deterioration envisaged must be specified; the court will have the discretion to specify a period within which a future application for damages is to be made but the period can be extended on application to the court; the rules on payment into court will apply to provisional damages and also a written offer of provisional damages will provide the same protection on costs; the plaintiff must give three months notice of his intention to apply for an additional award. All of this creates reserving problems for liability insurers but many claimants may prefer a once-and-for-all payment taking account of the possibility of future deterioration.

Administration of Justice Act 1969. Section 20 made provision for interim payments by interlocutory application in certain cases, eg defendant has admitted liability. Section 21 provides the means whereby an applicant can inspect documents, photographs or preserve property so, for example, an injured employee may obtain a consulting engineer's report relating to the machine that caused his injury. Section 22 makes it compulsory for courts to award interest on damages for personal injuries. In claims for pain and suffering and loss of amenities, interest covers the period from date of service of the writ (qv) to the date of judgment at a standard 2 per cent. For special damages the period covered is the date of accident to the trial at half the rate applicable to a current short-term investment. No in-

terest is payable on future losses. Interest is only awarded on those cases that proceed to judgment and payments into court should include interest. The House of Lords decision in *Pickett* v *British Rail Engineering* (1978) produced these guidelines.

administrator. 1. A person appointed by the court to administer the estate of another who died intestate or without an executor. Section 167 Judicature Act, 1925 obliges the administrator to enter into an administration bond (qv). 2. The person or persons regarded by the Superannuated Funds Office of the Inland Revenue and, where relevant the Occupational Pensions Board, as responsible for the management of a pension scheme.

admissible asset. An asset which, under the Insurance Companies Regulations 1981, may be brought into account in determining an insurance company's net assets to be compared with its required solvency margin. *See* ADMISSIBILITY.

admissibility. The Insurance Companies Regulations 1981 lays down which assets can be included in the Annual Return (qv) to the DTI and regulates how they should be valued. These admissible assets are brought into account for the purpose of determining an insurance company's net assets to be compared with its required margin of solvency (qv). Assets such as goodwill and stock-in-trade are not listed and cannot be brought into the return. There are rules (Regulations 37 to 49) for the valuation of each class of asset. *See* ASSET VALUATION RULES.

admission of age. In life insurance the insured may have the policy endorsed 'age admitted' by supplying the insurer with his birth certificate. This may be done at the outset or subsequently during the currency of the policy. When the age has been admitted, the insured or his representatives will not to have prove the insured's age when a claim is made.

admission of liability. 1. An admission (qv) by an insurer or reinsurer that they are liable for claim within the terms of their contract. 2. An admission (qv) by an insured that he is liable for injury or damage caused to another. In a liability policy the insured must not admit liability or negotiate with the claimant without the consent of the insurer. This is a condition precedent to liability.

admissions. Statements, oral, written or inferred from conduct made by or on behalf of a party to an action, and admissible in evidence, if relevant, as against his interest. Formal admissions for the purpose of a trial may be made on the pleadings, eg admission of negligence or the admission may be informal before (eg at the scene of an accident) or during the proceedings. As liability insurers may be prejudiced by the insured's admissions they seek to control the situation by the inclusion of a conduct of proceedings clause (qv), and a non-admission liability clause (qv). *See also* WITHOUT PREJUDICE.

admitted insurer. An insurer authorised to transact business from within a foreign country. The insurance transacted is known as establishment business (qv).

admitted liability insurance (automatic personal accident cover). Admitted liability insurance is basically a personal accident insurance for aircraft passengers offering benefits in return for a waiver of any rights they may have at law. The maximum sum payable usually corresponds with the limits of either the Warsaw Convention, the Hague Protocol or the 1967 Carriage by Air (Applications and Provisions) Order. Normally the cover is provided as an extension of the passenger liability policy the limits of which are expressed as being in excess of those in the admitted endorsement.

ad valorem. According to value. Many property insurance premiums are related to value by applying a rate per cent to the sum insured.

Advanced Financial Planning Certificate (AFPC). *See* FINANCIAL PLANNING CERTIFICATE.

advance freight. Unless otherwise agreed, English law insists that freight is payable only on right delivery of the goods. Consequently shipowners normally demand payment by the cargo owner in advance which is 'not repayable in case of loss'. The risk is carried by the cargo owner who therefore normally insures his advance freight by merging it with the value of the goods. Similarly where a charterer pays advance freight he too is able to insure it.

advance payment bond. Similar to a performance bond (qv). It safeguards the principal, who has made advance payments to the contractor, against loss due to poor performance or default by the contractor.

advance profits. A form of business interruption insurance (qv) relating to a new business or a new activity at an existing business. Immediate turnover is expected when the business or project is launched. Advance profits insurance covers the financial loss resulting from a delay in starting production or the activity due to damage to: (a) the new works, extension, or machinery; (b) suppliers' premises; (c) machinery in transit. Risks covered are normally fire and additional perils, and accidental damage to plant in transit. The normal business interruption wording is used but the indemnity period commences on the date production was intended to start and continues until it does actually start, but any increase in cost of working is calculated from the date of loss.

advance rent insurance. An insurance by a property owner against loss of rental income due to an insured event causing a delay in the letting of his property. The sum insured is the annual rent multiplied by the number of years in the maximum delay period. If a loss occurs an amount representing the loss of rent is payable to cover the period from when the tenant should have moved in to when he actually moves into the premises. Insurers require detailed information to cover these risks. *See also* INTEREST COVERS.

adverse selection. Selection against the insurer (qv) or anti-selection (qv).

advice. Legal liability may arise as a result of injury or loss-inducing advice or treatment given by the insured. Public liability insurers exclude advice for which a fee is normally payable as such risks are insurable under professional indemnity policies. Advice in other circumstances is not generally excluded but it does not follow that any liability due to negligent advice will be within the policy which generally operates only when the loss takes the form of liability for accidental bodily injury or property damage. Pure financial loss will not be covered unless the policy has been specially extended.

aerial devices. This means balloons, rockets, space vehicles and space satellites. The term refers to an additional peril (qv) of which the full wording is 'destruction or damage to the property . . . by Aircraft and other Aerial Devices or articles dropped therefrom'.

age admitted. *See* ADMISSION OF AGE.

age attained. The age last birthday of a proposer for life insurance.

age limits. The ages above or below which the insurer will not offer cover or admit to special schemes. Renewal of an existing policy may not be invited once the policyholder has reached the upper age limit. Also the premium to be charged may depend on the age of the proposer. In personal accident insurances proposers generally have to be in the age range 16–65 male, 18–60 female. Life insurers also apply age limits, the effect sometimes being to exclude older lives from non-medical schemes. In motor insurance, young drivers, variously defined but commonly under 25s, have to pay higher premiums for cover which generally carries higher excesses for accidental loss or damage.

agency inspector. Insurance company employee who liaises between the company and its intermediaries (brokers and agents). He opens new accounts and assists the intermediaries in negotiating for business. Some part-time agents (*see* AGENT 2.), who lack insurance knowledge, may simply introduce prospects and leave it to the inspector to complete the business.

agent. 1. The *legal or general definition*: Anyone allowed to act for another known as the principal. 'A person invested with the legal power to alter the principal's legal relations with third parties' (*Towle & Co.* v *White*). An agent: must obey the principal's instructions; exercise skill and care; perform duties personally (with exceptions); act in good faith towards the principal; account for money received on behalf of the principal. **2.** *Average agent* who acts as claim or settling agent involved with the assessment of cargo claims and the surveying and

treatment of damaged goods. **3.** *Cash agents.* Intermediaries with limited powers who receive a commission on business introduced. They cannot accept business or grant cover or give credit. Transactions are for immediate payment. **4.** *Claim agent (marine).* Someone authorised by the insurer to survey and certify casualties and losses but not pay claims. **5.** *Credit agent.* Despite the growing importance of insurance brokers, a large amount of business is still transacted through part-time insurance agents. Their main profession or business (estate agents, accountants, garages etc) enables them to introduce business to the insurer in return for a commission. Unlike cash agents (3 above) they operate credit accounts with the insurers and may have limited powers to issue cover (eg garage proprietors are empowered to issue cover notes in certain circumstances). They are not expected to have detailed knowledge of insurance although professionals such as solicitors and accountants who fail to handle insurance matters properly could breach their own professional obligations. **6.** *General agent.* A general representative of an insurer often in a foreign territory. The authority of the agent will vary but may include the ability to accept business, settle claims and supervise other agents. **7.** *Lloyd's agent.* Firm or individual retained by Lloyd's to supply shipping and other business intelligence. No business is transacted but Lloyd's agents survey damaged cargoes and may be given the authority to settle claims. **8.** *Managing agent.* A company managing and underwriting business on behalf of another company which prefers not to operate the account itself. The term is also used in respect of a Lloyd's underwriting agency which forms, recruits members for and administers a Lloyd's syndicate (qv). It may perform the duties of active underwriter or appoint someone else to that role. **9.** *Members' agent/agency.* A Lloyd's agency which introduces members or names to a Lloyd's syndicate and administers their affairs but does not form or manage a syndicate. **10.** *Part-time agents.* See cash agents (3 above) and credit agents (5 above). **11.** *Settling agent.* A claim agent who has the additional authority to settle claims from funds provided by the insurer. 12. *Underwriting agent.* A firm authorised to accept business on behalf of another insurer. (also see 8 above) 13. *Home service (or industrial assurance agent).* A full-time employee of an industrial assurance company.

agent-owned captive. A captive insurance company (qv) formed in recent years in the USA by insurance agents singly or in groups to insure selected risks from their own accounts.

aggravated burglary. A person is guilty of this offence if he commits any burglary (qv) and at the time has with him any firearm or imitation firearm, any weapon of offence, or any explosive (Theft Act 1968, s. 10).

Aggregate excess of loss reinsurance. A form of stop loss treaty (qv) under which the ceding office (qv) seeks protection in excess of its retention up to a stated cash figure rather than up to a percentage of annual premiums. A treaty might cover annual losses in excess of £2m up to a further £1m. The ceding office therefore covers all losses up to £2m, the reinsurer covers all losses in excess of £2m up to £3m, and the ceding office all losses in excess of £3m unless additional reinsurance has been arranged.

aggregate limit of indemnity. The maximum amount that a liability insurer will pay for all claims made during the period of insurance. Such a limit is commonly applied to products liability and professional indemnity insurances.

aggregate mortality table. A table based on the rate of mortality according to age. No allowance is made for the duration of the insurance. Aggregate tables are used for the valuation of life contracts. *See* ELT13.

aggregation. The process of aggregating claims over a period as specified by an excess of loss reinsurance (qv) for the purpose of establishing the amount recoverable under the reinsurance.

'agony of the moment'. In cases where the defendant pleads contributory negligence, the plaintiff may be excused for his contribution to the accident if he acted 'in the agony of the moment'. In *Jones* v *Boyce* (1816) the plaintiff, fearing that a fast-driven coach would overturn, jumped for safety but broke his leg in doing so. The fact that the coach did not overturn was irrelevant as his action was justified in the circumstances. This so-called principle of alternative danger applies to emergencies generally and may apply even when property is under threat.

agreed return. Marine insurers often insert a clause agreeing to return a certain part of their premium in return for a subsequent improvement in the character of the risk or in respect of a reduction in their potential liability under the policy. For example, cargo may by carried by a safer route than the one initially contemplated.

agreed value policy. *See* VALUED POLICY.

agricultural and forestry vehicles. Vehicles in these categories, including trailers when attached, are separately rated and insured by motor insurers depending on the nature of the machine and its value.

agricultural produce. The value of stocks held by farmers fluctuates. Fire insurers mitigate the penalty that an under-insured farmer would suffer following the normal application of pro rata average to adjust a partial loss. The under-insurance is ignored (ie no average is applied) provided that at the time of loss the sum insured is at least equal to 75 per cent of the value at risk. *See* AVERAGE and the SPECIAL CONDITION OF AVERAGE (THE 75% RULE).

AIDS (Acquired immune deficiency syndrome). Experience to date is that AIDS kills and it is probable that anyone who is HIV positive will contract it. They must in life or other insurances of the person supply the insurer with full information in response to questions relating to health. Members of the Association of British Insurers (qv) ask (i) whether the proposer has been counselled or medically advised in connection with AIDS or any sexually-transmitted disease; (ii) if they have had any blood test and, if so, to supply details including dates and results. Once a life policy has been effected, having an HIV blood test will not affect its validity. Having such a test is in itself no bar to obtaining new life insurance but new life cover cannot be provided for anyone who has AIDS or is HIV positive.

aircraft perils (aircraft or aerial devices). These perils can be added to a standard fire policy to cover damage to property caused by aircraft and other aerial devices including damage caused by articles dropped therefrom. Damage caused by sonic booms is excluded.

airline personnel and aircrew exclusion. A standard exclusion in a personal accident catastrophe excess of loss reinsurance. The nature of the employment causes regular exposure to a high risk activity where death and severe injury have a high incidence among accident victims. In addition there is an accumulation of risk and the personnel concerned tend to purchase high amounts of cover.

airliner. A large passenger aircraft plying in an airline on scheduled services over regular routes. Travel as a passenger on such aircraft is not normally excluded under personal accident insurance policies.

airport coupon and ticket business. Personal accident insurance purchased by individuals in respect of air travel at an airport from a machine or with a flight ticket. There is likely to be an accumulation of risk which cannot be controlled and, as a result, losses arising from these insurances is excluded from personal accident catastrophe excess loss of cover.

airport owners and operators liability policy. An aviation policy covering: (a) Premises legal liability to protect the insured against claims arising out of the use of his premises by third parties or passengers. (b) Hangar-keepers' legal liability in respect of the insured's liability as a bailee for aircraft and equipment on the ground. (c) Products legal liability to cover the risk associated with servicing or repairing aircraft or sale of fuel. 'Control tower liability' is also covered.

'airside'. Airside means being on the 'apron' of an airport and being in a position where there is a possibility of contact with aircraft. Some motor insurers exclude all liability where the motor vehicle is airside. In contract works insurance (qv) where the site of the work is at an airport insurers will take a more stringent view of work that is airside than work is landside (no contact with aircraft).

air travel. Travel as a fare paying passenger with recognised air lines is not excluded under personal accident policies. Private flying is, however, excluded but cover can be arranged.

Airworthiness Requirements Board (ARB). ARB advises the Civil Aviation Authority (qv) on 'design, construction, and maintenance of aircraft and all related matters'.

alarms. When insuring hazardous business risks (eg jewellers, tobacconists) theft insurers often require that the insured should install and maintain an intruder alarm. Failure to comply will mean that the insurance will not be granted or, if granted, invalidated by subsequent non-compliance. The insurer may additionally require that the installation and maintenance is undertaken by a company on the current role of Approved Installers published by the National Supervisory Council for Intruder Alarms (Queensgate House, 14, Cookham Road, Maidenhead, Berks, SL6 8AJ).

'alarm system in operation'. In *de Maurier (Jewels) Ltd* v *Bastion Insurance Co Ltd and Coronet Insurance Co Ltd* (1967), the following warranty in a jewellers' 'all risks' insurance stated 'road vehicles . . . fitted with lock and alarm system in operation'. This was held to mean that the system must be switched on in circumstances where the user has reason to believe that switching it on makes it fully operative. The words do not mean 'fully operative'. If because of an unknown fault, it fails to operate there will be no breach by the insured whose policy requires him to have an 'alarm system in operation'.

aleatory contract. Any form of contract involving chance. As insurance contracts involve chance they are of an aleatory nature but the legal requirements as to insurable interest (qv) prevent them from being used for wagering.

alien. An alien is a person who is neither a Commonwealth citizen nor a citizen of the Republic of Ireland nor a Protected British Citizen. Insurance contracts made with an enemy alien during a state of war are void.

all-in policy. An alternative name for an in and out insurance policy (qv).

all other contents clause. A phrase which appears in the basic specification wording of the standard fire policy to extend cover to forms of property otherwise excluded. The term includes money and stamps, national insurance stamps, documents, manuscripts and business books, computer systems records, patterns, moulds, plans and designs, employees' pedal cycles and personal effects. Monetary limits are usually applied to the majority of these items and cover in respect of plans, documents etc is limited to the cost of clerical labour in writing them up and not their alternative values.

all other costs and expenses. *See* OTHER COSTS AND EXPENSES.

all other perils. The words 'and of all other perils' concluded the words of the perils in the body of the now outdated SG marine insurance policy. The *ejusdem generis rule* (qv) applied. The words extended only to include perils of a similar kind to those already mentioned, ie perils of the sea. Any additional perils required the consent of the insurer. The words have been omitted from the new Institute Cargo Clauses as it was felt that the words could lead the insured to believe that he had more extensive cover than actually applied.

'all practicable steps'. This means something 'possible of accomplishment regardless of cost but dependent on the state of knowledge at the time'. The Factories Act 1961, s. 19 provides that 'all practicable steps shall be taken to ensure that no person employed shall be in the space between any moving part of a self-acting spinning mule and any fixed part of the machine towards which it is traversing'. Compare with properly maintained (qv) and reasonably practicable (qv).

all risks. All risks is the insurance term used where cover is not restricted to specific events like fire, storm and tempest, flood, theft, etc. The cover is loss, destruction or damage by any cause not specifically excluded. The exclusions depend partly on the type of property being insured but the following exclusions are typical of a business 'all risks' insurance on equipment: gradually operating causes: inherent vice, latent defect, gradual deteriora-tion, wear and tear, frost, corrosion, rust, wet or dry rot, shrinkage, evaporation, loss of weight, dampness, dryness, change in water table level, vermin or insects, pollution or contamination. Other exclusions: mechanical or electrical breakdown or derangement; heave or landslip or the normal settlement or bedding down of new structures; change in temperature, colour, flavour, or finish; money bullion, jewellery, precious stones or furs; theft from unattended vehicles unless there is evidence of forcible and violent entry into the vehicle; the first £25 of each and every loss unless resulting from fire, lightning or explosion. Valuables and personal effects are often insured on this basis either separately or as an extension of a household contents policy. Other policies are hybrids (eg the comprehensive section of a motor policy) adding all risks cover to a variety of other insurances, notably third party risks.

allocated premium limit. The limit as to the premiums that may be accepted on behalf of a Lloyd's underwriting member, ie Name (qv). The level is governed by his means (qv) and the amount of his deposit. *See* OVERWRITING OF PREMIUMS.

allocation of surplus. The allocation and division of a life insurer's divisible surplus to shareholders and eligible policyholders (ie those holding with profits policies).

allotment of bonus. The apportionment or division of a life office's surplus amongst its policyholders.

alphabet brokers. The commercial broking market in the USA is dominated by a limited number of firms who are usually referred to by their initials (eg Marsh McLennan are known as M.M.). Others include Alexander & Alexander and Johnson & Higgins. They are collectively known as the alphabet brokers. Much of their business comes to London by direct placing or in the form of reinsurance ceded on behalf of their American insurance company clients.

alteration of risk. An increase in risk after the contract has been made may be the result of structural alterations in premises, the introduction of hazardous trades, new methods of production etc, but in the absence of a policy condition the policy is not avoided by such alterations so long as the identity of the subject-matter insured (qv) remains, and provided there is no fraud (*Pim v Reid* (1843)). There has to be a real alteration in risk to relieve the insurer. This means either (a) alterations in the subject-matter of insurance, (b) changes of locality, (c) changes in circumstances, eg in the use of the subject-matter in the trade or business carried on by the insured. The description of the risk must be affected. As a protection the insurer may include a condition requiring the notification of any alteration which increases the risk which is insured. The fire policy contains an alterations condition to enable them to avoid the insurance if: there is alteration by removal; or increase in risk; or cessation of the insured's interest except by will or operation of the law. Temporary alterations not amounting to a breach of warranty do not terminate the policy but may suspend it. For example, property insured in the UK may not be covered when moved outside the UK with cover running again on its return.

alterations to the policy. The general rule is that any material alteration must be agreed by both the insurer and the insured. *See also* ASSIGNMENT and RECTIFICATION.

alterations bordereaux. These may be provided for under a reinsurance treaty. They serve a dual purpose. First they notify of all cessions on the preliminary bordereau (qv) which are eventually not completed. Secondly, they advise of subsequent alterations in risks reinsured where the amount of the premium is affected. It is not necessary under the treaty to advise of other alterations

alternative accommodation clause (loss of rent). A clause which appears in both household comprehensive buildings and contents insurances to provide cover in the event of the insured's home becoming uninhabitable as a result of destruction or damage insured by the policy. The buildings insurer will pay the reasonable cost of any necessary alternative accommodation, loss of rent due to the insured, and a maximum of two years ground rent for which the insured is liable, subject to a maximum of the 10 per cent of the amount insured. The contents insurer covers the cost of alternative accommodation and rent payable by the insured up to 20 per cent of the sum insured.

alternative basis clause. A business interruption policy clause to provide the insured with an alternative basis for adjusting a claim when the interruption is short and the turnover method impractical. The practice is for the insurer and the loss adjuster (qv) to calculate the loss on a 'sales value of output' basis, provided that the lost output cannot be regained within the indemnity period. Insurers are sufficiently flexible in their approach to allow this practice to be adopted even if the clause is not included.

always open. A term used in connection with open covers (qv) to signify that the insurance will remain continuously in force until ended by cancellation.

ambiguity. Wording is interpreted against the drafter. *See* CONTRA PROFERENTEM RULE.

American agency system. Well established US system under which insurance companies grant to independent contractors the right to effect all insurances and generally represent insurers in their areas or localities.

American Bureau of Shipping. A New York based classification society which sets standards relating to ship construction, surveys ships, and publishes a register of ships. The record, like Lloyd's Register of Shipping (qv) provides detailed information of each vessel, such as date of construction, builder, type, size, construction, machinery and fuel used and whether or not it has been surveyed by the Bureau. The information is invaluable to underwriters.

American exposures. Liability insurers regard any exposure to claims arising in the USA as material and any such exposure should, if known to the insured, be disclosed. The exposure may arise as a result of: (a) having employees and/or representation in the USA; (b) products exported to the USA; (c) USA business trips. The USA has been a cause for concern for the following reasons: (i) strict liability in many states; (ii) jury awards; (iii) contingent fee system (lawyers work on the basis that they will be paid a proportion of their client's award if successful but nothing otherwise); (iv) punitive damages often being awarded; (v) liberal interpretations of policies; (vi) reluctance to take contributory negligence into account.

American forms. Marine policy forms and clauses which are the USA equivalent of Institute Clauses (qv). They are approved and issued by the American Institute of Marine Underwriters, New York.

American Institute of Marine Underwriters. An association of marine underwriters with headquarters in New York. They meet to discuss problems common to their business and operate many technical committees which produce marine forms and clauses.

American trust fund. A fund established in New York to hold all Lloyd's dollar premiums, whether originating in the USA or not, and from which dollar claims are met. It was created when World War II was imminent. The fund is managed for Lloyd's underwriters by Citibank and makes Lloyd's one of the largest customers of one of the world's largest banks. Most of the fund is invested in US Treasury Bonds and this makes Lloyd's the largest private investor in the US Government.

amortisation. Periodical reduction in the value of a fixed asset until the asset is written down to nil.

amount at risk. The difference between the face value of a life policy and the mathematical reserve which has accrued. The net amount at risk declines throughout the duration of the contract while the reserve and its cash value increase. The amount at risk is the sum that an insurer would have to draw from its own funds rather than the policy reserve in the event of having to pay a claim for death.

amounts made good. The sums contributed as general average contributions (qv) to make good the loss of the party, whose act has saved the adventure from probable total loss, are known as the amounts made good. The allowances or amounts to be made good in respect of general average sacrifices are based on a formula to ensure equity in the adjustment. With expenditure, the amount made good is the expenditure itself.

amounts paid in error. The payment of a claim in error because an insurer has made a mistake of fact or a mistake of law. In the former instance the insurer is usually entitled to make a recovery but cannot do so when mistaken as to the law. Failure to deduct excesses or apply average are mistakes of fact and the resulting overpayments can be recovered.

ancillary activities. Activities that are ancillary or subsidiary to the main actitivities of the business. They arise from the business and are usually so closely connected with it that they properly constitute business activities. For the purpose of clarification it is the practice in liability policies to give an extended definition of 'Business' that includes ownership, maintenance and repair of premises; the provision and management of canteens, social, sports or welfare organisations for the benefit of employees and the insured's ambulance, first aid and fire services. One aspect of the definition which brings in a non-business situation is the cover in respect of the execution of private duties by employees for any director or senior official of the insured.

'and arrival'. In marine insurance practically all return premiums by agreement (eg to return –per cent if packed in tin-lined cases) are 'and arrival'. This means although a return may be due, the underwriter will not be liable to pay if the vessel becomes a total loss before expiry of the policy.

anglers insurance. A special policy enabling anglers to insure liability for accidents to the public, personal accident benefits for the angler himself, and loss or damage to tackle up to a specified limit. Where the angler engages a gillie he should effect employers' liability cover.

Animals Act 1971. The Act provides that where damage is caused by an animal of a dangerous species (qv) the keeper, subject to limited exceptions, will be strictly liable. In the case of an animal of a non-dangerous species (qv) (ie not of a dangerous species) the keeper will be liable for the damage which that particular animal to the keeper's knowledge is likely to cause (s. 2). A trespasser cannot generally recover damages (s. 5(3)). The keeper of a dog is strictly liable for killing or injuring livestock subject to certain defences. *See also* CATTLE TRESPASS and STRAYING.

annexes clause. The name given to the clause in a standard fire policy which brings within the scope of the cover outbuildings and the like.

annual exemption from capital transfer tax. Each individual can transfer to others up to a certain amount annually free of capital transfer tax. Unused amounts can be carried forward from one year to the next.

annual percentage rate (APR). This is the official formula for measuring the price of money—the true interest rate. APR is the total credit cost expressed as an annual percentage rate of charge.

annual premium method. A method of determining the premiums payable under an insurance contract with the object of keeping the premium of each member of a pension scheme at a constant rate until there is a change in circumstances.

annual report. A document completed by the managing agent of a syndicate for its underwriting members. The report contains: the underwriting accounts; a balance sheet; a seven year summary; a disclosure of interests statement; and such other information as is necessary for a proper understanding of the annual report (eg statement of accounting policies). The report and the information contained therein must be supplied in accordance with the Lloyd's syndicate accounting rules.

annual return. The activities and solvency of authorised insurers (qv) are monitored by a system of annual returns to the DTI within six months of the end of the year. The format and regulations regarding the returns are laid down in the Insurance Companies (Accounts and Statements) Regulations 1983. There is variation in detail in the returns as between life assurers engaged in long-term business and general business insurers. In life business the rules for asset recognition (*see* ADMISSIBLE ASSETS) and liability quanti-

fication are very detailed. Also the return must include a detailed valuation report and statement of long-term business prepared by the appointed actuary.

annual solvency test. Formerly called the Lloyd's audit, it is the annual check to ensure that the underwriters can meet their commitments. The Insurance Companies Act 1982 requires a solvency certificate in a prescribed form in respect of the underwriting accounts of every Name. The certificate declares that the available assets are sufficient to meet the liabilities as shown in the books. Each year Lloyd's lays down minimum reserves for each class of business in its first, second, third and subsequent years of development. The underwriters calculate their reserves by reference to these minima and increase their reserves if the claims record requires it. The solvency returns for each syndicate are amalgamated so the total exposure of each Name (qv) is ascertained. A certificate must be signed by an approved auditor in respect of each Name to certify that he has sufficient assets to cover his liabilities. Those assets comprise the Name's premium trust fund, deposits and personal reserves. If any default is made good the certificate will be signed otherwise the Name will be declared in default and central funds earmarked to cover the deficiency. When every Name has been accounted for the Department of Trade & Industry is notified as well as those overseas regulators who demand an annual proof of solvency from Lloyd's. In accordance with statute the solvency certificates have to be checked by an accountant approved by the Committee of Lloyd's.

annual subscriber to Lloyd's. A person, who although not a member of Lloyd's, is admitted to Lloyd's on payment of annual subscription. Such a person is not permitted to underwrite any risks.

annual turnover. This is defined in a business interruption policy as the turnover during the twelve months immediately before date of damage (where the indemnity period is for 12 months or less).

annuitant. Any person in receipt of an annuity (qv).

annuity. A periodic payment (often under a pension arrangement) for the lifetime of the annuitant (or any agreed shorter period) in return for cash subscribed as a lump sum or series of premiums. An annuity is not strictly life insurance but in one sense it is an insurance against a person outliving his capital. Life insurers issue the following annuities: (a) *Annuity-due.* An annuity under which the payment is made at the beginning of each period. (b) *Annuity for life.* A payment which, after it commences, eg pension age, continues until the death of the annuitant. (c) *Annuity certain.* No life element is involved. The annuity is payable for a definite period. It stops at the end of the period and is unaffected by any earlier death of the annuitant. (d) *Deferred annuity* which can be purchased by a single payment or periodic premiums (as in pension arrangements). The annuity commences at some future time, either a fixed date or at a date selected by the annuitant between two known dates (eg between ages 60 and 65). In the meantime the office invests the premiums and accumulates interest thereon. In the event of death of the annuitant before the annuity commences premiums may be returned with or without interest or they may be forfeited depending on the agreement made. (e) *Guaranteed annuity.* The payment is guaranteed for a certain period (eg 5 years) or until the annuitant dies, whichever comes the later. Sometimes the annuity is guaranteed until the purchase money has been refunded regardless of the number of years. (f) *Immediate annuity.* An annuity which is purchased by way of a lump sum with the first payment coming at the end of the first interval, eg quarter or half-year as agreed. (g) *Joint life annuity.* An annuity on two or more lives that ceases on the first death. (h) *Joint life and survivor annuity.* An annuity on two or more lives under which the annuity continues until the death of the last survivor. (i) *Reversionary annuity.* Payments to the annuitant begin on the death of another specified person. If the proposed annuitant dies first, there is usually no return of premium. (j) *Temporary annuities.* These are rarely used annuities under which the annuity is to continue for a fixed period of time or until the earlier death of the annuitant. They should be distinguished from annuity certain (see above). All of the above annuities can be considered under two basic categories—immediate or deferred. They may also be categorised as: 1. apportionable (complete) annuities—involving final proportionate payment calculated up to the date of death. 2. non-apportionable (or curtate) annuities.—ceasing with the final payment before the date of death.

annuity damages. Damages payable to a plaintiff in the form of life annuities rather than as a lump sum. Compensation can be arranged in this way only if the defendant's insurers agree. This type of structured settlement may occur when the plaintiff is disabled for life, is in need of ongoing care and capable of outliving the lump sum settlement. The annuity is index-linked and is purchased out of a high proportion of the damages that would have been awarded as a lump sum.

anti-selection. This occurs where the insured has a special motive for insurance that is opposed to the principles used by an insurer in the selection process. (*See* SELECTION OF LIVES.) In life insurance anti-selection appears to be greatest where the insurer is committed to the largest sum for the least premium. The tendency increases as the sum insured increases. In non-life business the tendency is to single out and insure only the more hazardous features of the risk.

'any driver policy'. A motor insurance policy that has been issued without special restriction as to the persons entitled to drive. The standard policy form permits driving by the insured and any other person driving on his order or with his permission. *See* PERMITTED DRIVERS.

'any member of the assured's household'. This phrase was construed as meaning 'any member of a household of which the assured is head'. A 20-year-old male effected a motor policy. He lived with his father and sister. His negligent driving injured his sister but the insurers denied liability relying on an exclusion of liability for 'death of or injury to any member of the assured's household'. They contended that the exclusion applied to any member of the same household of which the insured was a member. The Court of Appeal held that the words could mean 'any member of a household of which the assured was the head'. In view of the ambiguity they applied the *contra proferentem rule* (qv) and granted an indemnity to the insured (*English v Western* (1940) 2 A.E.R 515).

'any one accident'/event/original cause/ occurrence. A clause in a public liability policy restricting the insurer's liability to the sum of '£250 in respect of any one accident' was held to apply separately to each of 40 tramcar passengers injured in the same incident. The insurer contended that one accident had occurred and that the limit of £250 applied to the aggregate of all claims. The Court of Appeal rejected this argument and treated the word accident in 'the sense of mischief to an individual' (*South Staffordshire Tramways Co v Sickness & Accident Assurance Association* (1891). Where the word occurrence is used the outcome appears to be viewed from the insurer's standpoint and the limit embraces the number of claims made by the insured (*Allen v London Guarantee & Co Ltd* (1912). Modern public liability policies use an any one event or original cause (or occurrence) wording limiting their liability 'for all claims made in respect of or arising out of any one accident or series of accidents occurring in connection with or arising out of one event (or original cause etc) shall not exceed . . .'. This wording would have protected the insurer in the *South Staffordshire Tramways* case as all 40 individual accidents were linked by a single event or original cause. The event in such a case is readily identified but that is not always the situation. The words accident, cause, or occurrence relate to the earliest cause which is directly linked to the loss or losses involving multiple claimants. The intention appears to be to aggregate only those losses linked to the same event, error, act or omission etc that set the train of events in motion but terms like 'event' are open to more than one interpretation. In products

liability a 'bench error' could lead to a batch of defective products sooner or later causing injury to multiple claimants. If each claim is linked to the same 'bench error' the insurer would seem entitled to apply any single event/occurrence limit to the aggregate of the claims but in any event it is customary for the insurer to use a batch clause (qv). If the same bench error is repeated and further injuries result it has to be decided whether there are two or more events, or, as it is a repetition of the same manufacturing failure, still traceable to a single cause justifying the application limit to all claimants affected by the error regardless of the batch. It is often a question of how far to go back in the causal link and courts have tended to equate 'event' with the original cause. The problem is greatest when the product, or substance, causing the harm has latency characteristics, ie there is a long interval between exposure to the harm and the manifestation of the resultant disease. Failure to observe safety procedures could be the cause of multiple asbestosis claims spread over time becoming apparent many years later. But where the disease is progressive, each year of exposure or gradual operation of the disease could possibly be regarded as a new event each year in relation to an individual or group of individuals and in any event any aggregate limit may be applied in each of the years involved. Similarly, seepage or contamination can take place over time to create problems for the insurer of pollution risks. Each year of the undetected damage might constitute a new event and cause the stacking of the limits of indemnity. Reinsurers face problems with natural events like earthquakes and have to decide if it is the time or location which determines whether all losses stem from a single event. For example, an excess of loss reinsurer covering an aviation account may be adversely affected by a major earthquake which strikes in a number of places along an earthquake zone causing buildings containing aircraft to collapse in two or three towns many miles apart. It can be shown that all damage to aircraft had a common cause so that when the losses are aggregated the excess of loss reinsurer finds himself paying for a range of widespread and individual losses with a common cause. However, shock waves travel at various speeds and there might be some differences, albeit slight, to the times at which the damage occurs in these different locations. Insurers and reinsurers have attempted to resolve these problems by excluding certain risks, writing the coverage on a claims-made basis (qv), defining how the limit is to be applied, eg batch clauses (qv) in products liability and hours clause (qv) in reinsurance on property, using an aggregate extension clause to define how any series of claims is to be treated. In liability insurance it may be impossible to determine the event but the effects can be demonstrated and therefore accounted for in a suitable definition.

'any one cause'. See ANY ONE ACCIDENT ETC.

'any one disabled mechanically-propelled vehicle'. Under commercial vehicle policies it is customary for insurers to exclude the towing of trailers other than any one disabled mechanically-propelled vehicle unless the insurer has specifically agreed to provide such cover. The special section called Towing gives third party cover and keeps the insured within the law when lending assistance to a vehicle that has broken down and is not at the time capable of self-propulsion. Generally vehicles in need of tow have suffered from a mechanical defect, eg broken parts, damp plugs, flat batteries and, probably, even vehicles out of petrol will be regarded as mechanically disabled being incapable of self-propulsion for want of fuel. However, where a vehicle capable of self-propulsion and not mechanically broken is towed for convenience, it may well be that such a vehicle is not within the intended meaning of the term. For example, where an insured decides to tow a fork-lift truck to other premises for use there, or for servicing at other premises, and an accident occurs en route the insurer would appear well placed to argue that the section does not apply. The way is always open for the insured to arrange cover for the fork-lift truck as a trailer (qv). By virtue of a provision in the Road Traffic Act

when, in consequence of a breakdown, an articulated vehicle (unit and unladen trailer) is being towed it is treated as a single trailer and will therefore be within the term any one disabled mechanically-propelled vehicle.

'any one occurrence'. See ANY ONE ACCIDENT ETC.

applicant's form. The form used in fidelity guarantee insurance by the person, eg the employee, against whose dishonesty insurance is sought by the insured, eg the employer. The form elicits details of name, address, age, salary, present post within the firm and financial status of the employee. Details are also obtained on the form about previous employment history and any previous guarantees.

appointed actuary. A person appointed as actuary to a company carrying on long term business, as required by Insurance Companies Act 1982, s. 19. The appointed actuary must be at least 30 years old, hold a prescribed professional qualification, and must carry out a periodic valuation (see ACTUARIAL VALUATION) of the company's long-term business liabilities.

appointed adviser. This term is defined in some legal expenses insurances (qv) as 'the solicitor, accountant, counsel or other expert appointed under the terms and conditions of the policy to represent the insured's interests'.

appointed company representative. Individuals who, although not under a contract of employment, hold an agency either to sell the product of only one life assurer or to introduce clients exclusively to that insurer. They are also known as tied agents. See FINANCIAL SERVICES ACT 1986.

apportionable annuity. See ANNUITY.

apportionment of value. In cargo insurances different species may be insured under a single valuation. In a partial loss of cargo the insurer is liable for such proportion of the insured value as the insurable value of the part lost bears to the insured value as a whole (Marine Insurance Act 1906, s. 72). In practice, the apportionment of the insured value is normally based on the invoiced value of the various goods.

appropriate personal pension plan. One which satisfies certain conditions under the Social Security Act 1986 and is approved by the Occupational Pensions Board (qv) which enables the contributor to the plan to be contracted-out of SERPS (qv).

'approved alarm systems'. Unless the underwriter expresses a contrary intention it is sufficient that the alarm system in question has been approved by underwriters generally. In *De Maurier (Jewels) Ltd.* v *Bastion Insurance Co. and Coronet Insurance Co. Ltd.* (1967) the plea of the insurers under a jewellers' all risks policy that they had not themselves approved the system failed.

approved pension scheme. *See* APPROVED SCHEME.

approved policy. In the terms of the Employers' Liability (Compulsory Insurance) Act 1969, s.1(3)(a) an approved policy is a policy that is not subject to 'prohibited conditions' (qv). These are certain conditions (specified in the General Regulations), which would, if not complied with by the insured employer, allow the insurer to repudiate a claim under the policy. There is no objection, however, to conditions that enable the insurer, in specified circumstances, to reclaim from the insured the amount of any compensation (including incidental costs and expenses) paid by the insured to the injured employee. The insurer issues a certificate to indicate that the policy is approved in accordance with the Act. *See* AVOIDANCE OF TERMS AND RIGHTS OF RECOVERY.

Approved repairers. Motor vehicles garages listed by certain of the larger motor insurers as having been approved by them for the purpose of repairing damage the subject of claims under their policies. Policyholders are encouraged to take their vehicles to approved repairers and only one or two insurers use a contractual term to enable them to compel their policyholders to do so. The insurer can usually negotiate better terms in return for the greater volume of business a repairer can expect. It also assists the insurer in rationalising the work of its staff engineers.

approved scheme. A retirement benefits scheme approved by the Inland Revenue under Chapter I of Part XIV of the Income and Corporation Taxes Act 1988, including a free standing AVC scheme (*see* ADDITIONAL VOLUNTARY CONTRIBUTION). The term is also used to describe a personal pension scheme approved under Chapter IV of that Part.

a priori. A term describing a situation where all possible outcomes of an event are known in advance enabling their respective probabilities to be calculated, eg throwing a die, tossing a coin.

arbitration. A method of determining disputes by the decision of one or more persons called arbitrators. Where there are two arbitrators differences between them are settled by an umpire. An agreement to refer a dispute to arbitration is called an arbitration agreement. The arbitrator's decision is called an award. Businessmen often use their contracts to substitute arbitration for litigation but the courts have retained a measure of control over arbitration by the Arbitration Acts, 1950, 1975, 1979. For methods of settling disputes in consumer type insurances, *see* INSURANCE OMBUDSMAN BUREAU and the PERSONAL INSURANCE ARBITRATION SERVICE.

arbitration clause. A standard express condition in most fire and accident policies providing that, if any difference as to the amount to be paid arises, the matter shall be referred to arbitration. The arbitrator is to be appointed in accordance with the current relevant statutory provisions. The condition is restricted in scope as it applies only to the amount of the claim. Any difference as to liability of the insurer will go to the courts. The condition does not appear in liability policies or policies relating to the person, eg personal accident.

architects', surveyors' and consulting engineers' fees. These fees are not covered under the standard fire policy. It is customary to cover them by an extension of the sum insured or a special item. The fees are those payable by the insured for plans, specifications, etc, and general supervision of rebuilding in the event of fire or other insured perils. Cover is often provided by increasing the buildings sum insured by 12.5 per cent and the machinery sum insured by 7.5 per cent but insureds with very large sums insured may insure the fees on a first loss basis. Fees paid by the insured for preparing the claim are not covered.

arising out of and in the course of employment. Arising out of . . . 'means arising out of the work the man is employed to do and what is incident to it—in other words out of his service' 'in the course of . . . means . . . the work which the man is employed to do, and what is incident to it— in other words, in the course of his service', Lord Finlay in *Charles R. Davidson & Co* v *M'Robb* (1918). Acts incidental to employment, eg going to wash a tea-cup have been covered by the term (*Davidson* v *Handley Page Ltd* (1945), using a staircase on arrival (*Bell* v *Blackwood Morton & Sons Ltd* (1960). A lunch-break injury while playing darts was held to have occurred in the course of employment (*Knight* v *Howard Wall Ltd* (1938)) The act in question needs only to be reasonably incidental to the employment (a workman taking a meal on the employer's premises in accordance with the employment terms is in the course of service by being there at meal-times) but the course of employment can be interrupted when the employee goes on a frolic of his own (qv) or does something entirely for his own purposes provided he is not simultaneously doing something for his employer (eg smoking while working). The phrase, 'arising out of and in the course of employment' appears in the operative clause (and in the Employers' Liability (Compulsory Insurance) Act 1969) of the employers' liability policy. Injury sustained outside the employment is a matter for the public liability insurer. Travel to or from work in the employer's car is in the course of employment if the employee is obliged by the terms of employment to travel in that vehicle (*Vandyke* v *Fender* (1970)). Also where travel home is from a place other than the normal base in the employee's own car and in the employee's own time, then he is in the course of employment if the employer knows of and authorises the journey and, being entitled to order that travel should not take place on that day, fails to so order (*Smith* v *Stages & Anr.* (1987)). The employer was vicariously

liable for the injury caused to an employee-passenger by the negligence of an employee-driver. An employer is vicariously liable for the torts of his employee committed in the course of employment, the test for which is 'was the employee performing a class of act he was employed to do, or was he doing something he was not employed to do?' A bus conductor is not employed to drive buses and the employer was not liable for the injury caused when a conductor drove a bus (*Beard* v *London General Omnibus Co* (1900)).

arrests, restraints and detainments. 'Arrests, restraints and detainments of all kings, princes and people, of what nation, condition, or quality whatsoever' are defined in the Rule for Construction of the Policy (No. 10) as referring to political or executive acts, and not including a loss caused by riot or by ordinary judicial process. As goods were held to be lost when they could not be forwarded to their destination because of these perils (eg siege of a city), insurers introduced the Frustration clause (qv), the effect of which is to relieve the insurer of liability for a claim based on 'arrests etc.'

arrival, arrived (arrd.). A note on a report or claim to indicate that the vessel has completed the voyage or part-voyage, or cargo has reached its destination after the transit covered by the policy. Sometimes the term is used colloquially to refer to the successful completion without loss or claim of a non-marine cover.

arrived damage value. The depreciated value of cargo on arrival at the place where the voyage terminates following damage in transit. A formula is used to establish the percentage depreciation.

arrived sound value. Gross wholesale value after freight, import charges, duty etc to represent the value that cargo would have had if it had arrived safely at the place where the adventure ended.

arson. The criminal act of deliberately setting property on fire. The resultant damage is covered by a fire policy provided always that the victim is someone other than the arsonist. The Association of British Insurers gives advice on how the risk can be reduced including some useful suggestions in a leaflet, Home Safety.

Articles of Association. Regulations governing the internal working and management of a limited liability company (see the Companies Act 1948, ss. 6–10). The First Schedule of the Act consists of a set of specimen Articles applicable to a company limited by shares. A company may adopt the specimen set or draw up its own Articles of Association. The duties owed by directors and officers to the company have their origin in the Articles. *See* DIRECTORS' AND OFFICERS' LIABILITY INSURANCE.

asbestos. *See* CONTROL OF ASBESTOS AT WORK REGULATIONS 1987.

Asbestos Claims Facility. Established under the Wellington Agreement (qv) in the USA to enable certain asbestos manufacturers and insurers to respond to asbestos-induced injury claims in a manner intended to reduce litigation and its associated costs while accelerating the payment of claims to the victims. The Facility was created in 1985 but dissolved following internal disagreements in 1988. In consequence the Centre for Claims Resolution (CCR) was formed.

as expiry. A term that indicates that an insurance should, on expiry, be renewed on its pre-expiry terms.

as original. A term used to denote that the terms and conditions of a reinsurance follow those of the underlying insurance.

assessment. A US term applied in two different ways. In the context of mutuals it refers to the amounts policyholders may be called upon to pay in addition to their premiums if the insurer is unable to meet its claims liabilities. The term also describes a premium levy on all admitted insurers (qv) within a state to form a centrally run fund to pay the claims and other outstanding liabilities of insolvent companies and those with impaired capital (qv). All USA states now have guaranty funds.

assessmentism. An alternative term for 'pay as you go' it is a method of calculating life insurance risk premiums on a year-by-year basis. Each premium reflects the chance that the policyholder will die in the following year plus an allowance for expenses. It is suitable where the insurance is purchased as term (temporary) insurances (qv) on a year-by-year basis as is usually the case with group life insurance (qv). On any individual life the premium increases each year as the mortality rate worsens. This failure to take account of the increasing death risk usually renders it unsuitable for the insurance of individual lives. *See* the LEVEL PREMIUM SYSTEM.

assessor. *See* INDEPENDENT AUTOMOTIVE ASSESSOR, LOSS ASSESSOR and STAFF ENGINEER.

asset. Any property, cash, or financial claim that can be converted into cash (eg money owed by debtors). *See* ADMISSIBLE ASSETS for the purpose of the supervision and control of authorised insurance companies.

asset valuation rules. The assets of an insurance company have to be stated on Form 13 of the DTI return. Separate forms are required for: (a) Assets representing long-term funds, in total, and for each fund to which assets are separately appropriated. (b) Other assets (general business assets) and shareholders' funds. Each of the above is then further divided into assets: (i) deposited with the Accountant General, (ii) maintained in the UK, (iii) maintained in the European Community. The basic rules for valuation of the assets are contained in Regulations 37 to 49 of the Insurance Companies Regulations 1981. They are intended to give 'break up values' and not, as is usually the case with financial statements, 'going-concern' figures. In this context no value can be placed on goodwill or stock-in-trade After valuation, the next stages for the purpose of the DTI return are: Admissibility (qv); Matching (qv); Localisation (qv).

assigned risk. A US term to describe a risk that is not ordinarily acceptable to insurers and therefore by law assigned to an insurer participating in an assigned risk pool or plan. Each insurer in the pool accepts its share of all of the pooled risks.

assignee. The party to whom a policy is assigned. He may be an assignee for value, who has given a valuable consideration for the policy, or a voluntary assignee to whom the policy has been assigned by way of gift. The term assignee also applies to the party to whom a lease on premises is transferred. *See* ASSIGNOR'S LEASEHOLD LIABILITY POLICY.

assignor. The party who transfers (ie assigns) his rights in a policy, property or rights to another party called the assignee (qv).

assignment. The general rule is that only the parties to a contract can acquire rights or be made subject to obligations under it. However, rights or benefits may be assigned by legal assignment, equitable assignment, or operation of the law (see below). Liabilities can only be assigned if 'non-personal', and the other party agrees (novation (qv)). A legal right to enforce payment of money, such as payment of an insurance claim, is a 'chose in action'. Choses in action are assignable. In insurance there may be assignment of: (a) *the subject-matter of insurance, such as a motor car.* In all cases (other than life or personal accident insurance), the insured may part with all or part of his interest in the subject-matter such as when he sells his car. On disposal the insurable interest (qv) ends and the insured cannot claim for any subsequent loss. (b) *The insurance policy.* The position varies and may be governed by policy conditions. (i) In marine insurance, by s. 50 of the Marine Insurance Act 1906, marine policies are freely assignable unless expressly prohibited by policy terms. Thus an assignee is entitled to sue the insurer in his own name while the insurer is able to use against the assignee any defence (eg breach of utmost good faith (qv)) available against the original assured. Section 51 of the Act forbids assignment unless the assured agreed to it before or at the same time as parting with interest in the subject-matter. In practice, marine cargo policies are freely assignable but hull policies contain terms prohibiting assignment unless the insurer consents. (ii) In life assurance the Policies of Assurance Act 1867 (qv) renders consent of the insurer unnecessary but the assignee has no right to sue the insurer unless he has given the insurer written notice of the assignment. In the event of failure to comply, payment by the insurer to someone else in good faith will be valid against the assignee. The policy must be endorsed or the assignment must be by separate instrument as prescribed by the Act. (iii) Other cases. Purported assignments are ineffective unless the insurer has consented as insurances are personal contracts (qv) covering the insured's interest in the subject-matter of insurance. Where permitted by the policy, the assignment must be simultaneous with the transfer of the subject-matter. Assignment by operation of the law (death, bankruptcy) is valid unless the policy stipulates otherwise. (c) *Assignment of the proceeds.* With a valid assignment, the assignee substitutes for the original insured. Where only the proceeds of the policy are assigned, the contract continues between the original insured and the insurer with the former transferring his right to the sum payable under the policy. The insurer's consent is not required for assignment of the proceeds even though assignment of the policy may be prohibited. This right may be assigned before or after a loss either absolutely or by way of mortgage. So-called assignments of life policies are commonly assignments of the proceeds. N.B. Methods of assignment. There are two kinds: Legal assignments which permit an assignee to sue in his own name, eg assignment under Policies of Assurance Act 1867. A legal assignment is also one under the Law of Property Act 1925 (s. 136) which permits absolute assignments in the prescribed form of choses in action (a right of proceeding in a court of law to procure the payment of a sum of money such as that due on a bill of exchange or an insurance policy). Equitable assignments do not give the assignee the right to sue in his own name. No particular form is necessary; it need not even be in writing, eg the insured when borrowing from a bank hands over his life policy with the intention of giving a charge over it. Notice to the insurer is advisable as there may be successive assignees. Persons contemplating lending money on a policy should enquire whether the insurers have had notice of assignments. Where an insurer is in doubt as to entitlement to proceeds it may pay money into court under the Life Assurance Companies (Payment into Court) Act 1896, leaving the court to decide the entitlement.

assignment by operation of the law. The assignment of rights and obligations under a contract which arises not as a result of the acts of the parties to the contract but automatically by operation of the law without the consent of either party to the contract (eg on death or in the event of bankruptcy).

assignor's leasehold liability insurance. A policy designed to cover the ongoing liability of a tenant to landlord after assignment of the lease by the tenant. When a tenant sells or assigns the lease, the tenant may still be liable to the landlord for any default by the person to whom the lease has been assigned. The policy can be effected by an original tenant or subsequent assignee. The standard policy is for one year but payment by the insured of 200 per cent of the current premium normally secures a 24-month extension to make a total period of 3 years. The policy covers legal liability to pay rent, interest on rent, damages and costs for breach of any covenant or condition contained in the lease relating to the premises committed after the assignment and during the period of insurance. Claimant's costs and the insured's own costs incurred with the insurer's written consent are covered. The indemnity limits are usually in the range of £50 000 to £250 000 for all claims made during the period of insurance. The policy excludes liability connected with any premises not mentioned in the policy schedule. To assess the premium the underwriter requires a completed proposal form, a copy of the lease plus such financial information as is available in respect of the assignee, and a copy of the assignment. In the case of a limited company assignee the financial information should be the last two years' accounts. In the case of an individual it should be a copy of the references being supplied to the landlord.

assignor's liability insurance. See ASSIGNOR'S LEASEHOLD LIABILITY INSURANCE.

assistance to the insurer. In liability insurances it is an invariable rule to require by condition that the insured should assist the insurer in the enquiry into, or conduct of the defence of, any claim made against the insured. The insurer cannot make unrealistic demands by calling for information or assistance that the insured cannot reasonably be expected to supply. Some aspects are relatively straightforward, eg passing on any intimation of claim to the insurer including written communications upon receipt of them. As far as is reasonably practicable the insured must not alter or repair any machinery connected with the occurrence until the insurer has had the opportunity to inspect it. A condition in a fidelity guarantee insurance requiring an insured to prosecute a defaulting employee must be complied with unless waived by the insurer. In *London Guarantee Co* v *Fearnley* (1880), the insured's refusal to co-operate was fatal to his claim under the policy. *See also* CONDUCT OF PROCEEDINGS CLAUSE.

associated operation. A transfer of value by two or more operations affecting the same property. 'Same property' means property which represents directly or indirectly the property or income arising from it. Also operations which facilitate or provide for other operations will be associated with them. Where the associated operations rule (Inheritance Tax Act 1984) applies the effectiveness of back-to-back arrangements (qv) is reduced. In practice policies taken out for the benefit of another and annuities are not regarded as being affected by the associated operations rule if the policy was issued on full medical evidence of the insured's health and it would have been issued on the same terms if the annuity had not been bought. (25. E4 Inland Revenue Statements of Practice). If the transferor pays, either directly or indirectly, a premium on a life insurance on his life and an annuity on his life is purchased at any time, the premium will not be treated as part of his normal income unless it can be shown that the operations rule does not apply.

Associateship of the Chartered Insurance Institute (ACII). The ACII has been the principal qualifying examination of the Chartered Insurance Institute (qv) open to students with GCE 'A' level (or equivalent) qualifications. Up to 1991 candidates took nine subjects three of which were broad based and common to all candidates. For the remaining six a choice existed and a point came where the candidate chose a general or specialist route (life, pensions, marine or aviation). Successful 'ACII's' were able to proceed to Fellowship status (FCII) by further examinations. From 1992 there is one examination comprising ten demanding subjects leading to the Associateship. The Fellowship will subsequently be awarded to Associates who satisfy certain criteria relating to professional experience and other criteria set at an appropriately high standard of achievement. In combination with three compulsory foundation subjects, a menu of technical subjects is provided to give the candidate maximum choice in pursuing their studies. Election to the new Associateship involves the payment of a fee, passing all the necessary papers, two years experience of insurance work, and membership of the CII or eligibility to become a member.

Association of Average Adjusters. An association of independent fee earning practitioners with its own examination scheme engaged in marine insurance as average adjusters (qv). It was founded in 1869 and seeks to promote the 'correct principles in the adjustment of Averages and uniformity among Average Adjusters'. The Rules of Practice are: (a) rules of practice which concern the adjustment of averages and other related duties; and (b) uniformity rules under which uniformity is sought on less important issues. The Rules of Practice are followed in the adjustment of general average (qv); the York-Antwerp Rules (1974); damage to and repairs to ships; particular average on goods. The association has established expert committees to serve the marine insurance community, and may, by a panel of referees act as arbitrators in the case of dispute. Membership is optional but all members are practising average adjusters. *See also* UK SOCIETY OF AVERAGE ADJUSTERS.

Association of British Insurers (ABI). The trade association for insurance companies, with 450 members transacting all classes of business. Membership is open to companies authorised by the Department of Trade and Industry to transact business in the UK, Friendly Societies, brokers or other intermediaries, but not to individuals. Member companies transact over 90 per cent of the world-wide business of the UK insurance company market. The ABI is not a regulatory body although members must comply with certain codes of conduct and practice. For example, there is the ABI's Code of Selling Practice for General Insurance. Registered brokers have their own code but all other intermediaries have to follow the Code. *See also* STATEMENTS OF INSURANCE PRACTICE agreed between the ABI and other bodies. The ABI's main objectives are: (a) to protect and promote the interests of members. (b) To take concerted measures whenever the interests of members may be affected by the action of the government or other agency. (c) To co-operate with any other association having similar objectives. The ABI's Board is supported by management committees for general insurance and life insurance together with a wide-ranging committee structure drawn from the member companies. There are committees covering: Government relations; investments; European Com- munity; overseas; statistics; and technical. The ABI's public relations role embraces: regional offices; consumer information; education; public service (eg road and home safety campaigns).

Association of Burglary Insurance Surveyors (ABIS). A group of individuals, the majority from the insurance industry itself, who aim to improve the security of premises to reduce the losses arising from theft and attempts thereat. They are involved with research into theft protection and disseminate information with a view to improving standards and establishing both awareness of the risks and good practices.

Association of Futures Brokers and Dealers. A Self-Regulating Organisation (SRO) (qv) which regulates firms who advise and deal in futures, options and contracts for differences, and manage portfolios of these types of investments.

Association of Insurance Risk Managers in Industry and Commerce. Established in 1963 AIRMIC provides a forum for the exchange of data and opinion between insurance and risk managers in industry and commerce. It updates members on technical matters and current practice. It promotes the understanding of the nature and purpose of risk management and represents a body of informed opinion in dealings with trade and market associations and with Government.

Association of Lloyd's Members. A company formed to improve understanding of Lloyd's amongst its members and prospective members. It was formed by Names (qv) and has been involved in the publication of 'league tables' based on the syndicate's accounts that could be obtained.

'as soon as possible'. The insurer may specify in the notice of loss condition that any loss should be notified as soon as possible. It is a question of fact whether the insured has complied with this requirement which has to be interpreted in all the circumstances of the case. The Statement of Non-Life Insurance Practice (qv), which applies to UK non-life policyholders insuring in their private capacity, provides that regarding notification of a claim 'the policyholder shall not be asked to do more than report a claim and subsequent developments as soon as reasonably possible' except in the case of legal processes and claims which require a third party or the policyholder to notify within a fixed time, where immediate advice may be required'. A similar statement is included in the Statement of Long-term Business (qv).

assumed liability. See CONTRACTUAL LIABILITY.

assurance. The term insurance relates to an event which may, or may not, happen. Assurance relates to an event which is certain, eg death, survival of a given term of years, or attainment of a given age. The terms are, however, used interchangeably. In a Lloyd's policy both words occur and have the same meaning.

assured. Means the same as insured but is most commonly used in life assurance/insurance, and marine insurance. Either term is valid.

assurer. Means the same as insurer but is most commonly used in life assurance.

'at and from'. The printed wording of the discarded SG policy form referred only to voyages and rarely applied as ships were as a rule insured under time policies. Under the SG form for hulls the risk commences 'at and from' the specified place and ends when the vessel 'hath moored at anchor twenty-four hours in good safety'. A ship may be said to be 'at' a port when she has safely arrived within the limits of the port (Rule of Construction No. 3). When a ship is insured 'from' a specified place, the risk attaches as soon as the ship leaves that place with the intention of prosecuting the voyage insured (Rule of Construction No. 2).

Atomic Energy Authority. A Government body which with its licensees incurs a strict liability for injury, loss or damage arising from the operation of nuclear establishments. See NUCLEAR PERILS.

attach. In regard to the policy it means its inception, ie coming into force or starting its term. In regard to legal liability, liability attaches when a party is responsible for some injury, loss or damage.

attachment date. The date on which the risk attaches, ie begins to run. See INCEPTION DATE.

attendance expense cover. A form of cover available under legal expenses cover. It covers cost of time lost by the insured and employees having to attend court or tribunal as defendants or witnesses on behalf of the insured. The amount payable is based on a stated fraction (eg a 250th part for each day's absence) of the person's annual salary.

'attending to business'. The phrase 'attending to business' in the context of a temporary total business disablement benefit in a personal accident does not necessarily mean attending to all business. The insured's policy stated that a weekly sum would be paid for 'temporary total disablement from attending to business of any and every kind'. The insured normally travelled all over the country as a buyer but motor accident injuries severely restricted his activities and he attended to only a minor part of the work. Looking at the phrase in its context the court was satisfied that he was disabled within the meaning of the phrase. The test, according to the court, was 'is he fit to attend there and play a worthwhile part in the conduct of it (the business)?' If, 'no', the clause applied.

attestation clause. The final part of a policy signed by certain officers of the insurance company according to the Deed of Settlement or Memorandum and Articles of Association by which the company is constituted and business transacted. Also known as the Signature Clause.

audit. A USA term referring to the right of an insurer under a policy written on a reporting form or adjustable basis to scrutinise the insured's books to verify the accuracy of the premiums paid. In the UK audit refers to Lloyd's accountants' annual scrutiny of the syndicates' business conduct, results, solvency and reserves ratio. *See also* ANNUAL SOLVENCY TEST.

auditor's charges. *See* ACCOUNTANTS CLAUSE.

authorisation. The Insurance Companies Act 1982 states that no company may carry on insurance business in the UK unless authorised by the Secretary of State for Trade and Industry to whom an application must be made. Authorisations are granted for specified classes of business. The purpose is to minimise the risk of insolvency among insurers and so protect the public. 1. Life assurers. The applicant must first decide whether to operate as a UK branch or as a UK company incorporated under the Companies Act 1985. The DTI need to be satisfied, *inter alia,* that: (a) the margin of solvency (qv) will be met given the applicant's financial plans and resources. (b) Industry regulations will be complied with (eg membership of LAUTRO). (c) Appropriateness of investment strategy having regard to the circumstances of the applicant. (d) Suitability of intended managers and controllers. The DTI may, at its discretion, grant authorisation subject to conditions (eg restrictions on rate at which premium income is allowed to grow). 2. General

business insurers. Initially the applicant must form a branch of an EC or other foreign company in the UK or incorporate under the Companies Act 1985. Authorisation depends largely on the financial resources of the company in relation to the solvency requirements. The DTI will also be influenced by the suitability of the proposed reinsurance arrangements and the suitability of intended managers and controllers. Authorisation may be subject to compliance with certain conditions. Subsequently authorised insurers are monitored in terms of their activity and solvency by means of annual returns (qv).

authorised insurer. A company authorised by the Department of Trade and Industry (DTI) to operate as a life assurer or a general business insurer. For this purpose the Insurance Companies Act 1982 divides general business into 17 general business classes and seven long-term classes (*see* DTI CLASSES). It is not possible to gain a single authorisation to transact both life and general business. To secure authorisation stringent financial requirements, supervised by the DTI, have to be met. *See* AUTHORISATION.

authorised unit trust. *See* UNIT TRUST.

automatic cover. A clause in engineering insurance policies that provides automatic cover for a period, eg 180 days, in respect of additional plant of a similar class or type to that already insured installed at any address to which the policy refers. This cover does not apply to mobile plant unless specially arranged.

automatic escalation clause. *See* ESCALATION CLAUSE and INDEX-LINKING.

automatic personal accident cover. *See* ADMITTED LIABILITY COVER.

automatic reinstatement clause. Also called a self-renewing clause. A clause under which the sum insured or limit of indemnity is automatically restored to its original level following a claim.

automatism. An involuntary act done by a person who is not aware of what he is doing or who is unable to control his muscles. It may render a driver incapable of conscious control of his vehicle. If this can be proved by or on behalf of a driver accused of negligence it may be a good defence.

average. The meaning varies according to the circumstances. 1. *In non-marine insurance.* It is a device to penalise and deter under-insurance. The rate of premium is normally fixed on the understanding that the sum insured on property, to which the rate is applied, represents the full value at risk. As most losses are partial rather than total insureds may seek to fix the sum below the true value at risk. The insurance system will not work if adequate contributions are not made to the insurance fund. Most property and pecuniary insurances are subject to some form of average. Average is not a principle of law and applies only if specifically introduced into the insurance contract. (a) Pro rata condition of average. This is the most common and applies almost universally to fire and theft policies. If, when a loss occurs, the total value at risk exceeds the sum insured, the insured is his own insurer for the difference and has to bear a rateable proportion of each and every loss accordingly. (b) The special condition of average (the 75 per cent condition of average). This is applied to agricultural products at farms as values at risk will vary and the rigid application of the pro rata rule, in the circumstances, might be harsh. Accordingly if the sum insured is 75 per cent (or greater) of the value at risk no deduction for average will be made in partial losses. If the sum is less than 75 per cent then pro rata average will apply. This special condition also applies to policies on ecclesiastical property (churches, Sunday schools etc). (c) The two conditions of average. This may be applied where property is insured under more than one policy one of which is specific, eg covering property in premises A, while the other is general covering property in premises A, B and C. The first of the two conditions is pro rata average (see (a) above). The second allows that the more specific policy pays first in the event of a loss. Any uninsured portion of the specific policy falls under the general policy which is itself subject to pro rata average. (d) Reinstatement average. When a policy is written on a reinstatement basis (qv), this clause provides that average will not be applied if the sum insured is at least equal to 85 per cent of the reinstatement value at the time of reinstatement. This provides a measure of protection for the insured whose sum insured becomes inadequate, up to a point, on account of inflation. (e) 'Day one' average. Under this form the declared sum is compared with the actual cost of reinstatement at the inception of the period of insurance. If the declared value falls short of the actual cost then pro rata average is applied. 2. *In marine insurance.* Except in the way described below 'average' is not used in the sense of relating actual values to sums insured. It has a specialised meaning, ie 'loss'. (*See* GENERAL AVERAGE and PARTICULAR AVERAGE). The word 'average' in this sense is believed to be derived from the Arabic word *awariya* meaning 'damaged goods'. However, the non-marine principle has in practice a limited application in marine insurance. For example, in the event of partial loss or damage under a cargo policy, the claim is assessed by calculating the percentage of depreciation on a comparison of the actual damaged value at destination with the actual sound value at destination and applying this percentage to the agreed insured value. This position is comprehensively defined in the Marine Insurance Act 1906 (s.71). The old Institute Cargo Clauses, ie those prior to 1 January 1982 contained average clauses. The phrase 'with average' referred to a policy covering particular average, ie partial loss. The phrase 'free of particular average' meant that partial loss was not covered.

average adjuster. Impartial specialist entrusted by the shipowner with the adjustment of general average losses. In practice these adjusters handle all types of marine claims except perhaps straightforward cargo claims. Underwriters pay the fee of the adjuster when they are liable for the claim. If no liability attaches the adjuster waives his fee. Adjusters may join the Association of Average Adjusters (qv).

average disbursements. General average contributions (qv) are levied on arrived values but if the ship and cargo are subsequently lost on the voyage, the party incurring general average expenditure will be unable to make a recovery. Consequently the shipowner, who incurs general average disbursements at the port of refuge or elsewhere, effects an average disbursements insurance. In the event of the subsequent total loss of the ship on the remainder of the voyage the expenses can be recovered under this insurance.

average earnings scheme. A pension scheme where the benefit for each year of membership is related to the pensionable earnings for that year.

average rate insurances. When dealing with very large risks fire insurers sometimes charge a flat rate for all buildings and contents. The rate—an 'average'—is presumed to take account of the good and bad features of each risk. Contrary to the practice with blanket policies (qv) separate sums insured are set against the separate risks.

aviation hull deductible insurance policies. A policy under which an airline insures the amount it has at risk as a result of a deductible under its hull policy. It insures losses up to an agreed limit, the level of the deductible, so it becomes an insurance of the deductible itself . The deductible policy is itself subject to a small deductible.

aviation insurance. A specialised field of insurance. The main policies available are: (a) AVN1A. This policy form, which can be adapted, covers hull, third party and passenger liability. It is suitable for general aviation risks. (b) Aerial form—an airport owners' and operators' liability policy (qv). (c) Air displays policy—principally a public liability policy sought by promoters of air meetings and displays. (d) Cargo policy. An 'all risks' cover that, like a voyage policy, runs from start to finish and is not confined solely to that part of the journey involving air travel. (e) Deductible policy. Deductibles (qv) on aircraft insurances can be so large that a demand has emerged for a market in which the deductible itself can be insured. A specialist market caters for this demand. (f) Loss of licence policy. This pays a benefit to commercial pilots who lose their flying licence (or have it suspended) following accidental injury or for other medical reasons. The cover can be provided by separate policy or being added to other policies. (g) Loss of use policy. To cover the decline in earning power when an aircraft is laid-up for repairs following accidental damage. (h) Personal accident insurance. Group personal accident cover can be arranged for both passengers and aircraft crew. Policies are often effected by employers for their aircrew staff who stand to lose good incomes through being 'grounded' by an accident. Policies effected by individual travellers for their own protection are often arranged in the accident department. A relatively recent development is that of satellite (or space) insurance (qv). One feature of aviation insurance has been the tendency for British insurance companies to operate aviation insurance in two pools alongside Lloyd's and the departments of non-pool companies.

AVN1A. The hull and liability aviation policy form. There are three sections. (a) Loss or damage to the aircraft by an insured peril. The insurers will pay the sum insured if the aircraft disappears and is unreported for 60 days. Insurers also pay for reasonable emergency expenses to safeguard the aircraft following an accident subject to a limit of 10 per cent of the sum insured. The section does not cover wear and tear and deterioration, breakdown or failure of any Unit and consequences thereof within the Unit. (b) Legal liability to third parties for death, injury, property damage or destruction caused by an aircraft or article dropped therefrom. The employer's liability risk is excluded as well as death or injury to passengers and custody property (qv). (c) Legal liability for death, injury to passengers subject to exclusions of employees and operational crew. There are also general exclusions including: illegal uses, use outside geographical limits, use by unappointed pilot, whilst aircraft is transported on a conveyance, take-off or landing at unauthorised airfield, contractual liability, passengers in excess of scheduled maximum number, war risks, radioactive contamination, and non-contribution clause.

Aviation Insurance Offices Association. This exists to promote, advance and protect the interests of companies transacting aviation insurance. It ensures joint action where necessary to draw up standard policy wordings and clauses in co-operation with other insurance interests concerned with aviation insurance.

avoidance of certain terms and rights of recovery. A clause under this heading appears in motor insurance and employers' liability policies. These insurances have been made compulsory (Road Traffic Act and Employers' Liability (Compulsory Insurance) Act 1969) to protect the victims of accidents or diseases with a right of claim against the motorist or employer involved. The legislation restricts the right of insurers to avoid 'Act' liability under the policy following a breach by the insured of certain policy conditions (eg admitting liability without the consent of the insurer). The insurer is entitled to recover his loss from the insured where payment is made solely because of the legislative provisions. *See* NON-AVOIDANCE OF COMPULSORY INSURANCE.

B

back-dating. *See* DATING-BACK.

back-to-back arrangements. An arrangement whereby a life insurance and an annuity are effected simultaneously on the same life. The aim is to restore capital to the annuitant's estate when death occurs, usually with the intention of minimising inheritance tax liability. The lump sum purchase of an immediate annuity reduces the purchaser's estate but gives him an income for life. A life insurance on the purchaser's life for the benefit of others is 'backed' on to the annuity. When the life policy proceeds are paid they are free of tax because they do not form a part of the purchaser's estate. If the premiums on the policy are paid out of the policyholder's normal income then they will be exempt from inheritance tax as an exempt transfer. If the associated operations rule applies to the arrangement the effectiveness of the arrangement will be reduced. In practice the policies and annuities are not regarded as being affected by this rule if the policy was issued on full medical evidence of the insured's health and it would have been issued on the same terms if the annuity had not been bought.

back-to-back loan. An alternative to direct overseas investment. It occurs where a unit trust manager (or other investor) deposits sterling with a UK bank, which then arranges for an associate bank overseas to lend them an equivalent amount of foreign currency.

back-service. The period of previous service in employment with which a new member of a company pension scheme can be credited.

bad debts. *See* CREDIT INSURANCE and LEGAL EXPENSES INSURANCE. Commercial contract cover under the latter covers legal expenses for pursuing or defending an action where one of the parties alleges a bad debt on the part of the other arising out of a dispute related to a commercial contract.

bad debts insurance. *See* CREDIT INSURANCE.

baggage insurance. 'All risks' cover on personal effects and luggage generally available under travel insurance policies (qv).

baggage liability limits. The liability of an air carrier for checked baggage of passengers is governed by the Warsaw Convention and the Hague Protocol.

bail bond. A bond guaranteeing the appearance of a person in court which secures the release of that person on bail. If the person fails to appear, the bondsman or bonding company is required to pay the amount of the bond to the court. Some countries, notably Spain, require visiting motorists to provide bail bonds from their insurers as a means of ensuring that funds will be available to meet any damages payable after road accidents.

bailee. A bailee for reward is a person who receives payment for taking possession of the property of another for later return or to be accounted for in a different way, eg delivered. Where the bailment is for the common benefit of both the bailor and the bailee (eg car repair for reward), the bailee is bound to use the ordinary care that a prudent man would use over his own goods. Bailees sometimes use exemption clauses to restrict or remove their common law liability. Where the bailment (gratuitous loan) is solely for the benefit of the bailee (ie a gratuitous bailee), the bailee must exercise the care that a vigilant person would use over his own goods. *See also* BAILMENT.

bailee clause. A shipowner or other carrier is a bailee responsible for the goods entrusted to him. Where loss or damage that is insured under a cargo policy occurs the insurer may acquire subrogation rights against the bailee.

However, the bailee may escape liability if the consignee is dilatory in lodging a claim or has not observed the conditions of the carriage or bailment. The bailee clause in the Institute Cargo Clauses (qv) obliges the insured to take steps to ensure that rights against carriers or bailees are not allowed to lapse by default. Expenses incurred in complying with this clause are payable by the insurers.

bailment. A contract or an agreement under which one person entrusts his property to another on the understanding that it will later be returned or otherwise accounted for, eg delivered to a prescribed destination. Possession gives rise to responsibility and the bailee, ie the party in possession of the property, can insure on a material damage basis, on a liability basis, or as agent or trustee on behalf of the owner. Under legal liability insurances it may be necessary to have the 'custody or control' exclusion (custody property) (qv)) overridden. Policies are suitably drawn for hotel proprietors, garage owners etc

bailor. One who entrusts goods or other property to a bailee (qv).

balance settlement. An arrangement under which the insurer keeps a record of premiums and claims payable with the balance being paid over to the creditor party at the end of the period.

balance sheet. A financial statement in which the assets and liabilities of a company or other organisation are marshalled to disclose the overall state of affairs at a given moment in time. It shows the assets of the company and how they are financed.

balance table. A table used to show the balance of pension that the employer has to purchase for each employee under a pension scheme.

balanced portfolio. Insurers may seek to so arrange their insurance and reinsurance that their total business constitutes a well balanced range of risks and so do not become unduly committed in a limited number of areas, activities, or types of risk. The aim is to spread the exposure by a selective underwriting approach.

balancing charge. A tax payable by a shipowner who receives a claim payment in excess of the book value of the ship.

The excess is deemed to be a profit which attracts the tax.

band earnings. Pay between the lower and upper earnings for national insurance.

banking policy. A reinsurance contract under which premiums are 'banked' with the reinsurer for later return with interest.

bankruptcy and liquidation bond. A bond to guarantee the trustee in bankruptcy appointed by the creditors. If the trustee, who controls the assets of the insolvent party, fails to carry out his duties properly, the surety (usually an insurer) will make good the resultant loss.

bankruptcy clause in lease. A lease often contains a clause forfeiting the leasehold interest should the lessee become bankrupt. A policy to protect the mortgagee can be effected; the loss is the deficiency on the mortgage account where the property comes into the possession of the mortgagee following default of the borrower.

bankruptcy of life policyholder. When a life policyholder is adjudged bankrupt, his policy and personal estate become absolutely vested in the trustee for the time being. Property vests first in the official receiver and in the trustee when appointed. They become statutory assignees and the policy vests in them subject to all equities existing at the date of the receiving order. Notice of the order is usually given to the assurer but there is no obligation to do so. Assignees subsequent to the date of the receiving order do not gain priority over the official receiver.

barratry. An insured peril under a marine insurance policy meaning any wrongful act wilfully committed by the master or crew to the detriment of the owner or charterer of the vessel.

base premium. A reinsurance term describing the cedant's (qv) premium to which the reinsurer's rate is applied.

base value. The value of property at the inception of a valuation-linked insurance.

basic rate. A fundamental rate applied to a whole class of policies of a given description and often published in rating guides. This rate is subject to modification depending on the characteristics of the particular risk under consideration.

basic state pension. The pension payable by the state and commencing for males at age 65 and for females at age 60. The amount payable depends on the individual's national insurance record. Those who have not paid or been credited with sufficient contributions over their working life may have to accept a reduced pension. The amount also depends on whether the individual is married or single.

basis clause. A clause at the foot of a proposal form which makes the proposal form and declaration the whole basis of the contract. It converts representations (qv) in the form into warranties (qv) so that any inaccuracy will entitle the insurer to avoid the contract whether the matter concerned is material or not (*Dawsons Ltd* v *Bonnin* (1922)). The insured's answers may be subject to his 'best knowledge and belief'. The insured agrees that the proposal form and declaration shall be the 'basis of the contract'. *See* STATEMENT OF LONG-TERM INSURANCE PRACTICE and STATEMENT OF NON-LIFE INSURANCE PRACTICE to see how insurers adjust their position in regard to private insurances.

basis of settlement. A statement in a policy as to the method or methods the insurer will adopt in settling a claim. Some material damage policies provide new for old (qv) as alternative for the indemnity basis.

basis of valuation clause. A clause in an open cover (qv) which sets out a basis for the valuation of cargo which has been declared and added to the policy and is the subject of a loss.

batch clause. A products liability policy clause which provides that all claims, whenever made, arising out of the same prepared batch or acquired lot of the product, shall be treated as resulting from one occurrence (or accident or event) and will be subject to the limit of indemnity which applies to any one occurrence (or accident or event). There are alternatives. The clause may state that all claims, whenever made, arising out of the same occurrence will be allocated to the policy year in which the first claim arising from that occurrence is made against the insured and the aggregate limit of indemnity for that year will apply. The 'occurrence' could be defective design, bench error, error in distribution etc. This type of clause safeguards the insurer against claims from numerous individuals, where their injuries have a common cause, being treated as separate accidents or occurrences or separate periods of insurance in terms of the single occurrence limit of indemnity or aggregate limit for the period.

bench error. A products liability insurance (qv) term which describes an error or omission that occurs in the manufacturing or assembly process. Such errors are covered under products liability cover.

beneficiary. The person to whom the proceeds of a policy are to be paid as set forth in its terms. It also refers to a person who will benefit under the terms of a will.

benefit. A term used to describe the amount to be paid upon the happening of the insured event when that amount is agreed at the inception of the contract. *See* BENEFIT POLICY.

benefit policy. A policy under which the amount to be paid upon the happening of the insured event is agreed at the time the contract is made. It is not a contract of indemnity. Life and personal accident policies are not usually contracts of indemnity and are more generally written as benefit policies. Individuals are free to put their own value on their own life and limb but indemnity is not entirely overlooked. The benefits purchased by an insured are restricted by his ability and willingness to pay and insurers are careful not to grant benefits that are excessive in relation to the insured's occupation or earning capacity.

Berne Union. This association, the official name is the International Union of Credit and Investment Insurers, operates under the Swiss Civil Code. The association is concerned with the co-operation of credit insurers and overseas investment insurers in the development of underwriting techniques and in exchanging information on payment experience and other matters of mutual interest. The members work for: (i) the international acceptance of sound principles of export credit insurance and the establishment and maintenance of discipline in terms of credit for international trade; and (ii) international co-operation in fostering a favourable investment climate and in developing and maintaining **sound** principles of foreign investment insurance. The Export Credit Insurance Committee and the Investment Insurance Committee are key groups through which the work of the association is conducted and information exchanged. UK members are the Export Credits Guarantee Department and the Trade Indemnity plc.

best advice. Following the Financial Services Act 1986 (qv) the Securities and Investments Board (qv) requires anyone selling life assurance to provide 'best advice' as to the most suitable product for his client from a range across the market or his own company, depending on his status (*see* polarisation under the Financial Services Act 1986). The advice is to be irrespective of other considerations, such as commission, and must be based on knowledge of the client's circumstances at the time of sale.

best execution. A term defined by FIMBRA (qv) as effecting a transaction on behalf of a client on the best available terms and paying due regard to matters such as the charges payable, the reputation of third parties, and the size of the transaction. It does not apply to life or pension contracts, or where the intermediary is acting on behalf of a person authorised under the Financial Services Act 1986 (qv), an authorised person's client or a professional investor whose client agreement expressly excludes the best execution rule.

betterment. An improvement in the condition of property after repair or reinstatement following damage caused by an insured peril under a contract of indemnity. For example, respraying a damaged car may eliminate pre-accident blemishes and generally improve the appearance of the car. Insurers may call upon the insured to make a 'betterment' contribution to allow for the improvement.

bicycle insurance. An 'all risks' insurance for replacing or repairing bicycles. Usually insured as an extension of a household contents policy but separate insurances are available. Cover can be arranged with some insurers on a 'new for old' basis. Other extra benefits can include personal accident cover and legal liability to third parties.

bid/offer spread. Bid is the price received by the holder of units in a unit linked policy or when sold back to the fund managers. Offer is the price at which the same units could be bought on the same day. The bid/offer spread is the gap between the two prices. Usually there is a difference of between 5 per cent and 7 per cent which covers the costs of the fund and its profits.

bid (or tender) bond. A conditional bond (qv) to satisfy a principal in the construction industry that the contractor's bid or tender is a reasonable one and that, if accepted, the contractor will enter into the contract and effect a performance bond (qv). The insurer as surety stands to pay the costs incurred by the principal in scrutinising another tender if the conditions are not met.

bill of exchange. The authorisation by the buyer for the seller to draw on the buyer's bank the sum stated (ie the price of the goods) on a due date, usually when the goods reach their destination. The bank will not discount the bill of exchange unless the specified goods are insured against marine risks and the policy lodged with the bank as collateral security.

bill of lading. The document evidencing the contract between a shipowner and a cargo owner for the carriage of goods by sea. It specifies the name of the shipper; the date and place of the shipment; the name and destination of the vessel; the description, quality, and destination of the goods; and the freight which is to be paid. A clean bill carries no qualifying endorsement but a dirty or claused bill carries qualifications, eg 'badly packed'. The bill is also the receipt for the goods. Copies are kept by the master, the shipper and the consignee. It is a document of title transferable by endorsement and delivery, giving the holder the right to sue thereon but is not a negotiable instrument so that a transferee has no better title than that enjoyed by the transferor.

bill of lading freight. The amount payable to the shipowner for the carriage of cargo. By common law it is earned only on completion unless otherwise agreed. *See* ADVANCE FREIGHT.

binding authority. An authority granted by an insurer (company, underwriter or reinsurer) to an agent to enable the agent to accept insurance business on behalf of the insurer or underwriter concerned within specified limits. The agent (sometimes called a 'coverholder') collects the premium, issues certificates of insurance, services claims, and is fully empowered to commit the insurer within the terms of the authority. Binding authorities have been particularly favoured by Lloyd's in the non-marine market, especially overseas where coverholders (qv) have been active in accepting risks on behalf of the syndicates. Binding authorities have been described as the only way of getting around the rule about writing business only in the Room (qv) at Lloyd's. A set of regulations, passed by the Committee of Lloyd's, lays down procedures for the registration of binding authorities and the approval of coverholders by a panel of underwriters.

birth certificate. A document certifying the birth of an individual and therefore the best proof as to a person's age. Ideally the certificate should be produced at the inception of a life insurance contract so that age is admitted and subsequent proof not called for, eg at time of claim. Shortened versions are normally acceptable. If a birth certificate is not available (eg life insured born overseas and records unobtainable) the insurer usually accepts the best available evidence (eg entry in family bible).

'blanket' motor insurance certificate. A motor insurance certificate describing the insured vehicle in general rather than specific terms, eg 'any private type car owned by the policyholder or hired to him under a hire purchase agreement and registered in his name'. Changes in vehicle do not necessitate the issue of fresh certificates but such changes must be notified to the insurer.

'blanket' motor insurance policy. A private car motor policy which describes the vehicles covered in general terms rather than specifying the vehicles. The policy refers to any motor vehicle details of which have been notified to the insurer. When a change of vehicles takes place the substitution does not have to be endorsed on the policy. *See also* BLANKET MOTOR INSURANCE CERTIFICATE.

blanket policy. A policy which, in a single sum insured, covers a number of separate items of property without subdivision of the amount. The approach is used in fire insurance for large risks and also in fidelity guarantee to cover the whole staff without mention of name or position, the premium being computed on the number of employees in specific categories (eg accounting officials, non-accounting officials).

blanket rate. *See* AVERAGE RATE INSURANCE.

blast furnace clause. A clause in employers' liability policy excluding work on blast furnaces. The clause is equally a gasometer clause, a towers clause, a hangar clause depending on the point at issue, given the extensive list of buildings in the clause. Essentially it is a restrictive endorsement (qv) in an employers' liability policy which excludes work on a variety of buildings because of their height and/or other physical hazard aspects. The buildings concerned are listed and typically include: gasometers, towers, steeples, bridges, viaducts, blast furnaces, colliery overhead winding gear, hangars, and roofs other than of private dwellings and/or shops, consisting of not more than three floors (including the ground floor) and attic.

blind treaty. A reinsurance treaty under which the reinsurer is not given details of the individual risks ceded under the treaty. Bordereaux (qv) issued by cedants under open treaties containing details of all business placed under the treaty are not used. 'Blind treaties' take the form of periodical summaries of premiums and claims. The reinsurer works, more or less blindly, placing reliance on the record and standing of the cedant. The reinsurer reserves the right, rarely used, to examine the books and papers of the cedant relating to any risk or claim within the treaty.

block limit. The limit used by a property insurer to put a ceiling on the maximum amount of business he will write in respect of any one block of buildings.

block policy. Sometimes used in marine insurance where a merchant has a number of small sendings periodically by rail, parcel post, or road conveyances for inland transit. It is prepared for a sum estimated to be sufficient cover for the sendings for the next twelve months. It covers all of the insured's business within its terms during the period subject, normally, to a limit per sending. A block premium is charged at inception.

block system. A system whereby industrial assurance companies divide the country into areas known as blocks with an agent in charge of each block. Existing policyholders moving into an area have their business automatically transferred to the agent for the area.

blood relative clause. A clause in industrial life policies which enables the assurer to discharge his liability by payment of the sum due under the policy to the spouse of the assured or relation by blood or marriage. It is also known as the Da Costa clause.

bloodstock insurance. An insurance designed for the bloodstock industry and racehorse owners. The insurance covers bloodstock for death from accident or disease including breeding. The policy may be extended in respect of stallions to cover congenital and accidental infertility.

blue list. A term referring to Lloyd's Shipping Index (qv).

boat insurance. This term covers various types of vessels (eg dinghies, yachts and motor boats) used for pleasure purposes by their owners. A number of insurers issue their own proposals and policies for yachts, dinghies, motor boats and speed boats but in some cases hulls are covered by the standard marine policy with one of the various standard clauses (eg Institute Yacht Clauses) attached. Generally cover operates while the vessel is in the water, on land, with third party cover added. Exceptions include loss or damage to sails and protective covers which are split or blown away by the wind and racing is not automatically included for all vessels—if a dinghy is so used it is necessary to add the Racing Risks Extension Clause. It is possible to add boat insurance to household 'new for old' contents policies with some insurers. This will not apply to dinghies and motor boats capable of travelling at more than a certain speed (eg 20 mph (17 knots) or over a certain age (eg 10 years) or over 5 metres long.

bodily (or physical) defects. Proposers for life and personal accident insurances must disclose any physical defects or infirmities. This is not only material to the assessment of the risk but also in personal accident insurance may necessitate an amendment in the schedule of benefits to ensure that the benefit (eg loss of limb or sight) is payable only when caused by an insured peril. Personal accident policies generally exclude disablement directly or indirectly consequent upon any bodily (or physical) infirmity which existed prior to the accident.

bodily injury. 1. *Personal accident insurance.* The term is used to exclude disease from natural causes, but disease proximately caused by accident is bodily injury for the purpose of an insured event unless specifically excluded. This is merely an application of the doctrine of proximate cause and is well illustrated by *Etherington* v *Lancashire & Yorkshire Accident Insurance Co* (1909) 1 K.B. 591. The policyholder was thrown from his horse while hunting and because of his injury was unable to walk. He laid in wet conditions before help came and his resultant cold developed into pneumonia and he died. The chain of causation was unbroken and the court attributed the death to the accident and not pneumonia. Mental shock, fright or grief, unless taking the form of a definite illness is not within the term. 2. *Liability insurance.* The term bodily is used in liability policies as a form of loss within the scope of the policy. The modern tendency is for the insurer to define the term in the policy. A particularly wide wording under public and products liability policies is: 'Bodily injury includes death, illness or disease or mental injury, mental anguish, shock, false arrest, invasion of right of privacy, detention, false arrest, false imprisonment, false eviction, malicious prosecution, libel, slander or defamation of character'. Clearly this brings injury to feelings within the term but as it is likely to be qualified by the word accidental, deliberate libels etc will not be covered. There is common ground among all liability insurers in defining bodily injury to include death, disease and illness. Some insurers use the term personal injury and proceed to define that as including illness. The intention is to cover bodily injury and not injury to feelings whether accompanied or unaccompanied by physical injuries. Older liability policies tended to use the term personal injury but most insurers abandonded it in favour of the narrower term 'bodily injury' which more accurately represents their intentions. The Road Traffic Act 1988 obliges the users of vehicles on a road to insure, inter alia, their legal liability for bodily injury to third parties.

boiler. A vessel in which water is heated or steam is generated. The explosion risk associated with steam boilers has attracted legislative control. Every part of a steam boiler, receiver or container must be of good construction, sound material, adequate strength and free from any obvious defect. The outlet of every steam container must be kept open at all times and free from obstruction. Every steam boiler and its attachments must be properly maintained and examined by a competent person at specified intervals (14 months) and after extensive repairs (Factories Act 1961, ss. 32–35). Explosion of boilers used for domestic purposes is covered under the standard fire policy. Explosion or collapse of steam boilers or other steam pressure vessels belonging to the insured is covered in the engineering insurance department in terms of material damage (including surrounding property) and public liability risks. Statutory inspections are carried out by the specialist staff of engineering insurers.

boiler and pressure plant. The type of plant insurable under a boiler and pressure plant policy includes: steam boilers; economisers; superheaters; steam and feed piping; hot water heating and domestic supply boilers; heating, piping, and radiators, and other ancillaries, such as calorifiers; hot water storage tanks, etc; steam jacketed pans; air heating and drying batteries; ironing machines and presses; hot plates; bakers' steam tube ovens; air receivers—in effect, any items under pressure or under vacuum.

bond. A single bond is a contract under seal to pay a sum of money (a common money bond), or a sealed writing acknowledging a debt, present or future. A double or conditional bond is where a condition is added that if the obligor does or forbears from doing some act the obligation is void. The person who binds himself is the obligor and the person in whose favour the bond is drawn is the obligee. Technically a bond is defeasible upon condition subsequent with the promise imposing a penalty for non-performance of the condition which is the real object of the bond. In a common money bond one person may bind himself to pay a given sum of money (eg £1000) at a stated time if he has not paid a smaller sum (say, £750) at an earlier time. In a conditional bond a person may promise another (the obligee) that he will pay a given sum of money on a certain date (eg date for completion of work) with the condition that if before that date a third party has completed the work the bond will be void. Performance bonds etc (qv) are conditional bonds along these lines. The insurer in these instances is the obligor or surety (qv) otherwise called guarantor. In fidelity guarantee (also called suretyship insurance) (qv) bonds are issued whereby the insurer pays a money sum if a person fails to perform his duties properly—*see* COURT BONDS, LOCAL GOVERNMENT BONDS and GOVERNMENT BONDS for examples. Life insurers sell so-called 'bonds' but these are generally in the nature of single premium life policies and deferred annuities. *See* INCOME BONDS, GROWTH BONDS, GUARANTEED BONDS, INVESTMENT BONDS, MINI BONDS, SECOND-HAND BONDS, and SINGLE PREMIUM BONDS. N.B. A bond is also an instrument of indebtedness issued by companies and governments to secure the repayment of money borrowed by them. Insurance companies invest substantial sums in the UK Government by purchasing its bonds.

bonds, single premium. A bond is an arrangement whereby in return for a lump sum (the minimum investment is usually £500 to £1000), the insurer provides either a guaranteed income payable monthly or annually (guaranteed income bond) or accumulates the interest in order to make a cash payment at the end of the term (growth (or single premium) bonds). In both cases terms of one to five years are common. The return on growth bonds may be linked to some form of equity, property or cash fund operated by the insurer. Usually the investor is permitted to initiate the switch of his investment between the various funds but in practice most money is held in a 'managed fund' and the insurer's fund manager decides how the money should be invested at any one time. Each year the investor is permitted to draw up to 5 per cent of the original investment without liability to income or capital gains tax. The liability to pay tax is deferred until the bond is encashed, matures, or the holder dies. The rate of tax is that which applies at the time of payment. The arrangement is attractive to higher rate taxpayers who can get a net return of 5 per cent on their original investment for up to 20 years while arranging for encashment to occur when their tax rate is reduced.

bond switching. The switching of money in a life insurance bond from one fund to another controlled by the life insurer. *See* SWITCHING FACILITIES.

bonded goods. Dutiable goods in respect of which a bond (qv) for the payment of the duty has been given to the Commissioners of Customs and Excise. *See* CUSTOMS AND EXCISE BOND.

bonded value. Where goods are normally sold in bond (*see also* BONDED WAREHOUSE) the bonded price is considered to be the 'gross value'. However, the Marine Insurance Act 1960, s. 71(4) defines gross value as the wholesale price or estimated value ruling on the day of sale after freight, landing charges and duty have been paid.

bonded warehouse. A warehouse for goods upon which excise duty has not been paid. The warehouse owner becomes the subject of a government bond (qv), ie a general or warehouse bond or a removal bond. This is to guarantee payment of the duty to HM Customs & Excise in the event that goods are removed from the warehouse without payment of the duty.

bonus. 1. In *life assurance* a bonus is an addition to benefits allotted periodically by the assurer to its 'with profits' policyholders from its surplus (ie profit). Life assurers decide upon the divisible surplus after carrying out the valuation annually to comply with the Insurance Companies Regulations, 1983. Once the periodic bonuses are declared they are guaranteed. They are generally reversionary, ie payable at the same time and in the same circumstances as the sum assured. Under a uniform bonus system the bonus rate is the same for all 'with' profits policyholders. Under a contribution system the bonuses reflect a policy's contribution to the surplus and therefore varies according to the policyholder's age, type of policy, term, and date effected. The principal methods of distributing the bonus include: (a) Uniform simple reversionary bonus. A uniform addition proportionate to the original sum assured alone and payable with that sum on death or maturity. (b) Uniform Compound Reversionary Bonus. A uniform addition proportionate to the sum assured and accrued bonuses at the date of declaration. Bonus thus earns bonus and is compounded. The bonuses are also payable with the sum assured. (c) Cash bonus. This method is not widely used. The bonus can be declared as a cash sum rather than a reversionary value. (d) Bonus in reduction of premiums. The bonus is declared as a permanent reduction in premium until the premiums payable are finally eliminated. Any subsequent bonuses can be cash or reversionary. (e) Tontine bonus system. A system under which bonuses are retained in a fund for periodic distribution among survivors. *See* TONTINE. (f) Guaranteed bonus. This bonus is not dependent on the earnings of the office which, under contract, increases the sum assured periodically. It is really a non-profit assurance with an increasing sum assured. (g) Interim bonus. A bonus added to a policy which matures or becomes a claim in the interval between two periodic declarations. (h) Mortuary bonus. In industrial life assurance surplus can be distributed by a mortuary bonus which is an addition to the sum assured under policies becoming death claims during the period. Such a bonus also applies to endowment policies maturing during the same period but is still called a mortuary bonus. It operates as a reversionary bonus. (i) Terminal bonus. A method of distributing surplus to policyholders without declaring it during the currency of the policy. The bonus is declared at the declaration date as an amount to be added to policies becoming claims by death or maturity before the next declaration date. The bonus is expressed as a percentage of the accrued bonuses. Life offices are prepared to allow terminal bonuses to go up or down to reflect their current investment position but prefer to maintain consistency and growth in regard to their reversionary bonuses. Consequently during periods of high inflation and high interest rates when they may accumulate large divisible surpluses, the offices can provide additional rewards for the 'with profits' policyholders by increasing the terminal bonus. This is generally preferred to making significant increases in the reversionary bonuses only to have to reduce them at the next declaration. 2. *See* NO CLAIM BONUS.

bonus declaration. A declaration by a life insurer as to the rate at which bonuses will be allotted to 'with profits' policies.

bonus distribution. The act of distributing profits among with the 'with profits' life policyholders. For methods of distribution see bonus (qv).

bonus loading. The amount added to a life insurance premium to distinguish 'with profits' policies from those without profits. The payment of this higher premium entitles the policyholder to participate in any divisible surplus available for bonus distribution at any bonus valuation.

bonus-malus system. A motor insurance system that gives discounts for claims-free driving and makes surcharges for claims. The system is widely used in Europe. For the UK system *see* NO CLAIMS DISCOUNT.

bonus-protected policy. An alternative to a whole life 'with profits' policy. It is a combination of a 'with profits' policy with a decreasing term assurance. The benefits under the term assurance are so calculated as to maintain the cover under the two policies at a chosen level, provided that the assumed rate of bonus is maintained on the whole life element. This type of policy is also known as a bonus-reinforcement policy, a term also applied to low-cost endowment schemes.

bonus reinforcement policy. *See* HOUSE PURCHASE SCHEMES (LOW COST ENDOWMENT).

bonus reserve. A reserve created by life insurers for the payment of future bonuses to with profits policyholders.

bonus reserve valuation. A method used to value a life insurer's liability.

book debts insurance. Insurance against loss due to the inability to trace and collect from debtors following the destruction of accounting records by fire or other insured perils. Cover includes (i) 'increase in cost of working' so that payment is made for reasonable efforts to reproduce the accounts and trace details of debts and debtors (ii) auditors charges. There is no cover for bad debts (*see* CREDIT INSURANCE). The sum insured, which should represent the maximum debt outstanding at any one time, is subject to average (qv). Each month the insured declares the total amount outstanding from his debtors (hire purchase or credit sales). The premium is charged at a rate per cent on the average outstanding balance. The premium is adjustable annually subject only to the retention by the insurer of 50 per cent. Book debts are not insured by a business interruption insurance (qv) as they will have been incurred before the date of the damage and not related to loss of turnover after that event. The insurance is otherwise known as loss of book debts insurance.

book reserve scheme. A pension scheme under which the employer is responsible for the payment of the benefits which are financed by a provision in the employer's accounts.

bordereau. A detailed list of premiums and claims prepared monthly or quarterly by cedants (qv) or coverholders (qv) for reinsurers or underwriters to advise them periodically of risks accepted and claims incurred under treaty arrangements or binding authorities. Bordereaux are no longer required under treaties as an invariable rule.

borrowed servants. Servants (employees) who are loaned or hired out by their general or usual employer to other employers for specific purposes. There is a strong presumption that the general employer will remain liable for the torts of that servant while hired or lent to the special employer unless the general employer can show that control has passed to the special employer (*Mersey Docks & Harbour Board* v *Coggins & Griffiths* (1947). See Condition 8 of the Contractors Plant-hire Association's Conditions (CPA) which makes the hirer responsible for all claims from the operation of plant by the driver/operator who is supplied with it.

both to blame collision clause. This is clause 3 of the Institute Cargo Clauses. It indemnifies the cargo owner against the costs of reimbursing the shipowner who, under foreign law, has been called upon to pay 50 per cent of a cargo loss to a third party shipowner following a collision in which both were to blame. In the USA if both are to blame, they are judged equally to blame and the cargo owner can recover any loss in full from the third party shipowner who can then recover 50 per cent from the ship carrying the cargo. Exceptions in the Running Down Clause (qv) prevent the shipowner from making a recovery from the hull insurers, nor is the Protecting and Indemnity Club liable. Consequently the shipowner passes the risk to the cargo owner under the contract of affreightment and the Both to Blame Collision Clause provides the latter with the necessary cover.

bottom painting clause. An Institute Time Clause that relieves the insurer in all circumstances from scraping or painting the vessel's bottom. This rec-ognises that these matters relate to running costs.

bottomry. A loan raised by the master of a vessel when money is needed for the voyage when other methods of raising money have failed. The loan, which is secured on the vessel or vessel and cargo, is not repayable if the venture is lost. The term is now of academic interest only but it illustrates an early form of risk transfer (qv). The creditor acquired an insurable interest in the loan (Marine Insurance Act 1906 s. 10) and this would extend to the interest payable.

box. The space occupied by an underwriter and his staff in the Room at Lloyd's (qv).

bracketed provisions. *See* EXCEPTIONAL CIRCUMSTANCES CLAUSE.

Bradley v Eagle Star Insurance Co. (1989). A Court of Appeal decision to the effect that no action will lie under the Third Parties (Rights Against Insurers) Act 1930 if the insured defendant has been dissolved. The plaintiff's employer had been dissolved in 1976 and liability under the Act could only attach against the insurer when a liability could be proved against the company. As the company had ceased to exist no liability against it could be established.

branch. 1. An autonomous overseas office, which has full underwriting authority, and is staffed by the insurer's own employees. 2. A local office of an insurance company. The degree of authority for underwriting varies among insurers and may depend upon whether the branch is subject to the control of a regional office or is directly responsible to head office.

breach of statutory duty. Breach of a duty imposed by statute (eg Factories Act 1961 (qv)). The breach may give rise to both criminal sanctions and civil liability. The main considerations in claims based on breach of statute are: (a) was the defendant in breach? (b) does the Act confer a right upon the plaintiff to sue for damages in a civil action? The statute may provide for criminal proceedings and it is not always clear whether a civil claim can be founded upon its breach; (c) proof that the plaintiff has suffered damage; (d) regulations may apply instead of the statute. (e) the plaintiff may be responsible for the breach and while this is not often a complete defence it may give rise to contributory negligence (qv).

breach of warranty. Failure to comply with a warranty by not doing something the insured has promised to do or doing something he has promised not to do or making a mis-statement. A mis-statement in a warranty invalidates the contract whether it arises from innocent mistake or fraudulent intent. Breach of warranty renders the contract voidable by the insurer, notwithstanding that a loss has no connection with the breach, or that the breach has subsequently been remedied during the currency of the insurance. Where the warranties are incorporated in the contract as a result of a declaration in the proposal form the insurer can avoid the contract *ab initio* (qv) and does not have to prove materiality—otherwise the contract is voidable from the date of the breach. The Report of the Law Commission 104 proposed that insurers should not be able to repudiate claims for breach of warranty where: (a) the warranty breached was not in any way related to the type of loss that has occurred; (b) the breach had no effect on the cause or size of the loss. Insurers have voluntarily met these requirements for private insurances by way of the Statements of Practice.

Breach of Warranty Clause. Institute Time Clause No. 3 (1/10/83) indicating that the insured is held covered for breach of warranty as to cargo, trade, locality, towage, salvage services or date of sailing provided notice is given and any additional premium paid.

breach of warranty insurance. Banks who fund the purchase of aircraft usually take a lien on the aircraft but may stand to lose substantial amounts if the hull insurance is invalidated by a breach of warranty by the insured. As a result they seek protection for the outstanding amount of their loans by a breach of warranty insurance which compensates them if the primary insurance is breached. The cover may be arranged by separate policy or endorsement of the hull insurance.

breach of warranty of authority. An action for damages may be brought by a third party against an agent who acts in excess of the authority granted to him by his principal (*Collen v Wright* (1857) 8 E and B 647). Professional persons who insure against liability for professional negligence can normally extend their policies to cover breach of warranty of authority.

breakage. Where caused by the named perils under Institute Cargo Clauses (B) and (C) the risk of breakage is covered. Institute Cargo Clauses (A) provide 'all risks' cover and so ordinary breakage will be covered subject only to the exclusions. In fixing the premium the underwriter will be influenced by the susceptibility of the subject-matter to damage and the method and quality of the packaging. Breakable goods (eg crockery) are sometimes insured 'excluding breakage unless caused by the vessel or craft being stranded, sunk, burnt or in collision'. As most breakage claims arise from negligence wider cover is usually required and the General Exclusion Clause (qv), unlike the Marine Insurance Act 1906, s. 55(2)(c), omits any reference to 'ordinary breakage'. The Act states that unless otherwise provided the insurer is not liable for breakage. Where machinery is insured it is customary to include the Replacement Clause (qv). This limits the insurer's liability to the cost of replacing and forwarding and refitting the broken part, thereby obviating any possible claim for total loss.

breakdown. *See* BREAKDOWN INSURANCE.

breakdown insurance. Electrical plant, oil engines, steam engines, pumps, and air compressors are the main items of plant insured under breakdown insurance by engineering insurers. Breakdown means the breaking or burning out of any part while the plant is running that causes a sudden stoppage which necessitates repair before resuming work. In the case of a lift or crane it also means the actual and complete severance of a rope but not the breakage or abrasion of wires or strands which may render renewal of a rope necessary. In the case of water-cooled engines the term breakdown is so defined as to include fracture of the cylinder, cylinder head, or water jacket by frost rendering the engine inoperative. The basic cover under breakdown insurance relates only to self-damage, ie actual damage to the insured item. The policy can be extended to cover damage to surrounding property and third party. Wear and tear and certain types of failure (according to the type of plant concerned) are excluded. Insurers add an inspection and report service to the insurance. There are a number of extensions to the standard breakdown policy. *See* BREAKDOWN RISKS EXTENSIONS. *See also* STOCK DETERIORATION INSURANCE.

breakdown recovery. The usual form of motor policy covers the cost of removing a vehicle from the scene of the accident when it has sustained damage insured under the policy. No such costs are covered when a breakdown (as opposed to an accident) has occurred. Consequently a supplementary scheme offered by Lloyd's and others covers the cost of vehicle recovery after breakdown. Some extended warranty insurances (qv) may include breakdown recovery costs.

breakdown risks (extensions). The engineering breakdown policy can be extended to include: (a) damage to bearings due to breakage or sudden overheating; (b) damage to minor parts of engines, air compressors, etc, such as piston rings, springs, etc; (c) wiring between electric motors and starters, and between generators and switchboards; (d) thermostats and the wiring between the thermostat, controller and starter; (e) loss of oil from transformer tanks as a result of breakdown; (f) damage to surrounding property arising out of breakdown; (g) liability for third party personal injury; (h) damage from extraneous causes; (i) damage to goods being lifted by specified cranes and other lifting-machines, or, in the case of a goods lift, to the contents of the cage; (j) disruption and explosion of turbines; (k) loss of refrigerant due to breakdown, damage to brine pipes by sudden breakage or bursting including loss of brine, deterioration of stock.

British Insurance (Atomic Energy) Committee. The body which set up the pool of insurers to cover nuclear perils (qv).

British Insurance and Investment Brokers Association (BIIBA). BIIBA was formed in 1977 and represents registered insurance brokers and authorised investment intermediaries. It aims to enhance the status and recognition of members through the maintenance of high standards, public relations, government and parliamentary contacts.

British Maritime Law Association. The organisation which co-ordinates the various sectors of the shipping industry and includes both the London marine market, underwriting hull and cargo business, and the Protecting and Indemnity Clubs (qv) underwriting shipowners' liabilities in mutual associations.

British Rainfall Organisation. An organisations whose members take rainfall measurements all over the country. In weather policies the insured event is a minimum level of rain in a given location as verified by the organisation.

broiler cover. A special damage/business interruption insurance for poultry farmers rearing chickens by broiler techniques. The premium is based on the value of birds being delivered for sale. The risks covered include: fortuitous damage to buildings, machines, plant and feeding; machinery breakdown; accidental failures of public supply of electricity or water; violent death of birds by accident caused by visible external means excluding poisoning or disease; theft following violent or forcible entry or exit from the premises. The interruption cover is not subject to a material damage warranty (qv).

brokerage. 1. The commission and fee income received by an insurance broker. Normally commission is received from the insurer in consideration for broking or placing the business with them but fees may also be charged by brokers to their clients. 2. A USA term to describe an insurance broking company, firm or office. 3. The fee paid to a broker who arranges reinsurance cover for a ceding office.

broker. *See* INSURANCE BROKER.

broker-oriented company. An insurance company that secures its business exclusively, or almost exclusively, through insurance brokers. This is often a feature of companies transacting large volumes of motor insurance and other personal lines business. Some may extend their facilities to consultants who are full-time insurance intermediaries.

Brokers' Code of Conduct. A code established by the Registration Committee of the Insurance Brokers' Registration Council to which registered insurance brokers are required to adhere in order to regulate professional standards. The code is administered by the Disciplinary Committee on behalf of the Council. The code calls upon a registered insurance broker to act objectively and, *inter alia*, with good faith. He must observe confidentiality unless acting with specific authority or in the course of negotiating with insurers. An insurance broker must not use information to his own advantage or that of a third party. Advertising is strictly controlled, eg the broker must avoid extravagant claims, advertisements for his own services must be factual only, must not promote the policies of a single insurer (except in justifiable circumstances), where benefits are advertised the advertisement must show the distinction between contractual benefits and possible benefits. Advice is to be given without bias and the broker must disclose his 'terms of trade' if he wishes to make a charge above his normal commission. In the event of a policyholder wishing to transfer an insurance to another insurance broker, he must co-operate to meet the needs of the policyholder. In the choice of an insurer the broker must use his judgment objectively and carefully and disclose the insurer to the policyholder.

broker's cover note. A note or document issued by an insurance broker confirming that an insurance has been effected in certain terms. It amounts to a warranty to his client that his instructions have been carried out and does not impose liability on an insurer who has not actually entered into any agreement and so if the cover note is issued in anticipation of making such an agreement which is not forthcoming the broker will be liable for breach of warranty. A broker's note is not binding on the insurer (*Broit* v *S Cohen & Son (NSW) Ltd (1926)*). The issue of a note does not make the broker an insurer.

broker's daily statement. A frequently issued statement issued by Lloyd's Policy Signing Office to brokers to inform them of insurances notified to the underwriting syndicates.

broker's lien. In marine insurance the broker is liable to the insurer for the premium regardless of his ability to collect it from the insured. Consequently, the Marine Insurance Act, s. 53(2) grants him a lien on the policy which entitles him to retain the policy until the insured pays the premium. The lien is valuable as: no claim can be collected without production of the policy; the insured may wish to deposit the policy with his bank; or pass it to another interested party. The lien applies not only to the premium on the policy but the balance of any insurance account due to the broker. The lien has been held to apply in other classes of insurance (*Busteed* v *West of England Fire and Life Assurance Co* (1857) (Life assurance) in respect of the premium but not the balance due on any insurance account.

broker's open cover. This is a variation of the ordinary facultative reinsurance (qv) method under which a reinsurer agrees in advance to accept reinsurance from a reinsurance broker. The reinsurer becomes obliged to accept a share of any business ceded to it through the broker who thus acquires a facility for automatic reinsurance.

brokers' slips. Slips used by brokers (following marine practice) when placing fire business. Slips contain details of the proposer's name, nature of risk and address, total sum insured, rate (if agreed) and term. If the insurers accept, they indicate the amount of their acceptance and initial the slip accordingly.

building rate. Fire insurances are often rated separately for the buildings and contents. The terms 'building rate' and 'contents rate' have emerged as a result.

building risk policy (marine). A policy effected by shipbuilders to cover the vessel against all risks whilst under construction, launching, trial trips, and until delivery to her owners.

Building Society block policy. A block or master policy under which a large number of buildings, mainly private dwellings, are insured on a 'household comprehensive' basis. The buildings insured at any one time are those listed in a schedule maintained by the society. Individual property owners are not given a policy but are supplied with full details of the cover. The insurance is index-linked (qv).

Building Society indemnities. Building Societies often work to a fixed percentage of the purchase price of a house (eg 90 per cent) when fixing the level of their mortgage advance but will lend more if an indemnity is obtained. The borrower pays a single premium for the indemnity to secure the guarantee of compensation for the Society if there is default in respect of the additional advance. These indemnities are sometimes known as mortgage guarantee insurance.

Building Society linked life assurance. One of a number of alternatives to a conventional 'with profits' policy. The investment element of the premium is concentrated in designated building society investments and not investments more generally.

buildings. The term is defined in material damage policies. 1. In household policies it is 'the private dwelling house . . . and all the domestic offices, stables, garages, outbuildings, greenhouses, swimming pools, terraces, patios, driveways, footpaths, being on the same premises and used in connection therewith including landlord's fixtures and fittings therein or thereon and the walls, gates and fences around and pertaining thereto.' The term dwelling house is followed by a description of the construction that conforms to the insurer's notion of a standard risk. This means a dwelling which is 'brick, stone or concrete built and roofed with slates, tiles, concrete, asphalt, metal or sheets or slabs composed entirely of incombustible mineral ingredients except as specially mentioned'. The premium is increased for buildings of non- standard construction. There is no reference in the policy as to the construction of the outbuildings etc which remain insured even though constructed differently, eg timber built, from the dwelling house. 2. Under the standard fire policy used by businesses buildings are defined as: buildings including the landlord's fixtures and fittings therein and thereon unless otherwise stated constructed of brick, stone or concrete and roofed with slates, tiles, metal, concrete, asphalt or sheets or slabs composed entirely of incombustible mineral ingredients. Unless specifically insured Buildings excludes annexes and small outside buildings and conveyors' trunks, lines, wires, service pipes, and other equipment the property of the insured or for which he is responsible, walls and (except in so far as the policy covers storm and tempest or flood) gates and fences. 3. For the purposes of the Theft Act 1968 (qv), buildings includes inhabited vehicles or vessels, entry into which as a trespasser with intent to steal is burglary.

buildings insurance. A property insurance covering the house, flat, factory, office, or other buildings owned and/or occupied by the insured.

bungalow insurance. A special householders' comprehensive policy offered specifically for one-storey buildings. It is really a marketing term aimed at attracting the business of bungalow owners away from insurers who do not offer preferential terms for single storey dwellings. The difference is in the rating which is lower than that charged for two-storey dwellings. The insurer offering the preferential terms does so on the basis that repair costs are lower for bungalows than multi-storey or two-storey buildings where extensive scaffolding and hoisting equipment is often required. Few insurers make this distinction between single-storey dwellings and others.

burden of proof. 1. *Losses.* The onus is upon the insured to prove that his loss is within the operative clause of the policy in terms of both its cause, ie caused by an insured peril, and its loss, ie a form of loss covered by the clause. It is for the insurer to prove that the loss has been caused by an excepted peril. If the insurer has cut down the scope of the operative clause by qualifying the insured peril (*see* QUALIFIED PERILS) the insured must prove that the loss was caused by the qualified peril and not just the peril alone. 2. *Other issues*. It is for the insurer to prove that the insured is in breach of the duty of utmost good faith (qv), or breach of condition or warranty, unless the policy is so drawn that the insured has to prove that he has not broken a policy condition (*Bond Air Services* v *Hill* (1955) 2 QB 417).

burglary. Defined in the Theft Act 1968, s. 9 as the offence where a person '(a) enters any building or part of a building as a trespasser and with the intent to commit any such offence as is mentioned in subsection (2); or having entered any building or part of a building he steals or attempts to steal anything in the building or that part of it or inflicts or attempts to inflict on any person therein any grievous bodily harm'. 'The offences referred to in subsection 1(a) above are offences of stealing anything in the building or part of a building in question, of inflicting on any person therein any grievous bodily harm or raping any woman therein, and of doing unlawful damage to the building or anything therein'. If the term burglary is used in a policy which does not define the term, the court will apply the same meaning as given in this section of the Theft Act. The usual practice is for the insurer to provide cover against loss following forcible and violent entry into or exit from the premises (qv). *See also* AGGRAVATED BURGLARY.

burglary distress insurance. The victim of a burglary may be so distressed by the event as to want to move from the scene of the crime. A special scheme exists under which the removal costs are covered up to £1000 in those cases where the outcome is such that the insured or a member of his family needs medical treatment, physical or psychiatric. The decision to move must occur within 12 months of the entry to the house.

burglary insurance. *See* THEFT INSURANCE.

burner policy. A term sometimes used in aviation insurance to describe a policy covering potentially exceptional risk situations, as with helicopters etc

burning cost. A method of calculating the premium for non-proportional reinsurances or large industrial risks insured on a direct basis. The premium payable is directly related to the claims experience. In reinsurance there are minimum and maximum levels of premium expressed as a percentage of the cedant's underlying premiums. The reinsurer reviews the previous experience (say over 5 years) of the cedant to ascertain what proportion of that premium income would have been 'burned up' by reinsurance claims. The reinsurer loads up the resultant percentage by a figure of, normally, 100/70 to allow for profit and administration. If the claims burn up 5 per cent of the premium income over the period, the adjusted figure will give the reinsurer a premium based on 7.14 per cent of the cedant's premium income. This provides the basis for a deposit premium which is adjusted when the actual premium is known. In UK fire insurance the ratio may based on claims cost to premiums or sums insured.

burning of debris condition. A liability insurer may use this condition to ensure that the burning of debris away from the insured's premises is properly conducted. Fires should (i) be in a cleared area and at a distance (eg at least 10 yards) from any property; (ii) not be left unattended. A suitable fire extinguisher should be kept available for immediate use. It may also be required that fires should be extinguished at least one hour before leaving the site at the end of each working day.

burning ratio. Claims costs as a percentage of premiums.

burning warranty. Where an insured is engaged in certain processes involving the application of heat while working away from his premises insurers may impose conditions as to how the work is to be done. For example, a public liability insurer may require that where electric oxy-acetylene or similar welding equipment or cutting equipment is used the area of work must be adequately cleared and combustible materials moved at least 20 feet from the work. The warranty may also require that a two-gallon fire extinguisher be kept available. There are also conditions as to the use of blow lamps and blow torches.

burnt. This means substantial burning. Burning avoided the now discarded memorandum (qv) in the marine policy for all losses with respect to goods actually on board, whether the loss arose before, after, or during the event.

burst pipes. *See* BURSTING OR OVERFLOWING etc.

bursting or overflowing of water tanks, apparatus or pipes. This 'wet peril', often referred to simply as 'burst pipes cover', is for damage caused by bursting or overflowing but excludes sprinkler leakage (qv). Losses are normally subject to an excess (£100). Cover is readily available as an additional (or special) peril (qv) added to a fire policy provided the property is kept in a good state of repair. 'Burst pipes' cover is included in household policies on buildings and contents. When the dwelling is insufficiently furnished for full habitation 'burst pipes' cover ceases to apply after 30 days. The phrase as a whole is commonly taken as referring to overflowing etc from the water supply and distribution service of a building.

buses. Passenger-carrying vehicles with a seating capacity exceeding twelve, including the driver's seat, are regarded as heavy risks by motor insurers and treated as 'special types'.

business. 1. Most policies define what they mean by this term in a definition clause and will state the actual business of the insured in the schedule. The nature of the business is the key indicator of the degree of hazard present and therefore has a major bearing on the rate of premium. Consequently, the cover is written to operate only in connection with the 'Business' as specified in the schedule of the policy. However, certain activities are so closely connected with the business that liability insurers use an extended definition of the term to remove any doubt that might exist and close possible gaps. Generally, this means that business includes: (a) the provision and management of canteens, social sports and welfare facilities, sponsorship, first aid, fire or ambulance and security services, and ownership and maintenance of the insured's premises; (b) private work for directors or partners or senior officials by any person employed by the insured under a contract of service or apprenticeship. 2. For the purpose of the Employers' Liability (Compulsory Insurance) Act 1969 the term business includes a trade or profession, or any activity carried on by a body of persons (whether or not they are incorporated). Many activities that might not normally be regarded as a business, but where staff are employed (eg in members' tennis clubs) will come within this definition but a domestic servant employed solely to assist in the running of a private household is not employed in business for the purpose of the Act.

business books. Books of accounts and other business books, documents etc can be insured under material damage insurances such as fire policies as a special item. The insurer restricts his liability to the cost of stationery plus the cost of writing up.

business cancellation. *See* ABANDONMENT OF EVENTS. Some businesses may be able to insure against delay or abandonment of certain events, eg royal visits, royal occasions, in respect of which they incur costs in advance, eg design and manufacture of souvenirs.

business interruption insurance. 1. Formerly known in fire departments as consequential loss or loss of profits insurance. It insures against losses due to an interruption in business occurring immediately after and in consequence of material damage to property. The insured peril, eg a fire, may not only cause material damage to property, but an interruption for a measurable period in the trading activities of the business. During the interruption the business suffers a loss of, or reduction in, turnover. As a result there is a loss of gross profit from which fixed costs (*see* STANDING CHARGES and net profit are normally found. The gross profit, calculated on the 'difference basis' (qv), represents the sum insured for the maximum indemnity period (time selected by the insured to resume trading and recover market share). *See also* MATERIAL DAMAGE WARRANTY, RATE OF GROSS PROFIT, INCREASE IN COST OF WORKING, SPECIAL CIRCUMSTANCES CLAUSE, TURNOVER, AUDITORS CHARGES, PAYROLL COVER, DENIAL OF ACCESS, SUPPLIERS' EX-

TENSION, CUSTOMERS' EXTENSION, MURDER, SUICIDE AND FOOD AND DRINK POISONING, INFECTIOUS AND CONTAGIOUS DISEASE. 2. Engineering business interruption (or consequential loss) insurance. Similar in principle to 1. above but it insures consequential losses resulting from breakdown or accidental damage to installed plant or machinery or the failure of the electricity, gas or water supply. The indemnity is based on a fixed rate per day.

'business liability'. A 'short-hand expression' often used to describe the scope of the Unfair Contract Terms Act 1977 (qv). The Act applies mainly to liability that arises out of a business context. It is concerned, *inter alia*, with consumer contracts (*see* CONSUMER SALES) and contracts where one party deals with another on the standard written terms of that other's contract.

business of the insured. Always a factor in the rating of insurance risks. Consequently policies, eg liability policies, cover legal liability for injury (as defined) arising 'in connection with the Business'. Reference to the policy schedule will reveal how the insured's business has been defined for the purpose of the policy. Cover will not operate in connection with any business activity that goes outside that description unless it has been disclosed to, and accepted by, the insurer. Insurers often issue rating guides for use by brokers which indicate the premiums that can generally be applied to particular businesses but such guides may also include a list of excluded businesses for whom no quotations are available.

business travel. Insurance for business people travelling abroad differs little from that required by the holiday traveller (*see* TRAVEL INSURANCE). However, the business traveller sometimes goes at short notice so annual cover can be arranged for all trips that may follow in a twelve month period. This saves time and expense and obviates the risk of insurance being overlooked when last minute journeys are made.

business use. In assessing the premium payable for private car insurance the insurer takes account of the 'use' of the car which is a guide as to the exposure to risk. Where the 'business use' element is not confined 'to the policy-holder in person', most insurers apply a class 2 (or equivalent rate) which is about 25 per cent above the class 1 rate where the use is for 'social, domestic and pleasure use and use by the policyholder in person in connection with his business or profession'. Class 2 excludes commercial travelling or use in connection with the motor trade. Such uses imply greater exposure and attract class 3 rates (about 50 per cent above class 1).

'but for test'. A test to assist in determining whether the plaintiff's injury was in fact caused by the defendant's negligence (qv). It assists the court in rejecting those factors that could not have had any causal effect and should therefore be regarded as being too remote. 'If the damage would not have happened but for a particular fault then that fault is the cause of the damage; if it would have happened just the same, fault or no fault, the fault is not the cause of the damage'. (per Denning LJ in *Cork* v *Kirby Maclean Ltd.* (C.A., 1952). In *Barnett* v *Chelsea & Kensington Hospital Management Committee* (H.C. 1969) a casualty officer failed to examine a patient who later died of arsenic poisoning, but this failure was not the cause of the death as the patient would have died in any event. The test does not work when there are two concurrent causes each of which is sufficient to cause the damage. The test would eliminate both causes and that cannot be correct as both could have produced the result.

'buy and sell' agreement. An agreement made between partners or directors in a private limited company whereby in the event of the death in service of one of them his legal personal representatives will sell the deceased's share in the business to the surviving partner(s) or shareholders who will be obliged to make the necessary purchase. The purchase itself is often financed by means of life insurance under a partnership assurance scheme. Compare with double option agreement (qv) which does not take the form of a binding contract for sale.

buy backs. A term to describe those risks excluded from insurance policies but which can generally be 'bought back' by the insured on payment of an additional premium (eg motor-cycling risks in a personal accident policy).

buyer risks. A term used in credit insurance in respect of certain risks covered under the ECGD's comprehensive short-term guarantee (qv), namely: insolvency of the buyer; the buyer's failure to pay within six months after the due date for goods accepted; the buyer's failure or refusal to accept goods despatched that comply with the contract.

buying insurance. A leaflet under this title is available from the Association of British Insurers, Aldermary House, Queen St., London EC4N 1TT. It outlines the ABI's Code of Selling Practice for General Insurance (qv).

byelaw. The means whereby the Council of Lloyd's (qv) lays down the rules of the Lloyd's community.

C

call. A payment made by a member of a protection and indemnity club (qv) in consideration of a right to indemnity. The 'calls' are based on the tonnage entered in the club by shipowners. The calls are intended to cover losses and management expenses. The initial payment may be followed by supplementary calls.

canallers. Small vessels carrying goods in the upper St Lawrence in Canada.

cancellation clause. A policy clause giving the right of cancellation to both parties or to the insurer alone. The clause specifies the form in which notice of cancellation is to be given. If the insurer cancels (and it is rare) it is customary to allow the insured a pro rata refund for the unexpired term of the policy. If the insured cancels any refund is less than pro rata as the insurer will make a short period charge for the time on risk. *See* CANCELLING CLAUSE for marine insurance.

cancellation notice. An alternative term for statutory notice (qv).

cancellation period. *See* CANCELLATION RIGHTS UNDER STATUTE and COOLING OFF PERIOD.

cancellation rights under statute. Otherwise called the cooling off period (qv), which is now governed by the Financial Services Act 1986 (qv). Proposers for most life and pensions products can cancel their policies without loss provided they give notice of cancellation within the prescribed period. This means 14 days from the later of the receipt of the statutory notice (qv) or the date the policyholder becomes aware that he has made a contract and the first (or only) premium paid. The period is extended to 28 days where the company sells the same or similar product on substantially better terms than those offered by the company representative. The cancellation provisions do not apply where: both parties are outside the UK; the investor is a business or professional investor, or an execution only customer (qv); the investor responded to an advertisement; a customer agreement exists and the client waives his right of cancellation; the customer is exercising an option under an existing contract. The right of cancellation applies to life and pensions products classed as investments except: contracts for defined benefit pension schemes; regular premium policies or unit savings plans entered into by varying an existing policy, where the premiums do not exceed 10 per cent of those previously payable; deposit based appropriate personal pension schemes (qv).

cancelling clause. This clause providing for a period of notice, usually 30 days, in respect of marine risks, is found in open covers (qv) so that either party may terminate the contract if he so desires. Where war and strike risks are covered, insurers may give 7 days notice (less in some cases) of cancellation without disturbing the tenure of the open cover itself. When the clause is invoked, shipments that have gone or will go forward before the notice expires remain covered until arrival. Cancelling clauses also appear in floating policies (qv).

cancelling returns only. When a marine policy is issued covering a vessel whilst navigating or in commission for whole or part of the period it is customary to allow an adjustment in rate if the vessel is laid up out of commission at a safe port or place for an agreed minimum period. The rates of return for cancelling or laying up are inserted in the Institute Time Clauses (Clause 22— Returns for Lay-up and Cancellaion). However, the insurer may offer a reduced annual rate for a twelve months in commission insurance on the understanding that returns will not be allowed for laying-up but only for cancelling the policy, eg in the event of sale. *See also* LAYING UP RETURNS.

CFR. This means cost and freight. The seller must pay the costs and the freight as far as the port of destination but the risk passes to the buyer as the goods cross the ship's rail in the port of shipment.

capacity. The maximum amount of insurance that an insurer or underwriter is permitted to underwrite or considers that it can prudently accept. The term is also applied to the market as a whole in terms of its ability to accept risks directly or by way of reinsurance.

capacity boosting. One of the functions of reinsurance is to boost the capacity (qv) of a direct office thereby permitting it to accept larger risks while minimising its net exposure. This is particularly important when a cautious approach is needed such as the entry of the direct insurer into a new class of business.

capital additions clause. A fire insurance provision to automatically accommodate within the policy the addition of new buildings and/or machinery up to a specified limit of the sum insured. The insured usually provides quarterly declarations of additions and premiums are adjusted at the end of the year.

capital at risk. This term is used in connection with life solvency margins to denote the amount payable on death less the mathematical reserves in respect of the relevant contracts.

capital benefit. The single payment of a lump sum as opposed to smaller, regular payments. In personal accident policies lump sums are payable for death or loss of limb, loss of sight or permanent total disablement (qv).

capital protected annuity (otherwise called a capital protected immediate annuity). An annuity (qv) under which the annuitant is guaranteed that the total gross annuity payments will equal the purchase price regardless of the date of death. It is a safeguard against the risk of loss of capital due to a premature death.

capital redemption policy. Although issued by life insurers it is not a life insurance as the terms of the policy have no relation to human life. Policies issued are classified as long-term business (qv) but are not a part of the life fund. The policy provides that the insurer will pay a stated sum at the end of a given term in return for a single or periodic premium. The purpose is to provide a capital sum at a given time to repay debenture issues or replace a 'wasting asset' such as leaseholds or machinery. These policies are also known as sinking fund or leasehold redemption policies depending on the object of the policy.

capital sum. The sum payable under a life insurance as the main benefit on death or maturity.

capital transfer tax (CTT). A tax on the transfer of wealth that has been replaced by inheritance tax.

capital unit. The managers of unit-linked policies charge for their services. The capital unit is one charging device. Premiums in the early years (eg up to three) are allocated to capital units to help recover the initial expenses.

captain's room. The restaurant at Lloyd's (qv).

captive. *See* CAPTIVE INSURANCE COMPANY.

captive agent. A US term referring to an agent who is contracted to give exclusive representation to one company.

captive insurance company. A company created by a business corporation to supply all or some of the insurances needs of the parent company; it is the most sophisticated form of self-insurance. The captive is a staffed and managed subsidiary of a company or of a group of independent companies or professional practitioners with common insurance problems (multi-parent captive). Usually but not necessarily the captive is registered and resident in 'tax havens' (qv). The creation of a captive produces tax advantages not available with other forms of self-insurance. Also premiums are retained to meet small losses while also being available for investment until needed for claims. Some captives have become substantial writers of third party business, ie business for insureds other than the parent company (market captive). Most captives operate in the reinsurance markets (inward and outward). Captives operating offshore are also run by insurers, intermediaries, or specialised underwriting management companies to provide re-insurance facilities. There are now a variety of captives with each type attracting a particular term. *See* PURE CAPTIVE, SENIOR CAPTIVE, GROUP CAPTIVE, CREDIT LIFE CAPTIVE, AGENT-OWNED CAPTIVE, and MULTI-PARENT CAPTIVE. *See also* RENT-A-CAPTIVE.

capture and seizure. Capture, a marine term, means the taking by an enemy in wartime or by rebels or insurgents at any time. Seizure is wider in scope and embraces every act of forcible possession. Both are 'war risks' and are covered when the Institute War clauses apply. *See also* FREE OF CAPTURE AND SEIZURE CLAUSE.

caravan insurance. Special policies covering loss, damage and liability.

cargo. Goods shipped for carriage.

cargo insurance. The insurance of goods and/or merchandise imported or exported to or from various parts of the world. Cargo is insured by marine insurers against all maritime risks and transit risks, including war risks. 'All risks' cover is available under Institute Cargo Clauses (A). Clause (C) is the most limited of the alternatives covering certain major casualties only. Clause (B) provides the same cover but adds named perils and thus lies somewhere between (A) and (C) in terms of the scope of cover. *See* INSTITUTE CARGO CLAUSES (1/1/82).

cargo interest. An insurable interest in the cargo that arises other than by way of ownership.

cargo rating. Fixing the premium for cargo insurances. The principal factors affecting the rate for cargo insurance are: the vessel; the voyage; the nature of the cargo; and the conditions of insurance.

cargo value. The value placed on the cargo by the insured for the purpose of insurance under a valued policy (qv). It normally extends to include all charges and profit.

Carriage of Goods by Air and Road Act 1979. Section 4 amends the CMR Convention in that compensation expressed in gold francs is replaced by special drawing rights (qv).

Carriage of Goods by Road Act 1965. The Act gives force of law in the UK to the provisions of the Convention on the Contract for the International Carriage of Goods by Road (CMR) so far as they relate to the rights and liabilities of persons concerned in the carriage of goods by road under a contract to which the Convention applies. The principal details of the Convention, which appear in the Schedule to the Act, are: (a) CMR applies to all international contracts for carriage of goods by road for reward when at least one of the countries involved is a party to CMR, except under the terms of any international postal convention, funeral consignments, or furniture removals. (b) The carrier is responsible for the acts and omissions of his agents and servants and any other persons whose services he uses during the carriage. (c) There are detailed requirements as to consignment notes. The sender is made liable for expense, loss or damage sustained by the carrier for inaccuracies in the particulars supplied and the carrier must check the accuracy of the marks and number of packages. The sender is liable for the consequences of defective packing. (d) The carrier is liable for total or partial loss of or damage to the goods from the time of taking over and the time of delivery but this liability may be limited or removed altogether in certain circumstances but the carrier must prove that one of the exceptions applies. (e) Delay in delivery is defined as the 'agreed time-limit', or in the absence of an agreement, 'the actual duration of the carriage having regard to the circumstances of the case'. If the goods have not been delivered within 30 days of the end of the agreed time limit, or, where there is no agreement, 60 days from the carrier taking over the goods, they may be regarded as lost and claims formulated. (f) Dangerous goods must be notified to the carrier and entered into the consignment note as such. (g) Rules for the calculation of compensation payable by the carrier, the payment of an agreed surcharge by the sender in connection with the declared value or a declared special interest, and interest on compensation payable are all covered by CMR (*see* CARRIAGE OF GOODS BY ROAD ACT 1979). (h) CMR outlines carriers liability and procedures for claims. (i) If successive carriers are involved in a carriage governed by a single contract they each become party to the contract of carriage and responsible for the whole contract. Goods in transit cover in respect of CMR attracts a higher premium but is considered by the transport industry worth while. The cover on CMR is 8.33 SDRs (*see* SPECIAL DRAWING RIGHTS) per kilogram. To convert to sterling reference can be made to the press on a daily basis. On 1 December 1990 1 SDR equalled £0.738243. This worked out at £6.1495 per kg.

car laid-up clause. *See* VEHICLE LAID-UP CLAUSE.

car ratings/groups. An important variable in the rating of private car insurance is the car described in the proposal which will be driven by those entitled drive under the policy. Cars are generally divided into nine groups but some insurers add a tenth for kit-cars or others that have been modified to give increased performance. The higher the group number the higher will be the premium but not all insurers hold to the same classifications (eg most insurers put the Volvo 340 into group 5 but others put it into 4 and one or two into 6). Ratings are generally in line with the purchase price of the car as that determines the cost of repairs. 'Difficult to repair' imports may attract a higher rating than a similarly manufactured car from the UK or principal foreign makers.

car sharing. The payment of a sum of money by a passenger towards the running costs of a car. The Road Traffic Act 1988, s. 150 allows the user of a motor vehicle to carry passengers, who share the cost of the journey, without this being regarded as use for hire or reward provided that: (a) the vehicle is not adapted to carry more than eight passengers and is not a motor-cycle; (b) the total amount paid does not exceed the running costs (which includes depreciation); and (c) the arrangement for payment was made at the beginning of the journey. In effect the passenger contributes to petrol, oil and maintenance costs and the motorist's normal certificate of insurance suffices even though it excludes use for hire or reward.

car telephones. If fitted into the car the telephone will be covered as an accessory in the normal terms of the loss/damage section of comprehensive policies. If portable or transportable it is covered under the rugs, coats and personal effects section of the same type of policy which provides cover against fire, theft and accident up to a limited amount. It can alternatively be insured under personal or business equipment 'all risks' policies subject to it being specified to avoid the limitations imposed by single article limits (qv). A special policy is needed to cover the risk of breakdown.

Carpenter plan. *See* SPREAD LOSS REINSURANCE which was first introduced into the USA by a broker named Carpenter.

Carriage by Air Act 1961. An Act giving the force of law in the UK to the provisions of the Hague Protocol (qv). It became operative from June 1967.

Carriage by Air (Supplementary Provisions) Act 1962. Deals with the term 'carrier' by giving the force of law in the UK to the Guadalajara Convention whose provisions are applied to all-international carriage to which the Carriage by Air Acts (Application of Provisions) Order 1967 relates. The Act enables the court to make any order it deems just and equitable to adjust the liabilities between the contracting carrier (qv) and the actual carrier (qv).

Carriage by Air Acts (Application of Provisions) Order 1967. This applies the Warsaw Convention (qv) as amended by the Hague Protocol (qv) to carriage not governed by that Convention.

Carriage of Goods by Sea Act 1971. An Act giving force to the Hague-Visby rules (qv) by specifying the respective responsibilities, liabilities, rights and immunities of carriers and cargo owners to create uniformity in regard to the conditions of contracts of carriage of goods by sea to which the Act applies. It came into force in June 1977 and applies to contracts of carriage covered by (a) a bill of lading, and (b) any receipt or non-negotiable document stating that the receipt is to be treated as a bill of lading for the purpose of the contract, where the port of shipment is in the UK. It also applies when the carriage takes place in two different states and the bill of lading is issued in a contracting state (ie one which has accepted the Hague-Visby Rules). Shipowners must produce bills of lading when the goods are delivered stating particulars of the goods and their apparent order and condition. Prior to shipment this is a received for shipment bill but the shipper may later demand a shipped bill after the goods have been loaded. This usually means entering the name of the carrying vessel and date of departure. The shipper must supply particulars of the goods and will be liable for any loss, damage or expense resulting from the particulars being inaccurate. Unless the value and nature of the goods are declared and inserted in the bill, liability is limited to a fixed amount per package or per kilo of gross weight. The benefit of this limitation is lost if the damage results from the carrier's act or omission done with intent to cause damage or recklessly knowing that damage was likely to result.

carrier. 1. In transportation, it refers to the railway, shipowner, or other transporter of the goods subject to insurance. 2. The insurer or reinsurer carrying the risk. The term is commonly used in this way in the USA. *See also* COMMON CARRIER.

carry back. A pension provision which enables premiums paid in one tax year to be offset against 'against net earnings in that year, the year before that'. This is very useful in the case of personal pensions for those people who do not know exactly what their earnings will be until after the end of the tax year. It is also useful if it is discovered that a lower rate of tax will be paid this year than last year which means it will pay to backdate the pension contribution.

case method. A method of arriving at a reserve for balance sheet purposes for outstanding losses that have been notified. A list of outstanding cases is prepared and they are valued individually on the information available at the time of the estimate and an aggregate is then produced.

case reserve. The amount set against an individual outstanding loss that has been notified. *See* CASE METHOD.

cash accumulation policy. A pensions term referring to an insurance policy under which contributions, net of expenses, are accumulated in a pool to which interest and bonuses are usually added. The proceeds are used to provide pensions and other benefits as they become due.

cash agent. An insurance intermediary who receives a commission for business introduced but who is not allowed any period of credit and has no authority to grant cover.

cash at retirement. Pension scheme benefits taken at retirement by commuting part of the benefits into a tax-free lump sum. The maximum cash commutation permitted depends on the length of service, but must not exceed one and a half times annual earnings at retirement or £150 000 whichever is the smaller.

cash basis. A pension term meaning a method of accounting under which the transactions are accounted for only at the time money is received or paid. This is in contrast to the accruals concept (qv).

cash before cover. Legislative provision proposed in several developing markets requiring insurers to start cover only on receipt of full premium.

cash bonus. *See* BONUSES.

cash flow underwriting. The use of rating and premium collection techniques by insurance companies with the aim of maximising interest earnings on the premiums. This form of underwriting is more prevalent during periods of high interest rates when premiums, which are payable in advance, are fixed at a competitive level to attract funds for investment. Losses on underwriting can be covered out of the interest earnings. The premiums make allowance for 'the time value of money'. The policy is dangerous during periods of fluctuating interest rates.

cash fund. Unit-linked life offices may launch a cash (or money) fund. The managers invest only in short-term deposits with banks and local authorities. The interest rate they obtain is usually better than that which could be achieved by the investors acting as individuals.

cash insurance. *See* MONEY INSURANCE.

cash-in value. An alternative term for surrender value (qv). Also, means the cash value of units in a unit-linked policy.

cashing-in. The majority of unit-linked policies contain one of two options on maturity: either the investor may defer taking the policy for a year or more (ie the policy continues in force with no more premiums payable) or he may take the units his premiums have acquired in cash value. The cash value in any given year is affected by both the market trends and fluctuations and by investment management decisions.

cash loss. An arrangement in a reinsurance treaty (or under a direct insurance) where large losses are settled immediately without waiting for periodic statements.

cash option. An option to take cash as opposed to some other benefit under a life insurance contract.

cash payment. A principal method of providing the indemnity or benefit to the insured. Unless, as is usually the case, the insurer reserves the right to meet his obligations in other ways (eg repair, reinstatement or replacement), the insured is entitled to demand a cash payment. In liability insurance, a cash settlement is the only practicable method.

Cassel Report. The publication of this report in 1937 led to the creation of the Motor Insurers Bureau (qv) in order to ensure that road accident victims, who sustained personal injury on a road through the fault of a motorist, should receive compensation even if payment was not forthcoming from the defendant's insurer. The failure of a number of small motor insurance companies, which left victims uncompensated despite the existence of compulsory insurance, resulted in the report entitled the Cassel Report on Compulsory Insurance.

Castellain v *Preston* **(1883).** The leading case on indemnity (qv). The defendant contracted to sell property to the tenant. After the signing of the contract, but before completion, the property sustained fire damage of £330 which the defendant recovered from his insurer. However, on subsequent completion, the defendant received the full purchase price from the purchaser even though he had not used the policy money to repair the damage. Consequently, the plaintiff, chairman of the insurer, sought the recovery of the £330 on the ground that the defendant, having received the full price, had suffered no loss and the fire policy was one of indemnity. The argument succeeded and the insurer was entitled to recover as no loss had been sustained.

casualty. A term to describe a loss, particularly used in the insurance of marine hulls. In the USA the term is used to describe liability insurance.

catastrophe. Substantial losses resulting from an event or series of events (hurricane, flood, earthquake, conflagration) in a short period of time. The risk of catastrophic losses is a major reason for the demand from direct insurers for reinsurance. *See* CATASTROPHE REINSURANCE.

catastrophe reinsurance. Catastrophe reinsurance (known as catastrophe covers) protects the ceding office (qv) against accumulated losses in the event of one catastrophe, eg earthquake or hurricane destroying a whole town or area. The retention on individual buildings under surplus treaties may be within the insurer's capability but when a catastrophe strikes at property on a widespread basis the aggregation of claims will create a serious threat to the insurer. The catastrophe cover operates on an excess of loss (qv) basis in regard to very large losses. The reinsurer agrees to reimburse the ceding office for an agreed proportion (usually 90 per cent) of the office's loss that exceeds the excess point up to an agreed limit. The contract warrants that the balance of 10 per cent will be retained by the cedant. By their nature, catastrophes are rare occurrences so reinsurers have no statistical pattern to provide a base for rating. The reinsurers rely on their own experience of treaties with similar characteristics and usually charge a flat rate for the whole year on a non-adjustable basis or a flat rate of gross premiums, with a minimum and deposit premiums.

catastrophe reserves. An insurer may create a catastrophe reserve as a matter of common prudence. Unlike other technical reserves (qv), it does not have to be maintained in order to comply with the law governing the supervision of insurance companies. The catastrophe reserve is a safeguard against exceptionally poor claims experience.

category. The term used by the DTI for a sub-division of treaty reinsurance business accepted.

cattle trespass. Entry of one person's cattle on to the land of another from his own land. The Animals Act 1971 (qv), s. 4 imposes a modern form of strict liability on a person in possession of livestock for (a) damage done to the land or to any property thereon in the possession of another person; (b) any expenses are reasonably incurred by the other person in keeping the livestock while it cannot be restored to its owner or keeper. Cattle trespass is no longer actionable *per se* and no strict liability arises for damage to goods of a person not in occupation of the land or for personal injuries suffered by any person.

causa causans. The immediate cause—the last link in the chain and although nearest in time it is not necessarily the nearest in efficiency so that it becomes the proximate cause (qv).

cause of action. The fact or combination of facts which give rise to a right of legal action.

causes classified. For the purposes of proximate cause (qv) the causes of loss can be classified under three headings, viz.: (a) concurrent; (b) consecutive in broken sesquence; (c) consecutive in unbroken sequence. Under (a) the dominant cause is the deciding consideration. *See* CONCURRENT CAUSES. Under (b) where there are consecutive causes in broken sequence the proximate cause must be regarded, not taking into account prior causes. Under (c) the cause proximate in efficiency and not necessarily time is relevant. *See* LAST STRAW CASES.

caveat emptor. A common law rule relating to the sale of goods and meaning 'let the buyer beware'. The basis of the rule is that the buyer had the opportunity of satisfying himself as to the suitability of the article purchased and therefore no liability attaches to the vendor. However, the Sale of Goods Act 1979 (qv) provides a measure of consumer protection and the Defective Premises Act 1972, s. 3 (qv) abolishes the *caveat emptor* defence to a claim against a vendor or lessor which is based upon his negligence in building or other work carried out on the land before the sale or letting took place. Insurance contracts are subject to the doctrine of *uberrimae fidei* or utmost good faith (qv) and not *caveat emptor.*

ceasing age. The age at which a permanent health insurance comes to an end.

cedant. An alternative term for ceding office (qv), reinsured or reassured.

cede. To purchase reinsurance.

ceding office (company). An insurer who has entered into a direct insurance and then transfers the whole or part of the risk by purchasing reinsurance (qv). The ceding office remains fully liable under the direct insurance but has a right of recovery against the reinsurer in accordance with the reinsurance terms.

centralisation. The concentration by an insurance company of the principal powers of control and decisions at head office. Branch offices are given little authority and are principally a point of contact for customers and agents.

central solvency. The method of expediting and simplifying the earmarking process at Lloyd's by means of a centralised computerised facility.

Centre for Claims Resolution (CCR). Formed following the dissolution of the Asbestos Claims Facility (qv) in 1988, CCR provides an alternative to litigation in respect of asbestos-induced injury or disease. It is organised by USA asbestos manufacturers and supported by insurers and in its first year increased the number of out-of-court settlements over that achieved under the Facility.

certificate of entry. The policy issued by a Protection and Indemnity Club (qv) when a vessel is entered in the club.

certificate of existence. Otherwise called a survival certificate, it certifies that an annuitant (qv) is still alive.

certificate of insurance. A document issued to provide evidence of the existence of insurance. Certificates are required in law as evidence of the following classes of insurance: Employers' liability insurance. Motor insurance (Road Traffic Act cover only). Oil carrying vessels with regard to pollution. *See also* MARINE INSURANCE CERTIFICATE.

Certificate of Proficiency. A certificate awarded by the Chartered Insurance Institute to successful examination candidates. The certificate is taken by persons ineligible to proceed directly to the CII's Introductory Examination (qv) or Associateship examinations. It provides a broad knowledge of insurance at a basic level. It is nationally recognised by employers and successful students can proceed to the Introductory Examination.

cessation of payment of premiums. The cessation of payment of premiums under limited premium life assurance policies.

cession. A specific item of reinsurance under a reinsurance treaty (qv).

cestui que trust. A person for whom another is a trustee; a beneficiary. *See* TRUST.

'chain of events'. A proximate cause (qv) term to refer to a sequence of events leading to a loss.

chain of indemnity. This refers to the right of a supplier of a product that has caused injury/damage to recover the amount paid in damages from the party who supplied the product to him. A retailer, held liable under the Sale of Goods Act 1979 (qv) for injuries caused to a customer by a defective product, may be able to make a recovery against the wholesaler or manufacturer who supplied it. The contractual relationship between the retailer and his supplier will also be governed by the Sale of Goods Act and the same implied terms (*see* FITNESS FOR PURPOSE and MERCHANTABLE QUALITY) will apply. This contract is, however, a non-consumer contract and an exclusion of these implied terms will be permitted provided always the supplier can show that they are reasonable. *See* the TEST OF REASONABLENESS which may not be easy to satisfy. If a wholesaler is involved the wholesaler in turn may look to the manufacturer for a breach of the implied terms under the Sale of Goods Act 1979 under which liability between the parties is strict.

chain ladder method. A term well known to claims reserving practitioners which is sometimes used in a particular sense but at other times very generally. In the latter case, it describes a wide range of reserving methods, which operate through comparing the claims development cohorts of different years of origin, and which tend to employ triangular arrays of data. This usage is criticised as it obscures the important question as to what data is actually being used—many different possibilities exist. Also, it tends to suggest: (a) that a triangular array must be used, and (b) anything that is in triangular form must necessarily be a chain ladder. Neither of these propositions are true. In its particular sense, chain letter method is used to describe one means, and one means only for evaluating the triangular array.

chance. The probability or likelihood that an event will occur.

Chancery bonds. Chancery bonds, a class of court bonds, are required where receivers or receivers and managers are appointed in relation to some matter which is the subject of an action in the Chancery Division of the High Court. The receivers and managers may be appointed to deal with the preservation of property or simply collect the revenue arising from property. Such receivership may be necessary: 1. pending litigation. 2. during the minority of an infant. 3. to prevent its dissipation by persons having immediate or partial interest in it, or to whom it is entrusted by law. The appointment is made in the Chancery Division of the High Court and the court fixes the amount of the guarantee and the remuneration of the receiver. The security is called a Chancery bond or Chancery guarantee.

change in temperature clause. A fire policy exclusion in respect of loss or damage to goods, usually of a perishable nature, caused by a change in temperature resulting from the total or partial destruction or disablement by fire or other perils of the cold store or refrigerating plant. It is usually possible to extend the cover to include this risk on payment of an additional premium.

change of interest. It is implied in contracts of indemnity that the insured should have an insurable interest at the time of loss. If the insured's interest in the subject-matter of insurance ceases, he will not be able to make a claim. However, subject to the insurer's agreement, the policy can be transferred to the party (by change of interest endorsement) acquiring an interest in the subject-matter (*see* ASSIGNMENT). Some material damage policies, eg fire, contain a condition making it clear that the policy will continue to run, notwithstanding the cessation of the insured's interest, in respect of changes by will or operation of the law (eg appointment of a trustee in bankruptcy).

change of interest endorsement. The name given to an endorsement to signify that the original insured's interest in the subject-matter of insurance has been taken over by a new party who is now substituted as the insured. The latter normally completes a new proposal form and if acceptable to the insurer a change of interest endorsement will be prepared. *See* NOVATION and PERSONAL CONTRACTS.

change of ownership clause. An Institute Time Clause enabling the insurer to cancel the policy in the event of the vessel being sold or transferred to new management during the currency of the policy if their written approval of the change is not forthcoming. A pro rata daily return of premium is made but if the vessel has sailed the cancellation is suspended until arrival at the port of final discharge.

Change of Underwriting Policy Clause. A clause in a reinsurance treaty requiring the ceding office to notify the reinsurer if any change in underwriting policy takes place. It is one of a number of clauses that give the reinsurer a degree of control given that premium and claims bordereau are not usually required.

change of voyage. The Marine Insurance Act 1906, s. 45(1) describes this term as: 'Where after the commencement of the risk, the destination of the ship is voluntarily changed from the destination contemplated by the policy, there is said to be a change of voyage. S. 45(2) Unless the policy otherwise provides, where there is a change of voyage, the insurer is discharged from liability as from the time of the change, that is to say, as from the time when the determination to change is manifested, and it is immaterial that the ship may not in fact have left the course contemplated by the policy when the loss occurs'. A change of voyage clause (qv) (Clause 10, of the Institute Cargo Clauses) provides that a change of voyage is held covered at a premium to be arranged subject to prompt notice being given to the underwriter.

change of voyage clause. *See* CHANGE OF VOYAGE.

changes in risk. 1. *See* ALTERATIONS. 2. A condition under the title 'changes in risk' appears in the personal accident policy (qv). It requires the insured to notify any change in his occupation or profession. It may extend to the notification of any physical defect or infirmity that arises during the currency of the policy. In the absence of such a condition the only requirement will be to give notification at renewal when the duty of utmost good faith (qv) revives.

chargeable event (life insurance). In relation to life policies this is defined in Taxes Act 1970, s. 394 as amended. In regard to single premium bonds (qv) and other non-qualifying policies this means: death; maturity; total surrender; assignment for money or money's worth; the occurrence of an excess of 'reckonable aggregate value' over 'allowable aggregate amount'. In the case of a qualifying policy (qv) it means death or maturity if the policy is made paid up within 10 years or three-quarters of the original term, whichever is the shorter and it also means surrender. The following events, if they occur within 10 years of inception, or, if sooner, three-quarters of the policy term, are also deemed to be chargeable events: assignment for money or money's worth; the occurrence of an excess of 'reckonable aggregate value' over 'allowable aggregate amount'. If a chargeable event occurs the gains made under the policy or bond will be subject to income tax at the higher rates if appropriate. *See* TOP SLICING (qv).

chargeable gains. The gains made on a chargeable event (qv). The gains are chargeable to income tax and not capital gains tax (*see* TOP SLICING). There is a charge to higher rate tax gains arising on payments under all non-qualifying life policies effected after 19 March 1968; qualifying policies (qv) in certain circumstances (*see* CHARGEABLE EVENT); capital redemption policies (qv) and annuities in certain circumstances.

chargeable lifetime transfer. A lifetime gift, such as one to a discretionary or flexible trust, that may attract inheritance tax. It is subject to tax immediately unless it falls within the nil-rate band and if not it will be taxable at half rate.

charter. An agreement for the hire of a vessel or aircraft. *See* CHARTER PARTY.

charter aircraft. Aircraft available for hire.

chartered freight. The freight payable by the charterer to the shipowner under the charter party (qv) whereby the vessel (or space therein) is hired for a voyage or period. *See* FREIGHT INSURANCE.

Chartered Institute of Arbitrators. The professional institute for arbitrators which, *inter alia*, operates the Personal Insurance Arbitration Service (qv).

Chartered Institute of Loss Adjusters (CILA). The professional association of loss adjusters (qv). It controls membership and standards of professional conduct. It holds examinations at both Associateship and Fellowship levels.

Chartered Insurance Institute. The insurance industry's professional educational body. Membership is open to individuals wholly or mainly engaged in insurance. Professional examinations lead to the award of Associateship diploma entitling holders to the designation, ACII and the award of the Fellowship diploma (FCII). The chief objective is to promote efficiency and improvement in insurance practice. The Institute publicises careers information and runs conferences for teachers and careers officers. There are 90 local institutes in the UK with 50 affiliated institutes from overseas.

Chartered Insurer. A member of the Chartered Insurance Institute practising in the insurance industry.

chartered loss adjuster. A loss adjuster (qv) who is a member of the Chartered Institute of Loss Adjusters.

charter party. A contract under which the shipowner lets an entire ship (or part thereof) to any person (the charterer) to carry goods on a specified voyage or over a specific period of time.

cherished number scheme. A contingency insurance paying a benefit following the irrecoverable loss of the personalised number plate in the event of the licensing centre with whom the vehicle is registered not permitting the number to be transferred to another vehicle following theft or destruction of the insured's vehicle. The scheme is underwritten at Lloyd's.

child's deferred assurance. A life assurance under which, until the child reaches 'vesting age' (18 or 21) the premium is paid by the parent. Then the child has the right to take a policy in his or her own name up to a fixed sum assured at the insurer's normal rate of premium without evidence of health. Where the original policy is an endowment the proceeds at the vesting age can be taken as cash or used as a single premium towards future insurances for the child. A number of other benefits are often offered, eg suspension of premium and/or an income benefit if the parent dies before the vesting age. In the case of a female minor, some contracts allow guaranteed insurability on the life of a future husband.

chose in action. A right of proceeding in a court of law to procure the payment of a sum of money (eg proceeds of an insurance policy or sum due under contract) or to recover pecuniary damages for a wrong or non-performance of a contract.

CIM Convention. A convention promulgated and signed in Berne in 1952 and updated in February 1961 with the aim of establishing a measure of uniformity in Europe for the international carriage of goods by rail. The UK ratified the convention but never passed legislation to make it law as the railway system was nationalised and the machinery existed to give effect to the convention. Consequently it is necessary in the case of rail imports or exports involving the UK to incorporate the terms of the convention into the contract of carriage as shown by the consignment note. The carrier's liability is similar to that of CMR (qv) with similar exclusion clauses. The carrier is presumed liable if there is a total or partial loss/damage of the goods and for delay exceeding the transit period. Monetary limits of liability are expressed in relation to the gross weight of the goods.

Civil Aviation Authority (CAA). The CAA regulates the British civil aviation industry as a whole. It is a licensing authority and can refuse to license anyone considered unfit to hold a licence for the carriage of passengers or cargo for hire or reward or who has inadequate financial resources or who is not a UK national (unless approved by the Secretary of State). The financial resource requirements may take account of the insurance arrangements in respect of liability to passengers. The licensing requirements apply to any flight in any part of the world by a UK registered aircraft. They also cover any flight beginning or ending in the UK by an aircraft registered in a relevant overseas country or associated country. The CAA is also responsible for the registration of aircraft and employs surveyors to inspect firms in the aircraft industry including repairers.

civil aviation risk. The life or personal accident term for the extra risk presented by a proposer who engages in a significant amount of flying as a passenger or any flying as a private pilot. No extra premiums are required for fare-paying passengers on commercial flights or for commercial aircrew.

civil commotion. A risk which is excluded under the standard fire policy and other property insurances along with riot (qv) and similar perils. It refers to people getting out of hand and creating a disturbance which could be described as severe and prolonged. Civil commotion denotes an intermediate state between a riot (qv) and civil war (qv). 'The element of turbulence or tumult is essential' (*London & Manchester Plate Glass Co* v *Heath* (1913)). Riot and civil commotion can be in-

sured as additional perils (qv). Strict time limits are laid down by the insurer for the supply of particulars of a claim. These limits follow those specified for riot (qv).

civil engineering. This includes the design and construction of roads, railways, bridges, aqueducts, canals, ports, harbours, moles, breakwaters, lighthouses and drainage works. The term originated in the distinction between these engineering activities and those associated with military operations, eg fortification, ordnance, etc. The General Conditions of Contract for Civil Engineering Construction lays down specific insurance requirements for civil engineering contracts.

Civil Liability (Contribution Act) 1978. An Act which replaces and extends the Law Reform (Married Women and Tortfeasors) Act 1935 which abolished the common law rule that a judgment in favour of a plaintiff against one of a number of joint tortfeasors (qv) barred any subsequent proceedings against the others. The 1935 Act also provided that actions may be brought by tortfeasors for contribution from other joint tortfeasors but this applied only in respect of torts. The new Act permits this right of contribution whether the legal basis of their respective liabilities lies in tort, breach of contract, breach of trust or otherwise. The new Act also abolishes the rule that if the plaintiff's action against one tortfeasor succeeded the award of damages set a limit for any subsequent actions that he might bring against other defendants.

civil war. 'War between two or more portions of a country or state, each contending for mastery of the whole and each claiming to be the legitimate government. The term is also sometimes applied to war or rebellion when the rebellious portions of the state are contiguous to those containing the seat of Government' (F.H. Jones, *The Law of Accident and Contingency Insurance*, Pitman).

claim. A demand by the insured for an indemnity or benefit under the policy. The claim will be met if the loss, injury, damage or liability is caused by an insured peril and is not excluded subject to the adequacy of the sum insured or limit of indemnity. The insured must also observe the procedures laid for notice of loss (qv). *See also* CLAIMS CONDITION.

claim file. The file that is created to record all of the detail and correspondence that needs to be recorded for the purpose of handling the claim.

claim form. The printed form prepared by the insurer for completion by the insured when the latter wishes to make a claim (qv). *See also* ACCIDENT REPORT FORM.

claiming cash. *See* CASH LOSS.

claims condition. A condition in an insurance policy setting out what the insured has to do in the event of a claim. It covers notice of loss (qv), assistance to the insurer (qv), proofs of loss (qv) and, in the case of liability policies, there is a control of proceedings clause.

claims co-operation clause. This may appear in a reinsurance treaty calling for early notice of possible claims and for consultation and co-operation in the handling of claims that may affect the reinsurer. The ceding insurer must not admit liability for such a claim without the consent of the reinsurer.

claims equalisation reserve. A reserve to smooth out fluctuations in the cost of claims where the incidence is of an uneven nature. This produces a greater level of consistency in the revenue account.

claims expenses. The direct costs of investigation and settlement as distinct from the payments of the claims themselves. These include loss adjusters' fees, court fees etc. *See also* CLAIMS HANDLING EXPENSES.

claims experience. The insured's claims history with regard to the cost and frequency of previous claims. It is material for an insured to disclose his claims experience when proposing for insurance. The term can also be used to describe the relationship between premium and claims experienced by an insurer for a particular class of business over a period of time.

claims handling agreements. Agreements between insurers involved in the same incidents or losses to settle matters between them by way of a prescribed formula rather than resort to litigation. The knock-for-knock agreement (qv)

and the common law agreement (qv) are examples. The purpose is to minimise costs.

claims handling expenses. The indirect expenses incurred in handling and settling claims having their origin in salaries and other overheads associated with staffing and running a claims department.

claims-made policy. A liability policy covering all claims first advised during the policy year. The time of the occurrence of the injury or damage is irrelevant unless the policy includes a retroactive date which provides that cover will not apply to occurrences that happen prior to a specific date. Professional indemnity policies (qv) are always written on a claims-made basis. Compare claims-made policy with a losses-occurring policy (qv).

claims notification clause. This is introduced into liability insurances which include an excess. For example, where the insured decides to self fund all public liability claims up to £100 000, the insurer may add a clause requiring the notification of all claims over £75 000.

claims-related method. A method of dividing the cost of insurance purchased for the organisation and apportioning it among the cost centres based on claims experience. The aim is to ensure that each part of the company contributes to total insurance costs in a manner which reflects its own claims record. If the charges made can be justified the cost centres will have an incentive to promote loss prevention.

claims reserve. The provision made in the accounts of an insurer in respect of claims notified but not yet settled.

classification clause (1/7/78). This is used with floating policies (qv) and open covers (qv) on cargo where the name of the carrying vessel is unknown when the risk is accepted. The purpose of the clause is to give protection to the insured and provide a fair premium basis. A risk accepted on the terms of this clause is valid, irrespective of the type of vessel, at the rate stated in the policy if the vessel carrying the cargo is a 'mechanically self-propelled vessel of steel construction and classes as specified without modification by one of nine listed classification societies. The vessel must not exceed 15 years of age but an exception is made for vessels over 15 but not exceeding 25 years which have 'established and maintained a regular pattern of trading on an advertised schedule to load and unload at specified ports'.

classification society. A society whose main purpose is to inspect ships for the purpose of describing and listing them in its own publication for the benefit of underwriters. Ships are graded (*see* A1) and a whole variety of symbols conveys quite detailed information. The classification clause (qv) lists nine societies including Lloyd's Register (qv) and the American Bureau of Shipping (qv).

class of use. A rating factor used by private car insurers to broadly reflect the extent of use of the car. Normally, there are three classes of use, the most lightly rated of which is use for social, domestic and pleasure use and use by the policyholder in person in connection with his business or profession. There are exclusions, eg use in connection with the motor trade, commercial travelling, racing etc. The middle category, class 2, does not restrict the business use element to the policyholder while class 3, the most highly rated, allows commercial travelling which is not permitted by the other classes. *See* SOCIAL DOMESTIC AND PLEASURE USE.

clause. A part of a policy or other form of contract.

Clause 21.2.1 (formerly 19.2 (a)). This clause is from the Standard Form of Building Contract published by the Joint Contracts Tribunal (JCT). The intention is to secure 'non-negligent' third party cover. The clause is one of insurance and not indemnity. The contractor arranges the insurance in joint names but for the benefit of the Employer, although the contractor is liable for the premiums and must comply with the warranties. The insurance has to cover the liability of the Employer and damage to property (excluding the contract works) thus including 'own damage' as well as third party property. The limit is left to be stated in the contract bills. The cover, which is subject to an excess, is against 'nuisance perils' only (hence the term

non-negligent) eg collapse, subsidence, vibration, weakening/removal of support, lowering of ground water, heave. Negligence of contractors and sub-contractors is excepted—these risks are covered under public liability insurance. The clause applies whenever a provisional sum is included in the contract bills or specification. The clause is most likely to invoked by an Employer when the work is likely to affect adjoining property rather than when the work is on a greenfield site.

claused bill. A bill of lading which has been endorsed to note some defect in the products or packaging of the goods to be shipped. Dirty bill is an alternative term.

clauses descriptive of the risk. *See* DESCRIPTION OF RISK CLAUSES.

clawback. 1. Under the Finance Act 1975 where a life policy, which qualified for tax relief on the premiums, is cancelled, or benefits taken within four years of inception, part of the tax relief will be clawed back by the Inland Revenue. The relevant sum must be deducted by the assurer from the surrender value or proceeds payable to the assured. The Finance Act 1984 removed the tax relief on premiums so the clawback provision will apply only to qualifying policies issued before March 1984. 2. *See* DELAYED TURNOVER.

clean cut basis. A method to reduce the expense and work involved in the preparation of reinsurance treaty accounts. When a treaty is cancelled or the share altered, the ceding company may withdraw premium portfolio from the outgoing reinsurer at the date of cancellation and this is given to the incoming reinsurer. The outgoing reinsurer remains liable only for its share of losses outstanding at the date of cancellation but this causes inconvenience as the ceding has to maintain two sets of accounts and the outgoing reinsurer is unable to close its books in respect of the cancelled interest. The latter makes 'a clean cut' by paying a lump sum to be relieved of its share of losses outstanding at the date of cancellation. The payment is termed a loss portfolio and varies between 90 per cent and 100 per cent of the outstanding losses and is subject to adjustment. *See also* HUNDRED PER CENT TREATY BASIS.

cleanliness. Accumulation of trade waste and other rubbish provides a source of fire and also denotes lax management or poor moral hazard (qv). Greasy waste is liable to spontaneous heating and should be removed daily.

clean-up costs. An indirect financial loss due to pollution (qv). Costs may include: cleaning up land, buildings, machinery, lakes, riverside or other water courses, and generally removing the effects of pollution. The heavy cost has created a demand for insurance. The insured may seek to cover his liability for clean-up costs incurred by a third party and/or for the cost of cleaning up his own property. It is possible to extend liability policies but one approach is to provide the cover under a separate environmental impairment policy (qv).

client agreement. FIMBRA (qv) rules require that a member cannot provide a service to a client unless a client agreement or terms of business/engagement letter has been issued. The agreement or letter must include: a statement as prescribed setting out the investment services for which the member is authorised; reference to the member being bound by FIMBRA rules; an undertaking not to transact any business in which the member has a personal interest without previous disclosure; the manner in which instructions may be given by the client for the transaction and how the member's authority may be terminated; the basis of assessment of charges; any mark up or commission; a statement indicating whether the member is permitted to handle clients' money; information about the arrangements for registration and identification of ownership and safe custody of documents in title; identification of the client's right to inspect records and a statement of the protection available against any loss suffered by the client. Under IBRC rules brokers are not required to have client agreements setting out the terms upon which they provide investment service but it is good practice to issue a terms of business letter (*supra*).

client information form. A form to assist an independent financial adviser (qv) to comply with the best advice rule (qv) of the Securities and Investments Board (qv). The form elicits information on such matters as the prospective client's income; mortgage repayments; existing life assurance policies; details of other investments, unit trusts etc; pension arrangements; family commitments; personal investment philosophy (attitude to risk); expectations; life style; and tax bracket. The form provides evidence that enquiries were made before giving the necessary advice.

client's money. Money paid over by a customer to a financial intermediary pending issue of the contract. The Financial Services Act 1986 (qv) requires that this money must be held in trust in a separate account for the benefit of the client.

closed fund. A life assurance fund maintained for a particular group of policies with no new business being accepted for the fund.

closed scheme. A pension scheme which does not admit new members.

closed year. Where the accounting basis is for a two-year period or longer, a closed year is the year of account for which a result has been ascertained. This can only be done after providing for all outstanding claims. At Lloyd's a year of account is normally closed after 36 months.

closing. Completion of an insurance.

closing instructions (or advice). An advice sent by a broker to an insurer who has taken a line on a slip to specify the actual proportion of risk allocated to the insurer and the actual premium receivable. If a slip is oversubscribed, the broker scales down and apportions the risk on a pro rata basis. *See* SHORT CLOSING.

closing slip. *See* CLOSING INSTRUCTIONS.

clubs. *See* MEMBERS' CLUBS.

cluster policies. They have their origin in the introduction of unit-linked life insurance. When an insured pays a given premium he receives not one policy but a number of policies of equal value which offers advantages for tax planning. Each one is issued in return for an equal fraction of the total premium payable. The life insurer issues one document as the 'contract of insurance' together with a number of separate schedule of benefits which when read with the principal contract constitutes a life policy. The separate schedules are expressly incorporated into the contract. For the purpose of the statutory notice (qv), one notice is sufficient if all policies are issued as evidence of one contract. A cluster policy facility can be offered in association with single premium bonds.

CMR Convention (*Contrat de Merchandises par Route*). A convention setting out conditions governing the international carriage of goods by road. CMR makes the carrier responsible for the goods up to a specified amount. The provisions of the Convention were incorporated into UK law by the Carriage of Goods by Road Act 1965.

code of selling practice for general insurance. Registered brokers have their own code. All other intermediaries have to follow this code laid down by the Association of British Insurers (qv), from whom full details can be obtained. It covers selling, explaining, completing forms, collecting money, documents and claims.

co-insurance. 1. Where two or more insurers, who share the risk in agreed proportions, are in direct contractual relationship with the insured they are 'co-insurers' of the risk. One insurer assumes the role of 'leading insurer' for the purpose of administration. A single collective policy (qv) may be issued scheduling the risk and the manner in which it is shared. If one insurer fails to meet his share of any claim, the other insurers are not responsible and the loss will fall on the insured. 2. The term also describes situations where the insured carries a part of the risk. Some policies carry co-insurance clauses (eg insured responsible for 10 per cent of each loss, an excess (qv) or deductible (qv)) but otherwise the application of average clauses (qv) in the case of under-insurance results in the insured becoming a co-insurer responsible for part of the loss. 3. A co-insurance, clause number 11 of the Institute Time Clauses for use with the SG policy form was introduced on 1/10/69 in respect of machinery damage claims to apply a 10 per cent deductible items recoverable under the Inchmaree Clause as an additional deductible. The Institute Time Clauses 1/10/83

do not contain such a clause, but the Institute Machinery Damage Additional Clause (1/10/83), used only with the 1983 clauses, allows for a negotiated amount as a first deductible.

co-insurer. 1. An insurer participating in a co-insurance (qv). 2. The insured when he bears a part of the risk by way of excess, deductible or other means (eg under-insurance leading to the application of average).

cold call. A call made by a Financial Services Act intermediary or company representative on a potential client without any express invitation to call. A call embraces both visits and telephone calls. Cold calls are allowed for life insurance, unit trusts, and personal pensions but the caller must present a business card stating his name, position, firm's name and address and the Financial Services Act authorisation logo. Telephone calls must not be made at an unsociable hour and no misleading information should be given. The caller must make it clear to the client that he will be entering into a contract for the purchase of investments. If the client so requests, the interview should be ended immediately and no undue pressure may be brought on the client or prospect.

cold explosion. An explosion caused by the sudden release of pressure as in the case of a ruptured steam boiler. The risk is generally covered under boiler and pressure plant policies by engineering insurers but cover exists under the standard fire policy for damage caused by explosions (including hot explosions) of domestic boilers.

cold storage clause. *See* CHANGE IN TEMPERATURE CLAUSE.

collapse. 1. A risk covered under a boiler and pressure plant insurance. It means 'the sudden and dangerous distortion (whether or not attended by rupture) of any part of the plant caused by crushing stress by force of steam or other fluid pressure (other than pressure of chemical action or chemical action or ignition of the contents of ignited flue gases)'. 2. When insured under a buildings policy as a named peril, collapse has been defined as 'falling, shrinking together, breaking down or giving way through external pressure, or loss of rigidity or support. Collapse cannot cover intentional demolition, and, as the demolition was in fact due to a settlement (qv) which occurred before the commencement of the insurance, there was not subsidence within that period'—*Allen (David) & Sons Billposting Ltd.* v *Drysdale* (1939). The case considered subsidence and collapse as insured perils under a Lloyd's policy.

'collapse' cover. A popular term to describe third party insurance for the building and allied trades for liability arising from loss or damage taking the form of collapsed buildings. The cover operates in respect of liability for loss of or damage to any land, building or other structure (or any movable property therein or thereon) caused by the removal or weakening of support to such land, building or other structure. A claim, for example, could be made against a builder engaged to modernise premises or carry out extension work on the fabric of the old property which work could entail the removal of a wall or partition. The risk also arises when the foundations are being prepared for a new building in close proximity to existing property. In some circumstances a hefty excess will be required. Cover can be put into effect by overriding the property worked on (qv) exclusion in the public liability policy and/or any exclusion relating to the contract works, materials, temporary buildings etc in so far as damage is caused by removal or weakening of support to any land, property or building.

collateral. The security offered by a borrower for a loan. Life insurance policies that have acquired a surrender value are generally acceptable to lenders as collateral security.

collecting book. The book used in industrial life insurance to record premium payments by policyholders.

collecting societies. Registered friendly societies which operate almost exclusively in the field of industrial life insurance.

collective policy. 1. A single policy on behalf of several co-insurers (*see* CO-INSURANCE) sharing the same large risk. Co-insurers signify their acceptance of the documentation and authorise the leading office to sign a collective policy on their behalf by the issue of a signing slip. The policy is issued by the leading insurer in the joint-names of all co-insurers and on renewal a collective receipt is issued. 2. A fidelity guarantee policy (qv) embracing a number of employees with a separate amount guaranteed for each.

collision. Within the Three-fourths Collision Liability Clause (qv) this is confined to forcible contact between two or more ships. Contact with the anchor or mooring chain of another vessel is a collision but damage so caused to the nets of a fishing vessel is not. *See also* COLLISION LIABILITIES.

collision liabilities. Liability may attach to a shipowner arising out of collision or negligent navigation. Liabilities may include third party property damage, and death or injury. These liabilities, including employers' liability in respect of the crew, are insured (except three-fourths of collision damage to another ship or vessel) under the Three-fourths Collision Collision Liability Clause (qv)) by Protecting and Indemnity Clubs (qv). Shipowners liabilities for loss of life or damage to property may be limited if application is made to the Admiralty to a scale based on tonnage of the wrong-doing vessel (Merchant Shipping Acts). *See also* CROSS LIABILITIES, SISTER SHIP CLAUSE, FREIGHT COLLISION CLAUSE, and BOTH-TO-BLAME COLLISION CLAUSE.

collusion. An agreement between two or more parties to deceive another or others. Theft insurers generally exclude the theft resulting from collusion when a member of staff is involved. Such a theft has little to do with the security of the premises and is more related to the character of the staff. Cover may be available under fidelity guarantee insurance (qv).

combined liability policy. A policy combining two or more types of liability insurance in one policy document eg public liability combined with products liability; employers' liability combined with public liability; a combination of employers' liability, public liability and products liability.

combustible materials. Materials likely to take fire and burn. The actual materials that insurers consider most commonly the first to ignite are: waste and rubbish; combustible elements in the structure and fittings; electrical insulation; textiles; flammable liquids; packing and wrapping.

commercial all risks insurance. *See* INDUSTRIAL ALL RISKS INSURANCE.

commercial guarantees. These are commercial fidelity guarantees required by employers to protect them against loss of money (and often stock) as a result of the dishonesty of their employees in the course of their employment duties. The following are the main types of policies issued by insurers: (a) individual policy relating to one employee only; (b) collective policy, embracing a number of employees with a separate amount of guarantee for each; (c) floating policy, under which a number of employees are bonded, but with one amount of guarantee over the whole; (d) excess floating policy is a collective policy (*supra*) subject to an endorsement to provide a floating guarantee as a protection against any loss in excess of the amounts set out in the schedule; (e) positions policy in which the persons guaranteed are not mentioned by name, but merely the 'position', so that any changes in personnel need not be notified to the insurers. The principal underwriting factor is the system of check operated by the employer. (f) blanket policy which covers the whole staff without mention of either names or positions, the premiums being calculated on the number of employees in specified categories (eg accounting officials, non-accounting officials).

commercial legal expenses insurance. A legal expenses insurance (qv) for businesses. It shifts the expense of going to law to the insurers and gives a commercial or industrial firm the assurance that when involved in legal disputes it will have the necessary legal assistance. Cover is available under a number of sections to deal with the various types of dispute that can arise out of commercial activities, viz: *contract of employment disputes; employment award cover* to indemnify the insured in respect of compensation or damages awarded by a court or tribunal (or agreed settlement) when unfair or wrongful dismissal is proved; *criminal prosecution (legal defence)*—failure to observe leglislation such as the Health and Safety at Work Act etc 1974, Data protection Act, Trade Descriptions Act etc can lead to prosecutions but there is no cover for deliberate offences by the insured or penalties or fines; *patent, copyright cover*—*see* INTELLECTUAL PROPERTY; *property protection*—covers costs of pursuing legal rights to obtain a remedy or to recover damages from a third party, plus legal costs of appeal, where the third party has caused or threatens to cause phsyical damage to the insured's property and/or pecuniary loss to the insured; *goods or services contract cover (commercial contract cover)*—primarily concerned with the cost of pursuing or defending contract disputes, eg debt disputes or disputes related to goods or services bought or sold; *attendance expenses cover* to meet the 'hidden cost' to provide a benefit to pay the wages of directors and employees while attending court or tribunal hearings. In addition some policies make provision for tenancy disputes, jury service, statutory licence protection, warranty and indemnity, personal injury damages recovery, Inland Revenue investigations and VAT tribunals. Indemnities are up to £50 000 each and every claim and a 24-hour legal advice service is often available.

commission. The remuneration paid to an intermediary (broker or agent) for introducing to, and/or handling of, the business for an insurer. Brokers generally earn higher rates of commission (sometimes called 'brokerage') than other types of agents. *See also* REINSURANCE COMMISSION.

Committee of Lloyd's. *See* LLOYD'S, COMMITTEE OF.

common carrier. A person who carries goods for 'all and sundry' willing to pay a reasonable charge. Such a carrier may be of a particular product over a particular route but if he limits the service to a particular sector he becomes a private carrier. A common carrier's liability at common law for the goods is strict subject only to the defences of: action of Queen's enemies, Act of God, fault of the owner, inherent vice. Restrictions on this liability are provided by the Carriers Act 1830 which enables the carrier in certain circumstances to limit his liability to £10 per article or articles. Railways are not common carriers and many road hauliers use standard conditions of contract.

common employment. The Law Reform (Personal Injuries) Act 1948 abolished the defence of common employment. Previously an employer was not liable for injury to an employee caused by the negligence of a fellow employee. The injured party was expected to accept the risk of such injury as a part of his employment. The defence prevented the employer from being held vicariously liable for such torts.

common humanity duty. This expression first appeared in *British Railways Board* v *Herrington* (1972) when the House of Lords established that an occupier's relationship with trespassers was that he must act in a humane manner towards them but was required to do no more. The duty of common humanity has now been given statutory force by the Occupiers' Liability Act 1984 (qv).

common inn. Defined in the Hotel Proprietors Act 1956 (qv). Essentially an establishment open to 'all and sundry' which does not pick and choose its guests. Special responsibilities attach to its proprietor.

Common Law. The law that has been founded upon immemorial usage, established custom, and legal precedents as distinct from statute law. The common law has been developed by broadening down from precedent to precedent.

Common Law Agreement. This operates where contribution (qv) could otherwise apply between a motor insurer and an employers' liability insurer. The former covers the vicarious liability of an employer for injury to a passenger-employee caused by the negligence of the driver-employee in the pursuance of a contract of employment. The latter covers liability arising out of and in connection with the employment. A claim could arise under both policies in respect of the same interest etc. Under the Common Law Agreement, the employers' liability insurer agrees to settle the claim without seeking contribution from the motor insurer.

community co-insurance. A risk is a part of a Community co-insurance if all of the following conditions apply: (a) it is direct and not reinsurance business. (b) It falls into general business authorisation classes 4 to 9, 11 to 13, or 16 (*see* DTI CLASSES). (c) It is situated within a member State. (d) It is covered by a single contract by two or more insurers; and (e) one of those insurers participates through a head office, branch or agency established in a member State other than that in which the leading insurer's head office is situated.

community company. An insurance company whose head office is within a member state of the European Community.

commutation. The conversion of part of the money invested in a pension into a tax free lump sum at the moment of retirement. There are limits as to the amount that can be commuted in this way. Usually the lump sum is about three times the remaining annual pension.

commutation clause. A clause which sometimes appears in Lloyd's reinsurance treaties to permit the reinsurer to estimate all liabilities and then discharge them by payment of a lump sum.

company reimbursement. See DIRECTORS' AND OFFICERS' LIABILITY INSURANCE.

company representative. A term that applies to a life insurance sales consultant who is employed by a particular company to sell that company's financial products. Compare with appointed company representatives (qv). *Also see* FINANCIAL SERVICES ACT 1986.

competent fellow employees (servants). An employer must take reasonable care to provide his employees with competent fellow workers. Now that the defence of common employment (qv) has been abolished claims under this head are rare.

complete annuity. See APPORTIONABLE ANNUITY.

compliance officer. A person appointed by a Self Regulatory Organisation (qv) to ensure that the members' activities are carried out in accordance with the rules. The appointment of a compliance officer is compulsory.

composite company. An insurance company which transacts all or several of the major classes of insurance.

composite policy. *See* COMBINED LIABILITY POLICY.

compound reversionary bonus. A life insurance bonus payable in the same time and the same circumstances of the sum insured which is declared periodically as an addition to the sum insured and accrued bonuses.

comprehensive. A term describing a policy which brings together a number of different types of cover in one document (eg a private car comprehensive policy has sections providing material damage cover, third party cover, personal accident cover, medical expenses etc). The term can also be used to describe the range of risks or perils which are covered, eg a householders' comprehensive policy covers fire and special perils while the standard fire policy covers fire, lightning and certain explosion risks only. A policy covering an 'extensive' range of perils often attracts the term comprehensive.

'comprehensive extended-terms guarantee'. A term applied to the credit insurance provided by the Export Credit Guarantee Department (ECGD) to short-term policyholders (*see* COMPREHENSIVE SHORT-TERM GUARANTEE) who also sell capital or semi-capital goods. This supplementary insurance normally covers credit up to five years but exceptionally can be for longer terms.

'comprehensive short-term guarantee'. A term applied to the ECGD's short-term guarantee when arranged on a whole turnover cover. It covers contracts for the sale of UK goods or of certain admissible foreign goods which are being re-exported from the UK. The contract must not provide for credit of more than 180 days, and the standard cover commences on despatch of the goods for export. Where the goods are specially manufactured or adapted and are easily disposable if the shipment is frustrated the cover can commence at the date of contract provided the cover applies to all contracts and not on a selective basis. The 'buyer risks' covered are insolvency, failure to pay within six months of the due date, and failure to accept goods already shipped. The special case of the public sector buyer who simply fails to fulfil the contract can be covered by agreement. The policy also covers country risks which are mainly political risks and include action by any overseas government which prevents performance of the contract (eg imposition of import or payment restrictions or withdrawal of a valid authority to import and pay for goods). Any general moratorium declared by the country's buyer or any country through which payment is to be made is also covered. War, civil war or disturbance, and natural disaster are covered where they are the proximate cause of the non-performance of the contract and provided they are not normally insured in the commercial insurance market. The cover is usually 90 per cent of the loss in cases of buyer default or insolvency and up to 95 per cent for the country or market risks. When the buyer fails to accept or take up the goods the exporter bears a 'first loss' of 20 per cent and ECGD bears 90 per cent of the balance. *See also* COMPREHENSIVE EXTENDED-TERM GUARANTEE.

compulsory insurance. Insurance which has to be effected to comply with the law. Failure to comply may result in criminal sanctions. All compulsory insurance legislation in the UK has been passed with a view to ensuring that accident victims entitled to compensation do not have to rely upon the wealth of those responsible for their injury or damage. *See* ROAD TRAFFIC ACT 1988, RIDING ESTABLISHMENTS ACT 1970, NUCLEAR INSTALLATIONS ACT 1965, EMPLOYERS' LIABILITY (COMPULSORY INSURANCE) ACT 1969, and MERCHANT SHIPPING (OIL POLLUTION) ACT 1971. Also insurance brokers (qv) have to effect professional indemnity insurance in order to secure registration.

compulsory third party damage. This refers to the third party property damage which became the subject compulsory insurance requirements from 31 December 1988. *See* ROAD TRAFFIC ACT 1988 (COMPULSORY INSURANCE REQUIREMENTS), MOTOR VEHICLES (COMPULSORY INSURANCE) REGULATIONS 1987, and the MOTOR INSURERS' BUREAU.

computer consultants insurance. A combined liability policy for computer consultants not engaged in manufacture, installation or servicing of hardware covering: professional indemnity insurance (qv), public and products liability, and employers' liability.

computer insurances. Policies issued by engineering insurers covering risks of varying size from desk-top microcomputers to large main-frame systems. Broadly similar insurances can be divided into two categories. Cover in both instances can be modified to meet particular requirements and the protection afforded by the maintenance/hiring agreements in force, if any. (a) *Large commercial computer installations insurance.* This means an insurance of a computer installation being a configuration comprising a central electronic machine capable of storing and retrieving information working with tape units, disc drive units, card/read punch machines, printers and similar units. The cover comes in three sections. (i) Loss/damage to the computer installation by sudden and unforeseen physical damage at the situation. (ii) Loss/damage to computer systems records similarly caused including, if required, the cost of reinstatement of information. (iii) Consequential loss or indemnity for additional expenditure by hired time on an alternative computer or carrying out work manually as a result of the damage, and, if required, breakdown of air conditioning plant, motor generator set, or accidental failure of the public electricity supply. (b) *Small commercial computer insurance.* Cover is in two sections as follows: (i) Accidental loss/damage to the computer equipment and records, including accidental or malicious erasure of programs and other magnetically stored information. (ii) Increased cost of working arising from loss/damage in (i); loss/damage recoverable under a maintenance agreement; accidental failure or fluctuation of the electricity supply; denial of access through damage to own or surrounding property or by action of police or public authority. Cover includes transit, breakdown (if not covered under the maintenance agreement), debris removal, temporary repairs, automatic cover (qv), and reinstatement as new.

concealment. The wilful failure to disclose a material fact (qv) by a proposer for insurance. It is fraudulent and the insurer, who can prove this breach of the duty of utmost good faith (qv), can sue for damages for the tort of deceit. If fraud is proved the insured is not entitled to a return of premium but generally the insurer is content to avoid on grounds of non-disclosure and return the premium.

concurrent causes. The doctrine of proximate cause (qv) enquires into all the circumstances of the case to see which of all the causes is the proximate cause of the loss. If two or more causes operate together, ie concurrently, and combine to produce the loss they are known as concurrent causes. If the effects cannot be separated, and one of the causes is an excepted peril, the insurer will not be liable nothwithstanding that another cause was an insured peril. The loss is as much due to the excepted peril as the insured peril and the insurer gets the benefit of the exception. However, if no excepted peril is involved and the other causes are simply uninsured perils then the insurer will be liable for all of the loss as long as one of the causes is an insured peril. Insurers sometimes modify the operation of proximate cause by insuring only those losses that are 'solely and independently' due to the insured peril. If the effects of the causes can be separated the insurer will be liable for the loss attributable to the insured peril only.

concurrent insurance. A concurrent insurance is one covering the same property under the same conditions and against the same perils as the policy with which it is 'concurrent'.

concussion damage. Damage caused by a violent shock. Concussion damage is the typical outcome of an explosion. The standard fire policy covers explosion damage if caused by domestic boilers (qv) or if the explosion of gas is used for domestic purposes or used for lighting or heating the building (provided it is not a part of a gas works).

conditional assignment. An assignment of a life policy that is not absolute but is dependent upon certain conditions. The most frequent example is that of a policy given as security for a loan or mortgage. When the loan is repaid and no interest is outstanding the original assured has the right to have the policy reassigned to him. Alternatively there may be an equitable assignment which occurs when the borrower deposits his policy with the lender who then acquires an equitable interest in the property mortgaged. In the event of a claim the mortgagee would have to prove his right in equity.

conditional bond. A bond (qv) where a condition is added that if the obligor does or forbears from doing some act the obligation shall be void. The person in whose favour the bond is drawn is the obligee. The condition sets out the acts on the performance of which the obligation is to cease. *See* PERFORMANCE BONDS and GOVERNMENT BONDS.

conditions. Policy conditions regulate the cover granted and demand certain standards of conduct and procedures from the insured (eg notice of claims). Conditions may be express (ie stated in the policy) or implied, ie not set out but read into the contract by the law. Express conditions can be sub-divided into general conditions or particulars conditions. The conditions implied in insurance contracts that: (a) the parties will observe utmost good faith in all material particulars both in the making of the proposal and in connection with any claim; (b) the subject-matter of insurance is in existence; (c) the subject-matter of insurance has an identity; (d) the insured has an insurable interest. Conditions can also be classified as: (i) Conditions precedent, eg things to be done before the contract comes into effect such as the disclosure of material facts by the insured. A breach renders the contract voidable by the insurer *ab initio* (qv). (ii) Conditions subsequent, eg the insured may be required to comply with certain requirements during the currency of the policy, such as maintaining certain standards of security on his premises. The contract is voidable from the date of the breach. (iii) Conditions precedent to liability. These relate to things that have to be done by the insured before the insurer can be liable for a particular loss, eg notification of claims as required. A breach entitles the insurer to avoid the loss to which the breach relates. The breach does not otherwise affect the policy which will continue to run. The burden of proving a breach of condition attaches to the insurer unless the insurer has used clear words to show that the burden has been shifted to insured to show that he has complied with the condition.

conduct and control of claims clause. *See* CONDUCT OF PROCEEDINGS CLAUSE.

conduct of proceedings clause. Liability policies invariably include a clause (i) restraining the insured from making an admission of liability to the party claiming against him (*see* NON-ADMISSION OF LIABILITY CLAUSE, and (ii) giving the insurer the right to take the absolute conduct and control of all proceedings including the defence or settlement of any claim that may be within the policy. However, the courts have seen fit to control the absolute discretion of the insurer. In *Groom* v *Crocker* (1939) it was held that the insurers have the right to decide upon the proper tactics provided that they do so in what they consider to be to the common interest of themselves and their insured but the limit on the insurer's discretion is not a strict or onerous one. Where an insurer made a payment to a third party with a denial of liability and sought to recover a £5 excess from the insured being his share of the third party loss, the insured refused to pay as he felt he was not liable for the third party loss. He was not upheld as the insurers had acted within their rights under the conduct clause (*Beacon Insurance Co* v *Langdale* (1939). In Groom's case the payment had been made with an admission of liability and this technically libelled the insured and put the insurer in breach of their contractual duty. The insurers must not use their rights to unjustifiably admit liability. Finally, the clause enables the insurers to use the name of the insured to enforce for their own benefit any claims against any third party. This enables the insurers to exercise subrogation rights (qv) before they have made any payment and so modifies the common law principle.

confirmation of renewal. Acknowledgement sent to the insured after payment of the renewal premium confirming the continuation of the policy for a future term.

Congenital Disabilities (Civil Liabilities) Act 1976. The Act provides that a person responsible for an occurrence affecting a parent, whose child is then born disabled but alive, shall be liable to that child if he would have been liable to the parent in tort. There is no liability for an occurrence before the time of conception if the parents knew the risk of their child being born disabled. Liability of the mother, though not of the father, to the child is expressly excluded except where the mother is driving a motor vehicle when she knows, or ought to know, that she is pregnant. Also a professional person is under no liability for treatment or advice given in accordance with contemporary professional standards of care. Damages for loss of expectation of life (qv) are not awarded unless the child survives for 48 hours. There is also provision for a claim under the Nuclear Installations Act 1965 (qv) where a child is born with disabilities attributable to a nuclear incident.

connected policies. One life policy may be written on the terms that it is to continue in force provided always another policy continues to run. The two are called connected policies. They do not rank as qualifying policies unless when combined into a single policy, the latter would have been a qualifying policy (qv).

consensus ad idem. Literally means of the same mind. There must be agreement between the parties although they will be judged by what they appeared to agree to and not what they later claim. The law excuses certain kinds of mistake only (mistake as to the existence of the subject-matter, as to the identity of the subject-matter, as to the identity of the other party, as to the contract itself). Rectification (qv) of a written document may be possible, and the contract can be invalidated by innocent or fraudulent misrepresentation, non-disclosure, and concealment, and duress and undue influence.

consequential loss. Loss of an indirect nature that is the result of some other loss. For example, the destruction of

property by fire is a direct loss but the loss of income due to the interruption of business at the place where the destruction occurred is a consequential or indirect loss. A material damage insurance on property does not cover consequential loss unless a relevant item is specifically included (Re Wright and Pole (1834). The normal practice is to insure these losses separately under business interruption insurance (qv) or engineering consequential loss insurance. In *Symington* v *Union Insurance of Canton* (1928) cork insured under a marine policy against loss by fire and stored on a jetty was jettisoned into the sea to prevent the spread of an existing fire. This was regarded as loss by fire and not a consequential loss as the insured peril had happened and was so imminent that immediate action was necessary.

consequential loss insurance. *See* BUSINESS INTERRUPTION INSURANCE.

consequential loss (satellites). *See* SATELLITE CONSEQUENTIAL LOSS INSURANCE.

constant amiable. *See* EUROPEAN ACCIDENT STATEMENT.

constant net repayment mortgage. Most building societies now provide this type of mortgage in lieu of the repayment (known also as gross profile or increasing repayment mortgage) mortgage. The proportion of capital repayment increases each year but the societies have so arranged it that the net repayments remain the same for the whole of the mortgage term. The mortgagor pays back higher amounts of capital in the early years than in the gross profile system, so that overall the amount of interest paid is less and the total cost of the mortgage is lower than under the old system. However, payments will vary if there is an interest change or a change in the tax position of the mortgagor.

Construction (Lifting Operations) Regulations 1961. The regulations apply to plant used for building operations or engineering constructions works. The statutory maximum inspection periods for the plant are: lifting appliances 14 months; lifting gear, 6 months; hoists, 6 months.

construction of buildings. 1. Fire insurers always enquire into the construction of buildings proposed for insurance. Two aspects of great significance are: (a) The materials used in the construction of the building, including ceilings, linings and partitions. These should not be capable of assisting the spread of fire. (b) The division of buildings into fire-resisting compartments by fire-break walls and floors making them less vulnerable to fire and may be cheaper to insure. 2. Theft insurers are also concerned with construction. Premises with brick walls and concrete roofs offer more resistance to intruders and vandals than those built with less solid materials such as asbestos sheeting, corrugated iron and timber.

construction of policy. 1. The rules governing the interpretation of a policy which include the *contra proferentem* rule (qv), the ordinary meaning rule (qv), the *ejusdem generis* rule (qv), the whole policy rule (qv), the technical words rule (qv), and the written words prevail rule (qv). 2. The First Schedule of the Marine Insurance Act 1906 contains the Rules for the Construction of the Policy.

constructive total loss. It is defined in Marine Insurance Act, s. 60 as a situation where the subject-matter is reasonably abandoned by the insured because either an actual total loss is unavoidable or to prevent a total loss requires an expenditure which exceeds the value saved. In either event there is commercially a total loss, although not destruction. A prudent uninsured owner would, in such circumstances, abandon his property and therefore the insured must act in the same manner, ie abandon and then claim a total loss because an insurer is liable only for a total loss when it is proved. The insured cannot, however, claim any benefit from what may be salved from the loss. *See* ABANDONMENT.

Consumer Credit Act 1974. This Act establishes a comprehensive code for regulation for the supply to individuals (including sole traders and partners) of credit not exceeding £5000 throughout the UK. It further provides for the licensing of those who conduct a business of granting consumer credit, and of ancillary credit businesses. Policy loans, 'topping up'

loans, and house purchase loans are within the scope of the Act which therefore is likely to affect life insurers, insurance brokers, and other agents. The Act also states that if the debtor under a consumer debtor–creditor–supplier agreement has any claim against the supplier in respect of a misrepresentation or breach of contract, he also has a claim against the creditor, ie the supplier of finance. This does not apply to a claim under a non-commercial contract, or to any item costing less than £30 or more than £10 000.

consumer (or personal) legal expenses cover. A legal expenses insurance (qv) giving the policyholder access to the cost of legal representation to defend certain legal actions brought against him or to pursue actions against others. The 'consumer section' of the policy covers, *inter alia*, disputes over holidays and the quality of goods and services. The cover extends to cover the cost of suing builders who construct extensions. The 'neighbourhood' or 'enjoyment of property' section covers disputes with neighbours, property and actions against those who damage the insured's home or contents, eg motorists, tenancy disputes, squatters etc The 'personal injury' section operates when the insured has been injured and needs to bring an action against the party alleged to be responsible. The policy may also assist the insured in employment and motoring disputes, including recovery of uninsured losses and defence of motor prosecutions.

consumer/investor protection. Everybody in insurance has to observe strict rules about how insurance is sold (*see* CODE OF SELLING PRACTICE) and about the way in which insurance companies handle claims. As far as personal lines insurances and the payment of claims are concerned insurance companies follow rules set out in a statement of insurance practice. Complaints can be referred to the Insurance Ombudsman Bureau (qv) or the Personal Insurance Arbitration Service (qv). The Association of British Insurers (qv) can also help by approaching the insurance company on behalf of the insured. In industrial assurance complaints can be referred to the industrial assurance commissioner (qv). In investment business (qv) the whole purpose of the Financial Services Act 1986 (qv) has been to protect investors including the provision of the investors' compensation fund (qv). Also, complaints can be taken up with the relevant Self Regulating Organisation (qv).

Consumer Protection Act 1987. This implements the EC directive on product liability by imposing strict liability on the producers of goods for death, personal injury or damage to private property valued above £275. The Act does not affect any existing civil laws governing product liability and imposes no liability in respect of products first supplied before 1 March 1988. An injured person, who must prove that his injury was caused by the product, must claim within three years of the injury (or knowledge thereof) but cannot sue under the Act ten years after the defective product was supplied (ie put into circulation) by the producer. A defective product is one where the safety of the product is not such as persons are generally entitled to expect. The term 'producer' includes the manufacturer, component manufacturer, raw material suppliers, processors, importers (meaning first importers into the EC), 'own-branders' (suppliers whose name is on the product giving the impression they manufactured it), and 'forgetful suppliers' (a supplier who fails to inform the injured party of the identity of the producer). Section 4 of the Act sets out six defences: (i) The defect was caused by complying with the law if the defect was the inevitable result of that compliance. (ii) The person sued did not supply the product (eg it was stolen or is a counterfeit of his products). (iii) The supplier is not in business with a view to making profit (eg this excludes sales of home-made toys to church bazaars). (iv) The defect was not in the product at the time of supply. (v) The state of scientific and technical knowledge at the time of supply was not such that a producer might be expected to have discovered the defect if it had existed in his products while they were under his control. (This is known as the 'state of the art' defence

(qv) or the 'development risks' defence.) (vi) End-product design, ie the producer of a component will not be liable if he is able to show that the defect was due either to the design of the finished product, or to the defective specifications given to him by the producer of the final product. Part II of the Act introduces a general safety requirement (qv) and makes it a criminal offence to supply unsafe goods in the UK. This part of the Act is restricted to consumer goods subject to exceptions (growing crops, water, food, aircraft, controlled drugs, medicinal products, and tobacco). Meanwhile, the regulations under the Consumer Safety Act 1978 (qv) setting out in detail how specific goods must be constructed and what instructions and warnings must accompany them will continue. Product liability policies provide legal defence cover in respect of prosecutions under this part of the Act.

Consumer Safety Act 1978. An Act enabling the Government to pass regulations to set the standards to be met in the manufacture of specific goods, ie those considered potentially dangerous, eg paraffin heaters, children's nightdresses. A person marketing goods that do not conform to the standards laid down is guilty of an offence and will be strictly liable for injury caused by the goods. The Government can also issue a prohibition order banning the sale or supply of specified products. The powers are now contained in the Consumer Safety Act 1987.

consumer sale. A sale when the person buying 'deals as a consumer'. Exclusion clauses of the implied terms of fitness for purpose (qv) and merchantable quality (qv) are not permitted (Unfair Contract Terms Act 1977). The Unfair Contract Terms Act 1977 (qv), s. 12 of the Act explains that a person deals as a consumer if: (a) he neither makes the contract in the contract in the course of a business nor holds himself out as doing so; and (b) the other party does make the contract in the course of business; and (c) the goods are of a type ordinarily supplied for private use or consumption.

consumer transaction. See CONSUMER SALE.

constant extra risk. A term used by life underwriters to describe an impaired life (qv) where the additional risk will remain unchanged, ie the proposer's medical condition will neither worsen nor improve as opposed to one that is increasing or diminishing. *See* INCREASING EXTRA RISK and REDUCING EXTRA RISK.

contact lenses insurance. An 'all risks' insurance in respect of a form of property easily lost or damaged.

contingency. An uncertain event.

contingent fee system. A system operated in many states of the USA under which lawyers are prepared to act for plaintiffs on the understanding that their fee payment will be a percentage of any award made to the plaintiff. If there is no award they will receive no payment. The system removes the risk of a plaintiff incurring high costs for unsuccessful legal action and consequently gives easy access to the courts. The system is in part responsible for the reticence of UK liability insurers towards risks with a US exposure.

contingency fund. A reserve fund set aside by an insurer as a safeguard against exceptionally heavy and unexpected losses that could not be covered out of other funds.

contingency insurances. A term describing those policies that do not fall naturally into one of the principal classes of insurance business. The term embraces insurances such as abandonment of events (qv), pluvius insurance (qv), twins insurance (qv), marriage insurance, memorial stone insurance (qv) and similar insurances, particularly those of an unusual nature.

contents. All insurers define what they mean by this term in the household contents policy. Typically, this means: household goods including furniture, furnishings, domestic appliances, pictures, clothing, personal effects and other possessions—and money up to £200, which together comprise the sum insured shown in the policy schedule as 'household goods'. Specifically excluded from the term are: motor vehicles, boats, caravans, trailers, gliders—and accessories belonging to any of these items; pets and livestock; any property more specifically insured by this or any other policy; securities, certificates or documents of any kind except those defined as 'money'; interior decorations; property owned or used for business. The property must belong to the insured or be property for which he is legally responsible or belong to members of his family or household permanently living with him. The 'household goods' of domestic servants are also included.

contents insurance. *See* HOUSEHOLD CONTENTS INSURANCE.

continental scale. A scale of benefits payable under personal accident and sickness insurances to provide an alternative to the normal fixed scale of benefits. The continental scale fixes a maximum capital sum to be paid on death or permanent total disablement and then specifies the percentage thereof to be paid in respect of the other injuries/sickness constituting insured events under the policy. The more serious the injury the higher will be the percentage payable.

continental use. *See* FOREIGN USE.

contingency loading. An element in the insurer's premium calculation to allow a margin for possible fluctuations in claims costs. It is one of a number of items added to the risk premium (qv) which covers the 'average claims' cost for the year. The greater the level of fluctuations in an insurer's actual claims experience the greater the cushion of the contingency loading will need to be. Other elements in the premium computation include expenses loading (qv) and profit loading.

contingent (or survivorship) annuity. Also known as a reversionary annuity. The annuity payments start on the death of a named person and are payable to another named person throughout their life. One spouse can use this type of annuity to make provision for the other spouse although life insurance is usually more attractive.

contingent (or survivorship) assurances. These provide for the sum assured being payable on the death of one person (the life assured), provided it occurs during the life-time of the another (the counter life). The ages of both lives must be proved but only the life assured has to be medically examined or otherwise prove the state of their health.

contingent liability cover. When one party depends on an insurance effected by another party there can be no certainty that when a claim occurs that the insurance will be effective. Contingent liability insurance is effectively a fall-back insurance. The insured may, for example, have breached a policy condition. The party, usually a business, relying on the other's insurance can safeguard his position by extending his own public liability policy to provide contingent liability cover or arranging separate contingent liability cover. The extended cover becomes operative upon the contingency that the primary insurance fails. The insurance may be required by principals who rely upon cover arranged by contractors, hire car operators who rely on hirers but most commonly by employers who rely upon the motor insurances effected by their employees who use their private cars on the employers' business. The private car policy provides an employers' indemnity but the public liability policy almost invariably carries a motor contingent liability extension to give the employer a fall-back situation.

continuation clause. Clause 2 in the Institute Time Clauses by which the vessel is held covered until arrival at her destination should she be at sea or a port of distress, at the time the policy expires. It rarely applies as the succeeding policy comes into operation immediately at the expiry date.

continuation option. An option to an early leaver to continue an insurance in his own name when leaving a group life assurance scheme (generally an ancillary to a pension scheme), usually on termination of employment, before a specified age, eg 60. The option is to effect a new insurance at the company's ordinary rates without medical examination for a sum not exceeding that which applied to the individual under the group insurance.

continuing warranties. A warranty (qv) whereby the insured agrees that a particular state of affairs will exist or not exist in the future, usually for the duration of the insurance contract. The insured may promise, for example, to remove waste from his premises daily. Unless the insurer uses words that make it abundantly clear that the warranty is to apply on a continuing basis it will be treated as one applying only to the state of affairs existing at the time it was made. In *Kennedy* v *Smith* (1976), a warranty in a proposal form 'I am a total abstainer from alcoholic drink', was held to apply to the past and the time at which it was made but not the future. However, some statements can only be read as being applicable to the future. In *Beauchamp* v *National Mutual Indemnity Insurance Co* (1937) 3 AER 19 the insured's statement that he did not use explosives in his work as a builder was held to apply to the future as it was clear he had not used explosives previously. Warranties as to the nature of premises and precautions taken against loss are prima facie taken to be continuing warranties. Continuing (otherwise called promissory) warranties are created by the proposal form and declaration or in the body of the policy. If created in the proposal and there is a breach the policy is voidable *ab initio* otherwise it will be voidable from the date of the breach.

contraband of war. Goods which a belligerent may lawfully seize on the way to his enemy's territory. When used in a marine insurance policy the term applies only to goods or merchandise. It does not extend to persons (officers of a belligerent power) even though their presence on ship may increase the risk of an attack. If a policy is warranted 'no contraband' the policy may be avoided if any part of the goods carried is contraband.

contract cover. A commercial legal expenses insurance (qv) providing for the legal costs and expenses incurred in: (a) Pursuing or defending any dispute with a customer or supplier in respect of goods and services including the enforcement of judgments. (b) Appeal or defence of appeal against judgment of the relevant court or arbitrator. Any costs awarded against the insured are also covered. The amount of the dispute must not be less than £150. Lease or tenancy matters and disputes relating to the construction, conversion or extension of buildings are not covered. Full contract cover is not available for every occupation, notably those where professional indemnity cover (qv) is more appropriate.

contract frustration. An insurance for exporters and overseas contractors to cover bank guarantees (wrongful calling), contract ratification/termination/repudiation, penalties for delay/performance, rejection, embargo or recourse indemnity. The scheme is available from both Lloyd's and the company market.

contract of employment award cover. A legal expenses insurance covering: (a) An award of compensation or damages made against the insured in court or tribunal in favour of an ex-employee in respect of his wrongful or unfair dismissal. (b) A payment of compensation or damages to an ex-employee in respect of his wrongful or unfair dismissal in an out of court settlement approved by the insurer. In both instances cover operates when the award or payment follows a claim under contract of employment cover (qv). No compensation or damages are covered in respect of: breach of a fixed term contract; failure to allow the return of a woman after maternity leave; dismissals on grounds of pregnancy, race or sex discrimination, or trade union activities or failure to join a trade union in a closed shop situation; failure to supply written reasons for dismissal within the 14 day time limit and withholding money due under the contract of employment or any statutory provision relating thereto.

contract of employment cover. A legal expenses insurance covering legal costs and expenses for: (a) Defence of civil claims arising from disputes with employees or ex-employees relating to their contract of employment. (b) Defence of civil or criminal proceedings arising from disputes with employees, ex-employees or prospective employees leading to civil or criminal proceedings under the Race Relations Act 1976 or the Sex Discrimination Act 1975 or any Acts amending them or replacing them. (c) Appeal or defence of appeal against sentence, conviction or judgment of the relevant court, tribunal or arbitrator. Costs awarded against the insured in civil cases in re-spect of any of the above are also covered. Claims by employees for personal injury or damage to property are not covered and cover does not apply to disputes which relate basically to the ownership of the business. *See also* CONTRACT OF EMPLOYMENT AWARD COVER.

contract of insurance. A contract whereby one party, an insurer, agrees in return for an agreed consideration, from another party, an insured, to pay the insured money, or its equivalent, on the happening of certain events. Insurance is a contract of *uberrimae fidei* (of the utmost good faith (qv)) and of indemnity (qv), except in the case of life and accident insurance, when an agreed sum is payable (*see* BENEFIT POLICIES). Three elements (the consideration (premium), payment to the insured, and a specified event) were cited as the elements that must be present in a contract of insurance in *Medical Defence Union Ltd* v *Department of Trade* (1979). The agreed consideration can be a premium (qv), the cancellation of an existing insurance or the waiver of a return premium. The event must not only be uncertain but it must be one in which the insured has an insurable interest (qv). The payment by the insurer must be obligatory and not voluntary (*see* MEDICAL DEFENCE UNION). There is no definition in statute of an insurance contract and yet insurance is regulated by the Insurance Companies Act 1982, is exempted from the Unfair Contract Terms Act 1977, and is the whole purpose of the Policyholders' Protection Act 1975. It has been suggested (J. Birds, *Modern Insurance Law*, Sweet & Maxwell) that for the purpose of regulation, anyone who, for a consideration, regularly enters into contracts to carry the risks of others related to uncertain events is carrying on insurance business.

contract price insurances. Loss settlements under indemnity contracts are normally based on the market value at the time of the loss. However, fire insurers sometimes agree to settle on the contract price. This is where the goods, for which the insured (the vendor) is responsible, have been sold but not yet delivered, are damaged by fire causing the contract to be cancelled.

Consequently the only true indemnity (qv) is the contract price. If the contract is not cancelled by fire, the insured can purchase goods to replace those lost in the fire and fulfil his contract. In this instance, a settlement based on market value is the measure of indemnity.

contract price repairs. A motor claims situation where the staff engineer (qv) and the repairer agree in advance the price to be paid for the repairs. This is beneficial to the insurer when the damage is extensive and there is the risk that during the repair work additional work may be discovered to make total repair costs uneconomic having regard to the value of the car.

contract signing scheme. A scheme run at Lloyd's Policy Signing Office (qv) whereby underwriters can receive bulk entries of items for which they do not require individual advices (eg where there is a large volume of similar risks).

contract works insurance. Otherwise known as 'contractors all risks' insurance. The insurance may be related to the contract requirements of the Institute of Civil Engineers (ICE) and the Joint Contract Tribunal (qv). Conditions of this type covering civil engineering and construction contracts specifically refer to the liability of the contractors for the safety of the contract works and to the insurances that should be effected. The policy is 'all risks' covering the 'Property' on or adjacent to the site. Policies can be arranged for specific projects or to cover all projects during the period of insurance. The 'Property' includes the contract works, temporary works and materials, constructional plant, scaffolding, tools etc, site huts and temporary buildings and their contents, hired property, and employees tools and personal effects. Insurers impose excesses for certain perils (eg £250 for storm, theft and malicious damage), exclusions and limits in respect of certain categories of property. Policy extensions available include transit, off-site storage, removal of debris, principal's clause and professional fees.

contract works insurance on machinery installation contracts. Machinery installation imposes heavy burdens on the contractor who is often bound by I.Mech. E./I.E.E. Conditions of Contract which make the contractor liable for most forms of damage until the work is taken over by the Employer which is not normally until after testing. The policy on machinery installation contracts protects both the Employer and the contractor and covers physical loss/damage to the machinery and plant and materials brought on the site (optional extensions, to include constructional plant tools and tackle, temporary buildings, transit (but not by sea or air) and most testing risks can be covered). Policies are arranged either for a single contract or for a period of time. Contractors may select the latter but owners sometimes arrange the cover which is also known as machinery movement insurance. Cover is needed by contractors who specialise in the erection and installation of new plant or who move re-erect existing plant.

contracting carrier. See GUADALAJARA CONVENTION 1961.

contracting in. This terms describes an occupational pension scheme that provides benefits on top of state provided pensions, both basic and earnings-related. Members of the scheme have not been contracted out of SERPS (qv).

contracting out. 1. This term describes an occupational pension scheme that is used to provide its members with a level of benefits in place of those of the state earnings-related pension scheme (SERPS) (qv). National insurance contributions from the member and the employer are reduced to take this into account. The benefits are in addition to the basic state pension. 2. The term may describe use of a term or clause in a contract whereby one of the parties exempts (ie contracts out of) himself from certain responsibilities. For example, a bailee (qv) might agree to hold the bailor's (qv) property subject to contracting out of responsibility for loss or damage. The effectiveness of such a clause will depend on the circumstances of the case and the Unfair Contract Terms Act 1977 (qv) where applicable.

contracting purchaser's clause. *See* PUR-
CHASER'S INTEREST CLAUSE.

contractors' plant policy. A policy for
contractors who own, hire-in or hire-
out plant. It is a simple declaration
policy with a general description of the
plant without itemising the individual
items. The policy covers the risks of
impact, fire, lightning, explosion, aircraft, storm, tempest, flood, earthquake, water damage, frost, theft,
malicious damage whilst at work or at
rest or during dismantling or erection,
loading, unloading or transit. For
hired-in plant the cover includes legal
liability for negligent breakdown and
continuing hire charges. For hired-
out plant the cover can be extended to
indemnify the hirer. The premium is
adjustable in accordance with an annual declaration.

**Contractors' Plant-Hire Association's
Model Conditions (1979).** Conditions
generally used when plant is hired out
by its owner for use by others, eg the
construction or civil engineering industries. Condition 4 makes the hirer
responsible for personnel lent by the
owner and involved in loading or unloading operations. This appears to be
an indemnity clause (qv) in respect of
third party claims. Condition 8 makes
the hirer responsible for all claims arising from the operation of the plant by
the driver/operator hired with the
plant. The clause appears to relieve
the plant owner of his public and employers' liability risks. Condition 13
makes the hirer liable for loss/damage
to the plant and for third party claims
without affecting clause 8. There is an
obligation on the plant owner to supply a competent driver but the hirer
stills becomes liable for his negligence.
The owner is responsible for damage
etc before delivery to site when in transit arranged by the owner who is also
responsible for erection of the plant if
under his exclusive control.

contractual liability. Liability that arises as
a result of a contract (ie legally enforceable agreement) between the parties involved as opposed to liability
imposed by common law or statute. It
was formerly the practice to exclude
contractual liability from liability
policies unless liability would have attached in the absence of the contract.

The modern practice varies and the
outright exclusion of contractual liability is no longer the invariable rule.
More commonly the current practice
is to exclude only liability for liquidated damages (qv) and penalties.

contra proferentem **rule.** Any ambiguity in
the wording of a contract will be construed against the person who drew up
the wording, ie in insurance against
the insurer. The rule will only be applied where there is real ambiguity. It
is an aid to construction and not an instrument for creating ambiguity.

contributing interests. The main contributing interests to general average expenditure (qv) are ship, freight and
cargo, including specie. The only exceptions are HM mails, crew's effects,
and the personal effects of passengers
not shipped under a bill of lading.
Otherwise the interests saved contribute on their net arrived values at the
place where the voyage ends, that is, at
the destination, or at an intermediate
port where the voyage is abandoned.

contributing values. *See* CONTRIBUTING IN-
TERESTS.

contribution. A corollary of the principle
of indemnity (qv). If there is more
than one contract of indemnity in
force covering the same interest,
against the same peril in respect of the
same subject-matter the insured is entitled to make his claim in full against
the insurer of his choice. The insurer
so chosen is then entitled to call upon
any other insurers liable for the same
to make a rateable contribution towards that loss. If the insured recovered from more than one insurer
he would, contrary to the principle of
indemnity, emerge with a profit. Once
he has recovered in full from one insurer he has no loss to recover from
another. In practice each insurer uses
a contribution clause under which
they limit their liability to their
rateable proportion of any loss where
contribution arises and so modify the
operation of the principle so that the
insured has to make a partial recovery
from all insurers concerned. The basis
of contribution may be in proportion
to the sums insured under the policies,
the maximum liability method or be
determined by the independent liability method (qv). Insurers sometimes

avoid becoming involved in contribution by the use of non-contribution clauses (qv), 'more specific insurance' clauses (qv), and market agreements (*see* COMMON LAW AGREEMENT). *See also* KING AND QUEEN GRANARIES CASE. The term double insurance is used in the Marine Insurance Act 1906, s. 32 in connection with policies giving rise to contribution.

contribution system. A system whereby a life office allocates a part of its surplus to its with profits policyholders to reflect the policy's contribution to the surplus. The contribution depends on the policyholder's age, the type of policy, the term, and when it was effected. As a result of these variables different bonus rates will be declared. Compare with uniform bonus system.

contributory negligence. This is the failure by a plaintiff to use reasonable care for his own safety or that of his property so that he is partly the author of his own misfortune. It was once a complete defence to an action for damages (*see* LAST OPPORTUNITY RULE). Following the Law Reform (Contributory Negligence) Act 1945 where the injury or damage is partly the result of the plaintiff and partly that of the defendant, the damages recoverable by the plaintiff are reduced having regard to the claimant's share of blame, ie blame is apportioned between the plaintiff and defendant.

contributory pension scheme. A scheme to which both employers and members are required to make a contribution, usually as a percentage of pay.

Control of Asbestos at Work Regulations 1987. These regulations require the selection of methods of work which minimise exposure to asbestos dust as far as is reasonably practicable (regardless of any respirators being worn by workers). Methods of limiting exposure include: (a) removing asbestos materials before starting work. This prevents accidental exposure to asbestos; (b) wet methods or removal (to suppress asbestos dust); (c) prompt removal of waste asbestos; and (d) segregating asbestos work areas from other general work areas. Failure to comply is an offence and a conviction may be evidence in a civil action.

'controlled foreign company'. A term applied to offshore companies which, under provisions of the Finance Act 1984, have to pay UK corporation tax on profits whether remitted or not unless the company complies with certain conditions. The majority of captives (qv) can meet only two of these conditions, viz. 50 per cent of the profits to be remitted annually so that the other 50 per cent can be retained offshore; the captive gets less than 50 per cent of its business from its parent company. These provisions plus the disallowance of tax relief on premiums paid to a pure captive (qv) in the USA make group or multi-parent captives more attractive than pure captive arrangements.

controlled funding. This method of costing a pension scheme recognises that an individual's pension need not be secured until such time as he is entitled to receive payment. Each year the employer pays a premium to secure the total expected benefits at normal pension date for the oldest employees as far as the premium will extend either individually or in age groups. The life office and the employer agree the level of funding desired over a period of years. This level must be such that pensions for members due to retire within the period of assessment will be sufficient to fully secure their pensions by the pension date.

Control of Pollution Act 1974. This makes it an offence to deposit waste on an unlicensed site or in breach of the conditions of the licence. The dumping must constitute an 'environmental hazard', ie subject persons or animals to a material risk of death, injury or impairment of health or threaten the pollution of any water supply. If an offence leads to damage caused by poisonous, noxious or polluting waste which has been deposited on land, any person who deposited it or knowingly caused it to be deposited, is civilly liable for the damage subject only to the following defences: (i) Reasonable reliance on false information. (ii) Reasonable action taken on instructions from the polluter's employer. (iii) Reliance on steps to ensure compliance with the licence. (iv) Fault solely that of the person suffering the injury/damage. (v) Volenti (qv). (vi) Contributory negligence (qv).

Control of Substances Hazardous to Health Regulations 1988 (COSHH). These regulations came into full effect on 1 January 1990 to protect employees and others from exposure to substances that may damage their health. Employers have duties in five broad areas. (a) To carry out a suitable and sufficient assessment of the health risks arising from any substance hazardous to health. (Substance is defined as 'any natural artificial substance whether in solid or liquid form or in the form of a gas or vapour (including micro-organisms').) (b) To prevent exposure and, if this is not practicable, control exposure to substances hazardous to health. (c) To establish a suitable system of monitoring any controls and otherwise for the purpose of protecting the employees. The Health and Safety Executive have issued a guidance note (EH42) as to what may constitute an adequate system of monitoring. (d) To institute a system of health surveillance (ie a system of health checks) on employees where (i) the process involves the use of substances specified in Schedule 5 (those with a known deleterious effect); (ii) the exposure to a substance hazardous to health is such that an identifiable disease or adverse health effect may be related to disease or effect occurring in the particular circumstances of the work and there are valid techniques for detecting indications of the disease or effect. (e) Education—employees must be sufficiently informed for them to know the risks to their health created by their particular exposure and the relevant precautions. Failure to comply with COSHH, in addition to exposing employers to possible legal liability for injury or disease, constitutes an offence and is subject to penalties under the Health and Safety at Work etc Act 1974. COSHH regulations cover virtually all substances hazardous to health. Only asbestos, lead, materials producing ionising radiations and substances below ground in mines, which all have their own legislation, are excluded.

convention. A convention in the sense of those seeking to establish uniformity of law practice in the operation of activities such as air carriage and travel (eg Warsaw Convention (qv)) is a provisional treaty between sovereign states. It has no force of law until ratified by a minimum number of the signatories.

conversion. 1. A tort (qv), committed by someone dealing with goods not belonging to him in a manner inconsistent with the rights of the owner. By s. 1 of the Torts (Interference with Goods) Act 1977 conversion of goods, trespass to goods, negligence resulting in damage to goods and any other tort resulting in damage to the goods are classed as wrongful interference with goods. An action for damages may lie for loss or destruction of goods which a bailee has allowed to happen in breach of his duty to the bailor. Insurance is available including insurance for motor traders who may unwittingly sell on stolen vehicles in which they have acquired no title. See WRONGFUL CONVERSION. See also RETROSPECTIVE OWNERSHIP. Professionals, such as solicitors and accountants, handle documents which constitute 'goods' capable of wrongful conversion by refusal to surrender them or wrongful delivery. Certain protection is gained by extending the professional indemnity policy to cover loss of documents (qv). An auctioneer's professional indemnity policy is extended to cover conversion of goods submitted for sale by auction. 2. The change of a policy from one form to another. In life insurance convertible term policies can be converted to either whole life or endowment policies without further evidence as to health. Whole life policies can be converted into endowment policies. Also existing policies that have a surrender value can be converted to paid-up policies (qv) for reduced sums with no further premiums payable.

convertible currency. In the Lloyd's market this means any currency other than sterling, United States dollars and Canadian dollars. In the company market it means any currency other than the main currencies in which the business is transacted. Convertible currency is normally accounted for in sterling.

convertible term life policies. These are term assurances (ie sum assured payable on death within the policy term with no survival benefit) giving the option to convert to a permanent policy without further evidence as to the state of health. The policy enables young people to buy high sums assured when income is low but commitments high with the certain opportunity of permanent cover later. On conversion the new premium is that applicable to the age next birthday of the life assured at the time of conversion. If the option is not exercised the policy lapses at the end of the term. Sometimes convertible term assurance is combined with whole life or endowment in a single policy.

cooling off. A consumer protection measure enabling investors to cancel policies without loss within 14 days or longer if an extension applies. *See* CANCELLATION RIGHTS UNDER STATUTE.

co-ordinating agent. Underwriting members at Lloyd's who conduct their business through more than one agent must appoint one of them as a co-ordinating agent. This agent is then responsible for keeping the underwriting member informed on all aspects relating to his membership and keeping the Committee of Lloyd's advised as to how the member's premium limit is allocated.

coroners' courts. Courts that enquire into unnatural deaths or deaths in unusual circumstances. The coroner can summon and examine on the death anyone believed to have knowledge of the circumstances of the death. Liability insurers pay for the cost of the insured's representation by a solicitor at any inquest or fatal inquiry.

correspondent. A USA or other intermediary who acts as a sub-agent for a Lloyd's broker. Coverholder and producer are alternative terms.

cost, insurance and freight (CIF). A form of sale contract whereby the seller's price includes the cost of goods and insurance and freight charges through to the agreed destination. Consequently the seller must effect marine insurance for the entire transit.

costs inclusive limits of indemnity. These occasionally appear in product liability or professional indemnity policies or may be applied in respect of USA liability risks. The costs and expenses (incurred in defending a claim with the insurers' consent) are part of the total limit of indemnity, including all damages awarded. Normally these costs are payable in addition to the limit of indemnity. *See* INDEMNITY LIMITS.

Council of Lloyd's. *See* LLOYDS, COUNCIL OF.

counter guarantor. A counter guarantor is a party who, in addition to the insurer, may have guaranteed the person who is the subject of the guarantee. In a claims situation, the insurer must exercise care to ensure that its rights of recovery from the counter guarantor are not prejudiced. The insurer should keep the counter guarantor informed as he proceeds and only request reimbursement when the claim has been settled.

counter-indemnity. An indemnity obtained by a surety from the party whose performance or activity is the subject of the bond. For example, an insurer who has issued a performance bond (qv) in respect of a contractor may require a specific indemnity form to be sealed by that contractor. This is the counter indemnity and may be obtained even though the surety has a common law right of indemnity against the bonded party in respect of losses incurred under the bond. The counter indemnity is in effect a written undertaking by the bonded party, eg a contractor, that in consideration of the surety, eg the insurer, issuing a bond to the principal, to repay to the surety all losses, costs, charges, and expenses etc which the surety may be called upon to pay as a result of the bond.

counter life. *See* CONTINGENT INSURANCE.

counter selection. *See* ANTI-SELECTION.

country risks. A broad heading embracing the following risks which are covered, together with buyer risks (qv), under the ECGD's short-term guarantee: Difficulties and delays in transferring money from the buyer's country (due, perhaps, to a moratorium on external debt by the relevant government, or a third country through which payment must be made); any other action of the government of the foreign country which wholly, or partly prevents performance of the contract; political events or economic, legislative or administrative measures occurring outside the UK which prevent or delay transfer of payments; war, civil war and the like, outside the UK preventing performance of the contract, where the cause of loss is not normally commercially insurable; cancellation or non-renewal of an export licence or the imposition of new restrictions on export, after the date of contract; and when the ECGD confirms that the buyer is a public buyer, the buyer's failure or refusal to fulfil any of the terms of the contract.

coupon insurance. This is offered by newspapers or journals to their subscribers, or by the sellers of 'proprietary goods'. It is valid and gives an enforceable right to the person accepting the offer. The offer is usually accepted by the completion of a form and submitting it to a specified address but simply buying the publication or article concerned could be enough to create the contract.

court bond. A bond issued to a court of law to guarantee the performance of certain duties (accounting for income, preservation of property etc) by a principal.

Court of Protection Bond. Issued to the Court of Protection to guarantee the performance of a person responsible for the affairs of a mentally incapacitated person.

covenants. *See* RESTRICTIVE COVENANTS.

cover. The insurance provided by the insurer for the insured or reinsurer for the reinsured.

coverholder. The person authorised to grant cover so as to bind the underwriters. *See* BINDING AUTHORITY. It is any intermediary other than the final Lloyd's or other placing broker.

cover note. A document that may be issued by insurers pending preparation of the policy. It may issued as evidence of more permanent cover or it may be an acknowledgement of temporary cover pending the insurer's final decision. *See also* BROKER'S COVER NOTE.

cracking, fracturing, and failure of welds. These risks can be covered as an extension to a boiler and pressure plant policy (qv) but the insurance is limited to self damage. The risks of cracking and fracturing apply to plant of cast-iron construction and failure of welds to items with welded or brazed seams. Plant such as heating boilers, ironing machines, and air heating batteries would require the extension. The cause can be internal pressure, low water, water hammer, frost etc, but a valid claim only arises when the crack or weld failure gives rise to leakage of the contents.

craft risks. The risks to cargo during transshipment or landing in small vessels.

cranes and lifting machinery. The range of such items is very wide and includes: blocks, conveyors, cranes of all kinds (eg cantilever, derrick, gantry, jib, overhead travelling, scaffold, tower, transporter), dumpers, elevators, erection masts, escalators, excavators, fork-lift trucks, grabs, graders, hook hoists, jacks, lifting cradles, lifting magnets, lifting tackle attachments, loading shovels, lowerators, pallet trucks, platform trucks, piling frames, retort chargers, safety curtain equipment, scales, sheer legs, sideloader trucks, stacking trucks, stillage trucks, straddle carriers, tailboard loaders, teagles, telphers, track (monorail, overhead, crane, runway), tractors, traxcavators, vehicle loaders, waste disposal units, weighbridges, weighers, winches, window cleaning equipment, working platforms. The relevant policy form for these and similar items is the crane and lifting machinery policy.

cranes and lifting machinery policy. In addition to the periodical inspection service (compulsory for most items in this category), the policy covers breakdown (qv) but may be extended to cover sudden and unforeseen physical damage (qv) at the premises or while temporarily at other premises including the transit risk, and damage to goods lifted (excluding installed plant and machinery) and own surrounding property. Damage by extraneous causes is generally included. Optional extensions of cover include: public liability risks (the risk may be excluded under some public liability policies); physical damage to plant hired out; indemnity to insured and any hirer; physical damage during dismantling and erection; physical damage to property in the insured's custody or control; cost of hire of a similar item following insured loss or damage to any fork-lift truck during the period of repair up to an agreed time or sum.

The policy carries an excess (qv) in the range £25 to £100. Exclusions are: explosion; cutting edges, tools, glass porcelain, trailing cable, flexible pipes, driving belts, and chains or conveyor belts; rubber tyres by the application of brakes or by punctures, cuts or bursts; loss/damage when a single load is shared between two or more lifting machines; waterborne vessels or craft or machinery mounted on such vessels or while being loaded or unloaded thereon or therefrom.

crash helmets. Failure to wear a crash helmet may amount to contributory negligence (qv) by a motor-cycle rider injured by the negligence of a third party (*O'Connell* v *Jackson* (1972)). The plaintiff may be in no way to blame for the accident but may have contributed to his own injury.

credit card insurance. Insurance of losses arising through the misuse of a credit card by a third party.

credit insurance. This covers businesses against losses due to 'insolvency' or 'protracted default' (failure to pay within 90 days of due date) of their customers to whom goods have been delivered or work done on credit terms. It is, in effect, bad debts insurance. Policies usually cover between 75 per cent and 85 per cent of the risk, the balance being retained by the insured. The percentage varies according to the quality of the risk. There are two main policies: 'Whole turnover' or 'Specific account'. The former covers the whole of an insured's business whereas the latter deals with one or more named customers.

credit life assurance. A form of decreasing term assurance (qv) to cover the outstanding debt under hire purchase and credit sale agreements. Cover is provided under a collective policy to the creditor, eg finance company, to facilitate repayment on the death on any hirer or debtor. Arrears are not covered. Limits are placed on the age attained (eg 60 or 65) of any hirer or debtor and the length of the finance agreement (eg 3 years). Premiums are based on the average outstanding debt in accordance with returns supplied by the assured.

credit life captive. A captive insurance company (qv) formed by banks to insure loans to clients.

creditors. 1. Persons to whom money is owed. A creditor has an insurable interest (qv) in the life of his debtor up to the amount of the debt. More commonly, the creditor requires the debtor to effect a policy in his own name and then assign to the creditor. 2. Amounts owed by a pension scheme in accordance with the accruals concept, ie amounts due but not paid.

Criminal Injuries Compensation Scheme. This is administered by the Criminal Injuries Compensation Board which considers personal injury claims for compensation when the injury is directly attributable to: crimes of violence; injury while trying to stop a crime or apprehend a suspect after a crime or help the police apprehend someone; an offence of trespass on a railway (this applies only to incidents after 31 January 1990). The Board also considers applications from people who suffer mental injury after witnessing suicide on railway tracks. The Board does not pay for the cost of legal advice or representation. It considers claims from dependants or relatives of someone who died from criminal injuries or who was injured but died from some other cause.

critical illness (or dreaded disease) policy. This originated in South Africa and is a recent innovation in the UK. If the insured is struck by one of a number of specified diseases or illnesses (eg heart disease, stroke, cancer, multiple sclerosis) the insurer will pay a lump sum. This has some advantages over a regular income (which can be secured under permanent health insurance (qv)) and would enable a disabled person to take long convalescent periods or adapt their home to help them cope with their disability. It can be sold as an extension of a life policy with the sum payable on death being reduced if there has been an earlier critical illness claim.

crop insurance. Insurance effected by farmers against failure of, or reduction in output, due to specified peril (eg hailstorm) or a wider range of perils (eg adverse weather conditions).

cross-assignment. A method used in partnership insurance (qv) whereby each partner takes out a policy on his own life for the amount required, pays the premium himself and assigns the policy to his partners in order to put the money into their hands on his death or retirement. A disadvantage is that any gain under the policy is subject to capital gains tax.

cross-frontier business. *See* SERVICES BUSINESS.

cross liabilities. 1. An Admiralty rule provides that, where two vessels are to blame for a collision, the resultant damages between the shipowners are settled on a single liability basis, ie only the balance passes. This favours insurers at the expense of shipowners as the receiving shipowner, although liable for damage done would be unable to recover from the insurer because, as a result of the set-off, he had made no payment. To overcome the problem, a clause is included in the Three-fourths collision clause(qv) whereby if both vessels are to blame, claims are settled on a cross-liability basis, as if each shipowner had been compelled to pay the other owner his proportion of the latter's damage. Two payments are assumed. Cross liabilities cannot be applied where their amounts of damages have been limited. 2. Where a liability policy covers more than one party the position may arise where one becomes legally liable for injury or damage to the other. A cross-liabilities clause makes it clear that for the purpose of a claim arising from such injury or damage the policy will apply as if a separate policy had been issued to each party comprising the insured. Consequently claims can be brought by one party against another under the same policy. The parties could include subsidiary companies within the same group.

cross (or double) option agreement. Shareholders in small companies agree that on death or retirement of a shareholder the continuing shareholders have an option to purchase the outgoing shareholder's shares. Life assurance is often used in order to put money into the hands of the continuing shareholders at the relevant time to enable them to fund the purchase.

Crown Proceedings Act 1947. Under the Act a person may now sue the Crown, by ordinary process and under the normal rules of court, in all of those cases where previously he could only have proceeded by Petition of Rights or one of the other abolished procedures. With certain exceptions, the Crown is liable in tort as if it were a natural person of full age and capacity.

cumulative bonus. This is a now rarely used feature of personal accident policies. It is a bonus by way of increased benefits to secure the renewal of the policy. The capital sum benefits are automatically increased by 5 per cent at each renewal up to a maximum increase of 50 per cent above the original sum irrespective of any claims under other sections of the policy.

cumulative losses. *See* SUCCESSIVE LOSSES (qv).

curtailment. Cover under holiday or travel insurances (qv) to compensate for the curtailment (ie cutting short) of the trip due to specified causes (eg injury to the policyholder or close relative).

curtate annuity. *See* NON-APPORTIONABLE ANNUITY.

custody and control exclusion. *See* CUSTODY PROPERTY.

custody property (custody and control exclusion). Liability policies that cover the insured's legal liability for damage to property invariably exclude liability for damage to 'property belonging to or held in trust by the insured or in the custody or control of the Insured other than . . .'. The reference to the insured's own property is not necessary as the policy is based on legal liability and the question of a liability claim for 'own property' simply does not arise. However, property controlled by the insured is akin to an 'own property' situation in that it has a higher exposure to the risk of loss or damage than third party property in view of its continuing close proximity to the insured and his activities. It is excluded from the cover on the grounds that such property should be covered under material damage insurances. The words 'other than' at the end of the above extract from the policy serve to override the exclusion in regard to: directors, employees and visitors effects (including vehicles and their contents); premises (including contents thereof) not owned or rented by the insured but temporarily occupied by him for the purpose of work therein or thereon; premises (or fixtures and fittings thereof) leased or rented; property not belonging to the insured at premises or situations other than the insured's premises. It is doubtful if an insurer could hold that the property of directors, employees and visitors came under the insured's control just because they were on the insured's premises but modifying the exclusion makes this point clear. The work away aspect (qv) of a public liability risk will inevitably take many insureds into and onto other people's premises often for short periods of time and the act of work there will not necessarily bring the premises into a custody situation but the overrider of the exclusion in regard to premises and other property clarifies the point. In any event the risk is not usually akin to a first party one and is more suitable for liability than material damage insurance. Where the insured leases or rents premises the custody exclusion will apply so some insurers write this type of property out of the exclusion to safeguard the insured by providing legal liability cover subject to an excess of £100 (not applicable to fire and explosion claims) and subject to the exclusion of liability under an agreement which would not otherwise have attached. Where such agreements increase the liability above the tort level material damage cover should be arranged. For a judicial interpretation on the meaning of custody or control *see* OWNERSHIP OR OCCUPATION OF LAND under which an account of *Oei* v *Foster* (*formerly Crawford*) *and Eagle Star* (1982) is given. Where the insured is a bailee for reward (qv) the exclusion may have to be deleted or a special policy issued if adequate cover is to be given. This affects persons who trade as dry cleaners, hauliers, motor vehicle repairers, hoteliers, watch repairers etc.

customers' extension. An extension to a business interruption insurance (qv) which protects the insured against loss in consequence of loss of demand for the insured's output after damage at a customer's premises. The cover is expressed as a percentage of the gross profit based on the significance of the customer concerned.

Customs and Excise Bond. There are a number of distinct forms of bonds, all in the nature of indemnities, in respect of loss through fraudulent dealing with dutiable goods. Customs duties are duties or taxes on imported or exported goods. Excise duties are those taxes imposed on goods produced and consumed at home. The bond required is security taken by the Government for the due payment of customs and excise duties, together with the performance of specified conditions in the carrying on of business in dutiable goods. Fidelity guarantee insurers are in the business of issuing bonds. Among the distinct bonds provided are: (a) *Warehouse bond.* Dutiable goods are stored in bonded warehouses under the control of HM Customs and Excise Department. The proprietor of such a warehouse normally obtains a bond, the condition of which is that the proprietor and his sureties are liable if he fails to observe the legal provisions applicable to approved warehouses. (b) *Removal bond.* Covers one specific removal of dutiable goods, on which duty has not been paid, from a ship to a warehouse or one warehouse to another. The risk to be covered is (i) deficiency in goods, and (ii) non-payment of duty. (c) *General removal bond.* Covers any number of removals as above. (d) *Sufferance bond.* Provides cover against (i) loading or unloading at a particular wharf without special leave or sufferance of the Customs and Excise Department; (ii) defrauding of Customs; (iii) hindrance or molestation of customs officers. (e) *Licensed lighterman's bond.* A lighter is a large open boat used in loading and unloading ships and carrying goods. Lightermen are licensed to convey by water certain dutiable goods and must give a bond with sureties for the due and faithful delivery of the goods to the proper office of HM Customs and Excise at the vessel or quay for exportation. They also agree that the official locks or seals on the goods or the hatches of the ship in which they are conveyed shall not be broken or interfered with, and that the regulations imposed on lightermen will be observed. (f) *Licensed carman's bond.* Similar to lighterman's bond but covering removal by land. (g) *Transshipment bond.* Covers transshipment from importing ship to exporting ship. Risk: (i) disposal of goods in the UK without payment of the duty. (ii) Delay in transshipment beyond prescribed period. (h) *Industrial methylated spirit bond.* Bond required to ensure: (i) restrictions of use to manufacture of specified products. (ii) Observance of regulations regarding possession and use of methylated spirit. Chief risk is purification and use as a beverage. The amount of the bond is fixed by HM Customs and Excise and is related to the annual consumption of the spirit.

customs duty contingency. Loss due to the payment of customs duty by the insured following his inability to bring his vehicle back into the UK following a period of foreign use. This inability may be due to actual total loss by destruction or theft. Motor insurers provide an indemnity in respect of this loss usually by way of a clause in the foreign use section (qv).

cut-off. The termination provision of a reinsurance contract providing that the reinsurer shall not be liable for loss as a result of occurrences taking place after the date of termination.

cut-through clause. A reinsurance clause providing that, in the event of the insolvency of the ceding office, the reinsurer will be liable to the insured for his share of the loss and not to the ceding office's liquidator.

D

DTI return. *See* ANNUAL RETURN.

da Costa clause. This clause, otherwise known as the 'blood relative clause' or 'receipt clause' appears in industrial life policies where the sums assured are small. If the estate of the deceased is small, it frequently happens that no grant of representation is obtained and in such case the office generally pays the next of kin or the beneficiary under the will (if any) without further formalities. The Da Costa clause sets out this procedure which enables the assurer to handle small cases without having to adhere to strict legal requirements.

dangerous pets. Snakes, alligators and other such pets which are normally classed under the Animals Act 1971 as dangerous wild animals. Liability for injury caused by them is strict. Possession of such animals is a material fact (qv) to be disclosed when seeking cover, including household contents cover in view of the public and personal liability cover available to the occupiers of private dwellings. Specialised cover is available from Lloyd's. Legislation affecting American pit-bull terriers and Japanese tozers is pending and possession of such animals also constitutes a material fact. *See also* DANGEROUS WILD ANIMALS ACT 1976.

dangerous species. Defined in the Animals Act 1971 (qv) as an animal (a) not commonly domesticated in the British Isles; (b) which, when fully grown normally has such characteristics that it is likely, unless restrained, to cause severe damage or that any damage it may cause is likely to be severe. It is question of law whether a species belongs to this category. The characteristics of the individual animal are irrelevant. Animals dangerous to property only may be of a 'dangerous species'. Liability is strict and the test appears to be that of directness and not foreseeability.

Dangerous Wild Animals Act 1976. Anyone who keeps a dangerous wild animal as a pet must obtain a licence from the local authority who may reject any application on such grounds as safety, nuisance, or inadequate or unsuitable accommodation. Failure to comply is a criminal offence punishable by a fine. No licence may be granted to a keeper of a dangerous wild animal (as listed in the Act) unless he holds a pubic liability insurance against or for death, injury or damage to property. Zoos, circuses, pet shops (if licensed under the Pet Animals Act 1951) and research laboratories are exempt from the provisions of the Act.

damages. Compensation or indemnity for loss suffered owing to a tort (qv) or breach of contract or breach of some statutory duty committed by some other person. The principle is to put the injured party back, so far as money can, in the same position as if he had suffered no injury or loss. Damages from the same cause must be recovered once and for all. The measure of damages varies between different classes of action. Nominal damages are trifling amounts for the plaintiff who has made out his case but suffered no actual pecuniary loss. Nominal damages are never awarded in actions for negligence, in which proof of pecuniary loss is essential, but they may be awarded, for example, in actions for trespass. Real damages, intended as compensation for injury actually suffered, are divided into general damages and special damages. General damages aim to make good the plaintiff's loss as far as money can. They include awards for pain and suffering, future disability, personal inconvenience, and future loss from items in the special damages, eg continuing loss of wages. Special damages are damages the plaintiff can prove he has suffered in the particular case, eg medical expenses and loss of earnings.

data. Information in digital form the loss of which could be costly to the users of the information. Insurance can be arranged under reinstatement of data (qv). *See also* DATA PROTECTION.

data protection. 1. *Data Protection Act 1984.* The Act defines data as any information recorded in a form in which it can be processed by equipment by which it can be processed automatically (eg computers). The Act gives the individual four basic rights: (a) The right to see a copy of the information which forms the personal data held by the data user (public or private sector). (b) Recourse to the law to seek compensation for financial or other injury because of the loss of personal data by the data user or unauthorised disclosure of personal data. (c) The right to take action to have inaccurate personal data corrected or erased. (d) The right to complain to the Registrar if unhappy about the way the data user is collecting or using appropriately recorded information about the individual concerned. Those who hold computer (or similarly stored information) records on individuals must abide by eight Data Protection Act principles: (i) Obtain and process the information accurately and lawfully. (ii) Not use or disclose the information in a way contrary to those purposes. (iii) Hold only accurate information and, where necessary, keep it up to date. (iv) Hold only information which is adequate, relevant and not excessive for the purpose. (v) Not hold information any longer than necessary. (vi) When requested give individuals copies of the information about themselves, and, where appropriate, correct or erase the information. (vii) Take appropriate steps to keep the information safe. (viii) Register the purpose for which the information is held with the Registrar. The Registrar's address: Office of the Data Protection Registrar, Springfield House, Water Lane, Wilmslow, Cheshire, SK9 5AX (Tele: 0625 535777) 2. *Insurance aspects.* Breaches of the Act expose the data user to both criminal and civil actions. Potential liabilities (other than fines and penalties) can usually be covered in one of the following ways: (a) Extension of the public liability policy. The type of third party loss may be purely financial. A policy that only covers bodily injury and property damaged will have to be extended to cover pure financial and other intangibles, eg injury to feelings, that may arise in the context of a civil action. Insurers may wish to reduce the limit of indemnity and introduce a measure of co-insurance (qv) before granting the cover. Payment of fines and penalties will be excluded together with the cost of replacing or rectifying any personal data. Insurers also exclude deliberate or intentional acts, the effects of which the insured was aware of at or before the commencement of the cover. The policy could also extend to cover legal defence costs where a criminal prosecution is brought against the insured. (b) Legal expenses insurance (qv) can provide cover in respect of fees, expenses, compensation awards and witness attendance costs in defending any claim or legal proceedings arising out of the Act. (c) Professional indemnity insurance (qv) is a third way. Any claims, however, would have to arise out of any negligent act, error or omission arising in connection with the provision of the professional services the subject of the basic insurance.

dating back. Life insurers normally charge a rate applicable to the 'age next birthday' of the life insured. Where the proposal is made shortly after a birthday, the insurer is normally prepared to back date the commencement, usually to the day preceding the birthday. The insured pays for cover he has not had but the insurer loses interest on the premium.

datum line cover. Cover provided under credit insurance whereby the risk relating to a specific debtor does not attach until the level of indebtedness has reached a certain level known as the 'datum line'.

day (in hospital). Hospital cash plans (qv) and private medical insurances define this term as the benefit(s) payable and may be expressed as a sum per day in hospital. A typical definition is 'Day (in hospital) means a continuous period of confinement in a hospital which includes an overnight stay. It does not include out-patient treatment not involving an overnight stay'.

'day one' average. A form of average (qv) that allows for the special circumstances of the 'day one' basis of reinstatement cover (qv). It compares the declared value of the property at the commencement of the period of insurance with the actual cost of reinstatement at that time. If the actual cost exceeds the declared value pro rata average will apply in the settlement of any claim.

'day one' basis of reinstatement cover. A method used by fire insurers to provide reinstatement cover (qv) with due allowance being made for inflation from day one of the period of insurance. At the inception of each period the insured declares the full reinstatement value of the subject-matter. This should be adequate as otherwise average will be applied on this figure. The premium is calculated on this declared reinstatement value but the sum insured is established at a percentage in excess of this figure in the range 115 per cent – 150 per cent. If set at 150 per cent the insured can pay a flat rate of 15 per cent above normal terms for the cover or a rate of 7.5 per cent above normal adjustable at the end of the policy period on the increased declared value. See 'DAY ONE' AVERAGE.

days of grace. A number of days (usually 15) for which the insurance cover continues beyond the expiry date of the normal term to allow for the payment of the premium and achieve continuity of cover. This constitutes a privilege offered by the insurer but it will be forfeited if the insured rejects the terms of renewal or by his conduct indicates that he does not accept the offer of the renewal invitation. There are no days of grace in motor or marine insurance. In life insurance a privilege condition (qv) allows 30 days of grace for the payment of the premium (other than for monthly premiums) and if the event insured against occurs within 30 days of the renewal date, the premium not having been paid, the sum assured and bonuses (if any) will be paid subject to the deduction of the unpaid

premium. Some life offices allow 15 days of grace for monthly premiums. See RENEWAL.

'deals as a consumer'. See CONSUMER SALE.

death in service. Most pension schemes are supplemented by group life assurance which provides a tax free 'death in service' benefit up to four times the members' annual salary. The benefit is payable as long as the member concerned is still in the employ of the employer at the time of death. There is no requirement that death should arise out of the work. Employees leaving the service of the employer acquire the right to continue a policy in their own name without evidence of health. See CONTINUATION OPTION and GROUP LIFE ASSURANCE.

death strain. The mortality risk above the level of the ceding office's (qv) retention for which reinsurance may be required. On a risk premium basis this is the difference between the sum assured and retention in the first one or two years.

debentures. Securities issued by companies in return for long-term loans— usually 10 to 40 years; debenture holders are entitled to a fixed rate of interest each year whether the company to which they have made the loan is making profits or not.

debt. 1. An underwriting measure, which reduces the sum payable on death, imposed by life insurers in respect of substandard lives. See DIMINISHING DEBT and FIXED DEBT. 2. A sum of money due from one party to another. Trade debtors are an asset to a business and exposed to the risk of loss through insolvency etc and inability to trace debtors following destruction of records. See CREDIT INSURANCE and BOOK DEBTS INSURANCE.

debris. See REMOVAL OF DEBRIS.

debtor. A person who owes money to another, ie his creditor. The creditor has an insurable interest in the life of the debtor.

decennial insurance. A ten year latent defects insurance. The policy protects the owner against physical damage to the premises caused by an inherent defect in the design, materials or construction of the structure. The policy also covers the remedial costs which arise when, even in the absence of physical damage, an inherent defect threatens the stability and strength of the building. Thirdly, it covers damage caused by subsidence, heave or land-slip provided it is accompanied by damage to the structure. Inherent defect means a physical defect existing from the outset but not discovered until after completion of the building. The policy carries an excess (£5000 to £10 000) to eliminate minor problems. The policy, which is assignable, is a single term of 10 years and is primarily intended for commercial, industrial and public buildings but others can be considered. Insurers are prepared to take account of contract conditions and will normally be prepared to include a waiver of their subrogation rights against those actually responsible for the defect.

decentralisation. A system quite the opposite to that of centralisation (qv). Much decision-making and power is devolved to a network of branch offices. Head office exercises overall control and lays down the broad policies to be pursued by the company as a whole.

deck cargo. Cargo carried on deck during a voyage. By Rule 17 of the Rules for the Construction of Policy (qv) in the absence of any usage to the contrary, deck cargo and living animals must be insured specifically, and not under the general denomination of 'goods'. The insured will be excused on proof of a usage in a particular trade, or generally, to carry on deck goods of a particular kind. The insurer is bound to know of the existence of such usages and the mere description of the goods gives the necessary intimation (*British & Foreign Marine Insurance Co.* v *Gaunt* (1921)).

declaration. 1. A statement made by the insured in respect of the details he has submitted regarding the risk to be insured. Normally this declaration appears at the foot of the proposal form where the insured declares that his answers are true and correct (sometimes to his best knowledge and belief) and will form the basis of the contract. *See* BASIS CLAUSE. 2. Periodic declarations are made by the insured under declaration policies (qv) and adjustable policies (qv).

declaration-linked basis. A basis upon which business interruption insurance (qv) can be arranged as an alternative to the standard approach. The premium is based on the insured's estimate of the gross profit for the financial year nearest to the year of insurance subject to an adjustment up or down at the year end when the actual gross profit is known. Meanwhile the policy automatically allows for a 33.3 per cent increase in the estimated gross profit so that the insurer limits his liability to 133.3 per cent of the declared amount. Unlike the usual sum insured basis claims are not subject to proportional reduction on the grounds of under-insurance.

declaration of health. If a proposer, who has been offered life insurance, fails to pay the first premium in the time specified in the acceptance letter, the insurer may require a declaration of health. This is a statement by the proposer that his health has not altered and he has not consulted a doctor since completing a proposal form or being medically examined. The declaration may also be required in connection with the revival of policies that have lapsed through non-payment of the renewal premium.

declaration of value. A declaration at the foot of a proposal form that the sum insured represents the full value of the property at risk. The declaration forms part of the basis clause (qv) and is commonly used in the insurance of private dwellings and their contents as an alternative to using an average clause. *See* DECLARATION (qv).

declaration policies. 1. *Fire insurance.* These policies are designed to allow an insured to maintain full insurance on stocks of fluctuating values without over-insuring. The policy is effected for the maximum sum likely to be at risk at any one time during the year. The insured pays an initial premium based on 75 per cent of that figure. At the end of the year, following an adjustment based on average value at risk, the insured pays an additional premium or receives a return. The maximum additional premium or return is 33.3 per cent of the deposit premium charged. Each month the insured must declare the value of stock on a given date and this declaration must be given within 30 days. The average value at risk is calculated on the basis of these declarations. 2. *Goods in transit insurance.* The policy insures property up to agreed limits without restriction as to vehicle upon which it may be carried. The premium is based on an estimate of the annual value of goods despatched (for insureds carrying their own goods) or estimated carriage charges (for carriers of the goods of others). The insured keeps a record of the actual amounts involved. At the end of the year the insured pays an additional premium or receives a return depending on whether the estimate exceeds or falls short of the actual figure which is declared by the insured either monthly or annually. 3. *Travel insurance.* Declaration in arrears policies. A travel insurance (qv) for employers who declare at quarterly intervals trips made abroad. This obviates the need for individual policies. Cover is automatic and cannot be varied. (*See also* PRIOR DECLARATION and REGISTRATION POLICIES.

declared value. A term used in fire insurance to refer to the total cost of reinstatement as declared by the insured (*see* 'DAY ONE' REINSTATEMENT BASIS OF COVER). The cost will include re-building, re-equipping, plus due allowance for professional fees, public authority requirements, and debris removal.

declinature. An insurer may decline to offer cover (i) in respect of a proposal for insurance or (ii) at renewal or expiry of an existing policy. There is no obligation on an insurer to invite the renewal of an annual contract but when the insurer declines to renew, it is customary to give the insured adequate notice of the decision.

decoy policy. A policy obtained by fraud or collusion with a view to inducing other insurers to accept the risk. The insurer accepting the risk on the strength of such a representation of the existence of another insurance is able to avoid the policy (*Whittingham* v *Thornborough* (1690)).

decreasing term assurance. A term insurance (qv) under which the sum payable on death decreases each year in accordance with a fixed scale. If the insured survives the whole of the pol-

icy term nothing is payable by the insurers who retain all premiums. *See* FAMILY INCOME BENEFITS and MORTGAGE PROTECTION. The decreasing term insurance is an important component in low cost endowment schemes (qv).

deductible. A deductible is 'the portion of an insured loss borne by the policyholder'. The amount or percentage is specified in the policy. Normally application of a deductible reduces the insurer's limit of indemnity by the amount specified, ie an insurance for £10m with a £1m deductible means that the insurer is liable for £9m in excess of £1m. An excess (qv), on the other hand, sits below any sum insured and does not erode it so that a £10m insurance subject to a £1m excess means that the insured pays for the first £1m and the insurer is liable for any sum in excess of that up to a further £10m. The terms excess and deductible are not therefore interchangeable and should be used with care. Deductibles are often used when substantial amounts are involved and they enable the insured to secure large premium reductions. The deductible can be on an individual loss or event basis or an aggregate basis for all claims in the period of insurance.

deductions 'new for old'. According to the Marine Insurance Act 1906, s. 69 where a partially damaged vessel needs repair, for which the marine insurer is liable, the insurer is entitled to make deductions 'new for old'. When new material replaces old material, which has depreciated by ordinary wear and tear, the shipowner must bear part of the cost of the new material. A deduction of one-third or one-sixth is made from the amount otherwise payable. In practice all Institute Hull clauses provide that average, whether particular or general, shall be paid without deductions 'new for old'. However, wear and tear repairs not due to an accident must not be charged to the insurer.

'deep pocket' theory. A USA liability term to describe the situation where the recovery of damages by a plaintiff from a number of co-defendants with joint and several liability is based on ability to pay (ie the defendant with the 'deepest pocket') rather than the degree of negligence. If defendant 'A' is 90 per cent to blame and has no assets but defendant 'B', who was 10 per cent to blame, has wealth or insurance the claimant will reach into the 'deepest pocket', ie that of 'B' for the full amount of damages.

defamation. The tort consisting in the publication of a false and derogatory statement respecting another person without lawful justification. It may constitute libel or slander. Libel occurs where the defamation is by means of writing, print or some permanent form, such as broadcasting by wireless telegraphy. It is actionable without proof of special damage. It is a defence to a libel action that (a) there was no publication; (b) the words were incapable of a defamatory meaning; (c) that the words were true in substance and in fact (justification); (d) the publication was privileged (eg statements in Parliament, or qualified privilege as with references). Libel is a crime. Slander is defamation by the spoken word. It is a tort, not a crime and is not actionable without proof of special damage, subject to a few exceptions, such as imputing a crime punishable with imprisonment and imputing a contagious venereal disease. *See* LIBEL POLICY for the provision of cover against liability at law for libel or slander.

defeasible interest. This is an interest that may cease to exist after the commencement of the adventure for reasons other than maritime perils. For example, a merchant, who is entitled to reject goods because of default by the seller, has a defeasible interest. This amounts to an insurable interest. (Marine Insurance Act, 1906, s. 7).

defective design. See: 1. As an exclusion under a contractors' all risk policy *see* FAULTY DESIGN. 2. Design risks (qv) in regard to public liability, products liability and professional indemnity insurances. 3. Design warranty clause (qv). Under the *Standard Form of Building Contract with Contractors Design* 1981 edition the contractor is responsible for the design of the building.

Defective Premises Act 1972. Section 1 imposes a duty on builders (and others in the building process, eg architects, local authorities) to build dwellings (including the conversion etc) in a workmanlike and professional manner with proper materials so that it will be fit for human habitation. The duty does not apply to dwellings subject to the National House Builders Registration Scheme. The duty is owed to the purchaser and his successors in title. The limitation periods run from the time of completion of the dwelling. Section 3 removes '*caveat emptor*' (qv) in selling property (this requirement is not restricted to dwellings) and makes vendors and lessors liable for defects caused by their negligent work on the property carried out before the sale. Section 4 makes landlords with repairing rights or obligations liable for defects of which they know or ought to know so widening the duty that existed under the Occupiers Liability Act 1957, s. 4. The Act was not given force of law until 1 January 1974 to allow insurers time to adjust to the new situation. All public liability insurances for individuals and businesses now carry a Defective Premises Act extension (qv).

Defective Premises Act 1972 extension. An extension to public liability and household insurances to insure liability arising under the Defective Premises Act 1972, s. 3 or the Defective Premises (Northern Ireland) Order 1975, s. 5. The extension does not cover the cost of remedying any defect and will not operate if the insured is entitled to an indemnity under any other insurance.

defective product. For the purpose of the Consumer Protection Act 1987 (qv), such a product is one where the safety of the product is not such as persons generally are entitled to expect. This provides an objective test and refers neither to the particular injured person nor the particular producer. A product is not considered defective merely because it is of poor quality or because a safer version is put on the market. When deciding whether a product is defective, a court will take into account all the relevant circumstances including: the manner in which the product is marketed; any instructions or warnings that are given with it; what might reasonably be expected to be done with it; the time the producer supplied the product.

defective title. A contingency insurance to cover defects in title to land which can arise because certain documents of title are missing or because of an error in existing documents. A prospective purchaser will require protection against any adverse claims of true owners or persons with rights over property. Where possible full particulars of errors or missing documents must be given and in the case of possessory title statutory declarations may be required before the risk will be accepted.

'defective vision'. In the context of a question on a proposal form for motor insurance this means a defect affecting the competence of the proposer as a driver that has not been corrected by glasses or other means. A proposer was asked if he suffered from defective vision. He replied 'no' and was not guilty of misrepresentation as his eyesight was sufficient for the purpose of driving even though he wore 'thick glasses' when driving (*Austin* v *Zurich General Accident & Liability Insurance Co. Ltd* (1944)).

defective workmanship. 1. *Motor vehicles.* Negligent workmanship on a customer's vehicle or the sale of a defective part by a motor vehicle repairer may be the cause of an accident. The resultant liability can be insured by or under a motor trader's comprehensive road and garage policy or as an extension of the internal risks policy (qv). For the purposes of the cover 'workmanship' means 'repair, servicing, or maintenance' and includes the pre-delivery check of a new vehicle and MOT tests. Various forms of cover are available. The widest cover embraces: negligent workmanship, sale of spare parts, and liability for damage to the customer's vehicle. 2. *See* PROPERTY WORKED ON.

defects in ways. Proposers for employers' liability and public liability insurances are commonly asked in the proposal form if there is any defect in the condition of ways. The term 'way', in this context, means the course ordinarily taken in going from one part of the premises to another.

defendant. The party sued in a legal action. *See* PLAINTIFF.

deferment of benefits. *See* DEFERMENT PERIOD.

deferment of bonus. A life assurance underwriting method for slightly impaired lives proposing for 'with profits' life assurance. Acceptance is at ordinary rates on condition that bonuses shall not vest until maturity, or until attainment of the normal expectation. The method is seldom used, and when it is, it is usually applied only to endowment assurances for comparatively short terms, say, up to 20 years, where the extra premium that would otherwise apply is relatively modest.

deferment period. In permanent health insurance policies (qv) it is the period that must run in respect of an insured event before the insurer will start paying the disablement benefit. The lengths of deferment periods vary but the longer the period the greater will be the premium reduction allowed. The high levels of premium under permanent health insurances creates a particular interest in the deferment of benefits, especially if the insured through his financial resources or conditions of employment can carry the risk of short periods of disablement from working without recourse to insurance. In these insurances deferments for 13 and 26 weeks are common but could extend to two years.

deferred acquisition costs. Acquisition costs (qv) which are carried forward to a subsequent accounting period in order to match such expenses with the income generated.

deferred annuity. *See* ANNUITY.

deferred premium. That part of a premium which is payable in instalments. Premiums are normally payable in advance but sometimes the insurer agrees to accept payment by instalments, half-yearly, quarterly or monthly.

deferred premium clause AVN5A. An aviation insurance clause that applies when the premium is payable by instalments. If an instalment is not paid the clause provides that the cover will terminate at midnight on the day concerned. Also in the event of a claim on the policy exceeding the premium paid the outstanding balance is payable immediately.

deficit clause. A clause in a reinsurance or other agreement that specifies that deficits shall be carried forward and offset in arriving at profit commission.

defined benefit pension scheme. A scheme under which the pension benefits at retirement are fixed (usually ⅟₆₀th or ⅟₈₀th of final pensionable pay for each year of pensionable service) with the employer undertaking to make whatever contributions are necessary in addition to any members' contributions (which is usually a fixed percentage of pensionable pay). Also known as final salary scheme (qv).

defined contribution pension scheme. An alternative term for a money purchase scheme where the rate of contribution is specified in the rules. Employees who are contracted into the state earnings related pension scheme (SERPS) (qv) can secure additional benefits by such a scheme. The benefits on retirement are not geared to final salary but to the accumulated (tax free) fund which has accumulated from employers' and employees' contributions during the service period of the employee. The fund is used to purchase an annuity normally from the open market. These arrangements require exempt approval from the Inland Revenue in the same way as final salary schemes and are subject to similar limits on benefits and employee's contribution.

definition clause. A clause used by insurers to define as precisely as they can the meaning to be assigned in the policy to a particular word or phrase, particularly when the ordinary meaning of the word is not appropriate. For example, the term employee (qv) is very widely defined in public and employers' liability policies.

delay. 1. Some holiday policies pay a sum of money if the insured's departure is delayed beyond a specific period as a direct result of strike, industrial action, adverse weather or mechanical breakdown of the aircraft or sea vessel. The amount depends on the length of the delay but will usually be limited to £60 per insured person. 2. In marine insurance, the Marine Insurance Act 1906, s. 48 provides that 'in the case of a voyage policy the adventure insured must be prosecuted throughout its course with reasonable despatch, and if, without lawful excuse, it is not so prosecuted, the insurer is discharged from liability, as from the time when the delay became unreasonable'. Unreasonable delay after the commencement of the risk has the same effect as deviation (qv). There is an implied condition that the risk attaches within a reasonable time unless the insurer knew the circumstances at the time of accepting. See DEVIATION for the circumstances in which delay or deviation will be excused. Under the transit clause the insurance attaches from the time the goods leave the warehouse or place of storage named for commencement of the transit. This Institute Cargo Clause (1/1/82) also states 'this insurance shall remain in force . . . during delay beyond the control of the Assured, any deviation, forced discharge, reshipment or transshipment and during any variation of the adventure arising from the exercise of a liberty granted to shipowners or charterers under the contract of affreightment'.

delayed launch insurance. An insurance to cover the extra expenses arising from the delay in launching a satellite.

delayed turnover. Postponed trade that a business interruption insurer is entitled to take into account when adjusting a claim. After the material loss has been reinstated and trading is resumed, turnover may rise above the normal level as some orders will have been postponed as opposed to being lost. Provided this occurs within the maximum indemnity period (qv) the insurer can make due allowance in his calculation of the reduction in turnover. This adjustment is sometimes called 'clawback'.

del-credere risk. The risk of financial loss due to the insolvency or default of a debtor. See CREDIT INSURANCE.

'delegable' duties. Where a principal delegates work to an independent contractor and his duty in respect of that work is no higher than a duty to take reasonable care to see something is done, he discharges that duty by taking care to select a competent contractor. Such duties are known as 'delegable' duties. Certain duties are 'non-delegable' (qv).

delivered docks (DD). The contract price covers delivery to docks at port of dispatch, but not dock handling charges.

demonstration and tuition. The demonstration of motor vehicles to potential purchasers by motor traders often calls for driving by the potential customer. Motor traders' road risks cover can be extended to include driving by persons (eg prospective purchasers) other than the insured or employees. Where tuition is given, the policy needs to be similarly extended allowing also the use of the vehicle during the driving test. Demonstration and tuition risks are invariably provided together under the same extension.

demurrage. 1. A shipowner's loss of hire of his vessel. 2. The damages payable to the shipowner if the days allowed by the charter party (qv) for loading and discharging are exceeded.

demutualisation. This occurs when a mutual company becomes a proprietary company (qv).

denial of access. An extension to a business interruption (qv) insurance to protect the insured against loss of turnover following the physical inability of either the insured or customers to gain access to the premises. Cover operates in connection with the perils insured. For example, a fire at neighbouring premises that prevents access to the insured's premises will trigger the policy when fire is the insured peril.

Department of Trade & Industry—Insurance Division. This division is concerned with the administration of the Insurance Companies Act 1982 (including the authorisation of insurance companies and the supervision of insurers by the examination of their accounts and returns); the Policyholders Protection Act 1975 and the Insurance Brokers (Registration) Act 1977; general questions affecting the insurance industry (insurance companies, Lloyd's, insurance brokers and other insurance intermediaries) in the UK including enquiries and complaints; insurance interests in legislation other than supervising insurers; matters affecting the overseas interests of UK insurers including work in inter-governmental institutions eg EC, OECD and UNCTAD.

dependant. 1. For the purposes of the DTI (qv), this is a company in respect of which an insurance company, either alone or with associates, controls one third or more of the voting rights. A dependant of such a company is also regarded as a dependant. In calculating the insurance company's admissible assets, the value of shares in the dependants and the amounts due from them are based on the underlying assets and liabilities determined in accordance with valuation regulations. 2. A person reliant upon another for financial support, most commonly a spouse or child living at home. 3. A person who is financially dependent on a member or pensioner or was so at the time of death or retirement of the member or pensioner. For the purposes of the Superannuation Funds Office a spouse qualifies automatically as a dependant and a child of the member or pensioner may always be regarded as a dependant until reaching the age of 18 or ceasing to receive full-time educational or vocational training, if later.

dependants' income benefit. A form of group life assurance which is an alternative for, or addition to, a lump-sum payment. It provides a benefit in the form of an annuity certain (qv) ceasing at a fixed date, the fixed date coinciding with the date on which the member of the scheme would have been expected to retire. The premium is generally paid wholly by the employer and the income benefit is normally graduated by reference to a salary or wage classification. A beneficiary may elect to defer payment of the life insurance benefit until the cessation of the income benefit.

deposit. The amount deposited at the Court Funds Office by an external direct insurer which has a UK branch or agency through which business is transacted.

deposit administration scheme. An alternative term for a cash accumulation policy. It can be used for a group of employees or for personal pensions. Each premium is guaranteed to earn interest at a variable rate linked to a key rate interest rate, eg the building societies' mortgage lending rate. Each contribution earns interest at this level for the period of the investment. The final lump sum at retirement is converted into an annuity. The annuity rate at retirement is not guaranteed.

deposit against third party risks. *See* MOTOR VEHICLES (THIRD PARTY RISKS DEPOSITS) REGULATIONS 1967.

deposit back arrangement. An amount deposited by the reinsurer with the cedant.

deposit company. An external direct insurer carrying business in more than one member State of the European Community that has lodged a single deposit in accordance with s. 9(2)(b) of the Insurance Companies Act 1982. The deposit can be lodged in either the UK or another member State. Depending on the location of the deposit, the insurer will be either a UK deposit company or a Community deposit company.

Deposit of Poisonous Waste Act 1972. The Act contains a general prohibition against the depositing of poisonous and other dangerous waste, imposes a duty to notify responsible authorities before removing or depositing waste, designates local authorities and their functions, and in general creates stricter liability than exists at common law.

deposit premium. A premium paid at the inception of an insurance or reinsurance which is subject to adjustment at a later date when all of the relevant rating facts are known. Any adjustments are normally subject to the insurer's minimum premium requirements.

deposit (or interim) receipt. The acknowledgement of a deposit of premium and generally incorporates a cover note (qv) to acknowledge any temporary cover arranged.

deposits retained by a cedant (reserves). Amounts deposited by reinsurers with cedants to help finance the reinsurers' proportion of claims. The amount retained is usually such proportion of the premium that the parties agree at the time of the contract. The release of the deposit is normally made annually in arrears.

depreciation. The difference between the value of property new and the value at any subsequent time resulting from the use, wear or obsolescence of that property. Depreciation is not covered under contracts of indemnity (qv) but insurers are prepared in some cases to

issue 'new for old' (qv) and reinstatement policies which in effect modify the principle of indemnity to meet particular circumstances. It is not necessary for an insurer to exclude depreciation under a contract of indemnity although frequently such an exclusion appears to make the position clear.

description of use. *See* CLASS OF USE. Motor policies state the insurer will not be liable for loss whilst the vehicle was 'being used otherwise than in accordance with the 'Description of Use' contained in the policy. This description is also printed on the certificate of insurance. Where the vehicle is being used for two purposes, one of which falls within the description and one outside it, and a loss occurs, the insurer will not be liable (*Passmore* v *Vulcan Boiler & General Insurance Co. Ltd* (1936)).

description of risk clauses. In *Farr* v *Motor Traders Mutual Insurance Society Ltd* (1920) the court distinguished between a warranty (qv) and a clause descriptive of the risk. The proposer had stated in the proposal form that his lorry would be used for 'the delivery of coal' and warranted the truth of this statement in the customary way. The statement was not rendered untrue simply because the vehicle was on occasions used to carry other goods in addition to coal. The clause amounted to a description of the risk and operated in the manner of an exception in suspending cover when the vehicle was being used otherwise than in accordance with the description of the risk.

design risks. Liability for injury, loss or damage arising out of the design, plan, formula or specification of goods. The tendency is for public liability and products liability policies to exclude these risks where the work is done for a fee. The payment of a fee is an indication that the risk is more properly insured under a professional indemnity policy. Where a fee is not normally payable the exclusion does not operate and 'non-professionals' remain covered provided always there is third party injury or damage as defined in the policy. This cover is important as liability may arise under contract or statutes such as the Sale of Goods Act 1979 or the Consumer Protection Act 1987. *See also* PATTERNS, MODELS, MOULDS, AND DESIGNS.

design liability (or design warranty) insurance. *See* DESIGN WARRANTY CLAUSE.

design warranty clause. Under the *Standard Form of Building Contract with Contractors Design* 1981 edition the building contractor is responsible for the design of the building. Clause 2.5.1 seeks to put the contractor's design liability on the same footing as that of the architect or other professional, ie on the basis of a duty to exercise reasonable care. Doubt has been expressed as to whether this attempt to limit liability will succeed as under a design and build contract the contractor has to meet the fitness for purpose requirement. The contractor could also incur a liability for negligent statements (*see HEDLEY BYRNE V HELLER* (1964)) about the design. The clause does not call upon the contractor to effect insurance but the contractor's design liability can be insured in the professional indemnity market. Cover is in respect of the contractor's liability for neglect, error or omission in the exercise of the 'professional duty'. Insurance is not available for inadequate designs (*see* FAULTY DESIGN). Cover is on a claims-made basis (qv) and 'run-off' cover for periods of up to six years can be arranged. The policy is usually subject to a deductible of at least £5000. The indemnity limit is either on the basis of 'any one occurrence' or an aggregate for the period of insurance.

destination clause. The term is used to describe the life policy clause identifying the persons to whom the policy moneys are payable—the insured or his executors, administrators or assigns; or possibly the representatives or assigns of the assured. In other words, the clause identifies the payees.

deterioration of freezer contents (household). Insurance of stock stored in a freezer and/or refrigerator against the risk of loss through deterioration following (a) breakdown of plant, (b) non-operation of thermostatic or automatic controlling devices, (c) action of escaping refrigerant fumes from any cause, or (d) failure of the public electricity supply. Cover is usually expressed as a given amount per machine and there is a small excess (eg £15 to eliminate small claims) which increases for machines more than a certain age (5 to 10 years old). Insurance is not usually available for older machines (eg those over 15 years old) while in some cases insurers will not insure a machine over 5 years old unless it is the subject of a maintenance agreement. Cover can be arranged for householders as an extension of the household contents policy or by separate policy.

deterioration of stock. An engineering insurance covering stock (anything from soft fruit to frozen meats in units as small as domestic refrigerators to custom-built warehouses) in the cold chambers of refrigerating sets at premises. The widest form of cover available is in respect of physical loss or damage to stock in the cold chamber of the refrigerating set by deterioration or putrefaction caused by a rise or fall in the temperature within the chamber. A more restricted form covers loss/damage to the stock in the cold chamber by deterioration or putrefaction caused by (a) rise or fall in temperature from (i) breakdown of motor and/or compressor, (ii) non-operation (from any inherent cause) of any thermostatic or automatic controlling devices, (iii) accidental failure of the public electricity supply; and (b) action of refrigerant fumes which have escaped from the refrigerating set. In both cases 'stock in the cold chamber' includes stock which at the time of the occurrence is elsewhere on the premises but which would in the normal course be placed in the refrigerator. Policy conditions require that temperature readings should be taken twice daily (once on non-working days) and that a maintenance contract should be in force. *See* DETERIORATION OF FREEZER CONTENTS (HOUSEHOLD CONTENTS).

development hazard. Risk assessors and surveyors are not only concerned with the likelihood of a loss occurring (the inception hazard) but also the development of the loss (development hazard) which could be far-reaching or quite restricted.

development risks defence. The name

given to one of the six defences under which a producer or importer can avoid liability under the Consumer Protection Act 1987 (qv). If, at the time of supply, the state of scientific and technical knowledge was not such that a producer of products of the same description might have been expected to discover the defect if it had existed while the products were under his control, there will be no liability under the Act. The onus is upon the producer or importer to show that the defence applies. The term 'state of the art' defence (qv) is also used to describe this most controversial of all of the defences.

deviation. This occurs where the vessel leaves the stated or customary course of the voyage with the intention of returning to that course and completing the voyage. The liability of the insurer ceases immediately the vessel leaves the stated or customary course of the voyage (s. 46, Marine Insurance Act, 1906) without lawful excuse. Section 49, M.I.A. sets out seven lawful excuses (eg *force majeure*, authorised by a policy term, reasonably necessary to comply with warranty, to save human life or rendering assistance where human life may be in danger, for the safety of the ship or subject-matter, caused by barratry if the ship is insured against this risk, to obtain medical or surgical aid for a person on board). After excusable deviation the vessel must return to its course with reasonable despatch. The policy authorises the vessel to call at the customary calling ports en route. To protect the interests of cargo owners, the transit clause (qv) of the Institute Cargo Clauses Clause holds covered during all deviations beyond the control of the insured. A similar but more strongly worded Deviation Clause appears in the Institute Hull Voyage Clause. In time policies the clause does not appear, as deviation does not arise when the ship is insured for a period of time and not a voyage.

difference basis. A business interruption insurance (qv) term used when 'gross profit' is defined as the amount by which the sum of the amount of the turnover and the amounts of the closing stock and work-in-progress shall exceed the sum of the amounts of the opening stock and the amount of the specified working expenses (qv).

difference in conditions insurance. A master policy purchased by a multinational company to fill the gaps in cover that may arise through differences arising in insurances purchased locally in different overseas countries. In this way the company standardises its insurance cover.

difference in limits. A policy which supplements either previous or existing insurance by providing cover, up to a limit, for that part of any claim not met under the other insurances because of the inadequacy of indemnity limits.

diminishing debt. An underwriting measure used by life insurers in respect of sub-standard lives often as an alternative to an additional premium. The sum assured is reduced by the amount of the debt in the event of death within a given period. Under this scheme the debt is reduced by a predetermined amount each year and reaches nil at the end of a stated period after which the full sum becomes payable. It is most appropriate in those cases where the extra risk is heaviest in the early years but gradually diminishes with increasing age. *See* REDUCING EXTRA RISK.

diminishing risk. *See* REDUCING EXTRA RISK.

dinghies. *See* BOAT INSURANCE.

'dip down' proviso. A provision in an excess (qv) or umbrella liability (qv) insurance to pick up gaps in the underlying policy. It may apply to gaps in cover and also pay the shortfall brought about the exhaustion of the underlying limit.

diplomatic immunity. An ambassador or other public minister exercising diplomatic functions and accredited to the Queen by a foreign State or Sovereign is not within the jurisdiction of the English courts during his term of office. The immunity also extends to subordinate officials of the embassy but can be waived by the ambassador. Where an insured, who might have claimed diplomatic immunity, submits to the jurisdiction of the Court and is held liable for third party injuries, the insurer must indemnify him accordingly (*Dickinson* v *Del. Solar (Mobile and General Insurance Co. Ltd, Third Party)* (1929)).

direct business. Insurance transacted directly with the insurer without the involvement of an intermediary such as a broker or agent. The term is also used to describe insurance transacted by a direct insurer (qv) as opposed to the business of a reinsurer.

direct damage. Damage caused by the direct action of a peril as distinct from indirect or consequential loss or damage (qv). For example, fire may damage a building and machines within it. This is direct damage insurance under material damage insurance such as a fire policy whereas the loss of production occasioned by this damage is indirect damage or consequential loss. *See also* BUSINESS INTERRUPTION INSURANCE.

direct dealing. An arrangement which enables certain motor syndicates at Lloyd's to deal directly with non-Lloyd's brokers. However, the premiums payable have to be guaranteed by, and paid through, a Lloyd's broker.

direct insurer. An insurer as opposed to a reinsurer who is often said to write indirect business. In the USA the term is also used for an insurer dealing direct with their policyholder and not through brokers or agents.

direct liability clause. An alternative term for cut through clause (qv).

direct loss. *See* DIRECT DAMAGE.

direct mail insurance. Life and other forms of personal insurance can be sold by circulating details of packages and other schemes to individuals by post. Life offices may circulate existing policyholders who are offered a single type of policy without evidence of health. Other direct mail schemes are the result of an arrangement with an organisation that has a large list of members. The organisation negotiates a package of benefits with a single company or Lloyd's. The life packages are usually based on protection rather than investment. The advantage is that the organisations can budget their costs and reach many potential clients at much lower costs than an insurer could achieve through its own outlets. The savings are reflected in the premiums.

'directly or indirectly'. Where the policy refers to loss or damage, directly or indirectly arising from the excepted perils, the limitation is severe. In such circumstances both proximate and remote causes are excluded. *See Coxe* v *Employers' Liability Corporation* (1916) under PROXIMATE CAUSE.

directors. There is no statutory definition of this term. Anyone can be a director unless disqualified by law or prevented by the company's Articles of Association and the actual title has no effect on whether a person who exercises a company's powers is a director within the meaning of the Companies Acts. The term shadow director has been used of a person or company under whose instructions the directors of the company are accustomed to act—the facts of the situation outweigh the legal obligations. Similarly a director who has been invalidly appointed is subject to the same liabilities as validly appointed directors. A director need not be a natural person so that one company may be the director of another.

directors' certificate. The certificate required by Regulation 26(a) of the Insurance Companies (Accounts and Statements) Regulations 1983 to form part of the Annual Return (qv) to the DTI.

directors' liabilities. *See also* DIRECTOR'S AND OFFICER'S LIABILITIES. Whether or not a director has exercised reasonable care and skill will take account of his knowledge and experience. A greater burden is placed on 'expert' directors, such as solicitors or accountants, who are required to show a degree of care and skill commensurate with their professional qualifications. Directors (and officers) have responsibilities to the company, the shareholders, prospective shareholders and investors, employees and creditors. Claims most commonly arise after takeovers and when a company is in liquidation. The need for a 'professional indemnity' type policy is met by directors' and officers' liability insurance (qv).

directors' professional liability insurance. This is an insurance scheme set up by the Institute of Directors for its members. It provides a measure of cover for individual directors with a limit of £100 000.

directors' statutory duty. There are a number of statutory obligations imposed on directors and non-compliance may give rise to a fine or in cases of persistent default, disqualification or even imprisonment. The overriding legislation is the Companies Acts 1948-81 governing: prospectuses; accounts; interests in contracts; loans; meetings and resolutions; disclosure of directors' payments; disclosure of loans to directors; disclosure of shareholding; duty to have regard to employees' interests as well as shareholders'; inside information. The directors are also responsible for ensuring compliance by the company with numerous pieces of legislation imposed on all kinds of businesses and which relate mainly to employees and business premises such as the Health & Safety at Work etc Act 1974 (qv).

directors' and officers' liabilities. These usually result from breach of: fiduciary duties to the company (qv); duties of skill and care to the company; contract; statutory duty (*see* DIRECTORS' STATUTORY DUTY); duty to shareholders; and common law. Also in the event of compulsory winding-up there may be a personal liability of the directors for wrongful trading (qv) to persons who have dealt with the company. The skill and care duties are founded in the common law concepts of principal and agent, the company being the principal and the director being the agent. In a general way the duties of non-executive directors are less onerous than those of an executive director. The test of reasonable care is judged against the standard of care an ordinary person might take of his own affairs. Also it depends on whether a director has exercised the reasonable care and skill expected from a person of his knowledge and experience. 'Expert' directors (solicitors, accountants etc) carry a greater burden as they must act with the degree of care commensurate with their professional status.

directors' and officers' liability insurance. A two-part insurance: (a) *The directors' and officers' liability insurance/section.* The policy covers the liability at law of directors and officers for claims made against them by reason of any wrongful act (qv) committed by them or alleged to have been committed by them in their capacity as director or officer of the company or in their capacity as director or officer or trustees of the company's pension fund. In addition to damages the policy covers claimant's costs and other costs (including the cost of representation at an official investigation into the company's affairs). Principal exclusions relate to: dishonesty by the individual; employers' and public liability risks; claims for which the company is responsible; fines, penalties and punitive damages (qv); liability for national insurance debts; claims based on directors or officers making personal gain; and liability under a guarantee or warranty (other than a warranty of authority) given by directors or officers. Breach of professional duty is also excluded as the risk is insurable under professional indemnity insurance (qv). Policies are written on a claims-made basis (qv). An aggregate limit of indemnity applies to all claims in the year of insurance on a costs inclusive basis. Territorially the policy applies to UK and Republic of Ireland based companies and an excess of £500 or upwards applies unless an additional premium is paid. The policy contains a Queen's Counsel clause (qv). About 10 per cent of the total premium pays for this part of the cover with the major share paying for company reimbursement insurance. (b) *Company reimbursement section.* This indemnifies the insured company against any payment they may elect to make and are legally entitled to make arising out of any claim against any director or officer during the period of insurance for which the director or officer would otherwise have been entitled to indemnity under the policy. This provision arises because a director who is sued is entitled to indemnity from the company under the Articles of Association (qv) but only in respect of the successful defence of a claim. The Companies Act 1985, s. 310 precludes any agreement to indemnify a director unless the director is successful. The Companies Act 1989 introduced a new section 310 (3) into the 1985 Act which states that nothing within s. 310 prevents a company 'from purchasing or maintaining for any such officer or auditor insurance against such liability'.

dirty bill. Same as claused bill (qv).

disability benefits. The term used in respect of 'disablement' type benefits added to life or permanent health policies. Such benefits include: (a) waiver of premium, for which an additional premium is charged. Payment of the premium under the main contract is waived during periods of disability from following the insured's normal occupation subject normally to a deferred period of 26 weeks. The benefit ceases at age 60 or 65 and medical evidence is required to support a claim. (b) Periodic benefits while disabled—this is in effect permanent health insurance (qv) added to a life contract. (c) Total and permanent disablement benefit—when total and permanent disablement occurs the assurers pay the sum assured and terminate the contract. The definition for total disablement etc is usually inability to follow one's own occupation. This benefit is generally only linked to whole life or endowment policies and not term assurances.

disablement benefit. The benefit payable under a personal accident or permanent health insurer when the insured is either permanently or temporarily disabled. *See* PERMANENT TOTAL DISABLEMENT and TEMPORARY DISABLEMENT.

disbursements. Prior to the sailing of a vessel, money is spent on supplies, labour etc and this will be lost if the vessel does not complete its voyage. Insurance of 'disbursements' reimburses the shipowner for these expenses in the event of total loss before the ship reaches its destination.

disbursements warranty (Clause 21, Institute Time Clauses). By market agreement this warranty, from the Institute Time Clauses, is embodied in hull insurances. In the absence of this warranty, the shipowner, recognising that most losses are partial rather than total, would be inclined to fix low insured values on hull policies but still benefit from valuable partial loss cover which takes no account of the insured value apart from fixing a ceiling on the claim. Simultaneously he could effect a total loss only cover at a very cheap rate of premium. The main object of the warranty is to cause the insured to fix realistic values under hull policies by restricting the sums that the insured can insure on more limited conditions at much lower rates. The warranty prevents the shipowner from effecting disbursement policies for a sum exceeding 25 per cent of the insured value of the ship and warrants that no insurance including total loss only shall be effected. A breach will enable the insurers to avoid the hull policy. The warranty also restricts the sums which may be insured for periods of time under freight policies because these policies follow the settlements on hull policies in the event of the total loss of the ship.

discharges. Upon settlement of a claim insurers obtain a receipt from the insured to acknowledge a full discharge of the insurer's liability arising from the event which resulted in the claim for injury, loss, damage or settlement of liability. However, if settlement is by way of reinstatement or replacement, the receipt is normally signed by the repairer and the insurer obtains a satisfaction note from the insured to the effect that the work or replacement has been to his full satisfaction. In third party claims or claims by employees against the insured, the insurer pays the claimant and obtains an acknowledgement to absolve the insured from all liability for the event concerned whether arising now or in the future.

disclaimer notices. Notices displayed in hotels, garages, and similar places, often operated by bailees (qv), frequented or visited by members of the public or where they leave their property. Generally the bailee or occupier of premises seeks to restrict or contract out of responsibility for loss or damage to property left in their care or on their premises. Since the Unfair Contract Terms Act 1977 it has not been possible to contract out of liability for death or personal injury resulting from negligence. Contracting out of liability for loss/damage to property resulting from negligence is allowed provided it is reasonable. The disclaimer notice, however, will not be effective unless it has been brought to the attention of the bailor before the contract of bailment is concluded.

disclosure. The Financial Services Act 1986 (qv) legislates for disclosure to enable the investor to make an informed decision and protect him from biased advice. The Insurance Brokers Registration Council and FIMBRA (qv) require the intermediary to disclose to his client (a) the remuneration and commission he will receive as a result of any transaction; (b) information about the product, ie the life policy or units, details of the client's financial commitment, taxation, surrender values, consequences of early termination, and charges (where identifiable). For most investment products disclosure of the amount of commission is compulsory but in regard to life assurance and unit trusts there is soft disclosure of commission, ie there is a commission agreement and it is sufficient to state that the commission is within the LAUTRO agreed rate unless the client insists on knowing the exact amount. Also commission in excess of the LAUTRO rate must be disclosed in full. A key requirement for any commission agreement, arising from the rule of product bias published by the Securities and Investments Board (qv), is that it shall not be so framed that it influences salespersons to sell one type of product rather than another. There are moves pending towards a hard disclosure of commission, ie disclosure of the exact amount of commission in money terms.

Disclosure of Information Regulations 1986. The regulations oblige the trustees of pension schemes, with the exception of public service schemes, to make available each year copies of an annual report containing: a copy of the audited accounts for the scheme year in question; a copy of the latest actuarial statement, a reasonable amount of detailed information including, the names of the trustees, actuary, auditor and solicitors; the percentage increases made to pensions, a statement concerning the cash equivalents of accrued benefits paid out during the year, and if the auditors' statement shows that contributions have not been properly paid the reason for the discrepancy and how it

is likely to be resolved. In addition, trustees must obtain each year audited accounts from a properly qualified person.

disclosure of interests. The manager and executives of a Lloyd's underwriting agency, which provides recruitment and administration services for a syndicate, must disclose their interests in the insurance transactions of the syndicate in the annual report. A similar disclosure is also required of members' agents.

discontinuance. The cessation of contributions to a pension scheme leading to the scheme being wound-up or becoming a frozen scheme.

discontinued products. A product the production of which has been discontinued by the manufacturer. In product liability insurance (qv) such products need to be identified and brought within the business description to ensure that the 'run-off' risk is covered. This is important because the insurance usually operates on a 'losses-occurring' basis (qv) or, less frequently, a claims-made basis. The time of damage or the time of claim respectively trigger these policies, not the time of manufacture.

discounted gift schemes. These schemes are aimed at reducing the impact of inheritance tax by setting up inheritance trusts. A discounted gift scheme involves a package of two policies, a single premium pure endowment (qv), from which income withdrawals are taken, and a single premium term policy written in trust. The death benefit under the term policy is equal to the endowment at the time of the holder's death. Since this is a gift scheme, advantage is taken of the nil-rate band and the 10-year cumulation period. It gives an immediate tax saving according to the amount by which an estate is deemed to be reduced.

discounting. When a life policy is surrendered, the actuary calculates the surrender value, if any, by working back from the sum assured assumed to be payable on death at the date corresponding to the average life expectancy. This is the process of discounting and works like compound interest in reverse so the longer the period to elapse before payment of the relevant sum, the smaller will be the surrender value. A reduction is also made for the insurer's expenses.

discounting of reserves. *See* TIME AND DISTANCE POLICIES.

discovery of ship's papers. A process whereby, following a loss, an insurer can apply to the court for the production of relevant ship's documents. An order will not be made automatically and will not be made where the insurance covers land transit only. The order can be issued against the shipowner, a mortgagee, the insured in the case of a policy on cargo, insurers in the case of reinsurance, an agent who sues on behalf of his principal, an insured where the insurer seeks a return of money allegedly obtained by fraud, an assignee of policy proceeds, and other interested parties.

discovery period. 1. In fidelity insurance the term describes the period between the act of fraud or dishonesty and its discovery. It is usually limited to not more than six months after the resignation, dismissal, retirement or death of the defaulting employee, nor later than three months after the termination of the policy whichever shall occur the first. The object is to exclude stale claims which would be difficult to investigate and where the insurer's right of recovery might be prejudiced. 2. Professional indemnity insurance and other claims-made policies. In the event of a policy lapsing, the insurer normally allows a period of three months (or longer) after the date of lapse for the discovery and notification of new claims resulting from negligence occurring during the period of insurance.

discretionary trust policies. An approach to partnership assurance to minimise the number of policies necessitated under individual trust policies (qv). Each partner effects one policy on his own life under a discretionary trust in favour of the other partners who are normally the trustees in whom the proceeds are vested. When a claim arises they are then able to apportion the proceeds among themselves to repay the deceased or retiring partner's share of the business.

disposal of abandoned vehicles policy. An insurance available to local authorities to protect them in respect of their legal liability to vehicle owners whose vehicles they have removed as abandoned.

disputes. 1. If unable to resolve a dispute with the insurance company concerned private policyholders can, before resorting to legal action or sacrificing a possible right, use the Insurance Ombudsman Bureau (qv) or the Personal Insurance Arbitration Service (qv). It is also possible to get advice from the Association of British Insurers Consumer Information Department, Aldermary House, 10–15, Queen Street, London, EC4N 1TT. *See also* ARBITRATION which may apply to both private and business policyholders. 2. Section 32 of the Industrial Assurance Act 1923 provides that in all disputes between a society or company and a policyholder, the latter may apply, notwithstanding anything in the rules of the society or company, for a settlement of the dispute to: the County Court, or a Court of Summary Jurisdiction, if the amount does not exceed £25 and at least 14 days' notice of the application has been given to the society or company. If the amount does not exceed £50 and the legality of the policy is not questioned and fraud or misrepresentation is not alleged, the dispute may be referred to the Industrial Assurance Commissioner, by either party without the consent of the other. As an alternative, by consent of both parties, any dispute may be referred, without restriction as to amount or nature of the question to be decided, to the Industrial Assurance Commissioner. Although there is no appeal from a decision of the Commissioner he may, at the request of either party, state a case for the opinion of the Supreme Court in England, or the Court of Session in Scotland, although he cannot be compelled to do so.

district (or area) of use. A factor in the rating of motor insurance premiums. The incidence of vehicle accidents varies directly with the density of the population in given areas or districts. Consequently, motorists who live in urban areas pay more than those who live in rural communities. Private car insurers generally divide the country into six districts for this purpose while commercial vehicle insurers use three districts for goods-carrying vehicles. The district to be applied for rating purposes is fixed by reference to the place where the vehicle is kept as this indicates where it will be most frequently used.

divisible surplus. The surplus is the profit of the life assurer found on valuation (qv). The divisible surplus is that part of the surplus that will be distributed as dividend to shareholders (if any) and in the form of bonuses to with profit policyholders.

doctrine of priority. When a deed assigning a life policy has been executed notice should be given. The Policies of Assurance Act 1867 (qv) provides that the notice must be in writing to the office's principal place of business and must state the date and purport of the deed. Until notice is given the assignee has no right to sue under the deed and the Act provides that the date on which notice is received shall regulate the priority of all claims—this is known as the doctrine of priority. *See* ASSIGNMENT.

documentary bill. A common method of financing a shipment. The shipping documents (bill of lading, insurance policy or certificate, and invoice) are transferred when a bill of exchange for the contract price is accepted or paid by or on behalf of the buyer. An accepted bill of exchange can then be discounted with recourse and the seller thereby puts in funds immediately. The bank's security is the accepted bill.

documentary credit. The buyer's bank instructs their correspondent's bank nearest to the seller's place of business to pay against or accept in exchange for the shipping documents (bill of lading, insurance policy or certificate, invoice) a bill of exchange drawn by the seller on the correspondent for the price of the goods. After payment has been effected, the correspondent bank debits the buyer's bank which is reimbursed by the buyer.

documents. *See* LOSS OF DOCUMENTS for both cover available and a definition of documents for the purpose of professional indemnity insurance.

domestic agreement. *See* MOTOR INSURERS' BUREAU.

domestic boilers. Boilers not used in trade processes but this does not preclude their use in business premises exclusively for 'domestic' purposes such as central heating, supplying hot water for hand washing or use in the works canteen. The term is important as the standard fire policy provides cover for explosion damage caused by 'boilers used for domestic purposes only'.

domestic purposes. The words appear in the standard fire policy in reference to explosion of boilers (*see* DOMESTIC BOILERS) and of gas used for domestic purposes. This means gas as normally supplied to premises for heating etc and not gas created on the premises by a manufacturing process (*Stanley* v *Western Insurance Co.* (1868)).

domestic servants. Liability for injury to domestic servants is covered under the household contents policy as a standard feature. The liability is for an unlimited amount. It is not compulsory to insure this legal liability.

'doomed from the start'. An expression used by Lord Fraser in the House of Lords case of *Pirelli* v *Oscar Faber & Partners* (1983). The case decided that the cause of action in property damage claims against third parties for negligence accrued at the time of the damage and not the time of discovery or discoverability for the purpose of the limitation period of six years. Lord Fraser qualified this by saying that a building could be so defective as to be 'doomed from the start' so causing the time to run from completion. These matters were particularly relevant in the case of latent defects and Lord Fraser's qualification created the risk that persons with properties with serious but latent defects faced the prospect of running out of time even before they had sustained or discovered damage. The difficulties have been resolved by the passing of the Latent Damages Act 1986 (qv).

'doorstep' sales of cars. A term used by the Insurance Ombudsman Bureau to describe the sale of motor vehicles to strangers who take the vehicle but provide no honest means of payment. Policyholders are advised to retain possession until cheques, banker's drafts etc have been cleared, particularly as they are unlikely to be insured in respect of any ensuing loss (*see* LOSS OF CAR). The Insurance Ombudsman Bureau (qv) has advised all motor insurers to print appropriate warnings in their brochures.

double accident death benefit. A life insurance clause that doubles the sum insured if death is due to bodily injury caused by accidental violent external and visible means. The benefit is terminated at age 60 or 65 and death must occur within a stated time of the accident, eg 90 days.

double benefits. *See* DOUBLE INDEMNITY and DOUBLE ACCIDENT DEATH BENEFIT.

double endowment. An endowment assurance (qv) under which the amount payable on maturity is twice the amount payable on death within the policy term. It is a combination of an endowment assurance and a pure endowment (qv) for a similar sum. Alternatively it amounts to a term assurance for a particular sum combined with a pure endowment for double that sum. As the sum payable on death is limited the policy can be offered to sub-standard lives as an alternative to extra premiums.

double 'indemnity'. Certain personal accident policies (qv) pay twice their normal benefits if the injury or death has been caused under specified circumstances which normally means an accident during conveyance by road or rail.

double insurance. *See* CONTRIBUTION.

double option agreement. *See* CROSS OPTION AGREEMENT.

dreaded disease policy. *See* CRITICAL ILLNESS POLICY.

dredgers. Vessels involved with sprinkling or suction which normally work in ports or inland waterways. Cover normally granted: usually Institute Port Risk Clauses covering (a) Loss or damage. (b) Third party liabilities except in respect of employees. A dredger proprietor with a registered office in London is obliged to effect an employers' liability insurance to comply with the Employers' Liability (Compulsory Insurance) Act 1969. However, insurance is not compulsory for injury or disease suffered or contracted outside Great Britain.

drilling rigs. Off-shore installations whose insurance needs are formulated by the London Drilling Rig Committee.

drink convictions. Drink and driving are regarded very seriously by motor insurers. Convicted motorists returning to the road generally face premium increases of at least 100 per cent. The level of insurance may also be reduced, for example, from comprehensive to third party fire and theft. The higher premiums and cover restrictions are likely to be imposed for a number of years.

drive-in centres. Centres to which motorists can take their vehicles for the inspection and assessment of damage. After the check the insurer's engineer may issue a voucher for the insured to take the vehicle to a repairer of his own choice with a view to settling any claim direct less any excess (qv) or VAT that may apply. Some UK insurers operate this scheme but it is more popular in the USA. More generally, motor insurers use their own staff engineers or appoint independent engineers to appraise the vehicle damage at premises chosen by the insured.

drive-in damage checkpoints. *See* DRIVE-IN CENTRES.

driving licence. The word licence appears on a number of occasions in most motor policies without actually being defined. However, the word seems to be given the widest of interpretations and will therefore cover any kind of licence to drive, full, provisional, or foreign. In *Rendlesham* v *Dunne* (1964), Dunne, a provisional licence holder, was committing an offence in driving without being accompanied by a full licence holder in the course of which he negligently damaged the plaintiff's property. His insurers refused to grant him an indemnity but the judge found it 'impossible to construe the policy so as to restrict the meaning of the term licence to a full licence'. He did not think it possible to say that a man did not have a licence to drive a car on the road merely because he failed to comply with a condition on which the licence was granted. Permitted drivers under the third party section of the policy lose the benefit of the policy if they do not hold a licence to drive such vehicle or have not held such a licence or are disqualified. A general exception excludes the insurer's liability first in respect of driving by the insured 'unless he holds a licence, has held a licence, and is not disqualified from holding or obtaining such a licence', and secondly, in respect of driving by a person 'who to his knowledge does not hold a licence to drive such vehicle unless such person has held and is not disqualified from holding such a licence'. Nowhere in the general exceptions or in the third party section is the word licence qualified in any way. However, in the excess clause under the loss or damage section of the comprehensive policy the excess is made applicable, *inter alia*, to provisional licence holders, drivers 'who have not held for a period of one year a licence other than a provisional licence'. The special reference to provisional licences appears to indicate that the word licence when it stands alone covers all licences. It is always open to an insurer who wishes to deny an indemnity to an unaccompanied provisional licence holders to find a form of words to make his intention clear.

driving of other cars (DOC). A clause in the third party section of a private car policy which permits the insured to drive private type cars or motor cycles not belonging to him and not hired to him under a hire purchase agreement. If the insured parts with the car described in the policy, the extended indemnity ceases to apply as the main indemnity then terminates. Occasionally, as an underwriting measure (eg sports car owners) the insurer deletes the extension from the policy.

driving of other cycles. The same as driving of other cars (qv) but applies instead to motor cycles. For rating purposes the extension is sometimes deleted from the cover but can be reinstated.

dry-docking expenses. The costs of entering and keeping a vessel in dry dock for repairs form a part of the repair costs. However, where repairs, for the shipowner's account are needed to make the ship seaworthy, are executed concurrently with those for the insurer's account, the dues common to both repairs must be divided equally between the shipowner and the insurer. Nonetheless, the owner may take advantage of the ship being dry-docked for insurer's repairs to effect repairs for his own account (eg scraping and painting the ship's bottom or classification survey), not essential for seaworthiness without incurring any liability for any part of the dock dues.

dry perils. Additional (or special) perils (qv) can extend the range of perils covered under a fire policy. The following perils are categorised as dry perils: aircraft, explosion, riot and civil commotion, malicious damage and earthquake.

DTI classes. These classes of general business are the subject of regulatory control. The Insurance Companies Act 1982 divides them into 17 classes of business as follows:
1. Accident. 2. Sickness. 3. Land vehicles. 4. Railway rolling stock. 5. Aircraft. 6. Ships. 7. Goods in transit. 8. Fire and natural forces. 9. Damage to property. 10. Motor vehicle liability. 11. Aircraft liability. 12. Liability for ships. 13. General liability. 14. Credit. 15. Suretyship. 16. Miscellaneous financial loss. 17. Legal expenses.

To transact any of the general business classes authorisation (qv) by Department of Trade and Industry (DTI) is necessary. Each class embraces both commercial and personal line insurances. For the purpose of compiling accounts and returns for the DTI the classification is reduced to 10 classes as laid down by the 1983 Insurance Companies (Accounts and Statements) Regulations. These accounting classes comprise eight for direct and facultative business plus separate classes for treaty reinsurance as follows:

Accounting class	Corresponding general business
1. Accident and health	1,2.
2. Motor vehicle	3, 10.
3. Aircraft damage and liability.	5, 11.
4. Ship, damage and liability.	6, 12.
5. Goods in transit	7.
6. Property damage	4, 8, & 9.
7. General liability	13.
8. Pecuniary loss	14, 15, 16, 17.
9. Non-proportional treaty reinsurance.	
10. Proportional treaty reinsurance.	

DTI return. *See* ANNUAL RETURN.

dual wages basis. For many years this was the standard way of providing wages cover under business interruption insurances (qv) and has been superseded by payroll cover (qv). The policyholder insured 100 per cent of his wages for an initial limited period, eg 4 or 13 weeks, but only a percentage, eg 25 per cent, for longer terms. The percentage chosen was usually based on the amount needed to retain specialised staff who would have been difficult to replace on return of the business to normal activity if discharged in the early stages of a period of interruption.

duration of policy. Where an insurance is expressed to cover the period from one particular day to another, the insurance expires at midnight on the last day unless a contrary intention is stated. However, a policy may not run its full course for the following reasons: (a) payment of the full sum under the policy discharges it; (b) agreement between the parties; (c) termination by the insured in the case of permanent contracts (life and permanent health), normally by non-payment of the premium; (d) withdrawal from contract within the time allowed in long-term insurance after receipt of the statutory notice (qv); (e) determination for breach of condition subsequent (qv).

duration of risk. A marine insurance term to denote the period during which the insurer will be liable under the policy. This may mean the duration of a voyage or the completion of a period of time depending on the type of policy concerned, voyage or time. The insurer's liability under a voyage policy on a hull continues until the ship has moored at anchor in good safety for 24 hours at the port of destination named in the policy but the

policy may extend this period. In the case of goods the risk terminates when they are safely landed but this is usually extended by a transit clause. The contract may terminate early if the adventure is not commenced within in a reasonable period of time (Marine Insurance Act 1906, s. 42(1)). This implied condition may be negatived by showing that the delay was due to circumstances known to the insurer before conclusion of the contract or by showing that he waived the condition. The risk may also be terminated before running its full course by change of voyage (qv); deviation (qv); delay (qv).

duty to satisfy judgments. Under the Road Traffic Act 1988, s. 149 insurers must satisfy judgments against their insured in respect of third party liability as defined and emergency treatment notwithstanding any provisions in the policy entitling them to avoid or cancel the policy. The insurer is relieved of these obligations if able to bring the case within sub-section 2. This is concerned with matters about adequate notice of proceedings, appeals, cancellation of the policy before the event subject to certain procedures, and a declaration within three months of commencement of proceedings as to the insurer's right of avoidance for misrepresentation or non-disclosure. *See* AVOIDANCE OF CERTAIN TERMS AND RIGHTS OF RECOVERY and NON-AVOIDANCE OF COMPULSORY INSURANCE.

dwellinghouse. A permanent structure in which the owner or tenant (or his family or servants) habitually lives and sleeps at night. A caravan or anything similar does not come within the definition. In *Quinn v National Assurance Co.* (1839) it was held that dwellinghouse is not an apt term to cover a building in the course of erection.

E

each and every loss. A phrase used when some restriction, such as an excess, will be applied for every separate claim. Where there is more than one claim pending they will not be aggregated and any excess (qv) will be deducted from each claim.

'each for his own part and not one for the other'. A fundamental maxim which describes the basis on which a Name (qv) accepts a share of the risk. It highlights the fact that Names act as sole traders, albeit for convenience and practicalities on a syndicate basis.

early leaver. A person who ceases to be an active member of a pension scheme, other than on death, without being granted an immediate retirement benefit.

earned-incurred basis. A basis for calculating the insurer's loss ratio. The claims cost estimated for a period is compared with the premiums earned for the period and expressed as a percentage thereof.

earned premium. The proportion of premium related to the period of insurance that has already run.

earnings related pension. *See* SERPS (STATE EARNINGS RELATED PENSION SCHEME).

earthquake. The risks of earthquake and subterranean fire (fire of volcanic origin) are excluded from the standard fire policy. The risk from these causes varies with the locality (insurers designate some areas as 'earthquake zones' for the purposes of rating and control). Earthquake cover can be obtained for either fire damage or earthquake shock damage or both. This is usually arranged as an additional peril (qv). Earthquake is classed as a 'dry peril'. Subterranean fire, classed as a miscellaneous peril, can also be insured as an additional peril.

earthquake zone. A geographical area particularly prone to earthquakes.

ecclesiastical property. This consists of churches, chapels and their equivalents, halls, Sunday school buildings etc As sums insured are not easy to assess the fire policies covering these properties are made subject to the special condition of average (qv) rather than the pro rata condition of average. Another point of importance is the obligation placed on the Church Commissioners by the Ecclesiastical Dilapidations Measures 1923 to insure property, including the parsonage house, belonging to the benefice.

eco-labelling. A labelling scheme for consumer products. A product gets a label if it meets certain environmental criteria. A UK scheme is due to be introduced by the end of 1991.

economic loss. An alternative term for financial loss. 1. *Legal aspects.* (a) Negligent acts. If the loss (eg lost production/earnings) flows directly out of personal injury or damage to the plaintiff's property the defendant will be liable and will be indemnified under liability policies. If the negligently caused loss is purely economic, ie is unconnected with any personal injury or property damage, the plaintiff will not be able to recover except in very rare circumstances (*Junior Books Ltd* v *The Veitchi Co. Ltd.* (1982)). (b) Negligent statements. Economic loss is the most common form of damage resulting from negligent statements. Liability arises under both contract (eg solicitor/client relationship) and tort if a special relationship exists between the plaintiff and the defendant and there is no disclaimer—the leading cases are *Hedley Byrne* v *Heller & Partners* (1963) and *Caparo PLC* v *Dickman and others* (1990). (c) Nuisance. In public nuisance the plaintiff who suffers particular injury has a right of claim against the defendant. The injury could be to economic interests such as extra expense (eg taking detours when confronted with obstructions), loss of trade (eg obstruction preventing access to premises). 2. *Insurance aspects.* Public and products liability policies cover legal liability for accidental bodily injury and accidental damage to property and this will include the financial losses flowing from such injury or damage. Pure economic (ie financial) loss is not covered unless the policy definition of 'property damage' has been widened or the policy includes a financial loss extension. The wider definition often brings within the policy pure economic loss which results from accidental obstructions and similar accidental nuisances.

economy wording. Co-insurance (qv) often involves numerous properties resulting in lengthy specifications of individual properties and sums insured. To reduce the number of copies the specification is attached to the policy of the leading office but not those of the co-insurers. The policies of the co-insurers are worded to cover, for a stated proportion, the property set out in the specification attached to the leading office's policy and any endorsements thereon. This economises on the number of copies of both specifications and endorsements.

'EC' territorial limits. All British motor policies must include cover against those liabilities which are compulsorily insurable in all other member states of the European Community and non-EC countries, Austria, Czechoslovakia, Finland, Hungary, Sweden, and Switzerland. It is an offence to use a vehicle or trailer that is not insured in this way even though the vehicle or trailer may never leave Great Britain. The inclusion of these territorial limits in the certificate means that a green card (qv) is not strictly required but in practice they are still issued. If comprehensive cover is required the foreign travel (qv) section of the motor policy should be invoked. *See also* BAIL BOND.

educational endowment assurance. An endowment on the life of the parent with the benefits payable in instalments over the schooling period of the child.

effective date. An alternative term for the starting date or inception date (qv) of a policy. It is the date upon which the insurer first becomes liable to meet a loss.

effects. When referred to in policies, usually as the subject-matter insured, this means goods and chattels.

efficacy risk. The risk that a product will not work or perform to specification. A products liability insurer excludes liability resulting from failure of the insured's product to correctly fulfil its intended function (eg failure of cattle feed to fatten up the cattle, or machine part failure). To cover the risk would be tantamount to guaranteeing the efficacy of the product. There is a limited market for products guarantee insurance (qv). The failure of the product to perform may result in financial loss only or it may lead to property damage and/or injury. The exclusion may be so drawn that the resultant damage to property is also excluded but this is not an invariable rule as practice varies among insurers.

'egg-shell skull rule'. The test of causation in *negligence* is that of reasonable foreseeability so that the defendant will be liable for the damage if it is reasonably foreseeable. If the chain of causation is not sufficiently continuous to link the act of negligence with the damage, the damage will be too remote. However, if the type of damage is reasonably foreseeable then liability will attach to the defendant notwithstanding the fact that the extent of the injuries may be entirely unexpected because a pre-existing physical or physic abnormality exacerbates the injury. The defendant must take his victim as he finds him. In *Smith* v *Leech Brain & Co* (1961) an employee suffered a burn on the lip when splashed by molten metal. The type of injury was foreseeable but it was not foreseeable that cancer would ensue at the site of a burn because of a pre-cancerous condition. The defendants were liable. The 'egg-shell skull' does not apply where the plaintiff's loss is aggravated by his own lack of financial resources (*Liesbosch Dredger* v *S.S. Edison* (1933)). A line is drawn between physical and psychic peculiarities on the one hand and lack of financial means on the other. The lack of finance can increase consequential losses through inability to replace property, expedite repairs etc.

ejusdem generis rule. This means 'of the same kind'. It is a rule of construction which can be applied to descriptive phrases in insurance documents. If a specific phrase is followed by a general expression then the latter will be interpreted as meaning 'of the same kind' as the specific words. For example, if a policy refers to 'jewellery, plate, silver, gold, or any articles', the last three words mean 'any articles of the same valuable kind as jewellery, plate, silver and gold' and do not mean 'any articles of any kind'.

electronic networks. These interlink various electronic data processing systems to facilitate the communications and exchange of information without resort to the spoken word and written communications. In 1988 Lloyd's Policy Signing Office, the Institute of London Underwriters, the Policy Signing and Accounting Centre, and LIBC came together to launch LIMNET (London Insurance Market Network) (qv). This permits electronic data interchange between brokers, underwriters, the respective policy signing and claims processing bureaux and other bodies.

elemental perils. Perils of the elements, namely storm and tempest (qv), earthquake (qv), windstorm (qv) and flood (qv).

ELT13. A mortality table which is an aggregate table based on the mortality experience of the population of England and Wales during the 3 years 1970–1972 inclusive. Calculations were based on the deaths in each of these years and on the population recorded in the 1971 census. Given its wide scope the table is appropriate for use by Government Departments in connection with work on national insurance schemes and the like.

electrical breakdown exclusion. *See* MECHANICAL BREAKDOWN EXCLUSION.

electrical clause. A special fire insurance policy clause which excludes loss or damage to dynamos, motors or other electrical apparatus, caused by its own over-running, self-heating etc Such losses are not due to accidental fire

but are incidental to the running of electrical apparatus. The exclusion refers to the electrical apparatus only— other property damaged as a result thereof is still covered. Losses so excluded can be brought into the policy on payment of an additional premium.

electrical plant. This main engineering insurance category includes alternators, air conditioning plant, blowers, bulk milk storage plants, cables, capacitors, condensers, electric motors, extraction plant, fans, frequency changers, furnaces (industrial electrical), gearing/gear boxes, generators, hydro extractors, oil/gas burners, printing machines, pumps, rectifiers, refrigerating plant, space heating units, starting plant, stem turbo generating sets, switchboards, switchgear, transformers, turbines, welding machines, and X-ray plant. Generally the term covers all types of plant powered by electricity. It includes process machinery which together with power producing and generating plant can be insured under an electrical plant policy (qv).

electrical plant policy. The insurance follows that of engine plant (qv). Traditionally cover is against breakdown (qv) (while at the premise or while temporarily at other premises or working sites including transit thereto or therefrom) and damage to surrounding property by fragmentation (qv). Broader cover can now be obtained by extending the breakdown cover to sudden and unforeseen physical damage. This type of plant does not usually require statutory inspection (electrical installations in mines and quarries, power presses, and dust extraction plant are important exceptions) but it is customary for the insurer to include an inspection service with the insurance under which periodical inspections are made including any which are necessitated by statutory provisions. An excess (qv) is applied to all claims. Third party risks are not covered as cover is available under general public liability policies.

eligibility. The conditions which govern a person's right of entry into a pension scheme or right to receive a particular benefit. The conditions may relate to such matters as age, service, status and type of employment.

embezzlement. The felony consisting of the conversion to his own use by a clerk or servant of property received by him on behalf of his master (Larceny Act 1916, s. 17 (1)). It now falls within the definition of theft (Theft Act 1968). The risk is insurable under fidelity guarantee and not theft insurance. Limited cover is given under money insurance policies in respect of cash stolen by employees.

emergency treatment. In order to comply with the compulsory insurance requirements of the Road Traffic Act 1988, s.145, the policy must, *inter alia*, insure any liability for the payment of emergency treatment fees. Section 158 of the Act imposes liability on the user of a vehicle to pay £15 plus travelling expenses (29p per mile) to a registered doctor for each person involved in a vehicle accident on a public road who is given emergency treatment by that doctor. Where more than one doctor attends the fee is payable only to the first one who attends. The third party section of the motor policy covers emergency treatment payments and provides that any payment under this section will be disregarded for the purpose of no claim discount entitlement. The amounts payable for the treatment and the travelling expenses are varied from time to time to take account of inflation.

employees. For the strict legal approach on the term employee *see* EMPLOYER/EMPLOYEE. 1. For the purpose of the employers' liability policy employees are: (a) 'persons under a contract of service or apprenticeship with the insured'. To overcome problems of workers whose status is difficult to determine a wider definition is used to bring within the term 'employees' those listed in (b) to (f) below: (b) any labour masters or labour only sub-contractors or persons supplied by them. (c) self-employed persons. (d) persons hired or borrowed by the insured. (e) persons on work experience schemes. (f) volunteers. The public liability policy excludes liability for injury to employees as defined above. This prevents a duplication of cover. 2. Employers' Liability (Compulsory Insurance) Act definition. 'an individual who has entered into or works under a contract of service or apprenticeship with any employer, whether by way of manual labour, clerical work, or otherwise, whether such contract is expressed or implied, or oral or in writing' and they may be full or part-time. Certain employees are exempt in that an employer is not required to insure his liability to them. *See* EXEMPT EMPLOYEES.

employee/passengers. The third party section of all motor insurance policies excludes liability in respect of death or injury to employees, ie any person arising out of and in the course of such person's employment by the person claiming to be indemnified. The risk is not required to be insured under Road Traffic Act provisions but is insured under employers' liability policies. Under the common law agreement (qv) an employers' liability insurer will not seek to recover his outlay from negligent drivers or their insurers. The 'course of employment' for employee/passengers has been held to include situations where, under the terms of employment, they are provided with travelling facilities, to and from their place of work, which they are obliged to use. A contrary view has been taken where travelling facilities are available for any workman to accept or reject. The test was applied in *Vandyke* v *Fender* (1970) when the obligation to travel made the employer vicariously liable for the negligence of the driver who injured a fellow-employee. In *Smith* v *Stages and Another* (1987) the Court of Appeal modified the rule. Where travel is from a place other than the normal base and is in the employee's own time and own car, it will be within the course of employment, notwithstanding the availability of alternative transport, if the employer knows of the journey and authorises it, and, being entitled to order that travel should not take place on that day, fails to so order.

employer and employee. Liability insurers have to be able to distinguish the employer/employee (master and servant) relationship from that of principal and independent contractor. The distinction is a legal one and is important as: (a) Certain duties are owed by an employer to an employee. The same duties are not owed to independent contractors; and (b) the employer is vicariously liable for the torts of an employee. To succeed against the employer, the plaintiff has to show (i) that the relationship of employer/employee existed and that the tortfeasor was an employee; and (ii) that the latter's tort was committed in the course of employment. An employee is employed under a contract of service but a contractor is employed under a contract for services. In the latter case there is no vicarious liability. To help decide whether an individual is an employee or a contractor, the courts have developed three tests (they are not principles of law): 1. The control test under which a person is a servant if the employer retains the right to control the actual performance of the work. The test usually works well but employers are not always capable of exercising control over some highly skilled people. For example, hospital authorities cannot control the work of their surgeons who often work as employees. In such cases the control seems to be of 'when' and 'where' rather than 'how'. *See also* BORROWED EMPLOYEES. 2. The integration test. 'A person is a servant when his work is an integral part of the business, whereas under a contract for services, his work is not integrated into the business but is only an accessory to it'. A chauffeur is integrated in the business, a taxi driver is an accessory to it. This test asks whether the worker is doing the work on his own account or not. Indirectly, the extent of 'control' of the work becomes an important element of the test. 3. The multiple test builds on the other two by asking if there are any aspects of the relationship which are inconsistent with the individual being an employee. Three basic elements are required to constitute a contract of employment: (a) the employee provides work for the employer for wages; (b) the employee accepts that the employer will exercise control over him; (c) their relationship is consistent with that of employer/employee. The intention of the parties is considered but even if they have expressed it as an employer/em-

ployee relationship, the courts may take a contrary view having regard to the real nature of the relationship not simply what the parties have said. In *Ready Mixed Concrete (South East) Ltd* v *Ministry of Social Security* (1968), the requirement that a driver had to make a vehicle with driver available at his own expense throughout the contract term and the allocation of financial risk to him made the contract inconsistent with one of employment. N.B. In view of the difficulty which arises in distinguishing employees from self-employed sub-contractors, the term 'employee' (qv) is widely drawn up in the employers' liability and public liability policies. This introduces a degree of precision at least as to how insurers wish to treat this issue.

employers' liability at common law. An employer's common law duty to employees may be founded in contract and tort. In the absence of specific terms, some of which may not be allowed by statute, the duty is measured by the obligations imposed by the law of tort which means that an employer is liable only for injury or disease that he has caused by his own or another employee's fault. The duty, which is personal and non-delegable, is to take reasonable care and although general in nature is conveniently considered under four heads. The duty is to take reasonable care to provide: a safe place of work (qv); adequate plant and machinery, properly maintained (qv); a safe system of work (qv); competent fellow employees (qv). An unsafe system or place of work, etc does not *per se* make an employer liable at common law, there has to be negligence.

employers' liability insurance certificate. A certificate that must be issued under the compulsory insurance requirements of the Employers' Liability (Compulsory Insurance) Act 1969 (qv). The certificate must be displayed by the insured at each place of business. The certificate must show: name of insured; policy number; dates of commencement and expiry of the insurance; wording that satisfies the Act; signature of the insurer and an indication that the insurer is authorised to transact this class of business.

employer's form. In fidelity guarantee insurance, where a commercial guarantee is sought a form must be completed by the applicant (ie the employee to be guaranteed) and a separate form must be completed by the employer. The employer's form is actually the proposal form and will form the basis of the contract.

Employers' Liability (Compulsory Insurance) Act 1969. An Act making employers' liability insurance compulsory and obliging insurers to issue policies and certificates. The insurer issuing the policy must be authorised and policies must be in an approved form. The limit of indemnity must be a minimum of £2m for any one occurrence. Regulations under the Act prevent insurers from relying on certain conditions in order to avoid claims. These are conditions precedent to liability relating to matters such as claims notification and conduct, reasonable care, compliance with enactments, and the keeping of records. The restricted right of avoidance applies only for the purpose of the Act and is intended to secure the position of the victim. The insurer who pays a claim because of his inability to rely upon the policy breach has a right of recovery against the insured.

Employer's Liability (Defective Equipment) Act 1969. An Act making an employer liable for injury caused by equipment supplied by him even though the injury is wholly or partly the fault of a third party whether identified is not. At common law the employer who had acquired equipment from a reputable supplier was not liable for injury caused by a latent defect in such equipment. Where the supplier could not be traced or had gone out of business the victim went uncompensated. The employer's liability under the Act is strict and is simply triggered by the act of supply of defective equipment that causes injury but there may be a right of recovery against the supplier or manufacturer. This right may become subrogated to the employers' liability insurer.

employers' liability insurance. An insurance to indemnify the insured in respect of his legal liability to pay compensation to employees in respect of bodily injury or disease caused during the period of insurance and arising out of or in the course of employment by the insured in the business. The indemnity is unlimited in amount. In addition to damages the policy covers: (a) Claimant's costs and insured's own costs if incurred with the insurer's written consent. (b) Solicitor's fees for representation (i) at any Coroner's inquest or fatal accident enquiry or (ii) defending any proceedings in a Court of Summary jurisdiction where the death or proceedings relate to acts or omissions which may be the subject of indemnity under the policy. (c) Indemnity, in the event of the insured's death, to his personal representatives. The cover does not generally apply to injury or disease caused elsewhere than in Great Britain, Northern Ireland, the Isle of Man, the Channel Islands, and offshore installations around Great Britain and its continental shelf. This restriction does not apply to employees temporarily employed elsewhere if they normally reside in the territories stated. For the purpose of this form of insurance the term 'employees' is drawn up in wide terms. *See* EMPLOYEES. *See also* EMPLOYERS' LIABILITY (COMPULSORY INSURANCE) ACT 1969.

Employment Medical Advisory Services (EMAS). EMAS forms part of the Health and Safety Executive's Health Policy Division. It is responsible for providing advice to employers and others about all aspects of health at work.

empty buildings clause. A clause added to a fire policy covering unoccupied buildings. It requires the insured to notify the insurer when the building becomes occupied and to advise how the building will be occupied. The insured is also required to pay any extra premium that may be demanded.

endorsement. A clause appended or affixed to the policy embodying some alteration to the policy terms. Endorsements may be added at inception or afterwards to record a change agreed by the parties.

endorsement charge. A small fee sometimes charged by a broker for altering a policy at a time other than renewal.

endowment assurance. A life assurance policy under which the sum assured (qv) is payable on death or at the end of a given term of years whichever shall occur the first. Policies are typically arranged for periods ranging 10 to 40 years. They combine savings with life assurance protection. The endowment is probably the most popular form of life assurance in the UK. The policy can be used to repay mortgages and other loans, provide a lump sum at a future for pension provision or simply a 'nest egg' while providing life cover in the interim. The policy generally acquires a surrender value and loan value after a period of time and can therefore be used in connection with the payment of school fees. The policy can be with 'with' or 'without profits' (qv).

endowment mortgage. *See* HOUSE PURCHASE SCHEMES.

engine plant. This category of plant for engineering insurance (qv) can be insured against breakdown (qv), while at the premises and temporarily elsewhere and in transit, and damage to surrounding property by fragmentation (qv), ie flying fragments under a relevant policy. Insurers issue a steam engine policy, gas and oil engine policy, or diesel engine policy according to the type of engine. The cover can be extended so that the principal insured peril becomes sudden and unforeseen physical damage (qv) including breakdown. In regard to the diesel engine, the air compressor is included in the insurance. Extensions of cover are available—*see* BREAKDOWN RISKS (EXTENSIONS)—to cover additional risks, eg damage to minor parts, which are excluded under the policy, and damage to the plant by extraneous causes. The situation on inspection services is the same as that for the electrical plant policy (qv). All claims are subject to an excess (qv). Third party risks are not covered as they fall under the general public liability policy. In addition to the type of plant named, refrigeration equipment is insured under this type of policy. *See* REFRIGERATOR INSURANCE.

engineering insurance. Insurance of plant which can be grouped under four main headings: boilers and pressure plant (qv); engine plant (qv); electrical plant (qv); and lifting machinery. In addition to insurance inspection services (qv) are provided. The insurances available cover such losses that take the form of self damage (qv), damage to surrounding property, third party risks, and engineering interruption insurance. Also cover is provided in connection with deterioration of stock (qv), computer risks (qv), contractors' plant (qv), and contract works insurance on machinery installations contracts (qv) and other miscellaneous insurances. The principal risks against which insurance is sought are explosion and collapse (qv), breakdown (qv), sudden and unforeseen physical damage (qv), fragmentation (qv), and extraneous risks (qv).

engineering interruption loss. A form of business interruption insurance (qv) issued in the engineering department to provide an indemnity in respect of interruptions following damage to specific machines. The insured perils are: sudden and unforeseen damage and failure of the public utilities (gas, water, electricity, or effluent services). There are excesses and franchises applied to the indemnity period to avoid small losses, particularly temporary losses of services.

engineering surveys. Detailed surveys regarded as necessary by insurers for the underwriting of high-risk situations, eg pollution or environmental impairment liability cover in high risk industries. The cost is borne by the insured directly or indirectly through higher premiums.

engineer-surveyor. An engineer employed by an engineering insurance company to carry out the inspections under the contracts of insurance or special commissions.

enhanced ordinary charges. The extra charges for the handling of insured cargo because of its damaged condition.

enrolled body corporate. An insurance broking company which has been enrolled in the list maintained by the Insurance Brokers Registration Council. A majority of the directors of an enrolled body corporate must be registered insurance brokers (qv).

entrepreneurial risks. Risks of a speculative nature that do not lend themselves to insurance as they centre on the flair, intuition and self-confidence and similar qualities of the entrepreneur. They are not insurable but may be controlled by sound business practices, eg market research, cost control etc, and/or forming a limited liability.

'entry'. Theft insurances generally, subject to qualifications (*see* FORCIBLE AND VIOLENT ENTRY), cover theft following 'entry' into the insured's premises. Actual entry means the insertion of any part of the body, even if it is only a finger, into the premises. Thus, the person who breaks a window and reaches in to gather and remove an object has effected an actual entry even though he stands outside the premises. It is an entry just as much if the window is open but the absence of force and violence would be fatal to a claim under the usual form of theft policy on business premises. The insertion of an instrument to remove property is also an actual entry. A constructive entry occurs when the breaker of the defences of the premises induces someone else to enter on his behalf.

environmental emission limits (EML). Limits set under the Environmental Protection Act 1990 (qv) relating to the concentration in the air of pollutants emitted from processes. Different types of limits for air pollutants are set under the Act and health and safety legilsation. *See also* OCCUPATIONAL EXPOSURE LIMITS (OEL).

environmental impact assessment (EIA). A formal assessment of the total environmental effect of a project, process, product or development. It is a legal requirement for some specific projects.

environmental impairment liability. A special form of pollution insurance covering: (a) third party claims for bodily injury and damage to real property and for the impairment or diminution of any other right or amenity protected by law; and (b) preventive clean-up costs. The insurance may apply only to losses arising other than from 'sudden and accidental' pollution, which is generally covered under public liability insurance. The costs of cleaning at the insured's own premises and elsewhere are covered. The market is fairly limited with demand coming mainly from high risk industries and insurance being granted only after a survey of the risk.

Environmental Protection Act 1990. An Act consisting of eight parts the most important of which is the introduction of integrated pollution control (qv). The Act also includes a local authority air pollution system, a new requirement for a number of industries which create atmospheric pollution to obtain authorisations from local authorities. Another major change to environmental law is a tightening up of control over waste. All waste producers are subject to a duty of care and are liable for their waste even when it is in the hands of a disposal contractor. Other parts of the Act cover; statutory nuisance; litter; radioactive substances; genetically modified organisms; reorganisation of countryside bodies; and miscellaneous matters (trade and waste, dumping at sea, hazardous chemicals, straw and stubble burning). The Act strengthens the powers of pollution control authorities by establishing in legal frameworks the concept of Integrated Pollution Regulation. Her Majesty's Inspectorate of Pollution is responsible for the statutory regulation of those industrial processes that discharge significant quantities of harmful non-radioactive waste. It is also the regulatory agency for all radioactive waste.

equalisation reserve (or fund). The amount set aside to prevent exceptional fluctuations in the amounts charged to revenue in subsequent years in respect of claims of an exceptional or irregular nature (eg catastrophes).

equitable interest. A legal term referring to interests in property originally created and enforced by the Court of Chancery. Such an interest can arise in a number of ways such as where money has been advanced on property but no formal mortgage deed drawn up. The lender has an equitable interest and this is enough to create an insurable interest. Similarly, a person on whose behalf property is held in trust has an insurable interest in that property.

equity. Unlike the common law, equity is not a complete system of law that would stand alone. It consists of rules that modify the harshness of the common law, and takes precedence over the common law when in conflict with it.

equity-linked life policies. Life insurance policies that aim to combine the advantages of life insurance with investment in equities, ie ordinary shares. Life insurance is linked to equity investment either through an established unit trust (qv) or unitised fund (qv) administered by the life office itself. Usually a large part of the premium is invested in the unit trust or equity portfolio, the balance being used to provide the life cover which is generally on a term insurance basis. The sum insured payable on death is usually a guaranteed minimum but this may increase with the growth in the value of the shares that have been allocated to the individual policy. On expiry of the policy term, the life office either pays the insured an amount equal to the value of the shares standing to his credit on maturity or transfers the units allocated to the policy. *See* UNIT-LINKED POLICIES.

equivalent pension benefit. The benefit which must be provided for an employee who was contracted out of the former graduated scheme.

erection all risks insurance. An insurance in the satellite insurance market covering the assembling and subsequent testing of launchers, satellites and their component parts. The testing comprises functional tests or simulated launchings, ie static firing of engines. The manufacturer may also be able to insure against the loss of the incentive payment normally included in the contract price as a reward for the satisfactory operation of the satellite. The manufacturer faces the risk of losing this payment in the event of unsuccessful operation.

errors and omissions. 1. An insurance effected by Lloyd's underwriting agents in accordance with the rules of Lloyd's. A Name may be able to sue his underwriting agent if the latter's negligence or breach of professional duty has caused a loss. The insurance, which is normally placed in the Lloyd's market, ensures that an agent who is sued will be able to meet any resultant liability. 2. Errors and omission insurance is used as an alternative term for professional indemnity, particularly for insurance brokers, investment managers, and others who can carry out their activities without necessarily being qualified by a recognised examination. 3. An errors and omissions clause appears in proportional reinsurance treaties. Its purpose is to make the treaty watertight and ensure that the contract will not fail through inadvertence. The general intention is to protect the ceding office against accidental omission, either to cede any share of a risk which could properly be ceded or to make the requisite entry in the reinsurance register or to furnish the proper particulars by bordereaux (qv), by providing that the reinsurer shall remain liable for its share of the particular risk affected by the omission. The ceding office can repair the omission as soon as it is discovered by back-dating the cession to the time at which it should have been made. Also it must retain its retention at its usual level if the risk has been affected by a loss. The reinsurer has the right to inspect the books and documents of the ceding so far as they relate to matters falling within the treaty.

escalation clauses. These permit the insurer to automatically raise the level of benefits or sums insured in line with inflation. Many household policies on buildings operate in this way in order to avoid under-insurance as inflation proceeds. Such clauses often appear in family income benefits or in permanent health policies subject to a ceiling of, say, 5 or 7.5 per cent per year. Pension schemes (dynamic or dynamised pensions) can also provide for an automatic increase in the pension on a specified basis by reference to a particular index or an annual increase at a predetermined rate, eg 5 per cent. An escalation clause also appears in a builders' risk marine risk policy providing for a possible increase in the insured value of the vessel under construction because of inflation or rising costs.

escape clause. A clause inserted into sliding scale treaties (qv) to permit the reinsurer to give notice of termination should a maximum rate become payable in any year and the cedant has the same facility if the minimum rate becomes payable in any year.

establishment business. Overseas insurance business obtained by an insurer as a result of establishing a local agent, branch office, subsidiary or associated company in foreign territories. The business is transacted in the foreign country by admitted insurers (qv) unlike non-admitted insurers (qv) whose foreign business is transacted as services business (qv). Shareholders of UK insurance companies receive their profits from establishment business through dividend payments. These payments increase the UK's income from invisible exports. Companies sometimes create 'establishments' as services business is prohibited in certain countries.

estimated future liability. In the Lloyd's annual solvency test on an open year of account, an estimate has to be made of the provision required by a syndicate to cover claims and other adjustments likely to arise from risks accepted during that year. The basis for calculation is laid down in the instructions for the guidance of auditors.

estimated maximum loss (EML). The underwriter estimates the amount of risk the office is able and willing to retain before ceding any surplus to a reinsurer. The estimate has a significant bearing on the profitability of the account. The risk factors influencing a fire underwriter's decision include: division of the risk; values at risk; construction of the property; occupation and use of premises; nature of contents and susceptibility to fire; fire protection measures.

estoppel. The rule of evidence or doctrine of law which precludes a person from denying the truth of some statement formerly made by him, or the existence of facts which he has by words or conduct led others to believe in. Estoppel can be classified in a number of ways including estoppel by conduct which is the one most likely to affect insurance. Where an insurer continues to deal with a claim despite knowing of a breach giving him the right of avoidance, he may later be estopped from

denying liability under the policy. (*Evans* v *Employers Mutual* (1936)).

European accident statement. This statement is an English translation of the widely used 'Constat Amiable', a form issued by motor insurers to their policyholders taking their vehicles to the continent. In the event of an accident, the policyholder and any other party involved write down as much as they are able to agree on the form while events are still fresh in their minds and without admitting liability. The form should be signed by the parties involved and submitted to the insurer with a claim form.

evidence of age. Life insurance premiums are based on the age next birthday of the life insured. It is therefore desirable that evidence in proof of age be supplied at the outset. The policy is then marked 'age admitted' and no subsequent proof, eg at the time of claim, will be demanded.

evidence of health. Life and permanent health insurers require evidence of good health from proposers and from policyholders seeking to revive lapsed policies. Proposers unable to meet the good health standards of the office concerned will be regarded as impaired lives (qv) and face declinature or the imposition of special terms. Under non-medical schemes the proposer provides evidence of health in the proposal form and declaration but the insurer may call for a private medical attendant's report or a medical examination. A declaration of continued good health may be required from proposers who fail to pay the first premium within a stipulated time (eg thirty days) of the letter of acceptance and from policyholders seeking to revive lapsed policies. Life policies sometimes contain options to effect additional policies or convert existing ones without evidence of good health (eg convertible term policies). Evidence of good health is not usually required for members of group life schemes. Selection against the office is avoided in a variety of ways, eg stipulating a given percentage of all the lives in the group must be included in the scheme (this secures an average mortality experience in accordance with the basis of the calculation).

exceptional circumstances clause. *See* SPE-
CIAL CIRCUMSTANCES CLAUSE.

exceptions. *See* EXCLUSIONS.

excess. The specified sum which the insured must bear before the insurers
pay their liability. In the event of liability exceeding the limit of indemnity
specified the insurers pay the limit specified providing the insured has borne
the limit of his policy excess. Unlike a
deductible (qv) the excess sits below
any sum insured, eg an excess of £1 m
and a sum insured of £10 m means
that the insurer is liable for £10 m
once the insured has paid the first £1 m
of any loss otherwise covered by the
policy. Compare with deductible (qv).
Often excesses are for quite small
sums, eg £25 accidental damage excess
under motor insurances. Excesses may
be voluntary to secure premium reduction or compulsory as an underwriting
measure or simply to eliminate small
claims. Compare with franchise.

excess aggregate reinsurance. *See* AGGRE-
GATE EXCESS OF LOSS REINSURANCE.

excess floating policy. A collective guarantee insurance to provide additional
cover on a floating basis to supplement
the specified sums insured in respect
of the individual employees.

excess insurance. An insurance that is designed to be in excess over one or
more primary insurances and does not
contribute to a loss until the limit of
the primary insurance has been
reached. Excess layers are common in
liability insurance where the limits of
indemnity available under primary insurances may not be adequate to meet
the requirements of the insured.

excessive (or exaggerated) claim. A claim
by the insured for an amount which
exceeds the loss he has incurred and
his entitlement to a recovery from the
insurer. The excessive claim may be
the result of an honest mistake or it
may be a fraudulent claim (qv) in that
the insured deliberately seeks to mislead the insurer in order to profit from
his loss. The claim is fraudulent where
the insured: (a) Clearly intended to
deceive the insurer. (b) The over-estimate of the loss is so excessive that the
inference is that the claim is not honest and the intention was to deceive
the insurer. (c) The over-estimate is
deliberately designed for the purpose

of fixing a basis upon which to negotiate with the insurer.

excess liabilities. This term describes certain liabilities for general average contribution, salvage, sue and labour
charges or collision liability that a shipowner may not be able to recover from
the hull insurers. The Marine Insurance Act 1906, s. 73 (1) provides that
the extent of the insurers' liability for
general average contribution is the full
amount of the contribution, providing
the contributory value does not exceed
the insured value. Where there is
under-insurance, the insurers' liability
is rateably reduced. It may happen
that a fully insured vessel may be in a
port where, owing to a rise in tonnage
values, the value on which she is assessed for general average contribution, etc exceeds the insured value. To
safeguard himself against having to
meet a proportion of the contribution
and other charges, the shipowner
generally effects an additional insurance covering Excess liabilities.

excess liability insurance. An insurance
arranged by tour operators in connection with fly-drive holidays to the USA
and Canada. The car companies supplying the vehicles effect third party
cover for limits in excess of the statutory minimum for the benefit of the
car users. Nonetheless the high level of
damages awarded to the victims of road
accidents in North America may exceed
the cover provided. The purpose of excess liability insurance is to cover the liability which is uninsured under the car
company's insurance arrangements.

excess of average loss reinsurance. A
form of excess of loss ratio reinsurance
(qv). The excess point is recalculated
each year as a moving average of the
loss ratio experienced over an agreed
number of preceding years. The ceding
office agrees to bear an agreed share of
any loss in excess of that average.

excess of line reinsurance. This is the
marine insurance equivalent of surplus
reinsurance, excess of line being the
term for surplus. As a rule the retention is based on a table of limits
graded according to the class of the
carrying vessel. Retentions are based
on total sums insured and not maximum probable loss as in fire insurance.

excess of loss cover. Aircraft fleets can be insured on the basis that the excess (or deductible) is so large that the owner is virtually his own insurer except for very large losses or catastrophes. The schemes can take a variety of forms, eg: (a) The insurer paying if the claims arising from any one accident exceed a figure which is an appreciable percentage of the value of the aircraft. (b) Similarly, but the excess is a percentage of the total value of the fleet. (c) The insurer paying only losses which, taken over the whole fleet during the course of the year, exceed a certain percentage of the value of the fleet.

excess of loss ratio reinsurance. This is also known as stop loss reinsurance. Like the excess of loss treaty it is non-proportional and is based on claims results. However, the claims ratio for the whole account is the key rather than individual claims. The aim is to assist the ceding office when its claims ratio rises above a specified percentage. The reinsurer agrees, for example, to pay 90 per cent of all losses in excess of an 80 per cent loss ratio up to 120 per cent. The reinsurer may also fix a monetary limit at which his liability will stop even though in percentage terms the maximum loss ratio has not been reached. This type of reinsurance rarely starts below 70 or 80 per cent and is therefore in the nature of a catastrophe reinsurance. Given loss ratios in excess of 70 per cent, the ceding office is usually in a loss situation before the reinsurance recoveries are possible. The ceding office is protected against substantial losses over the year.

excess of loss reinsurance. A non-proportional reinsurance where the insurer's liability only attaches when a loss exceeds a certain figure and then only for the excess of that figure up to an upper limit. The ceding office may accept liability for the whole of any loss up to the excess point, eg £50 000 with the right to recover the excess (or a percentage thereof) on any individual loss from the reinsurer up to say £150 000. Further layers of reinsurance may be added. The premium is based on a percentage of the ceding office's premium income for the class of business concerned. Cover is usually arranged by treaty (qv) but can also be on a facultative basis. Excess of loss treaties are used for working covers, ie they relate to individual losses and for catastrophe covers (qv).

excess point. In excess of loss reinsurance (qv), the insurer fixes a point up to which level he will retain losses for his own account. This is the excess point and losses above this level will be payable by the reinsurer. The reinsurer fixes an upper limit and this creates the first layer and constitutes the second excess point upon which further layers can be built. In this way there may be a succession of excess points.

excluded form of loss. An exclusion of a particular form or type of loss. For example, the fire policy excludes damage to property undergoing a heating process (qv). Damage caused by fire spreading to other property on the other hand is within the scope of the policy so the risk of igniting property in these circumstances is not excluded. Similarly, a public liability policy excludes liability for damage to property the insured is working on but does not exclude losses that flow from the initial damage.

exclusion. A part or clause of the policy that removes from the scope of cover a risk that might otherwise be insured having regard to the insured risks as set out in the operative clause (qv). Exclusions (otherwise called 'exceptions') can be found within the operative clause in the sense that they qualify the insured peril (*see* QUALIFIED PERILS), in which event the insured has to prove that his claim is not affected by the qualification, or under separate sections of the policy. In the latter instance the insurer who wishes to rely on an exclusion must prove that the exclusion applied to the loss. *See* BURDEN OF PROOF.

execution of policy. A policy under hand is a simple contract and is fully executed when it is signed. These days a facsimile signature is used. A policy under seal is a deed and operates from the time it is formally signed, sealed and delivered.

execution only client. A client who is placing no reliance on the advice or judgment of a financial intermediary in the matter of selecting an investment. He approaches the intermediary with his mind made up and asks for the transaction to be made on his behalf. *See* KNOW YOUR CLIENT, a requirement attaching to financial intermediaries as a result of the Financial Services Act 1986 (qv). Execution only clients have no right of cancellation under the Financial Services (Cancellation) Rules 1988.

executive pension plans. This term describes occupational pension schemes set up for the selected individual employees. These plans are normally associated with senior executives and directors, hence they are sometimes described as 'top hat' schemes, but any employee is eligible for such a scheme.

exemplary damages. Also known as 'punitive' damages they are particularly a phenomenon of the USA. They are often excluded in products liability risks where there is a North American exposure. Such damages are not in any event within an operative clause (qv) where the insurer promises to pay damages 'as compensation'. These damages are rarely awarded in the UK but have been known in statutory awards, cases of wrongs done by civil servants, or serious libel or defamation leading to undue profit.

exempt employees. This refers to people who are not employees for the purpose of the Employers' Liability (Compulsory Insurance) Act 1969. They are: independent contractors; people engaged in any activity that is not defined as a 'business' for the purpose of the Act, eg a domestic servant; people whose employer is related to them as their husband, wife, father, mother, grandfather, grandmother, stepfather, son, daughter, grandson, granddaughter, stepfather, brother, sister, half-brother or half-sister; people who are not ordinarily resident in Great Britain and who are working in Great Britain for fewer than 14 days. In the case of offshore installations, people not ordinarily resident in the UK who work on an installation for more than 7 days are not exempt employees.

exempt(ed) company. Insurance company registered in Bermuda or similar financial 'haven' which is exempted from certain taxes and from many or most of the supervisory and disclosure requirements which apply elsewhere. Usually there is a condition that the company conducts only non-domestic or reinsurance business. Many captive insurance companies (qv) are registered in tax-advantaged territories (*see* TAX HAVENS).

exempt employers. Certain employers are exempted from the compulsory insurance requirements of the Employers' Liability (Compulsory Insurance) Act 1969. Section 3 of the Act exempts: (a) any local authority (other than a parish council); (b) any joint board or committee whose members include representatives of any such local authority; (c) any police authority; (d) any nationalised industry and its subsidiaries; (e) certain bodies financed out of public funds; (f) employers of crews covered by insurance with a mutual insurance association of shipowner.

exempt transfers. Transfers of money or money's worth that is free of liability to inheritance tax. *See* PREMIUM EXEMPTION and BACK-TO-BACK ARRANGEMENTS.

***ex-gratia* payment.** A 'claims payment' made by the insurer 'out of favour' even though there is no legal obligation to pay. Such payments are only made in exceptional circumstances viz: to preserve goodwill; where legal right to refuse payment is founded only on a technicality; costs of defending a claim exceed the claim itself. As the payment is in the nature of a gift, the insurer acquires no subrogation rights (qv).

exhibition insurance. An insurance in respect of loss or damage to exhibits, stands and furnishings while at the exhibition with the option of covering loss or damage occurring in transit to and from the exhibition. Public liability cover can be added. A further option is cover in respect of exhibition expenses wholly or partly lost following damage to property on the exhibition premises or due to abandonment or interruption due to damage by fire, lightning, aircraft or explosion at the exhibition premises.

expectancy. A mere expectancy does not create an insurable interest (qv). A beneficiary under a will may have good reason to expect to collect the inheritance but this is no more than an expectancy and creates no insurable interest in the life of the benefactor (*Lucena* v *Craufurd* (1808)) but the purchaser of an expectancy has an insurable in the life of the beneficiary as there will be financial loss if the death of the beneficiary frustrates the bequest.

expectation of life. The average life expectancy of a person at a given age according to mortality tables.

expected claims cost. The cost of claims which policyholders make on average each year. The annual average of previous years' claims experience adjusted for inflation is the usual basis for this figure which must be covered by the risk premium (qv).

expense loading. The amount added to a premium calculation to secure an appropriate contribution from the policyholder to the insurer's administrative expenses (eg salaries, rents, rates, heating, stationery etc). Some of these are fixed costs (qv) and others are variable costs. Other items in the premium computation are: contingency loading (qv), risk premium (qv), and profit loading.

expense ratio. The fraction arrived at by dividing the amount of premiums into the amount of expenses incurred in connection with a particular class of business. It is generally expressed as a percentage of the premiums and is monitored carefully by the insurer.

experience rating. A method of calculating rating based on previous claims experience of the individual insured.

experience refund. The term used by life reinsurers to describe the profit commission that they pay to the ceding office as a refund based on the profitability of the business.

expiry. The completion of the period of insurance.

explosion (engineering insurance). In engineering insurance explosion means the sudden and violent rendering of the plant by force of internal steam or other fluid pressure (other than pressure of ignited flue gases) causing bodily displacement of any part of the plant, together with forcible ejectment of the contents. The risk is insured by using the term explosion or collapse (qv) as a way of specifying the insured perils.

explosive nuclear assemblies clause. *See* NUCLEAR PERILS.

explosion. 1. *Fire and special perils insurance.* The standard fire policy covers the risk of explosion to a strictly limited extent, ie concussion damage following the explosion: (i) of boilers used for domestic purposes. (ii) In a building not forming part of a gasworks of gas used for domestic purposes or for lighting. No other concussion damage is covered under the standard fire policy. However, as fire and explosion may arise sequentially, the rules of proximate cause (qv) are amended. The following combinations show the effect of the policy modifications set out in Condition 3 (Exclusions): (a) Explosion followed by fire. No concussion damage unless (i) or (ii) above but fire following explosion is specifically covered. (b) Fire followed by explosion. Fire damage is covered but concussion damage even though proximately caused by fire is specifically excluded. Explosion cover in excess of the limited cover ((i) and (ii) above) can be added by way of additional perils (qv) insurance. When added the cover is not limited to explosion arising on the insured's premises. To prevent overlap with engineering policies, the cover excludes the explosion of boilers and steam pressure vessels under the control of the insured. 2. *Engineering policies.* Explosion and collapse are the principal risks covered in respect of boilers and steam pressure vessels under the control of the insured.

explosive nuclear assemblies clause. A clause in material damage and public liability policies excluding liability directly or indirectly caused by or contributed to by or arising from the radioactive toxic explosive or other hazardous properties of any explosive nuclear assembly or nuclear component thereof. If nuclear explosives were ever used in the UK, it would be under the control of the Government who would take responsibility.

exposure. A term used in three senses. 1. The state of being subject to the possibility of loss. 2. The extent of risk as measured by turnover, payroll etc 3. The possibility of loss to property caused by its surroundings.

exposure theory. A theory concerned with the problem of when the injury or loss occurred in the context of 'long-tail' claims liability for which may be the subject of indemnity under a liability policy. The exposure to the injury-inducing risk may have its origin in one significant event which causes no further problem or it may arise out of an exposure over a long period to a harmful product or environment. As most liability policies (with employer liability the law permits no alternative) are written on a 'losses-occurring' basis, the problem is deciding when the loss occurred. The exposure theory advocates that the occurrence took place during the whole period of exposure to the harmful situation. If the insured has changed insurers over the years, the resultant claim will be apportioned among the insurers concerned. The manifestation theory advocates that the occurrence took place when the injury or damage became known to the claimant so that the insurer on risk at that time alone becomes liable. *See also* TRIPLE TRIGGER THEORY.

exposure to loss premium rating. A method of rating working cover excess of loss reinsurance treaties (qv) for property risks. The ceding company's portfolio is analysed according to sums insured in relation to the treaty deductible. Policies with sums insured below the deductible expose the reinsurer to no risk of loss and facilitate the use of a mathematical formula to calculate a rate of premium commensurate with the degree of exposure.

express conditions. 1. *Insurances generally.* Conditions that are expressly stated in the policy. They may be general conditions or particular conditions (otherwise called 'special conditions'). The general conditions are printed on the policy and are common to all contracts on that form. They usually reinforce implied conditions (eg non-disclosure), deal with alterations that require notification, claims procedures, privileges and rights, and modify the common law principles of contribution (qv) and subrogation (qv). Particular conditions apply to matters affecting the individual policy and may extend or restrict the cover or control the risk by the application of warran-

ties. 2. *Life insurance.* The general conditions include privileges (qv) consisting of clauses covering such matters as provisions for paid-up policies (qv), surrender values (qv), loans (qv), days of grace (qv) and non-forfeiture (qv). Typical conditions imposing restrictions are embodied in clauses relating to suicide (qv), foreign residence/travel (qv), occupation (qv), and war risks (qv). The practice varies—some insurers treat them as general conditions while others may treat them as particular (or special) such as foreign travel or occupation where they feel a special risk arises. Other matters, eg premium instalments, are included and classified as special conditions.

express warranty. A warranty (qv) set out or incorporated in the policy requiring the insured to do or not to do something or stating that a certain state of affairs will or will not be maintained. The Marine Insurance Act 1906, s. 35 (1) provides that an express warranty 'may be in any form of words from which the intention to warrant is to be 'inferred'. Section 35(2) adds 'an express warranty must be included in, or written upon, the policy, or must be contained in some document incorporated by reference into the policy'. Section 35(3) states that 'An express warranty does not exclude an implied warranty, unless it be inconsistent therewith'.

expropriation cover. An insurance against the risk of losing property or rights in property when the property is seized by the government of the country in which the property is located.

extended definitions. A definition introduced into an insurance contract when the normal meaning of a word or phrase does not give full effect to the insurer's intention. Such definitions are often used in liability policies. For example, the term 'employee' (qv) is taken to include self-employed persons and 'business' includes the rendering of first-aid, canteens, and private work by employees for directors or partners.

extended reporting period. A specific period allowed by insurers at the end of a contract to bring claims that would otherwise be out of time within the policy. A 'tail' is often added to liability insurances written on a claims-made basis to bring within the cover of lapsed policies claims first advised during a specified period, eg three or six months, from the date of expiry provided that there is no other policy in force.

extended terms insurance. A credit insurance where the credit term exceeds 180 days.

extension clause. A clause in a policy that introduces additional cover.

extended warranty insurance. 1. Purchasers of electrical and electronic equipment may wish to extend the one year guarantee which is frequently provided by the manufacturer or supplier. The extended warranty insurance extends the guarantee of one year to five years in return for a single premium. As it stretches the original guarantee, it is restricted to items covered by that warranty which usually means cover against faulty manufacture and faulty workmanship. The insurance is usually arranged by the retail store selling the product. An alternative form of cover is an annual breakdown insurance (qv). 2. This operates in a similar way to the scheme in 1 above in respect of new cars carrying a manufacturer's warranty for 12 or 24 months. The cover runs from the time the manufacturer's warranty expires and ends when the car reaches a stated age, eg 4 years. The premium is payable annually.

extensions away from insured premises. The intention of most material damage policies is to cover property in fixed locations. However, property may be temporarily removed for specific purposes. In order to obviate the need for separate negotiations extension clauses are added to provide automatic cover for these temporary removals. Under householder comprehensive policies on contents property temporarily removed from the dwelling is covered up to 15 per cent of the sum insured. Property removed to furniture depositories and for sale or exhibition is not covered under this extension. For the treatment of business risks *see* TEMPORARY REMOVAL CLAUSE, the METALWORKERS' EXTENSION and the FARMING INSURANCE EXTENSION.

external company. An insurance company whose head office is situated in a country outside the European Community.

external dependencies. The risk that attaches to a business as a result of its relationship with, and dependency on, outside bodies from the public or private sectors. For example, a business may be exposed to the risk of loss by occurrences, eg fires, at the premises of customers and/or suppliers. Risk management involves a close scrutiny of external dependencies and internal dependencies (qv). Business interruption policies can extend to cover loss of trade due to damage occurring at the premises of customers and/or suppliers.

'external means'. A personal accident policy insures the insured against bodily injury caused by 'violent, accidental, external and visible means'. The intention of 'external means' is to make it clear that the bodily injury must be due to some outside event as distinct from physical defects. The words are used as the antithesis of 'internal means'. The qualification 'external and visible' applies to the means only and not the injury itself which may be internal and invisible. Where a person suffered an injured spine through lifting a heavy weight there was an internal injury with an external cause entitling the insured to a benefit under the policy (*Martin* v *Travellers' Insurance Co* (1859). Similarly the dislocation of the internal cartilage of the knee involved an external agency when the insured stooped to pick up a marble (*Hamlyn* v *Crown Accidental Insurance Co* (1893)). When the insured was drowned after becoming insensible due to a fit, his death was caused by water, an external means (*Winspear* v *Accident Insurance Co* (1880)).

external member. A Lloyd's underwriter who does not fall within the definition of a working member.

extinguishment damage. This is the damage caused by water and other extinguishing agents used to put out and limit the effects of a fire. Such damage is the natural and probable consequence of the fire. Damage caused in attempts to mitigate the loss are a part of the loss so water damage can be regarded as fire damage even though there is no actual ignition of the property concerned.

extra charges. A marine insurance term referring to the expenses incurred by the insured in proving a loss, eg survey fees, auction or sale charges. They are paid by the insurer only if the claim is admitted. However, where a survey is carried out on the instructions of the insurer, eg by the Salvage Association, this will always be paid by the insurer.

extraneous risks. Certain additional, or extraneous, perils brought into marine insurance policies to extend the cover provided in the discarded SG form of policy. The extra risks were aimed at 'negligent handling' rather than casualties during transport and the Institute Cargo Clauses (A) (1/1/82) now provide the necessary cover. In hull policies this is achieved by the Inchmaree clause (qv).

extra perils. An alternative term for additional perils (qv) or special perils.

ex-turpi causa non oritur actio. 'An action does not arise from a base cause.' The rule prevents a criminal from recovering under a liability policy for injury or damage that otherwise would be within the policy. However, in *Hardy* v *Motor Insurers Bureau* (1964), the plaintiff, through a right conferred by the Road Traffic Act, had a direct right of action against the insurer. Recoveries can also be made for mere acts of negligence even though criminal.

EXW (ex-works). This indicates that the price of the goods in a contract of sale is their cost at the factory gate. The purchaser assumes responsibility for the goods from that point and pays all movement costs including insurance. The contract specifies if packing is included.

F

Factories Act, 1961. An Act consolidating and extending many of the common law duties of employers towards employees employed in factories. Generally, the duties stipulated in this statute are strict; ie employers are not merely required to take reasonable care that the precautions are adopted; they must in most circumstances ensure that they are observed to the letter. Liability is on the occupier of the factory, unless, in some particular circumstance, the relevant section provides that the owner shall be liable. *See* FACTORY (qv), and FENCING OF MACHINERY.

factory. The term 'factory' has a very wide meaning as given in the Factories Act 1961 (qv), s. 175. It consists of any premises, including open air premises, where people are employed in manual labour for gain in order to: (a) make an article; (b) adapt an article for sale or altering, repairing, ornamenting, finishing, cleaning, washing, breaking-up or demolition of any article; (c) slaughter certain cattle and confine them on premises other than a farm or market; (d) construct, repair, refit or break-up ships or vessels in any yard or dry dock; (e) sort any article; (f) wash, fill bottles or containers or pack any articles; (g) hook, plait, lap, make up or pack yarn or cloth; (h) carry on a laundry as ancillary to another business or public institution; (i) construct, reconstruct or repair locomotives, vehicles or other plant used for transport purposes except where the premises are used solely for housing the vehicles, washing, cleaning, carrying out running repairs, and minor adjustments; (j) print by letterpress, lithography, photogravure, or similar process, or carry out bookbinding; (k) make, adapt, repair dresses, scenery or properties, except in the stage or dressing rooms of a theatre where only occasional work is done; (l) make or mend fishing nets; (m) use mechanical power for making or repairing articles of wood or metal; (n) produce cinematograph films; (o) make or prepare articles incidental to the building and construction industries provided they are not premises in which such operations or work is carried on; (p) store gas in a gasholder where the storage capacity is not less than 5000 cubic feet (q) use as a line or siding (not being a part of railway or tramway) in connection with the factory; (r) carry on work in any workplace in which two or more persons work with the permission of, or under agreement with, the owner or occupier.

facultative obligatory treaty. Often called 'fac-oblig', this permits the cedant (qv) to choose which risks to cede to the reinsurer who is obliged to accept the chosen risks provided that they are within the terms of the treaty. It is normally arranged after a surplus treaty and provides automatic cover to the cedant when the capacity of the surplus treaty has been exhausted. It differs from a further treaty only in that the cedant can exercise a choice. It in effect provides a method by which the cedant obtains an automatic facility for its facultative reinsurances (qv).

facultative reinsurance. The reinsurance (qv) of an individual risk on terms and conditions agreed with the reinsurer specifically for that risk. It is the oldest form of reinsurance under which particulars of each risk are submitted by the ceding office (qv) to the reinsurers who may accept or decline at will. Treaty reinsurance (qv) eases the administrative burden. Facultative reinsurance is useful when dealing with risks outside the ceding office's treaty arrangements. *See* FACULTATIVE OBLIGATORY.

failure of consideration. If a risk, for which the insurer has received a premium, fails to attach (eg for innocent misrepresentation), there is a failure of consideration on the part of the insurer and, in the absence of fraud by the insured, the insurer must return the premium.

failure of main services insurance. An engineering policy which pays a specified amount per day in respect of losses caused by accidental failure of the public electricity, gas or water supplies.

falling trees. 1. Most household policies provide cover for damage to the insured property caused by falling trees or part thereof. Loss/damage caused by tree felling or lopping by or on behalf of the policyholder is excluded. There may be a small excess in respect of the buildings cover and damage to gates, hedges and fences is excluded. *See* IMPACT DAMAGE. 2. Injury or damage to a third party caused by a falling tree may give rise to a liability in negligence or nuisance. Liability cover is provided for owners under an extension of the buildings policy and for occupiers' liability there is an extension under the contents policy.

family car. A term popularly used to describe a car shared by members of a family. The term has no legal status. In *Morgans* v *Launchbury* (1973) the House of Lords rejected the contention that almost any journey with either spouse as a passenger had a joint matrimonial purpose. In that case the car owned by the wife was driven by someone nominated by the husband. The attempt to hold the wife vicariously liable for the negligence of the driver of her husband's choice failed. There was no agency between her and the driver.

family income benefits. A decreasing term assurance (qv) under which an annual sum is payable on death of the life assured within the policy term for the remaining part of that term. For example, the benefit may be £1000 per year for 20 years giving an initial cover of £20 000 reducing to nil. The amount of cover decreases by £1000 per year and if the life assured survives the term, the policy runs out and there is no survival benefit. The chief use is for the family man who wishes to protect his family against the risk of his early death by guaranteeing an income during a selected period, eg up to and just beyond school leaving age of his children. They can also be used as an alternative for mortgage protection by linking the term of the policy to the term of the mortgage and the amount to the mortgage repayment. These benefis can be provided in a separate policy or combined with whole life or endowment assurances (qv).

farming insurance extensions. Various kinds of farming stock are covered by appropriate extensions while temporarily removed anywhere in Great Britain, Ireland and Northern Ireland as follows: (a) Vehicles and implements and utensils of husbandry if not otherwise insured. (b) Grain (removed for drying or dressing) if not otherwise insured. Other extensions include: Agricultural produce, farming stock, implements and utensils of husbandry and livestock while in transit; Livestock in the open or in buildings elsewhere than on any farm in the insured's occupation.

F.A.S. (Free alongside ship). This signifies that goods are 'delivered free alongside ship'. The seller must carry goods to the named loading port at his own expense and deliver alongside the vessel so that they can be handled by the vessel. He must provide the customary dock or wharfingers' receipt if required under the contract. He will be responsible for all loss/damage until the goods are placed alongside ship. The buyer is responsible for all loss/damage after the goods have been placed alongside the ship.

Fatal Accidents Act 1976. The Act consolidates earlier legislation which created exceptions to the common law rule that no action lies in tort for another's death. Section 1(1) provides that where the death is caused by the wrongful act, neglect or default which (if death had not ensued) would have entitled the person injured to maintain an action for damages, the person, who would have been liable had death not ensued, shall be liable to an action for damages. Section 1(2) provides that the action shall be for the dependants of the deceased. Dependants are: deceased's husband, wife, children, grandchildren, stepchildren, parents, step-parents, and grandparents and any person who is the issue of a brother, sister, uncle or aunt of the deceased (s.1(3), (4)). The relative concerned must show that he or she suffered a pecuniary loss as a result of the death. Spouses (not former spouses or cohabitors) may claim for bereavement (the sum can be varied by statutory instrument but the aim is to award one-half of the average annual earnings). Parents of a minor who has never married may claim under this head but in the case of an illegitimate child only the mother may claim. Otherwise the claim is for loss of prospective pecuniary advantage meaning the loss of the direct financial contribution to the dependant. The gain to the dependant, which may have been based on a legally enforceable right or been entirely gratuitous, must have accrued from a family and not business relationship. In fixing damages no account is taken of a widow's re-marriage prospects. Claims must be brought within three years of the death or relevant 'knowledge' of the claiming relative whichever is the later. Extensions may be granted under the Limitation Act 1980 (qv).

fatal accidents policy. A personal accident policy under which the only benefit payable is a lump sum (or annuity) for death following an accident. The policy may be useful for a person whose income is not at risk of loss through accidental injury but who wishes to provide for his dependants in the event of accidental death. There may be a special motive for effecting such a policy, eg foreign travel or engaging in a hazardous activity.

fatal claim. A claim following accidental death under a personal accident or the relevant section of some other policy, eg personal accident sickness policy, or other travel policy. It is customary for the insurer to obtain the Coroner's report (known as Depositions) but it is not binding in law and is not necessarily sufficient proof of a claim under the policy. The doctor's death certificate is also obtained. The death benefit is payable only if death has occurred within twelve months of the accidental injury.

fatal enquiry. The Scots term for inquest (qv) and for this reason both terms are mentioned in liability policies. The insurer can arrange for legal representation of the insured at the relevant proceedings and a copy of the coroner's depositions can be obtained. The insured is required by policy conditions to give notice immediately he has knowledge of any impending inquest or fatal enquiry.

fault. For the purpose of the Law Reform (Contributory Negligence) Act 1945 fault is defined as 'the negligence, breach of statutory duty or other act or omission which gives rise to liability in tort, or would apart from this Act, give rise to the defence of contributory negligence'. For the purpose of the Employers' Liability (Defective Equipment) Act 1969 fault means 'negligence, breach of statutory duty, or other act or omission which gives rise to liability in tort in England and Wales or which is wrongful and gives rise to liability in damages in Scotland'.

fault liability system. A legal system under which a party who has sustained injury or damage must prove fault on the part of another in order to recover compensation. In the UK, for example, the victims of road and industrial accidents have to prove that the respective motorists and employers involved were either negligent or in breach of some other duty. In the absence of fault (or proof thereof) the injured party will only receive such limited compensation as is available through the social security system. The onus of proof of fault is sometimes shifted to the alleged wrongdoer—see *res ipsa loquitur* (qv) and there is a tendency to use legislation to give greater protection to potential victims by making liability strict, eg Consumer Protection Act 1987. *See also* PEARSON COMMISSION.

faulty (or defective) design. In the context of the exclusion in the contractors' all risks insurance, this means (i) a design which fails to meet the standards expected of design engineers; and (ii) a design that proves inadequate but without blame or negligence attaching to the design engineer

(*Queensland Government Railways* v *Manufacturers' Mutual Insurance Co. Ltd* (1969)). It is generally regarded as a professional indemnity risk to be insured by any engineer whose duties include designing structures and buildings. However, some contractors' all risks policies insure the cost of making good damage to property other than the permanent works consequent upon defective design or specification.

faulty workmanship. A risk that is normally excluded under public liability insurance. *See* PROPERTY WORKED ON. *Also see* DEFECTIVE WORKMANSHIP.

fees. Professional fees are insurable in a variety of circumstances. Architects', surveyors', and consulting engineers' fees (qv) incurred in connection with the rebuilding of property after a fire etc may be added to the cover as a separate item or included with the buildings and contents items. Accountants fees payable by the insured for preparation of a business interruption insurance claim can also be insured under the policy. Also the major aim of legal expenses cover (qv) is to cover legal defence costs and, under appropriate sections, the fees incurred in connection with Inland Revenue and VAT investigations.

fees recovery extension. An extension of a professional indemnity insurance to indemnify the insured (usually up to 80 per cent) in respect of the costs of recovering or attempting to recover professional fees due to him under contract for work performed. Generally, the insurance is subject to the proviso that the insured has instituted legal proceedings and the party sued has intimated that he proposes a counter-claim that would be covered under the operative clause of the professional indemnity cover.

Fellowship diploma of the Chartered Insurance Institute (FCII). Until 1991 the diploma was awarded to holders of the ACII diploma who had completed five examination subjects provided that the candidate had been in insurance for at least four years. From 1992 there will be no examinations leading to the Fellowship award. The FCII will in future be awarded to those Associates who satisfy certain criteria relating to professional experience and other criteria set at a high standard. Election involves a minimum waiting period of three years after the Associateship award, demonstration of what has been learned and development within the employment situation, commitment to the educational activities of the Chartered Insurance Institute, and submission of a 5000 word dissertation.

female lives. The mortality rates for women are more favourable than for men and this enables life insurers to offer policies at lower rates of premium than those charged for male lives. Typically, insurers will deduct 4 years from their tabular rates (based on male lives) to find the rate for a female life (eg a 44-year-old female is rated as per a 40-year-old male).

fencing of machinery. The Factories Act 1961 (qv), ss. 12–16 lays down the principle that every part of transmission machinery and every dangerous part of any other machinery must be securely fenced, unless it is in such a position or of such construction as to be safe to every person employed or working on the premises as it would be if securely fenced. The regulations do not apply to machines in the course of manufacture (*Parvin* v *Morton Machine Co Ltd* (1952). The danger to be guarded against is the contact of worker with the machine. The fence is not intended to keep the machine or its parts in (*Nicholls* v *Austin* (1946)). Section 12 governs prime movers (eg motors, generators, water-wheels, water turbines, rotary converters) and flywheels directly connected to them. They are presumed to be dangerous. Section 13 relates to transmission machines (appliances that take the power to production machinery via shafts, belts, and pulleys). In the case of transmission machinery devices enabling power to be cut off promptly must be provided. Section 14 refers to all other machinery every dangerous part of which must be securely fenced unless the fencing would not make it safer. Section 16 provides that except during examination, lubrication or adjustment, all fencing or other safeguards must be of substantial construction, maintained, and kept in position while those parts which must be safeguarded are in motion or use. The obligation to fence is absolute and the fact that compliance makes the machine unusable does not excuse the use of an unfenced machine (*Summers & Son Ltd* v *Frost* (1955)). In civil claims based on breach of statute the fence must give protection against such dangers as might reasonably be expected and the employer must make allowance for the fact that employees act carelessly from time to time.

FGU (from the ground up). A term describing all of a primary or ceding company's losses over a period of time, including losses for their own account (retained). This enables the reinsurer to assess the effect of shifts in direct underwriting experience on future reinsurance claims.

fianza. The Spanish term for a bail bond (qv).

fidelity guarantee insurance (suretyship insurance). Indemnity contracts to protect one party against loss due to the dishonesty of another or the failure of that other to carry out his duties in the proper manner. There are four main sections of fidelity guarantee insurance: (i) Commercial guarantees (qv). These protect employers from loss due to the dishonesty of employees. Policies can be issued on individual employees, or in respect of a number of them by collective or floating policies. Under a collective policy a separate sum is guaranteed in respect of each named employee. Under a floating policy one amount covers all named employees. The 'positions policy' is one which guarantees the position (eg accountant) and not the individual. The 'blanket policy' gives protection against dishonesty of the staff generally. (ii) Local government guarantees. Similar to (i) above but cover is wider. It extends to include losses due to mistakes. (iii) Court bonds. The guarantee of the performance of individuals appointed by the courts to handle the money and assets of others. See COURT BONDS. (iv) Government bonds. The guarantee of the performance of individuals in a position of trust given to government departments. A Customs and Excise bond, for example, protects HM Customs and Excise Department against loss through default in the payment of duty on dutiable goods. See CUSTOMS AND EXCISE BONDS.

fiduciary duties. The relationship of one person to another, where the former is bound to exercise rights and powers in good faith for the benefit of the latter, eg as between trustee and beneficiary. Similarly a director (qv) must act in the best interests of the company in good faith, honestly and without ulterior motive. Unless the company's Articles of Association permit and he makes a full disclosure, he may not be party to any contract made by his company. If he acts in breach of this duty he is liable to the company for any gain. The duties are owed to the company and not individual shareholders. Conflicts of interest and duty may arise in relation to contracts of employment, property transactions, loans and insider dealing. Directors will be liable to pay losses suffered by the company following any act which is illegal, outside the company's authority, or beyond their powers. If a director acts as a trustee of a pension fund he owes a separate fiduciary duty to the members of that fund. Officers (qv) owe the same duty to the company as directors.

field staff. The field staff is the sales force of an insurer or insurance broker.

fifteen per cent extension clause. A clause in householders' comprehensive policies on contents allowing the insured to remove temporarily—without notice—property up to 15 per cent of the sum insured anywhere in the UK. The extension does not operate in connection with property removed for sale or exhibition or to a furniture repository. Some policies now offer cover up to 20 per cent of the sum insured.

film producers' indemnities. A contingency insurance against pecuniary loss due to the interruption or abandonment of film through the death or incapacity of named actors or actresses. A limited specialist market caters for these risks and insures 'non-appearance'. The contingency insured is the non-appearance of a film or television star at a public event where the takings will be affected in consequence.

final earnings scheme. See FINAL SALARY SCHEME.

final pensionable salary. This is defined in a pension scheme and is calculated in a specified way (e.g. averaged over a period prior to the retirement date). The actual pension is determined by reference to the final pensionable salary (n 60ths, n representing the number of years of pensionable service subject to a maximum of 40/60ths).

final salary scheme. A pension under which the pension payable is based on the final pensionable salary (qv). Defined benefit pension scheme is a commonly used alternative term. Final earnings scheme is another alternative.

Financial Intermediaries, Managers and Brokers Regulatory Association (FIM-BRA). A Self-Regulating Organisation (qv) which regulates intermediaries who mainly advise upon and arrange life insurance, pensions and unit trusts (and similar collective investment schemes) as well as financial management services to retail customers. There are a number of membership categories some of which do not permit the intermediary to handle the client's money. To secure authorisation the intermediary has to satisfy the Council of the Association that he is a 'fit and proper person' to carry on investment business (qv). In the case of a company any person with authority has to be 'fit and proper'. It has to be shown that the business will be conducted in a proper and prudent manner. In addition the Council requires references, audited accounts, and details of how the business will be conducted in the event of a single authorised intermediary being disabled through accident, sickness etc. Unregistered insurance intermediaries and registered insurance brokers who earn more than 25 per cent of their income from life business, pensions and collective investment schemes apply to FIMBRA for authorisation. Registered insurance brokers and enrolled bodies corporate (qv) earning not more than 25 per cent of their income from the foregoing activities should seek certification through the Insurance Brokers Registration Council (qv), which is the relevant Recognised Professional Body (qv). Professional indemnity insurance (qv) is compulsory for FIMBRA members. Indemnity varies according to turnover. *See also* INDEPENDENT FINANCIAL ADVISER; SECURITIES AND INVESTMENTS BOARD.

financial loss cover. The insurance of legal liability for pure financial loss (ie financial loss unaccompanied by physical injury or damage) by way of an extension to public liability and products liability policies. Cover under those policies is limited to liability arising from bodily injury or property damage including any financial loss resulting from such injury or damage. Basic policies do not generally cover pure financial loss. It can be arranged by way of a policy extension but limited cover is often given by adopting a wide definition of property damage in the body of the policy. A wide definition may cover liability arising from 'nuisance, trespass and impairment or diminution of or interference with any right of light or air or way or easement or other environmental right or amenity or any likely cause'. Liabilities arising in such ways often relate purely to financial losses as they are concerned with events that may prevent a third party from enjoying the uninterrupted use of his premises, eg an escape of gas could temporarily close his business or a road obstruction could deny access to him or his customers. Cover is subject to the policy's normal terms and this will generally mean that the nuisance, trespass etc has to be accidental. Fuller cover is given by a policy extension which extends property damage to include Financial Loss meaning 'a pecuniary loss cost or expense incurred by any person other than the insured'. The extended cover is subject to the policy's normal terms and conditions but insurers generally introduce additional exclusions to apply to the financial loss cover. Typically, the cover will be on a claims-made basis (qv) notwithstanding that the main cover is losses-occurring (qv). Cover will not apply to breach of professional duty, passing-off, breach of copyright and other intellectual property, payments by reason of statute etc, liquidated damages and fines, contractual liability, making good defective products, or product recall expenses. The limit of indemnity is usually a separate one on an aggregate for the year basis and there is invariably a co-insurance clause (eg insured responsible for 10 per cent of all claims). The products liability extension operates only in connection with products supplied and the contractual liability exclusion will not strike out any liability that would have attached in the absence of any agreement. The financial loss extension of the products policy overlaps with products guarantee insurance (qv) in so far as the latter covers the financial consequences of the failure of the product to perform its intended function.

Financial Planning Certificate (FPC). A certificate issued by the Chartered Insurance Institute (qv) to provide an accepted market qualification for those engaged in financial services. The CII liaises with the Self-Regulating Organisations (qv) to ensure that their syllabus and course meet the requirements of the SROs. The FPC has three papers: (a) Marketing, salesmanship and investor protection; (b) Life assurance; (c) Pensions. Paper (a) must be passed plus one out of (b) and (c). The next step, currently being developed, is the introduction of the Advanced Financial Planning Certificate to build on the knowledge gained from the FPC. It will include modules on Investments and Trusts; Corporate Investment Planning and Taxation; Mortgages.

Financial Services Act 1986. The Act regulates those undertaking investment business, which includes life assurance, pensions business and unit trusts, in the UK. The Act regulates the activities of, *inter alia*, insurers and intermediaries. Also within the scope of the Act are those who arrange transactions and individuals who give advice in the choice of company or product. Although certain aspects of the business of life assurance companies continue to be regulated by the DTI, such companies need additional authorisation through membership of either: a SRO (Self Regulatory Organisation); or a RPB (Recognised Professional Body); or through direct authorisation from the SIB (Securities and Investments Board). The SRO for life companies is LAUTRO (Life Assurance and Unit Trust Regulatory Organisation). LAUTRO regulates the selling practices of companies and their representatives (direct sales force and appointed company representatives, ie tied agents (qv). IMRO (Investment Management Regulatory Organisation) regulates fund management activities. FIMBRA (Financial Intermediaries Managers and Brokers Regulatory Association) regulates independent financial intermediaries and brokers. Smaller brokers can secure authorisation by membership of the Insurance Brokers Registration Council (IBRC) which is recognised as an RPB (see above). A smaller broker for this purpose is one who does not handle client monies and whose brokerage from investment business activities does not exceed 25 per cent of total income. *See* POLARISATION.

Financial Services Compensation Fund. A fund set up following the Financial Service Act 1986 to protect private investors against fraud. As a result anyone buying an investment from an authorised person is able to seek compensation from a central body, called the Financial Services Compensation Manager Ltd. It provides compensation if the investor loses money in the event of the firm going out of business or in the event of fraud. Investors may receive 100 per cent of the first £30 000 and 90 per cent of the next £20 000 to give a maximum payment of £48 000.

fine arts insurance. The insurance of works of art. In the USA it is usually underwritten by inland marine insurers on an 'all risks' and a 'valued basis'.

fire. 1. *General meaning.* Fire, for the purpose of fire insurance, occurs where there is actual ignition which is accidental or fortuitous in origin as far as the insured is concerned. Something must be on fire which was never intended to be so. The term does not include a fire lighted for a specific purpose while confined to its normal limits (eg in a grate) but does include destruction or damage when such a fire goes outside its normal limits. It also includes the burning of something in a deliberately lighted fire that does not break its bounds if property is ignited accidentally by the fire. In *Harris* v *Poland* (1941) the plaintiff as a precautionary measure concealed jewellery beneath the fuel in a grate and later, forgetting this precaution, lit the fire and destroyed the jewellery. As there had been no intention for the jewellery to make contact with the fire, there had been a fortuitous occurrence no different, in the court's view, from a fire breaking its bounds to destroy property. Damage to property accidentally thrown into a fire will therefore be covered. Unburned property may still be damaged by fire. For example, property damaged by water or other extinguishing agents introduced to combat a fire is damage by 'fire'. This is a straightforward application of the doctrine of proximate cause (qv). *See* EXTINGUISHMENT DAMAGE. Similarly, damage caused by the fire brigade in the execution of its duty and damage caused to property by rain or theft after removal from a burning building is loss by fire. The fire need not originate on the insured's premises; a fire in neighbouring premises causing blistering to the insured's property is a fire for the purpose of the insured's policy. 2. *Liability for fire.* Liability for fire damage under nuisance, negligence or a principle analogous to *Rylands* v *Fletcher* (qv). A person is liable where the fire is caused by negligence, spreads through negligence or where it starts or spreads as a result of a non-natural user of land in which case negligence does not have to be proved which is an application of *Ryland* v *Fletcher* (*Mason* v *Levy Auto Parts of England Ltd* (HC, 1967).

fire and theft cover. Loss or damage to motor vehicles resulting from fire and theft is within the 'loss or damage' cover of the 'own damage' section of a comprehensive policy. (Section 1 is on an 'all risks' basis.) The accidental damage excess under comprehensive policies applicable to 'young and inexperienced drivers' does not apply to fire and theft claims. An insured who chooses third party cover may, however, extend the policy to include loss or damage to his vehicle when caused by fire or theft as named perils. Loss or damage caused in other ways remains uninsured. It is possible for an insured who has taken his vehicle off the road to insure against the risks of fire and theft only.

firebreak doors warranty. A fire insurance warranty that all firebreak doors are closed at the end of business each day.

fire certificate. *See* FIRE PRECAUTIONS ACT 1971.

fire insurance duty. A duty imposed on every fire insurance policy between 1782 and 1896. It was levied in accordance with the sum insured. The purpose was to raise revenue but it had a useful outcome in providing records of the volume of fire insurance transacted. The duty was charged in addition to stamp duty.

fire insurance rating. The system used to fix premiums for individual fire insurance risks. The insured is required to contribute in proportion to: (a) the value at risk; (b) the degree of hazard present. The premium is the product of the rate per cent multiplied by the sum insured which should represent the total value at risk unless the insured is to be penalised for under-insurance. The rate is directly related to the degree of hazard and will take account of: (i) Trade classification; groupings that bring together trades or sections of trades that have broadly similar experience in terms of the incidence and severity of fires. (ii) Discrimination, ie the differentiation of individual risks within a specified class having regard to the particular features present in any individual risk. (iii) Experience, meaning the relationship of losses to premiums in a given class over a period of years.

fire map. A visual record of the distribution of insured properties in a given area to identify the possibility of catastrophic fire losses.

fire mark. In the early days fire insurers owned their own fire brigades. They affixed plaques or medallions, known as fire marks, on buildings in respect of which they insured the building and/or contents. The intention was to indicate, in the event of a fire, which fire brigade should be called. Fire marks are now collectors' items.

Fire Offices Committee (FOC). The FOC was the tariff association (qv) that pooled statistics, produced rates and laid down a standard policy wording. It liaised with other interested organisations and produced standards of construction, operation of extinguishing appliances and methods of operation. It ceased to operate on 30 June 1985. From that date its technical work has continued under the Loss Prevention Council (qv)—ie the Loss Prevention Council Technical Centre (qv). For over 100 years the FOC provided 'rules' and approved equipment with the object of reducing fire waste (qv). Lists of approved equipment are now published annually in January. Equipment and companies gaining recognition in the course of a year receive a certificate detailing the product or service recognised and the date from which the LPC/FOC recognition takes effect.

fire plate. The successor to the fire mark (qv) used in the 19th and early 20th century.

Fire Precautions Act 1971. An Act which applies to four main categories of premises: (a) places of amusement, recreation, and public resort (theatres, cinemas, dance halls, and the like); (b) residential establishments, such as hotels, boarding houses, hospitals, and residential institutions for the care of the elderly, the young, and the handicapped; (c) educational establishments; (d) certain private dwellings, chiefly high-rise blocks of flats. The Act empowers the Secretary of State to make fire certificates compulsory for premises devoted to the use or uses designated in the order. Certain premises are excluded either because adequate fire precautions are enforced through other legislation or because there are special conditions relating to them. Applications for a fire certificate have to be made to the fire authority which is under a duty to inspect the premises and, if satisfied as to the means of escape and other relevant fire precautions issue a certificate. If the authority is not satisfied it must inform the applicant what it considers should be done to bring the premises up to the required standard. Order 1972 (no. 238) had particular reference to hotels and boarding houses. If sleeping accommodation is provided for more than six persons, whether guests or staff, or there is sleeping accommodation above the first floor or below ground-floor level a fire certificate must be obtained.

fire prevention. Measures taken to eliminate the cause of loss by fire.

Fire Prevention (Metropolis) Act 1774. Section 83 requires insurers, in the event of damage to insured buildings in England and Wales, to ensure that, any money due in respect of a claim, be spent, as far as it would go, on rebuilding or repairing the building, where (i) there is a suspicion that the insured has been guilty of fraud or arson or (ii) a person interested in the building, eg a tenant, requests it. The insurers are relieved of this duty if, within 60 days of the claim of adjustment, give security to the insurers that the money will be spent on reinstatement or where the money has been disposed of among the contending parties to their satisfaction. Section 86 states that where an accidental fire (qv) occurs the occupier of premises shall not be liable for the resultant damage to third parties.

fire protection. Measures taken to protect property against loss by fire and to keep the loss to a minimum.

Fire Protection Association (FPA). A constituent part of the Loss Prevention Council (qv), the FPA aims to advance the science of fire protection. It investigates the causes and spread of fire, provides technical advice on fire protection, publishes information and generally seeks to educate in the matter of fire protection. A large number of FPA publications provide both general and specific advice. It also cooperates with Government Departments and other interested bodies.

Fire Research Station. This is a part of the Department of the Environment's Building Research Establishment. It carries out investigations on buildings, building materials, fire protection devices and fire extinguishment systems. They also collect statistics on all fires attended by fire brigades.

fire resurveys. A further survey of premises by a fire surveyor after his first survey has been carried out. It may be necessary to ascertain if suggested improvements have been carried out; to see that accumulated waste has been removed; to check new features, eg new machinery, not installed at time of first survey; look at changes notified to the insurer since the first survey. When a resurvey is carried out, the surveyor usually checks the whole of the premises and not just the feature necessitating the resurvey.

Fire Safety and Safety of Places of Sports Act 1987. An Act following the Bradford City stadium fire and the Popplewell Report to extend the requirements of the Safety of Sports Ground(s) Act 1975 which applies only to sports stadia to other sports grounds. As a result general safety certificates are required for any sports ground so designated by the Secretary of State. Prohibition notices restricting or prohibiting admission can be served when there is a serious risk of injury to spectators. Other provisions include: local authorities to arrange 12 monthly inspections of sports grounds; safety certificate required from local authority for each stand providing covered accommodation for 500 or more spectators but the authority can designate stands of smaller capacity to be subject to regulation but appeal against this is allowed; criminal sanctions can be imposed for a breach of the regulations especially permitting spectators into a regulated stand not having the necessary certificate—defences are available. The Act makes no provision for civil actions so injured spectators have to rely upon proving negligence but a conviction under the Act would provide evidence in support of an action in negligence.

fire survey report. A report prepared by a fire surveyor for consideration by the fire underwriter to assist in the underwriting of the risk. The report will describe the premises and include a plan. The report will cover: fire hazards; fire protection; management; claims history; recommendations for risk improvement; reference to any special perils that may be required and the susceptibility of the risk to those perils.

fire waste. The absolute economic loss to the community caused by fire. It embraces the direct loss of property and material damage in general, plus the time and cost in manufacture, plus consequential losses and any unemployment that may follow. Fire insurance provides an indemnity to individuals for their own losses and distributes these losses over the community by means of premium. Fire insurers endeavour to reduce fire waste by penalising unsatisfactory features of a risk and rewarding good features (eg discounts for fire extinguishing appliances). Also the Association of British Insurers and Lloyd's work closely with the Loss Prevention Council (qv).

firm. The title under which a company or partnership transacts business. The concept of the firm is important in professional indemnity insurance which covers the insured, often a firm, and predecessors in business. The term firm is not usually defined but the insured is identified in the schedule of the policy. An indemnity is provided to both the business firm (or professional practice) and the individual partners, including those, ie predecessors, who are no longer a part of the business, for breach of duty etc committed in the practice of the business. The firm continues to be insured in respect of claims made against it because of any alleged breach of duty by partners now out of the business. The former partners themselves are not covered once they have left the firm but they can purchase 'run-off' cover.

first aid services. When provided by the insured for the benefit of his employees, these services are stated to be a part of the 'Business'. *See* ANCILLARY SERVICES.

first loss policies. An insurance under which the insurer pays up to the sum insured without consideration of the total value at risk. The insured property may be of such a type that it could virtually never all be lost in one claim. For example, in a theft risk it might be impossible for the thieves to remove the total of a large stock of metal at one time. The insurer may agree to fix the sum insured below the amount at risk but at a sum intended to cover the maximum probable loss at any one time. First loss policies can also be issued in respect of water perils (storm, flood, burst pipes, and sprinkler leakage (qv)). The principle is that only the bottom piles of stock would be affected by water damage and therefore there is no need to cover the total amount at risk. First loss policies are cheaper than full value policies but the actual rate charged is higher. The insured must still declare the full value at risk as this is a rating factor. A form of average (qv) applies to ensure that the full value is declared:

$$\frac{declared\ full\ value}{actual\ full\ value} \times first\ loss$$

first party insurance. An insurance to provide benefits or indemnity directly for the insured person as distinct from covering his liability to third parties. For example, a material damage policy effected by a property owner to secure his own financial protection is a first party policy.

first surplus treaty. A surplus treaty (qv) which participates in cover in respect of the first band or layer in excess of the ceding office's retention up to a stated limit. The reinsurer shares the risk with the ceding office on a pro rata basis. As the treaty covers the layer above the retention up to an agreed amount, the ceding office may find it necessary to arrange second or third treaties and so on.

FIS (Free into store). The seller must pay all charges, including import duty, freight and other costs including insurance to time of delivery of the goods into buyer's warehouse.

fitness for purpose. The Sale of Goods Act 1979, s. 14(3) implies in to contracts of sale where the seller is in business, and the buyer makes known, expressly or by implication, the purpose for which the goods are being bought, that the goods will be reasonable for the purpose intended. The seller is only liable if the goods are not reasonably fit for the purpose supplied. Where the use is unusual the seller will be liable for the adverse consequences if he has indicated that the goods will be suitable for that purpose. The seller is not liable if the buyer shows that he does not rely, or it is unreasonable for him to rely, on the seller's skill and judgment. The seller cannot contract out of these obligations in consumer sales (qv) and in non-consumer sales (qv) any exclusion of this implied term will be subject to the test of reasonableness (qv). The injurious consequences of any breach constitute a products liability risk while losses relating to the goods themselves can in some instances be insured under a products guarantee insurance (qv). Although merchantable quality (qv) is defined in terms of 'fitness for purpose', often causing the two implied terms to overlap, there are situations when a product is of 'merchantable quality' but is not fit for its intended purpose as made known to the seller, eg paint for an article to be exposed to extreme temperatures. Also a product may be fit for its purpose but not be of merchantable quality, eg new car with scratch on wing. If the goods are bought from a private individual the implied term does not apply.

fitness screening. A term applied to the process of checking that officers of insurance companies seeking to transact business are deemed suitable and proper. The check applies to controllers (chief executives or the owners of at least one-third of the share capital, directors and managers). The requirements are necessitated by the Insurance Companies Act 1982 which lays down the procedure and requirements for the authorisation of UK based insurers. Fitness screening has been extended to main agents in the case of general insurers.

fixed costs. These are costs of production which do not vary directly with the level of output in the short run—they are incurred on a once and for all basis for a given period of time. They usually include such things as the cost of land, buildings and capital equipment. In insurance the main component of costs is a variable one, claims. Also most business is obtained through intermediaries remunerated by way of commission, a variable cost, only paid on business transacted. Consequently, an insurer's fixed cost usually forms only a small proportion of total costs. This is especially so for Lloyd's underwriters, whose method of operating through Lloyd's brokers, enables them to handle large volumes of business with relatively small staffing levels. Similarly companies that rely upon a network of brokers will avoid the fixed expenses associated with staffing and maintaining a network of branch offices. Staff costs can be fixed or variable depending on the policy of the insurer but generally a high proportion of staff costs, excluding overtime, will be fixed as insurers have to employ specialist staff who cannot be easily hired and fired in response to short term changes in the volume of business. In business interruption insurance the gross profit item is so calculated that there will be an indemnity in respect of fixed costs as they will have to be met out of a reduced turnover following material damage at the premises. *See* STANDING CHARGES.

fixed debt. A fixed debt is an arrangement whereby the sum payable on death is reduced by a fixed amount if death occurs within a specified term of years. If the life assured survives the specified term the full sum assured is payable. The fixed debt has largely been superseded by the diminishing debt (qv). *See also* DEBT.

fixed objects. In marine insurance this refers to harbours, wharves, piers, and similar 'fixed objects'. By means of a proviso inserted after the Running Down Clause (qv) in the Institute Hull Time Clauses insurers exclude liability for damage to such objects and goods or property thereon. These (and other) liabilities are insured by Protecting and Indemnity Clubs (qv).

fixed rate treaty. An excess of loss reinsurance treaty (qv) under which a flat rate is agreed. The rate is applied to the cedant's original gross premium income less only reinsurances paid out by the company which operate in priority to and for the benefit of the excess of loss treaty. The burning cost method (qv) is used to calculate the rate. Compare with sliding scale treaty (qv).

fixed share treaty. Another name for a quota share reinsurance treaty (qv).

flash point. The temperature at which a liquid gives off a flammable vapour when a standard test is carried out under standard conditions. *See* HIGHLY FLAMMABLE LIQUIDS REGULATIONS.

flat line (or first interest) reinsurance. An arrangement in marine insurance whereby the reinsurer receives all of the cedant's interest up to a predetermined amount. For example, if an underwriter accepts £50 000 on a vessel and reinsures £25 000 on a first interest basis, any amount 'closed' up to £25 000 will be ceded to the reinsurer. If only £40 000 is closed to the underwriter it is his share of the risk that goes down as the reinsurer's line holds good in the sum of £25 000.

flat-premiums. When, as in most material damage insurances, a sum insured is fixed, the premium is calculated by applying a rate per £100 to the sum insured. Where there are limits of indemnity instead of sums insured, the insurer often charges a flat or unit premium for the risk. Motor insurers construct tables indicating their flat premiums which vary according to age of the driver, district of use, type of car, and class of use. There may be additional charges for 'excess values', ie cars where the car is valued in excess of a stated upper limit. Flat premiums are also applied to combined policies sold on a 'package deal' basis to small retailers and other traders.

flat-premium method. A simple numerical method of apportioning indirect insurance costs (eg premiums paid for facilities etc shared by all cost centres) among the cost centres. The cost of these insurances is aggregated and then apportioned on a basis that is equitable and lends itself to a measure that reflects the degree of activity or use made of centrally provided insurance. For example, the common measure could be number of employees, turnover, payroll, floor area occupied etc. If a premium is incurred solely because of property or an activity run in particular cost centre apportionment does not apply as the premium can be charged, ie allocated, wholly to the cost centre concerned.

flat sharers (or students) insurance. An insurance effected by flat sharers, students or their parents on their behalf. It provides an indemnity or partial indemnity if possessions (eg clothes, records, hi-fi equipment or other items normally kept in flats or halls of residence) are stolen or damaged by fire, storm, flood, or burst pipes. Cover can be limited to the place of lodging or hall of residence or apply wherever the insured is staying or while travelling to or from college. Some schemes cater only for students.

fleet insurances. An insurance contract

that applies to a number of vehicles operated by the same insured and rated on an experience basis (*see* FLEET RATING). Usually five or more vehicles constitute a fleet. The fleet itself can comprise vehicles of different classes, eg private cars, goods-carrying vehicles etc. Aircraft and ships can also be insured as fleets.

fleet rating. 1. *Marine insurance.* The underwriter and shipowner agree an insured value for each vessel in the fleet. The rate is based on ownership, past claims experience, and other underwriting considerations. The leading underwriter, and those who follow, write a 'line' on the highest valued vessel on the slip (qv) and a pro rata line on all other vessels in the fleet. The subsidiary insurances on freight and disbursements are also effected on a fleet basis. 2. *Motor insurance.* A fleet rating system is used when a number of vehicles (they do not have to be all of the same type) under the same ownership are proposed for insurance. The minimum number of vehicles for this purpose is often ten but some insurers will accept five, particularly for heavily rated vehicles such as coaches and large goods-carrying vehicles. The larger the spread of risk the more viable it becomes to achieve the insurer's aim of making each risk pay for its own losses. The insurer compares average gross premium (ie before deduction of no claim discount) per vehicle with the claims cost per vehicle/year during the previous years. If the resultant loss ratio is materially under a certain percentage, eg 60 per cent, the gross average premium may attract a fleet discount. If the loss ratio exceeds, say, 62.5 per cent, then the gross average premium will be increased. The discount or loading will be based on the insurer's tabular rate for each vehicle in the fleet necessitating the maintenance of a complete and detailed schedule of all vehicles covered. A favourable loss ratio will not attract a discount if the underwriter observes an adverse trend. Insurers offer advice to fleet owners on maintenance schemes, driving bonuses, and good discipline. An alternative rating approach is to charge the same flat premium for each vehicle

within a given class. The insured makes periodic declarations of the number and type of vehicles covered with due allowance being made for premium adjustment. Blanket certificates are issued, ie one for each class of vehicle. Administrative savings make it possible for insurers to work with higher loss ratios than would otherwise apply. A well-managed fleet can benefit from lower premiums. For large fleets with premiums over £100 000 rating is by burning cost or is on a retrospective basis. This usually means a system of relating premiums to known claims costs over a period of time after payment of an initial deposit premium.

flexible endowment. An endowment assurance (qv) which provides guaranteed surrender values after ten years to allow the whole or part of the policy to be encashed.

flight. This is defined in policy form AVN1A (qv) as meaning 'from the time the aircraft moves forward in taking off or attempting to take off, whilst in the air, and until the aircraft completes its landing run'.

flight risks. The risks attaching to an aircraft whilst airborne as opposed to those whilst on the ground.

floater. An insurance or item within an insurance that covers property in a number of locations or situations in a collective sum insured without any breakdown of that sum according to the different risks. Such items are usually effected to top-up sums insured on specific items of insurance. The floater is made subject to the two conditions of average so that in the event of a claim the specific insurance contributes first and the floater second. Thus, the floater tops up, subject to average, any shortfall in one of the more specific insurances across which it 'floats'. Floaters are commonly used in fire insurance. An insured may be able to estimate the total value at risk at any one location but be uncertain as to how the goods will be distributed among his warehouses at that place at any one time. He can protect his position by using a floater to top up his specific insurances but he will be penalised for under-insurance.

floating policy. 1. *Marine cargo policy.* A policy which defines the insurance in general terms with the actual shipments to be defined by subsequent declarations (Marine Insurance Act 1906, s. 29). The policy runs until the sum insured is exhausted by the declarations. The declarations are made in chronological order unless the policy provides otherwise. The insured is bound to declare all shipments within the scope of the policy. Errors and omissions made in good faith can be rectified even after loss or arrival. The policy contains a basis of valuation clause for the purpose of computing the insured value of shipments where the loss occurs before the declaration has been made. Where the policy covers a number of different kinds of goods and voyages a scale of rates is embodied in the policy. *See* OPEN COVERS. 2. *Floating insurance for builders and contractors.* The property insured consists of buildings of normal construction in course of erection and completion (including outbuildings, walls etc) on the site of any contract on which the insured is engaged. This obviates the need to arrange separate insurances for each contract. The policy excludes contracts in excess of a specified value on any one site and property otherwise insured. The sum insured at the commencement is not less than twice the insured's estimate of the turnover for the forthcoming year. An initial premium is paid and adjusted at the end of the year following the submission by the insured of the turnover during the year with a separate statement for each category, eg houses; extension; other contracts. The rate charged varies with each category. The sum insured is reinstated after the payment of any loss and the insured pays an additional premium accordingly.

flood. This has been said to be a natural phenomenon which has some element of violence, suddenness or largeness about it—and does not include seepage of water from an underground watercourse which covers the floor to a depth of 3 inches—(*Young* v *Sun Alliance* (1976) 2 Lloyd's Report 189). *See* FLOOD INSURANCE.

flood insurance. Insurance against damage caused by the escape of water from the normal confines of any natural or artificial water course (other than water tanks, apparatus or pipes) or lake, reservoir, canal or dam in addition to inundation from the sea. Losses are normally subject to an excess of £100 which is increased for hazardous risks. The risk is normally insured as one of the additional (or special) perils (qv) added to a fire policy. Flood cover is usually grouped with storm and tempest and burst pipes but can be covered independently of those perils.

flotsam. A maritime term originally defined in the Merchant Shipping Act 1894 as wreckage floating on the sea.

flour 'all risks' clauses. Marine insurance clauses drafted by the Institute of London Underwriters for the insurance of flour as cargo. Cover is in respect of 'all risks' whatsoever but excludes damage by weevils, inherent vice, etc.

flue gas explosion. An explosion of gases in boiler flues (ie pipes). This type of explosion is the result of ignition and not of the sudden release of internal pressure as in the case of a steam boiler explosion. The boiler and pressure plant policy (qv) can be extended to cover the explosion of gas in the furnaces or flues of the plant. Cover follows the terms of the boiler policy and therefore covers self damage and the consequences thereof in terms of surrounding property and third party risks.

flying risks. A term used by personal accident insurers in connection with the risk of accidental bodily injury arising from flying: (a) As a member of the crew of an aircraft. (b) As a passenger. Personal accident insurers do not usually provide cover for (a) above. The risk is closely related to the type of aircraft, routes travelled, the person's duties, and experience etc, all of which is more readily assessed by an aviation insurer. Hence the risk is usually underwritten in the aviation market which also caters for persons flying their own or club private aircraft. In regard to (b) cover is freely available for fare-paying passengers on a scheduled air flight. Such travel is commonplace and those operators, who provide scheduled services, usually have the highest possible standards of safety in terms of their aircraft, crew, and ground organisation. Other forms of passenger travel are excluded but cover can be arranged by agreement with the insurer.

foaling policy. A livestock policy which may be either short period (thirty days) or for several months (six or twelve months). The policy stipulates that all in-foal mares shall be insured and cover not only includes the mare herself but also the foal.

follow the fortunes. Under proportional reinsurance treaties the doctrine is for the reinsurer to 'follow the fortunes' of the reinsured. It means that the treaty will cover all losses within the proper terms of the original policy but will not cover the following: *ex-gratia* payments (unless agreed); punitive damages or interest; acts outside terms of policy or fraud by the reinsured. A clause in the treaty may modify the doctrine to allow for, *inter alia*, the payment of *ex-gratia* losses.

food spoilage. *See* DETERIORATION OF STOCK.

football. 1. *Insurance for individuals.* Most personal accident insurance underwriters consider that playing football is a hazardous pursuit which should attract an additional premium. Consequently the risk is excluded from the policy but those who run the risk can 'buy it back'. The amount of the extra premium may depend upon whether the insured plays Association football, Rugby union, or Rugby league. 2. *Insurance for teams.* Club officials may effect group policies to provide personal accident benefits for any of their members sustaining injury while playing or training and while travelling to or from an away fixture provided they are club activities.

forced sale of cargo. The sale of cargo to obtain funds needed to prosecute the voyage for the common good. Any loss arising is admitted as a general average (qv) sacrifice. However, this only applies when cargo can be forwarded in no other way and it is preferable to remaining on board until the voyage can be completed.

forces' kit insurance. A policy devised to meet the needs of members of the armed forces (all ranks) and civil ser-

vants. Such personnel are often provided with furnished accommodation in barracks, etc and a householders' comprehensive policy may not be appropriate. The forces' kit insurance covers loss or damage to civilian or service clothing, uniforms and equipment, mess kit, household and personal effects worldwide. Legal liability cover is added to protect the insured as occupier of property charged to him plus personal liability cover. Loss of money cover is also available. Another optional extra is 'all risks' cover (as per the principal section) in respect of individual items of property valued in excess of £500 in view of a limitation under the main section of cover which treats no single article as being worth more than that figure.

forcible and violent entry. The insured event under a theft (business premises) policy is 'theft following upon forcible and violent entry or followed by forcible and violent exit'. Sometimes the insurer limits the cover to theft following entry only. The insurer is concerned to limit his cover to theft where there has been some breaking down of the defences of the premises. The wording came into general use after the Theft Act 1968 replaced the Larceny Act 1916 whose legal definitions of burglary and housebreaking had previously been imported into policies by theft insurers. The new Act afforded no such opportunities unless the insurer was to give unduly wide cover as the definition of theft embraces theft of all kind, including pilferage, eg shoplifting which occurs without any attack on the premises. Under the old law the phrase breaking and entering was interpreted in the widest possible sense and even the slightest degree of force, eg turning a door handle, was sufficient to constitute breaking within the meaning of the 1916 Act. In *Re Calf and Sun Insurance Offices* (1920) the court held that the sliding back of a latch lock by means of an instrument was supposed to constitute a forcible and violent entry. The Court of Appeal construed the phrase, forcible and violent entry in *Nash* v *Prudential Assurance* (*The Times, November 1988*). The court held that the word violence was used in its ordinary sense: as accompanying an entry where otherwise force might have been minimal by a physical act characterised as violent. The trial judge had found for the insured by awarding him an indemnity under a combined policy in respect of a loss sustained following the theft of his car keys from his car by the thief who used them to open the door of the premises. The trial judge construed the words by reference to the character of the act by which the entry was made. It was accepted for the insurers that forcible was defined as 'the application of any energy', following a meaning attributed to it in a different context by Lord Justice Donaldson in *Swales* v *Cox* (1981), so that minimum force was sufficient. The submission on behalf of the plaintiff was that the phrase meant forcible and unlawful as relating to the means of entry. The Court of Appeal rejected that submission as the ordinary word violent bore a different meaning from unlawful and because the context in which the phrase appeared in the policy already contemplated a state of unlawfulness, namely a theft by virtue of entry. The inclusion of the word violent seems to be the key and implies that there must be some actual attack on the defences of the premises.

for declaration only. Policies are sometimes issued 'for declaration only'. No charge is made and no specific insurances are stated but the insured then makes subsequent declarations as to insurances within the policy description and premiums are charged accordingly.

forecast mortality table. A mortality table which takes account of anticipated changes in mortality. It indicates expected future mortality.

Foreign General Average Clause. 1. *Cargo policies.* This Institute Cargo Clause binds British insurers to pay general average adjusted according to foreign law, or if the contract of affreightment so provides, according to the York-Antwerp Rules (qv). In the absence of any provision in the contract of affreightment, the law governing the general average adjustment is that of the place where the adventure terminated. The insurer is not a party to the contract

and, while accepting as accurate a statement drawn up in accordance with foreign law, is not bound to accept the law governing the statement. British insurers, are normally bound by British law, but render themselves liable through the clause for any properly prepared general average adjustment to accommodate cargo owners who usually have qualifications in bills of lading regarding general average imposed upon them. 2. *Hull policies.* The corresponding clause in the Institute Time clauses is more restrictive. Shipowners have the power to introduce into contracts of affreightment terms that prejudice the underwriter but favour themselves in the adjustment of general average. Accordingly, the Foreign General Average clause provides general average is to be adjusted in accordance with the law and practice at the place where the voyage ends, as if the contract of affreightment made no reference thereto, but where the contract so provides, the York-Antwerp Rules shall apply.

foreign residence and travel. Life assurers used to charge an additional premium where there was a prospect of an assured travelling or residing outside the 'free limits' (ie temperate zones) (qv). In some instances foreign travel or residence, eg residence in unhealthy areas or travel to areas of political unrest, may amount to material facts that should be disclosed.

foreign use (motor vehicles). The use of a motor vehicle outside the territorial limits specified in the policy. A foreign use section is included in private car and commercial vehicle policies. The territorial limits of the motor policy are Great Britain, Northern Ireland, the Channel Islands, the Isle of Man and sea transits between any of these territories of not more than 65 hours duration in normal conditions. The insurance certificate, however, provides evidence of cover for the minimum third party liability in any EC countries (*see* EC TERRITORIAL LIMITS). If the territorial limits are not extended and the insurer has to meet a claim by virtue of this EC extension the insurer may include a pay-back clause giving them the right to recover claims paid under the EC extension. More usually, the foreign use clause is invoked by the insured notifying the insurer of the countries to be visited and the period involved. The amount of premium charged to extend the insurance on its full terms is usually based on the period involved. Insurers issue a green card (qv) for up to three months. Motor cycle policies do not usually have a foreign use clause except to comply with EC requirements. *See also* CUSTOMS DUTY CONTINGENCY.

foreseeability. The test of 'reasonable foreseeability' is applied in determining liability in the tort of negligence and contract. The case known as the Wagon Mound (no. 1) made the rule that damage following negligence will not be too remote if it is reasonably foreseeable. Thus foreseeability is the test and not directness so that there will be no liability for direct but unforeseeable consequences of the defendant's act. The test, however, applies to the type of damage and not its extent (*Smith* v *Leech Brain & Co. Ltd* (1961)) so the tortfeasor, who could foresee that his negligence might injure the plaintiff but could not foresee that cancer might ensue from a burn, was liable for all the injury including the cancer.

forged transfer indemnity. An indemnity in respect of a loss attaching to a public company or local authority through registering a transfer of stock and shares on a forged certificate. The company or authority may have to reinstate the name of the true owner in its register without redress under the Forged Transfer Act. The policy also covers the insured's legal liability for errors, omissions and other losses relating to the register.

form. A description of policy terms and conditions applying to insurance of specific risks or closely related group of risks or to other matters (salvage, loss prevention measures etc) of direct relevance to such insurances. The form may be a separate document attached to the policy or included in it.

fortuitous cause. An accidental cause. A happening by chance.

forum. A place where disputes are heard. It usually refers to the particular court or courts having jurisdiction in the matter.

forum rei. The court of the country in which the thing or person, the subject of the action is situated. *See* FORUM SHOPPING.

forum shopping. The selection by a plaintiff of a country where he prefers his action to be heard. In certain circumstances he can choose the forum (qv) and 'shops around' in order to select the country where he is most likely to win his action and/or secure the highest level of compensation. For example, a plaintiff who can choose between the USA and the UK may find the law and level of awards in the USA more favourable to his case.

forwarding charges clause. Institute Cargo Clause 12 provides that where, as a result of an insured peril, the transit is terminated at a port or place other than the port of destination, the underwriter will reimburse the insured for any extra charges properly and reasonably incurred in unloading, storing and forwarding the goods to their destination. The clause does not apply to general average (qv) or salvage (qv). There is also a specific exclusion of forwarding charges if they arise from the insolvency or financial default of the owners, managers, charterers, or operators of the vessel.

foundations clause. A clause added to a standard fire policy to exclude cover in respect of any damage to any part of the building below ground-floor level. The incentive is to save premium as the sum insured will be reduced. The extent to which this is advisable depends very much on the construction of the premises concerned and whether explosion and earthquake are insured perils.

fragile property exclusion. The breakage of fragile property is commonly excluded from 'all risks' policies (qv) but some cover can be bought back by the insured. Insurers will generally be prepared to insure breakage due to fire and theft.

fragmentation. The risk that flying fragments from plant and machinery may impact upon surrounding property. The risk is insurable under the principal engineering insurance policies (boiler and pressure vessels, cranes, lifts, and electrical and machinery) and is defined as 'damage by physical impact . . . resulting from fragmentation of any part of any insured item of plant'.

fragmentation policy (impact damage cover). An engineering insurance that combines cover in respect of damage to own surrounding property following fragmentation (qv) of the plant with an inspection service. Cover is normally up to £20 000 for any one accident but higher sums can be arranged. The policy excludes fire, lightning, storm, flood, inundation, leakage from sprinklers, aircraft and aerial devices, theft, direct application of tools, modification and maintenance etc, loss of use and consequential loss. Also there is no cover for the contents of the plant or its load or damage resulting from lack of heat, light, power, steam, refrigeration or air conditioning or damage caused by any fluid. The fragmentation risk can otherwise be insured as a named peril under broader forms of cover such as policies relating to boilers and pressure vessels, cranes and hoists, and electrical and mechanical plant. The fragmentation policy can be applied to all inspected classes (qv) and is generally used when the insured arranges material damage insurance on the plant under blanket policy.

franchise. 1. A clause stating that no claim is payable unless the amount involved exceeds a stated amount. Once the claim exceeds that amount the entire claim is payable. The franchise eliminates small claims but unlike an excess (qv), which can also be used to eliminate small claims, does not reduce the cost of all claims by the amount of the excess. The franchise originated in marine insurance. 2. The amount by which a Lloyd's syndicate is permitted to exceed its syndicate allocated capacity.

fraudulent claims. A claim where the insured has: (a) made false statements of fact in his claim, or (b) made statements, knowing them to be false, or not believing them to be true, or that he made them recklessly without caring whether they were true or false. The onus of proof is on the insurer who can avoid the policy whether the policy contains an express condition to that effect or not. Good faith, which is implied in all insurance contracts, requires that any claim by the insured shall be honestly made. If the insured submits a fraudulent claim all benefit, including the premium, under the policy is forfeited. *See also* EXCESSIVE CLAIM.

fraudulent misrepresentation. This is a breach of the duty of utmost good faith (qv) occurring where the person making the statement knows it to be false, does not believe it to be true, or makes it recklessly without due regard to its accuracy. The Road Traffic Act 1988 makes it a statutory offence for a person to make a false statement or to withhold material information for the purpose of obtaining a certificate of motor insurance required by the Act.

fraudulent withdrawals and forged signatures insurance. A policy to indemnify building societies and similar institutions against losses incurred as a result of payments made in connection with fraudulent withdrawals and forged signatures. The annual premium is adjustable and is based on the annual amount of withdrawals.

free cover. The maximum amount of death or disability cover which an insurer covering a group is prepared to insure for each individual without production of evidence of health (qv).

free from particular average (FPA). A marine cargo insurance term referring to the former Institute Cargo Clauses (FPA), a restricted form of insurance mainly used for bulk cargo commodities. It insured all maritime perils but underwriters were not liable for particular average (qv), ie partial loss, except where there had been a major casualty on the voyage, eg following fire, stranding, sinking or when caused by the vessel or conveyance being in collision or contact with any object. The equivalent set of conditions is now the Institute Cargo Clauses (C) which also covers major casualties only.

free limits. Life policies are generally issued without restriction as to where the assured resides or travels. The former practice was to designate certain geographical areas as 'free limits' being areas within which the life or permanent health policyholder is covered without extra premium. If at the time of entry the assured shows an intention or prospects of travelling outside the 'designated regions' (temperate zones) an additional premium might be charged for a limited period but these days foreign residence or travel is unlikely to concern the assurer unless the area is one of unrest or upheaval. In any event once cover has been granted, it will operate worldwide and the assurer will be able to claim no extra premium.

free of capture and seizure (F.C. & S). A clause that excluded war perils from the SG policy form. It has now been superseded by the War Exclusion Clause of the Institute Cargo Clauses and the Institute Time Clauses.

Free on Board (FOB). A form of sale contract whereby the seller is responsible for the goods until they are on board the vessel and the buyer is responsible for all charges (including marine insurance) thereafter.

free reserves. A term describing the difference between an insurance company's assets and its technical liabilities. The size of the reserves is dependent on the strength of valuation of the assets and liabilities. If the technical reserves (qv) have been calculated to exactly equal the payments to current policyholders, the free reserves amount to the residual assets belonging to the company's shareholders. Alternatively, the free reserves can be described as the sum of share capital, general reserves, and insurance funds less technical reserves, plus possibly hidden reserves such as the excess over book values of market value investments. Free reserves provide a cushion against random fluctuations in claims; adverse claims experience; losses on investments; catastrophes, failure of reinsurance and other miscellaneous risks; losses from poor management. The adequacy of the 'cushion' provided by the free reserves is crucial to an insurance company's solvency. As a result the Government has used legislation to set a minimum level of free reserves known as the margin of solvency (qv).

F.O.T. ('free on trucks')/F.O.R. ('free on rails'). In both cases the seller must deliver goods free on truck, obtain a waybill from the transport agents if required by contract, and be respon-

sible for loss/damage until the truck carrying the goods is delivered to the railway or other public carrier. The buyer is responsible for loss/damage after such delivery and for the freight and transportation charges. The buyer is also responsible for all subsequent movements of the goods.

freedom of establishment. The right to set up a branch, subsidiary office or similar establishment to transact business in a foreign country. Freedom of establishment business (qv) for reinsurance was implemented by an EC Directive in 1964 from which time reinsurers were subject only to supervision in their country of establishment.

freedom of services business. The right to transact business across national frontiers with those domiciled in another country without having an establishment in that country. Freedom of services business (qv) is still to be achieved in the EC.

freedom with publicity. A term used to describe the British approach to the supervision of insurance.

free-standing AVCs. Additional voluntary contributions (AVCs) (qv) which a member of a pension scheme can make to an insurance policy or building society outside his or her own pension.

freight. The reward that a shipowner earns from the use of his ship for the carriage of his own or other peoples' goods or moveables but it does not include passage money (Marine Insurance Act 1906, s. 90). The contract of affreightment is evidenced by a bill of lading (qv) for the goods of others or a charter party (qv) for the hire of the ship or space within it. At common law freight is only earned by completion of the carriage but the shipowner normally requires the cargo owner to pay in advance either wholly or in part 'not repayable in case of loss'. The advance freight (qv) is at the risk of the cargo owner and is merged in the value of the goods for insurance purposes. The amount payable by a charterer to a shipowner is chartered freight and is insurable by the shipowner unless paid in advance when it is at the risk of the charterer.

freight waiver clause. Clause 20 of the Institute Time Clauses (1/10/83) provides that in the event of total or constructive total loss the underwriter will not make any claim for freight whether notice of abandonment has been given or not. In law where the ship is abandoned the underwriter is entitled to the freight in the course of being earned, and which is subsequently earned, less the expense of earning it (Marine Insurance Act 1906, s. 63(2)). The waiver clause in effect is a recognition that the exercise of these legal rights would be unfair to the insured.

freight insurance. The insurance of the profit derivable by the shipowner from the use of his ship to carry goods. Where freight is insured at and from a specified place, the risk attaches pro rata *as the goods are shipped, provided that if there be cargo in readiness which belongs to the shipowner, or which some other person has contracted with him to ship, the risk attaches as soon as the ship is ready to receive such cargo (Rule for Construction No. 3d). When chartered freight is insured at and from a specified place the risk attaches as soon as the ship arrives there in good safety. If the ship is already there when the charter party is concluded the risk attaches immediately. Shipowners could insure their freight voyage by voyage but more usually they insure it for twelve months by fixing an amount that could be earned on any one round voyage during that period. Bill of lading freight is normally paid in advance and added to the value of the goods. The insurable value of freight is the gross value of freight receivable by the shipowner plus the cost of insurance. *See also* FREIGHT and FREIGHT COLLISION CLAUSE.

Freight Collision Clause. A clause incorporated into freight policies to cover three-fourths of the shipowner's liability for collision damages that may attach to freight. The clause is used only where freight is liable to be called upon to contribute to collision liability, ie where certain foreign laws may apply to the settlement. In English law freight is not taken into account in assessing the shipowner's liability for collision.

fresh contract. A term applied to an annual contract when renewed. There is no obligation on the insurer to invite renewal or the insured to accept. Usually the renewal notice constitutes an offer and payment of the premium is the acceptance of the new or fresh contract.

freshwater damage. Cargo may be damaged by freshwater without the operation of a maritime peril. This risk, together with other extraneous risks such as damage by other cargo, hooks, oils, and sweat need to be brought into the policy when governed by Institute Cargo Clause (B) or (C). Clause (A), which is 'all risks' is already sufficiently wide in scope to take account of the risk. The loss or damage caused by freshwater must be the result of a fortuitous happening by reason of some external cause.

friendly societies. Organisations otherwise known as 'collecting societies' who, like industrial life companies, are authorised to transact industrial life assurance as defined in the Industrial Assurance Act 1923. Friendly societies started as local organisations, distributing benefits to sick and bereaved members. They have to be registered under the Friendly Societies Act 1974 and are subject to the supervision of the Industrial Assurance Commissioner who: (a) Receives their statutory returns. (b) Can investigate their accounts and returns, particularly in respect of the valuation of the fund. He can, if necessary, require the accounts to be modified. (c) Can petition the Court for the winding up of a Society for insolvency or breach of statutory obligations. These requirements also apply to industrial life offices.

fringe company. An insurance company, not regarded as one of the 'majors', by whom or for whom business is written in one of the underwriting rooms near Lloyd's.

'frolic of his own'. It means an act 'for one's own purposes'. The term is used to describe circumstances when an employer is not vicariously liable for the tort of his employee because the latter was not acting in the course of employment as he was 'on a frolic of his own'. This means he was engaged in an activity on his own account and not on account of his employer. In *Hilton* v *Thomas Burton (Rhodes) Ltd* (1961) demolition workers left the site in the employer's van to go to a café. The driver, an employee of the defendants, was negligent and the foreman was killed. The defendants were not liable as the men, not engaged in their employment, were pursuing a 'frolic of their own'.

from. When a ship is insured 'from' the port of departure, the insurance commences when she breaks ground intending to proceed on her voyage.

fronting. The acceptance of insurance or reinsurance with the intention of passing it wholly to another insurer or reinsurer. Fronting is disapproved of in USA jurisdictions for tax and supervisory reasons unless the fronting company (qv) retains a reasonable share of the risk.

fronting company. An insurer or reinsurer engaged in fronting (qv) by placing business with another insurer or reinsurer. The term is also used in respect of insurance companies formed offshore by foreign brokers and/or insurers to handle large risks arising in countries which lack domestic insurance facilities and markets.

frost. 1. *Fire and additional perils policies.* Frost is not an insured peril under a household policy whether or not frost damage is specifically excluded under the storm damage clause. Where frost is the cause of the bursting of pipes etc the policy will operate as the insured peril is 'burst pipes'. A few insurers cover frost as an insured event in its own right but generally restrict the cover so that it does not apply to tennis courts, swimming pools, drives, pathways, gates, hedges, and fences, or apply at all if the premises are unoccupied. 2. *Motor policies.* Comprehensive policies cover loss or damage and not named perils in respect of the insured vehicle. Consequently frost damage, unless specifically excluded, is insured. Some insurers may add a requirement that the insured should use a recognised brand of anti-freeze in accordance with manufacturer's requirements in the cooling system. The question also arises that failure to use anti-freeze during cold spells may be a breach of the reasonable care condition (qv). Claims when they occur are costly as they may involve the cracking of the cylinder block and the fitting of a reconditioned engine, which would

normally lead to the insured being required to make a contribution for betterment (q.v). Frost damage is not insured under the standard motor trader's road risks policy (qv) but is usually included where a road risk comprehensive policy and an internal risk (damage and third party) (qv) are in force and run concurrently.

frozen meat clauses. Marine insurance clauses drafted by the Institute of London Underwriters for the insurance of frozen meat. A variety of clauses exist with the differences mainly concerning attachment and cessation of the risk and the average clauses. Under the principal set (clause 'A') set cover is provided against defective condition from any cause except bone taint, improper dressing, cooling and freezing, stoppage of machinery through shortage of fuels or labour during strikes, lockouts etc. The risk attaches when meat is passed into the meat chambers and terminates 60 days after arrival at the UK destination.

fruit growers' insurance. A comprehensive insurance for growing apple and/or pear crops against weather damage caused by frost, hail and windstorm.

fruit storage insurance. An engineering insurance against loss of hard fruit (apples and pears) in cold storage arising from sudden and unforeseen physical damage to refrigerating machinery or failure of public electricity supply.

frustration clause. This appears in the Institute War Clauses (Cargo) among the general exclusions to exclude 'any claim based on upon loss or frustration of the voyage or adventure'. The exclusion is made of paramount importance by Clause 7 which stipulates that anything contained in the contract which is inconsistent with the frustration clause shall, to the extent of the inconsistency, be null and void. The clause prevents the recovery of any claim depending entirely on the loss of the adventure when the goods are still within the control of the insured and when delivery at the destination port is denied by a blockade, embargo or sanctions. The frustration clause also appears in the Institute Strike Clauses (Cargo).

full particulars of loss. The requirement that an insured should furnish full particulars of the loss has been held to be 'the best particulars the insured can reasonably give which must be sufficient to enable the insurer to ascertain the nature, extent and character of the loss' (*Mason* v *Harvey* (1853)).

full reinsurance clause. This clause is an essential part of the facultative reinsurance policy (qv) stating that 'being a reinsurance of warranted same gross rate terms and conditions as and to follow the settlements of the company'. This clause binds the reinsurer to follow the fortunes of the reinsured provided settlements are within the terms of the original policy and the reinsurance. The reinsured's retention is normally warranted to be on identical interests, ie the retention and the cession (qv) must be on identical interests. If the cession refers to buildings and contents the retention must also do so and be based purely on the buildings with contents only ceded. Minor changes not affecting the reinsurance risk or adversely affecting the information on which the reinsurance is based do not affect the validity of the contract.

full value insurances. Insurances based on a signed declaration in the proposal form that the sum insured represents the full value of the property that forms the subject-matter of insurance. Household policies are invariably arranged in this way and, if at the time of effecting the policy, the sum insured is less than the full value the insured is guilty of breach of warranty giving the insurer the right of avoidance. However, under the Statement of Non-Life Practice (qv) insurers have undertaken not to take advantage of breaches of a mere technical nature. A negotiated settlement which imports pro rata average is possible only after the policy has been repudiated as the legal position is that the insurer pays in full or repudiates. These problems do not generally arise as average applies to most insurances.

fully insured scheme. A pension scheme where the trustees have effected an insurance contract in respect of each member which guarantees benefits corresponding at all times to those promised under the rules.

fully paid up policies. *See* PAID UP POLICIES.

fund. A provision or reserve. Each class of insurance business has a fund based on the balance of premiums less claims and expenses after taking into account any transfer to or from the profit and loss account.

fundamental risks. These are risks of wide-ranging effect that affect society as a whole or large segments thereof rather than individuals. They are of a catastrophic nature; examples include war, famine, earthquake, widespread pollution, and unemployment. The effects are so far reaching that they are generally outside the scope of private enterprise insurance. They are problems for society as a whole and as such responsibility for them is usually undertaken by governments. Compare with particular risks (qv)

funeral expenses insurance. 1. The Assurance Companies Act 1909 legalised the issue by friendly societies and industrial life assurers of policies to defray the cost of funeral expenses following the decease of near relatives. The Industrial Assurance and Friendly Societies Act 1948 in withdrawing the authorisation of these policies permitted, instead, the issue of policies on the life of a parent, grandparent, or step-parent for a sum not exceeding £20. The Industrial Assurance and Friendly Societies Act 1948 (Amendment) Act 1958 increased this to £30. Each brother and sister can effect policies of up to £30 on the same life. The £30 limit excludes, *inter alia*, bonuses, returns of premium, and any assurance where there is a valid insurable interest, ie an insurable interest other than that created by the foregoing legislation. 2. The above sums are now wholly inadequate to fulfil the intended purpose. Consequently, pre-payment schemes enable those who participate to pay by lump sum or instalments to undertakers who in effect safeguard the participant's estate against the effects of inflation by offering a future funeral of a given standard at current prices. More traditionally, whole life without profits policies can be used and, for marketing purposes, are sold as 'funeral expenses' insurances, often through magazines or newspapers.

gambling policies. The Marine Insurance (Gambling Policies) Act, 1909, makes it a criminal offence to enter into a contract of marine insurance without a bona-fide interest, or possibility of such interest, in the subject-matter insured. It is also an offence for a shipowner's employee, not being a part-owner, to effect a policy on PPI (qv) terms. The Act is to prevent gambling in marine insurance.

Gaming Act 1845. The Act makes all wagering or gaming contracts null and void. An insurance on goods without insurable interest is, in effect, a wager and it is unenforceable because of the provisions of the Act.

gas. The standard fire policy covers explosion of gas used for domestic purposes (qv) or for lighting or heating premises. In *Stanley* v *Western Insurance Insurance Co* (1868) 'gas' was said to mean 'ordinary illuminating coal gas and not vapour given off in the course of extracting oil from shoddy'. Vapours given off in the course of manufacture are clearly not gas for the purpose of the clause but the term gas now covers town mains gas, whether manufactured from coke retorts, obtained from the North Sea or imported in liquid form.

gas cylinders insurance. An engineering policy covering physical damage to gas cylinders, bottles or tanks of solid drawn construction, on hire from recognised suppliers including damage to other property belonging to the insured and liability to third parties for property damage or personal injury, directly consequent on and solely due to explosion of an insured item.

general average (GA). A general average act may be either a sacrifice or expenditure, extraordinary in nature, voluntarily and reasonably incurred, in time of general peril, for the common safety of the maritime adventure. When all of these essentials are present, there is said to be a general average act, and the loss to be made good by the contribution of all concerned, when the adventure is saved (Marine Insurance Act 1906, s. 66). A similar definition is given in the York-Antwerp Rules (qv). 'All concerned' includes those interested in the ship, the cargo and the freight. Examples of general average losses include: (i) jettison of cargo to lighten the ship to facilitate refloating after stranding; (ii) water damage to cargo or ship when extinguishing a fire; (iii) expense of discharging and reloading cargo to lighten the ship after stranding; similarly any damage to such cargo occasioned thereby. The party suffering the loss or expense is entitled to a contribution from all other parties involved. A general average claim under a marine insurance may arise from: (a) General average sacrifice. The prudent sacrifice of property for the common safety of the maritime adventure. The owner of sacrificed property may claim under the Institute Cargo Clauses directly against his insurer or, if the vessel arrives safely, seek general average contributions from the interests which have been saved. The insurer settling a claim for a general average sacrifice takes over the right to the general average contributions. (b) General average contribution. The general average contribution towards the sacrifice or expenditure of others is a loss that the party upon whom it falls can recover under the Institute Cargo Clauses. Such contributions will be paid by insurers when the final amount is ascertained and apportioned. This can take years so a general average deposit (qv) is requested but is subject to an eventual adjustment.

general average adjustment. The adjustment of a general average loss (qv) is normally carried out by an average adjuster(qv) appointed by the shipowner. A statement of losses, values and proportionate contributions is prepared. The cost of the adjustment is part of the general average.

general average agreement. *See* GENERAL AVERAGE BOND.

general average bond. Besides paying the general average loss the consignees of the cargo sign an average bond binding themselves to pay the general average contribution (*see* GENERAL AVERAGE) and agreeing, if required, to deposit a sum as security for this purpose. The bond also provides authorisation for the shipowner to draw on the trust funds up to the amount of the cargo's liability to defray any reasonable general average disbursements. The bond is sometimes referred to as the 'general average agreement'.

general average contribution. The rateable contribution under maritime law from the parties interested in a maritime adventure to the parties suffering a general average loss. *See* GENERAL AVERAGE (Marine Insurance Act 1906, s. 66(3)). The liability to pay the contribution is recoverable under insurance.

general average deposit. *See* GENERAL AVERAGE above where it was noted that ascertainment of final contributions may take years. The shipowner has a particular possessory lien over goods which enables him to obtain security for payment by the cargo owners. The payment of a deposit serves as a condition of releasing the lien on cargo that is subject to a general average contribution. Average adjusters advise as to the level of these deposits.

general average expenditure. Against the essentials of general average (qv) various types of expenditure become general average. The expense of hiring craft to lighten a ship a vessel when ashore and the cost of restowing shifted cargo caused by heavy weather are general average expenditure. Any damage to cargo during these operations is general average sacrifice. If a vessel is towed to a port of refuge by hired tugs, the cost is treated as general average expenditure; it is an expense incurred for the safety of the whole adventure. Port of refuge expenses (qv) are the most common form of general average expenditure.

general average fund. The accumulated general average deposits (qv) which are available for general average expenditure and, in due course, payment of the contributions.

general average loss. A loss by way of sacrifice or expenditure caused by or directly consequential upon a general average act. Unless specifically agreed the insurer is not liable for any general average loss where the loss was not incurred for the express purpose of avoiding an insured peril or in connection with the avoidance of such a peril (Marine Insurance Act 1906, s. 66(6)). Where the ship, freight and cargo, or any two, are owned by the same insured, the liability of the insurer for general average loss is to be determined as if those interested had been separately owned (Marine Insurance Act 1906, s. 66(7)).

general business. Any insurance business that is not classified as long-term business (qv). The Insurance Companies Act 1982 divides general business into the following 17 classes:
1. Accident.
2. Sickness.
3. Land vehicles.
4. Railway rolling stock.
5. Aircraft.
6. Ships.
7. Goods in transit.
8. Fire and natural forces.
9. Damage to property.
10. Motor vehicle liability.
11. Aircraft liability.
12. Liability for ships.
13. General liability.
14. Credit.
15. Suretyship
16. Miscellaneous financial loss.
17. Legal expenses.

general conditions. *See* EXPRESS CONDITIONS.

general exceptions. A list of exceptions found in a comprehensive or hybrid policy to indicate the exceptions which will apply to all sections of the policy. In addition each section generally has exceptions specific to that section.

General Exclusions Clause (Institute Cargo Clauses) 1/1/82). The Marine Insurance Act 1955, s. 55 specifies certain losses as being excluded but the practice is to use this clause to set out the exclusions. The General Exclusion Clause in Clauses B and C excludes: wilful misconduct of the insured; ordinary leakage and wear and tear; insufficient/unsuitable packing or preparation; inherent vice; delay; insolvency or financial default of owners/charterers; deliberate damage by the wrongful act on the part of any person or persons; nuclear weapons or war. The General Exclusion Clause in Institute Cargo Clauses (A) is identical save only for the fact that no reference is made to 'deliberate damage by the wrongful act of others' so this 'all risks' version of the cover affords protection to the insured against deliberate damage. The exclusion of deliberate damage is particularly aimed at removing liability for arson, scuttling, sabotage or any form of malicious act involving the goods. The clause can be deleted on payment of an additional premium to incorporate the malicious damage clause.

general insurance company. A company underwriting a number of classes of business. The term is also used to describe a company which does not transact long-term business. *See* COMPOSITE COMPANIES.

general removal bond. *See* CUSTOMS AND EXCISE BONDS.

general representative. A person resident in the UK designated as the representative of an insurance company with a head office outside the UK, who is authorised to act generally and accept the service of documents.

general safety certificate. A certificate required in connection with any sports ground designated by the Secretary of State as requiring such a certificate. *See* FIRE AND SAFETY OF PLACES OF SPORTS ACT 1987.

general safety requirement. Consumer goods have to be reasonably safe having regard to all the circumstances which include: the manner in which the goods are marketed and any instructions or warnings given with the goods; any published safety standards for those goods; and the means, if any, and the cost of making them safer.

'Safe' means reducing to a minimum the risk of death or personal injury. The requirement is defined in the Consumer Protection Act 1987 (qv) which makes contravention a criminal offence. The safety of a range of goods has for some time been controlled under regulations setting out in detail how specific types of goods must be constructed and what instructions and warnings must accompany them (Consumer Safety Act 1978). As it is not practical to make such regulations for every type of consumer product the general safety requirement closes a gap. The requirement applies to anyone who supplies the goods but retailers may be able to plead that they neither knew nor had reasonable grounds for believing that the goods failed to comply with the general requirement. The general requirement does not apply to growing crops, water, food, aircraft, motor vehicles, controlled drugs, medicinal products and tobacco. There are certain defences including one in respect of second-hand goods. Trading standards officers can issue suspension notices prohibiting the sale of goods which they believe contravene the legislation and can apply to the magistrates for an order that such goods be destroyed. These sanctions give rise to the need for legal defence cover which can be provided under a products liability extension or legal expenses insurance.

general transshipment bond. *See* CUSTOMS AND EXCISE BONDS.

general warehouse bond. *See* CUSTOMS AND EXCISE BOND.

general works damage insurance. An engineering insurance covering physical loss or damage caused by accidental external impact including falling, swinging, collision, overturning or dropping in respect of: (a) machinery and plant permanently installed in a factory or workshop or identifiable department or section thereof. (b) Goods of an engineering nature produced within the factory or workshop premises. (c) Machinery and plant (not being the property of the insured) brought on to the factory or workshop premises for repair, overhaul or similar work. Extensions available include: customers' property undergoing repair or renovation at the premises; loading and unloading and transit risks of new products (in certain cases only). The policy carries an excess (qv), fire and special perils risks (qv) are excluded as well as theft, direct application of tools, electrical or mechanical breakdown of the insured property, loading for despatch and the initial installation or final removal from the premises, and faulty workmanship.

geographical distribution. Insurers and, in particular, reinsurers can benefit from the law of averages by drawing their business from as many different countries as possible. Reinsurance is essentially of an international character and it is generally most successfully conducted by extending the risk-spreading process as far as possible but the reinsurer must always be guided by the circumstances which will inevitably call for the exercise of discretion and selectivity in underwriting.

glass insurance. Originally limited to the insurance of panes of plate glass, this insurance is available for all types of glass (eg wired and embossed plate, silvered glass (mirrors), figured glass, bent glass, non-reflecting windows and pavement lights). The glass is insured against breakage following which the insurers will either make good the glass or pay the full replacement value. The option lies with the insurers but replacement is the usual course of action. The policy excludes any breakage insurable under a fire policy or caused by explosion, earthquake or war. The insurance can be extended to cover the cost of repairing damage to the window frames or the cost of removal and subsequent replacement of fixtures and fittings in the window. Damage to stock caused by the breakage of glass can also be insured. The insurance is available for businesses as a separate policy or, in the case of small shops, as a part of a combined or package policy. Fixed glass in private dwellinghouses is insured under householders' comprehensive policies.

Glass's Guide. A monthly publication setting out estimated current values of motor vehicles. The values indicated are usually taken by motor insurers as the basis for negotiating total loss claims in the case of unvalued policies (qv). Caravan insurers use *Glass's Guide to Caravan Values.*

glider policy. A policy on a glider (ie engineless aircraft) covering loss/damage during launching, flight and landing, all subject to an excess; loss/damage while in a picketed hangar or not left unattended in the open at an approved launching site or in transit; third party injury and damage; passenger liability.

global excesses. An excess of loss reinsurance to cover the reinsured's entire operation or at least a number of different departments or classes. The global excess pays losses in excess of the aggregate net losses sustained by the reinsured in all of its departments (eg motor, aviation, marine, property etc) following one major loss or disaster. The demand for this type of reinsurance arises from catastrophes like Hurricane Betsey (qv) which are capable of producing losses on ships, aircraft, property on land, etc at the one time. The policy wording is similar to an excess of loss catastrophe reinsurance. Global excesses can provide cover for specific risks as well as catastrophes and large risk accumulations.

global insurance programme. A worldwide insurance programme which aims to establish the same level of production in a number of different countries to meet the needs of a business enterprise which owns assets or conducts business across national boundaries. At one extreme a global insurance programme could consist of a master policy issued in the home country which results in a totally non-admitted insurance programme. No policies, premiums or claims are issued or paid locally. At the other extreme is a totally admitted programme with all local entities being issued with policies and all premiums and losses being dealt with locally. In practice a global insurance programme consists of (a) a master policy arranged in the home country uniform for the whole group, and (b) local policies arranged on an admitted basis according to local needs and usages. The purpose of a master policy is to fill gaps in the local policies and so secure for the insured a consistent level of cover across the group as a whole. Generally the insured can, through the master policy, purchase cover on a wider basis than is possible through individual fragmented buying. The master policy is subject to a difference in conditions (qv) clause and a different in limits clause (qv).

global return. The statement required by the Department of Trade and Industry covering the activities of all Lloyd's syndicates. Accountants approved by the Council of Lloyd's prepare a return dealing with all their syndicate clients. The returns are consolidated by Lloyd's who then publish Lloyd's market underwriting results.

'goods'. In the context of a marine insurance policy this means goods in the nature of merchandise. It does not include personal effects or provisions and stores for use on board (Marine Insurance Act 1906, Schedule, Rules for Construction of Policy, rule 17). This rule also provides that deck cargo and living animals must be specifically insured and not insured as goods unless it is customary to do so.

goods in transit insurance. The insurance of goods, or liability for goods, during transit by road, rail or other means except for transit more appropriate for marine insurance. Where road transit is involved policies can be on a specified vehicle basis under which a sum insured is fixed for each named vehicle (average (qv) applies). Under declaration policies the policy operates in respect of transit by road or rail in unspecified conveyances with the premium being based on an estimate of the value of goods carried or haulage charges earned subject to adjustment at the end of the year after a declaration of the actual amount involved. Hauliers can insure for the full value of the goods or merely their legal liability for loss or damage. Policies operate while goods are on the vehicle, including loading and unloading, and during transit including temporary housing en route. Policies, other than those on a legal liability basis, provide cover on an 'all risks' basis or, occasionally are restricted to loss or damage caused by fire, collision, overturning or derailment. Exclusions include: explosives, acids, bullion, cash, currency, deeds, bonds, securities, jewellery, precious stones, clocks, watches, curios, antiques, design and livestock.

'Goods . . . in trust or on commission'. The phrase 'goods in trust' when used in an insurance policy does not in any sense imply a technical trust. It includes goods with which the insured is entrusted as bailee (*Waters* v *Monarch Fire and Life Assurance Co* (1856)). The phrase 'goods held on commission' has a more restricted meaning and refers to property entrusted to the insured for the purpose of sale. In the *Waters* case it was held that the phrase as a whole was wide enough to not only cover the insured's interest but was sufficient to cover the full value of the goods. Any sum recovered in excess of the insured's own interest is held in trust by the insured for the benefit of the owners. It was a first party (qv) not third party insurance. *See also* GOODS . . . in trust or on commission for which the insured is responsible and on goods.

'goods in trust or on commission for which the insured is responsible'. The addition of the phrase 'for which the insured is responsible to goods in trust or on commission' (qv), has the effect restricting the cover to the interest of the insured and does not extend to cover the proprietary interests of other persons in the goods. In *North British and Mercantile Insurance Co* v *Moffat* (1871), the property in the goods held by the insured as wholesale tea merchants had passed with the risk to the purchasers who were not protected when a fire occurred at the insured's warehouse. *See also* ON GOODS.

government bonds. Government bonds are required for special managers in bankruptcy, trustees under deeds of arrangement, liquidators, and those concerned with dutiable goods (*see* CUSTOMS AND EXCISE BONDS).

graded schedule scheme. A pension scheme under which benefits are related to earnings in each year of membership. An alternative term is salary grade scheme.

gradually operating causes. Causes which result in loss over a period of time.

Examples include rust, corrosion, and normal wear and tear. No fortuitous element is present and to compensate property owners for the reduction in value due to these causes would be contrary to the principle of indemnity (qv). Wear and tear, etc is specifically excluded from 'all risks' policies. However, policies issued on a 'new for old' (qv) and reinstatement basis are a modification of the principle of indemnity.

grammatical construction rule. A rule of construction (qv) to the effect that in construing a policy the ordinary rules of grammar and punctuation will apply, although a court has a discretion to correct obvious slips. The draftsmen of policies and other legal documents endeavour to avoid reliance on punctuation to convey their meaning.

grant of probate. This is the name of the document issued under seal by the court which grants title to legal personal representatives of the deceased. There are two kinds: (a) probate when a will has been left; (b) letters of administration when no will has been left. Under a grant of probate the executors derive their title from the will. Any acts carried out by the executors before the probate is granted are binding on the estate, but they cannot sue until probate is granted. Probate is specific evidence that the will is valid and is the last will.

Great Fire of London. London's largest fire occurred in 1666, started in Pudding Lane and prompted the development of fire insurance in the UK. Previously compensation for fire damage was obtained by way of charitable donations and collections from guilds of craftsmen and churches. The Fire Office was formed in 1680 and is generally regarded as the first fire insurance company although records suggest that some fire insurance was transacted in 1667. For other historical aspects *see* FIRE MARKS, FIRE INSURANCE DUTY and the TOOLEY STREET FIRE.

green card. Otherwise referred to more officially as the international motor insurance certificate. It is issued to motorists travelling on the continent of Europe to produce as proof that they have insurance to comply with the minimum requirements of the states they enter. Each country has a bureau on the lines of the Motor Insurers Bureau (qv) to guarantee the certificates issued by them. The certificates have to be green in colour and contain the kind of information found in a normal motor insurance certificate, eg persons entitled to drive, restrictions as to use, etc but also shows the countries to which it applies. Under EC Directives insurers in member countries such as the UK must include within their policies the minimum third party cover required by all member states. Consequently green cards are no longer a legal necessity within EC territories but they continue to be used as they have acquired a recognition in their own right which makes negotiations easier if they are produced following an accident. For travel outside the EC the card remains necessary as failure to produce it will oblige the motorist to buy insurance locally in the state or states concerned. It should also be noted that the insured who wants cover in excess of the statutory minimum when travelling on the continent should notify the insurer. The countries in which a green card is acceptable include all those in Western Europe, most of those in the Eastern Europe plus Malta, Gibraltar, Israel, Morocco, and Tunisia.

gross fund. A fund that is not liable to tax on income or capital gains. Annuity funds are treated in this way.

gross line. The amount of insurance the insurer has accepted on a risk before deducting the amount reinsured. Net lines plus reinsurance equals gross lines.

gross premium income. Total premium income (gross or written, ie face value) before deducting outgoing reinsurance premiums or other deductions.

gross profit. The amount by which sales revenue exceeds the cost of sales, ie costs incurred in getting the goods ready for sale and in a manufacturing concern this will include direct labour costs and other direct costs. It is the principal item insured under a business interruption insurance (qv) which usually provides cover on the difference basis (qv). The policy actually defines gross profit on this basis.

An older way of calculating gross profit for the purpose of business interruption insurance was to add the net profit to the standing charges (qv) of the business.

gross proceeds. *See* GROSS VALUE.

'gross value'. This is defined in the Marine Insurance Act 1906, s. 71 (4) as the wholesale price or estimated value ruling on the day of sale after freight, landing charges and duty have been paid. 'Gross proceeds' is the price obtained at a sale, all charges on sale being paid by the seller (Marine Insurance Act 1906, s. 73).

ground heave. The upward pressure of the ground which pushes up the foundations and causes damage to the structure of the property. Damage caused by ground heave is not covered by the peril subsidence (qv). Ground heave can be caused by the natural movement of earth and rock.

ground risks. An aviation insurance term describing the risk of damage to the aircraft while stationary on the ground.

grounding risk. A risk insurable under an aviation products liability to indemnify a manufacturer against loss incurred following the grounding of the aircraft pending investigation and repair of an alleged defect.

group insurance. The insurance of a number of persons under a single contract or, by way of agreement, under individual contracts. Usually the persons are all employed by a single employer or members of a particular association. Group cover can be applied to various kinds of insurance, eg group life (qv), group accident, group legal expenses etc.

group captives. A captive insurance company (qv) formed by an association to insure the risks of its members.

group life insurance. A life insurance policy covering a group of people as distinct from individual lives. The group must exist for some purpose other than the insurance, eg employees in a firm or a particular part of the firm or members of an association. The cover is most often provided as an ancillary benefit to a pension scheme but can be provided without accompanying pension benefits. Most policies are written on the basis of one-year term insurance (qv) with the automatic right of renewal each year suubject to the terms of the contract.

group underwriting. This may be used where a parent company controls other insurance companies within its group. Group underwriting is an alternative to interchange of business among companies in the group. It involves each acceptance of business being reported to a central control where a retention is observed in accordance with a scale of group limits having regard to the group's commitments, the limit and the merits of the risk. The accepting office may be instructed to effect any reinsurance or it may be obtained centrally. The retention is a group one and the centralising of underwriting enables the group to maximise its underwriting capacity.

growth bonds. A guaranteed bond (qv) providing capital growth on maturity. The guarantee is expressed as a net percentage increase at the end of the term. The bond is usually based on a single premium endowment or occasionally a deferred annuity. In both cases, the gain on the original lump sum is subject to tax at the higher income tax rates (there is no capital gains tax) but with a single premium endowment top slicing (qv) is allowed in determining the liability. On a deferred annuity contract basic rate income tax is chargeable on the gain, and this cannot be top-sliced. The essence of a growth bond is the re-investment of income to produce the capital growth on death or maturity. The return on the bond may be linked to a unitised fund (qv) operated by the insurer. Bond switching (qv) may be permitted but usually the fund manager decides which investments to favour as relatively few investors exercise these rights.

Guadalajara Convention 1961. A convention to unify certain rules relating to the international carriage by air undertaken by a person other than the contracting carrier. Where the actual carrier performs the whole or part of carriage, which is international carriage according to the contract made by the consignor or passenger with the contracting carrier, the contracting carrier will be subject to the Warsaw Convention (qv) for the whole of the carriage, and the actual carrier will be similarly placed in relation to that part of the carriage that he performs. If a passenger is injured or baggage or cargo lost or damaged the option arises of claiming against either or both parties. Contracting carrier means the person who as a principal makes an agreement for carriage governed by the Warsaw Convention with a passenger or consignor or someone acting for them. Actual carrier means someone, other than the contracting carrier, who is authorised by that contractor to perform the whole or a part of the carriage but who is not with respect to such carriage a successive carrier within the meaning of the Warsaw Convention. The Convention was given the force of law by the Carriage of Goods by Air (Supplementary Provisions) Act 1962 (qv).

guarantee. A collateral engagement to answer for the debt, default, or miscarriage of another person. The person giving the guarantee is the guarantor or surety, the person to whom it is given is the guarantee or creditor, and the person whose debt, default, or miscarriage is the foundation of the guarantee is the principal debtor or, more simply, the principal. A guarantee is unenforceable unless evidenced in writing. A fidelity guarantee policy may be either insurance by way of indemnity only, or a combination of both indemnity and guarantee. In the first instance only the law of insurance will apply. In the second instance this is still the case as between insurer and insured with the law relating to guarantee applying to the relationship between the insurer and the debtor. *See* INSURANCE-GUARANTEE and PURE GUARANTEE. The policy is one of insurance only if effected without the constructive knowledge and consent of the person guaranteed.

guarantee fund. A solvency indicator, defined as one third of the required margin of solvency. If a company's net assets fall below the guarantee fund, it must submit a short-term financial scheme to the Department of Trade and Industry.

guaranteed annuity option. The right to use the proceeds of a pension plan or insurance policy to purchase an annuity at a rate which is guaranteed in the contract. *See also* OPEN-MARKET OPTION (qv) and GUARANTEED ANNUITY OPTION (qv).

guaranteed bonds. Life policies normally in the form of single premium life policies which guarantee certain benefits. *See* GROWTH BONDS and INCOME BONDS.

guaranteed bonus. A life insurance policy under which the insurer guarantees a bonus, usually a reversionary bonus, as a periodic addition to the basic sum insured at a guaranteed rate. The insurer is committed under contract to increase the sum payable on death or maturity and the bonus is not dependent on the divisible surplus. This is really an increasing insurance and not a with profits insurance.

guaranteed insurability. A life insurance term describing the insurer's offer to provide new policies without further evidence of health. The offer is usually confined to existing policyholders and often features in selling by direct mail (qv).

guaranteed minimum pension (GMP). The minimum level of pension which a pension has to provide in order for its members to be contracted-out of SERPs (qv).

guaranty fund. *See* ASSESSMENT.

Guard Dogs Act 1975. Section 1 provides that a guard dog is not permitted to be used on premises unless under the control of a handler while being used except while it is secured so that it is not at liberty to go freely about the premises. A warning of the guard dog's presence should be exhibited at each entrance to the premises. The Act imposes criminal sanctions but a conviction would be of value to a plaintiff as evidence in a civil court. In *Cummings* v *Granger* (*The Times*, 29 May 1976), the Court of Appeal held that there was no liability under the Animals Act 1971 (qv) when a woman as a trespasser entered a breakers' yard at night knowing of the presence of the dog. She was held to have voluntarily accepted the risk of injury.

guest. A person who comes to stay at the property of another. In the context of certain hotels, ie those operating as inns (qv), it is someone who books sleeping accommodation. The innkeeper becomes strictly liable for loss or damage to the property of a guest subject to the limitations introduced by the Hotel Proprietors Act 1956 (qv).

guests' effects. Property and effects belonging to, or the responsibility of guests, ie persons staying overnight at hotels and similar establishments. The proprietor of the establishment can insure the effects under a material damage policy or his legal liability for loss or damage to it.

H

Hague Convention 1970. A Convention that ruled that hijacking occurs when a person on board an aircraft has unlawfully committed, or is about to commit, by force or by threat of force, an act of interference, seizure, or other wrongful exercise of control of an aircraft in flight. The convention required every ratifying state to introduce domestic legislation to acquire jurisdiction over this new offence. The state which apprehends the offender may either extradite him or her or refer the case to its own prosecuting authority, eg the Director of Public Prosecutions in the case of the UK. *See the* HIJACKING ACT 1971.

Hague Protocol. An international meeting at the Hague in 1955 called to update the Warsaw Convention (qv). It redefined certain terms; extended the protection to servants and agents of the carrier who had been sued as individuals by plaintiffs dissatisfied with the limits of the Warsaw Convention; reduced the amount of detail required on tickets and the consequences of non-compliance with the terms by the carrier moved in favour of the passenger or consignor to make avoidance of liability more difficult. Also the defence available to the carrier concerning pilot error or negligent navigation was removed. The limit for passenger liability was doubled to 250 000 gold francs. The provisions of the protocol were introduced into the UK by the Carriage by Air Act 1961 (qv).

Hague-Visby Rules. A set of rules drawn up as a result of the Brussels Protocol of 1968 to replace the Hague Rules of 1924. They are now appended as a Schedule to the Carriage of Goods by Sea Act 1971 (qv). The rules have been adopted by several countries.

hail insurance. The insurance of property against damage caused by hailstorms. It is written on buildings and their contents and on growing crops.

hail reinsurance. The reinsurance of hail insurance (qv). Reinsurance can be by quota share and surplus treaties but when excess of loss is required it is normally excess of loss ratio (qv). This is because excess of loss centres around losses from any one occurrence but with serious loss from hailstorm it is extremely difficult to say what is 'one occurrence', ie where one storm ends and another begins.

half system. A method of calculating an insurer's earned premium for the year. It assumes that half of all written premium income in any one year is earned during the year. Consequently 50 per cent of written premium income is treated as earned premium income. The method lacks precision as it assumes that the average annual policy incepts half-way through the year.

halving agreement. A claims-settling agreement under which two insurers agree to divide claims equally when the claim covered by the agreement is made against one or both of them.

Hancock annuity. An annuity purchased by an employer for a former employee. Provided that the employer clearly shows his intention to provide an irrevocable pension for an employee who has already retired when the purchase price is paid, the purchase price will attract tax relief. This follows the judgment in *Hancock* v *General Reversionary & Investment Co. Ltd* (1918).

'hands' insurance. A form of personal accident and sickness (qv) designed for persons whose earning capacity depends on their manual detexerity (eg pianists, musicians, surgeons). The benefits payable for injury to the insured's arms or hands (as defined) are increased so that, for example, a pianist will receive 100 per cent of the lump sum for permanent damage to the ends of his fingers. Other benefits follow the normal pattern for the type of insurance concerned.

hangarkeepers' liability insurance. *See* AIRPORT OWNERS' AND OPERATORS' LIABILITY INSURANCE.

hard disclosure of commission. *See* DISCLOSURE.

hard market. A market in which the supply of insurance is restricted in relation to the demand. The reduced supply may be in both the primary and reinsurance markets with the result that premiums increase and terms and conditions harden as insurers endeavour to move into more profitable situations.

hazards. The aspects of a risk considered by an insurer as likely to increase to influence the occurrence or severity of a loss, including the attitudes and conduct of the people associated with the risk. *See* PHYSICAL HAZARD AND MORAL HAZARD.

hazardous pursuits. Certain sports and activities are excluded from personal accident insurances (qv) because of their hazardous nature and because they relate to risks that are not common to all policyholders. However, the policy can usually be extended to provide the cover in respect of the risks actually run by the individual insured provided he pays an additional premium. The pursuits concerned include: aviation (other than as a passenger on normal flights which is not regarded as 'hazardous'); hunting and polo; football; motor-cycling; mountaineering involving the use of ropes; winter sports.

hazardous wastes. Wastes containing any substance which may create danger to (a) the life or health of people or animals when released into the environment or (b) to the safety of humans or equipment in disposal plants if incorrectly handled. Hazardous waste may be toxic (most pesticides, lead salts, arsenic compounds, cadmium compounds, cattle dip); flammable (eg hydrocarbons); corrosive (eg acids or alkalis); oxidising (eg nitrates or chromatic). Insurers will regard involvement by the insured with any hazardous waste as a material fact.

heading. The name and address at the top of the policy form whereby the insurer is identified.

Health and Safety at Work etc Act 1974. The Act provides a legislative framework to promote high standards of health and safety at work. The Act is an enabling measure superimposed over earlier health and safety legislation. The earlier duties under the Factories, Shops and Railway Premises and the Mines and Quarries Acts, etc, remain in force but will gradually be replaced by regulations under the Act. It deals with the health and safety of all 'persons at work' (qv) and the protection of the public where they may be affected by the activities of persons at work. The Health and Safety Commission (qv) and the Health and Safety Executive (qv) administer the legislation. In addition to its regulation-making power the Act imposes duties of a general nature on employers, manufacturers, employees, and the self-employed and others. Employers must safeguard so far as is reasonably practicable the health and safety of employees. This applies in particular to the provision of safe plant and systems of work, and covers all machinery and appliances used. An employer employing five or more must prepare a written statement of his general policy, organisation and arrangements for health and safety. Employers must also have regard for the health etc of self-employed or contractors' employees working close to their own employees and for members of the public affected by work activities. A similar duty to that placed on employers attaches to the self-employed. Designers, manufacturers, importers and suppliers of articles or substances for use at work must ensure that as far as is reasonably practicable they will be safe when used. Employees have a duty to take reasonable care to avoid injury to themselves or to others and to co-operate with employers and others. Also they must not interfere with or misuse anything provided to protect their health, safety or welfare in compliance with the Act. Contravention of the Act may lead to the issue of a prohibition notice (qv), an improvement notice (qv), and/or a prosecution, or the seizure, the rendering harmless or destruction of any substance that the inspector considers to be the cause of imminent danger or serious personal injury. Health and Safety Executive inspectors are responsible for enforcing health and safety legislation in industrial undertakings (factories, mines, building sites, and farms). Environmental health officers are responsible for commercial premises (eg offices, shops, and warehouses). The enforcement measures have brought a demand for legal defence cover which is provided either as an extension of employers' and/or public liability policies or under legal expenses insurance. *See also* EMPLOYMENT MEDICAL ADVISORY SERVICE.

Health and Safety Commission. The Commission and the Health and Safety Executive (qv) administer the Health and Safety at Work etc Act 1974 (qv) and are a focus of initiative for all matters relating to health and safety at work. The Commission consists of representatives of both sides of industry and the local authorities. It is responsible for developing policies in the health and safety field, and for making proposals for new health and safety regulations to the appropriate minister.

Health and Safety Executive. This is a separate statutory body appointed by the Health and Safety Commission (qv) which works in accordance with the advice and guidance given by the Commission. The Executive also enforces legal requirements and provides an advisory service to both sides of industry. The major inspectorates in the health and safety field are within the Executive.

heating processes. Any process involving the applicaton of heat such as drying, baking, cooking and the like. The term is significant in the context of the fire policy which excludes damage to any property undergoing a heating process. This is an excluded form of loss (qv) and not an excluded risk as any fire damage that flows from the damage to the heated property will be covered by the policy.

heave. *See* GROUND HEAVE.

Hedley Byrne v. Heller & Partners (HL1964). A case that became the leading authority on the law of negligent mis-statement. It altered the law and established that one party can be liable in negligence for the economic loss sustained of another party as a result of the defendant's negligent mis-statement, provided always a 'special relationship' exists between them and there has been no disclaimer of liability. Previously there could be no liability in the absence of dishonesty (essential for the tort of deceit) or a contractual or fiduciary relationship. The 'special relationship' creates a duty of care on the part of the defendant and arises when the defendant knew or should have forseen that the plaintiff would rely on his skill and judgment and that it was reasonable in the circumstances for the plaintiff to do so. In *Caparo* v *Dickman* (1990) the House of Lords has defined the limits of liability by stating that the advice given must only be used in relation to the matter about which the advice was given. Professional persons or bodies can insure their liability for negligent mis-statements under professional indemnity insurance (qv).

height clause or warranty. A restrictive endorsement (qv) in public and employers' liability insurances which may operate as an exclusion or a warranty to regulate the height at which work may be undertaken. For example, the policy may exclude work at heights in excess of 40 feet. If the clause is written as a continuing warranty all cover ceases from the date the warranty is breached. The insurer is not prohibited by the Employers' Liability (Compulsory Insurance) Act 1969 (qv) and regulations thereunder from relying upon any breach of such a condition or warranty. As an alternative to, or in addition to, a specific height restriction the policy may exclude work on particular types of buildings. *See* BLAST FURNACE CLAUSE.

held covered. 1. Insurers may confirm that a risk is 'held covered' pending completion of the formal arrangements. 2. A marine insurance term applied to shipments of cargo in certain vessels not acceptable to insurers at rates agreed for the purpose of the Classification Clause (qv) embodied in open covers. (qv). Shipments in these vessels (see below) are not excluded from the cover. They are 'held covered' at rates to be arranged. The vessels to which the held covered provision applies are steamers, other than liners, which are over 20 (25 years by agreement) years old, or which have not been assigned the highest classification of a ship classification society. 3. The held covered clause appears in the Breach of Warranty Clause, ie number 3 of the Institute Time Clauses. Marine insurers use express trading warranties (see INSTITUTE WARRANTIES) without which the insured vessel would be free to proceed to any corner of the earth. This freedom would attract high rates of premium in view of the potential exposure to high risk areas and would often lead to shipowners paying for risks that they did not run. Shipowners therefore accept the warranties, eg vessel not to proceed to northern regions in the winter, quite readily. However, by the held covered clause the cover continues to operate in the prohibited areas provided the insurer is notified and any additional premium paid. The clause applies only to breach of warranty as to cargo, trade, locality or date of sailing.

hidden reserves. The reserves, undisclosed in amount, deducted from assets or added to liabilities by an insurance company which is exempted from some of the detailed disclosure provisions of the Companies Act.

Highly Flammable Liquid Regulations. Regulations controlling the use and storage of all substances with a flash point (qv) below 32°C (excluding cellulose solutions which are regulated separately).

highway authorities. The Highways Act 1959 transferred the duty to repair highways to the Secretary of State for the Environment or the appropriate local authority according to the classification of the road. Formerly, a local authority was not liable for injuries caused to users of the highway by its own non-feasance (eg non-repair of the surface) but this rule was abolished by the Highways (Miscellaneous Provisions) Act 1961, s. 1. Previously there had been liability for misfeasance only.

hijacking. The forcing of a pilot to fly aircraft to an unscheduled destination. See the HAGUE CONVENTION 1970 for the first legal definition. The normal aircraft policy is on an 'all risks' basis but specifically excludes hijacking. Politically motivated hijacking and sabotage can be insured by a separate war risks policy. Hijacking of lorries has been a concern for goods-in-transit insurers but the risk is not excluded.

Hijacking Act 1971. An Act to ratify the Hague Convention 1970 (qv) in the UK. The definition of hijacking closely follows that of the convention. The Act makes hijacking an offence regardless of the offender's nationality or the state in which the aircraft is registered or whether the aircraft is in the UK or elsewhere, unless the flight on which the offence takes place begins and ends in the state of registration of the aircraft. The Act does not apply to aircraft used in military, customs, or police service except when the offence is committed by a citizen of the UK or colonies, or by a British subject, or if the hijacking takes place in the UK, or the aircraft is registered in the UK or used in UK military, customs or police service. The Act makes provision for extradition or return of anyone committing or attempting to commit the offence. The penalty on conviction is life imprisonment.

hire purchase. A hire purchase agreement is technically a contract of hire with the hirer having the option to purchase. In practice the hirer selects his own product, eg a motor-car, and the seller thereupon sells it to a finance house which enters into a hire purchase contract with the buyer. In such a case the interest of the finance house is protected by a hire purchase clause in the motor policy. The policy is in the name of the hirer/buyer and the operative clause of the loss or damage section is specifically worded to cover the interests of the owners. The buyer gets the benefit of the implied terms of fitness for purpose (qv) and merchantable quality from the finance house as 'sellers'.

hit and run drivers. See UNTRACED DRIVERS.

Hold Harmless Agreement. An agreement by one party to indemnify another against certain losses. For example, the principal in a construction project may call upon the main contractor to 'hold him harmless' (ie indemnify him) against claims against him arising arising out of the contractor's negligence. As a result liability insurances generally include a principal's clause.

'hold-up' cover. *See* PERSONAL ASSAULT COVER.

holiday insurance. *See* TRAVEL INSURANCE.

home business. Business underwritten in the UK for UK residents.

home foreign business. General insurance business underwritten in the UK relating to risks situated outside the UK. Marine, aviation and transport business and treaty reinsurance is normally excluded from this definition. *See also* SERVICES BUSINESS and NON-ADMITTED INSURER.

home income plans. Schemes to assist elderly home owners raise loans on their property for the purpose of purchasing immediate annuities in order to increase their incomes. The loan (up to 80 per cent of the value) is provided by an insurance company or building society on the security of the property. For a couple the money would be invested in a joint life and survivor annuity. Interest on the loan would be paid, net of tax relief, from the annuity payments leaving a surplus for the annuitants. To secure tax relief, 90 per cent of the loan must be invested in the annuity. The borrower is often given the option of taking the remaining 10 per cent as a lump sum. On death (the second death in the case of a joint life and survivor annuity), the house is sold to repay the loan. Depending on the amount borrowed and the current state of the property market, there will be an amount left over for the dependants of the deceased. The viability of the scheme in terms of increasing the income of the property owners depends on their age(s) at entry.

home letting. Legal expenses insurance is available for those who let their homes temporarily. It covers the legal costs incurred in pursuing rights under tenancy agreements (non-payment, damage, eviction etc), legal costs of unauthorised tenants (squatters) and costs of hotel accommodation while the legal proceedings are completed.

home reversion plan. Like home income plans (qv), this plan is used by elderly property owners to increase their incomes. The house is sold outright to the insurance company in return for an immediate annuity and a life tenancy. The sale price is below market value and the insurance company or institution purchasing the property benefits from the capital appreciation attaching to the property. After death nothing remains for the dependants. The scheme is therefore generally more likely to attract those without dependants but it is important in all cases for those interested to get professional advice with this and similar schemes.

home service assurance. An alternative term to industrial life assurance (qv).

home rescue. *See* ROAD RESCUE COVER.

honour policies. *See* POLICY PROOF OF INTEREST (PPI).

hops growers' consequential loss insurance. An engineering policy covering loss of hops arising from sudden and unforeseen physical damage to hop-picking machines, oil-burning units, fans, presses or failure of public electricity supply.

horse riding. Liability arising from horse riding in a private capacity is within the scope of personal liability insurance (qv). It may be regarded as a hazardous pursuit (qv) by personal accident insurers with cover available as a buy-back (qv). *See* RIDING ESTABLISHMENTS.

hospital. The term is generally defined in private health insurances and hospital cash plans as meaning a privately owned or National Health Service hospital with facilities for medical and surgical treatment registered in the UK with a local authority in accordance with the Public Health Acts. Insurers also list a number of types of establishment that are not included in the definition. These include all or some of the following: residential nursing homes, convalescent homes, hospices, health hydros, nature cure clinics and similar establishments or private beds registered as nursing homes.

hospital cash plan. A low cost insurance which offers the policyholder a fixed sum (eg £50 per day) for each day he is in hospital. The object is to contribute to the extra expenses, or replace lost income, that arise during the hospital period. Exclusions under the plan include: Pre-existing medical conditions (qv); war; intentional injury to self; alcohol or drug abuse; pregnancy or childbirth; mental diseases, disorders or breakdown; nuclear radiation; cosmetic surgery; treament for infertility or pregnancy termination; AIDS; confinement for domestic reasons.

hospital payments. The payment of certain hospital treatment fees by an insurer who has made a third party payment to the victim of a road accident. The Road Traffic Act 1988, s. 157 obliges the insurer to make payments to the hospital where treatment as an outpatient or in-patient has been given regardless of whether an admission of liability has been made or not. The amount to be paid is based on 'expenses reasonably incurred' not exceeding £2000.37 for each in-patient or £200.04 for each out-patient. Section 157 also applies to vehicles owners who have made deposits against third party risks (qv) or obtained securities against third party risks (qv).

'hostilities'. This term does not imply war but means acts of hostility or operations of hostility. They must be carried out by persons acting as agents of an enemy government or of an organised rebellion and not by individuals acting on their own initiative.

hot explosion. The sudden release of energy from an extremely rapid combustion of chemicals, gas or a cloud of dust.

Hotel Proprietors Act 1956. An Act which defines an inn (qv), restricts strict common law liability for property to the property of a guest (qv), sets limits of liability at £50 on any one article and £100 for any one guest, and provides that there will be no strict liability for vehicles and their contents, horses or other animals, their equipment or harness. The innkeeper loses the benefit of the limits of £50 and £100 if he fails to display the notice in the Schedule to the Act in a conspicuous place at or near the reception desk. Displaying the notice is not an admission that the establishment is an inn. The financial limits do not apply to property which has been deposited, or offered for deposit, for safe custody.

hours clause. A clause used in catastrophe excess of loss reinsurance treaties to overcome the difficulties of applying the term 'any one event or occurrence' to multiple losses or losses occurring over a period of time all associated with the same phenomenon such as riot, earthquake and flood. The reinsurer promises an indemnity in respect of a proportion of each and every loss occurrence above the excess point (qv). Loss occurrence is defined as meaning 'all individual losses arising out of and directly occasioned by one catastrophe'. However, the duration and extent of any loss occurrence is limited to 72 consecutive hours as regards a hurricane, typhoon, windstorm, rainstorm, hailstorm and/or tornado. Similar provisions are made in regard to other catastrophes, eg earthquakes. Where riot and civil commotion and malicious damage are concerned the loss occurrence is based on the individual losses occurring within 72 consecutive hours within the limits of one town, city or village. In other circumstances the period is 168 consecutive hours. The reinsured is permitted to choose the date and time when any period of consecutive hours shall commence. If any one catastrophe exceeds the specified period the reinsured is allowed to divide that catastrophe into two or more loss occurrences provided no two periods overlap.

House of Lords. The highest court in the land. It is the Supreme Court of Appeal from the Court of Appeal in England and the Superior Courts of Scotland and Northern Ireland. Appeals are heard by the Appellate Committee, which usually consists of five, or three, Law Lords. They give written judgments. Since its Practice Statement in 1966 it is not bound by its previous decisions but they bind the lower courts.

house purchase schemes. Life insurance is used in a variety of ways in connection with house purchase. (a) Full endowment mortgage. A mortgage advance is made by a building society or bank and the insured effects an endowment policy for the same term as the mortgage. During the term he pays interest to the mortgagee and premiums to the insurer. At maturity or earlier death the policy proceeds are used to repay the mortgage. If the endowment is 'with profits' then at maturity, or even before, the proceeds normally exceed the mortgage debt to provide a balance for the insured. (b) Low cost endowment also known as bonus reinforcement policy. The insured effects an endowment with profits insurance for an amount appreciably less than the mortgage. The amount insured under the endowment policy, the guaranteed sum payable on death or survival, is fixed in the expectation that bonuses will accrue over the policy term at a rate that by maturity will be sufficient, when added to the guaranteed sum insured, will be sufficient to repay the mortgage loan. Generally the bonus additions exceed the initial estimates so that at maturity a balance is available for the insured. If death occurs in the early stages then the sum assured and accrued bonuses will be insufficient to clear the debt. Consequently, a decreasing term assurance is also effected at the outset so that at any point in time the aggregate of the sums payable on death from both insurances will be sufficient to repay the mortgage. The combined cost of the endowment and the decreasing term policy is lower than that of cost of a full endowment, hence the term 'low cost'. The saving element of the full endowment is much stronger. N.B. In neither case is any capital repaid during the period of the loan. (Compare with the normal repayment method—see decreasing term assurance below.) The introduction of MIRAS (Mortgage Interest Relief at Source) (qv) in 1983 has increased the popularity of both full and low cost endowment schemes. (c) Decreasing term assurance. (qv). This is used to cover the amount outstanding on death at any time during the mortgage term. The policy is known as a mortgage protection policy. In a normal repayment mortgage the mortgagor pays regular instalments comprising part capital and part interest. The capital outstanding gradually reduces as the period progresses. Consequently a policy with an initial sum payable on death that reduces to nil by the end of the term ensures that if the mortgagor dies before repayment is complete, the outstanding mortgage will be repaid.

House Rebuilding Cost Index. A recognised index of movements in the cost of rebuilding houses produced by the Royal Institute of Chartered Surveyors. It is used by insurers of buildings under household insurances as the basis of automatic increases in the sum insured on renewal where the policy concerned is subject to indexation (qv).

household insurances. Household insurances meet the needs of individual owners and occupiers of private dwellings by providing cover in respect of buildings and contents. Policies are invariably 'comprehensive' which means that an extensive range of named perils provide the insured perils. Both the buildings and contents insurances can be extended to cover accidental damage (qv) as an insured peril. 'New for old' cover is available in connection with contents. Various extensions of cover are available including: property owners' liability, occupiers' liability, personal liability, domestic servants, cost of alternative accommodation (loss of rent), professional fees and other costs, fatal accident insurance, all risks on personal effects and valuables, money, and deterioration of freezer contents.

household removal insurance. A special insurance to cover the contents of a house during the process of removal to another property. Cover under the normal householders' comprehensive policy on contents applies only to property 'temporarily removed' and therefore special arrangements are necessary. Neither does the householders' policy apply to furniture removed to a depository. Cover under the extended or special insurance can be arranged on an 'all risks' basis and it is usually a condition that the removal or the packing is carried out by professional removers. Cover can be arranged for up to seven days but some insurers restrict cover to 48 or 72 hours.

Hovercraft (Civil Liability) Order 1979. An order under the authority of the Hovercraft Act 1968 which replaces and amends the Order of 1971. The amendments are concerned with, *inter alia*, the application of the Carriage of Goods by Sea Act 1971 (qv) to the carriage of cargo by hovercraft. The new limit of the carrier's liability is £434.14 per package or unit or £1.30 per kilo of gross weight of the goods lost or damaged whichever is the higher. The limit of liability (the Carriage by Air Act 1961 and the Carriage by Air (Supplementary Provisions) Act 1962 apply) for injury to passengers and damage to their baggage has been increased from £12 000 to £30 000 and the limit for baggage to £216. The carrier will be liable for such damage unless he can prove that he took proper care. The Merchant Shipping Act 1894 (amended by the Merchant Shipping (Liability of Shipowners and Others) Act 1958) applies to hovercraft and limits the total liability of their owners for damage caused (other than to passengers and their baggage) to a figure related to the weight of the hovercraft. In respect of death or injury to person not aboard the hovercraft the new, higher figure is £5.50 per kg and for damage to property it is £1.57 per kg.

hovercraft insurance. Hovercraft are insured in the aviation market under special air cushion vehicle policies with separate forms for hull and liability risks.

hull. The frame or body of a ship, boat, aircraft, and hovercraft.

hull policy. This covers the vessel and its machinery (marine insurance) or aircraft (aviation insurance) as distinct from the goods carried. In marine insurance hulls are normally insured for periods of time (ie 12 months) and consequently the term 'time policy' (qv) is used. *See* INSTITUTE TIME CLAUSES (HULLS).

hull syndicate. A marine insurance syndicate which specialises in hull insurance to the exclusion of other forms of insurance.

hundred per cent treaty basis. A method to reduce the work and expense in preparing reinsurance treaty accounts. It obviates the preparation of separate accounts each showing the reinsurer's individual proportion of premiums and losses. Instead a statement shows the hundred per cent treaty amounts of every item on the account with a copy submitted to each reinsurer with the only its proportion of the final balance shown thereon. *See also* CLEAN CUT BASIS.

hurricane. A violent windstorm covering a large area. It usually originates at sea, with winds circulating at tremendous velocity around a 'centre' which in itself moves fairly slowly. In view of its range in time and space, hurricanes are brought within the hours clause (qv) in catastrophe excess of loss treaties.

Hurricane Betsey. A severe American windstorm causing heavy losses at Lloyd's amounting to 8 per cent of premium income in 1965. Losses were also incurred in 1966 and 1967. Resignations from Lloyd's doubled and the number applying for membership halved. In 1968 Lord Cromer chaired a committee to examine, *inter alia*, the required growth in Lloyd's capacity. Membership increased dramatically as it became more accessible as a result of proposals which included opening membership to women and foreigners.

IBNR. *See* INCURRED BUT NOT REPORTED.

identification clause. A clause in a policy stating that the policy and schedule will be read together and that any word or expression to which a specific meaning has been attached shall have the same meaning wherever it appears. Consequently one definition of a particular expression is sufficient for the whole policy form.

illegal 'contracts'. All illegal contracts are void, but all void contracts are not necessarily illegal. Otherwise stated, illegal contracts comprise a comparatively small class of contracts within the large category of void contracts (qv). Contracts by way of gaming or wagering illustrate the distinction between an illegal contract and one which is simply void. By the Gaming Act 1845 (qv), all such contracts are void, but they are not illegal; thus, collateral transactions are valid. For instance, if a man borrows money to make a bet, the lender can recover that money by legal process in the normal way. Illegality stands in the way of insurance against the consequences of the commission of a criminal offence but a motor policy is not invalidated because of a statutory offence such as speeding. It is possible to insure against negligence (public liability etc) and against wrongful acts committed innocently (libel insurance). It is also possible to insure against losses due to being the victim of the crime of another, eg arson (fire insurance), embezzlement or theft (fidelity guarantee). Where the insurer pleads illegality he has to discharge the burden of proof.

illuminated electrical signs insurance. An insurance issued by engineering insurance departments against physical loss of or damage to illuminated electrical signs from accidental cause.

illustration. A statement sent to a person seeking details of an insurance he is considering. The illustration is a part of the preliminary negotiations and does not usually constitute an offer to insure. In legal terms it usually ranks as 'an invitation to treat'. It indicates the approximate premium and the benefits of the policy and is usually supplied with a proposal form. The term 'illustration' is most commonly used in life insurance.

immediate annuity. An annuity (qv) that commences to the annuitant (qv) at the end of the first interval. If the annuity is payable quarterly this means that the first payment will be three months after payment of the purchase price. Immediate annuities are always bought by a single premium or purchase price.

immediate cause. This means the proximate cause (qv), ie the nearest cause in efficiency and not the nearest in time. Bacon summarised this by saying, 'it were infinite for the law to consider the cause of causes, and their impulsions one of another, therefore, it contenteth itself with the immediate cause, and judgeth of acts by that, without looking to any further degree'.

immediately. The insurer may require notification of a claim immediately and, under liability policies, require the insured to forward every writ, notice, letter or other document served on him immediately on receipt. Immediately has been held to mean 'with all reasonable speed considering the circumstances of the case (*Re Coleman's Depositories Ltd and Life and Health Assurance Association* (1907). In *Farrell* v *Federated Employers Insurance Association Ltd* (1970) a writ served on 7 January 1966 was not given to the insurer until 3 March 1966. Lord Denning MR said that 'with all reasonable speed' would mean by the end of January at the latest'.

immobile property agreement. An agreement entered into between insurers and other insurers, and insurers and local authorities, in respect of damage to property (eg walls, street lamps) caused by vehicles. It is usually provided that the vehicle insurer will pay two-thirds of the cost of repairs or replacement.

immobiliser clause. A goods in transit (qv) clause requiring vehicles to be fitted with an approved anti-theft device which is put into effective operation when the vehicle is left unattended. The particular wording of the clause is important. See ALARM SYSTEM IN OPERATION.

impact damage agreement. This agreement, designed to save administrative costs on claims, operates when a motor vehicle is in collision with immobile property (eg buildings and fences) which may be insured against such impact damage. The terms of the agreement vary between insurers but it is customary for the motor insurer to pay 75 per cent of the damage to immobile property regardless of actual liability.

impact damage cover. 1. An engineering insurance term to describe a form of cover available as a part of a broad insurance or as a separate insurance. The risk insured is 'damage by physical impact to surrounding plant or property belonging to the insured or held in trust by the insured or on commission or for which the insured is responsible resulting from fragmentation of any part of any insured item of plant'. The cover can be applied to: boilers and pressure plant; cranes and other lifting machines; lifts and hoists; and electrical and mechanical plant. 2. An additional peril (qv) which covers impact damage by any motorised vehicle, horses or cattle, and it can include damage arising from the insured's own vehicles for the payment of an extra premium. Some insurers cover impact damage caused by falling trees, telegraph poles, and lamp posts subject to the exclusion of damage to gates and fences.

impaired capital. A USA term describing the financial position of an insurer whose net current assets are less than its fully paid-up shares.

impaired lives. Persons with health defects that may limit their life expectancy. Such persons cannot secure life insurance on normal terms and conditions.

implicit items. Certain types of unusual asset, namely future profits, zillmerising and hidden reserves which may be admitted to a specified extent under Regulation 10(4) of the Insurance Companies Regulations 1981 in computing a company's net assets if the company has obtained an appropriate Section 68 Order.

implied conditions. Contractual terms that do not have to be expressly stated but are implied to give effect to the presumed intention of the parties. In the sale of goods in the course of business certain conditions and warranties are implied by statute (Sale of Goods Act 1979 (qv), see also SUPPLY OF GOODS AND SERVICES ACT 1982). The following conditions are implied in insurance contracts: (a) that the subject-matter of insurance is in existence at the date of effecting the policy; (b) that the insured has an insurable interest; (c) that the parties observe utmost good faith towards each other at all material times and in all material particulars; (d) that the subject-matter of insurance is so described as to clearly identify it and define the risk undertaken by the insurers.

implied warranty. A warranty (qv) which by law is tacitly understood to be binding and does not have to appear in the policy. The Marine Insurance Act 1906, ss. 39 and 41 imply the following: (a) that under a voyage policy (qv) the vessel will be seaworthy at the commencement of the voyage; (b) legality of the insured adventure. In a voyage policy on goods or other moveables there is an implied warranty that at the commencement of the voyage the ship is not only seaworthy but also that she is reasonably fit to carry the goods or moveables to their intended destination (s. 40).

improvement notice. A notice issued by Health and Safety Executive inspectors ordering that contraventions of the Health and Safety at Work etc Act 1974 (qv) be remedied within a specified time. The notice is served on the person who is deemed to be contravening the legal provision, or it can be served on any person on whom responsibilities are placed, whether he is an employer, an employed person, or a supplier of equipment or materials. Any person contravening a relevant statutory provision may be prosecuted instead of, or in addition to, being served with a notice. These matters give rise to the demand for legal expenses insurance (qv).

imputed knowledge. Knowledge which one party is deemed to possess because it is within the cognisance of another party. An insured, for example, may wish to impute knowledge to the insurer on the grounds that their agent actually possesses that knowledge. In insurance the position is complicated by the fact that for some purposes the intermediary acts as agent of the insurer (eg collecting the premium) and for other purposes (eg carrying out instructions to effect the insurance) is agent of the insured. It is therefore incumbent on the party who seeks to rely upon the doctrine of imputed knowledge to prove the existence of agency in relation to the point at issue.

'inability to attend to business of any kind'. *See* ATTENDING TO BUSINESS OF ANY KIND.

inadequate design. *See* FAULTY DESIGN.

in and out policy. A special type of fidelity policy for banks and other financial institutions, eg stock brokers dealing in securities. The subject-matter of insurance may include all or some of: bonds, debentures, stocks, scrip, shares, transfers, certificates, coupons, warrants, cash, cheques, banknotes, bills of exchange, promissory notes, title deeds, or other valuable documents. Cover is in respect of loss arising from dishonesty by employees, customers, or others. This is otherwise called an All-in policy.

'in an efficient condition'. Motor insurers require their insureds to take 'all reasonable steps to safeguard from loss or damage and maintain in efficient condition the vehicle described in the Schedule'. The insured will be excused if, having taken reasonable steps, a defect remains to cause an accident as the condition requires no more than reasonable steps. It does not ask the insured to guarantee the condition of the vehicle so, for example, the casual negligence of a garage employee does not breach the condition unless there was negligence by the insured in delegating the work to an incompetent (*Liverpool Corporation* v *T & H.R. Roberts* (1964)). What is 'reasonable' depends on the facts of the case. In *Conn* v *Westminster Motor Insurance Association* (1966) the insured drove a London taxi with two bald tyres and a brake defect. He certainly knew of one bald tyre and the Court of Appeal held on these facts he had not taken reasonable care and his plans for overhaul in two weeks time were not good enough (*see* REASONABLE CARE CONDITION). The trial judge had tipped the scales in favour of the insured as the vehicle was being used mostly in an area subject to a 30 m.p.h. speed limit as opposed to being a high-powered car driven hard and long on motorways. Using a car without tread on the tyre or a footbrake that does not work (*Jones and James* v *Provincial Insurance Co Ltd* (1929)) are clear breaches as it is hard to imagine that a reasonable insured would not know about them. Conn's car ought not to have been driven at all until the defects were remedied but in theory at least there remains the possibility that an apparently 'inefficient car' might be efficient for a particular use. The insurer's case will always be strengthened by showing that not only was the car 'inefficient' but that it was inefficient for the particular use to which it was being put at the time in question. The condition will not save the insurer in the face of a claim for a third party claim which is the subject of the compulsory insurance legislation but there will be a right of recovery against the insured. The condition is one which is precedent to liability (qv). *See also* UNROADWORTHY.

inception date. The date on which the insurance becomes operative.

Inchmaree Clause. Clause 7 of the Institute Time Clauses of 1970 named after the ship Inchmaree. The SG policy form covered only perils of the sea and the clause added cover for loss or damage to the ship by a number of different events, eg bursting of boiler, latent defects etc which became known as Inchmaree perils (qv). Under the new MAR form no perils are mentioned in the policy and so Clause 6 of the Institute Time Clauses, the Perils Clause, brings together the Inchmaree perils and the marine perils of the SG form. The Inchmaree clause was first adopted in 1887 after the Inchmaree case (*Thames and Mersey Marine Insurance Co.* v *Hamilton, Fraser & Co*, 12 App Cas 484). A negligent crewman left a donkey valve to an engine closed causing damage to the boiler. The damage was not covered and led to additional perils being added to the policy by a new clause named after the ship concerned. Other perils were added over the years.

Inchmaree perils. Loss or damage to the ship caused by: accidents in loading, discharging or shifting cargo or fuel; bursting of boilers, breakage of shafts or any latent defect in the machinery or hull (damage to the defective part is not covered only the resultant damage); negligence of master, officers, crew, or pilots; negligence of repairers or charterers provided such repairers or charterers are not the insureds. These perils are now covered under the Perils Clause, number 6.2 of the Institute Time Clauses (Hulls) (1/10/83). There is a proviso that the damage shall not have resulted from the want of due diligence on the part of the owners or managers. Clause 6.2 includes barratry of master, officers, or crew. Certain perils, 'contact with aircraft', 'explosion on board ship or elsewhere', and 'earthquake, volcanic eruption and lightning' are covered under clause 6.1 of the Perils Clause.

incidental business. Business written by a Lloyd's syndicate formed to write one class of business but which falls into another class. This is permissible within specified limits.

incidental non-marine. Non-marine insurance underwritten by a marine insurer which is supplementary or incidental to his marine business.

income benefit. 1. An amount paid annually (or more frequently) under a family income benefit policy (qv) from the time of death to the end of the agreed term. 2. An amount paid monthly (or weekly) under a policy covering disablement from working due to accidental injury or sickness. *See* SICKNESS BENEFITS (qv).

income bonds. A guaranteed bond (qv) that expresses the guarantee in terms of income and lump-sum benefits. Normally purchased by a single premium they give a guaranteed income with a death or maturity value approximating to the initial lump-sum investment. The policy is non-qualifying and normally has maturity periods of 5 to 10 years, but could run 1 to 15 years. The bond is normally based on endowment assurance (but whole life can be used) with the encashment of bonuses at yearly or half- yearly intervals providing the income. There is no liability to basic rate income tax or capital gains tax but any income over 5 per cent (the amount that can be withdrawn each year for up to 20 years free of income tax) and the 'profit' on maturity will be subject to higher rate tax spread over the term by the top slicing method (qv). A high rate tax-payer can enjoy a tax free income (the 5 per cent) and arrange encashment years later when his income and tax rate will be reduced. Some income bonds, mainly those for longer periods, are based on the combination of a deferred and immediate temporary annuity with the former providing the return of the original capital at the end of the term while the latter provides the income (the capital element is tax free) in the intervening period. The proceeds of the deferred annuity are subject to basic rate and higher rate tax but the bulk of the single premium is used to produce the income payments. The benefits under the bond may be linked to a unitised fund (qv) and bond switching (qv) may be permitted.

'in connection with'. In *A. Hatrick & Co Ltd* v *R*(1923) this phrase was said to mean 'connected with, subserving and being ancillary to'. The test was applied in *Kearney* v *General Accident* (1968) when an employee fell while painting roof trusses of a building. The employer's liability policy excluded 'any work *in connection with* roofs other than of private dwellings and/or shops . . . of not more than three floors'. The judge considered that the painting of the trusses and the underside of the outer cover was 'connected with, subserving or ancillary to' work in connection with the roof.

incoterms. Standardised contract terms used in international trade to define the obligations in a contract of sale. These terms deal, *inter alia*, with the important questions such as 'who will bear the risk if the operations cannot be carried out?' 'who will bear the risk of loss or damage to the goods in transit?' Examples include free on board (qv), cost, insurance and freight (qv), EXW (qv).

increase in cost of working. An expense that is insured under a business interruption insurance (qv). It is the additional expense necessarily and reasonably incurred for the sole purpose of reducing the shortfall in turnover during the indemnity period (qv). For example, alternative premises may have to be hired and/or overtime paid to make up for lost production. The insurer will not pay for increased costs in excess of the loss of the gross profit which the extra costs have served to avoid.

increasing extra risk. A life insurance term to describe an extra risk which increases with the passing of time, eg being overweight or chronic bronchitis.

increasing term (or temporary) insurance. A term (temporary) insurance (qv) particularly suitable for individuals uncertain as to their future life insurance requirements. In one version this type of policy affords maximum cover, maximum flexibility, and protection against inflation at modest cost. It is written as a five year policy with the following options (or similar) which are available to the policyholder without further evidence of health: (a) Renewal option—to extend the policy beyond five years at the rates applicable at that time (but renewal may be granted at level premium throughout with an adjustment of the sum insured); (b) Increase option—when the option is effected the sum insured can be increased by up to 50 per cent; (c) Conversion option—conversion in whole or part to whole of life or endowment insurance at any time during the five year term but not later than age 60. Some policies may be written simply on the basis that the death benefit increases as the policy runs. For example, the sum payable under a 20-year policy may increase by a fixed amount at the end of every five years in return for a premium which is level throughout the contract.

incurred but not reported (IBNR). At the end of an accounting period, the insurer creates a reserve to cover the estimated cost of losses that have occurred but have not yet been reported. The 'IBNR' reserve is quite significant in liability insurance as many claims have a 'long tail' (qv). The Insurance Companies Act 1982 prescribes the form in which IBNR claims must be included in the statutory returns.

incurred claims or losses. The total of paid and outstanding claims arising in a period. The term is also used, for the purpose of claims statistics, where for given accident (qv) or policy years (qv), the incurred claims (sometimes excluding IBNR (qv) are compared to earned premiums in order to assess the underwriting profitability for each class of business.

incurred loss ratio. Incurred losses (qv) stated as a percentage of earned premiums (qv).

indemnification aliunde. This doctrine simply means indemnity elsewhere. It must be distinguished from subrogation (qv). If the insured receives any sum either before or after a loss settlement in diminution of that loss, he must account for it to the benefit of the insurer. For example, an employer holding salary otherwise due to a defaulting employee must deduct the relevant sum from any claim under a fidelity guarantee policy (qv).

indemnity. 1. A fundamental principle of insurance whereby the insured, who has sustained a loss, is restored to the same financial position after the loss that he enjoyed immediately before it. It means an 'exact financial compensation' and prevents the insured from turning the loss into a gain. An inadequate sum insured (qv), indemnity limit (qv), excess (qv) or franchise (qv) may prevent an insured recovering a full indemnity. The principle is difficult to apply to insurances of the person. Consequently, life insurance (qv) and personal accident (qv) policies are termed 'benefit policies' in that payment is made by reference to predetermined benefits specified in the policy and not the principle of indemnity. The leading case on indemnity is *Castellain* v *Preston* (1883) (qv).

2. A contract of indemnity arises where one party agrees to make good the loss of another. Insurance is but one kind of such contracts. In the construction industry under JCT Contracts, the contractor undertakes to make good certain losses for the principal. Insurers need to vet contracts for the insurance implications arising.

indemnity commission. Commission advanced by a life company to a broker or agent on the understanding the company can clawback the whole or part of the commission if the policy on which it was paid lapses within a specified period of time.

indemnity limits. These are imposed by liability insurers to put a ceiling on their potential liability. Under public liability insurers limit their liability in respect of the damages or compensation including claimant's costs arising from any 'one occurrence' but otherwise impose no limit for the period of cover (usually one year). In addition the insurers will pay the insured's own costs if incurred with their written consent but *see* 'COSTS INCLUSIVE LIMITS OF INDEMNITY'. Under products liability and professional indemnity policies it is usual to impose aggregate limits for the year of insurance.

indemnity period. In a business interruption insurance (qv) this is the period beginning with the occurrence of the damage and ending not later than the maximum indemnity period thereafter, during which time the trading results of the business are affected by the interruption occasioned by the damage. The maximum indemnity period is chosen by the insured, eg 12 months, and is stated in the policy. The insured should take account not only of the time for repairing the damage but also the time needed to restore the turnover to its former level. The formal definition is: 'the period beginning with the occurrence of the damage and ending not later than—months thereafter during which the results of the business shall be affected in consequence of the damage'.

independent assessor. *See* INDEPENDENT AUTOMOTIVE ASSESSOR and LOSS ASSESSOR.

independent automotive assessor. A motor vehicle engineer carrying out the work of a staff engineer (qv) on an independent fee-earning basis. *See* INSTITUTE OF AUTOMOTIVE ENGINEERS ASSESSORS.

independent financial adviser (IFA). A category of financial intermediary created by the Financial Services Act 1986 (qv). Such an intermediary has to be authorised in order to carry on investment business (qv) and advise consumers which products from the market as a whole are best suited to their individual needs. Independent financial advisers include insurance brokers, members of FIMBRA (Financial Intermediaries, Managers, and Brokers Regulatory Association (qv)), accountants, solicitors, and major corporations. These corporations are authorised by the Securities and Investments Board (qv) or the Investment Management Regulatory Organisation (qv). The other advisers seek authorisation from FIMBRA or certification by a Recognised Professional Body (RPB) (qv) such as the Insurance Brokers Registration Council (IBRC) (qv), the Law Society, The Institute of Chartered Accountants etc. Registered insurance brokers and enrolled bodies corporate (qv), who do not handle clients' investment money, but whose income from life insurance, pensions and collective investment schemes does not exceed 25 per cent of total income, normally rely upon certification by the Insurance Brokers Registration Council. Unregistered insurance intermediaries (eg consultants) and brokers whose income, as above, exceeds the 25 per cent figure apply to FIMBRA. Not all independent financial advisers are able to transact the same sort of business (*see* INVESTMENT BUSINESS for the four main areas). An adviser cannot offer himself for a wider range of business than that for which he is authorised. All independent financial advisers contribute to the financial services compensation fund (qv). Also many firms will have professional indemnity cover (qv) but this is not mandatory. It is a criminal offence to carry on investment business without authorisation.

independent liability method. When contribution (qv) arises the insurers contribute 'rateably' to the loss. One way of apportioning a loss among the insurers involved is the independent liability method. Each insurer's liability for the loss is calculated as if the other policy was not in existence. The insurers then calculate their contribution to the loss in proportion to their individual liabilities. This method is commonly used in liability insurances or in property cases where the insurances are non-concurrent (qv). For example, liability insurer A had issued a policy with a limit of indemnity of £100 000 and insurer B had issued a policy for £10 000. The loss amounted to £4400. Independently each insurer was liable for £4400 and each therefore contributed £2200 to the loss. Insurer B contended unsuccessfully that the loss should be apportioned in the ratio of 10:1 to reflect their respective limits of indemnity. This is the maximum liability or pro rata method (qv).

indexation. *See* INDEX-LINKING.

index-linking (indexation). Methods of keeping sums insured or benefits up to date by means of automatic increases by linking them to a relevant index which represents an appropriate rise in money values. 1. *Family income benefits* (qv). The benefit escalates at a predetermined annual rate or, alternatively, in line with a specified index such as the RPI (Retail Price Index). The escalation may be from the date of inception or from the date of death. 2. *Permanent health insurance* (qv). The weekly benefits payable increase at a predetermined rate to protect the insured against the effects of inflation. The increase may be at an agreed fixed rate or at a rate which is in line with a specified index, eg RPI, subject to a maximum limit equal to three times the initial weekly benefit. 3. *Household insurance* (qv). Sums insured on both buildings and contents policies can be increased automatically at each renewal by an amount which represents the increase that has taken place in some recognised index. In the case of buildings the House Rebuilding Cost Index is commonly used

while for contents the consumer durables section of the RPI is often the link. 4. *Liability excess of loss reinsurance treaties.* A clause is inserted in the treaty which links the treaty limits to an appropriate earnings or price index. *See* STABILITY CLAUSE.

indirect business. 1. Business transacted with the insurer through an intermediary such as a broker or agent. 2. Business accepted by way of reinsurance.

indisputable policies. A policy under which the insurer cannot dispute liability except on the grounds of fraud. A life policy may be declared to be indisputable once it has been in force for a specified period of time. The insurer cannot repudiate the policy on the grounds of non-fraudulent misstatement, non-disclosure or breach of warranty. It is not necessary for the insurer to include a proviso to enable him to dispute the policy on grounds of fraud. This is an application of the equitable rule that no one should profit from fraud.

individual bonds. *See* MINI BONDS.

individual insured pension arrangement (individual arrangement). An occupational pension scheme with only one member which can be set up by a letter of exchange. An employer may have several individual arrangements for different employees.

individual trust policies for partners. Each partner effects life insurance on his own life in trust for his partners. A separate policy is required for each partner to ensure that each has funds with which to purchase a share of the deceased (or retiring) partner's part of the business. Large partnerships involve a large number of policies.

industrial accident. An accident to an employee that has arisen out of his employment. There must be a connection between the accident and the injury, but the accident need not be the only cause or even the main cause. The definition is important because someone who is unable to work due to injuries caused by an accident at work does not have to satisfy the national insurance contributions conditions for statutory sick pay or sickness benefit. The payment is automatic upon the claim being made and, if after a 28-week period, the employee is still unable to work, he goes on to an invalidity benefit.

industrial all risks insurance. Otherwise called commercial all risks insurance or difference in perils insurance, it provides the widest available material damage cover for commercial and industrial properties. One approach is to cover accidental loss or damage with no reference to specified perils but with exclusions, the other is to add the risks of accidental loss or damage to the normal fire and special perils cover. The exclusions found in a fire and perils policy will apply plus the additional exclusions of: faulty design, materials, and workmanship and inherent vice or defect; the gradually operating causes (qv) invariably excluded from all risks policies; change in temperature, nature of property etc; disappearance or shortage; pollution or change in the water table; subsidence, settlement or shrinkage; storm damage to property in the open. Some of the other excluded risks may be bought back by the insured or cover will be restricted to specified perils (fire and the customary range of additional perils). These may include: theft, fraud, engineering risks, brittle articles, money, computers, livestock and growing crops. The policy is often issued on a first loss basis (qv).

Industrial Assurance Commissioner. *See* INDUSTRIAL LIFE ASSURANCE.

industrial chimneys insurance. An engineering insurance covering physical damage to industrial chimneys of brick, concrete or steel construction, by sudden and unforeseen cause and to insured's surrounding property consequent thereon.

industrial disease. A disease or illness suffered by an employee as a result of working on an industrial process not as a result of an accident. Benefits are payable to the victims by the state under the Social Security (Industrial Injuries) (Prescribed Diseases) Regulations 1980. In addition the victim may have a right of action for damages against the employer for negligence or breach of statute. These diseases are often latent for many years and their long-tail nature has created particular problems for insurers. These diseases include asbestosis and mesothelioma

(associated with ships, boilers, motor trade); silicosis (mines and quarries); byssinosis (respiratory, cotton); tenosynovitis (conveyor work, pottery); lead poisoning (glass, scrap metal, lead); cancer; dermatitis; occupational deafness including tinnitus.

industrial life insurance/assurance. This is the business of effecting assurances on human life, the premiums in respect of which are received by means of collectors at intervals of less than two months. The most distinctive feature is the employment of agents (home service representatives) to collect premiums from the homes of the policyholders. Relevant legislation is the Industrial Assurance Act 1923, the Industrial Assurance and Friendly Societies Act 1948 (with a similar amending Act in 1958). The 1923 Act created the Industrial Assurance Commissioner, who is also the Registrar of Friendly Societies. The Registrar decides on disputes.

inevitable accident. An accident which cannot be avoided by the exercise of ordinary care, caution and skill. It therefore amounts to a defence to negligence or refers to a situation where negligence cannot be proved against the defendant.

infectious disease, murder and closure extension. An extension clause to a business interruption policy (qv) to protect the insured against interruption or interference with the business by infectious and contagious disease (AIDS is not covered), discovery of vermin at the premises causing restricted use, closure due to defective drains and sanitation, murder or suicide, or food poisoning affecting persons at the premises. The 'closure' aspect refers to closure by order of a competent authority due to defects in the drains or other sanitary arrangements at the premises. This extension is particularly relevant to hotels, etc. It also covers cancellation of bookings due to an outbreak of notifiable infectious or contagious diseases in the area.

'inflammable'. It means easily set on fire. Any property which by its presence in premises increases the risk of fire in those premises is inflammable. It has to do with the inherent nature and qualities of the goods.

in force. A policy is in force from the time of inception until the time of expiry unless previously cancelled.

ingestion damage. Damage caused when foreign objects (eg stones and grit from runways) are drawn into the airtake by the suction of the engine of an aircraft and are rotated around in contact with the rotating compressor blades. The risk applies mainly to turbo-jet and turbo-propeller engines. Even slight damage necessitates the complete stripping of the engine which often represents the major cost of repairs. Cover is normally included subject to a sizeable excess but damage caused by progressive deterioration over a period is usually excluded. Cover then applies to sudden damage attributable to a single recorded incident.

inhabited vehicles or vessels. For the purposes of burglary (qv) as defined by the Theft Act 1968 (qv), inhabited vehicles or vessels are 'buildings'.

inhabited vessels. *See* INHABITED VEHICLES.

inherent defect. *See* DECENNIAL INSURANCE.

inherent vice. The quality that something has to deteriorate or damage itself by natural processes without the operation of any external agency (eg food may rot). The resultant damage or reduction in value is not fortuitous and is therefore outside the scope of insurance. Under many property insurances, particularly those on an 'all risks' basis, the risk is excluded to put the matter beyond all doubt.

inheritance tax (IT). A UK tax on capital wealth or assets transferred to other persons (except a spouse) within seven years preceding the benefactor's death. There are certain exemptions from IT, eg gifts out of income; gifts to support certain relatives in need. Life insurance can be used to both minimise and pay the tax. The latter is important in that it provides liquid funds and obviates the forced disposal of assets, including business assets, as the means of raising the money to meet the tax liability.

injury to the environment. A definition that has its origin in an EC Directive. It means an important interference with the environment caused by a modification of the physical, chemical or biological conditions of water, soil and/or air in so far as these are not to be considered to be damage to property or death or physical injury. The intention is to make the polluter pay (qv) on a strict liability basis for this injury and for other forms of injury and damage.

injury to working partners clause. A clause in an employers' liability policy which brings injury to the proprietors of a partnership within the terms of the policy. It is relevant when two or more individuals jointly own and actively work in a partnership, ie they are unincorporated and do not run as a limited liability company. If a partner is injured at work due to the negligence of an employee or another partner, a standard employers' liability policy will not operate but the clause brings such injury into the policy subject otherwise to the terms and conditions of the policy. As a result the premium is calculated as if all partners were employees, ie their earnings must be included in the estimate and declarations relating to wages and salaries.

inn. Defined in the Hotel Proprietors Act 1956, s. 1(3), as an hotel, ie 'an establishment held out by the proprietor as offering food, drink and, if so required, sleeping accommodation, without special contract, to any traveller presenting himself who appears able and willing to pay a reasonable sum for the services provided . . . and who is in a fit state to be received'. The words 'without special contract' are important. In effect an inn is an establishment that is open to all and sundry and does not pick and choose its guests. The proprietor of such an establishment assumes special legal responsibilities (*see* INNKEEPER'S LIABILITY). Consequently for legal purposes hotels are either inns or private hotels (qv).

innkeeper. The proprietor of an inn (qv).

innkeeper's liability. An innkeeper (qv) cannot refuse food, drink or, if required, sleeping accommodation, to any traveller unless he appears unable or unwilling to pay or is unfit to be received. At common law the innkeeper's liability for the property of any traveller is strict but there is no liability for loss caused by the traveller himself, Act of God (qv), or action of Queen's enemy (war). The Hotel Proprietors Act 1956 (qv) limits this strict liability to £50 for any one article and £100 for any one guest provided the notice in the schedule of the Act is conspicuously displayed. Also the innkeeper will be fully liable for losses where (a) the property loss is due to fault of the proprietor or his staff, (b) the property had been deposited for safekeeping, (c) the property was offered for safekeeping but refused. There is no strict liability (liability could still arise in tort or under contract) for loss/damage to vehicles, the contents thereof, or any horse or other live animal or its harness or equipment. The Act also modifies the common law by confining the strict liability rule to the property only of those people who book sleeping accommodation, guests (qv). Others are mere travellers and liability for their property will depend on the ordinary rules of law, ie contract and tort.

'innocent' capacity. The acceptance of insurance or reinsurance business at very favourable but inadequate rates without a proper study or understanding of the risks involved. New and inexperienced insurers have been accused of providing innocent capacity and the naive acceptance of whole portfolios of business.

inquest. A judicial enquiry before a jury into any matter, particularly violent or sudden deaths. Liability insurers pay for the solicitor's fee for representation at any inquest or fatal enquiry (qv) in respect of any act causing or relating to any event that may be the subject of indemnity under the policy. A policy condition calls upon the insured (or his legal personal representatives) to give immediate notice once they have knowledge of an impending inquest or fatal enquiry. Proper representation of the insured is important and the insurer can also obtain copies of the coroner's depositions.

'in respect of'. Under liability policies the insured is indemnified in respect of accidental bodily injury and accidental property damage. This means that any damages and costs payable to a claimant must be related to the claimant's injury or damage but will include the financial losses flowing from the direct injury/damage, eg loss of earnings, loss of use etc.

'in respect of any one accident'. *See* ANY ONE ACCIDENT.

in-scheme AVCs. Additional voluntary contributions (qv) by a member of a pension scheme to an insurance company or building society chosen by his pension scheme, or to the scheme itself.

inspected classes. This expression refers to the different types or classes or plant and machinery in connection with engineering insurers provide an inspection/examination service. Broadly, this means: boiler and pressure plant; lifts, cranes and lifting machinery; and electrical and mechanical plant. *See* INSPECTION SERVICES and STATUTORY EXAMINATIONS.

inspection of records clause. A clause in a treaty reinsurance giving the reinsurer the right to inspect the records of the ceding office. The rights arising under this clause continue to apply after the termination of the contract and for as long as liability exists. The clause is used to give the reinsurer a degree of control now that it is no longer the usual practice to require premium and claims bordereaux.

inspection service. Engineering insurance normally includes an inspection service by engineer surveyors. There are detailed statutory requirements that call for periodic inspections of boilers and pressure vessels, lifts, cranes and other lifting plant etc. Engineering insurers provide this service in conjunction with insurance on the plant or item concerned. The insured can opt for more than the basic service that is just sufficient for statutory purposes. A full technical service, which will include advice, reports, tests and the like, is available from specialist insurers.

instalment monthly premium. In life insurance this is treated as an instalment of an annual premium so that, if a death occurs before all twelve instalments have been paid for the current year, the outstanding balance will be deducted from the claim payment. A loading is added to the annual premium to compensate for the loss of premium which is calculated on the assumption that it will be paid in advance. This approach is seldom used in view of the complications that arise under the Consumer Credit Act 1974.

Institute Agent. An agent appointed by the Institute of London Underwriters with authority to settle claims payable abroad.

Institute Clauses. Standard sets of clauses drafted by the Technical and Clauses Committee of the Institute of London Underwriters (qv). They are all used in the main forms of marine insurance and air cargo insurance written in London. The clauses are also adopted by many underwriters outside the UK. In marine insurance the clauses override many of the provisions of the Marine Insurance Act 1906 which otherwise governs the extent of the insurer's risk. On 1 January 1982 new clauses to be used with the new MAR form were introduced to replace more traditional clauses used with the SG form. The new cargo clauses are: the Institute Cargo Clauses (A) similar to the old Institute Cargo Clauses (All Risks); Institute Cargo Clauses (B) similar to the old Institute Cargo Clauses (With Average) but no longer tied to the memorandum (qv); the Institute Cargo Clauses (C) similar to the old Institute Cargo Clauses (Free from Particular Average). All these clauses exclude 'war' and 'strike' risks which are insurable under Institute War Clauses (Cargo) and Institute Strike Clauses (Cargo) also dated 1 January 1982. New Institute Time Clauses (Hulls), including those Total Loss Only, and Institute War and Strikes Clause (Hulls-Time) were introduced on 1 October 1983. Individual clauses have their own name, eg the Running Down Clause (qv). Similarly each group of clause in the Institute Cargo Clauses has a definitive title as follows:—(a) risks covered; (b) exclusions; (c) duration; (d) claims; (e) benefit of insurance; (f) minimising losses; (g) avoidance of delay; (h) law and practice.

Institute of Automotive Engineers Assessors. This is the professional organisation and qualifying body for those practising the profession of automotive engineer assessor. The Institute is incorporated and has the following objects: (a) to promote and develop for the public benefit the science of the design, manufacture and related technology of motor vehicles, and the science of repair of and risks arising from the use of road vehicles, and to further public education therein. (b) To advance the study of the said sciences, to promote research work therein and in related subjects, and to publish the results of such research. (c) To regulate for the public benefit the conduct of its members. (d) To make available to the public for the benefit thereof the expertise of its members in the said sciences.

Institute of Insurance Consultants (IIC). The IIC aims to enhance the status and ethical standards of insurance consultants and encourage, through advertising, the public to deal with its members. It can act as an arbitrator in disputes between members and act on behalf of a member in disputes with others. The council also arranges educational courses, lectures and social events.

Institute of London Underwriters. Founded in 1884 and the ILU has a world-wide influence but membership is confined to companies underwriting in the London market. The Institute acts as Secretary for the Technical and Clauses Committee which compiles and revises the standard Institute Clauses (qv). Lloyd's Underwriters Association and the Liverpool Underwriters Association are also members of the joint committee. The Institute is Secretary to other joint committees of Lloyd's and non-Lloyd's marine insurers. The Institute uses a combined policy form and a policy department signs policies on behalf of all members. The department also checks extra premiums and returns and provides central accounting. The Institute is an underwriting centre, a servicing office, and a trade association.

Institute of Risk Management. The Institute of Risk Management was set up in 1986 with a Court of Governors comprising nominees of the Association of Insurance and Risk Managers in the Industry and Commerce, the Institute of Chartered Secretaries and Administrators, the Health and Safety Executive, the Institution of Fire Engineers, the Institution of Occupational Safety and Health, the Institute of Industrial Security, the Chartered Insurance Institute and University and College risk management and insurance faculties. Its major objectives are to delineate a corpus of knowledge; to provide learning facilities; to hold examinations leading to professional qualifications; to promote post-qualification research and continuing professional education; to promote and safeguard the professional standing of its members.

Institute Warranties. Clauses designed by the Institute of London Underwriters and accepted as standard trading limits for shipping which is not engaged in regular services. Shipowners' insurances are invariably effected for periods of twelve months, and unless some stipulation were inserted in the policy, the insurer would be obliged to give world-wide cover and could become involved unwittingly in ships travelling in most hazardous waters. The alternative is that a full charge could be made for such travel to the detriment of shipowners not normally involved in such high risk situations. Accordingly trading warranties are introduced into shipowners' policies on hulls and other interests for the benefit of shipowners and underwriters. Such warranties may, for example, specify that the vessel is not insured while in the Great Lakes or St Laurence Seaway west of Montreal but cover can be arranged when it is required. Also a held covered (qv) provision in the Institute Time Clause No. 3 protects the insured in respect of breach of warranty as to cargo, trade, locality, towage, salvage services or date of sailing, provided notice is given and any additional premium paid.

instructions for the guidance of Lloyd's auditors. A document issued annually by the Council of Lloyd's with the approval of the Department of Trade and Industry. It provides instructions and guidance concerning Lloyd's solvency test and is accompanied by a covering letter which amplifies and explains the Instructions.

insurability. See INSURABLE RISK.

insurable interest. Insurable interest is an essential requirement for the validity of an insurance contract. Without such interest, the person insuring is 'wagering'. The Gaming Act 1845 makes wagers unenforceable in a court. The essentials of insurable interest, the legal right to insure, are: (a) there must be life or limb, property, potential liability, rights or financial interest capable of being covered; (b) such life or limb, property etc (as above) must be the subject-matter of the insurance; (c) the insured must be in a legally recognised relationship with the subject-matter of insurance whereby he benefits by its safety or absence of liability and is prejudiced by its damage or destruction or creation of liability. In order to preserve the principle of indemnity (qv), the insured must have an insurable interest, ie be out of pocket on the happening of the insured event. In marine insurance insurable interest must exist at the time of the loss but does not have to exist at inception (Marine Insurance Act, 1906). In life assurance the interest must exist at the inception but does not have to exist at the time of loss (*Dalby* v *The India & London Life Assurance Co.* (1845)). The general rule for other insurances is that interest should exist at the inception and the time of loss. See ASSIGNMENT for transfer of interest *and also see* LIFE ASSURANCE ACT 1774.

insurable risk. A risk that is capable of being insured. A risk is insurable when it contains the following elements: (a) it is measurable in financial terms (*see* SENTIMENTAL VALUE for an uninsurable risk); (b) an insurable interest (qv); (c) it exists in large homogeneous groups (*see* RISK COMBINATION); (d) it is possible for the probability of loss to be calculated; (e) it is a pure risk (qv); (f) it is of an entirely fortuitous nature; (g) it is not against public policy (qv) to insure it; (h) its transfer can be achieved at a reasonable premium in relation to the financial risk of the individual; (i) it is not so widespread as to be beyond the scope of private enterprise insurance (certain fundamental risks (qv) eg property damage on land during war are not insurable. An uninsurable risk (qv) is one which fails to meet these or nearly all of these elements.

insurance. Insurance is both a system of risk transfer (qv) and risk combination (qv). By combining a large number of exposure units into a group the insurer can predict the probability of loss relating to uncertain events with a reasonable degree of accuracy for the group as a whole and so spread the loss evenly over the group. The degree of uncertainty for the group is reduced but simply combining individuals in a group does nothing to change the uncertainty for the individual. The insurer can through knowledge of the probable incidence of loss for the group offer each individual the opportunity of risk transfer (qv). The individual can transfer the risk of a possibly large loss to the insurer by payment of a premium and so convert the uncertainty of a possible large loss into the certainty of a smaller but fixed annual cost. Not all risks are insurable. See insurable risks (qv) to see the essential elements of an insurable risk. *See* CONTRACT OF INSURANCE for the legal definition.

insurance agent. *See* AGENTS and IMPUTED KNOWLEDGE.

insurance broker. A full-time specialist intermediary offering a service on the basis of a reasonable standard of professional expertise and competence. The broker offers advice and arranges the insurance normally as agent for the insured but is usually remunerated by a commission from the insurer. It is illegal for anyone to use the term 'insurance broker' unless registered with the Insurance Brokers Registration Council (qv).

Insurance Brokers (Registration) Act 1977. This created the Insurance Brokers Registration Council which regulates the insurance broking industry. The Act restricts the use of the term 'insurance broker' (reinsurance broker) to individuals and companies that have respectively registered and enrolled with the Council. To secure registration an individual must have a recognised qualification (ACII or FCII) or have had relevant employment for at least 5 years (2 years if previously a full-time agent). In addition the individual must have had 'suitable work experience'. To trade as a broker an individual or a company must effect

(i) professional indemnity insurance; (ii) observe certain accounting practices and conditions designed to ensure the solvency of the undertaking; (iii) observe a code of conduct; (iv) be independent. In the case of limited companies (enrolled bodies corporate (qv)) at least half of the directors must be registered brokers.

Insurance Brokers Registration Council. *See* INSURANCE BROKERS (REGISTRATION) ACT 1977.

Insurance Broking Account. A trading insurance broker or an enrolled body corporate (qv) must maintain a bank account (IBA) for the receipt and payment of insurance transactions monies. Each such account must be designated 'Insurance Broking Account', the use of which is restricted by rule 6 of the Insurance Brokers Registration Council (Accounts and Business Requirements) Rules 1979 or, in the case of a Lloyd's broker, by the rules governing Lloyd's brokers.

insurance companies. Insurance suppliers who are constituted as companies. This includes: (a) Proprietary companies. These are limited liability generally constituted under the Companies Act with a subscribed share capital. The shareholders have the ultimate rights to the profits but in the case of a life insurance company provision has to be made for a share of the profits to go to 'with profits' policyholders. (b) Mutual companies. These are notionally owned by the policyholders who share in the distributable profits in proportion to the sums assured and conditions of their policies. Such companies are fairly common in life assurance. Otherwise, the policyholders expect to take their profit in the form of lower premiums. Many mutual companies are now organised as companies limited by guarantee.

Insurance Companies Act 1982. The major statute governing insurers, the Act specifies the requirements a company must fulfil to gain authorisation, the annual accounting and disclosure standards that must be met, 'fit and proper' criteria for directors and controllers and the margin of solvency (qv) requirements. There are also wide ranging supervisory powers and sanctions enabling the Secretary of State to require an insurance company to disclose information and records, the power to restrict new business, order an actuarial investigation and report and, in the extreme, to order a company to cease trading. The Act embraces two sets of regulations: Insurance Companies Regulations 1981 (qv) and Insurance Companies (Accounts and Statements) Regulations 1983 (qv).

Insurance Companies (Accounts and Statements) Regulations 1983. These set out the rules for the completion and submission of annual returns to the Department of Trade and Industry. With the shareholder accounts, the DTI returns are subject to audit and are filed by the DTI at the Registrar of Companies to be available for inspection.

Insurance Companies (Advertisements) (Amendment) Regulations 1983. This regulates that where an insurer trades in another member state of the EEC but its UK activities are not authorised, its advertisements must carry a warning that the Policyholders' Protection Act 1975 (qv) cannot be invoked.

Insurance Companies Regulations 1981. These cover: authorisation; solvency margins and deposits; the matching, localisation and valuation of assets; determination of liabilities; rules governing advertisements.

insurance cycle. The swing that occurs periodically between hard and soft markets (qv). In a hard market premiums are high and terms are stringent and underwriting may be profitable. These conditions attract new entrants into the market and the increased competition eventually drives rates down and terms of cover become less onerous. Eventually when business has ceased to be profitable capacity is withdrawn from the market and the cycle is reversed. The situation can be affected by high interest rates which draw companies into the market to gain access to funds with which to earn good financial returns from the use of the cash (see CASH FLOW UNDERWRITING). Losses become more tolerable in the short run and the soft market conditions extend for longer periods of time.

insurance-guarantee. In fidelity guarantee insurance (qv) three parties are involved: The insurer, as surety (guarantor), the insured, the party, eg an employer, for whose protection the policy or bond is given, and the person guaranteed (qv) whose fidelity or undertaking is the subject of the policy or bond. The relationship between the insurer and the insured is based on an insurance-guarantee and the duty of utmost good faith (qv) is the same as that applicable to ordinary insurance contracts. This is not so with a pure guarantee (qv) which is the nature of the contract between the insurer and the person guaranteed. If the insured is a party to or privy to the application of the person guaranteed then the insured will assume responsibility for any information that is withheld.

insurance history. The previous insurance record of the insured or proposer. Adverse or unsatisfactory insurance history attaching to a proposer is material (see UTMOST GOOD FAITH and must be disclosed to the insurer. Where proposal forms are used it is customary for the insurer to include questions enquiring as to present insurances; previous declinatures; imposition by previous insurers of special terms or increased premiums; refusals to renew; cancellations. Each question focuses on typical responses that may have been made by previous insurers to an unsatisfactory record or history. The information is material and has to be disclosed irrespective of whether proposal forms are used or whether particular questions are asked.

Insurance Ombudsman Bureau. The bureau—IOB—was created by a number of leading composite insurance companies to provide an independent body to arbitrate upon claims disputes between 'personal' policyholders and member companies. It is a consumer protection measure and does not entertain disputes on business insurances. Industrial life policies are also excluded from the scheme (see INDUSTRIAL ASSURANCE COMMISSIONER. Member companies accept the Ombudsman's decision as binding up to £100 000 provided always the policyholder suspends legal action. The policyholder is not precluded from subsequent legal action if dissatisfied with the decision. Not all insurers are members of this voluntary bureau. Some companies belong to the Personal Insurance Arbitration Service.

insure. To buy or supply insurance.

insured. The party who has acquired the insurance and will be entitled to enforce a claim under the policy as a party to the contract. The insured is also known as the assured and policyholder.

insured's representative clause. A clause appearing in liability policies to the effect that in the event of the insured's death the insurers will continue the cover in favour of the deceased's personal representatives subject to compliance by them with the terms of the policy. *See* PERSONAL REPRESENTATIVE.

insurer. A body or person authorised to supply insurance.

insurer concerned. Insurers who, under the Motor Insurers' Bureau's (qv) Domestic Agreement, settle a third party claim because at the time of the accident a policy issued by them was in force in respect of the defendant. The payment is made notwithstanding that the defendant, by reason of breach of policy, had no valid right to indemnity under the policy. As insurer concerned the insurers carry the loss and are not reimbursed by the MIB although they have a right of recovery against the uninsured motorist himself.

insurer's option. Under material damage insurances the insurer reserves the right to provide the indemnity by monetary payment, repair, reinstatement or replacement. In the absence of a clause to this effect the insured is entitled to demand a cash payment. The insurer loses the option if he fails to exercise his alternative rights in a reasonable period of time. An insurer who, by a course of action, has indicated that he favours a particular course of action, may be estopped from choosing any alternative course.

In motor insurance the insured may be able to demand a new car where a new for old clause is included (eg when repair costs of cars less than 12 months old exceed a certain percentage (eg 50 per cent) of the list price).

insuring clause. An alternative term for operative clause (qv).

insurrection. This implies 'combination with a view to understanding government authority'. (F.H. Jones, *The Law of Accident and Contingency Insurance*, Pitman). It was defined in *Lindsay and Pirie* v *General Accident, Fire and Life Assurance Corporation Ltd* (1914) as a 'rising of the people in open resistance against established authority with the object of supplanting it'.

integrated pollution control (IPC). This is established by the Environmental Protection Act 1990. IPC is operated by Her Majesty's Inspectorate of Pollution (HMIP). It regulates the major polluting processes. About 3500 sites are subject to IPC and include oil refineries, major iron and steel works, and large chemical works. IPC represents the replacement of the present system of separate pollution controls by a single system covering discharges from major industrial processes to all environmental media. The aim is to anticipate changes in pollution control technology, risk assessment and public concern. It provides industry with 'one-stop' authorisation. Once an operator gets a certificate of authorisation for an IPC process then he needs no other form of authorisation and will not have to deal separately with other regulatory agencies.

intellectual property. This means the exclusive rights over the use of patents, copyright, trademarks, service marks, merchandise marks, registered designs, intellectual property secrecy or confidentiality agreements. Some of these risks can be included under commercial legal expenses policies (qv) if it includes an intellectual property section. The cover may include the legal costs of pursuing or defending the insured's legal rights, including appeal or defence of appeal against judgment in respect of disputes relating to (a) any licence agreement disclosed to the insured relating to intellectual property; or (b) registered trademarks, registered service marks or registered designs disclosed to the insured, or copyright or passing-off, where the matter is not the subject of a licence agreement between the insured and the other party involved in the dispute.

intention of parties rule. A rule of construction to the effect that where possible the words of the policy must be construed liberally so as to give effect to the intention of the parties. The object of the parties is to make a contract of insurance and consequently any construction that leads to a result which is absurd or otherwise manifestly contrary to the real intention of the parties is not to be adopted. (An exception is a personal accident policy of wilful exposure to unnecessary danger which, if literally interpreted, would exclude the majority of accidents as everyone who travels by land, sea or air exposes himself to danger and if he does so in the course of a holiday, he does so unnecessarily.) The words must be construed with qualifications. But the words are not to be extended beyond their ordinary meaning in order to embrace a case which is within the object of the parties.

interest clause. A clause in a reinsurance contract under which the reinsurer and the reinsured share any interest awarded on damages in proportion to their respective shares of the actual loss in those cases where the reinsured's net loss exceeds £200 000. In long-tail liability business large claims may take years to settle and interest may be awarded.

interest covers. An insurance that goes one stage further than advance rent insurance (qv) by providing cover in respect of loss related to interest payable or receivable by the developer whose additional loss stems from having capital tied up in the project.

interim bonus. A life insurance bonus calculated and paid at the time of a claim on with profits policies maturing or becoming the subject of a death claim during the interval between two bonus declarations. The bonus is usually the

last declared bonus or even less.

intermediary. A 'middleman' through whom the insurance is arranged. Intermediaries are agents some of whom are registered brokers who take on a professional responsibility in advising, arranging and placing the insurance, while others do little more than provide introductions between the insurer and the insured. Financial intermediaries have to be authorised under the Financial Service Act 1986 (qv). *Also see* AGENTS AND INTRODUCERS.

internal dependencies. The risks of loss to a business or other organisation that have their origin in internal activities and situations, eg production runs. *See also* EXTERNAL DEPENDENCIES.

internal risks insurance. The name given to the motor trader's version of a public liability policy. Custody and control of customers' cars and the nature of the work renders the general policy form unsuitable. Cover may or may not exclude loss or damage to customers' cars, depending on the option chosen by the insured, as well as general third party risks. Defective workmanship and sale of parts can be included in the cover.

international motor insurance certificate. *See* GREEN CARD.

International Union of Aviation Insurers. The official body that represents the interests of aviation insurers. It provides a central office for the circulation of information between members. The Union also seeks to provide a better understanding and conduct of international aviation. Membership is open to pools, groups, or associations whose participants are engaged in aviation insurance on a direct or reinsurance basis. In exceptional circumstances aviation insurance companies may be considered for membership.

interruption reports. Reports that set out the findings of surveys of the potential interruption of a business as a result of fire, breakdown or any other peril covered or to be covered. They are the business interruption (qv) equivalent of a fire survey. Broadly, the report covers three aspects: (a) the effect of 'damage', (b) how long it will take to recover from the interruption, (c) how the insured might be assisted to keep the business going during the period of interruption. The report will assist in fixing the rate, the assessment of the estimated maximum loss (EML), and provide opportunities for risk improvement. The report should take account of the effect of interruption at all premises that will affect the interruption risk such as suppliers and customers.

intervening cause (*novus actus interveniens*). A new cause that intervenes into a sequence of events which is not the reasonable, natural or probable consequence of the cause which precedes it. It is an independent cause which breaks the chain of causation. Even if the chain started with an insured peril there will be no liability for losses occurring after the occurrence of the intervening cause which changes the outcome and destroys the cause and effect relationship between the insured peril and the loss. *See* PROXIMATE CAUSE.

intervention in the affairs of an insurance company. The act of the Secretary of State in pursuance of powers under the Insurance Companies Acts in intervening into the affairs of an insurance company and imposing conditions as to the conduct of that company's business. He may do so when he feels it is desirable for the protection of policyholders, or future policyholders, against the risk that the company may not be able to meet its liabilities or, in the case of long-term business, fulfil their reasonable expectations. Other reasons for intervention are belief that the company has not complied with a statutory provision; it has supplied misleading or inaccurate information; unsatisfactory reinsurance arrangements; loss of eligibility for authorisation; substantial departure from planned operations; cessation of authorisation in EC where the company has its head office or made its deposit. The Secretary of State can petition the court for a winding-up order, impose limits as to premium income, call for actuarial investigations, accelerate the provision of accounting information, call for specified information and the production of documents, impose requirements about investments which cover liabilities, require that assets be maintained in the UK, prohibit the writing of new business, etc.

'in transit'. It is the primary intention of the goods in transit insurer to cover goods while in transit and temporarily housed during the course of transit. Transit begins when the goods start to move, ie when they are loaded. The insurer, who contended, when a loss occurred after loading but before commencement of the journey, that the goods were not yet in transit failed in that contention. The transit started with movement of the goods (*Sadler Bros. Co.* v *Meredith* (1963). In *Crows Transport* v *Phoenix* (1965) it was held that, unless the policy otherwise provides, transit commences the moment the carrier accepts the goods. Transit does not end when the vehicle reaches it destination. In *Tomlinson* v *Hepburn* (1961) it was held that transit only came to an end when the unloading was completed.

introducers. In terms of the conduct of investment business (qv) following the Financial Services Act 1986 (qv) an introducer is a person, firm or corporation whose role is simply to introduce a client to an authorised independent financial adviser (qv) in return for a commission. The introducer must not give any investment advice except discreet advice to the effect that the client should consider making an investment and recommending a suitably authorised individual or firm he may consult.

introductory discount. A discount allowed to a proposer for private car insurance who has a claims-free driving record but not gained a no claim bonus (qv) in his own right. Usually such persons have gained experience driving cars other than their own and therefore had their own policies.

introductory examination. An examination designed by the Chartered Insurance Institute for those wishing to sit the ACII examination but who lack the necessary direct entry requirements.

For this reason it does not provide a professional qualification in its own right. From 1992 students will take the Certificate of Proficiency (qv).

invalid 'contracts'. *See* ILLEGAL CONTRACTS , UNENFORCEABLE CONTRACTS, VOID CONTRACTS, VOIDABLE CONTRACTS.

invalid carriages. Mechanically-propelled vehicles with an unladen weight not exceeding 5 cwt, which have been specially designed and constructed for the use of persons suffering from some physical defect or disability and used solely by such persons. They do not have to be insured in respect of the compulsory insurance requirements of the Road Traffic Act. Motor insurers offer special rates for these vehicles, area of use is immaterial, and driving of other cars (qv) is excluded.

inventory and valuation clause. A clause that may be attached to a household contents policy to provide a basis for the settlement of losses and obviate the later production of evidence of value by the insured. At the inception of the policy the insured supplies a list (ie an inventory) of his household goods and personal effects and a value is assigned to each item by an independent valuer. It provides evidence of value at the policy date, but in the event of a claim due allowance will be made for depreciation if the policy is on a normal indemnity basis.

investment agreement. An agreement to provide services regulated by the Financial Services Act 1986 (qv). The Act prohibits intermediaries from entering into such an agreement with any client by way of an unsolicited call. This type of call, subject to some exceptions, includes mail shots, telephone calls, visits, and advertisements (except the 'off the page'). The exceptions which arise under IBRC and FIMBRA rules relate to the sale of collective investments; life insurance policies; pension contracts; and management contracts for pension funds. These exceptions are, however, covered by strict rules relating to communications and visits.

investment bond. A unit-linked single premium bond (qv).

investment business. A wide definition is given in the Financial Services Act 1986 (qv) (Part 1, Schedule 1). It includes investment in: company stocks and shares; debentures; Government and other public securities; units in collective investment schemes; long-term life insurances; options, futures, etc. The 'business' activities governed by the Act (Part II, Schedule 1) include: dealing in shares; arranging investment deals; managing investments; providing investment advice; establishing, operating or winding up a collective investment scheme. For most consumers 'investment' is putting money into a life policy, a pension, a unit or investment trust, and stocks and shares. Excluded from the definition of investment business are shares in building societies, straightforward banking instruments (cheques, bank accounts, letters of credit, leases and normal property dealings. Certain policies, ie most non-convertible level or reducing term insurance are not regarded as investment. Permanent health insurance is likewise outside the scope of the Act unless they contain a profit element or have a surrender value. Income from such policies is therefore excluded from the IBRC's assessment of the intermediary's income from investment activities. Not all independent financial advisers are able to transact the same sort of business. There are in fact eight categories which can be grouped into four main areas: advising on investments; arranging and transacting life, pensions and unit trust contracts; arranging and transacting other types of investment; and managing investments. All advisers must have to have printed copies of their status available.

investment income. The part of an insurer's income that comes from the interest and dividends on its investments in financial assets (eg equities and government bonds) and the return on any other investment (eg property) into which it has put its funds.

Investment Management Regulatory Organisation (IMRO). A Self-Regulatory Organisation (qv) which regulates investment managers, eg firms where the sole or main activity of the member firm or where the member firm holds itself out as offering discretionary management services distinct from other activities. Other investment managers in this SRO include firms engaged in:

the management and operation of collective investment schemes; acting as trustee (or the overseas equivalent of trustee) of regulated collective investment schemes (eg authorised unit trusts); in-house pension fund management and acting as pension fund trustee (in so far as authorisation is needed); investment advice (other than corporate advice) to institutional or other corporate customers; and advising on and arranging investment deals where this is incidental to the main investment management activity of the member firm.

investment trust. A company that invests in stocks and shares bought with the capital subscribed by shareholders, retained profits and loan finance. The shares of the trust are available only to the extent that existing shareholders are prepared to sell the whole or a part of their holdings.

investors' compensation fund. *See* FINANCIAL SERVICES COMPENSATION FUND.

issue risk policy. A reversioner (the owner of property which will revert to him on the determination of a particular estate, eg death of a life tenant) or someone else with a reversionary interest (a right in property, the enjoyment of which is deferred) may suffer loss for instance by the birth of a child or children to the life tenant. An insurance to cover this and other losses arising from the birth of a child is called an issue risk policy and is issued in the life department sometimes as a contract of indemnity.

J

Jamaica earthquake. A term applied to the proximate cause (qv) case of *Tootal, Broadhurst, Lee Co* v *London and Lancs* (1908) which concerned a claim for fire damage following an earthquake in Jamaica in 1907. Fire broke out in premises occupied by Curphey, allegedly due to an earthquake, and fire spread naturally to burn down the insured building. The policy excluded fire due to earthquake. It was held that as the fire spread naturally, the proximate cause was the earthquake and the indemnity, therefore, did not operate.

Jane's 'All the World's Aircraft'. An annual publication containing information of value to underwriters. It contains photographs, descriptions, and performance details of the majority of civil and military aircraft and engines in current production and/or under development.

Janson clause. A clause that applies an excess (qv) to a marine policy. It is most likely to be applied when insuring hazardous goods or where hull particular average (qv) claims are likely to be frequent.

jettison. The throwing overboard of part of the cargo or gear of the ship to lighten the load and save the ship when endangered. The owner of jettisoned goods is entitled to 'general average' (qv), but without prejudice to the insurer's liability for a loss by jettison. When cargo is carried on deck it is usual to state specifically that the risk of jettison is covered as, unless the goods are so carried in accordance with trade custom (eg timber), insurers assume them to be stored in the hold.

jeweller's block policy. Broad policies covering jeweller's stock and goods in trust on an 'all risks' basis subject to exceptions.

joint and several liability. Where two or more parties are liable jointly and severally for the loss or obligation, each party is liable severally, ie on an individual basis, for the whole of the loss but at the same time all are liable jointly. A plaintiff can sue one or more severally, or all jointly, at his option. *See* JOINT TORTFEASORS.

Joint Cargo Committee. A committee of Lloyd's and insurance company underwriters concerned with the general welfare of marine cargo insurance in connection with which it makes recommendations to the market to provide a framework for the underwriting of cargo business.

Joint Contracts Tribunal (JCT). A group representing various bodies with an interest in building contracts, notably the Royal Institute of British Architects, that has combined to produce the standard form of building contract and variations thereof. The principal contracts are: JCT Standard Form of Building Contract 1980 edition (qv) amended in 1986; the Nominated Sub-Contracts NSC/4 and NSC/4a 1980 edition; the Standard Form with Contractor's Design 1980 edition; the Intermediate Form of Building Contract 1984 edition; JCT Management Contract 1987; the Standard Form of Sub-Contract Conditions for Named Sub-Contracts under the Intermediate Form—NAM/SC edition. All contain clauses relating to obligations and insurance matters.

JCT 80 Standard Form of Building Contract with 1986 amendments. The principal clauses affecting insurers are: (i) *Clause 20.1.* This is an indemnity clause (qv). The Contractor indemnifies the Employer for personal injury claims unless the Contractor can show that they were caused by the Employer's negligence. The indemnity is unlimited in amount. If an Employer is partly at fault, he will be indemnified to the extent that he was not at fault. Under 20.2, except for certain loss/damage (eg damage to the contract works the subject of clause 22C), the Contractor must indemnify the Employer against property damage claims provided that the damage has been caused by the negligence of the Contractor or his sub-contractors. In this instance the onus of proof is on the Employer. The Employer can recover to the 'extent' that the loss/damage is due to the Contractor's negligence so that contributory negligence by the Employer is not fatal to the Employer's indemnity. (ii) *Clause 21.1.* This is an 'insuring clause' obliging the Contractor to insure his liabilities under 20.1 and 20.2. The clause does not require the insurance to indemnify the Employer directly. The Contractor must also ensure that his sub-contractors arrange suitable insurances. (iii) *Clause 21.2.* A property developer (*Gold* v *Patman & Fotheringham* (1958)) was unindemnified when damage was caused to property adjoining the property worked upon by his contractors who were guilty of no negligence. 21.2 seeks to close the gap by securing 'non-negligent' third party cover. The Contractor is obliged, when the contract so directs, to effect an insurance in joint names but for the benefit of the Employer alone. The limit of indemnity is stated in the contract and the cover is against 'nuisance' perils only, eg collapse, subsidence, vibration, weakening/removal of support, lowering of ground water, and heave. (iv) *Clause 22.* This concerns insurance of the contract works. 22A applies to the erection of new buildings where the Contractor is obliged to effect 'All Risks' (defined in JCT 22.2) in joint names. 22B applies to new buildings where the Employer has elected to effect the All Risks insurance in joint names. This is mainly used when the Employer is a local authority or large corporation capable of securing cover more cheaply than through the Contractor. 22C applies to alterations or extensions to existing structures and causes the Employer to effect insurance on the existing structures and contents against Specified Perils while insuring the new work on an All Risks basis. (v) Clause 22D is an 'insuring clause' which may be required by the terms of the contract in respect of the Employer's loss of liquidated damages (qv). The Contractor may be obliged to obtain quotations and then effect the insurance. The aim is to protect the Employer for losses due to delays in completion caused by specified perils (fire, lightning, explosion, storm, tempest, flood, bursting or overflowing of water tanks, apparatus or pipes, earthquake, aircraft and other aerial devices or articles dropped therefrom, riot and civil commotion). Architects commonly grant the Contractors an extension of the contract date given delays caused by these perils with consequent loss of liquidated damages to the Employer. The amount spent by the Contractor on this insurance are added to the contract sum (clause 22D.4).

JCT intermediate form of building contract (IFC 84). This is intended for building works of a simple nature. It involves recognised basic trades but no service building installations or specialist work. This form is used for contracts too large to be categorised as minor works but without the complexities that normally demand the use of the JCT 80 standard form of contract. Clauses are similar to those of JCT 80. Clause 6 deals with indemnities and insurance.

JCT agreement for minor building works. This is used for uncomplicated works where the contract value at 1981 prices does not exceed £50 000 and the Employer appoints an architect or supervising officer. Clause 6 deals with indemnities and insurance.

JCT other contracts forms. These include JCT with Contractors' Design for design and build contracts and the JCT Management Contract 1987. The latter is the result of the procurement of building contracts by management contracting. All forms contain insurance provisions.

Joint Hull Committee. A committee of Lloyd's and insurance company underwriters concerned with problems related to, and the development of, marine hull insurance. It makes recommendations on rating and conditions to the market. The Committee administers the Joint Hull Understandings (qv). It also issues a Scale of Returns that underwriters can apply in respect of returns of premium for certain vessels which have been laid up or where the insurance has been terminated before expiry.

Joint Hull Returns Bureau. A bureau under the auspices of the Joint Hull Committee (qv) which handles and approves applications from shipowners for returns of premium, eg laid-up returns.

joint hull survey. A hull survey undertaken jointly by a surveyor representing the insurer and another surveyor representing the insured.

Joint Hull Understandings. A market agreement to provide a framework for the underwriting of hull business in London. The agreement is administered by the Joint Hull Committee (qv). The aim is to achieve some uniformity of practice by means of recommendations but the understandings do not provide rates or a basis of rating. The understandings are reviewed annually and, *inter alia*, give guidance on the treatment of renewals of business where the results have generally been regarded as unsatisfactory.

joint insured clause. A clause stating the contract of insurance is made between the insurer and more than one other party. The other parties will be jointly insured. In liability insurance it is customary to add a cross-liabilities (qv) clause.

Joint Liability Committee. Established in 1974 as a joint committee of the Institute of London Underwriters it was originally called the Joint Carriers' Liability. It co-ordinates the work of market representatives on a number of bodies, such as the International Chamber of Commerce, dealing with maritime liabilities and documentation. It was active in the consultations that preceded the adoption of the Hamburg Rules in 1978, and the adoption of the multi-modal convention (regulating the contractual relationship in transport involving more than one mode of carriage) by UNCTAD in 1980. The committee also participates in the work of the British Maritime Law Association (qv).

joint life annuity. *See para (g) under* ANNUITY.

joint life and survivor annuity. *See para. (h) under* ANNUITY.

joint life insurance. Life insurance policies dependent on two or more lives that become payable on the first death. Policies may be whole life, endowment or term.

joint surveys. Fire surveys are sometimes undertaken by two surveyors. Where a risk is very large and shared by two or more insurers (co-insurance) the lead insurer normally undertakes the survey but on some occasions may involve the insurer holding the next largest proportion. A joint survey may occur where one insurer surveys the building and another company the contents. It may also occur where a fire surveyor is accompanied by a specialist surveyor (eg sprinkler leakage specialist). In other instances, the company surveyor may be accompanied by the broker's surveyor.

Joint Technical and Clauses Committee (JTCC). Formed by the Aviation Insurance Office Association (AIOA) and Lloyd's Aviation Underwriter's Association (LAUA). It is mainly concerned with the drafting of wordings and clauses.

joint tenancy. The ownership of property in common by two or more persons where there is a right of survivorship, ie where on the death of one joint owner the property as a whole vests in the survivor(s) and can only be disposed of by will of the last survivor. Joint tenancy is assumed unless there is evidence to the contrary. Joint life policies (qv) are usually owned as joint tenants. *See* TENANCY IN COMMON.

joint tortfeasors. Persons are joint tortfeasors (wrongdoers) when liable for the same tort (qv). Examples are: (i) Vicarious liability where a master is liable for the tort of his servant. (ii) Agency where the principal is liable for the agent's tort. (iii) Common action where two or more people join forces to commit the same wrongful act. Joint tortfeasors attract joint and several liability (qv). At common law a judgment obtained against one joint wrongdoer released all others liable jointly for the same tort, even if it was unsatisfied. This rule was abolished by the Law Reform (Married Women and Tortfeasors) Act 1935, s. 6(1)(a). At common law no joint tortfeasor had any right of indemnity or contribution from another. This rule was abolished by the above Act, s. 6(1)(c). The position is now governed by the Civil Liability (Contribution) Act 1978 (qv). Any person liable for damage suffered by a third party may recover a contribution in respect of that damage whether the other person's liability is joint with the first party's liability or not. (Act of 1978 s. 1(1).) Where the liability is not joint the parties are several concurrent tortfeasors and this arises where separate torts result in one unit of damage, eg in the *Koursk* (1924) the separate negligent acts of two ships combined to inflict damage on a third. The amount recoverable is the amount that is equitable having regard to each party's share of responsibility for the damage (s. 2(3)).

joint torts. Damage may result from the torts of two or more defendants who may be (i) joint tortfeasors (qv) or, (ii) several concurrent tortfeasors (*see* JOINT TORTFEASORS).

judicial delay. A special scheme insuring against the additional costs incurred by a litigant following the delay or postponement of a court hearing. Cover operates for non-appearance of the judge, a presiding official or counsel due to illness or for any other reason.

jumbo risk. A risk accepted by an insurer that is far greater than normal. The term appears to have originated in the USA when reinsurance first enabled fire insurers, as a matter of common practice, to write much larger gross lines. As far as the individual insurer is concerned a jumbo risk is any risk that is inconveniently large and potentially dangerous on account of its size.

jurisdiction. 1. The power of a court or judge to entertain an action, petition or other proceeding. 2. The district or limits within which the judgments or orders of a court can be enforced or executed. The territorial jurisdiction of the High Court of Justice is over England and Wales. *See also* JURISDICTION CLAUSE.

jurisdiction clause. A clause in a policy specifying which nation's laws will apply to a dispute and in whose courts any action will be heard. Liability policies often specify that any action for damages against the insured, even though the injury or damage occurred in overseas territories, must be brought in a court of law in Great Britain, Northern Ireland, the Channel Islands or the Isle of Man (eg the employers' liability policy which covers liability for injury to employees while temporarily working outside the stated geographical limits).

justification. A defendant may plead that the actions that form the basis of the case against him were justified. In a libel case, the plea of justification admits the publication of the words said to be defamatory but pleads that they are true in substance and in fact.

K

keeper. The person upon whom liability is imposed under the Animals Act 1971, s. 2. (qv). The keeper is the person who owns the animal or has it in his possession, or is the head of the household of which a member under the age of 16 owns it or has it in his possession. If a person ceases to own or have possession of the animal he will remain the keeper until such time as another person becomes the keeper. A person who takes possession of an animal to prevent it from causing damage or to return it to its owner does not, merely by so doing, become a keeper.

keyman insurance. A life or 'accident or health' insurance effected by a business on a person whose death or disablement would adversely affect the profitability of the business. In theory an employer's interest in the life of an employee is limited to the employee's salary for the period of notice but in practice insurers are prepared to issue policies on key employees for far greater sums. The policy sum then compensates for such as: abandoned projects, restarted projects, cost of recruitment and training, diminution in profits following the interruption caused by death or disablement.

keys clause. A clause in a theft policy stating the 'cash in safe' cover will not operate if the safe keys are left on the premises when the premises are closed for business.

kidnap and ransom insurance. A form of cover thought by some to be contrary to public policy. Policies are required only by those who see themselves as 'target risks' and inevitably this means some selection against the insurer. It is a condition of the policy that its existence is never disclosed and cover is made subject to a substantial excess or co-insurance clause (eg 10 per cent of the ransom sum). It is illegal to effect this type of cover for any organisation in Ulster. Kidnap and ransom cover is also available at Lloyd's for valuable bloodstock.

King and Queen Granaries case. The name by which the leading case of *North British & Mercantile Insurance Co.* v *Liverpool, London & Globe Insurance Co.* (1877) is known. Following trade custom wharfingers, Barnett & Co., effected insurance with the L.L. & G. on grain held by them, in trust or on commission, for which they were responsible. Part of the grain belonged to Rodocanachi & Co. who insured it with the N.B. & M. Both policies contained a contribution clause under which each insurer sought to limit its liability to its rateable proportion of any loss in the event of contribution (qv) applying. A fire occurred and both policies were sufficient to cover their respective insured. In the ensuing action it was held that: (a) the wharfingers, being primarily liable, must bear the whole loss and, in the event of the merchants receiving indemnity from their insurers, the latter would be entitled to recover from the party primarily liable; (b) contribution did not apply as this arises only when more than one policy covers the same interest. In this case two separate interests were covered—therefore the insurers covering the person primarily liable must bear the whole loss. As a result of this decision some insurers entered into claims sharing agreements to disregard the respective rights and liabilities of the insured parties and put contribution into effect.

knock-for-knock agreement. A forbearance agreement between two motor insurers designed to reduce administrative expense and avoid legal action. If two vehicles are in a collision each insurer agrees to pay for the damage to the vehicle of its respective insured (provided it is liable under a comprehensive policy) without regard as to who was to blame for the collision. Special provisions exist in respect of: emergency treatment fees (qv); accidents to vehicles in the custody of motor traders; fleet vehicles insured on a third party basis—the partial indemnity clause. Under this clause if a fleet vehicle insured for third party collides with a comprehensively insured vehicle, the fleet insurer pays 50 per cent of the other insurer's repair costs. If cover is comprehensive with an excess greater than £100 regardless of liability, the insurer of the fleet-rated vehicle will pay 50 per cent of the repairs to the other vehicle up to 50 per cent of the excess. If cover is comprehensive with an excess less than £100, the knock-for-knock agreement will operate in the normal way. As many fleets are insured third party only, this clause addresses the problem of imbalance between insurers that arises where one has a greater preponderance of third party insurances than the other and would unduly benefit from the knock for knock agreement. Claims paid solely because of the agreement do not normally affect the insured's entitlement to no claim bonus (qv).

'know your client'. A specific requirement placed on independent financial advisers (qv), company representatives (qv), and appointed representatives (qv). They are required to take all reasonable steps to elicit from the clients the personal and financial information needed to enable them to discharge their services properly from the client's point of view. In practice this means obtaining a profile or client information form (qv) with the assurance to the client that all information supplied is totally confidential. The form can also be used to note instances where the client has declined to give information. It is not usually necessary to make these enquiries if the client is a professional investor or an execution only client (qv), but clear written instructions should be obtained from such clients. Also the enquiries do not have to been made where a client enters into a transaction as a result of an advertisement which sells 'off the page'. These advertisements are subject to tight controls and are rarely placed by financial intermediaries. Where the intermediary has been approached by a third party to effect a transaction for that third party's client, the circumstances may be such that the intermediary can reasonably assume that neither the third party nor his client is relying upon the intermediary to advise the client or exercise judgment on his behalf. In these circumstances the know your client and best advice (qv) requirements are not so demanding.

L

labour gangs. Groups of individuals who work in gangs, often appointing one of their members as the gang leader, known as a labour master, to negotiate work and payment on behalf of the gang with an Employer. The payment is then divided among the individuals. Difficulties as to the status of these workers made it uncertain whether injuries to them involving an allegation of liability against the Employer should be dealt with as an employers' or public liability claim. As the labour master and his gang often use the employer's tools and work side by side with his own staff, the risk is seen by insurers as being akin to an employers' liability risk. Consequently, the term employee (qv) is widely drawn and includes labour masters and persons supplied by them, labour only sub-contractors, and self-employed persons. Liability to them for injury is insured under the employers' liability policy and excluded under the public liability policy.

landslip. A small landslide—'a rapid downward movement under the influence of gravity of a mass or rock or earth on a slope'—(*Oddy* v *Phoenix Assurance Co. Ltd* (1966)). Landslip is specifically excluded from storm and tempest cover (qv). The risk is automatically insured as an additional (or special) peril in its own right (together with subsidence (qv)) under household comprehensive policies on buildings subject to a sizeable excess (£500 or £1000 or a percentage of the sum insured) and excluding fences, boundary walls etc unless the house is damaged at the same time. It is insured under household contents policies free of excess and special exceptions. In commercial and industrial insurance landslip cover, bracketed with the subsidence contingency, is available subject to a satisfactory survey. It is customary to exclude normal land settlement, coastal erosion, and damage to boundary walls, gates and fences unless the buildings are damaged at the same time.

lapse. A policy lapses when, after running its term, the insured fails to pay the renewal premium or where renewal is not invited by the insurer.

lapse ratio. The number of policies not renewed as a percentage of the number of renewals invited. The insurer who has to constantly replace lapsed policies with new business will face a higher expense ratio than an insurer of a similar size but with a lower lapse ratio. This ratio also varies according to the class of business. In the private car insurance market there are many insurers transacting their business through insurance brokers and this may cause a higher lapse ratio than in other classes of business.

'last opportunity rule'. A common law rule which now rarely applies in negligence cases. It was otherwise known as the rule in *Davies* v *Mann*, an 1842 case in which both parties were negligent but the whole of the blame was attached to the person who had the last opportunity of avoiding the accident. The defendant drove into the plaintiff's donkey which was negligently tethered in the highway but the driver's final act of negligence was considered decisive. Under the Law Reform (Contributory Negligence Act) 1945 liability is apportioned between the parties according to the degree of blame. However, if there is a sufficient separation in time between the respective faults of the two parties, the one who could have avoided the accident could be held wholly liable. This is another way of saying that the earlier act of negligence was inoperative.

'last straw' cases. A term used in the doctrine of proximate cause (qv) to describe a chain of events in which the final link is merely the closest in time to the outcome but is not the nearest in efficiency and is not therefore the proximate cause of the loss. In *Leyland Shipping Co.* v *Norwich Union* (1918) a ship was torpedoed and some time later it sunk following a storm. The storm was the 'last straw' but the proximate cause of the loss was the torpedo damage and therefore the insurer was not liable as the policy excluded war risks. An undamaged ship would probably have survived the storm and so the war damage continued to be the dominant influence on the course of events. The term death blow cases is an alternative for last straw cases.

last survivor assurance. A life assurance on two or more lives under which the sum assured is payable on the last death. They are usually effected in connection with leases granted during the lifetime of several people. Policies can be with or without profits on a whole of life, endowment or, less frequently, a term assurance basis. The more lives the smaller will be the premium.

Latent Damages Act 1986. An Act which partially nullifies the House of Lords decision in *Pirelli* v *Oscar Faber & Partners* (1983) to the effect that when property damage occurs the time runs from the time of damage. It adds a further limitation period of three years from the date the damage was reasonably discoverable subject to a 'long stop' provision of 15 years from the act of negligence. The plaintiff's knowledge of the damage or capability of reasonably discovering follows the lines of the 'knowledge' required in personal injury cases. *See* LIMITATION ACT (1980).

latent defect. A defect that is not immediately apparent although it is in existence.

latents defects insurance. A 10-year non-cancellable insurance issued by insurers to the building owner indemnifying him against the cost of remedying the defect. It is alternatively called decennial insurance (qv).

latent disease. A disease that is not immediately apparent though it is in existence. In many cases it may be a matter of years before the disease affecting a person is discovered. It is any disease

that is not immediately apparent. *See* LONG TAIL.

launch insurance. An insurance to cover a spacecraft during the launch phase. The cover is material damage on an 'all risks' basis and includes the risk of malfunctioning. The policy runs from the initial ignition until the spacecraft reaches its correct and final orbit and its systems are fully checked before it begins the commercial operations for which it was intended.

launderettes (self-operated laundries). Certain local authorities have introduced legislation for a compulsory inspection service of certain installations and plant used in launderettes and coin-operated dry cleaning establishments and a certificate must be produced by the owner before trading will be permitted. The statutory maximum period for inspections is 14 months. Engineering insurers offer an inspection service combined with insurance against the risk of fragmentation (qv) giving cover up to £20000 on any one accident in respect of physical damage to own surrounding property but wider cover can be granted. As well as the boiler and main electrical service installations, plant such as hydro-extractors, tumbler dryers, coin-operated washing machines, and dry cleaning machines can be included.

law of large numbers. A statistical law stating that the larger the number of exposure units considered the more closely will the losses occurring match the underlying probability of loss. Insurance has a statisitical base and is dependent on the law of large numbers in order that future losses can be predicted with an acceptable degree of accuracy and so facilitate the risk spreading function of insurance. A mathematical value can be given to risks provided there is a sufficiently large sample of exposures. Reinsurance (qv) is a further application of the law of large numbers as insurers can reduce their own uncertainty (a much narrower band than for individuals) by spreading their risks on an even wider basis.

Law of Property Act 1925. This Act affects fire insurers as follows: 1. *Rights of mortgagees* (s. 108). (a) A mortgagee may insure the mortgaged property against fire and charge the premiums to the mortgagor. The amount of insurance is not to exceed the amount of insurance specified in the mortgage deed or, if no amount is specified, two-thirds of the replacement value. These provisions apply only where the mortgage is by deed and there is no stipulation therein to the contrary. Also if the mortgagor maintains the insurance according to the deed, the mortgagee has no rights. Any money recovered under a fire policy may be applied at the instance of the mortgagee to discharge the mortgage debt. (b) Section 108 (2) gives mortgagees the right to compel a mortgagor who has received insurance moneys to expend it on reinstatement of the building. 2. *Rights of a purchaser of real property* (*s.*47). After a contract for sale has been made, the equitable interest vests in the purchaser and the property is at his risk. On completion of the contract the vendor shall pass any insurance moneys payable to him in the interim to the purchaser provided that (a) there is no stipulation in the contract to the contrary; (b) the purchaser bears any premiums for the period after the date of the contract; (c) the consent of the insurer is obtained. In practice the insurer usually provides a purchaser's interest clause (qv) and the vendor holds moneys in trust for the purchaser.

Law Reform (Miscellaneous Provisions) Act 1934. At common law claims did not survive the death of an individual (*see* ACTIO PERSONALIS MORITUR CUM PERSONA). Survival of causes of action is permitted under the Act which provides that on the death of any person all causes of action subsisting against or vested in him, survive against, or, as the case may be, for the benefit of his estate. The estate can claim damages for the period between the accrual of the cause of action and the date of death and can thus include damages for pain and suffering, loss of amenity etc. Damages are calculated 'without reference to any loss or gain to the estate consequent upon the death' so annuities previously payable to the deceased and life insurance monies now payable are disregarded. Awards

under the 1934 Act are the same regardless of claims under the Fatal Accidents Act (qv), under which there is to be no duplication of damages.

layers. A term used in insurance and reinsurance to describe a stratum of cover where the risk is placed in sections, ie layers. For example, a civil engineering contractor might require public liability cover up to £30m. The primary insurer may take a first layer up to £5m with the next layer providing cover in excess of £5m up to £15m and so on. Different insurers are normally involved and the rate of premium in liability insurance is in inverse proportion to the level of the layer. Layers are also used to arrange excess of loss treaty reinsurance in which successive treaties come into operation only when those preceding it have been exhausted.

lay-up return. Sometimes called laid-up (or lying-up) returns, this is the return of premium by marine insurers when the insured vessel is out of use. *See* RETURNS CLAUSE.

leading underwriter/insurer (leader). 1. A Lloyd's underwriter or company recognised as a specialist or as having the greatest capacity in a particular class of business. They are first to take a portion of the risk and quote a rate of premium. The broker normally seeks out a specialist in the class of insurance concerned as the reputation of the underwriter will give other underwriters confidence to follow the lead by accepting portions of the risk on their own account. On large risks it may be necessary to select two or three specialists to lead. 2. The insurance company on a co-insurance policy who has accepted the largest share of the risk and accepts responsibility for the survey and administration of the insurance.

leading underwriter clause. A clause to the effect that all underwriters with a share of the risk will follow the rates and terms agreed by the leader (qv). It is introduced into the slip (qv) by the broker in order to economise on the administration involved in dealing with a number of underwriters on large risks. Underwriters not prepared to accept this requirement are not invited to share in the risk. The clause is not a part of the insurance contract. It is an agreement between the broker and the underwriters for administrative convenience.

leakage. 1. *Marine.* Where leakage is caused by maritime perils the policy operates to cover the loss. The policy is normally extended to cover leakage however caused but the insurer pays only for claims in excess of a certain figure or percentage as a certain amount of shrinkage or evaporation during the voyage is inevitable. When liquids such as palm olive or molasses are shipped in bulk or, as with wine, in casks, there will be a certain trade loss or 'ullage'. 2. *Household.* Leakage of oil from any fixed heating installation under both buildings and contents insurances is covered without special exceptions.

leasehold redemption policy. A form of capital redemption policy (qv).

leaving service. A pensions term referring to an employee leaving an employer's employment, for any reason.

'left unattended'. Goods in transit insurers commonly restrict cover when the vehicle is left unattended. Whether a vehicle is left unattended is a question of fact. In *Ingleton of Ilford v General Accident* (1967) 2 Lloyd's Rep. 179 it was held that a driver who was in a shop for 15 minutes was in no position to watch over his vehicle which was therefore unattended. In *Starfire Diamonds v Angel* (1962) 2 Lloyd's Rep. 213, the Court of Appeal held that a car was left unattended when the driver left his car in a lay-by while urinating behind some bushes some 37 yards away. He kept the car in view and had a partly obscured view of a man on the far side of the car walking away with a suitcase containing rings from the car. The car was not attended as the driver was not in a position to attempt to frustrate any attack on the vehicle. *See* ORDINARY MEANING RULE.

legal costs and expenses. *See* OTHER COSTS AND EXPENSES.

legal defence clause. An extension to a professional indemnity clause to indemnify the insured in respect of costs incurred in respect of legal representation at proceedings not directly related to a claim. Cover is usually limited to 80 per cent of the costs. The proceedings may be at a court of law or tribunal but not a disciplinary body representing the insured's professional association. The insurers provide representation if they feel that the cause of the proceedings might be relevant to an existing or possible claim or prejudice the insured's professional reputation.

legal expenses insurance. An insurance for individuals, families and businesses to enable them to meet the cost of defending or pursuing certain civil actions. Cover is also available for defending prosecutions and an allowance is made for attendance expenses in connection with court hearings or similar proceedings. *See* COMMERCIAL LEGAL EXPENSES INSURANCE.

letter of credit. A document normally issued by a banker authorising the person to whom it is addressed, normally another bank, to pay the agreed sum to the person specified in the letter. The risk is borne by the drawer whose account becomes charged. Letters of credit are sometimes used to guarantee the performance of a reinsurance contract or provide financial support for a Name (qv) underwriting at Lloyd's. Reinsurers may use letters of credit as a substitute for cash when they wish to create loss reserves, premiums reserves, or perhaps a reserve for IBNR (qv). These instruments are widely used in the USA and Canada.

level premium system. Virtually all life insurance premiums are charged at the same rate each year and do not increase as the likelihood of death increases with age. Consequently the premiums charged in the early years are more than sufficient to cover the mortality risk. In this way a reserve is created to compensate for the later years when the annual premium is insufficient to cover the mortality risk.

liability insurance. The insurance of legal liability to pay the compensation and costs awarded against the insured in favour of another party in respect of particular loss or damage sustained by that party. The Insurance Companies Act 1982 classes the following liability insurances as general business: motor liability; aircraft liability; ships liability; and general liability. Liability may arise through negligence; nuisance (qv); trespass (qv); strict liability (qv);

breach of statute (qv); defamation (qv), and conversion (qv).

libel. *See* DEFAMATION.

licence. *See* DRIVING LICENCE. *Also see* LOSS OF LICENCE.

licensing. The licensing requirements of the Consumer Credit Act 1974 (qv) are likely to affect life insurers under the four categories: consumer credit business; credit brokerage; debt-adjusting and debt counselling. A licence issued to an insurance company will cover all its employees and any 'tied agents'.

lien. The right to hold the property of another as security for the performance of an obligation such as the payment of an account. Thus, when a broker as agent of the insured pays the premium and receives the policy from the insurer, he may retain it until the amount of the premium has been refunded. This is known as the broker's lien. These rights depend on due and proper performance by the agent of his duties on behalf of his principal, ie the insured. The lien does not usually apply to money due from another broker or sub-agent. Also there is the carrier's lien which operates in a similar way to protect a carrier when freight is payable at destination.

life assurance/insurance. A term applied to the insurance of persons' lives where the contract is not one of indemnity but of an ultimate claim. In the UK there are two kinds of life insurance: (a) ordinary life assurance/insurance which means all life business that is not within the term industrial life assurance. Ordinary life business is supervised by the Department of Trade and Industry as long-term business (qv). (b) Industrial life assurance is the business of effecting cover on human life where the premiums are collected at intervals of less than two calendar months. This business may be conducted by friendly societies or authorised insurance companies. Industrial life assurance is regulated by the Industrial Assurance Act 1923. The most common types of life insurance contracts are: endowment (a fixed term policy with the sum insured payable on death or at the end of the term whichever occurs first); whole life (sum insured payable only

on death); term (or temporary insurance) sum insured payable only if death occurs during the policy term; decreasing term as per term insurance except that the amount payable on death decreases each year; convertible term (a term insurance with the option to convert to whole life or endowment without evidence of health provided the option is exercised before expiry). The permanent policies, ie whole life and endowment, may be 'with profits' (qv) or 'without profits'. *See* BONUS and EQUITY-LINKED POLICIES. Note: The terms assurance/insurance are interchangeable with the former being more traditional but there is now a tendency for greater use of the term insurance.

Life Assurance Act 1774. This made insurances on the lives of persons or events (other than insurances on ships or merchandise) null and void if the person benefiting from it had no interest. It also made it unlawful to issue policies without the name of the person for whose benefit the policy is issued appearing in the policy. It further provided that no greater amount than the value of the interest could be recovered under the policy. Case law has shown this to be the amount of the interest at the time of making the contract not the time of claim (*see* INSURABLE INTEREST).

life assurance contract. 'That in which one party agrees to pay a given sum upon the happening of a particular event contingent upon the duration of human life, in consideration of the immediate payment of a smaller sum or certain equivalent periodical payments by another' (Bunyon, *Law of Life Assurance*).

life assured/insured. The person whose life is the subject-matter of the life assurance contract. Such a person is often but not always the policyholder. Some policies are issued on a life of another basis.

life fund. *See* LIFE INSURANCE FUND.

Life Insurance Association (LIA). The LIA has four main objectives: (a) to promote communication, participation, and education within the life insurance industry; (b) to improve business standards by illuminating malpractices and heightening the professionalism of all those involved in selling life insurance; (c) to sponsor courses, seminars and lectures to increase awareness of the range of activities encompassed by the life insurance industry; (d) to promote mutual respect with Government and other bodies regarding life insurance.

Life Insurance Council (LIC). The LIC operates as part of the Association of British Insurers (qv) dealing specifically with the life insurance industry. It has an elected management committee of 12 people reporting back to the full council which in return reports to the Board of the ABI.

life insurance (satellites). Life insurance (generally an alternative for life assurance) in the satellite insurance market refers to an 'all risks' insurance in respect of total or partial loss during the operating life of the satellite.

life insurance funds. The life insurance funds represent the accumulated savings and contributions of policyholders. They are held against the life insurance companies' liabilities to pay future claims. The amounts of the funds are increased year by year by premiums paid by policyholders and investment income received, less payments made to policyholders, management expenses (including commission), taxation and transfers to shareholders' funds (qv), where appropriate. It is common practice to credit to the life insurance funds all or part of any capital appreciation in the value of the assets.

Life Assurance Premium Relief (LAPR). The income tax relief allowed to policyholders on premiums in respect of qualifying policies (qv) issued before 14 March 1984. There is no relief on premiums in excess of £1500 or 1/6th of total income whichever is the greater. Eligibility for tax relief is only in respect of policies providing a capital sum on death; the policy must be on the life of the policyholder or his/her spouse by whom premiums must be paid; the pair must reside in the UK at the time of payment. The relief entitlement is one half of the basic rate of tax and this granted by permitting the policyholder to deduct the appropriate sum (currently 12.5 per cent) when paying the premium. Alternatively a policyholder can elect to pay the gross premium and reclaim the tax. For policies surrendered in the first four years the Inland Revenue will 'clawback' (qv) some of the tax relief.

Life Assurance and Unit Trust Regulatory Organisation (LAUTRO). A Self-Regulating Organisation (qv) whose member firms are, for the most part, insurance companies and friendly societies engaged in retail marketing of life assurance products, pensions and unit trust products. An important LAUTRO rule obliges advisers, whether independent or representing a particular company, to issue a Buyer's Guide which, *inter alia*, points out the essential difference between an independent adviser and a company representative.

life of another policy. A life policy taken out by one person on the life of another in whom he has an insurable interest.

lifts and hoists. The cover provided under a lift policy (qv) is applicable to items such as: electric or hydraulic passenger and goods lifts, manual goods lifts and service lifts, paternosters, motor vehicles lifting tables, and builders, coal, coke, cupola and like hoists. These can be found in schools, universities, offices, flats, restaurants, hotels, nursing homes, hospitals, shops, garages, warehouses, factories, and elsewhere.

lift policy. The policy covers breakdown (qv) but can be extended to cover sudden and unforeseen physical damage (qv) to the plant at the premises, temporarily elsewhere and in transit between the two. It also covers damage to own surrounding property resulting from fragmentation (qv), damage to goods being lifted (excluding installed plant and machinery), and third party risks. An excess (qv) applies to all claims, usually 5 per cent of the cost subject to a minimum in the range £25 to £100 depending on the form of the loss. Optional extensions include: third party risks (the choice depends on the cover available under the general public liability policy); physical damage to property in the insured's custody or control; and physical damage to goods being lifted.

lightning. An insured peril added to a standard fire policy to cover damage by lightning. It is independent of the fire peril and no ignition is necessary in order to bring a claim within the policy.

LIMNET. An acronym derived from the computerised London insurance market network set up to improve business efficiency. It enables brokers, underwriters and clearing houses to exchange premium and claims transactions electronically. Ultimately 'electronic slips' will be initiated by brokers for scrutiny by underwriters on their own terminals when considering acceptance of the risk. Any newcomers to the London insurance market must be prepared to equip themselves appropriately.

limit of indemnity/liability. The maximum sum that a liability insurer will pay for any event, occurrence, or accident, or in aggregate in any one year. Public liability policies generally have a 'single occurrence' limit but no limit as to the claims in the year, while products liability policies have an aggregate limit for all claims during the year. Employers' liability insurances provide indemnity without limit. The indemnity limit generally applies to all sums payable as compensation, ie damages and claimant's costs. The insured's own costs incurred with the insurer's consent are payable in addition to the limit of indemnity. Where aggregate limits apply, the limit can be reinstated to its former level after a claim. *See also* COSTS INCLUSIVE LIMITS OF INDEMNITY.

Limitation Act 1980. The right to sue lapses if the writ is not issued within the period specified in the Act—the claim becomes statute barred (qv). The Act allows three years from the accrual of the cause of action in the case of personal injury but the court can at its discretion extend this period where it is equitable to do so. Twelve years are allowed for disputes as to title to land and six years for other actions (eg property damage cases). By s. 11 of the Act the time begins to run at the date the cause of action accrues or, if later, the date of knowledge. This is the date on which the plaintiff first realised that the injury was significant, knew the de-

fendant's identity, and knew that the injury was attributable to negligence, nuisance, or breach of duty, and, if the injury was caused by a person other than the defendant (eg defendant's employer), knew the identity of that person. The Latent Damages Act 1986 deals with the problem of latent property damage by allowing three years from the date on which the plaintiff discovered or ought reasonably to have discovered significant damage. 'Knowledge' in this situation closely follows the foregoing description referring to personal injury cases. Section 14(b) of the 1986 Act provides a 'long-stop' by barring all claims brought more than 15 years from the date of the defendant's negligence. If, when a cause of action accrues, the plaintiff is a minor or of unsound mind, the time (three, six years etc) runs from the date their disability ends.

limited comprehensive cover. A policy offered by some private car insurers which combines the own damage cover (qv) which appears in the usual form of comprehensive policy with the third party section of that form of cover. It does not include the supplementary or 'fringe sections' covering personal accident, medical expenses, or rugs, coats and personal effects. The premium is reduced and the cover is concentrated on the key concerns, namely damage to the car and liabilty for third party injury or property damage.

limited premium life policy. A life policy under the premium will be paid by the insured for a limited period only and not the full duration of the policy term. For example, a whole life policy may be written with premiums terminating at age 65. Thereafter the policy remains in force without further payment of premiums.

'liner allowances'. *See* OVERTIME and TEMPORARY REPAIRS.

line. 1. The proportion of risk accepted by an insurer or reinsurer. In reinsurance the cedant's retention is termed a line and the capacity of a surplus treaty can be expressed as a multiple of the retention. For example, if the cedant's retention is £10 000 a ten-line surplus treaty creates a reinsurance capacity of

£100 000. The amount accepted by an underwriter when signing a slip is called the written line. 2. The term also describes a type or category of insurance. For example, 'personal lines' refers to those insurances effected by individuals in their private capacity (eg household, private car etc).

line of credit. A method of risk financing (qv) which involves the agreement of a bank to provide finance as required to fund losses as they occur. Contingency funds arranged in this way may reduce a firm's borrowing capacity and restrict its investment potential but there may be advantages for firms with a good credit rating. The only charge levied by the lender is made for guaranteeing the standby line of credit which may or may not be used. If not used there will be no additional charge.

line slip. An arrangement whereby underwriters and a broker agree, for a specified type of risk, that the broker only needs to approach the leading and second underwriter who will accept or reject each risk on behalf of all the underwriters concerned in their agreed proportions. This is used when a broker is placing a large number of similar risks with the same group of underwriters. It is prompted by administrative convenience.

lines to stand. A condition whereby a broker secures a commitment from an underwriter as to the monetary amount of his acceptance, even though on closing, this line may represent an increased percentage of a reduced limit. This will happen if the placement is not completed. This allows the broker to place 100 per cent of a smaller monetary amount and is an approach that will be adopted when the broker has doubts about the availability of the capacity available for full placement.

linked assets. Long-term business (qv) assets by reference to which linked benefits are determined. These assets are separated from the other long-term business assets of the company.

linked benefits. The value of the rights conferred under a life policy by reference to the value of specific assets.

linked-life insurance (or life-linked). Investment schemes offered by life insurers in which premium by the policyholders as investors is used partly to purchase life insurance and partly to purchase units in a unit trust (qv) or unitised fund (qv). The proceeds or benefits payable will be the greater of the guaranteed sum insured or the value of the units accrued. *See* UNIT-LINKED LIFE INSURANCE.

Linked Life Assurance Group (LLAG). The LLAG was established in 1972 to advance the interests of ordinary long-term life assurance business by ensuring high standards of professional conduct by codes of conduct as appropriate; to provide a forum for discussion among member companies and to represent them in discussion with Government Departments and other bodies.

liquidated damages. A genuine pre-estimate of damages for an anticipated breach of contract, provision for which is made in the contract. Any amounts fixed as liquidated damages are recoverable by the aggrieved party but penalties are not. Liability insurers specifically exclude any liability to pay liquidated damages or penalties. See also clause 22D of the Joint Contract Tribunal Standard Form of Building Contract 1980 as amended.

Liverpool Underwriters Association. Formed in 1802 membership is open to marine insurers and brokers in the Liverpool area. It collaborates with the Institute of London Underwriters (qv) and informs Lloyd's of sailings, arrivals and casualties to ships of Liverpool ownership.

livestock insurance. An insurance of livestock against death through accident or disease. Insurances usually relate to horses and cattle but pigs and sheep can be covered. Policies are issued on a yearly basis but it is customary for insurers to obtain a fresh proposal each year in order to remain up to date. The main categories of risk are: horses; hunters and polo ponies; foaling risks; bloodstock; cattle; transit and show risks; castration.

Lloyd's. The name of the major insurance market-place based in Lime Street, London. It originated from a coffee house (proprietor Edward Lloyd) in Tower Street within a year or two of the Great Fire of London in 1666. It became a meeting place for persons interested in shipping and marine insurance. Lloyd's became incorporated by statute in 1871 and is now controlled by the Lloyd's Act 1982 (qv). Lloyd's as a corporate body does not undertake risks. The risks are accepted by underwriting members known as Names (qv) through their agents. The Names act as sole traders but combine into syndicates to share the risks. Lloyd's syndicates (qv) do not transact business directly with the public who can only insure at Lloyd's through Lloyd's brokers (qv). Lloyd's organises the market, provides ancillary services and supervisory control. The Corporation of Lloyd's is directed by the Council of Lloyd's (qv) of 28 and is funded largely by the rents paid for 'boxes' (qv) and by the annual fee paid by underwriting members (otherwise called 'names'). The Council is empowered to delegate the day-to-day regulation of the underwriting members, brokers, underwriting agents and syndicates to the Committee of Lloyd's (qv). The solvency of individual members is a matter for self-regulation by the Committee but the Insurance (Lloyd's) Regulations 1983, issued under the Insurance Companies Act 1982 apply to Lloyd's membership as a whole general insurance solvency regulations broadly similar to those applicable to insurance companies.

Lloyd's Act 1982. The Act resulted from an enquiry into the constitution and the effectiveness of Lloyd's powers of self-regulation, and led to the formation of a new body, the Council of Lloyd's (qv) to assume the rule-making and disciplinary functions previously vested in Lloyd's membership as a whole. The Act is based on the Fisher Report and incorporates the proposal that Lloyd's brokers should divest themselves of their interests in underwriting agencies within five years.

Lloyd's agent. Lloyd's have a worldwide network of agents who supply shipping intelligence for Lloyd's Intelligence Department and publication in *Lloyd's List* and *Lloyd's Shipping Index.* The agents also arrange for inspections and reports in connection with reported losses and sometimes negotiate settlement on behalf of the underwri-

ters concerned. They also get involved with non-marine insurances, notably aviation and travel claims. There are over 1500 agents and sub-agents throughout the world. A Lloyd's agent is not an agent of the underwriters and is not authorised to receive notice of abandonment (*Vacuum Oil Co* v *Union Insurance Society of Canton Ltd* (1926).

Lloyd's American Trust Fund. This is a trust fund maintained in the USA by Lloyd's underwriters since 1939. Under the trust all premiums received in respect of policies issued by the underwriters in US dollars are vested in Citibank as trustee for the benefit of the holders of such policies.

Lloyd's Aviation Underwriters' Association (LAUA). A specialist group of aviation underwriters who combine to represent their common interests in consultation with the Committee of Lloyd's, government departments etc. It maintains close links with company market and aviation insurers throughout the world. It publishes Lloyd's policy forms and is represented on the joint technical and clauses committee.

Lloyd's broker. A partnership or body corporate permitted by the Council to broke insurance business at Lloyd's. A broker who has been approved by the Council of Lloyd's and thus entitled to enter the underwriting room at Lloyd's to place business direct with underwriters. The general public cannot place insurance direct with Lloyd's underwriters. The broker or body corporate must meet the Council's demanding requirements in terms of integrity and financial stability which includes filing an annual report regarding their financial position.

Lloyd's Canadian Trust Fund. A trust fund created in November 1971 into which Lloyd's underwriters must pay all of their Canadian dollar premiums. The fund is held by the Royal Trust Corporation of Canada.

Lloyd's Central Accounting. A facility provided by the Lloyd's Policy Signing Office (qv) which enables syndicates and brokers to receive or pay money centrally on a fixed day each month. This, in effect, gives the syndicates a brokers' ledger accounting service since all business signed each day is processed for the account of each syndicate and each broker.

Lloyd's Central Fund. A fund created to meet any underwriting deficit of a Lloyd's underwriting member whose Lloyd's deposit, premium trust fund balance, reserves and personal assets are inadequate to meet his liabilities to policyholders. All Lloyd's underwriters make an annual contribution to this fund based on premium income. The fund is huge and constitutes a valuable form of extra security for policyholders.

Lloyd's central resources. These are financial resources forming a part of the security underlying policies issued at Lloyd's. Lloyd's Central Fund (qv) may be earmarked as part of the solvency procedure to enable underwriters to pass the solvency test if necessary. Earmarked assets are available to discharge the underwriting liabilities of members should they become due and the earmarkings lapse when a member discharges his liability. The Central Fund and, in addition, the assets of the Corporation of Lloyd's therefore exist as the ultimate safeguard and protection for the Lloyd's policyholder.

Lloyd's, Committee of. A body comprising the 16 working members of the Council of Lloyd's (qv), which is representative of the members and controls the business of its members according to the provisions of Lloyd's Acts. This involves the provision and maintenance of suitable premises, the running of Lloyd's Policy Signing Office and Claims Bureau, and the provision of intelligence services. Its powers and functions are delegated to it by the Council of Lloyd's.

Lloyd's, Corporation of. The society of Lloyd's incorporated under the Lloyd's Act 1871 to provide services and facilities for the transaction of insurance business.

Lloyd's, Council of. The body responsible for the regulation of the Lloyd's market and management of the Corporation of Lloyd's. Sixteen members are elected from working members of Lloyd's, eight elected from external members, three nominated members whose appointments are subject to confirmation by the Governor of the Bank of England, and a chief execu-

tive. The Council took office on 1 January 1983, the day the Lloyd's Act 1982 acquired the force of law.

Lloyd's deposit. Persons wishing to become underwriting members of Lloyd's must first deposit cash, approved securities, bank or insurance company guarantees or letters of credit. The deposit is then held in trust for policyholders by the Corporation of Lloyd's under a trust deed. Meanwhile the member is entitled to receive the dividend or interest. The amount of the deposit determines the level of the premium income a member is permitted to write. Overseas members are required to deposit more than UK members.

Lloyd's Fire Policy. This policy varies from the standard fire policy in that fire caused by explosion is covered.

Lloyd's Form. This is Lloyd's standard form of Salvage Agreement.

Lloyd's (General Business) Regulations 1979. Regulations made under the European Companies Act 1972 to apply to Lloyd's the solvency provisions of the EEC Directive 73/239/EEC on the taking up and pursuing direct insurance business other than life. The effect is to require the Corporation of Lloyd's to meet, on behalf of all its members who conduct general insurance business, the solvency requirements applicable to insurance companies under the margin of solvency requirements subject to certain exceptions allowed because of the special position of Lloyd's.

Lloyd's Information Services. The information gathering and processing service that supplies information for publication by Lloyd's of London Press Ltd (qv). The headquarters at Colchester are open at all hours of the day and night. The reports are processed on a computer and passed immediately for publication.

Lloyd's Insurance Brokers Association (LIBA). Represents the interest of Lloyd's brokers.

Lloyd's Insurance Brokers Committee. All Lloyd's brokers must be members of the British Insurance and Investment Brokers Association. Lloyd's interests within BIIBA are represented by a 15 strong committee elected from the brokers themselves.

Lloyd's Introductory Test. An examination introduced at Lloyd's by Bye-law No. 8 of 1985. Each new entrant to the Room must take the test soon after starting at Lloyd's.

Lloyd's Life Assurance Ltd. A separate company established in 1971 by Lloyd's underwriters to offer life insurance schemes through insurance brokers.

Lloyd's List International. A daily newspaper read in over 120 countries by management engaged in transport and associated industries. Shipping movements, marine and aviation casualty reports, and details of fires, strikes and riots are published daily. Regular reports appear on ship sales and purchases, launchings, charterings, offshore industry and the tanker and dry cargo markets.

Lloyd's Loading List. This provides exporters with a valuable guide to cargo-carrying services available from UK and European ports.

Lloyd's Log. A magazine produced for the members of Lloyd's by the Corporation's public affairs department.

Lloyd's Market Certificate. A certificate for underwriters to be introduced into Lloyd's in 1992 which has been devised in association with the Chartered Insurance Institute. The certificate will be compulsory for all underwriters wanting to practise.

Lloyd's membership. Membership is in two categories, Lloyd's brokers (qv), who are the intermediaries, and Lloyd's underwriters (qv), who are the insurers. Underwriting membership is open to men or women who must satisfy stringent conditions to qualify. They must: (a) Be recommended by other members. (b) Transact business with unlimited liability (qv). (c) Meet the financial requirements of the Council of Lloyd's (qv), including means of £250 000 on entry. Members must also lodge funds in an approved form equivalent to 30 per cent of their gross premium underwriting limit. The maximum gross premium underwriting limit is £2m. (d) Pay all premiums into premium trust funds (qv) under deeds of trust approved by the Department of Trade and Industry and the Council of Lloyd's from which only claims, expenses and profit may be paid. (e) Subject underwriting accounts to an annual solvency test as at 31 December which requires underwriting assets to be sufficient to meet their liabilities for all classes of business. (f) Contribute by means of a levy on premium income to the Central Fund which is intended to meet the underwriting liabilities of any member in the unlikely event of their security and personal assets being insufficient for their commitments. *See also* LLOYD'S MEMBERS' MEANS.

Lloyd's members' means. A part of the security underlying policies issued at Lloyd's these means consist of (a) Lloyd's deposits (qv) which must be held in trust until all of a member's liabilities have been fully reinsured by other Lloyd's underwriters; (b) additional underwriting reserves in the form of personal reserves (qv) held in trust by their underwriting agent or held in joint trust by Lloyd's and the agent in the special reserve fund scheme (qv) approved by the Inland Revenue; (c) personal wealth (*see* MEANS TEST) evidence of which is demanded by the Council of Lloyd's that he or she has a minimum level of wealth (known as the qualifying means); (d) total declared resources of members either in the form of assets held in trust at Lloyd's or representing their means confirmed to Lloyd's (the 1989 figure was £18 345 m.). As the figure includes only the amount of the members' confirmed means, it is a conservative valuation of the total resources of Lloyd's members.

Lloyd's Motor Underwriters' Association (LMUA). An association that works on behalf of motor syndicates to place motor-cars into groups according to the degree of hazard and cost of repair for the purpose of rating motor risks. The LMUA obtains information on vehicle characteristics from the Motor Conference which represents the interests of the motor-car industry and obtains the necessary information from motor manufacturers. The LMUA's motor vehicle groups are recommended to their members but there is no obligation for those recommendations to be followed. The same work is carried out by the Motor Committee of the Association of British Insurers.

Lloyd's of London Press Ltd. A subsidiary of the Corporation of Lloyd's it collects, processes and publishes the enormous volume of information received from Lloyd's agents (qv) and other world-wide connections. Information on ships leaving ports every day for destinations throughout the world is processed by Lloyd's Information Services (LIS). The details are important to insurance and shipping communities and the governments of many countries. Other information passed on by LIS for publishing concerns ship arrivals, departures, port congestions, labour disputes, vessels under construction, and casualties. The best-known publication is *Lloyd's List International* (qv). Other important ones include: *Lloyd's Shipping Index* (qv), *Lloyd's Shipping Economist* (qv), *Lloyd's Loading List* (qv), *Lloyd's Ship Manager* (qv), and *Lloyd's Log* (qv).

Lloyd's Policy Signing Office (LPSO). Policies are prepared by Lloyd's brokers but checked and signed on behalf of the underwriters in the LPSO. This office performs a number of other administrative functions including the operation of Lloyd's Central Accounting (qv).

Lloyd's Register of Shipping. A classification society (qv) known as 'Lloyd's' Register but controlled by an independent body consisting of underwriters, shipowners, shipbuilders and marine engineers. The publication is valuable to underwriters as it classifies all vessels, oil rigs etc submitted to it for the purpose and records details of other vessels whether classed by Lloyd's or not. The comprehensive information embraces vessels built for special trades, the names of shipowners and the vessels owned by them, the names of shipbuilders and details of docks. There is a strong link with Lloyd's strengthened by the pooling of the computer-based shipping information of the Register and Lloyd's of London Press Ltd.

Lloyd's security controls. The security underlying policies issued at Lloyd's is based on both financial resources (*see* TECHNICAL RESERVES, MEMBERS' MEANS, PERSONAL WEALTH, TOTAL DECLARED RESOURCES OF MEMBERS and LLOYD'S CENTRAL RESOURCES) and security controls. These controls comprise premium income limits (qv), the annual solvency test (qv), and the statutory solvency margin (qv).

Lloyd's Ship Manager. The leading international maritime monthly publication.

Lloyd's Shipping Economist. A monthly publication giving a comprehensive analysis of world shipping produced from computer-generated statistics.

Lloyd's Shipping Index. A unique daily record of the details and latest world-wide movements of more than 21 000 merchant vessels.

Lloyd's solvency test. The annual test of the solvency position of each underwriting member. Under s. 83 of the Insurance Companies Act 1982 a certificate must be supplied to the Secretary of State.

Lloyd's syndicates. In the early days each Lloyd's underwriter accepted risks wholly on his own account but the limitations of personal wealth resulted in the underwriting members combining in groups to form syndicates. Each syndicate is represented by an active underwriter (qv) whose signature binds the members of the syndicate. In this way the expertise of one underwriter becomes available to many and larger volumes of business can be transacted. Each person in the syndicate takes an agreed share of the risks accepted by the active underwriter. Each syndicate member is directly liable to the policyholder for his share of any loss to the full extent of his personal wealth, ie liability is unlimited. No liability attaches to an individual member for any part of any other member's loss, ie liability is several and not joint. In 1990 some 28 700 Lloyd's members grouped into approximately 400 syndicates varying in size from relatively few Names to those comprising more than one thousand Names. The affairs of each syndicate are managed by an underwriting agency which appoints an active underwriter for each class of business.

Lloyd's underwriter. Otherwise called an underwriting member or Name (qv). These are the members who accept the risks but operate within syndicates (*see* LLOYD'S SYNDICATES) on a sole trader basis with unlimited liability for their own portion of the risks. They come from all walks of life but have in common access to sufficient wealth to satisfy the Lloyd's deposit and other requirements to secure membership (*see* LLOYD'S MEMBERSHIP). Members have to be elected and must appear before the Committee of Lloyd's. The Committee satisfies itself as to the status, responsibility and financial standing of the applicant before voting on the application. The underwriter is not actively engaged in underwriting business as this function is carried out by the active underwriter.

Lloyd's Underwriters Association. Formed in 1909 it is concerned with the underwriting, technical and administrative problems that arise in Lloyd's marine market. It liaises closely with Lloyd's Insurance Brokers Association, the Institute of London Underwriters and the Liverpool Underwriters Association.

Lloyd's Underwriters Non-marine Claims Office (LUNCO). Most non-marine Lloyd's syndicates belong to this organisation whose scheme simplifies the settlement of claims. Where several syndicates are involved the broker shows the claim to the leading underwriter before presenting it to LUNCO which, for claims within certain limits, will act on behalf of the remaining underwriters who are kept informed of their individual liabilities by means of LUNCO cards and a summary known as the LUNCO printout.

Lloyd's underwriting procedure. Business is transacted at Lloyd's in the Underwriting Room (the 'Room') in Lime Street, London where the underwriter acting on behalf of a syndicate sits at a 'box' (qv). Business is presented to the underwriter by a Lloyd's broker on a 'slip' giving material features of the risk. The underwriter may decide to refuse or accept the risk in whole or in part. If accepting and the broker agrees, the terms are recorded on the slip which the underwriter initials for the amount of his acceptance (note the origin of the term 'underwriter'). If the portion is less than 100 per cent the broker approaches other underwriters until the risk is fully subscribed. The completed slip is then passed to Lloyd's Policy Signing Office (qv).

loading. The meaning varies according to the context in which it is used. 1. An addition to the pure premium (qv) to cover expenses, profits and adverse fluctuations. 2. An increased charge on the premium levied by the insurer in view of some adverse feature of the risk. 3. The act of placing goods on a vessel or vehicle. The term is relevant to the following insurances: marine, goods in transit, commercial vehicle, and public liability. In some instances, the acts of loading and unloading may signify the moment that the risk attaches or terminates. 4. In reinsurance (qv) it is the practice of quoting and calculating additional amounts of premium above the underwriter's normal rating to allow for future administration expenses, loss escalation, and a reasonable profit margin on non-proportional contracts. One effect is to provide a safety loading which facilitates transfers to the underwriting reserves to provide for such developments.

loading and unloading (of motor vehicles). The loading and unloading of goods-carrying motor vehicles are activities capable of causing accidental injury to others or damage to their property. The cover for any resultant liability may fall under either the commercial vehicle policy or the public liability policy depending on the circumstances. The commercial vehicle policy gives no cover beyond the limits of the carriageway (this normally means beyond the pavement bordering the highway) unless the loading or unloading is performed by the driver or his mate. The cover operates throughout the whole loading/unloading process when undertaken by the driver or mate including accidents occurring on the premises of others. The normal public liability policy wording picks up the excluded risk while excluding the risk as covered by the motor policy. *See also* 'IN TRANSIT' for the relationship between loading and unloading and the term 'in transit'.

loanback. A term describing the loan facility that is generally provided in connection with personal pension schemes. The size of the loan depends on the amount of the annual contribution, the amount already contributed, or size of the expected tax-free lump sum at retirement. Common uses of the loan include purchase of house or business premises, new machinery, or meeting short-term requirements such as school fees. The policyholder has to provide security for the loan as the pension policy cannot be used for this purpose. A first or second charge on property is normally taken but the lender may take other forms of security. The loan does not have to be repaid until retirement at which time it is financed out of the tax free lump sum available at that time. The loan may be provided by an insurance company, bank or finance house.

loan facility. A risk financing method. *See* LINE OF CREDIT.

loan protection policy. A policy that pays a benefit to help the policyholder meet his loan obligations during periods of incapacity through sickness or accident or through unemployment following redundancy.

loans (life policies). Life policies (endowment or whole life) sometimes include a privilege clause undertaking to grant a loan up to 90 per cent or 95 per cent of the surrender value (qv). The rate of interest may be expressed but more usually is determined at the time of the loan. Repayment can be made at any time or the loan allowed to remain as a permanent charge on the policy provided that premiums and interest are paid as they fall due. An alternative way of securing a loan on a life policy is to use it as collateral security (qv) when borrowing from a bank or other financial institution to which it may be legally or equitably assigned.

localisation. *See* MATCHING AND LOCALISATION.

location clause. Shipments declared under open covers (qv) may accumulate at one port. The aggregate exposure creates a far heavier liability than the insurer anticipated when fixing a limit per bottom to control liability in any one vessel. This clause limits the liability of the cargo insurer to an amount for any one loss in any one location.

London Insurance and Reinsurance Market Association (Lirma). Lirma came into being on 1 January 1991 as the result of a merger between the Reinsurance Offices Association (ROA) and the Policy Signing and Accounting Centre (PSAC). The ROA was formed in 1969 by UK reinsurers to represent the interests of reinsurers transacting business in the London market, to study and advise on reinsurance issues and to provide a forum at several levels where member companies could discuss matters of mutual interest. The ROA negotiated with the Government and acquired trade association status. The ROA also had an important overseas role; two-thirds of the members were overseas companies. PSAC was formed in 1976 as a company limited by guarantee to provide a central bureau to process premiums and claims entries, to check and sign policy documents and to prepare the relevant accounting documentation between companies and brokers, giving a service similar to that of Lloyd's Policy Signing Office (qv). Many companies were members of both ROA and PSAC and the overlap has led to the merger. The new association covers both reinsurance and slip written business. The majority of the business passing through the Lirma bureau is reinsurance, but the insurance and reinsurance interests of the company non-marine slip market are handled.

London insurance market. The term is often used but rarely defined. It refers to the international insurance business written in London and consists of the following segments: (a) Home foreign (qv), namely direct overseas business written in the UK. (b) International reinsurance (large volumes of business generally comes from the USA). (c) Marine and aviation. Sometimes the London share of the international market has exceeded 50 per cent. (d) US excess and surplus lines business. London market premiums earn a gross income about equal to that derived from UK 'domestic' commercial business and UK personal lines business.

London Underwriting Centre (LUC). The LUC, due to open in March 1992, will bring together a large number of non-marine company underwriting rooms. It will stand beside Lloyd's and the marine-oriented Institute of London Underwriters (qv) and so will help the process of centralisation. It will accommodate both insurance companies and reinsurance companies in a centre that will serve the company market with the advantage that all insurance and claims functions will be dealt with under one roof. Companies take leases in the centre which for some will become the main London office. Computer-based communications will supply a link to the world market, with an infrastructure incorporating full computer network facilities and all electronic systems, including LIMNET (qv).

'long tail' business. Classes of business where claims take a long time to be notified or to be settled. Most liability insurances are written on a losses-occurring basis (qv) and the victims of certain industrial diseases (eg asbestosis) may not discover for many years that they are suffering from the disease. The interval, ie the tail, between exposure/causation can be anything from 10 to 20 years or even longer. Once notified the claim may take a long time to settle. Long-tails may also arise in connection with pollution and some professional indemnity claims, although the latter policy is written on a claims-made basis. Insureds face the problem of having to trace the insurer on risk at the relevant time (*see* RETROSPECTIVE COVER).

long-term agreements. Once a policy has been issued it is to the insurer's advantage to maintain renewal as this is cheaper than issuing new policies. Long-term agreements are separate contracts where in return for a discount off premium, the insured agrees to renew the policy with the insurer for a specific number of years (eg 5 per cent for 3 years, 7.5 per cent for 5 years). As long as the insurer maintains the same terms and conditions of cover at renewal the insured is contracted to renew the policy. The insurer is not bound to offer renewal terms and if amended terms are offered the insured can avoid renewal. These agreements are most common in fire insurance.

long-term business. The Insurance Companies Act 1982 classes insurance business as long-term or general (qv). The following seven classes make up the long-term business. 1. Life and annuity. 2. Marriage and birth. 3. Linked long term. 4. Permanent health. 5. Tontines. 6. Capital redemption. 7. Pension fund management. Each is a separate class but the life business is sub-divided into industrial life and ordinary life business. *See* LIFE ASSURANCE/INSURANCE.

long-term business amount. A figure defined by the Insurance Companies Regulations 1981 in connection with the valuation of assets. The value which may be placed on certain assets or categories of assets in determining a company's available assets for long-term business is restricted by reference to a specified percentage of the long-term business amount.

long-term care insurance. An insurance which, in return for a regular premium or a single premium, will meet all or part of the cost of personal or nursing care consequent upon the insured event. A policy dedicated to funding long-term care has proved popular with elderly people in the USA and is now available in the UK. Alternatively, cover can be added to an existing life policy. Policies can cover care provided by institutions or in the insured home. The insured event is a disability which may be defined as a 'professional opinion that the insured is in need of care'. Alternatively, the benefit may become payable at a specified level of disability with claims being based on the care needed in connection with the activities of daily living (ADLs), eg bathing, dressing, using the toilet, continence, getting into or out of bed, and eating and drinking. If the insured needs assistance with, say any three of these ADLs, the benefit becomes payable.

loss. The essence of a contract of indemnity is the recovery of a loss suffered by the insured. Not all losses will be within the policy but the insured will recover under the policy if the loss has been caused by an insured peril. If the insured can show that he has suffered in a pecuniary way (*see* INSURABLE INTEREST) he has sustained a loss within the policy but a sentimental loss (qv) will not be covered. Even when the policy promises to indemnify the insured for his loss without qualification the policy will not cover all pecuniary losses, eg the term all risks of loss does not cover inherent vice as that is a certainty and not a risk (*British & Foreign Marine Insurance Co* v *Gaunt* (1925)). The Marine Insurance Act 1906, s. 55(2)(c) provides that 'unless the policy otherwise provides, the insurer is not liable for ordinary wear and tear'. Generally then, loss is a term for a claim or an event giving rise to a claim under the policy. It is necessary in some insurances and reinsurances to refer to the particular policy to see how the term has been defined. In property reinsurance catastrophe excess of loss treaties the hours clause (qv) is used. With cargo reinsurance damage between the point of sending and final destination constitute one loss. In directors' and officers' liability the operative clause simply refers to loss and then defines the term at length in the definitions. In liability insurance there are certain kinds of injury or damage where the effects can be identified more readily than their causation. This has resulted in the use of batch clauses (qv) and aggregation of losses over the policy term. Particular problems in relation to the term loss have arisen in respect of loss relating to missing goods (qv), loss relating to irrecoverable goods (qv), and loss of car (qv), and loss of proceeds (qv). *See also* ACTUAL TOTAL LOSS, CONSTRUCTIVE TOTAL LOSS, GENERAL AVERAGE LOSS, and PARTICULAR AVERAGE LOSS.

loss adjuster. A highly trained and independent claims expert engaged by insurers on a fee-paying basis to investigate claims and assess the true extent and value of any loss. Loss adjusters are not engaged for smaller, routine type losses which can be handled by the insurer's own staff. The relevant professional body is the Chartered Institute of Loss Adjusters.

loss assessor. A person, sometimes called a public loss assessor, with specialist knowledge, appointed by the insured to assess his claim and negotiate a settlement with the insurer or insurer's representative, eg loss adjuster (qv).

loss occurrence. 1. Occurrence of a single loss. 2. An occurrence of several losses arising out of the same incident or catastrophe (*see* HOURS CLAUSE).

loss of attraction. An extension to a business interruption policy (qv) where the volume of business transacted is affected by another business or activity which acts as an attraction and enables the insured to benefit from 'passing trade'. For example, fire damage causing the closure of a main department store in a shopping mall could seriously affect the business of a small shop nearby entirely unaffected by the fire itself but suffering a loss of trade due to the interruption in activities at the main store.

'loss of car'. The own damage section of a comprehensive motor policy covers 'loss of or damage to the insured motor car'. This is 'all risks' cover and there is little doubt about the vast majority of claims made under this clause. However, the meaning of the term loss has called for the deliberation of the courts on more than one occasion, particularly where confidence tricksters have been involved. In *Webster* v *General Accident* (1953) a policyholder entrusted his car to a dealer for sale at an auction where the car failed to achieve the reserve price. The dealer falsely claimed to have a private buyer and this induced the policyholder to leave the car with the dealer who then sold it at another auction and kept the proceeds. The dealer sent cheques to the policyholder but all of these were dishonoured. The court decided that the moment the dealer decided to send the car to the auction for his own purposes, he effectively deprived the owner of his title. The car passed through a number of hands and although Webster reported the matter to the police and motoring organisations he had little prospect of recovering his car. He was the victim of conversion (qv). There was a loss within the meaning of the indemnity. *Eisinger* v *General Accident* (1953) involved a direct sale to a rogue who took the car and logbook in return for a cheque that was dishonoured. However, Eisinger had parted with both title and possession and all he had lost were the proceeds of the sale. Unlike Webster, Eisinger had entered into a contract of sale intending to pass title to the person with whom he had negotiated notwithstanding the dishonesty of that person. There was no claim for loss under the policy. The policy is not intended as a form of guarantee of the creditworthiness of anyone to whom the policyholder might sell a car and that can never have been intended by the insurer. See DOORSTEP CAR SALES.

loss of documents. 1. *Material damage policies.* Fire, theft and similar policies enable professional people, eg solicitors, to insure against loss or damage to documents caused by the perils concerned. The indemnity is limited to the value of the documents as stationery and the cost of clerical labour in rewriting the documents. See ALL OTHER CONTENTS. 2. *Professional indemnity policies.* A 'loss of documents' extension covers the insured against legal liability to third parties following loss/damage to documents which are the property of the insured or those entrusted to him. The cover includes actions against the insured for conversion (qv), trespass (qv), eg erasing a tape-recording, and negligence. Cover is also provided in respect of the cost of replacing or restoring the documents provided they are not otherwise insured. The policy operates only in respect of loss/damage occurring in the UK. The policy excess applies only to the legal liability cover. The policy exclusion relating to losses caused by dishonesty, malicious acts, criminal acts etc of the insured, his predecessors or employees applies to all claims under the extension. Documents are defined in the extension as 'Deeds, Wills, Agreements, Maps, Plans, Records, written or printed Books, Letters, Certificates or written or printed Documents and/or Forms of any nature whatsoever used in connection with the Insured's business or practice, but excluding any Bearer Bonds or Coupons, Bank or Currency Notes or other negotiable paper or any computer records'.

losses-occurring policies. In liability claims there may be a separation in time between the act of negligence, the loss or damage, and the submission of the claim. Policies, therefore, need a 'trigger'. Most liability policies operate on a 'losses-occurring' basis, ie the policy applies to all losses occurring during the policy period. The time of negligence and claim are ignored for this purpose. Compare with claims-made' (qv) policies.

loss of expectation of life claims. A person injured by the negligence of another could recover, as a separate head of damages, for loss of his normal expectation of life (*Flint* v *Lovell* (1935)). The personal representatives of the deceased were also able to claim under this head (usually an award for a conventional amount was made—*McCann* v *Sheppard* (1973)). As a separate head of claim it has been abolished by the Administration of Justice Act 1982, s. 1 (qv). See also LOST YEARS. However, if the plaintiff's expectation of life has been reduced, any award for pain and suffering may take account of the plaintiff's anguish caused by his awareness of this reduction.

loss of hire insurance. An insurance for shipowners who may lose a charter as a result of a casualty. The insurance is expressed as an amount per day approximating to the charter rate for a certain number of days (eg 90, but could be as much as 360) in excess of an initial fixed period which is often 14 days. Cover follows the Institute Time Clauses—Hulls but excludes total loss.

loss of licence policy. A policy to cover commercial pilots against the risks of being temporarily grounded or loss of licence on medical grounds. The sum insured for each pilot is usually a multiple of his annual salary. The underwriting factors are: type of flying done; geographical limits; flying experience and type of aircraft flown; previous health record; previous licence invalidations.

loss of liquor licence. An insurance for those who run licensed premises. Cover is against the depreciation in value of the premises and loss of gross profit in the event of the suspension, refusal to renew or the forfeiture of the licence for the sale of excisable liquors. Cover applies if the cause of the loss or forfeiture etc is beyond the control of the insured. The costs and expenses incurred in connection with an appeal against such suspension, forfeiture or refusal are sometimes included in the cover.

loss of market. The inability to sell a product or complete a contract as a result of delay or damage. It is a consequential loss and not generally covered under insurance contracts but there are exceptions, eg contract price insurance (qv).

loss of proceeds relating to the proceeds of the sale of property. *See* LOSS OF CAR.

loss of profits insurance. A term that has largely been superseded by the term business interruption insurance (qv).

loss of specie. This arises when the subject-matter of insurance (qv) is so badly damaged that it so loses its identity that it ceases to be the type of thing that was insured (eg a bicycle crushed by a steam roller, or a shipment of food so damaged by sea perils it ceases to be fit for human consumption).

loss of use. Inability to use property, eg a motor-car, during the period of repair or replacement following loss or damage. The risk is not covered under the standard motor policy but even where there is no specific exclusion there is no cover under the policy. One or two insurers offer a replacement car for a short period and some will provide loss of use cover at an additional premium. An insurer who elects to repair and causes the repair car to be unreasonably delayed may be liable in damages for the delay (*Davidson* v *Guardian Royal Exchange Assurance* (1979)). Often loss of use is an uninsured loss and, if a third party caused the damage, a claim may be made against that party. The cost of pursuing such claims is covered under motoring legal expenses insurance.

loss of use policy (aviation). An insurance to safeguard an aircraft owner against loss of earning capacity when laid-up for repair following an accident. The benefit is expressed as an amount per day as agreed between the parties. The policy is normally subject to a time excess (qv). Cover operates only when a claim is admitted under the hull policy.

loss portfolio. *See* CLEAN CUT BASIS.

loss prevention. The measures taken to eliminate or minimise the probability of the occurrence of a loss and the effects of losses that do occur. *See* POST-LOSS MINIMISATION and PRE-LOSS MINIMISATION.

Loss Prevention Certification Board. The part of the Loss Prevention Council (qv) that provides approvals and a quality assurance service within the criteria set by the National Accreditation Council for Certification Bodies for loss prevention equipment, building construction materials and maintenance and installation services.

Loss Prevention Council (LPC). Established in 1986 the LPC provides a total fire and loss prevention service. It works closely with the Association of British Insurers and Lloyd's and acts as an approvals body on their behalf. The LPC assumes responsibility for the approvals schemes, rules and recommendations formerly issued by the Fire Offices' Committee (qv). It is also concerned to raise the standard of performance, reliability, and quality of fire protection and buildings and structures in the UK. The LPC incorporates the following organisations: the Loss Prevention Council Technical Centre (qv), the Loss Prevention Council Certification Board (qv), and the Fire Protection Association (qv).

Loss Prevention Council Technical Centre. The centre is the outcome of relocating the technical department of the Fire Offices' Committee (qv) alongside the Fire Insurers' Research and Testing Centre. It carries out tests and evaluates fire protection equipment, materials and structures in accordance with procedures required by insurers, standards organisations, and the requirements of FOC/LPC standards. Development and research work is conducted and a consultancy service is available.

loss ratio. The ratio of claims to premiums.

'loss' relating to irrecoverable goods. In *Morley* v *Evans* (1918) shortly before the first World War a jeweller forwarded goods to his bailees in Frankfurt and Brussels on a sale or return. The Germans then occupied Brussels and for four years both sets of jewellery were irrecoverable. The insured's claim for loss was rejected as, although temporarily irrecoverable, there was no suggestion that the German authorities had interfered with or seized the property. The jewellery did not apparently leave the custody of the insured's authorised bailees and accordingly the pearls were not 'lost' to him although he had suffered temporary deprivation. Complete deprivation is a different story but that is not a necessary requirement to establish a loss within the meaning of the policy. If, after all reasonable steps have been taken, the property has not been recovered, it seems that a loss has occurred. In *London & Provincial Leather Processes Ltd* v *Hudson* (1939) theoretical legal remedies, which are difficult to enforce in practice, against persons without proper title to goods made it unlikely that a recovery would be made.

'loss' relating to missing goods. Missing goods will be deemed lost for the purposes of an insurance covering loss if, after a reasonable lapse of time to allow for a diligent search, they have not been recovered. The subsequent discovery of the missing property does not disprove the loss. In *Holmes* v *Payne* (1930) 2 K.B. 301 jewellery was missed on 24 November and this was reported to the insurers on 25 November. On 4 December an agreement to replace the property was proposed and in December and February replacement articles were selected. The missing jewellery was found on 27 February and the insurers were bound by the agreement to provide replacements. Their contention that the jewellery was not *lost* was rejected for the reasons stated. The insured was not, of course, entitled to retain the recovered jewellery. It was important that a diligent search had been made so where the insured makes little or no effort to find the missing goods it will be difficult to prove a loss within the policy.

loss reserve. 1. An amount set aside to provide for outstanding claims, both reported and not reported. 2. A reserve deposited by a reinsurer with the reinsured to cover outstanding claims. It is often done by way of irrevocable letter of credit in connection with USA treaties and contracts.

lost motor insurance certificate. A certificate issued to the insured in accordance with the Road Traffic Act which has been lost or destroyed. The insurer, if satisfied as to the loss, must replace it at the request of the insured. In the case of defaced certificates the insurer can delay issue of the new certificate until the defaced document is returned.

lost or not lost. Most marine insurances were formerly effected 'lost or not lost'. This meant (Rule for Construction No. 1) where the subject-matter (qv) had been lost before the contract was concluded, the risk attached unless, at such time the insured had been aware of the loss and the insurer was not. The term lost or not lost is no longer used in the Institute Cargo Clauses (1/1/82). Clause 11.1 (the Insurable Interest Clause) specifically provides that the insured must have an insurable interest at the time of the loss. Clause 11.2 provides that, subject to 11.1, the insured is entitled to recover for insured loss occurring during the period of insurance, notwithstanding that the loss occurred before the contract was concluded, unless the insured was aware of the loss and the insurer was not.

lost policy. Loss of a policy does not invalidate a contract and in non-life business duplicates can be issued without difficulty. In life insurance, the insurers are more cautious as life policies can acquire a surrender value, be used for loan purposes or become assigned. If pressed and satisfied that there have been no unrecorded dealings with the policy most insurers will issue a duplicate provided that the insured completes a statutory declaration giving the history of the loss and stating that the policy has not been dealt with in any way.

'lost years'. The years by which a person's life expectancy is reduced following an accident or disease caused by another person. The plaintiff is able to recover as a separate head of damages for the loss of earnings during the 'lost years' (*Pickett* v *British Rail Engineering Ltd* (1980) A.C. 136). The legal personal representatives of a deceased person could also recover damages under this head for the benefit of the estate (*Gammell* v *Wilson* (1981) 1. A.E.R. 578 H.L.) but by virtue of The Administration of Justice Act 1982 (qv) this particular right of claim no longer exists.

lowering of ground water. A 'nuisance' peril that can give rise to liability for damage to third party property even though there may have been no negligence. The risk, which can also cause damage to the contract works and the insured's own property, is faced by members of the construction industry. Insurance can be arranged under JCT clause 21(2)(1). Ground water is the water that occupies the pores and crevices of rock and soil as opposed to surface water. Where the work of the contractor or his sub-contractor lowers the ground water the stability of buildings may be undermined leading to a common law liability for the tort of nuisance if third party damage is caused.

low cost endowment. *See* HOUSE PURCHASE SCHEMES.

low start endowment insurance. An endowment policy (qv) under which the premiums in the early years are set at a

low level on the understanding that later premiums will be at a higher level to compensate the insurer for the loss of premium in those years.

lump sum. A method of settlement where the claimant or beneficiary receives the entire proceeds of the policy at once rather than in instalments. Life policies are most usually settled in this way.

Lutine Bell. The bell from H.M.S. *Lutine* a French vessel lost in 1799 when carrying bullion much of which was recovered in 1857/8. The bell now hangs in the 'Room' at Lloyd's above the Caller's Rostrum and is rung to call attention to very important announcements such as casualties and arrivals of missing ships. It is rung once for bad news and twice for good news.

M

machinery consequential loss insurance.
An engineering policy covering loss of
profits, increased costs of working and
continuing overheads due to a reduction or complete stoppage of production following sudden and unforeseen
damage (including breakdown) to
plant and machinery. The risks of accidental failure of the supplies of electricity, gas or water can be also be
included. There are excesses and franchises applied to the indemnity period
(qv) to avoid small losses particularly
as a result of temporary breaks in service.

machinery erection insurance. An engineering insurance catering for contractors and others involved in the
movement, erection or installation of
plant and machinery. The cover enables the contractor to meet his contractual obligations and, depending on
the circumstances, can be extended to:
testing operations; maintenance period liability; constructional plant and
equipment used in connection with
the contract; manufacturers' guarantee for repairs or replacements from
manufacturing defects.

**magnetic and dye penetrant flaw detec-
tion.** A service available from engineering insurers. Magnetic testing is used
to locate minute surface imperfections
by spraying a suspension of magnetic
oxides on the surface of the part
under test and applying a magnetic
field. This causes particles of oxide to
accumulate around the small cracks or
flaw cavities. Dye-penetrant testing replaces magnetic testing on non-mag-
netic materials. A highly penetrative
dye is applied to the surface of the part
under test.

maintenance bond. A type of performance bond (qv) under which the
surety guarantees that the contractor
will fulfil his obligations during the defects liability period.

maintenance payments plan. *See* MARRIAGE
INSURANCE.

maintenance protection plan. *See* MAR-
RIAGE INSURANCE.

maintenance warranty. This, sometimes
included in a fire policy, requires the
insured to maintain the premises in a
good and substantial state of repair
during the currency of the policy.

malicious damage. Unlawful damage
committed by individuals motivated by
ill-will in circumstances not amounting
to a riot (qv). Some cover is available
as an extension of the riot contingency
in that damage caused by malicious
persons acting on behalf of a political
organisation is covered. Wider material damage cover can be obtained, subject to an excess and the exclusion of
loss by theft, as an extension of the
normal 'riot' cover. A theft or burglary
policy covers malicious damage after
violent and forcible entry into the
premises (or as otherwise stated in the
operative clause). The commission of
actual malicious damage is an offence
under the Criminal Damage Act 1971
and may otherwise be called criminal
damage.

malicious product tamper. A crime that
concerns the contamination of goods,
or the threat thereof, but which is not
accompanied by any demand for
money. The resultant expenses incurred by a victim can be insured
under malicious product tamper insurance. Food manufacturers and retailers are the most likely victims. They
can also avail themselves of specialised
consultancy services under the policy.

malpractice insurance. The USA equivalent of professional indemnity insurance (qv). The term is occasionally
used in the UK.

Malta Group 1974. An informal group of
West European governments with the
aim of encouraging countries to adopt
higher limits of liability for death or

personal injury in their general conditions of carriage. The UK made it a condition from October 1975 that every air transport licence issued by the Civil Aviation Authority (CAA) should oblige the holder to enter into a special contract with every passenger to be carried to increase the carrier's limit of liability to not less than £25 000 including costs. The CAA now requires 100 000 special drawing rights (qv), about \$100 000.

manageable risks. Risks which can be handled by the process of risk management (qv) and the term may be applied to any risk that is not regarded as an entrepreneurial risk (qv).

managed fund. A unit-linked fund in which transactions in the underlying assets are made upon the decision of the fund manager. Normally the fund managers invest in a spread of all types of assets as opposed to a specified type of asset, eg a Japanese fund which invests exclusively in Japanese companies.

management expenses. The normal day-to-day expenses incurred in administering an insurance company, or syndicate or its business, excluding the commission payable.

manifestation. The term used in connection with a latent disease which identifies the date at which the disease becomes evident. Liability policies often operate on a losses-occurring basis (qv) and in these cases liability of the insurer is triggered by the occurrence of the disease and not its manifestation.

manual (or) group premium rating. Similar units of exposure (qv) are grouped together in order that the risk premium (qv) to be applied to the group, whose constituent units have similar underwriting factors, can be calculated with an acceptable degree of accuracy.

MAR form. A policy form introduced in 1983 by the Institute of London Underwriters and Lloyd's Underwriters Association to replace the S.G. form (qv) to simplify policy wordings. The new form states the agreement to insure in simple terms and the detailed cover is set out in the Institute Clauses which are attached.

margin of solvency. The Insurance Companies Act 1982 requires all authorised insurance companies to meet certain solvency standards. Key requirements are set out in Part II of the Insurance Company Regulations 1981 and requirements relating to the minimum guarantee fund (qv), which companies must maintain, are set out in the 1982 Act. The margin of solvency is the excess of the company's total assets over the solvency requirement. A company transacting general business or reinsurance business must maintain a minimum margin of solvency at least equal to the minimum guarantee fund for the classes of business it transacts. Companies writing direct long-term business (qv) must maintain a minimum margin of solvency according to an annual actuarial valuation of its assets and liabilities for different types of long-term business. In addition UK companies writing long-term business must maintain a minimum guarantee fund (qv) amounting to one-third of their minimum solvency margin. *See* MARGIN OF SOLVENCY (GENERAL BUSINESS) and MARGIN OF SOLVENCY (LONG-TERM BUSINESS) for details on the calculation of the margins of solvency.

margin of solvency (general business). A general business company must maintain a minimum margin of solvency (qv) at least equal to the minimum guarantee fund for the classes of business it transacts. The solvency margin is calculated by two methods, the premium basis and the claims basis, and the prescribed margin is the greater of the two sums so calculated. The calculations follow set formulae. In the premium basis the company's gross premium income (no deduction for reinsurance ceded) is converted into ECUs at the current rate of exchange and a percentage of 18 per cent applied to the first 10 m ECUs and 16 per cent to the balance. The resultant figure is multiplied by the net ratio of claims incurred to gross premiums incurred in the last financial year, subject to a maximum deduction for claims recoverable from reinsurers of 50 per cent. This gives the solvency requirement on a premium basis. The claims basis uses the average gross claims incurred in the last three financial years. Twenty-six per cent is applied to the first 7 m ECUs and 23 per cent is applied to the balance. The resultant figure is multiplied by the ratio of net claims incurred to gross claims paid in the last financial year, subject to a maximum deduction of 50 per cent for claims recoverable under reinsurance facilities.

margin of solvency (long-term business). The margin of solvency (qv) for long-term business varies according to the class of business. Where more than one class is involved, the solvency margin for each class is aggregated to find the required margin of solvency. The minimum margin for long-term business is the aggregate of two calculations. Calculation (i): 4 per cent (1 per cent only for certain linked contracts where the company bears no investment risk and nil where there is no limit on management charges) of the mathematical reserves (qv) for direct business and reinsurance acceptances without deduction for reinsurances ceded. The figure is then multiplied by 85 per cent. Where the percentage of 'net' mathematical reserves (ie after subtracting reinsurance ceded) exceeds 85 per cent of the gross figure the higher percentage figure is used for the multiplication. Calculation (ii). 0.3 per cent of the gross capital at risk (the sum payable on death less the mathematical reserve in respect of relevant contracts). Where a policy providing death benefits is valid for less than five years and more than three years the figure is 0.15 per cent and if it is valid for less than three years the figure is 0.1 per cent. The rules allow for a deduction of reinsurance cessions from the gross capital at risk subject to a maximum of 50 per cent of the gross. The solvency requirements for all long-term business are related to these calculations as follows: life and annuity business the sum of (i) and (ii); marriage birth the sum of (i) and (ii); linked long-term (i) plus (ii) for death risks only; permanent health (i) only; tontines 1 per cent of the assets of the tontine; capital redemption (i) only; pension fund management (i) plus (ii) for death risks. The margin of solvency must be at least equal to the minimum guarantee fund (800 000 ECUs). In addition UK companies must maintain a minimum guarantee fund level (qv) equal to one-third of the minimum solvency margin. If this level is not covered the company must prepare and implement a short term financial scheme to remedy the position otherwise the DTI may intervene. The margin of solvency must be covered by specific items consisting of: share capital and reserves not attributable to general business; the excess of fund assets over liabilities. All of these requirements are in accordance with the EC Life Establishment Directive.

marine and aviation risks exclusion. An exclusion in a public liability policy of risks more suitably insured in the marine and aviation markets. The exclusion refers to the liability arising out of the ownership or possession or use by or on behalf of the insured of aircraft, hovercraft, or watercraft other than barges, motor launches and non-powered craft used on inland waterways. If the insured owns or uses small craft this risk is covered under the policy. Also the insured may seek a modification of the exclusion so that any contingent or vicarious liability associated with craft not owned or operated by the insured is within the policy. Non-owned craft may be used for the purposes of entertaining, eg river trips etc.

marine cargo certificate of insurance. Evidence that an individual consignment is insured. Banks will only discount bills of exchange on the production of this certificate.

marine clause. A fire insurance clause excluding from the cover property which is insured or would but for the existence of the fire policy be insured by a marine policy except for any excess beyond the amount which would be paid by a marine policy.

Marine Insurance (Gambling Policies) Act 1909. *See* GAMBLING POLICIES.

marine insurance. Defined by the Marine Insurance Act, s. 1 as 'a contract whereby the insurer undertakes to indemnify the assured, in manner and to the extent thereby agreed, against marine losses, that is to say, the losses incident to marine adventure'. A policy written in the form of a marine insurance against a total loss in the event of peace not being declared between

Great Britain and Germany on or before 31 March 1918 was not a marine insurance and accordingly the Act did not apply (*Re London County Commercial Reinsurance Office Ltd* (1922)).

marine insurance certificate. A document that may be issued in respect of shipments declared under floating policies (qv). The purpose of a certificate is to replace the policy when this document is lodged is required by the bank or consignee. Certificates may be issued by Lloyd's, companies or brokers.

marine reinsurance commission. Reinsurance commission (qv) in the context of marine insurance. The commission can be charged either on the original gross premiums paid by the insured or as an overriding deduction from the net premiums received by the cedant (qv). On the gross premium basis it is fixed at a level to cover the company's average expenses of acquisition plus an allowance to cover the cedant's administrative expenses. The total cost varies according to the way in which the original business was acquired and a fair average must be agreed. On the 'net basis' the calculation provides for the acquisition costs to be deducted from the original premiums. The reinsurance company's overriding commission (qv) then has to only take care of the cedant's own expenses. Whichever method is used the cedant can expect account to be taken of the quality of its business and so commission terms will vary according to the business and the type of protection offered.

maritime adventure. Defined in the Marine Insurance Act 1906 as existing where (i) tangible property is exposed to loss by maritime perils, (ii) any pecuniary interest etc. is thereby endangered, (iii) any third party liability may thereby be incurred. To be insurable, such adventure must be lawful.

market agreement. An agreement among insurers to establish practices beneficial to the interests of those participating in the agreement. Most commonly, insurers enter into claims agreements to avoid expensive debates and arguments about liability when each insurer insures a party involved in an accident. The agreements are voluntary and work well when each insurer writes a similar account so that, overall, the net amount that one insurer would owe another under normal legal processes is insignificant when compared to the savings gained by avoiding administration, legal and investigation costs. *See* KNOCK FOR KNOCK AGREEMENT and COMMON LAW AGREEMENT. Market agreements are also made by underwriters at Lloyd's in given sections of insurance business.

market capacity. The total amount of insurance capable of being undertaken by all insurers operating in the relevant market.

market captive. The parent of a captive insurance company (qv).

market overt. Market overt (ie open market) in the City of London is held every day except Sunday and in every shop where goods are exposed for sale in the ordinary course of the trader's business. The sale must be made openly between sunset and sunrise (*Reid* v *Commissioner of Police of the Metropolis* (1973)). Market overt elsewhere is only held on the special days at the particular places provided for by charter or prescription. The doctrine is of significance to insurers who seek to recover property insured under theft policies. If stolen goods are sold in market overt, the purchaser, if acting in good faith, acquires a valid title to them against the true owner (Sale of Goods Act 1979, s. 22(1)) but the court has the power to make orders for restitution or for compensation (Theft Act 1968, s. 28; Criminal Justice Act 1972, s. 6, Schedules 5,6). This means, *inter alia*, that even a bona fide purchaser must return the goods if the thief is prosecuted to conviction. Insurers who have paid for losses by theft acquire the title to them. This is usually made clear in a policy condition which enables the insured to reclaim the property on refunding the claims payment.

market share liability. A principle of liability the concept of which has been accepted in certain US courts in response to the problems caused by the delay in toxic tort claims between the time of exposure and the time of manifestation (qv) of the injury. It may be difficult to discover whose product caused the injurious exposure and, when applied, the market share liability theory enables the plaintiff to proceed without proof as to the specific product or manufacturer. The theory requires the plaintiff to join as defendants a substantial number of manufacturers and shifts the burden to the defendants to show that they could not have made the substance that caused the plaintiff's injury. Each defendant is held liable for the proportion of the judgment represented by their market share unless they can disprove their involvement. The theory has been denied in some cases brought in respect of asbestos actions partly because injury caused by asbestos exposure is not restricted to asbestos products. *See the* WELLINGTON AGREEMENT.

'marriage insurance.' A two-part insurance devised by a Lloyd's broker. The first part, the maintenance protection plan, enables a man to insure against a fall in the income of his ex-wife through illness, disability, redundancy or unfair dismissal, all of which could increase the maintenance payments he has to make. The second part, the maintenance payments plan , enables a woman to insure against a fall in her ex-husband's income.

Married Womens' Policies of Assurance (Scotland) Act 1880. The Scottish equivalent of the Married Womens' Property Act 1882 (qv).

Married Womens' Property Act 1882. Under this Act s. 11, a married woman can effect a policy on her own life or the life of her husband for her separate use. No similar power is given to a husband but the Act further provides that a policy of assurance effected by a man on his own life, and expressed to be for the benefit of his wife and/or children, creates a trust (qv) in favour of the stated objects. Any moneys payable under such a policy do not form a part of the husband's estate or become subject to his debts. The same situation applies when a policy is effected by a wife for the benefit of her husband and/or children. The Act creates a trust of life policies where, apart from the Act, they would not be created and gives special protection against creditors.

martial law. 'The exercise by armed forces of the ordinary power of the executive to suppress disturbances. It can come into existence only in time of war or rebellion. It does not rest upon a proclamation which is a statement of an existing fact rather than the legal creation of that fact, the proclamation of martial law being in effect a declaration by the executive government that ordinary law is inadequate to cope with the circumstances, and a provision of exceptional means of arrest and punishment of persons who resist the government or aid the enemy. Martial law is, therefore, the suspension of ordinary law, rendered necessary by circumstances of war and rebellion. It is not a law in the proper sense of the term, but the exercise of the will of a military commander, who takes the responsibility of suspending ordinary law in order to ensure the safety of the state. Martial law is illegal in time of peace, but is, by inference, declared lawful in time of war and internal commotion'. (F.H. Jones, *The Law of Accident and Contingency Insurance*, Pitman).

master policy schemes. A scheme under which an insurance company or Lloyd's syndicate permits a broker to issue cover to eligible insureds on terms and conditions laid down in a master policy. Individual insureds are issued with certificates of insurance which set out the principal features of the cover and incorporate all of the terms of the master policy by reference. These schemes are well known in the professional indemnity market. Brokers are not empowered to vary the standard terms and conditions of the master document.

matching and localisation. Regulations within the Insurance Companies Regulations 1981 lay down that an insurance company must match part of its technical reserves by assets denominated in the same currency and to hold such assets either in the UK or the country of the currency concerned. The requirements come into effect whenever the liabilities in any particular currency exceed 5 per cent of that company's liabilities in which event the company must hold assets capable of realisation into that currency without exchange risk to cover at least 80 per cent of the liabilities in that currency. The regulation applies to all insurance business except: (i) Business carried on outside the UK. (ii) Marine and aviation insurance. (iii) Business of a pure reinsurer who does not write facultative business. (iv) In some cases where the liability is for property-linked benefits.

material damage insurance. The insurance of tangible property as distinct from the insurance of persons (life and limb), rights, pecuniary interests, and liability. Fire, theft, motor, cargo and hull policies are all policies which are entirely or partly of a material damage nature where the subject-matter of insurance takes the form of tangible property. The property can be insured against named perils or on 'all risks' basis depending on the type of property concerned.

material damage warranty. This appears in a business interruption insurance (qv) and provides that, before a claim can be admitted, there must be a material damage policy in force under which a claim has been paid or liability admitted.

material fact. Any fact that influences the judgment of a prudent underwriter (qv) in his assessment of the risk. Such facts have to be disclosed. *See* UTMOST GOOD FAITH. Certain facts do not have to be disclosed unless there is a specific inquiry. The Marine Insurance Act 1906, s. 18(3) sets these out: facts which diminish the risk; facts the insurers may be presumed to know; facts as to which information is waived; facts superfluous to disclose because of policy conditions. In addition the proposer does not have to disclose facts capable of discovery from information disclosed and facts that the insurer should have noticed on a survey.

maternity cash benefit. A benefit payable under some private health insurances at a specified rate, eg £100 for each child, after the policy has been in force for at least 10 months.

mathematical reserves. The provision made by an insurer to cover liabilities (excluding liabilities which have fallen due) arising under or in connection with contracts for long-term business.

mature drivers. Drivers over the age of 55. Some private car insurers seek to attract mature drivers by the offer of a special discount on the basis they are experienced and have fewer accidents than those below that age. In some instances the mature drivers' discount is at one level for drivers aged 55–59 and a higher level for those aged 60–70.

maturity. The end of the term of an endowment insurance.

maximum possible loss (MPL). A factor taken into account by the insured when fixing the ceiling on the cover required and by the insurer when deciding how much cover they will grant or retain. MPL is the largest possible loss which it is estimated may occur in regard to a particular risk given the worst combination of circumstances.

means test. The test to demonstrate that a person applying for underwriting membership of Lloyd's has sufficient personal wealth to meet the requirements of the Council of Lloyd's. Only certain assets qualify for inclusion in the test, eg the funds held at Lloyd's in the form of deposits, personal reserve, and special reserve funds, the object being to ensure that a high proportion of the wealth is in the form of readily realisable assets.

measure of exposure. *See* UNIT OF EXPOSURE.

mechanical breakdown exclusion. Motor insurers exclude from the own damage section of a comprehensive policy mechanical or electrical breakdowns or failures or breakages. A motor policy is not a maintenance contract obliging the insurer to replace worn parts, but really this is an excluded form of loss (qv) rather than an excluded peril. If the breakdown, eg brake failure, causes an accident with both own damage and third party damage, the own damage will be covered (but not the repair of the brake) and the insured will also get the benefit of the third party section of the policy. However, if the breakdown is the result of the insured's failure to observe the reasonable care condition (qv) he may get no benefit under the policy.

medical aid insurance. The term, private medical insurance is an alternative, describing the various insurances aimed at providing cover in respect of the cost of private medical and related treatment. The principal benefits available in a complete package or some combination falling short of that are: (a) Cash benefits. A payment at a fixed rate for each day in hospital (qv) as per hospital cash plan (qv). Maternity cash benefit (qv). Personal or out-of-pocket expenses (to cover newspapers, telephone calls, visitors' meals)—in all instances at a fixed rate per day in hospital. (b) Treatment. eg Accommodation and nursing charges, surgeons,' anaesthetists' and operating theatre fees, X-rays, dressings and drugs while an in-patient, consultants' and physicians' fees, radiotherapy, chemotherapy, physiotherapy, private ambulances and other specialist treatment. Full refunds are provided by the insurer, usually subject to a maximum amount for each benefit. Out-patient and day-care treatment is also covered if linked to a stay in hospital. Overseas treatment is also covered if the insured or a member of his family (under family policies) is involved in holidays or business trips when treatment is needed. The treatment must be given by, or under the control of, a specialist and the insured must have been referred to the specialist by his own general practitioner. The exclusions follow the lines of those of the hospital cash plan (qv) and the Finance Act 1989 gives income tax relief on premiums paid by individuals over the age of 60. If premiums are paid by an employer, the employee pays tax on it as a benefit in kind if earning above a certain salary.

medical attendant's report. A life insurer may call for a private medical attendant's report under non-medical schemes (qv). The report elicits details of the proposer's medical history and assists the underwriter where, because some medical point needs further enquiry, a decision cannot be made simply based on the proposal form details.

Medical Defence Union, Ltd. An association formed into a limited liability company whose members are medical practitioners and dentists. The services provided include the conduct of legal proceedings for members, an indemnity in whole of part against claims based on breach of duty, and advising on matters of a professional or legal nature. Payment of the membership gives the member access to professional indemnity insurance but the union is not an insurance company within the the the terms of the Insurance Companies Act 1974 (*Medical Defence Union, Ltd.* v *Department of Trade* (1978)). Since January 1990, the Department of Health has required health authorities to meet damages and costs incurred by their employed doctors and dentists in cases of negligence.

'member of a household'. *See* 'ANY MEMBER OF THE ASSURED'S HOUSEHOLD'.

member to member liability. *See* MEMBERS' CLUBS.

members' agent. A Lloyd's underwriting agency which introduces members to a syndicate but does not manage one.

Members' Agent Information Report (MAIR). Each Lloyd's underwriting agent is required to prepare a Members' Agent Information Report showing, *inter alia*, its average performance for each year of account. The average performance is derived from the sum of the aggregate results of the Names for whom the agent acts, expressed as a percentage of the total allocated capacity of those Names. The market average return can be compared with the average performance required to be calculated and disclosed by members' agents. The return for each year of account is restated at successive year ends to take account of calendar year movements on run-off years of account.

members' clubs. A voluntary association of individuals for social or other purposes. It is not a partnership and must sue or be sued in the names of the members of the committee, or the officers, on behalf of themselves and all other members of the club. Members are liable only to the extent of their subscriptions. Clubs commonly effect public liability insurances on ordinary terms and conditions but can extend cover to include the personal liability of members as well. A further extension is member to member liability which means that the policy will operate to indemnify one member when a fellow member brings an action against him as an individual for injury or damage that is within the scope of the policy.

members' means. *See* LLOYD'S MEMBERS' MEANS.

Memorandum, The. A clause referring to particular average (qv) used in connection with the now discarded SG form. Broadly the object of the clause was to free underwriters from liability for particular average in respect of certain classes of goods which were particularly susceptible to damage by insured perils and in respect of other goods, also the ship and the freight, and to apply a franchise or a percentage of damage which had to be reached before a particular average claim could be recovered from the insurer.

Memorandum of Association. A deed that must be completed as a part of the process in creating a company to be incorporated under the Companies Acts. Two or more persons may by subscribing their names to a memordandum, and complying with the other statutory requirements, form an incorporated company with or without limited liability (Companies Act 1948, s. 1; Companies Act 1980, s. 2). The memorandum must state (a) the name of the company, (b) situation of registered office, (c) the objects of the company, (d) that, in the case of a company limited by shares or guarantee, the liability of members is limited, (e) the amount of any share capital and its division. The memorandum cannot be varied by the company itself (except in special circumstances) but only by application to the court. The memorandum delimits the powers of the company so that any act that is in excess of the powers conferred by the objects clause will be *ultra vires*, ie beyond the power, and therefore invalid.

memorial stone insurance. An insurance purchased by a 'single' premium offering all risks cover in respect of a memorial stone at the head of a grave. Few schemes are available but cover is usually provided for a period of five years at the end of which a further 5 years cover can be obtained, and so on. Third party insurance is included and a 5 per cent escalator operates to help keep the benefits in line with inflation.

merchantable quality. In terms of the Sale of the Goods Act 1979 (qv) s. 14 (2) merchantable quality means that the goods must be as fit for the purpose for which goods of that kind are commonly bought as it is reasonable to expect (having regard to any description applied to them, the price and all other relevant circumstances). So a person buying a new pair of shoes would not expect the soles to come away within days of purchase but a person buying a 10-year-old car from a dealer could not reasonably expect it to perform like a new car, although he could expect that kind of service that the average car of that mileage and make would give. A purchaser has no right to reject goods in respect of defects brought to his attention before the sale. Also, if a purchaser examines goods before buying them, this right does not apply to defects he should have seen during the examination. The seller can use an exclusion clause (qv) in respect of this implied obligation if the buyer is not a consumer (*see* NON-CONSUMER SALES, subject to the test of reasonableness (qv), but cannot do so in consumer sales (qv). Sellers who breach this implied duty will be liable in damages in respect of the goods themselves and their injurious consequences. These consequences constitute a products liability risk while damages relating to the goods themselves are in some instances insurable under products guarantee insurance (qv). The implied term does not apply to goods bought from a private individual. *See also* 'FITNESS FOR PURPOSE'.

Merchant Shipping Act 1979 (Commencement No. 6) Order 1982. The order enables the Secretary of State to hold an enquiry or an investigation, or both, into incidents producing, or capable of producing, a casualty. The latter is extended to include cases of serious personal injury. These results are produced by the links between this Order and the relevant sections of the Merchant Shipping Acts 1970 and 1979.

Merchant Shipping (Oil Pollution) Act 1971. As amended by the Merchant Shipping Act 1974 this states that certain oil carrying vessels must have a certificate of insurance before they can enter or leave port.

'Merle Oberon' Clause. The clause in the third party section of a private car policy indemnifying persons other than the insured. Such persons, who are indemnified as though they were the insured, are: any driver; any user; any passenger; the insured's employer or partner. Such persons are bound by the terms and conditions of the policy. The clause acquired its name from the case of *Digby* v *General Accident* (1942). Film star Merle Oberon sustained injury while travelling as a passenger in her own car driven by her chauffeur. She claimed against the chauffeur who sought an indemnity from the insurer as a person permitted to drive. The insurer contended that Miss Oberon could not constitute herself as a third party under her own policy and that it was not their intention to create a new class of claimant. Their argument was rejected by the House of Lords who found in favour of Digby.

Metal Workers' Extension. An extension applying the insured's fire policy to the premises of any machine maker, engineer, metal worker, customer, agent or sub-contractor and whilst in transit by road, rail or inland waterway in Great Britain and Ireland but excluding premises occupied by the insured, subject to a maximum liability under this extension and also a maximum any one location.

military or usurped power. 'This includes not only the acts of foreign enemies engaged in warfare within the realm or of subjects of the Crown engaged in internal warfare, but also the acts done by forces of the Crown in repelling the enemy or suppressing a rebellion. There must be something in the nature of warfare, something more in the nature of war or civil war than of riot or civil commotion.' (F.H. Jones, *The Law of Accident and Contingency Insurance.* Pitman.) The risk of damage caused by this risk is usually excluded in property insurance together with similar risks such as riot and civil commotion. Liability for damage caused in these ways rests with the authorities responsible for maintaining law and order and not with insurers.

mini bonds. A special application of a single premium bond (qv) to meet the desire of an individual investor to pursue specific investment objectives. A separate fund is created within the insurer's funds for the benefit of the individual who gets life cover and the tax advantages while being able to control the assets underlying his investment. Mini bonds are also called individual or personalised bonds.

minimum contributions. Contributions payable to a personal pension scheme or to a free-standing additional voluntary contribution (qv) scheme by the DSS in respect of a member who has elected to contract out. The contributions consist of a partial rebate of National Insurance contributions, together with the 2 per cent incentive where applicable. The term is also used to describe any minimum amount which a member is required to contribute in order to be a member of an occupational or personal pension scheme, or in order to make additional voluntary contributions (qv).

minimum guarantee fund (MGF). Minimum reserves required by insurance company solvency regulations (Insurance Companies Act 1982). Companies must maintain a margin of solvency at least equal to the minimum guarantee fund which is the sterling equivalent of 200 000, 300 000 or 400 000 European currency units, depending on the class of business a company is authorised to transact in the case of a general business company. In the case of life business it is 800 000 ECUs. In both general and life business this is reduced by 25 per cent in the case of a mutual. If a company's net assets are less than the minimum guarantee fund,it must submit a short-term financial scheme to the Department of Trade and Industry.

minimum premium. The administrative costs of handling and processing policies have to be recovered regardless of the size of the risk. Consequently insurers usually prescribe a minimum premium for particular classes of risk (eg personal insurances and small 'shop' insurances) where small insurances are common.

minimum reserve. A nominal amount reserved against a claim that has been reported to an insurer but without sufficient information to enable the insurer to make a reasonable assessment of his potential liability on that claim.

Minus-30 club. One of two categories to which major international groups are commonly assigned for the purpose of rating. It means that the collective loss experience of a group over ten or more years is less than 30 per cent of the premiums. Such companies have a major incentive to form captives as rating by class is more costly for them than rating by experience. The other main category is the 100-plus club (qv).

mirror syndicate. A syndicate with the same constitution as another syndicate managed by the same managing agent.

misfeasance. The improper performance of a lawful act, eg repairing a road negligently. Compare with nonfeasance (qv).

missing beneficiaries indemnity. Executors, administrators or trustees may wish to distribute an estate among the available beneficiaries even though a beneficiary may be missing. The indemnity enables them to proceed with the distribution knowing that they will be indemnified against claims if the missing person later reappears.

missing document indemnity. A transaction may depend upon a life insurance policy, share certificate or other document that is missing. An indemnity given by an insurer may enable the transaction to proceed as the insured is then covered against any loss resulting from another person subsequently producing the document and basing a claim upon it.

missing goods. See LOSS RELATING TO MISSING GOODS.

mixed policy. A marine policy covering the subject-matter for the voyage and a period of time thereafter, such as a period in port.

modified vehicles. Unless advised to the contrary a motor insurer will always assume that the vehicle described in the proposal conforms to manufacturer's specification. It is material for anyone to advise the insurer that their particular vehicle has been modified or adapted in some way, usually in order to give an increased performance. Insurers will be concerned that the work

has been carried out properly and will want details of any increased performance in order that they can apply the appropriate rate and not the one normally assigned to a vehicle of that description.

money. See MONEY INSURANCE.

money insurance. Money is insured on an 'all risks' basis in transit, in the custody of collectors, at the insured's business premises during business hours, in a locked safe out of hours, and at the dwellings of the insured or authorised employees. Various limits may be imposed. The term 'money' means 'cash, bank and currency notes, cheques, postal and money orders, postage, national insurance, national savings and holiday with pay stamps, luncheon vouchers, consumer redemption vouchers, gift tokens—belonging to the insured or employee while deposited with the insured. Cover extends to include damage to safes and strongrooms and damage to clothing following robbery or attempt thereat. The policy excludes, *inter alia*, losses recoverable under fidelity guarantee insurance.

money purchase scheme. A pension scheme under which the individual member's benefits are determined by contributions paid into the scheme in respect of that member, usually increased by an amount based on the investment return on those contributions.

Montreal Agreement 1966. An inter-carrier agreement drawn up in Montreal and later approved by the Civil Aeronautics Board of the USA following earlier reticence on the part of the USA which felt that the Warsaw Convention (qv) limits were obsolete and unfair. The 1966 agreement increased the carrier's limit of liability for passenger death or injury to US$75 000 (inclusive of legal fees) or US$58 000 (plus fees). It also obliged carriers to provide a legible notice of the increased limits on the passenger ticket.

moped. This term is legally defined in order to distinguish a less powerful form of machine from motor cycles more generally. The Road Traffic Act sets the minimum age for riding mopeds and motor cyles at 16 and 17 years respectively. For machines first registered on or before 31 July 1977, a moped is a machine (ie motor cycle) with an engine capacity not exceeding 50 cylinder capacity and which is equipped with pedals as a means of propulsion. If registered on or after 1 August 1977 it is a machine which has a maximum design speed not exceeding 30 m.p.h., a kerb side weight not exceeding 250 kg and an engine with a cylinder capacity not exceeding 50 c.c.

moral hazard. This is the hazard arising from the character and behaviour of human beings (eg the insured, his employees, associates, and third parties) connected with the subject-matter of insurance. Moral hazard can be good or bad and will be affected by honesty, carefulness, reasonableness, business aptitude and attitude, and financial standing. Standards of conduct and behaviour are also influenced by the 'trend of events', eg an adverse economic or political situation can increase the crime rate and cause unrest. Moral hazard is difficult to assess but in some instances the risk can be improved by persuading the insured to take more interest in his own claims experience by imposing an excess or limiting the cover. Compare with physical hazard (qv).

'more specific insurance clause'. It is a non-contribution clause. Two policies may cover the same property and same interest, one in specific terms and the other in general terms. To prevent the two policies from being brought into contribution (qv), this clause provides that the more specific insurance operates first in a claim situation. The term 'more specific' refers to the range of property covered and not the range of perils.

Mortgage Interest Relief at Source. A system under which the payments made by the mortgagor to his bank or building society are net of income tax at the basic rate. Higher rate tax payers can claim additional tax relief through adjustment to their PAYE code.

mortgage protection. The name often applied to a decreasing term assurance used to cover the amount outstanding at any time during the period of an ordinary repayment mortgage. In the event of death before repayment of the mortgage the sum payable should be sufficient to clear the loan. The reductions in the sum assured are designed to fall in line with the reductions in the amount of outstanding debt as repayments of capital are made over the years. If the life assured survives the mortgage period the policy comes to an end and there is no return of premium. The reductions in the early years are for modest amounts, as very little capital is repaid in the early stages.

mortality table. An instrument by which the probabilities of life and probabilities of death can be measured. The basis is the ratio of the number of persons dying at any age to the number of persons alive at the beginning of the year of that age. Mortality and interest rate factors enable actuaries to produce life assurance 'net premium' calculations.

motor accessories. Additional items on or in the vehicle. In the case of private cars the material damage cover provided under a comprehensive policy will apply to accessories while in or on the car or in the insured's private garage. In the case of goods-carrying vehicles the accessories have to be on the vehicle. Radio and cassette players are treated by motor insurers as being within the term 'accessories'. *See* CAR TELEPHONES.

Motor Committee of the Association of British Insurers. A committee that does for motor insurance company members of the ABI what the Lloyd's Motor Underwriters' Association (qv) does for the motor syndicates at Lloyd's.

motor cycle. A machine for which the minimum age for permitted drivers is 17 years. In a legal sense it is any form of motor cycle that is not defined as moped (qv). Current regulations restrict 'learners' to motor cycles not exceeding 125 c.c. engine capacity.

motor cycle rider insurance policy. A policy centred on the rider rather than the motor cycle. The policy operates while the insured is riding any motor cycle up to the engine size selected by the insured. The policy can remain in force even though the insured may not own a motor cycle.

motor insurance. The insurance of motor vehicles and liabilities arising out of the use thereof. The principal forms of cover available are: (a) *Comprehensive* covering loss/damage to the insured's vehicle, liability to third parties, and various other sections depending on the type of vehicle involved. In private car insurances the extensions include personal accident cover, rugs, coats and personal effects, medical expenses, and foreign use. Commercial vehicles do not have these extensions but include a towing of disabled vehicles section. In the private car market limited comprehensive cover (qv) is available. (b) *Third party fire and theft*. Third party risks plus damage to the insured's vehicle if caused by fire and theft. (c) *Third party only*. (d) *Act only cover*, ie cover in accordance with the compulsory insurance requirements of the Road Traffic Act 1988 (qv). Insurers produce different rating structures and policy forms according to the type or use of vehicle proposed for insurance. The principal types are: private cars (excluding hire cars); commercial or goods-carrying vehicles; agricultural and forestry vehicles; motor trade; motor cycles, private, business and trade; mopeds; and special types.

Motor Insurance Anti-fraud and Theft Register (MIAFTR). A register that logs all total loss and theft of vehicle claims on computer at the Association of British Insurers' office. Both companies and Lloyd's participate in the scheme which assists in the tracing and recovery of vehicles.

motor insurance certificates. The certificate is proof that the use of a vehicle is insured in accordance with the Road Traffic Act 1988 (qv) and is issued by the insurer in the form specified by the Motor Vehicles (Third Party Risks) Regulations 1972. Section 147(1) provides that a certificate must be delivered to the person or body effecting the insurance otherwise, for the purpose of the Act, the insurance is not effective. The insured can authorise an agent to receive the certificate on his behalf. When an insurance is cancelled the certificate must be surrendered to the insurer within seven days of the cancellation date. Where the certificate has been lost or destroyed a statutory declaration (qv) must be made to that effect.

Motor/Fire Agreement. Where one vehicle catches fire and spreads to another, the insurers concerned agree that the second insurer, if liable under his policy for fire damage, will not pursue any subrogation rights (qv) that may exist against the owner of the first car.

Motor Insurers' Bureau (MIB). Set up in 1946 after the Cassell Report (qv) the MIB, consisting of all authorised motor insurers, entered into an agreement with the Ministry of Transport whereby it undertook to satisfy judgments in respect of claims for personal injuries made by third parties under the compulsory insurance provisions of the Road Traffic Act where no policy was in force. This is called the Principal Agreement. In addition, each individual member has undertaken under a so-called Domestic Agreement that where at the time of the accident a policy is in force, it will deal with the claim as insurer concerned (qv). Consequently, the MIB deals only with cases where insurance was never issued, or cannot be ascertained, or where a non- member fails to meets its obligations. MIB reimburses itself by levies on its members but has a right of recovery against the negligent motorist. In 1969 the MIB entered into the MIB (Compensation of Victims of Untraced Drivers) Agreement to bring the victims of untraced drivers (qv) within the scheme. Under the Motor Vehicles (Compulsory Insurance) Regulations 1987 third party damage cover became compulsory. The MIB accepts such claims in respect of uninsured motorists subject to a £175 excess. It does not accept property damage claims involving untraced drivers. Membership of MIB became compulsory for all motor insurers under the Road Traffic Act 1974. The Bureau is also the issuing authority in the UK for Green Cards (qv) (International Motor Insurance Certificates) and administers the international agreements which are the basis of the Green Card system.

motor legal expenses insurance. Usually arranged as an extension of a private car policy, the insured is covered in respect of legal expenses associated with civil actions and motoring prosecutions. The policy covers legal expenses incurred in seeking to recover uninsured losses (eg own damage excesses (qv), hire of another car during repairs, loss of earnings) and compensation for personal injuries after a motor accident. There is also cover for the legal expenses associated with the pursuit or defence of disputes relating to the sale, purchase, hire, service, repair or testing of the insured's vehicle. Legal defence costs in respect of prosecutions are also insured. In addition many schemes include a 24-hour motoring legal advisory service by telephone hotline. Cover operates for sums up to £50 000 in any one claim.

Motor/Public Liability Agreement. An agreement whereby a motor insurer with possible subrogation rights against a public liability policyholder accepts half the cost of the vehicle repairs.

Motor Risk Statistics Bureau. The Bureau is a department of the Association of British Insurers. Its main objective is to produce market statistics useful for the management and underwriting of motor insurance business for its members who contribute to the scheme. MSRB reports are designed to show the way in which risk varies between different groups of policyholders and the relative costs incurred by each group. The Bureau accepts raw data on policies and claims for analysis. Over 20 offices submit data on their private car portfolio providing the Bureau with two computer files each quarter. The first lists details of all policies in force at the end of the quarter which is compared with the file submitted three months earlier. This enables the Bureau to estimate the exposure to risk during the quarter, subdivided by any combination of risk factors for which information is available. The second file contains information on outstanding or recently settled claims and this facilitates the creation of a master file on claims and their development. The two bases enable the Bureau to indicate the relative claims experience between different levels of risk factors and consider trend movements in the frequency and size of claims.

motor vehicle. A mechanically propelled vehicle intended or adapted for use on a road (Road Traffic Act 1988, s. 190 (1) and Road Traffic Regulations 1967, s. 99(1)). The term has been held to apply to a go-kart (*Burns* v *Currell* (1963) and a farm tractor (*Woodward* v *James Young (Contractors) Ltd* (1958).

motor vehicle assessor. *See* INDEPENDENT AUTOMOTIVE ASSESSOR and STAFF ENGINEER.

Motor Vehicles (Compulsory Insurance) Regulations, 1987. The regulations amend the compulsory insurance requirements of the Road Traffic Act 1988, s. 145 3(a) by extending them to include an insurance against liability at law to pay compensation for third party property damage up to £250 000 'any one accident' resulting from the use of a vehicle on a road. The policy does not have to cover liability in respect of: damage to employees' property; damage to the vehicle or goods carried for hire or reward; damage to custody or control property (qv); any contractual liability. The regulations also oblige the insurer to deal with judgments related to 'Act' liability claims even though the driver may be a thief, be unauthorised by the insured, or be unlicensed but they will have rights of recovery against any negligent person or the person who permitted the use of the vehicle. *See also* PERMITTED DRIVERS.

Motor Vehicles (Compulsory Insurance) (No 2) Regulations 1973 (SI 1973 No 2143) and Amendment (No 2) Regulations 1974 (SI 1974 No 2186). *See* ROAD TRAFFIC ACT 1988 (COMPULSORY INSURANCE REQUIREMENTS).

Motor Vehicles (Third Party Risks Deposits) Regulations 1967 (SI 1967 No 1326). These regulations provide an alternative to an insurance to comply with the compulsory insurance requirements of the Road Traffic Act 1988 (ss. 143-156). The user of a motor vehicle may deposit the sum of £15 000 in cash or securities with the Accountant General of the Supreme Court provided authorisation is granted by the Secretary of State for Transport. Normally such authorisation is only granted to public bodies and authorities and to major organisations with access to substantial funds.

'Movables'. In marine insurance this means 'any movable tangible property, other than the ship and includes money, valuable securities and other document' unless the context or subject matter indicates otherwise (Marine Insurance Act 1906, s. 90).

multi-insurers. A term used in marine and transit insurance for a single movement of goods where different insurers are involved in different parts of the transit.

multi-parent captive. A captive insurance company (qv) formed to meet the common needs of a group of independent companies or professional practitioners.

multi-peril. A USA term describing a policy covering a range of perils as opposed to one covering a single peril or restricted range of perils. The UK equivalent is comprehensive (qv).

multiple birth insurance. An insurance to secure a specified amount in the event of a multiple live birth. Insurers enquire closely into the history of multiple births in the family. *See* TWINS INSURANCE.

musical instruments. They are within the term personal effects (qv) and cover therefore arises under the household contents insurance on a specified peril basis. As many instruments are portable and susceptible to accidental damage wider cover is often arranged under an all risks policy or extension where its value will often necessitate that it is designated as a specified valuable with its own sum insured. It is usual for an insurer to exclude the breaking of reeds and strings, the effects of the climate, and theft from an unattended vehicle.

Mutual Indemnity Associations. Originally formed as trade associations to provide self insurance (qv) for the members with losses paid out of funds financed from members' contributions. Mutual indemnity associations have been regarded for many years as being primarily concerned with marine insurance through Protecting and Indemnity Clubs (qv). In recent years mutual clubs have started in professional indemnity insurance (qv) for solicitors, architects, and housing associations as well in the airline industry. Some of the older associations have widened their scope and deal with the public generally.

mutual insurance companies. An insurance company owned by its policyholders, ie having no shareholders, formed by Deed of Settlement (a form of partnership) or registration under the Companies Act as companies limited by guarantee. Funds are raised by premiums, the profits being shared among the policyholders in the form of lower premiums or higher life insurance bonuses than would otherwise have been enjoyed. An additional levy is imposed to meet losses if the premium contributions are insufficient. Mutuals may be established for any class of business or they may be limited to members of a particular trade. Some former mutuals have now registered under the Companies Act as proprietary companies but retained the word 'mutual' as a part of their title. Others who are constituted as mutual companies may have chosen not to put the word into their title.

'nail-sick' roofs. A term used by loss adjusters and others connected with claims to describe a situation where the nails holding down roof slates or tiles have rusted through causing the slates or tiles to slip in high winds. Consequently any indemnity payment following storm or tempest should allow for prior wear and tear.

Name. An alternative term for an underwriting member (qv) of Lloyd's.

named drivers. The persons named in a motor insurance policy as being the only drivers permitted to drive under the policy.

named driver basis. 1. A term used by motor insurers when issuing policies under which cover is restricted to drivers specifically named in the policy. 2. Motor traders' road risks policies may be arranged on a named driver basis. The method is popular where there is a small number of drivers who are fairly fully employed and where hiring is not a major element of the business. The policy operates only if a named driver is driving. The premium is based on a flat rate per named driver and varies according to the scope of the cover, comprehensive or third party.

narrative policies. A policy written in continuous prose with little or no clear-cut divisions into paragraphs or sections. The policy narrates the cover provided. It is an old-fashioned approach now largely replaced by scheduled policies. Until 1982 nearly all marine policies were issued in the narrative form, ie the SG policy form used at Lloyd's.

National insurance. A part of the state's social security system which in the UK comes under the control of the Department of Social Security providing benefits in various forms, namely, sickness, industrial injury, unemployment, pensions, maternity and death. Apart from contracting out (qv) provisions participation is compulsory for designated categories of people. The rates of contribution vary according to class but are standard within each class. Contributions are deducted from earnings. Disputes are handled by local tribunals and ultimately a National Insurance Commissioner.

National Supervisory Council for Intruders Alarms. The organisation that maintains a roll of approved installers of alarms who undertake to maintain a minimum standard of service, equipment and maintenance conforming to BS 4737.

natural premium method. An outmoded method of charging life assurance premiums. Each premium is related to the current risk of death and therefore increases year by year. At later stages the premiums become almost prohibitive. No reserve is built up and therefore there is no surrender value. It differs from assessmentism (qv) in that no allowance is made for expenses. The level premium system (qv) overcomes the problem of the natural premium system.

navigation risks. The risks arising when a vessel is navigating or at sea as distinct from the risks arising in port or when the vessel is laid up.

National Health Service (NHS) Cash Benefit. A benefit payable in cash to a person insured under a private health insurance policy who is treated in the public ward of an NHS hospital. This section of the policy operates if a medical specialist recommends particular hospital treatment covered by the policy.

negligence. A tort (qv) defined as 'the omission to do something which a reasonable man, guided upon those considerations which ordinarily regulate the conduct of human affairs, would do, or doing something which a prudent and reasonable man would not do'. It is simply the neglect of some care owed to others. The reasonable man has been described as the 'man on the Clapham omnibus'.

Negligence Clause. *See INCHMAREE CLAUSE.*

negligent statement. In *Hedley Byrne* v *Heller and Partners* (1964), the House of Lords ruled that whenever a special relationship exists, there is a duty to take care in the making of statements, a breach of which would find liability for the harm suffered unless there is a disclaimer of responsibility. Previously liability for negligent statements could only arise in contract. The key elements are 'special relationship' and 'no disclaimer'. In deciding whether there is a special relationship the following questions are relevant: Was it reasonable for the plaintiff to rely on the person making the statement because of his special knowledge or skill? Did the defendant claim special knowledge or skill or conduct a relevant business or profession? Did the defendant know, or should he have known, that his statement would be relied on by the plaintiff? Was the statement made in a 'business context'? In Hedley Byrne's case the defendant was protected by the disclaimer that his statement was made 'without responsibility'. Professional indemnity policies cover, *inter alia*, breach of duty and this includes negligent statements. Public liability policies exclude advice for which a fee is normally payable.

'neighbour principle'. A term referring to the general duty to take care formulated by Lord Atkin in *Donoghue* v *Stevenson* (1932). Lord Atkin said "you must take reasonable care to avoid accidents or omissions likely to injure your neighbour". Neighbours are 'persons so closely and directly affected by my act that I ought reasonably to have them in contemplation as being so affected when . . . directing my mind to the acts or omissions called into question'. Before 1932 many claims based on negligence failed because the plaintiff was unable to show that

the defendant owed him a duty of care. The law recognised certain 'duty situations' only, eg duties owed by occupiers to visitors, employers to employees and failure to bring the case within one of these situations was fatal to any claim based on negligence. However, Donoghue's case also created a new 'duty situation', the duty of care owed by a manufacturer to the user of his product.

net line. A USA term referring to the amount of risk that an insurer retains for his own account. More widely a 'net line' underwriter accepts business mainly with the intention of ceding all or nearly all of it by way of reinsurance. The underwriter acts in effect as a fronting company or agent.

net line underwriter. *See NET LINE.*

net premium income. This is usually taken as gross premium income less premium returns and rebates, reinsurance premiums, and often production costs, brokers'/agents' commission etc.

net relevant earnings. Earnings from self-employment or non-pensionable employment which, after deducting losses and certain allowances, determine the maximum contributions to retirement annuity or personal pension scheme that qualify for tax relief. Currently 17.5 per cent of 'net relevant earnings' is permitted for persons born after 1934 but special conditions apply to those who are older to enable them to build their pension rights more quickly.

net result. The bottom line of the personal account prepared for a Lloyd's underwriter in respect of a syndicate in which he participates. The net result is the member's share of profit or loss of closed year and any run-off account result for the year, adjusted for personal expenses.

net retention. The amount of business retained after allowing for reinsurance.

net risk. The remaining residual risk after the intrinsic hazards of the business or organisation have been reduced in terms of nature, scale and probability of occurrence by the precautions taken by the insured. Ascertaining the net risk is a part of the procedure of risk assessment and requires some skill on the part of insurance underwriters and surveyors.

new business strain. When an insurance company is expanding its business the unexpired premium reserve will be increasing faster than it is being released. If the claims experience follows the expectations upon which the premiums have been based this will cause the underwriting profit to be negative. This is the effect of the strain of building up the reserves to a higher operating level. In life business new policies coming on to the books have heavy initial expenses which, under the net premium valuation basis, are assumed to be spread evenly over all future premiums. Consequently the calculated reserves will be higher than the available assets and a 'new business strain' results. Zillmerization (qv) is one method of allowing for this by ensuring that the premium valued allows for initial expenses having been spent out of the first year's premium. Reassurance on a risk premium basis (qv) is one possible solution to the strain. If part of the business is reassured certain expenses (stamp duty, commission) will be shared and the reassurer may pay an overriding commission to contribute to the administration expenses.

new for old policies. A policy providing 'replacement as new' as the basis of settling claims as an alternative to the traditional indemnity cover. The insured receives the full cost of repairs for damaged items without deduction for wear and tear (qv) and the cost of replacing them with 'equivalent' new items if they are stolen or destroyed. If the new item is more sophisticated or superior in some way to the replaced item the insured pays for the betterment (qv). Cover on this basis applies to furniture, domestic appliances, televisions etc but not to household linen and clothing. The policy is the household equivalent of a business insurance policy with a reinstatement clause (qv). In the case buildings new for old means repairs or restoration without deduction for betterment. The sum insured must represent not less than the full replacement or rebuilding cost. The policy modifies the principle of indemnity.

'night'. A goods in transit policy warranted that vehicles would be in 'locked garages at night, except when employed on night journeys, but then never left unattended' (*A. Cohen & Co. Ltd.* v *Plaistow Transport Ltd (Graham, Third Party)* (1968)). McKenna J stated, *obiter*, that night should be construed by reference to lighting up time.

night risk clause. A clause applied to goods in transit policies to warrant that vehicles left loaded overnight must not be unattended unless locked and immobilised in accordance with any such provision in the policy. In addition it is customary to require that such vehicles are either left in a building or yard which is also securely closed and locked or in an attended official car park. *See* 'NIGHT'.

nipple leakage. Leakage through the failure of the nipple joints of boiler or pressure plant. The cost of repair can be covered as an extension to a boiler and pressure plant policy (qv). The extension covers 'self damage' only. Damage consequent upon the leakage is not covered as separate water damage cover is available under burst pipes cover (qv). *See* ADDITIONAL (SPECIAL) PERILS INSURANCE.

no claim bonus (or discount). A reduction of premium allowed at the time of renewal to an insured who has made no claim in the previous period or periods of insurance. They are very common in motor insurance but also used in some householders' insurances. The motor policy normally sets out a progressive scale which shows that the maximum bonus in private car cases will be reached after four years. If there is more than one vehicle insured under the policy, the no claim bonus is applied separately to each vehicle as if a separate policy had been issued for each vehicle. If an insured loses his no claim bonus following a claim for damage to his vehicle, he can include the loss as an item in any claim for damages against a third party whose negligence led to the claim (*Ironfield* v *Eastern Gas Board* (1964)).

no cure no pay. *See* SALVAGE.

no fault liability system. A system under which an injured person can receive compensation up to a specified amount without having to prove fault (eg negligence) on the part of another. In New Zealand the victims of road accidents are paid out of a socialised fund. In the UK certain industrial injury benefits are payable automatically under the social security system without reference to fault. In the USA many states permit the individual vehicle accident victim to collect directly from his own insurer sums for hospital and medical expenses regardless of who was at fault. Most states allow the injured party to sue the negligent party if the amount of damages exceeds a stated limit. *See* FAULT LIABILITY SYSTEM.

Noise at Work Regulations 1989. The employer must arrange for an 'assessment' whenever an employee is likely to receive a noise dose in excess of the prescribed level. The assessment must provide enough information to enable appropriate action to be taken.

nominations. A person may be nominated to receive the benefits of a life policy. This really amounts to an assignment (qv) of the proceeds whereby a nominated person has the right to claim and collect the policy benefits. Such nominations arise under the Married Womens' Property Act 1882 (qv).

Non-admission of liability clause. A clause in a liability policy prohibiting the insured, except at his own expense, from compromising or settling any claim or admitting liability without the written consent of the insurer. The clause is not contrary to public policy (*Terry* v *Trafalgar Insurance Co Ltd* (1970)) and the insurer does not have to show that he was prejudiced in order to rely on it. *See* ADMISSIONS.

Non-admitted insurer. An insurer who transacts services (or cross-frontier) business. It is not authorised to conduct business from within the foreign countries from which it receives its business.

non-apportionable annuity. Another term for curtate annuity. It is an annuity that ceases with the ordinary periodic payment immediately preceding the death of the annuitant. All life annuities are by law apportionable (or complete) unless the contrary is expressed in the annuity policy.

non-avoidance of compulsory insurance.

1. *Employers' liability insurance.* Regulation 2 of the Employers' Liability (Compulsory Insurance) General Regulations 1971 prohibits certain conditions in employers' liability policies for the purposes of the Employers' Liability (Compulsory Insurance) Act 1969. These relate to: things to be done or not done (eg admission of liability) after a 'claim' event; reasonable precautions by the insured; compliance with enactments; keeping specified records. *See* AVOIDANCE OF CERTAIN TERMS AND RIGHTS OF RECOVERY. There is nothing in this regulation that prevents an insurer from relying on a restrictive endorsement (qv). In *Dunbar* v *A & B Painters and Economic Insurance Co and Whitehouse & Co* (1986) the policy contained a clause excluding work carried on at more than 40 feet above ground level. The employee fell from 40 feet 7 inches and the insurers were held entitled to rely upon the exclusion although had that been the only point at issue it seems that they would not have pleaded it. 2. *Motor insurance.* The Road Traffic Act 1988, ss. 148(1-3) lists ten categories of policy conditions or exceptions that an insurer is unable to rely on in regard to claims that must be insured under the Act. These are: age and condition of the driver; condition of the vehicle; number of persons carried; weight, physical characteristics of goods carried; times or areas of use; engine size or value of vehicle; carriage of particular apparatus; carrying of identification of vehicle; requirement to do specified things after the happening of the event (eg notice of claim); limitation or exclusion of passenger liability (qv). Rights of recovery against the insured exist in all cases but the last.

non-commissioned office. A life insurance company that does not pay commission for the introduction of new business. Most offices pay commission to brokers and other intermediaries but there are one or two exceptions.

non-concurrent policies. These are policies covering the same property, but where one or more of them covers other property in addition, or where, although covering the same property, they are differently divided. Examples:

A and B are non-concurrent if A covers the dwelling-house and B covers the same dwelling-house and adjoining shop. If the house is damaged contribution between A and B may arise. Y and Z are non-concurrent if Y covers stocks of beer and other liquor, utensils and furniture in a public house, with separate amounts on each, and policy Z covers the contents of the same public house in one undivided sum.

non-consumer sales. A non-consumer sale takes place when the purchaser buys the goods for his business. In such a sale the seller is permitted to exclude his liability for the implied terms under the Sale of Goods Act 1979, fitness for purpose and merchantable quality, provided that the exclusion clause passes the test of reasonableness (qv). Compare with consumer sales (qv).

non-contribution clause. A clause which ousts contribution (qv) when it would otherwise apply. *See* MORE SPECIFIC INSURANCE CLAUSE.

non-contributory pension scheme. One to which only the employer makes contributions.

non-dangerous species. Animals not falling within the definition of dangerous species (qv). Animals which are commonly domesticated in the British Isles are therefore within this category. There is no strict liability (qv) in connection with such animals but where a plaintiff can show that a particular animal had abnormal characteristics and the keeper knew of these characteristics and their capability of causing damage 'likely to be severe', the keeper will be strictly liable subject only to the limited defences under the Act.

non-delegable duties. Duties of a personal nature. The person responsible has a duty to see that proper care is taken and even though he may engage a contractor to carry the duties he remains liable for any breach of duty. For example, a principal may engage a contractor to perform acts involving strict liability (qv) as in *Rylands* v *Fletcher* (qv).

non-disclosure of a material fact. *See* UTMOST GOOD FAITH.

nonfeasance. The failure or neglect to do some act which ought to be done, eg failing to keep the highway in repair.

The exemption that highway authorities enjoyed from civil liability was abrogated by the Highways (Miscellaneous Provisions) Act 1961, s. 1(1) but the absence of negligence is a defence, s. 1(2)(3).

non-forfeiture clause. A clause in a life policy under which the policy remains in force for a limited period after the expiry of the days of grace (qv) even though the premium remains unpaid. The surrender value (qv) of the policy, if any, is used to keep the policy in force for a stated period (eg one year) or until the surrender value is exhausted depending on the practice of the insurer. If the period is limited any balance of the surrender value remaining is paid to the insured or used to purchase a paid-up policy (qv). When the non-forfeiture period comes to an end a revival clause (qv) may come into operation.

non-insurance. A situation in which a person or business assumes a risk(s) without having made a conscious decision to do so and without having made any financial provision for it. Many risks are unwittingly assumed in this way, hopefully only those of an inconsequential nature. This is otherwise called unplanned risk assumption. *See* RISK ASSUMPTION.

non-invalidation clause. A clause which can be added without charge to a fire policy. The purpose is to protect the owner of property against a breach of warranty by a tenant provided that the owner was not aware of the breach and he advises the insurers as soon as he becomes aware of it.

non-natural use of land. The *Rylands* v *Fletcher* (1868) (qv) will apply only if the use of the land is non-natural. This is 'special use bringing with it danger to others, and must not merely be the ordinary use of the land or use which is for the general benefit of the community' (*Rickards* v *Lothian* (1913)). 'Ordinary use' goes beyond domestic or ordinary use. The storage in bulk of water, gas, and electricity have been held to be non-natural uses.

non-marine. General business other than marine, aviation and transport.

non-medical assurance. This is the same as ordinary life assurance except that normally no medical examination is required. The proposer must, however, give the name of his ordinary medical attendant to whom the assurer may, with the proposer's permission, refer if it is not satisfied with the particulars supplied in the proposal form. Life offices have their own non-medical limits expressed in terms of age and sum assured depending on the type of policy.

non-medical underwriting limits. Proposals for life cover on lives showing no adverse features can be accepted without further medical evidence, such as a medical examination, provided the total cover is below a predetermined limit. Limits are set by age and sum assured and depend on a particular office's size and past experience.

non-participating policy. An alternative term for a without profits life insurance policy or non-profit policy. The term is mainly used in the USA.

non-profit policy. A life insurance policy which does not participate in the divisible surplus so that the amount payable on claim is the sum insured only. No bonuses are added. Alternatively called without profits policy (qv).

non-proportional treaties. Reinsurances that protect the insurer against large individual losses or losses on the whole account. The reinsurer's liability on a loss is not in direct proportion to the insurer's loss as in the case of proportional treaties (eg surplus and quotas share treaties). See EXCESS OF LOSS and EXCESS OF LOSS RATIO (STOP LOSS) treaties for examples of non-proportional treaties.

non-tariff company. A company that does not join a tariff association and remains free to fix premiums below the tariff rate and adopt its own policy wordings.

'no risk no premium'. Where the risk has not been run by the insurer any premium paid by the insured must be returned to him (*Tyre v Fletcher* (1777)).

normal expenditure exemption. Expenditure which is regular, out of income, and such as not to reduce the transferor's normal standard of living, can be transferred from one person to another free of inheritance tax. Life insurance premiums normally qualify for this exemption.

'nose'. A colloquial term to describe the period between the retroactive date (qv) and the inception date of a claims-made policy (qv). Claims arising from occurrences within this period made during the policy period will be within the policy but occurrences preceding the retroactive date are not within the 'nose' and will not be covered notwithstanding that the claim is made during the policy period.

not to inure clause. Clause 15 (Benefit of Insurance Clause) of the Institute Cargo Clauses provides that the insurance is not to inure for the benefit of the carrier of other bailee. Contracts of carriage or bailment often provide that the carrier or bailee will have the benefit of any insurance on the goods. The aim of such a provision is to deny insurers any benefits available to them by way of subrogated rights against the carrier of bailee. The not to inure clause clause protects the insurer's position by negating this contractual provision.

notice of abandonment. Where the insured elects to abandon the subject-matter to the insurer and claim a constructive total loss (qv), he must give notice of abandonment. If he fails to do so, the loss can only be treated as a partial loss unless an actual total loss is proved (Marine Insurance Act 1906, s. 62). It is unnecessary if, when the insured receives information of the loss, the notice could be of no benefit to the insurer. An original insurer need not give notice of abandonment to his reinsurer. An insurer can waive the notice. If the insurer accepts the abandonment this is irrevocable unless there is a mistake as to fact and the loss has not been caused by an insured peril. The mere silence of the insurer after the notice is not an acceptance (s. 62 (5)). In practice the insurer will not accept the notice when tendered. He declines until he is in full possession of the facts but the rights of the insured are not to be prejudiced by this refusal (s. 62(4)) which means the insured can enforce his claim by legal process, ie the issue of a writ. It is the state of facts existing at the time of the issue of a writ that determines whether there has been a constructive total loss. Consequently the insured's broker sends two letters to the insurer, one giving notice of intended abandonment and claim for total loss, the other a reply to the insured refusing to accept the notice but agreeing to place the insured in the same position as if a writ had been issued. The latter is signed by the insurers. If a constructive total loss is proved the insurers accept the abandonment and pay a total loss. The waiver clause (No. 17 of the Institute Cargo Clauses) states that neither party will be prejudiced, ie considered as acceptance or waiver of abandonment, by any attempts to preserve the property, whether successful or otherwise.

notice of loss. *See* NOTIFICATION OF LOSS.

notification of loss. As an invariable rule the insured is required by policy condition to give notice of loss in writing otherwise an oral notification would suffice (*Re Solvency Mutual Guarantee Society, Hawthorne's Case* (1862)). Notice may be to the insurer's head office or simply to the insurer or agent of the insurer depending on the wording. Unless the condition so stipulates, the giving of the notice does not have to be the personal act of the insured (*Davies* v *National Fire and Marine Insurance Co of New Zealand* (1865) AC 485). The insurer requires notice not just of claims but, in liability insurances, of any occurrence likely to give rise to a claim, or of the receipt by the insured of any notice of claim or proceedings. The insurer may fix a time for the notice; it may be forthwith, immediately (qv), as soon as possible (qv) or within a specified period of time. If no time limit is prescribed the insured must give notice within a reasonable period of time. Any requirements of this sort must be complied with and the insurer does not have to show prejudice by non-compliance to avoid the claim, although in practice it is rare for the condition to be relied upon in that way, unless there has been some prejudice to the insurer's position. Also under the statements of practice, which apply only to private policyholders, the insurers agree to do no more than ask for a report of the claim as soon as possible, except in the case of legal processes and claims which a third party requires the policyholder

to notify within a fixed time where immediate advice may be required. In *Pioneer Concrete (UK) Ltd* v *National Employers Mutual General Insurance Association Ltd* (1985) contractors, who supplied plant to Pioneer, were insured under a public liability policy which provided—'the insured shall give written notice . . . of any accident *or* claim *or* proceedings immediately the same shall have come to the knowledge of the insured or his representative'. An accident occurred on 4 September 1978 and correspondence took place between Pioneer and the insurers from that month until March 1979. In the meanwhile the insured contractor, whose faulty workmanship had caused the accident, went into voluntary liquidation. Pioneer served a writ on 25 June 1979 but gave no notice to the insurers. No defence was entered and a default judgment against the insured was secured. P's solicitors notified the NEM of the judgment with damages assessed at £12 000 and when the insurers refused to pay P sought to recover from them under the Third Party (Rights Against Insurers) Act 1930 (qv). A third party's position under the Act is no better than that of the insured. The court held that notice had to be given of the accident and the claim and the proceedings. P had issued the writ but had failed to tell the insurers and this amounted to a breach of the notice requirement relating to proceedings. The insurers were entitled to rely on a breach of notification even if they had not been prejudiced because the condition expressed in clear terms that notification was a condition precedent to any liability to make payment under the policy, but there was in any event prejudice as the insurer was deprived of the opportunity of considering how to handle the claim. The insured may sometimes be able to plead that the insurer has waived compliance with the notification provision. Where a loss occurred on 26 February the insured's solicitor went to see the insurer's branch claims manager on 19 May and the manager agreed to report the matter to head office. The policy called for written notice of loss to head office as soon as possible after the loss but the manager's conduct led the insured to believe no written notice was required in regard to that particular loss (*Webster* v *General Accident* (1953)). Finally, the insured who notifies the accident in the form and manner required but chooses to give an inaccurate version of the events to mislead the insurer fails to comply with the notice provisions (*Cox* v *Orion Insurance Co Ltd* (1982)).

notification period. Otherwise called a discovery period (qv) it provides limited additional protection to policyholders whose claims-made policies (qv) have not been renewed and where no new insurance has been effected. Provided the negligence giving rise to the claims occurred during the period of insurance, claims reported after expiry will be treated as claims made within the policy term provided it is notified within a stated period of expiry (eg 6 months).

noting limit. An amount determined by the active underwriter (qv) of a syndicate as a criterion for determining whether records should be maintained of premiums, claims, etc which have yet to be taken down by Lloyd's Policy Signing Office (qv).

notional reinstatement value scheme. A mechanism adopted by property insurers to combat the effects of inflation. It provides for a sum insured in two parts—the declared value and the added provision for inflation during the policy and reinstatement periods. The declared value is the figure the insured fixes as adequate for reinstatement (qv) at the inception—the notional reinstatement value. The policy is prepared showing three figures—the sum insured, the declared value and a percentage figure for inflationary increase.

novation. Most contracts of insurance (life and marine contracts are the exceptions—*See* ASSIGNMENT) are personal contracts, ie entered into on the basis of personal confidence and trust. Consequently when the subject-matter of insurance changes hands (eg a motor car is sold) the policy is not automatically assigned with it. This would bring the insurer into a contractual relationship with a new person of whom they know nothing. The policy can only be transferred when the consent of the insurer is given. The effect is to create a new contract between the insurer and the assignee. This alteration is termed novation.

novus actus interveniens. A new act intervening. *See* INTERVENING CAUSE and PROXIMATE CAUSE.

Nuclear Installations Act 1965. The holder of a nuclear site licence must by insurance or some other means make provision against third party injury or property damage claims to an aggregate amount of £5m. The Government has made provision for compensation up to £43m per occurrence. *See* NUCLEAR PERILS.

nuclear perils. These are the risks of injury to persons or damage to property caused by radiation from nuclear reactor sites or by nuclear matter in the course of carriage. The Nuclear Installations Act 1965 provides that except under licence no one other than the UK Atomic Energy Authority can operate a nuclear reactor, an installation for producing or preparing atomic power or store, process or dispose of nuclear fuel or bulk quantities of other radioactive matter. 'Licensees' are strictly liable under the Act for injury or property damage to third parties resulting from the use of nuclear energy. The liability must be covered up to £5m (the government meets liability in excess of this sum) above by insurance or other approved means. Cover is available, including damage cover on the installations themselves, from a single atomic energy insurance pool set up by the British Insurance (Atomic Energy) Committee for the British insurance market as a whole. As a result most policies (marine, aviation and insurances of the person) contain a radioactive contamination clause. This excludes damage to any property, any loss, expense, consequential loss or legal liability arising from ionising radiation or contamination from nuclear fuel or nuclear fuel waste. The explosive nuclear assemblies clause excludes loss, liability etc resulting from the radioactive toxic explosive or hazardous property of any explosive nuclear assembly or its nuclear components. The latter clause was added in 1969 following air crashes when nuclear bombs were damaged on impact. These clauses do not apply to employers' liabilty policies in respect of indemnity to the insured but do apply to the contractual liability extension.

nuisance. Sir Frederick Pollock defined it as 'a wrong done to man by unlawfully disturbing him in the enjoyment of his property or, in some cases, the exercise of a common right'. There are two kinds of nuisance—private and public. The former is a crime and does not fall within the law of torts except that a particular case may constitute some liability in which event it is actionable by an individual if it causes him special damage over and above the inconvenience suffered by other members of the public. For example, a road obstruc-

tion constitutes a crime but the person who suffers injury as a result of colliding with it will have suffered special damage and may claim. Private nuisances are unlawful interferences affecting the owner's or occupier's use or enjoyment of property. Such nuisances commonly take the form of intangible invasions (eg noise, smell, vibration). Many incidents of pollution are nuisances. Liability arises when there is *injuria* (the wrongful act) and *damnum* (damage, loss or inconvenience actually suffered). There is a tendency for public liability insurers to provide cover for accidental obstruction and other accidental nuisances by broadening their definitions of 'property damage'.

O

obligatory treaty. A reinsurance treaty under which the original insurer must cede and the reinsurer must accept all risks falling into the class of business covered by the treaty.

obligee. The person or persons protected by a bond (qv).

oblige line. An alternative term for accommodation line (qv).

obligor. The person giving the bond (qv) to the obligee (qv).

obsolete buildings clause. A clause introducing a form of reinstatement insurance on buildings upwards of 50 years old. The design and construction of these buildings may make it difficult to rebuild them in a like manner after a claim and the insurer agrees that, in the event of substantial loss, they will replace with a new building or purchase an alternative building as a replacement. The sum insured should reflect this cost and partial losses can be dealt with on a reinstatement or indemnity basis.

obsolete parts clause. A clause applied by motor insurers when the subject-matter insured is a car that is no longer in production. The clause limits the liability of the own damage (qv) insurer for the cost of replacing any part unobtainable from stock to the maker's last list price plus the current cost of fitting.

'occupation'. Occupation means vocation, profession, trade, or calling in which the insured is engaged for reward or profit. Where there is an exception relating to particular occupations in an insurance on a person this does not preclude the insured from carrying out acts or duties connected with the ordinary daily acts associated with occupations in general. Occasional acts do not amount to an occupation (*Berliners* v *Travelers' Insurance Co* (1898)).

occupational classes. A method of rating whereby the usual premium is based on the insured's occupation. The method, otherwise called underwriting by occupation (qv), is commonly used in personal accident insurance (qv) where as many as five occupational classes or groups segment risks according to the degree of hazard present in the particular occupation. The lowest risks are class 1 and the highest risks class 5. The classes are usually published in the proposal forms so that the proposer can readily identify the premium that will apply unless in an extra-hazardous occupation which calls for special consideration by the insurer.

occupational deafness. An industrial disease caused by noise exposure. It is an insidious disease affecting the inner ear. Many workers are exposed to this risk and many years may pass before the victim becomes aware of the situation. The incidence of the disease and its long-tail potential have created serious implications for employers' liability insurers. The disease is incurable but preventable and has attracted more attention from the legislators. *See* NOISE AT WORK REGULATIONS 1989.

occupational exposure limits (OELs). Under Control of Substances Hazardous to Health Regulations 1988 the control of certain substances, which create a risk to health through inhalation, is only regarded as adequate if certain occupational exposure standards have not been exceeded. If the specified limits have been exceeded the employer must ascertain the cause and act as soon as reasonably practicable to remedy the situation. In pursuance of this control certain occupational exposure limits have been set and are published annually by the Health and Safety Executive in HSE Guidance Note EH 40, eg general nuisance dust, welding fumes, solvents and silica. Another kind of exposure limit—maximum exposure limits—is also published.

occupational hazard. A condition in an occupation that increases the peril of accident, sickness or health.

occupational pension scheme. A scheme organised by an employer or on behalf of a group of employers to provide pensions and/or other benefits for or in respect of one or more employees on leaving service or on death or retirement.

'occupation or ownership of land'. What amounts to occupation and control of property depends on the facts of the case but some insight can be gained from *Oei* v *Foster (formerly Crawford) and Eagle Star* (1982). During the absence from home of Mr and Mrs Oei their neighbours, the Crawfords, looked after their children and were allowed to sleep and eat in Oei's house. They spent the days in their own home. Mrs C negligently caused a chip-pan fire to damage the O's home and the O's claimed on their own insurance. Their insurers sued the C's in a subrogated claim. The C's sought an indemnity from the Eagle Star under the personal liability section of their householder's policy. Clause 15 covered negligence 'provided always that this indemnity does not apply to any claim . . . (b) for injury or damage arising directly or indirectly from . . . (ii) ownership or occupation of any land or buildings . . . ; (c) for damage to property held in trust by or in the custody or control of the insured or any member of his family. It was held: 1. that the insurers could not rely on clause 15(c). They were mere guests enjoying the right to use such parts of the house and such equipment as in ordinary life they required to use; that did not amount to control within the meaning of the the clause as they controlled neither the house nor contents; there was no custody since the C's had not been asked to look after the house but were only there to look after the children. 2. The C's were at the relevant time in occupation of the house so the exclusion applied. 3. The proximate cause of the damage was not the occupation but Mrs C's negligence but the occupation was an indirect cause

since cooking was a necessary and inevitable incident of the C's occupation of the house. The exclusion, because of its wording, operated whether the damage was the direct of indirect result of the occupation.

Occupational Pensions Board. A statutory body set up under the Social Security Act 1973, with functions derived from that Act and the Social Security Pensions Act 1975. The Board is responsible for issuing contracting out or appropriate scheme certificates for pension schemes which meet the statutory requirements, for supervising those schemes to ensure that guaranteed minimum pensions and protected rights are secure and for ensuring that equal access and preservation requirements are satisfied. The Board is required to report to the Secretary of State when he/she seeks their advice and to comment on draft regulations affecting occupational pension schemes.

occupier. The Occupier's Liability Act 1957 (qv) contains no official definition. The term is one of convenience to denote a person who has a sufficient degree of control over premises to put him under a duty of care to lawful visitors. Control is the decisive factor and it is immaterial that the occupier has no interest in the land. Occupancy gives control over, knowledge of, the state of premises but this does not preclude others from being liable, eg repairing landlords.

occupier's liability. The occupier's duty to visitors to his premises is set out in the Occupiers' Liability Act 1957 (qv) and the Occupiers' Liability Act 1984 (qv). The occupier must also: refrain from creating nuisances; prevent nuisances coming into existence; abate any nuisance (qv) subsisting on his land.

Occupiers' Liability Act 1957. Section 2 states that an occupier owes the 'common duty of care' to all lawful visitors except so far as his duty is modified by agreement. The duty is to 'take such care as in all the circumstances of the case is reasonable to see that the visitor will be reasonably safe in using the premises for the purpose for which he is invited or permitted by the occupier to be there'. The occupier must be prepared for children to be less careful than adults while 'tradesmen'—persons exercising their calling—can be expected to appreciate and guard against any risks incidental to their calling (eg the risk presented to an electrician by a 'live' wire). By s. 2(4)(a) a warning will absolve the occupier if it is sufficient to make the visitor reasonably safe. Section 2(5) preserves the defence of *volenti* but where there is business liability within the meaning of the Unfair Contract Terms Act 1977, s. 2(3) of that Act provides a person's agreement to or awareness of a notice purporting to exclude liability for negligence is not of itself to be taken as indicating his voluntary acceptance of any risk. Section 2(4) of the 1957 Act provides that the occupier is not liable for damage arising from the faulty work of independent contractors provided that it was reasonable to entrust the work to a contractor and that the occupier took reasonable steps to see that the contractor was competent and that the work was properly done. Where a person enters under a contract the common duty of care will be implied but if the contract provides a higher standard of protection the greater standard applies (s. 5(1)). The statutory provisions apply not only to personal injury but also to damage to property, including property of those who are not visitors which is nevertheless lawfully on the premises (s. 1(3)(b)).

Occupiers' Liability Act 1984. Section 1(3)(4) lays down a statutory duty of care owed by occupiers of premises to trespassers. A duty is owed if the occupier is aware (or ought to be) of danger and knows (or has grounds to believe) that the trespasser is or may be in the vicinity of the danger, ie the risk is one against which, in the circumstances, he may reasonably be expected to offer some protection. The duty is to take such care as in all the circumstances of the case is reasonable to see that the trespasser does not suffer injury. The duty may be discharged by giving appropriate warnings and it is effectively restricted to personal injury cases. The duty under the Act is not far removed from the common duty of humanity (qv) which took into account, along with the occupier's skill

and resources, his actual knowledge of the trespasser's presence or likelihood of it.

'occurrence'. The word occurrence is used sometimes as an alternative to accident (qv) or event. An occurrence, unlike an accident, does not have to involve something unexpected and fortuitous and can result from repeated or continuous exposure. Many liability policies operate on a losses-occurring basis (qv) ie they are triggered when the loss *occurs*. This may be months or years after the act of negligence which is the cause of the loss. For example, an act of negligence in the manufacture of a product may create the defect that sooner or later occasions the damage or injury. The injury or damage may not be apparent for some time as might be the case if the product is a pharmaceutical one. There are three separate occurrences in this example, the act of negligence, the sustaining of the injury (albeit unknown at the time) and the discovery but the only insurer to be liable will be the one on risk at the time of the occurrence of the injury. The problem arises when the damage or injury occurs over time and arises from repeated exposure to substantially the same injurious conditions. This is often the case with industrial diseases and pollution claims where there has been gradual seepage. The occurrence cannot be clearly fixed in time as could a motor accident or fire and a number of theories have emerged in the USA. The exposure theory calls for participation in the loss by all insurers throughout the period of exposure. The manifestation theory holds responsible the insurer on risk at the time where the injury or damage becomes manifest. The triple-trigger theory brings in all insurers, including those providing insurance at the time of the occurrence, at the point of manifestation, and throughout the period of exposure. By involving a number of periods of insurance the insurer or insurers concerned face the prospect of limits of indemnity for each year of the progressive injury being stacked (*see* STACKING OF

LIMITS). Insurers endeavour to overcome some of the difficulties by using batch clauses (qv), hours clauses (qv) and defining the limit of indemnity to apply to 'any one occurrence or series of occurrences consequent upon or attributable to one source or original cause shall not exceed . . . '. In the American case of *Hyer* v *Inter-Insurance Exchange* (Washington Supreme Court, 1956) the court said that 'where one negligent act or omission is the sole proximate cause there is but one accident (ie event or occurrence) even though there may be several resultant losses or injuries' but in *South Staffordshire Tramways* v *Sickness and Accident Insurance Association* (1891) an overturned tramway had but one proximate cause resulting in 40 passengers being injured and this was treated as 40 separate accidents but given the wording above they too would seem to be traceable to an original cause to give the insurer the benefit of the limit of indemnity against the claims in aggregate. To overcome the problem of the single claimant exposed to disease or injury progressively over the years the insurer could introduce a limit per claimant although in employers' liability insurance the practice is to issue policies which are unlimited as to amount. *See also* ANY ONE ACCIDENT.

ocean marine. A term rarely used in the UK describing the insurance of seagoing hulls, cargoes and liabilities. This distinguishes those insurances from inland marine and sometimes from inland waterway hull, cargo and liability insurances.

odd time. The majority of policies are issued for terms of one year but renewable annually. However, on some occasions the first period of insurance may be for longer than one year, perhaps to bring the renewal date into line with other insurances. The period by which that period exceeds one year is called the odd time for which a *pro rata* premium is calculated and added to the annual premium.

officers. The term is important in the context of directors' and officers' liability insurance (qv). There is no specific statutory definition but the title includes a director, a manager or secretary of a company. 'Manager' means someone who manages the affairs of the company as a whole (branch or local managers are not included). Ordinary employees are not *per se* officers. Any person purporting to be an officer must be empowered to transact the affairs of the whole company in a particular area of activity. Therefore an expert or 'professional' engaged to act in a particular instance is not an officer, but a salaried professional who undertakes functions and responsibilities as part of the management of the company's affairs may be a company 'official'. An auditor is also deemed to be an officer for some purposes of the Companies Acts 1948-1981.

Office, Shops and Railways Premises Act 1963. An Act applying health and welfare and safety provisions to specified types of premises. The health and welfare provisions cover such matters as: cleanliness, clothing, drinking water, eating facilities, floors, passages, stairs, and gangways, lighting, overcrowding, seats for sedentary work, siting facilities, temperature and ventilation. The safety provisions refer to heavy work, hoists and lifts, notification of accidents, machinery, washing facilities, and waterclosets. Criminal sanctions are imposed for non-compliance and a conviction could be used as evidence in a civil claim.

oil tankers. Vessels carrying oil in bulk. The risk of oil pollution has resulted in compulsory liability insurance for vessels carrying more than 2000 tons. The Merchant Shipping (Oil Pollution) Act 1971 as amended by the Merchant Shipping Act 1974 requires such ships to have a certificate of insurance before they can enter or leave a UK port or terminal.

'omission, error or negligent act'. This phrase was considered in the professional indemnity case of *George Wimpey & Co* v *Poole* (1984) and held to include any omission or error *without* negligence. The judge added a proviso that the omission or error must not be deliberate and had to be one capable of creating liability. Accordingly such a phrase embraces breach of warranty.

omnibus clause. An 'indemnity to other persons' clause in a liability policy.

The motor insurance policy, for example, indemnifies permitted drivers (qv), passengers, and employers. *See* MERLE OBERON CLAUSE.

one agent/one class rule. A rule introduced by the Committee of Lloyd's in 1904 to the effect that an underwriter could have only one underwriting agent for marine business. The same rule was subsequently applied to the other markets. For many years now the Names (qv) have sought to spread their business across a number of syndicates to spread overall risks. The one agent/one class rule means that a member can only gain access to the syndicates managed by another agent operating in the same market through the medium of a sub-agency agreement between his own agency and the agent of the syndicate he wishes to join. It is possible for the underwriter to go direct to the second agent if he has no other agent for business in that market. The rule has led to a plethora of sub-agency agreements beneficial to both agents, seeking access to the best syndicates for their Names, and those acting as managing agents in forming and recruiting members for their syndicates. In October 1984 a consultative document on membership requirements recommended the ending of the one agent/one class rule.

'one disaster or casualty' clause. A reinsurance clause incorporated in catastrophe covers (qv) to define what the reinsurer and the ceding office (qv) mean by 'one occurrence'. It is otherwise known as the hours clause (qv).

one eighth rule. *See* QUALIFYING POLICIES.

100-plus club. A major international group whose property insurance claims are double the premiums received by the insurer is categorised as belonging to this 'club'. The other category into which major international groups can be placed is the minus-30 club (qv). The phenomenon also exists in other classes of insurance.

one-third new for old. Where the ship has been repaired, the insured is entitled to the reasonable cost of the repairs, less the customary deductions, but not exceeding the sum insured in respect of any one casualty (Marine Insurance Act 1906, s. 69(1)). This means that when new material is supplied to replace old material damaged and taken out, the shipowner is required to bear part of the cost of new materials; a deduction of one-third or one-sixth is made from the amount payable. In practice the Institute Time Clauses, No. 14, New for Old, provides that claims are payable without deduction new for old.

'on goods'. An unqualified reference to insurance on goods covers both the beneficial interest of the insured and, if they belong to someone else, the liability of the insured to the owner. It does not serve to cover the proprietary interest of others. However, if the policy names the insured as commercial trustee and describes the property as belonging to a named third party, the inference is that the insured as trustee is insuring the proprietary interest of the owner even though the policy may not mention trusteeship (*Hepburn* v *A. Tomlinson (Hauliers) Ltd* (1966)).

'on the insured's order or with his permission'. The usual form of private car policy, unless overridden by a policy restriction, allows the insured to permit driving by others in terms of the above wording. The meaning of this phrase was considered in *Browning* v *Phoenix Assurance Co Ltd* (1960). It is a question of fact to be decided by the court as to whether the driver had the necessary 'order' or 'permission'. *See* PERMITTED DRIVERS.

onus of proof. The onus of proving that the loss arises from an event insured under the policy rests upon the insured. The insured discharges his duty if he presents facts from which it is reasonable to conclude that the loss has resulted from an insured peril. The insured must follow any requirements as to notice and details set out by policy condition. It is implied in every insurance contract that the insured will act in good faith, ie not make a fraudulent claim. Where an exclusion is given effect under the heading exclusions or exceptions, the burden of proving that the loss results from an excepted peril rests upon the insurer. If the exclusion is given effect by a qualification in the operative clause (qv) then the insured must prove that the exception did not operate. For example, in a personal accident policy covering 'injury unless due to suicide or attempt threat', the insured, or his representatives, must not only prove the injury but that it was caused otherwise than by a suicide attempt.

open covers. This is a marine insurance term. When there are regular sendings of goods it is usual to arrange an open cover to avoid the necessity of separate policies for each sending. The two most common methods are the *floating policy* and the *open cover*. The following features are common to both: (a) The assured is bound to declare and the insurer to accept all sendings coming within the scope of the contract. (b) The contract sets out the terms and conditions of the insurance, the goods and the voyages covered, the rates of premium and the limit which may be declared in respect of any one sending. (c) When War Clauses and Strikes Clauses are covered there is a provision that the rate current at time of shipment shall be charged, so that any alterations during the currency of the contract take effect automatically. (d) All contracts of this type are subject to cancellation at thirty days notice (War and Strike risks are subject to seven days notice). In neither case does the cancellation notice affect a risk that has already commenced when the notice takes effect. The floating policy and the open cover differ as follows: a floating policy is issued for a round sum sufficient to cover the estimated total value of sendings for some months. The insured declares all sendings which reduce the amount of the policy until exhausted when a further policy can be issued. There is normally no time limit. The premium is payable when the policy is issued but the policy may provide various rates for different commodities, voyages, etc, there may be an adjustment of premium on expiry. An open cover is in effect a permanent provisional cover note to take all sendings within its scope during a fixed period, usually twelve months. The insured must declare each sending and policies are then issued to cover these sendings. N.B. Both methods involve declarations of sendings. The floating policy is now less popular than the open cover but it can be issued in conjunction with it when the open cover is 'always open'. However, if the open cover has a time limit then the floating policy must have the same limit.

open-ended endowment policies. Otherwise known as flexible endowments, they are written as endowments maturing at age 65 but give early maturity options and incorporate guaranteed cash values at specific dates. The guaranteed cash value is a basic sum to which bonuses are added. Policyholders buy 'units' of cover in that they pay £5 or £10 per month or multiples thereof. Further flexibility is generally available in that policyholders are able to buy more 'units' of cover without evidence of health within certain periods and limits (eg one additional unit for every two if effected within the first five or ten years). Also a policyholder who has cashed in a 'unit' at any time can effect a new replacement 'unit' as long as he is under 55. This is called the 'cash and carry option'. The 'unit' principle enables the policyholder to acquire cash without having to surrender the whole of the contract. In effect, each 'unit' is a separate policy and can be treated separately. The main disadvantage is that the extra life cover given through the guarantees results in a reduction in the amount of premium available for investment.

open market. A term referring to a risk placed in the open market as opposed to one that is covered under a binding authority, line slip or treaty.

open-market option. The option to use the proceeds of a pension plan to buy an annuity at a current market rate from the insurer concerned or any other insurer. *See* TIED ANNUITY OPTION and GUARANTEED ANNUITY OPTION.

open year. Where a two year or longer basis of accounting is adopted, an open year is a year for which adjustments are still being made, no profit having been ascertained. (*See also* CLOSED YEAR.)

operating ratio. A measure and means of monitoring an insurer's overall trading performance and profitability. The ratio is made up of three components: (i) the loss ratio, ie total losses and claims handling costs as a percentage of net premium income; (ii) the expense ratio, ie underwriting expenses as a percentage of premium income; (iii) investment income ratio, ie net investment income on funds contributed by policyholders as a percentage of net premium earned. The operating ratio is the result of deducting the investment income ratio from the sum of the loss ratio and expense ratio.

operative clause. This, otherwise called the insuring cover, sets out the cover provided. It refers to the subject-matter of insurance and the perils that must operate to render the insurer liable under the policy. The onus is upon the insured to prove that the insured event, as described in the operative clause, has occurred. The clause can be very short, as in an 'all risks' policy or very long as with a motor-car comprehensive policy. In the latter case, the policy consists of sections each with its own set of exceptions (qv) and all subject to the policy's general exceptions (qv).

optional increasing benefit. Most permanent health insurance (qv) offers the option of a benefit which will increase automatically at some point in the future to combat the effects of inflation. The option may be to: (a) purchase an increased benefit at some later time without further evidence of good health; (b) pay a premium from the inception that secures an increase at an agreed level(s) or linked to an index periodically (eg every third year) throughout the contract; (c) pay a premium from the inception that secures an increase that begins to operate at an agreed level from the time of a claim (eg 5 per cent compound a year).

option in the matter of indemnity. *See* IN-SURER'S OPTION.

oral evidence. Means the same as parol evidence (qv).

ordinary meaning rule. A rule of construction stating that the words in a policy must be construed in their plain, ordinary and popular meaning, and not in their strictly philosophic or scientific meaning. However, the context may make it clear that the words must, to carry out the intention of the parties, be understood in some special sense. Legal and technical terms are to be given their strict legal meaning unless the policy shows a different inten-

tion. A fire policy on a building excluded liability while gasoline was 'stored or kept' in it. A fire was caused by a small amount of gasoline in a cooking stove. No other gasoline was in the building. It was held that the words 'stored or kept' must be construed in their ordinary meaning. The exclusion did not apply as the words implied a considerable amount of gasoline or at least stocking it for trade purposes—*Thompson* v *Equity Fire Insurance Co.* (1910) 103 L.T. 153.

original terms reinsurance. Reinsurance (otherwise called reassurance) of life insurance at the same rate of premium and subject to the same conditions as those of the ceding office. The reinsurer is liable for a proportion of the original policy throughout its duration. In the event of surrender or alteration of the original policy, the reinsurer follows the practice of the ceding office and the conditions of the underlying policy. The reinsurer also follows the rate of bonus declared by the cedant under with profits policy. Treaties on original terms are especially helpful to new life offices by minimising the risk of fluctuation in the mortality experience and in reducing its heavy initial costs. The retention of the cedant generally increases as the office's funds grow.

other costs and expenses. Legal liability policies invariably make provision for the payment by the insurer of the insured's own costs and expenses incurred with the insurer's written consent. These costs are generally borne by the insurer in addition to the limit of indemnity but see costs inclusive limits of indemnity (qv). As the insurer will ultimately pay for any policy liability that actually attaches to the insured, it is in their interests to see that claims against their insured are properly investigated and handled particularly from a legal point of view. Costs on the High Court scale are always considerable and even if judgment is given for the insured as defendant, he may not recover his costs from the unsuccessful plaintiff.

'other insurance'. This means an insurance which is in addition to the one issued, or to be issued, by the insurer to the insured. Legally the insured may effect as many policies as he wishes although his rights may be modified in the event of a claim (*see* CONTRIBUTION). In order to provide a safeguard against over-insurance and any attempt by the insured to profit from the situation the insurer takes two steps. A question in the proposal form requires the proposer to disclose any 'other insurances' existing at the time of completing the form plus those he plans to effect between that date and the inception of the proposed insurance. Secondly, the policy contains a condition requiring any such insurances effected during the policy term to be notified to the insurer. The condition may be a condition subsequent (qv) or a condition precedent to liability. To constitute 'other insurance', it must be one: (a) covering the same risk as the proposed insurance, ie the same interest, same subject-matter, same peril, otherwise it may simply be an overlapping insurance (qv); (b) which is valid and subsisting (void policies do not count); (c) which is in addition to the proposed insurance.

ouster of jurisdiction. A clause in an insurance policy that seeks to oust the jurisdiction of the court and substitute an alternative mechanism, eg arbitration (qv), for settling disputes. An arbitration clause does not necessarily take away an insured's right to legal action in respect of relevant matters. The clause, in the absence of anything to the contrary, is a mere collateral term for the purpose of providing a tribunal for the purpose of resolving disputes. If the insured commences a legal action the insurer can cross-sue for breach of the agreement or apply to the court under the Arbitration Act 1979 for the action to be stayed. Where an arbitration clause provides that an award is a condition precedent to any action on the policy, no cause of action arises until the requisite award has been given and then the action lies for enforcing the award only. To oust the jurisdiction of the court it is necessary for the clause to provide that in no circumstances shall the court deal with any dispute on the policy. In fact no clause of this type is found in practice.

outstanding claims advance. A payment made under a reinsurance contract or treaty whereby an advance payment is made in respect of outstanding claims that will come into account in a subsequent periodic settlement when the actual claim amount has been determined.

outstanding losses or claims. The total of losses or claims that have been notified but at a given time are still outstanding and as such are only estimated amounts.

outworkers extension. An extension to the business interruption policy (qv) available to members of the clothing trade who can suffer loss through material damage occurring at the premises of their outworkers. A limit is imposed. The premises are not specified to avoid the constant endorsements that would be needed to cope with the turnover that inevitably occurs.

overcarriage. A marine insurance term in reference to a situation where certain goods are not discharged at the destination port but are 'overcarried' and discharged on the homeward voyage. This can happen on voyages to the East or West coasts of Africa, island ports, or New Zealand. This amounts to deviation (qv) and the risk ceases when the vessel sails on from the port of destination still carrying the goods.

overclosing. The acceptance by an underwriter of a larger amount than originally agreed with the broker.

overdone slips. A slip (qv) where the acceptances exceed the total amount of cover available. At the close the acceptances are reduced on a proportionate basis.

overdue risk. An overdue ship. When a ship is overdue, the underwriter who has insured it, may seek a reinsurance with other marine syndicates. The premium is a heavy one. Both the insurer and the reinsurer have access to the latest shipping intelligence provided by Lloyd's.

overheating. Excessive heating. If a boiler or self-fired pressure vessel accidentally suffers a general deficiency of water while working, severe damage may be caused to the boiler shell, firebox etc. The risk is insurable as a whole or, in the case of a multi-tubular boiler, limited if desired to the overheating of the tubes only. The cover is for 'self damage' only and is put into effect as an extension of the boiler and pressure plant policy (qv). The cover is not usually required on cast-iron boilers (the equivalent risk is cracking, fracturing, and failure of welds (qv)) and in the case of a welded boiler, cover for failure of welds is normally a prerequisite to the overheating extension.

over-insurance. 1. Insuring property for more than its actual value. It can be inadvertent or fraudulent. The penalties for under-insurance can cause the insured to over-insure but the use of declaration policies (qv) enables insureds with fluctuating sums insured to overcome the problem. 2. Over-insurance in business interruption policies is guarded against by limiting the amount payable to an actual percentage of profits to turnover in the last financial year. Increase in the cost of working is limited to the amount necessary to maintain turnover or output during the period of indemnity at a level not exceeding that of the corresponding period in the twelve months immediately preceding the insured event.

overlapping policies. Two or more separate policies each covering a portion only of the same risk. A policy condition may require an insured to notify the insurer of any additional insurance effected during the currency of the policy. To constitute another insurance within the meaning of this condition, the additional insurance must cover the same interest, in the same subject-matter against the same peril. A subsequent insurance covering a portion of the same risk, which involves the possibility of accidental overlapping, is not another insurance within the meaning of the condition.

overriding commission. 1. An additional commission payable to particular intermediaries who introduce a large volume of profitable business to the insurer. 2. Discount granted by a reinsurer to an intermediary or cedant to cover the cedant's overhead expenses. To prevent a ceding office from writing business and reinsuring 100 per cent as a full-time activity for the sake of the underwriting commission, established reinsurers usually insist that the cedant retains a reasonable proportion of the business for his own account.

overriding of implied terms rule. A rule of construction (qv) to the effect that where there is a contradiction between express and implied terms the express words will prevail.

overseas deposits. Deposits required under local legislation to be made by insurers in overseas countries for the protection of locally-based policyholders.

Overseas Personal Liability. An extension to a public liability policy also called private personal liability (qv) as where the insured is an individual the personal liability (qv) cover applies to the UK as well as foreign countries.

overtime. When overtime is worked to merely expedite the repairs so that the owner may more speedily employ the ship, the excess cost is not recoverable from the insurer. However, where liners with advertised sailing dates are involved the overtime expenditure is admitted by the insurer. 'Liners' in this context means passenger and cargo vessels. The 'liner allowances' were formally established in an exchange of communications between the Institute of London Underwriters (qv) and the Association of Average Adjusters (qv) in 1954.

overwriting of premiums. This occurs where the volume of business underwritten on behalf of a Lloyd's underwriting member exceeds the level permitted by reference to the amount of security provided. Each underwriting member must furnish security as approved by the Committee, the amount of which varies according to the volume of business transacted. Each underwriting member contracts with his underwriting agent to write business up to his premium income limit. The security is held in trust by the Corporation. If the limit is exceeded Lloyd's will demand additional security to back the additional risks undertaken. This increase in obligations can be the result of the agent's failure through poor administration to cut off the flow of business at the right point, a fall in the £/$ exchange value, or coverholders (qv) writing larger volumes of business than expected under binding authorities (qv).

own account. Premiums, loss etc on or for own account are those retained by an insurer or reinsurer and not reinsured or retroceded.

'own branders'. Suppliers who put their own name on the product and give the impression that they are producers. Such suppliers are 'producers' for the purpose of the Consumer Protection Act 1987 (qv) and may be strictly liable for the damage as defined by the Act.

own damage. A term used to describe loss or damage to the insured's own vehicle under a motor insurance policy.

own damage excess. An excess (qv) under motor insurance policies which is applied to the material damage sustained by the insured vehicle and insured under the 'loss or damage' section of the policy.

own life policies cross-assigned. *See* CROSS-ASSIGNMENT.

owner only driving. A car insurance situation in which only the insured is permitted to drive the car. Where the insured volunteers for this restriction a 10 per cent discount is normally allowed. Where the restriction is imposed by the insurer no discount is granted.

'own surrounding property'. The term is used in connection with engineering insurance (qv) and refers to 'property belonging to the insured or for which he is responsible'. Such property is at the risk of damage through explosion, fragmentation etc of nearby plant and machinery.

P

PA(90). A select mortality table based on data collected by the CMI in recent years. It is based on data in respect of pensioners and is appropriate for use in pensions work.

package policy. A policy combining insurances of different types in one document for one insured. Examples include: householders' covers, shopkeepers' policies (property, business interruption, money, liability covers etc).

paid losses or claims. The total amount of losses or claims that have been settled during a given period (before adjusting for outstanding claims).

paid-up policy. A policy, sometimes called a 'free policy', granted by a life insurer for a reduced amount based on premiums already paid with no further premiums payable. The reduced sum is payable in the same event (eg death or survival of a given term) as the original sum. It is, in effect, the sum produced by applying the surrender value (qv) as a single premium. Paid-up provisions therefore apply only to those policies that may acquire a surrender value, ie whole life or endowment. In certain cases (eg whole life with limited endowment and pure endowment), the paid-up policy may be granted for a sum insured which bears the same proportion to the original sum insured as the number of premiums paid bears to the number originally payable. The practice of offices as regards participation in future bonuses varies. A paid-up policy clause is included in the policy.

paid-up value. *See* PAID-UP POLICY. The value of a paid-up policy is determined by actuarial calculation. Under endowment or whole life limited premium policies the reduced sum payable is sometimes that proportion of the original sum assured that the premiums paid bear to those originally payable provided no loan has been granted

and the conversion takes place within the days of grace (qv).

pair and set clause. Appears in certain property insurances, particularly those covering jewellery. It limits the insurer's liability in the event of loss or damage to any article forming part of a pair or set to the value of the particular part which is lost or damaged.

pantechnicon. A goods carrying vehicle with a large surface area which makes it susceptible to overturning in high winds. Motor insurers may wish to apply special rates as the carrying capacity (a principal rating factor) may not produce a sufficient premium to compensate for the increased risk.

parallel underwriting. The operation of two syndicates (*see* LLOYDS SYNDICATES) in the same market both of which are managed by the same managing agent.

paramount clauses/exclusions. Clauses 23 to 26 of the Institute Time Clauses (1/10/83) (qv) are stated to be paramount and override anything inconsistent with them. These clauses embrace exclusions of: war; strike; malicious acts; nuclear risks.

parents. 1. A parent has no insurable interest in the life of a child unless he has a pecuniary interest—education expenses and mere moral obligations confer no such interest. Exceptions are made in connection with industrial life insurance. 2. Parents are not liable for their children's torts unless the tort occurs by reason of the parent's negligence (eg inadequate instruction or supervision when the child uses a firearm) or authorisation.

Paris Convention 1919. This established rules governing flight over and between different states. It also affirmed the complete exclusive sovereignty of every state over the airspace above its own territory. The rules laid down concern: the fitness of the aircraft and the crew and navigation. The convention was superseded by the Chicago Convention 1944 and conseqently the Air Navigation Act 1920, which gave effect to the Paris Convention in the UK, was replaced by the Civil Aviation Act 1949.

parity clause. A marine insurance clause stating that where the contract is one of two or more such contracts and differing rates of premium apply, the lower rate shall prevail.

parol evidence. Evidence given in court by word of mouth. Such evidence is not generally admissible to contradict or vary the meaning of the policy, since, after the contract is reduced into writing, the parties are not at liberty to show, by giving evidence of their negotiations, that they contracted otherwise than in accordance with the terms they have used to express their agreement. There are certain cases in which such evidence is admissible. These are to prove: (a) the policy is void (eg obtained by fraud); (b) the policy does not set out the terms agreed (*see* RECTIFICATION); (c) the identity of the parties or subject-matter; (d) a parol condition which induced a party to enter the contract; (e) add collateral terms which were agreed upon, provided they do not contradict but merely supplement the written policy; (f) that a word is used in a special or peculiar sense (eg local or commercial term); to resolve any ambiguity which is obvious or patent. Where parol evidence is admitted, the matter in issue is no longer a mere question of construction but becomes a question of fact.

part of. A reinsurance term indicating that the reinsurer is accepting part only of the original risk and making it clear that in the event of a short closing (qv) will not be prepared to accept the whole of the risk.

partial disablement. An injury to the holder of a personal accident policy may leave him partially disabled (ie able to work but on a reduced basis) as opposed to totally disabled. Many such policies pay a reduced benefit for partial disablement.

partial indemnity clause. *See* KNOCK-FOR-KNOCK AGREEMENT.

partial loss. A loss within the limit of the sum insured and not therefore amounting to a total loss. It is a loss covered by the policy that does not completely destroy or render as worthless the insured property. *See also* PARTICULAR AVERAGE.

partially repaired damage. Where a ship is only partially repaired, the insured is entitled to recover the reasonable cost of such repairs plus an allowance for the reduction in the ship's market value because of the failure to effect full repairs. The aggregate must not exceed the cost of full repairs (Marine Insurance Act 1906, s.(69)2). *See also* UNREPAIRED DAMAGE.

participating policy. An alternative term for a with profits policy (qv).

particular average. A marine insurance term meaning partial loss affecting one particular interest (eg the hull, the freight or a particular consignment of cargo) caused by an insured peril but excluding general average (qv). If the policy is 'free from particular average' it excludes partial losses but cargo policies are sometimes claused 'each packet deemed to be a separate insurance' so that loss of a single packet is within the policy. Particular average on freight policies normally arises from partial loss of cargo by the insured perils. The measure of indemnity for hull particular average claims (Marine Insurance Act 1906, s. 69) is the reasonable cost of repairs, less the customary deductions 'new for old'. The term particular average does not appear in the new Institute Clauses (for use with the new MAR form), where the term partial loss is preferred but the term continues to be used by those engaged in marine insurance business and remains indelibly defined in the Marine Insurance Act 1906, s. 64(1).

particular charges. A marine insurance term to describe expenses (excluding salvage charges and general average) incurred by or on behalf of the insured for the safety or preservation of the subject-matter (Marine Insurance Act 1906, s. 64(2)). These charges are recoverable from the insurer if incurred to prevent or minimise a loss covered by the policy.

particular conditions. *See* EXPRESS CONDITIONS.

particular risks. A risk which has restricted consequences. A motor vehicle accident will normally only affect people within the vicinity or a fire may affect only the property owner, his employees, customers and suppliers. Most particular risks result in loss when they happen and are susceptible to some form of loss control. They are therefore usually insurable unlike fundamental risks (qv) which are generally not.

particulars of loss. Insurers provide within the claims condition that the insured should furnish full particulars of his loss. The requirement overlaps with proof of loss (qv). In property insurances such as fire policies the requirement may be set out in quite specific terms. The standard policy calls for delivery to the insurer within 30 days (or any longer period that is allowed) of the destruction or damage a written statement containing particulars of the property damaged and the amount of the damage. The insured must also give details of any other insurances on the property and such other proof and information as may be reasonably required. An insured, who ignored the insurer's repeated requests for details of his business bank accounts in his mother's name, was refused an indemnity as his conduct amounted to a breach of a condition precedent to liability (*Welch* v *Royal Exchange Assurance* (1939)). Where the condition calls for verification of certain details by third parties, their failure to co-operate may prevent the insured from complying with the condition so a breach occurs (*Worsley* v *Wood* (1796)).

partners and insurable interest. A business partner has insurable interest (qv) in the life of a co-partner to the extent of the capital invested by the co-partner in the business. *See* PARTNERSHIP ASSURANCE.

partnership insurance. This describes the use of life insurance to protect business partners against the withdrawal of capital and/or the costs of meeting the financial obligations to the dependants of the deceased on the death of one of them. Various combinations of life insurance can be used depending on the ages, financial interests, agreements etc relevant to the particular situation. The aim is always to make sure that the money gets into the right

hands, at the right time while minimising costs and taxation liabilities.

part-time agent. A person who, in addition to another activity (eg garage proprietor), introduces insurance business to an insurer in return for a commission.

party wall. A common wall between two buildings but not passing through the roof. It is not an effective fire shield. A perfect party wall is at least nine inches thick extending up to and through the roof. This is considered an effective fire shield.

passenger carrying vehicles. Motor insurers categorise these vehicles for rating purposes into (i) hire cars and (ii) coaches and buses. Hire cars are vehicles with not more than 12 seats including the driver's seat and used for carrying passengers for hire or reward. Hire cars are sub-divided into (a) private hire vehicles, ie hiring direct from the insured's premises; and (b) public hire vehicles which can ply for hire from the streets, eg taxis. Coaches and buses have seating capacity in excess of 12 including the driver. Some passenger carrying vehicles are not used for hire or reward (eg contractor carries own employees to work sites) while others are so used.

passenger indemnity. The indemnity granted at the request of the insured under the third party section of a motor policy to persons in, mounting into, or dismounting from, the motor vehicle. The indemnity is available under private car and commercial vehicle policies.

passenger liability. The liability of the user or driver of a vehicle, ship, aircraft or other conveyance towards passengers travelling in or upon that conveyance in respect of injury or damage to their property. Liability may be governed by common law, contract, statute or international convention. Passenger liability insurance for motor vehicles is compulsory. This requirement applies to all vehicles which are required by the Road Traffic Act 1988 to have third party insurance and the cover must extend to authorised passengers (other than employees in the course of employment), other non-farepaying passengers, and 'unauthorised passengers' (qv). *See also* PASSENGER TICKET.

passenger lifts. *See* LIFT POLICY for cover available from engineering insurers. Public liability insurers no longer as an invariable rule exclude liability caused in connection with passenger lifts, elevators and escalators owned by the insured or those for which the insured is responsible. However, it is usually material to disclose the existence of a passenger lift risk to the insurer and cover will be subject to compliance by the insured with the statutory obligations for inspection.

passenger ticket. The provisions of the Warsaw Convention 1929 (qv) which limit the liability of air carriers for death of, or bodily injury to, passengers operate only if the carrier issues a ticket to each person intending to travel. The ticket should contain: date and place of issue; place of departure and destination; scheduled stopping place; name and address of the air carrier or carriers; and an assurance that the carriage is subject to the Warsaw Convention.

passing off. This tort (qv) is the pretence by one person that his goods or services are those of another. The person whose business interests suffer has a right of action in damages or for an account, and for an injunction to restrain the defendant (qv) in the future. There is a limited insurance market in which a person may insure against his liability for having infringed the industrial property rights of another.

passive breaches of utmost good faith. These are non-disclosure and concealment. Both are concerned with a failure to disclose material facts, the former innocently and the latter deliberately. *See* UTMOST GOOD FAITH.

past service benefit. A pension scheme benefit allowed to a new member in respect of his previous service.

past service pension. A pension allowed to an employee at the inception of a pension scheme in respect of his years of service before the commencement of the pension scheme.

patent. The right conferred by letter of patent of the exclusive use and benefit of an invention capable of an industrial application. The normal duration of a patent is 20 years and this may not be extended (Patents Act 1977, s. 25).

patterns, models, moulds and designs. Under a material damage policy the liability for loss of such items is limited to the cost of reproducing them. The consequential loss is not covered unless special arrangements have been made.

Pawsey v *Scottish Union & National* (1907). *See* PROXIMATE CAUSE.

pay as may be paid. A reinsurance term indicating that the reinsurer will pay without questioning the insurer's liability under the original insurance.

pay as you go (PAYG). A method whereby pension scheme payments are financed as they fall due rather than by previous financial provision. The state pension scheme operates in this way.

payee policy. A term used by personal accident insurers when issuing a policy involving two parties (a) the subject-matter of the cover, (b) the person who is to receive the policy moneys. The first party is called the insured and the second the payee. The policy can be for any type of cover but they are normally restricted to death benefits. Examples: a wife insures a husband; a firm insures a 'keyman' (*see* KEYMAN INSURANCE).

'paying passengers'. Passengers who get a 'lift' in someone else's vehicle and make a contribution towards the running costs. Prior to the Transport Act 1980 motorists accepting such contributions invalidated their motor insurances policies which exclude use for hire or reward. The position is now governed by the Road Traffic Act 1988. *See* CAR SHARING.

payment of premium. The general rule is that the insurers must meet a claim which is within the terms of the policy, even if the premium has not been paid. The premium is payable immediately the contract is concluded but in the absence of an express provision, a stipulation as to time for payment will not be regarded as of the essence of the contract. There are exceptions to this rule, such as non- payment after many demands, since this may amount to repudiation of the contract; or failure to pay within a time limit; or where payment of the premium is expressly made a condition precedent to liability to indemnify. Payment of the premium within a fixed time is illustrated by a renewal premium where days of grace are allowed for such payment. As payment of the premium and liability of the insurer are separate and distinct, the insurers may, if necessary, commence proceedings for the recovery of the premium due to them irrespective of their obligations to indemnify.

payroll cover. A business interruption insurance (qv) term in respect of the insurance of the remuneration payable to staff. 'Payroll' includes salaries, wages and remuneration of all kinds including national insurance, bonuses, holiday pay, and other payments pertaining to salaries and wages. Payroll may be insured in either of the following ways: (a) the amount of the entire payroll is insured in full as part of the item of gross profit. (b) (i) initially for a selected limited number of weeks, (ii) then a selected percentage for the remainder of the indemnity period (qv), the sum insured being based on the annual payroll. Both the initial period and percentage are chosen on the basis of the insured's responsibilities under the Employment Protection Acts. The selected percentage is related to the remuneration of the employees the insured wishes to retain in the longer term. Others may be dismissed at the end of the initial period after the statutory obligations relating to periods of notice have been met.

pax. A common abbreviation of 'passengers' as used on aviation slips.

peak value clause. A clause applied to cargo insurances on cotton providing that the sum insured will be determined by reference to the highest value in the cotton market at the time of loss.

Pearson Commission (Report). The Royal Commission on Civil Liability and Compensation under the chairmanship of Lord Pearson reported in March 1978 (Cmnd 7054). It was set up in 1972 to enquire into the basis of civil liability for causing death or personal injury. Its main proposals were: 1. A no fault liability system (qv) for motor vehicle accidents on the road paid for by a levy on petrol: modelled on the industrial injuries schemes, the proposal however covered all members of the family but with improved benefits. 2. To retain the existing tort system so that the victim of a motor accident would have to be able to sue for damages in tort while also being eligible for a 'no fault' benefit, ie a new type of social security benefit. 3. To improve the industrial injuries scheme by providing higher benefits and extending its scope to cover the self-employed, contractors and additional cases of occupational disease. 4. Certain changes in the basis of calculating tortious liability by: (a) Offsetting the full social security benefits. (b) Applying a three months' 'excess' to damages in respect of pain and suffering to eliminate smaller claims. (c) Keeping damages for future pecuniary loss by death or protracted injury under review while paying the damages in the form of periodic payments unless the parties agree to a lump sum payment.

pecuniary loss. Pecuniary means 'relating to money' and pecuniary loss refers to the loss due to having to make unexpected payments or due to a loss or diminution of expected income. The risk of pecuniary loss is insurable in a variety of ways. *See* PECUNIARY LOSS INSURANCE.

pecuniary loss insurance. This is one of the 10 DTI accounting categories which combines the following DTI classes (Insurance Companies Act 1982): Credit insurance; Suretyship (ie fidelity guarantee); Miscellaneous financial loss (eg business interruption); Legal expenses.

pedal cycles. *See* BICYCLE INSURANCE.

penalty. 1. A punishment, particularly a fine or monetary payment. It is against public policy (qv) to allow a person to insure against fines but legal defence cover is available under liability and legal expenses insurances. Penalties along with liquidated damages arising under contract are commonly excluded under liability policies. 2. The nominal sum payable by an obligor on breach of a condition in a bond.

pension. A retirement annuity (qv) resulting in a regular lifetime payment to the pensioner whose rights may been acquired under a personal or occupational pension plan or scheme.

pensionable salary. Under many schemes the pension is based on the member's final salary on reaching retirement. This salary is defined within the scheme and is often the final salary.

pensionable service. Employment that counts as years of service towards a member's benefit entitlement from a pension scheme. Pension schemes define the period and type of service eligible for these purposes.

pensioneer trustee. An experienced person or company appointed in accordance with the requirements relating to the approval of small self-administered schemes under the Income and Corporation Taxes Act 1988 to act as a trustee of such a scheme.

pension fund. Strictly this means the assets of a pension scheme from which the pensions will be paid. Often the term is used to denote the pension scheme itself.

pension guarantee. An arrangement whereby on the early death of a pensioner the pension scheme continues to pay further sums until a guaranteed total has been reached or until a certain number of years have expired. Generally, this is achieved by fixing a total in relation to the late member's accumulated contributions or a multiple of the annual pension rate.

pension mortgage. A pension arrangement under which a proportion of the benefits can be used to repay the mortgage debt. The remaining benefits must be in the form of a pension so that tax relief will be allowable on both the interest payable to the mortgagee and the premiums payable. This is an attractive tax-efficient alternative to endowment or repayment mortgages (see HOUSE PURCHASE SCHEMES).

pension revaluation. Since January 1986, paid-up pensions for leavers have been required by law to be increased at least: (a) until state pension age (SPA), by the amount of any post leaving guaranteed minimum pension (GMP) revaluation; and (b) until the scheme's normal retirement date, the increase in retail prices (or 5 per cent if less) on pension in excess of GMP accrued since 1 January 1985. Also, the Social Security Act 1986 obliges contracted-out pension schemes to revalue from SPA, GMP and WGMP

(widow(ers)s guaranteed minimum pension) in so far as they have accrued from 6 April 1988.

pension scheme. This normally refers to an occupational scheme effected by an employer for the benefit of selected employees or the workforce as a whole. As a retirement benefit scheme it needs to be approved for tax purposes under Chapter I, Part XIV Income and Corporation Taxes Act 1908 (ICTA 88).

pensioners' right premium. The sum paid to the state by a private pension scheme when it ceases to be contracted-out (qv) to enable the state to provide the guaranteed minimum pension (qv) for its existing pensioners.

pensions managed fund. An occupational pension scheme not managed by the firm itself but either by an insurance company, which receives the premiums, invests them for the benefit of the fund, and pays out the pensions, or by external investment managers.

Per capita **premium basis.** *Per capita* means per head. There are some risks, eg public liability for a cinema (*see* PUBLIC ACCESS RISKS), where the number attending or the attendance capacity provides an adequate reflection of the magnitude of the risk. Consequently, the premium can be quoted on a *per capita* basis.

percentage adjustments. A term describing a percentage increase or decrease to give effect to changes in fire insurance premium rates to reflect changes in the experience of the various classes of risk.

percentage of fire loss insurance. A form of business interruption insurance (qv) now rarely used. It pays such percentage of the amount recovered in respect of the ordinary fire insurance loss as the sum insured under the interruption (or loss of profits) policy bears to the total sum insured under the fire policy. Example: If the loss of profits sum insured was 10 per cent of the fire insurance and the fire claim amounted to £50 000, then the amount payable for loss of profits would have been £5000. It is not a contract of indemnity, merely an excess fire policy.

performance bond. A conditional bond (qv) under which the obligor's obligations cease if the stipulated performance is carried out. Performance bonds are most commonly used in the construction industry. They protect the principal against the risk of default by the contractor due to insolvency or other reasons. If the contractor fails to meet his obligations, the principal (ie the obligee) can call upon the obligor (the surety), usually but not always an insurer, to pay damages (the additional cost of completing the contract) up to the amount of the bond. This amount is normally set at 10 per cent or 20 per cent of the contract price. The contractor and the surety combine to give the guarantee and the surety has a right to recover losses from the party guaranteed. For other types of bond affecting the construction industry *see* BID OR TENDER BOND; ADVANCE PAYMENT BOND; MAINTENANCE BOND; RETENTION BOND; STREET WORKS BOND.

peril. Whatever may cause a loss, eg fire or flood.

perils of the seas. This refers only to fortuitous accidents or casualties of the seas and does not include the ordinary action of the wind and waves (Marine Insurance Act 1906, Schedule 1, Rule for Construction 7), eg foundering of ship at sea, collisions, unintentional stranding, etc. Something which may happen at sea not something which must happen at sea is the criterion.

period of insurance (or risk). The period during which the insurer is liable to meet losses under the policy. (*See also* LOSSES-OCCURRING POLICIES and CLAIMS-MADE POLICIES.)

period policy. *See* TIME POLICY.

permanent contracts. Contracts for a specified term during which the insurer has no right to refuse the annual premium when tendered by the insured. Contracts of life insurance and permanent health insurance come under this category in that the insurer agrees at the inception that the policy will run for a given term (eg 30 years or up to age 65) subject only to the insured paying the annual premium when due. The policy will lapse, subject to non-forfeiture privileges (qv), if payment is not made when due.

permanent health insurance (PHI). This is long-term business written in the life department. The principal benefit is an income for the insured during periods of disablement from working. The insured effects the policy for a given period (eg to age 60 or 65) and provided always the premium is paid (usually annually) the insurer remains 'permanently' on risk for the entire period regardless of any changes in the state of health of the insured. Once the benefit commences, it continues to be payable for so long as the incapacitating illness or accident continues up to the fixed age. Health and age at entry are key underwriting factors. The level premium system (qv) operates and, in order to minimise costs, many insureds opt for deferred periods ranging from 4 weeks to 52 weeks or even longer. With long deferred periods the insurance becomes one against the 'catastrophe' disablement risk. Policies are issued to both individuals and employers who wish to effect group cover for their employees.

permanent selection. The exclusion from a group of lives of persons of a certain type with the result that the mortality rate of the group will differ when compared with the population norm. For example, persons suffering from chronic diseases may be excluded from a group of lives acceptable for life insurance at ordinary rates of premium with the result that the insured group will have an overall lighter mortality rate.

permanent total disablement. Most personal accident policies provide a benefit for permanent disablement caused otherwise than by loss of limb or sight for which separate provision is made. The benefit is normally in the form of a capital sum. A number of alternative definitions are used by insurers in the personal accident and sickness insurances. The principal ones are: (a) Permanent total disablement from gainful employment of any kind. This definition is narrow in that a policyholder must be very severely disabled before the benefit will be paid. A badly injured person who can take up sedentary work, even part-time, will not be entitled to the benefit. (b) Permanent total disablement from the insured's usual occupation and any other occupation for which the insured is suited by knowledge and training. An injured footballer forced into clerical work may be entitled to a benefit but would not be if he secured employment as a football writer. Cover is wider than in (a) above. (c) Permanent total disablement from the insured's usual occupation. In (b) above the footballer turned football writer would be entitled to a benefit and so this definition gives the widest cover.

'permitted drivers'. Any driver of a motor vehicle who is driving 'on the order or with the permission of the policyholder'. The standard form of motor insurance policy includes a clause to the effect, that subject to the terms and conditions of the policy, such a driver is indemnified under the third party section of the cover provided he holds a licence, has held a licence and is not disqualified from holding or obtaining a licence. The remaining sections of the policy are governed by the general exceptions and the policyholder will lose the benefit of the policy if, to his knowledge, the vehicle is being driven by someone who does not hold a licence, unless such person has held a licence and is not disqualified from holding or obtaining one (*see* DRIVING LICENCE). It is a question of fact as to whether the driver has had the necessary 'order' or 'permission'. In most cases the position on permitted drivers is obvious. A 'joyrider' or car thief is not a permitted driver and cannot claim the indemnity under the third party section but the general exception will not operate to the detriment of the policyholder in respect of any own damage (qv) that occurs as he will not knowingly have acquiesced to driving by an 'excluded' driver. At the other extreme there will be drivers given specific permission for specific journeys or specific periods of time. The driver who goes outside any precise limits laid down and in defiance of them may cease to be a 'permitted driver'. In *Browning* v *Phoenix Assurance Co Ltd* (1960) a garage employee was authorised by the insured to drive the car to warm it up before draining the oil. Nothing was said about driving after the oil change so the employee's subsequent driving was not permitted. It seems unlikely that a permitted driver can, without the express permission of the insured, give permission to another driver. In the Canadian case of *Minister of Transport* v *Canadian General Insurance* (1971) the policyholder's son, a permitted driver, allowed a friend to drive and the court held that he was not a permitted driver. Permission, once granted, can be withdrawn and so any continued driving by the person concerned after communication of the revocation would not entitle him to the indemnity under the third party section. However, where prior to his death the policyholder had given permission to his son, the continued driving during the current term of the policy was upheld by the House of Lords (*Kelly* v *Cornhill Insurance Co Ltd* (1964) 1 AER 321). Where the insured has sold his car the new owner is not a permitted driver for the purpose of the insured's policy (*Peters* v *General Accident* (1938) 2 AER 267). A permitted driver is entitled to an indemnity under the policy when the claimant is the policyholder (*Digby* v *General Accident* (1943) AC 121) *see* 'MERLE OBERON' CLAUSE. Following an amendment to s. 149 of the Road Traffic Act 1988 the insurer will have to meet any judgment in respect of an 'Act' liability regardless of who was driving. For this purpose it is immaterial whether the driver is a thief, is authorised, or holds a licence or not. The only 'excluded liability' is in respect of a passenger who knew or had reason to believe the vehicle was stolen. *See also* PERMITTED DRIVERS' STATUTORY RIGHT TO INDEMNITY.

permitted drivers' statutory right to indemnity. A permitted driver (qv) has a statutory right to enforce a motor insurance contract purporting to afford him an indemnity directly against the insurer. This right is not dependent on the approval or acquiesence of the insured. The Road Traffic Act 1988, s. 148(4) states that an authorised insurer must indemnify the person or classes of person specified in the policy in respect of any liability the policy purports to cover. This negates any problems that might arise if an insurer objects to an indemnity on the grounds that a permitted driver, who did not know of the insurance arranged for him, will be seeking to ratify a contract after a loss (*Williams* v *Baltic Insurance Association* (1924).

perpetual insurance. A fire insurance method under which the insured pays a deposit in a lump sum or in instalments based on a percentage of the value of the property at risk. The insurer invests the sum paid in order to accrue interest from which claims will be paid. The insured can terminate the arrangement by withdrawing his deposit.

persistency. The renewal quality of insurance policies, the term persistency is particularly applied to life insurance. High persistency means that a high percentage of policies stay in force to the end of the policy term. Low persistency means that a high percentage of the policies lapse through non-payment of premiums.

personal accident insurance. A policy (sometimes called 'accidents' only) which pays out capital sums following death or permanent disablement (loss of limb, sight etc as defined) and weekly benefits for temporary disablement (up to 104 weeks) from working following accidental bodily injury (qv). No cover is provided for death or disablement following illness or disease. The policy is normally renewable annually but short period policies can be arranged. Occupation is a key rating factor. Most packaged travel and holiday policies incorporate a personal accident section.

personal accident and sickness insurance. The same as personal accident insurance (qv) cover but adding a benefit for temporary total disablement (up to 52 weeks) following illness or disease. As the policy is renewable annually the insurer can decline to renew at any time. The risk of loss of cover in the event of a change in the state of health explains why some insureds prefer the higher cost permanent health insurance (qv)

personal account. Each underwriting member of a Lloyd's syndicate receives a statement showing how the member's net result was determined.

personal assault. A policy to provide personal accident benefits and some material damage cover. In the event of the insured or his employees sustaining injury as a result of personal assault committed during robbery or hold-up then capital sums are payable for death, loss of limbs, eyes, or other permanent total disablement, and a weekly benefit is payable for temporary total disablement. Cover also extends to include damage to clothing and personal effects up to £250 (or there-abouts) which occurs during the personal assault. Some policies include medical expenses incurred up to 15 per cent of the weekly benefits payable. The insurance is often included in traders' combined policies.

personal contracts. Most insurance contracts are personal contracts and as such they are not freely assignable. A contract is a personal one if the continued existence of it depends totally upon the insurer's knowledge of and confidence in the person who is the policyholder. The identity of the policyholder is so important to the insurer that the policy cannot be freely assigned by the policyholder and transfer it with the subject-matter of insurance. The new owner of a motor car insured under a motor policy may not be as acceptable as his predecessor. In such a case the permission of the insurer is needed if the policy is to be validly transferred. If the insurers give their consent they have effectively made a new contract. This is known as novation (qv). Marine and life policies are not considered to be personal contracts.

personal effects. Items belonging to and used by individuals. The term personal effects appears in household contents policies, 'all risks' policies, travel and a number of other policies. The term itself is not defined and the usual approach is for the insurer to specify the items that do not fall into this category although it would be hard for a person to bring some items of property, say a business machine used as such, within the term. The items of property excluded varies according to the insurer but they all require that the sum insured is the total value at risk. Where the cover is for unspecified personal effects a single article limit (qv) is applied. A household contents policy covers 'household goods and personal effects of every description' except deeds, bonds, bills of exchange, promissory notes, cheques, securities for money, and the like. The restriction of cover to specified perils at the dwelling of the insured and while temporarily removed creates a demand for alternative insurances such as all risks cover.

personal expenses. The expenses, including agent's salary and profit commission, directly attributable to an underwriting member of Lloyd's

personal injury (injuries). 1. A term used in policies and in legislation such as the Limitation Act 1980 under which actions for such injuries must be commenced within three years or whenever the time starts to run. It is normally intended to mean harm that takes the form of bodily injury to a person but on a strict interpretation includes injury to intangibles such as injury to feelings resulting from defamation. Insurers now have a tendency to use the term 'bodily injury' in preference to personal injury. 2. Personal injury legal expenses. The name given to a legal expenses insurance that provides legal expenses to pursue actions againt third parties from whom compensation is sought for personal injuries. The cover is often combined with property protection cover.

Personal Insurance Arbitration Service (PIAS). This is a low cost arbitration scheme to which a number of companies belong. Membership is voluntary and companies normally choose between this and the Insurance Ombudsman Bureau (IOB) (qv). The PIAS covers 'personal type' insurances only and provides policyholders, who have claims disputes, with a means of having their case heard without going to court. The proceedings are less costly and formal than court proceedings but more formal than the system operated by the IOB. The award is issued in accordance with the Arbitration Act 1950-79 and it is enforceable on both parties with only a limited right of appeal. Life insurances and insurances

effected by employers on behalf of employees are not covered by PIAS.

personalised bonds. *See* MINI BONDS.

personal legal assistance. A section of a commercial legal expenses insurance (qv) to provide similar cover for directors, partners, and key personnel and their families to cover private matters.

personal liability insurance. This indemnifies the insured (and members of his family who permanently reside with him) against legal liability for bodily injury to others or damage to their property resulting from their acts or omissions occurring in private capacity. The policy excludes liability arising out of: his business or profession; the ownership or occupation of land or buildings; or the ownership or use of motor vehicles. The cover is invariably included as an extension of a household policy on contents.

personal lines. A term imported from the USA to describe the kind of insurances bought by individuals in response to their personal insurance needs. Private car, household, holiday, and similar insurances are all within the personal lines description.

personal pension/personal pension plan. A new arrangement introduced under the Social Security Act 1986 and Finance Act (No. 2) 1987. It enables an employee or self-employed person to make contributions to his own pension plan. The benefits must be taken mainly in the form of an annuity although 25 per cent of the total fund can be taken as cash. The personal pension attracts the tax concessions generally associated with pension schemes, viz:—tax-free contributions if within 17.5 per cent of net relevant earnings (qv) with higher percentages for persons over 50; contributions accumulate in a tax-free fund; tax-free cash available on retirement (25 per cent of total fund); up to 5 per cent of net relevant earnings can be contributed towards widows' death in service benefits provided this is within the overall maximum. The benefits must be taken between ages 50–75, the amount of the annuity is unlimited, and an employer can contribute. Also a personal pension can be used for contracting out of SERPS.

personal possessions. Means the same as personal effects (qv).

personal property. Movable property; goods and chattels as distinct from real property.

personal representative. An executor or administrator. By s.55 (1)(xi) Administration of Estates Act 1925 the term means the executor original or by representation or administrator for the time being of a deceased person. The Law Reform (Miscellaneous Provisions) Act 1934 provides that on the death of any person all causes of action subsisting against him or vested in him shall survive against, or, as the case may be, for the benefit of his estate. This means, *inter alia*, that on the death of the negligent party damages may be awarded against the personal representatives of a deceased party and must be paid out of the deceased's estate. Consequently, liability policies contain a clause indemnifying the insured's personal representatives provided always they observe the terms and conditions of the policy.

personal reserve. A reserve held on behalf of an underwriting member (Name) of Lloyd's by his agent to provide a fund to meet future losses. A proportion of the Name's profits, in accordance with the underwriting agency agreement, are set aside to build up the fund, to which the Name can contribute from other sources. This reserve, which must be maintained in the premium trust fund (qv), is in addition to the Lloyd's deposit and to any amounts set aside in any special reserve fund on behalf of the Name.

personal wealth. The wealth that must be proved at a minimum level before an individual can be accepted as an underwriting member at Lloyd's. *See* MEANS TEST.

personal stop loss policy. A policy which can be effected by Names at Lloyd's to insure them against an overall underwriting loss. The insured pays an excess (qv) and the insurer pays over and above that amount up to an agreed limit. Cover can be for up to £250 000 with an excess of 10 per cent of the allocated premium income limit up to a maximum of £25 000 either on an excess basis for each year of the three year period of insurance or on a three-year aggregate basis. Under the second basis a claim made in the first or second years of insurance would reduce by the amount of that claim the cover available in the subsequent year(s). The excess amount always applies separately to each year of account. The scheme is underwritten at Lloyd's.

person guaranteed. The person, also called the principal, whose fidelity or undertaking is the subject of a fidelity guarantee or a bond.

persons at work. In terms of the Health & Safety at Work etc Act 1974 (qv) 'all persons at work', whether employers, employees, or self-employed, are covered with the exception of domestic servants in a private household. The Act extends to many not covered by the previous legislation, eg self-employed, those employed in education, health services, leisure industries, and in some parts of the transport industry.

petrol pumps. Loss or damage to petrol pumps may be covered under a separate material damage policy (which itself may be a section of a motor traders combined policy) or as an extension of a public liability or internal risks policy (qv). Note that under a knock for knock agreement (qv) where a petrol pump is damaged by the driver of a vehicle whose insurer is a party to the agreement, the pump insurer agrees to accept 50 per cent only of the damage in full settlement of recovery rights.

'physical defect or infirmity'. This was held to mean 'any malfunctioning or departure from a healthy state of any part of the body' (*Jason* v *British Traders Insurance Co* (1969)). A personal accident policy covered accident bodily injury resulting in and being the independent and direct cause of the injury or disablement. There was an exception of 'death, injury or disablement directly or indirectly caused by or arising or resulting from or traceable to . . . any physical defect or infirmity which existed prior to the accident'. The insured had a coronary thrombosis after a car accident, the clot blocking a coronary artery that had been narrowed by an existing disease. This was a physical defect within the meaning of the exception and operated as a concurrent cause (qv) with the motor accident. Consequently the exception applied.

physical hazard. The risk arising from the physical nature of the subject-matter and the inherent factors related thereto. It is any hazard arising from the material, structure, or operational features of the risk itself apart from the persons associated with the risk, particularly those involved with ownership or management (*see* MORAL HAZARD). Examples are: marine insurance—type of cargo, type of vessel, voyage and route. Fire insurance—construction and use of premises; life insurance—age and state of health of life insured.

pilferage. Theft unaccompanied by any form of attack on the premises often committed by persons with a lawful right to be on the premises (eg employees and customers). The risk is not covered under theft (business premises) policies. It is not possible to measure or rate the risk. Generally individual losses are for small amounts and the risk is widespread in the retail trade. These conditions favour risk assumption (qv) and risk prevention as suitable responses to the risk. Retailers also use their costing and pricing policies as a means of recovering these losses from customers in the same way that other recurring expenses are recovered. Pilferage by employees is often covered under fidelity guarantee insurance (qv). In the context of a marine cargo clause Donaldson J stated in *Nishina Trading Co Ltd* v *Chiyoda Fire and Marine Insurance Co Ltd* (1968), 'pilferage refers probably to the taking of a small part of the goods rather than of the whole'.

pirates. Loss/damage caused by pirates is a maritime peril (Marine Insurance Act 1906, s. 3) covered under marine policies. Pirates are marauders without allegiance to any recognised flag who, for their own gain, plunder ships, goods or other moveables at sea. The term includes passengers who mutiny and rioters who attack from the shore (Rule of Construction 8, First Schedule of the Marine Insurance Act).

The term pirates is synonymous with rovers.

place of work. *See* SAFE PLACE OF WORK.

placing. Effecting an insurance.

plain English. This refers to a 'campaign' by a number of insurers to combat criticism that policies are written in difficult, almost incomprehensible language. These insurers endeavour to use language that will be perceived by their policyholders as being in plain English, ie easier to understand.

plain form of policy. The standard form of marine policy, known as the SG (ie ships and goods) form, was adopted by Loyd's in 1799 and in use until 1983. In its 'plain' form it has no clauses attached. Despite its antiquated language it remained in use because the import of every one of its expressions has been clearly defined by the courts. Clauses were added to meet the requirements of the particular subject-matter or adventure. In 1982 the Institute of London Underwriters and the Lloyd's Underwriters Association drafted new marine forms and clauses to simplify policy wording and these have been operative since 1983. The new MAR form states in simple terms the agreement to insure and details of the cover is given in the various new Institute Clauses. There are separate MAR forms for Lloyd's, the Lloyd's Marine Policy, and for companies, the Companies Marine Policy.

planned risk assumption. A method of risk financing (qv) often used by businesses as a response to losses that may occur frequently, particularly where they have a spread of risk and the maximum probable loss is small. They treat the losses as normal operating expenses and recover them from their customers through their normal costing and pricing procedures. *See* RISK ASSUMPTION.

plant. For the purposes of engineering insurances (qv) this is defined in the relevant policies as follows: (a) Boiler and pressure policy—'all integral parts of any item but excluding foundations, brickwork, and ancillary or connected equipment unless specifically included'. (b) Cranes and lifting machinery policy (qv)—'all integral parts of any item (other than foundations, brickwork, fixing bolts, or appliances) but excluding tracks, stagings, gantries, grabs or magnets, unless specifically included'. (c) Lift policy (qv)—'all integral parts of any item including landing gates and signalling apparatus but excluding foundations, brickwork, lift-well enclosure, motor room and supporting structure'. (d) electrical plant (qv) and engine plant (qv)—'all integral parts of any item (other than foundations, brickwork, and masonry) and included all starters or starting switchgear for individual items and the wiring connecting them'. (e) refrigeration plant 'all integral parts of any item (other than foundations, brickwork, masonry, cold chamber structure and cooling tower). It includes condensers, evaporators, piping valves and other apparatus in the refrigerant circuit pumps and the starters or starting switchgear for individual items and the wiring connecting them. (f) fragmentation policy—'all integral parts of any item excluding foundations, masonry, brickwork, chimneys, supporting structures and any ancillary equipment'.

plate glass insurance. *See* GLASS INSURANCE.

plated weight. The unladen weight of a goods-carrying vehicle plus its carrying capacity. Vehicles manufactured since 1 January 1968 carry a plate on which the manufacturer marks the plated weight of the vehicle as agreed with the authorities. Intermediate (plated weight between 3.5 tons and 16 tons) and large vehicles (those over 16 tons) can only be used if the owner or user has an operator's licence. Small goods vehicles have a plated weight below 3.5 tons and can be run without such a licence. Use of the vehicle is a major factor and generally the larger the vehicle the greater will be the intensity of its use. Originally insurers used a table of rates based on carrying capacity of the vehicle but following the introduction of plating, plated weights have been used instead as a rating factor.

plurality of risk. This exists when a fire insurance covers more than one building or range of buildings each with its own separate sum insured.

plural tenancy. Premises occupied by a number of different tenants. The situation may present fire hazards due to: (a) Variety of different trades of widely different character under one roof. (b) Many different standards of cleanliness. (c) Frequent changes of tenants without notice to the insurer. (d) Poor upkeep of fire extinguishing appliances in the absence of clear responsibility for such matters. (e) Risk of insecure and badly kept heating appliances in some parts of the building.

pluvius insurance. *See* WEATHER INSURANCE.

pneumoconiosis. A generic term for insidious lung diseases caused by the inhalation of very fine dusts of metal, rocks, coal and the like. A variety of names are given to this condition according to the nature of the dust—anthracosis is a coal miner's disease and asbestosis is caused by asbestos fibres. Employees working in mines and quarries, refractory brick works, potteries, cutlery manufacturers and metal grinding are exposed to diseases of this kind. They are of the 'long-tail' (qv) variety and a matter of concern for employers' liability insurers.

Poincare' franc. A diplomatic unit of value also known as the French gold franc. It is used in the terms of the international conventions governing liabilities arising out of air travel and carriage. One gold franc is equivalent to 65 milligrams gold of millesimal fineness of 900. Millesimal fineness 900 means gold which is 900/1000ths pure. The sterling equivalent is determined by the Carriage of Air (Sterling Equivalent) Order.

points basis. A system of rating motor traders' road risks policies (qv) by allocating a certain number of points for each feature of the insured's activities (eg number of vehicles; number of persons permitted to drive; number of trade plates, etc). The insured submits an annual declaration in respect of these activities and the extent thereof for the coming year for which period the premium is adjusted.

polarisation. Persons selling life assurance must identify themselves as belonging to one of two distinct groups, ie the market is 'polarised'. They must be either wholly independent intermediaries, namely independent financial advisers (IFA) or representatives selling the products of one company and one company only. These representatives may be either: (a) appointed representatives (qv) authorised to give advice and sell the products of only one company. They are not employees and are known as tied agents; or (b) company representatives advising on and selling the products and services of one company by which they are actually employed. The agent with a strong commitment to one company but free to sell the products of others is a thing of the past. The agent must make it clear as to the category to which he belongs. The salesman must give 'best advice' (qv) based on knowledge of the client's circumstances at the time of sale. Many small agents have responded to the regulations by becoming tied to one company. *See* FINANCIAL SERVICES ACT 1986.

policies incepting basis. A reinsurance treaty may be written on the basis that the reinsurer's liability is based on when the underlying policy was effected and not whether the loss occurred or was notified during the reinsurance period.

Policies of Assurance Act 1867. Section 1 gives the assignee of a life policy the right to sue in his own name provided he has the equitable right to the policy proceeds. Section 3 provides that no assignment gives the assignee the right to sue until written notice of the date and purpose of the assignment has been given to the insurer. The assignee therefore has no title until notice is given. Section 4 specifies that every life policy must show the insurer's principal place of business where notices of assignment can be served. Section 5 provides that an assignment can be either by endorsement or by separate document. Section 6 states that when an insurer is served with a notice of assignment the insurer must on request and for a fee not exceeding 25p, supply a written acknowledgement of receipt of the notice. Section 7 provides that the Act relates to all policies of life assurance. *See also* 'PRIORITY OF NOTICE REGULATES THE PRIORITY OF CLAIM'.

policy. The document that is the written evidence of the contract between the insurer and the insured. The policy is drawn up by the insurer so any ambiguity will be construed against the insurer (*see* CONTRA PROFERENTEM RULE). If the policy fails to represent the in-

tention of the parties then it can be rectified by (i) mutual consent, or (ii) application to the court. The party seeking rectification (qv) will have to supply proof as to the real intention of the parties. *See also* PAROL EVIDENCE. The insurer under an annual contract issues the policy for the first period of insurance and provides for renewal in the policy wording.

policy fee. When fixing the premium under life insurance policies most companies incorporate a fixed annual charge on each policy. This is the policy fee and is intended to cover the office's administration costs which are fixed regardless of the amount of the insurance. It varies from one insurer to another and sometimes with the type of policy.

policyholder. The person in whose name the policy is issued. (*Also see* INSURED).

policyholders' equity. A large part of the investment earnings of non-life insurers comes from the administration of what is called the 'policyholders' equity' in the assets of the company covering the unearned premium reserve (qv) and outstanding claims.

policyholders' funds. Funds earmarked by insurers to cover outstanding liabilities to policyholders. Also known as technical reserves (qv).

Policyholders' Protection Act 1975. An Act to protect policyholders and others prejudiced by the failure of authorised insurance companies to meet their liabilities. When a company goes into liquidation, authorised insurance companies pay a levy up to 1 per cent of premium income to fund compensation payable under the Act. There are separate levies for long-term and general business. Compulsory insurances are fully secured. Others are secured up to 90 per cent. The Act is for the benefit of private policyholders, ie individuals and partnerships. Incorporated firms are not protected. The Act applies to 'general policies' excluding contracts of marine, aviation and transport (not motor vehicles) business and reinsurance contracts. The Policyholders' Protection Board (qv) can intervene to make interim payments to policyholders of companies in liquidation or in financial difficulties. The Board can also transfer the insurer's business to another insurer or cause it to reduce the liabilities or benefits of its policies.

Policyholders' Protection Board. Established under the Policyholders Protection Act 1975 (qv) to adminster the Act. Five members are appointed by the Secretary of State, of whom at least three must be selected from the management of insurance companies, and of whom there must be at least one able to represent the interests of policyholders.

policy proof of interest (PPI). A term which applies to a policy which agrees to pay the insured whether or not he has an insurable interest (qv). By s. 4(2) Marine Insurance Act 1906 such a policy is deemed to be a gaming or wagering contract and therefore unenforceable in a court. In practice, in maritime ventures it may be difficult to establish the existence of insurable interest at any given time. Consequently it has become the custom to attach a PPI clause to the policies to obviate the need to prove insurable interest. As these policies are legally void and unenforceable they are known as 'honour policies' as payment under them is dependent on the honour of the insurers. These policies are peculiar to marine insurance.

Policy Signing and Accounting Centre (PSAC). A London based organisation which provided a policy signing and central accounting service for its members in respect of non-marine business. It serves the needs of the London non-marine company 'slip' market in a similar way to the Lloyd's Policy Office served its underwriters and the Institute of London Underwriters serves the marine company market. From 1 January 1991 PSAC merged with the Reinsurance Offices Association to form the London Insurance and Reinsurance Market Association.

policy year. 1. The period between inception or renewal date and expiry of annual policy. 2. A term used for certain loss statistics, it relates to the calendar year or accounting year in which the commencement date of the policy falls and may include policies issued for varying periods of time.

political risks. Exporters or investors may not receive payment from their overseas customers because of the intervention of political changes, eg civil war in the overseas country, war between the nations of the contracting parties, exchange control restrictions, imposition of import restrictions in the buyer's country and similar matters beyond the control of the traders concerned. Exporters can normally obtain cover against such risks from the Exports Credit Guarantee Department. *See* COUNTRY RISKS and DEL-CREDERE RISKS.

polluter pays principle. A principle that equates the price charged for the use of environmental resources with the cost of damage inflicted on society by using them. The price charged may be levied directly, eg as taxes on the process which generates the pollution or as the purchase price of licences which entitle the holder to generate specific quantities of pollutants. If the producer or consumer can avoid the additional expenses by refraining from using the polluting item or changing consumption or production patterns and processes then he will have the incentive to do so. Non-market measures involve the promulgation of regulations governing the emission or effects of pollution with civil and criminal penalties for those who contravene the rules. One approach is to make polluters strictly liable for the injury/damage which they cause, leaving them free to carry the risk or insure it. The matter of compulsory insurance is currently a topic of debate.

pollution. Damage to the land, water, property or the atmosphere by the disposal of waste materials or the release of toxic, corrosive, ionising, irritating, thermal or other noxious or offensive substances. The environment can also be impaired by noise or vibration. Pollution imposes direct (bodily injury, damage to crops) and indirect (loss profits due to business interruption and clean-up costs) costs on society. Legal liability for pollution is becoming more onerous. Legislation (the Environmental Protection Act 1990) has introduced the concept of Integrated Pollution Control (qv). Meanwhile an

EC draft directive on waste and civil liability proposes a strict liability on the 'polluter pays' principle. The EC wishes to see the strict liability backed by mandatory insurance.

pollution insurance. Increasing levels of pollution in the late 1960s and 1970s led to liability insurers excluding pollution but, in some cases, adding back the cover where the pollution is 'sudden and accidental'. The intention is to exclude deliberate or gradual pollution. The term 'sudden and accidental' has been interpreted as 'fortuitous and unexpected as far as the insured is concerned', resulting in wider cover than the insurer may have intended. Where covered there still has to be damage (bodily injury or damage to property) to make the insurer liable unless a wider definition of property damage has been used to bring in some form of financial loss or loss of enjoyment of property, eg some policies extend property damage to include 'accidental nuisance'. Wider cover can be provided under a separate environmental impairment liability insurance (qv) which a few insurers offer subject to satisfactory survey. In one form the insurance provides an indemnity for claims (a) from third parties for bodily injury and damage to property, and for the impairment or diminution of any other legally protected right or amenity; and (b) for preventive clean-up costs. The policy does not cover losses resulting from 'sudden and accidental pollution' insurable under public liability policies. The argument to separate the whole of the pollution risk from other forms of liability insurance is currently under debate. The market is restricted and pools (qv) have been suggested. *See also* CLEAN-UP COSTS. Some cover for pollution is available under property insurances where the pollution is caused by a named peril, eg fire leading to smoke damage. Also the cost of decontaminating property after an insured peril is covered under the removal of debris clause (qv)

polychlorinated biphenyls (PCBs). The products of the chlorination of the hydrocarbon compound, biphenyl. There are in theory 210 different compounds that can arise from this reaction. Since the early 1930s they have been used in industrial applications. PCBs are chemically inert materials not hydrolysed by water and resistant to alkalis, acids and other chemicals. They possess boiling points in the range $278°C$ to $451°C$. They are not easily decomposed by the temperatures associated with the destruction of rubbish by combustion. There is ample evidence to indicate that PCBs are highly persistent chemicals which contaminate the environment. PCBs have found use in transformers and capacitators, as heat transfer fluids, hydraulic fluids, and as plasticisers in paints, varnishes, adhesives, inks and sealants. Satisfactory substitutes are available in some areas. The use of PCBs as a heating transfer fluid led to a major accident in Japan in 1968; PCB leaked from a pipe in food processing equipment, resulting in the contamination of rich oil bran. This resulted in the poisoning of about 1000 people who ingested the contaminated oil. Even at concentrations as low as parts per billion or less, PCBs can be lethally toxic to fish; however, they are only moderately toxic to birds and mammals.

pool (or pooling). A combination of insurers in a specific class of insurance in which they agree to share the premiums and losses in agreed proportions. Pooling is a risk spreading device mainly used for exceptionally heavy risks, eg atomic energy risks.

portfolio. A term describing the whole or a part of the insurance or investment business of an insurer or reinsurer.

portfolio transfer. 1. The transfer of liability for unearned premiums or outstanding claims from one insurer to another. The transfers generally take place at either the inception or the termination of a reinsurance treaty or where an insurer is withdrawing from a particular class of business or territory. 2. The carrying forward of part of a long-term premium to subsequent years of account when the risk spans more than one year of account.

port of refuge expenses. This is the most common form of general average expenditure (qv) arising when a ship enters a port of refuge following a casualty or general average damage to the ship. If the entry is in consequence of accidental damage, only the expenses of entry into port and discharging the cargo, if necessary for the purpose of repairs, are allowed in general average. If the entry follows general average damage then the undernoted additional expenses will also be allowed: warehouse rent while repairs are undertaken; cost of reloading the cargo; outward port charges.

port risks insurance. When a ship is laid up out of commission, or whilst being repaired, she may be insured under a port risks policy which, like the buildings risks insurance, covers 'all risks'.

positions policy. A fidelity guarantee insurance (qv) indemnifying an employer (public or private sector) against direct pecuniary loss through the dishonesty of persons in stated positions (eg chief cashier) in the organisation. The insurance covers the 'position' and not named individuals.

post-loss minimisation. The steps taken after a loss to ensure that the loss is contained to the minimum amount. The property salvaged from a fire may have a sale value and property can be removed from burning buildings and then protected against the elements and theft. Where personal injury or disease is concerned the provision of appropriate support, eg medical services and counselling, can shorten periods of disablement suffered following injury and trauma.

post-mortem. A medical examination of a corpse in order to discover the cause of death. Personal accident policies insuring against accidental death may contain a condition giving the insurers the option of a post-mortem examination which they may exercise if they suspect that death is from natural causes.

post-traumatic stress disorder (PTSD). A recognised psychiatric illness, the essential feature of which is the development of characteristic symptoms following a psychologically distressing event that is outside the range of normal human experience. It is a form of actionable nervous shock. Many vic-

tims of the Zeebrugge disaster (the capsising of the Herald of Free Enterprise in March 1987) suffered PTSD and were awarded damages under an arbitration procedure. PTSD may involve re-living the trauma, intense psychological distress brought on by events similar to the traumatic event, outbursts of anger, sleeping difficulties and similar disturbances.

'potentially exempt transfer'. A lifetime gift by an individual which is: a gift to another individual; a gift to an accumulation and maintenance trust; a gift to a trust for a disabled person. A 'potentially exempt transfer' is exempt at the time of the gift, but becomes chargeable if the donor dies within seven years.

pound-cost averaging. The gain made by an investor in a unit trust scheme is determined by the relationship between the average price paid for units and the actual unit price on encashment. The average acquisition cost of units is determined by market movements and the principle of pound-cost averaging applies. More units are purchased by a given premium at a lower price than a high one and consequently the average acquisition cost incurred by an investor will be below the average unit price over a period.

Power Press Regulations 1965. The regulated plant consists of power presses and safety devices. The compulsory maximum statutory periods for examination are: press with fixed guards, 12 months; all other presses, 6 months.

practising insurance broker. A registered insurance broker carrying on an insurance broking business as a sole trader or in partnership.

preamble. *See* RECITAL CLAUSE.

pre-existing condition or defects. Personal accident policies exclude death or disablement directly or indirectly consequent upon any pre-existing condition, ie any physical defect or infirmity (qv) which existed prior to an accident.

pre-existing medical condition. An exclusion which appears in hospital cash plans (qv) and similar health insurances. A pre-existing medical condition is an illness, injury or medical condition for which the insured has received medical advice or treatment during a specified period (eg two to five years depending on the insurer) before effecting the policy. If after a specified period (eg usually the period above) of continuous insurance and providing no treatment has been sought for any condition existing before the inception (qv), the exclusion will no longer apply.

pre-launch insurance. A satellite insurance providing 'all risks' insurance from the completion of the assembly until the launch. The policy operates while the satellite is in storage and transit and also covers third party risks. The cover continues until the intended time of the launch engine's ignition. If the launch is aborted the policy may become operative once again.

pre-loss minimisation. The steps taken by insurers before a loss-producing event to reduce the likelihood of that event and/or its severity if it does occur. Insurance surveys are undertaken with a view to not only risk assessment but also risk improvement. Pre-loss minimisation measures such as the installation of fire fighting equipment, improved security, better housekeeping etc which may be the result of the insurer's insistence or recommendation.

premises risk. An aspect of public liability insurance. Potential liability arises from ownership or occupation. The duty of an employer to provide a 'reasonably safe place of work' makes it relevant to employers' liability insurances. See also PUBLIC ACCESS RISKS.

premium. The consideration paid or payable by the insured in return for the insurance cover provided by the insurer. See also PAYMENT OF PREMIUM.

premium advice note. A note sent by a broker to an insurer or policy signing office when the broker's client has been debited with the premium or credited with a return premium.

premium debit note. A demand, ie a bill, for the payment of the premium.

premium earned. Most premiums are payable in advance and the insurer earns the premium as the time advances. For example, if the premium for a three-year policy is paid in advance, one-third is the 'premium earned' at the end of the first year.

premium exemption. Certain transfers of value during a person's lifetime may be regarded as normal expenditure out of income and so gain exemption from inheritance tax. A premium on a life policy on his own life paid directly or indirectly by the transferor is *not* a part of his normal expenditure if at any time an annuity was purchased on his life, unless it is shown that the annuity purchase and the making or varying of the insurance (or any prior insurance replaced by the current one) were not associated operations, ie back to back arrangements (qv). The practice is 'to regard policies and annuities as not being affected by the associated operations rule if, first, the policy was issued on full medical evidence of the insured's health, and, secondly, it would have been issued on the same terms if the annuity had not been bought' (Official Report, Standing Committee A, 5 February 1975 Col. 872).

premium/expense ratio. A ratio which relates expenses to net premium earned.

premium income limit. The amount of premiums at Lloyd's that a Name (qv) is permitted to underwrite in the course of a calendar year. The limit is related to the amount of the Name's Lloyd's deposit. If a Name exceeds his premium limit he must establish a special deposit with the Corporation of Lloyd's of a minimum of 50p for every £1 of the net excess. See OVERWRITING OF PREMIUMS.

premium overwriting. See OVERWRITING OF PREMIUMS.

premium receipt book. In industrial life insurance, a society or a company must provide premium receipt books and cause a receipt for each payment to be inserted in the book and initialled. The book must contain details of the policy number (if any), the date of the policy, name and age of the life insured, name of the proposer and the amount of the premium and the interval at which payable.

premiums trust fund. The trust fund into which all premiums received by a Lloyd's underwriter must be placed in accordance with s. 83 of the Insurance Companies Act 1982. The fund is available for the payment of claims, syndicate expenses and, when an account has been closed, for the payment of any profit due to the Name.

premium to be arranged. A term used when cover has been granted on the understanding that the actual premium will be the subject of later negotiation. The Marine Insurance Act 1906, s. 31 provides that a reasonable premium will be payable in these circumstances.

premium rate. The rate per unit of exposure (qv), eg an employers' liability rate will be £'x' per £100 of the payroll. The premium rate itself depends on the average claim frequency per annum per unit of exposure and the present value of the average size of claim. An increase in either will necessitate an increase in the premium rate otherwise the risk premium (qv) will prove inadequate.

premium spread rule. *See* QUALIFYING POLICIES.

preservation. This is governed by the Social Security Act 1973 which states that when an employee leaves the employer's service he must be granted preserved pension rights provided he is at least 26 years and has completed five years service. The preserved pension must be calculated in the same way as other pensions arising at normal retirement date and which have the same options. In the case of a contracted out pension scheme the preserved pension must be in accordance with the guaranteed minimum pension rights and they must be transferable.

preserved pension. Otherwise known as a frozen pension, it is granted to a person leaving a pension scheme in respect of his participation up to that time but to become payable when he attains retirement age.

pressure plant (vessels). Plant designed to contain gas or vapour, such as steam, under pressure. The majority of items have to be inspected under statutory provisions. The main statute affecting this type of plant is the Factories Act 1961 (s. 33(2)(3) and (4) – s. 35 (5) and (6) – s. 36 (4) and (5). A steam boiler is an example. The principal risk is explosion and/or collapse. *See* PRESSURE POLICY.

pressure policy. A policy on pressure plant (qv) covering: (a) damage to the plant and the insured's own surrounding property (including that for which he is responsible) due to explosion or collapse of the plant. (b) Third party liability (compensation, claimants' costs etc) for property damage or bodily injury due to explosion or collapse. (c) An inspection service. Items (a) and (b) are subject to the limit of indemnity stated in the policy. Broader cover is available in respect of: (i) Sudden and unforeseen physical damage to the insured. (ii) 'Impact damage cover' (which is primarily cover for damage to the insured's surrounding property, caused by fragmentation (qv). The material damage (not third party cover) is subject to an excess, normally 5 per cent of the cost of each claim. Automatic cover is provided for a period of 180 days in respect of any additional plant of the same type installed at the insured's premises.

Pressure Systems and Transportable Gas Containers Regulations 1989. The regulations replace and extend provisions made under the Factories Act 1961, the Quarries (General) Regulations 1956 and Miscellaneous Mines (General) Regulations 1956 in so far as they relate to the examination of pressure systems. The new regulations took effect from 1 July 1990 to be phased in over four years to introduce revised requirements for the installation, control and examination and certification of pressure systems. The user of an installed system must have a written scheme of examination, including the frequency of those examinations. The scheme must be certified as suitable by a competent person. The maximum statutory examination periods are likely to be those laid down in the Factories Act 1961.

presumption of death. Where a life insured has disappeared, it is usual for the court to permit presumption of death after seven years—if it is satisfied that all evidence points to death and that everything possible has been done to trace the missing person. It is not essential for seven years to elapse if the evidence of possible death is strong.

prevention of access. *See* DENIAL OF ACCESS.

primary exposure. An aviation insurance term to describe risks which, although serious, are not potentially catastrophic.

primary insurance. The first layer of insurance, ie the underlying policy, upon which additional layers known as excess layers are built to give the insured a greater amount of cover. This is common in liability insurance.

primary liability. The principle of primary liability is bound up with that of subrogation (qv) and operates where the same loss or damage is insured in different names with different insurers, one on a liability basis. It ensures that the insurer insuring the party primarily liable for the damage shall ultimately pay for the loss. There is, however, no direct right of action against the insurer of that party; the right of action lies against the party only.

primary reinsurance clause. A clause under which the reinsurer agrees to pay losses directly to the insured. The clause is rarely used.

principal. 1. One who authorises another, called an agent, to act on his behalf. If an agent purports to act on his own behalf, his principal is called an undisclosed principal. Usually the third party can sue the undisclosed principal when the latter's existence is discovered. 2. A principal debtor is one who owes a debt which is guaranteed by a surety. 3. A sum of money put out at interest. N.B. Insurers are particularly interested: (a) In the relationship of principal and agent for the purpose of (i) enquiring into vicarious liability and (ii) imputed knowledge (qv) when insurance is arranged through an intermediary such as a broker. (b) In the relationship of principal and contractor to ascertain where responsibility lies for certain forms of loss, damage or injury (*see* CONTRACT FOR SERVICES, PRINCIPAL'S CLAUSE.

principal's clause. A clause in a public or employers' liability extending the insured's policy to provide an indemnity, where any contract so requires, to any principal in like manner to the insured. The principal (qv) must observe the terms and conditions of the policy and agree that conduct and control of any claims shall be vested in the insurer. A principal (referred to in some contracts (eg Joint Contract Tribunal) as the 'employer') may seek his indemnity directly as a joint insured or request that the insured extends his policy to indemnify the principal as another party. Effect is given to the latter approach under the 'indemnity to other parties section' which operates 'at the request of the insured'.

principal's cover. A phrase used when the principal (ie the employer) and not the contractor arranges the insurance even though the standard form of contract, eg Joint Contract Tribunal, ICE Conditions normally place insurance obligations on the contractor. It often means a combined contractors' 'all risks' public liability being effected. The Americans describe this arrangement as wrap-up cover.

prior declaration policies. A form of travel insurance (qv) policy used by firms whose employees make frequent trips abroad. To avoid the issue of numerous individual policies, the insured makes a prior declaration of trips and cover required. This enables the insured to decide in each case the level of cover required. There is no automatic cover if a declaration is omitted. Other forms are declaration in arrears policies and registration policies (qv).

'priority of notice regulates the priority of claim'. A rule laying down that where there is more than one assignee of a life policy priority among them will be determined according to the order in which notice of the assignments was given to the assurer. There are exceptions to the rule, viz: a trustee in bankruptcy cannot claim priority over existing interests even where no notice was given of those interests, gifts, as between assignor and assignee, where the assignee was aware of a previous assignment and suspected or knew that notice had not been given, mortgages for unlimited amounts. *See* POLICIES OF ASSURANCE ACT 1867.

private cars. Motor insurers categorise private cars as a separate group for the purpose of rating. Different considerations apply to commercial and passenger carrying vehicles (qv).

private hire vehicle. Passenger seating vehicles having not more than 12 seats and used for the carriage of passengers for hire or reward but, not being authorised to ply for hire from the streets and designated places, are hired direct from the insured's garage. Their exposure is not considered to be as great as that for public hire vehicles (qv) but this type of risk still warrants careful selection and underwriting by the insurer, particularly where a two-way radio system is likely to increase the exposure.

private hotel. A term used as a matter of convenience in order that hotels in general can be distinguished from those run as inns (qv). It is an hotel (or similar establishment) which, unlike an inn, picks and chooses its guests. The proprietor's responsibilities for guests (qv), and their property is not governed by any special legal rules. The normal laws of tort, contract and bailment will apply.

private medical insurance. *See* MEDICAL AID INSURANCE.

private personal liability. An extension to a public liability to indemnify the insured and his employees in respect of their personal liability (qv) while outside their usual country in connection with the 'business'. The actual liability must arise otherwise than in connection with the business of the insured or the business of the person claiming indemnity. Where the insured is an individual the cover also applies within the usual country of residence.

private policyholders. In the context of the Policyholders' Protection Act 1975 (qv), this means 'individuals, partnerships, or other unincorporated bodies of persons all of whom are individuals'.

privilege conditions. These are life assurance policy conditions conferring concessions on the insured such as paid-up provisions (qv), surrender values (qv), days of grace (qv) and non-forfeiture (qv).

probability. The science of the measurement of chance. In the theory of probability, certainty is represented by unity. The probability of an event that is not certain is a fraction—the smaller the chance of the event happening the smaller will be the fraction. Insurance by combining large numbers of similar exposure units can predict the probability of the insured event with greater accuracy than is possible with small groups or individuals. *See* RISK COMBINATION. Actuaries, for example, can predict with a high degree of accuracy the probabilities of males and females dying at each age by observing a large number of lives. *See* MORTALITY TABLES.

product defect insurance. A term occasionally used for product liability insurance (qv). The term is less satisfactory as the goods do not have to be defective to trigger a products liability policy. The insured could be liable for injury resulting from products in themselves sound but applied to the wrong use as a result of misdelivery or negligent advice.

product liability exclusion. The exclusion of liability arising from any goods or products manufactured, constructed, altered, etc, sold, supplied or distributed by the insured appears in both public liability and professional indemnity policies. The risks are insurable under a products liability policy (qv). The dividing line between the products and public liability policies is an important one. In the public liability policy the exclusion is overridden in respect of products still in the insured's possession.

product tamper and extortion. *See* MALICIOUS PRODUCT TAMPER AND EXTORTION.

products guarantee insurance. A policy indemnifying the insured against his liability to pay damages and claimant's costs with regard to the removal, repair, alteration etc or replacement of any product, including consequential losses, if due to a defective or harmful product or failure of the product to perform its intended function. The insured's own costs incurred with the insurer's written consent are included in addition to the limit of indemnity which operates on an aggregate basis for the period basis. The policy is on a claims-made basis (qv) and some form of co-insurance is customary. Product recall insurance (qv) can be arranged as an extension. The indemnity applies irrespective of whether there is bodily injury or damage to property and fills the gap created by the exclusion of loss/damage in respect of goods supplied under products liability insurance (qv). The products guarantee policy is often written to meet the specific written guarantee given by the insured to his customer(s) for a selected or one-off product (eg aircraft or high value equipment) or products.

products liability insurance. This insurance may be by separate policy or be combined with public liability. Wherever possible both risks should be with the same insurer to obviate the risk of gaps in cover. The policy covers legal liability for damages and claimants' costs (and the insured's own costs incurred with the insurer's written consent) for accidental bodily injury or damage to property arising from 'products' supplied etc by the insured. The term 'products' (or goods) is widely defined and includes containers, faulty labelling, instructions or advice. It is not necessary that the product should be defective (eg wrong delivery leading to injury is covered). The policy operates on a 'losses-occurring' basis with an aggregate limit of indemnity for any one period of insurance. Most policies insure against liability for injury, loss or damage on a world-wide basis for goods manufactured etc from any premises of the insured in Great Britain, Northern Ireland, the Isle of Man and the Channel Islands. The exceptions include the employers' liability risk, loss/damage caused by products in the insured's custody or control, loss/damage to goods supplied (*see* PRODUCTS GUARANTEE), aviation products (can be overridden if the destination of the products is unknown or products do not affect safety or navigation), contractual liability (scope varies), inefficacy, design and specification (sometimes), exports to the USA, radioactive contamination and war risks. The effect of excluding loss/damage caused by products still in the insured's custody or control is to make that a public liability risk. The exclusion of exports to the USA obliges the exporter to negotiate cover with the insurer. The policy can be extended to provide retrospective cover

(qv), vendors' indemnity (qv) and other interests, financial loss (qv), but products guarantee and products recall normally necessitate separate insurance arrangements. Premiums are adjusted annually in accordance with turnover.

products liability (financial loss). It may be possible to extend the policy to cover pure financial loss. The loss must be the direct result of the defective or harmful condition of the product or its failure to perform its intended function. The cost of replacing or repairing the product is not covered and there is usually some form of excess or co-insurance. The extension is generally written on a claims-made basis.

products recall insurance. After manufacture and distribution, it may be discovered that the insured's products contain a dangerous fault making it necessary or prudent for the insured to withdraw all products containing the fault. The potentially high expense of withdrawal creates a demand for product recall insurance. After the death of a boy in the UK caused by incorrect earthing, the manufacturer recalled 250 000 table lamps. The market for such cover is very limited but it can be arranged, often as an extension of product guarantee insurance (qv). The cover is triggered by the decision of the insured to recall the product because its use or consumption may create a legal liability or where there is a risk of bodily injury. If the insurer disputes the decision, the matter is referred to arbitration in accordance with policy conditions. The expenses covered include the cost of publicity (eg newspaper, television and radio announcements), and costs relating to transportation costs, examination, and additional labour. The policy does not cover design faults and normally applies to accidental causes only. *See* PRODUCT RECALL PLAN.

products recall plan. A plan drawn up by a manufacturer to enable him to action a product recall (qv) situation with great speed upon becoming aware that it is necessary or prudent to withdraw a dangerous product. The ability to trace and identify products and particular batches of products is clearly important. It is an aspect of risk management and is needed by manufacturers regardless of their insurance position.

professional fees legal protection. A legal expenses insurance for professional fees (including those of a firm's accountants) for representing the insured's interests in the event of being subject to an in-depth investigation by the Inland Revenue. Also covered are appeals against VAT assessments made by HM Customs and Excise. This cover includes personal protection for individual directors, partners and the self employed where there is likely to be overlap of the investigation into the individual's own affairs. Cover usually extends to include the cost of fees that may be incurred by the insured in dealing with PAYE Audit Investigations.

professional indemnity insurance. This is to protect a professional person (eg doctor, solicitor, accountant) against the legal liability to pay damages and costs to persons sustaining loss through a breach of professional duty (breach of contact or liability in tort). The insured's own costs incurred with the insurer's consent are also covered and are in addition to the limit of indemnity which is an aggregate limit for any one period of insurance. The policy is 'claims-made' and cover is given in respect of the fault of any predecessors in title because when a practice is taken over the incoming owner assumes responsibility for the faults of predecessors if the claim is made against the firm or practice. A 'discovery period' of three or six months brings within the policy claims made after the policy has lapsed provided the negligence occurred during the period of insurance. The principal exclusions refer to dishonesty by the insured and libel and slander. However, extensions are available in connection with dishonesty of employees, libel and slander, loss or damage to documents, and breach of warranty of authority (qv). The outcome in professional indemnity cases is often pure financial loss but in some professions can cause injury or damage (eg medical profession).

'professional negligence'. The neglect of a professional duty of care that renders the professional person committing the act, error or omission of neglect liable in law to a client or some other third party (*see* HEDLEY BYRNE V HELLER & PARTNERS (1964) who suffers loss as a result of that neglect. *See* PROFESSIONAL INDEMNITY INSURANCE.

professional reinsurer. A reinsurer who transacts nothing but reinsurance and undertakes no direct business. Also called pure reinsurer (qv).

professional sports teams exclusion. Cover in respect of professional sports teams is a standard exclusion in a personal accident catastrophe excess of loss reinsurance cover. The high sums of cover purchased plus the accumulation factor that arises when they travel as a group are the factors that cause concern.

profit commission. A commission based upon a predefined formula. The principal examples are: (a) the commission received by an underwriting agent from the Names (qv) at Lloyd's as a reward for the profit made by them through the agent's activities on their behalf; (b) the commission received by a ceding office from a reinsurer as a reward for the ceding of profitable business.

profits insurance. Loss of profits insurance is now better known as business interruption insurance (qv).

prohibited conditions. Conditions in a compulsory insurance policy that are prohibited for the purpose of the insurance that has to be covered for the purpose of the Act.

prohibition notice. An order issued by Health and Safety Executive inspectors ordering those responsible for a place of work to discontinue unsafe processes or activities for the benefit of employees and members of the public. Contravention of the order risks prosecution for the employer or company officers responsible.

project insurance. A policy used occasionally in connection with large construction projects. The principal effects a policy on the project as a whole to avoid the multiplicity of policies that occurs when each party arranges his own insurance. The policy applies to the more conventional material damage and liability policies (except employers' liability and motor risks which are governed by legislation), but does not usually include professional indemnity risks.

promissory. This word may be included in the declaration at the foot of a proposal form in which the insured may agree that the proposal and declaration shall be 'held to be promissory and shall be the basis of the contract'. Where the proposal or policy specifically provides that the statements are of a promissory nature, they do not necessarily constitute continuing warranties (qv), rendering the contract voidable if contravened at any time during its currency. The term promissory emphasises that the proposal answers amount to express conditions (ie warranties in insurance parlance) as distinct from mere representations so that the replies are taken as statements of fact and not of intention. The expression may reinforce the fact that the completed proposal form and declaration constitute the basis of the contract (qv).

proof of loss. Policy conditions normally require the insured to furnish particulars of the claim and proof of the loss. This requirement is a condition precedent to liability of the insurer. The details required are almost always set out in a claim form issued by the insurer but additional information and supporting documents may be required. In some cases, the insurer may wish to inspect the books of the insured or call for medical evidence in appropriate cases. The insurer may impose time limits for the supply of the information required. To comply it is sufficient for the insured to produce such proof that would satisfy reasonable men. *See also* ONUS OF PROOF.

'properly maintained'. The Factories Act 1961, s. 28(1) provides that 'all floors, steps, stairs, passages, and gangways shall be of sound construction and properly maintained'. The obligation attaching to the factory owner is absolute. Other obligations in the Act expressed in this way will have the same meaning. Compare with all practicable steps (qv) and reasonably practicable (qv).

property damage excess. An excess (qv) which may be introduced into public liability policies in respect of particular trades or situations. For example, in those trades where the work is mainly carried out on the customer's premises the insurer may seek to use the excess to eliminate small claims where the insured has caused damage to third party property. This may be set at £100 for plumbers and heating and ventilation engineers, £50 for electrical contractors, etc and there may a £100 excess in respect of damage to underground services.

property damage limit. A limit of indemnity under a commercial vehicle motor policy in respect of the maximum amount the insurer will pay for third party property damage. Under compulsory insurance legislation the minimum permitted limit is £250 000. Legal liability for third party bodily injury is unlimited.

property insurance. A general business category of insurance defined by the Insurance Companies Act 1982. It is the 'business of effecting and carrying out contracts of insurance against risks of loss of, or damage to, material property, not being risks of a kind such that the business of effecting and carrying out contracts of insurance against them constitutes marine, aviation and transport insurance business or motor vehicle insurance business'.

property in the insured's custody or control. *See* CUSTODY PROPERTY.

property legal protection cover. This provides cover for legal costs and expenses incurred in pursuit of civil actions against third parties whose torts result in or could result in physical damage or interference to the policyholder's property and/or pecuniary loss to the policyholder. Cover is available for both individuals and businesses and may be purchased separately or as a part of a general legal expenses.

property linked benefits. *See* LINKED BENEFITS.

property owners' liability. A policy insuring the legal liability of the owner of property to third parties who may sustain injury or property damage. It is in effect a public liability insurance which meets the needs of those who own but do not occupy property. Where the owner and occupier are one and the same, the general public liability provides the cover to the insured as owner and occupier.

property worked on. Public liability policies generally exclude the insured's legal liability for damage to that part of any property being worked on where the loss or damage is the direct result of such work. The intention is to exclude defective workmanship and the clause effectively operates as an excluded form of loss (qv) and not an excepted risk because any consequential damage will be within the policy. Where a painter uses a blowlamp and sets fire to a timber window frame and the fire spreads to destroy the entire property, that part of the loss that takes the form of a damaged window frame is excluded but the rest of the property damage will be covered. In regard to property worked on the insured is expected to rely upon his own skill or knowledge and it may be open to him to attempt to use an exemption clause, arrange a first party insurance (qv), or, in exceptional circumstances, negotiate with the insurer. The case of *Pioneer Concrete (UK) Ltd* v *National Employers Mutual General* (1985) shows how this type of exclusion should be applied. The exclusion stated 'the policy does not cover . . . the making good of faulty workmanship'. A firm of contractors were engaged by Pioneer to dismantle, transport and re-erect an item of plant. Ten months later a part of the plant (a hopper) collapsed because the base of the metal support structure was inadequately secured to the foundations on which the hopper stood. The collapse caused damage to associated machinery and plant totalling just under £5500 while the cost of replacing the bolts to hold down the base (the wrong bolts had been used previously) came to £580. It was held that the exception applied only to the making good of the defective work and not the damage caused by it so only the liability for £580 was outside the policy.

proportional reinsurance. A reinsurance under which the ceding office and the reinsurer share the risk in agreed proportions which may be fixed or variable depending on the ceding office's retention and the sum insured. The reinsurer shares proportionally the premiums earned and the claims plus certain expenses incurred by the ced-ing office. Proportional reinsurances may be arranged facultatively or by treaty and they may include: quota share reinsurances (qv); surplus treaties (qv); facultative/obligatory treaties; reinsurance pools.

proportionate benefit. This benefit may be incorporated into a permanent health insurance (qv) as a feature or an option. It applies when a claimant returns to work but, because of the disablement, in a different occupation. The benefit is that proportion of the full benefit that the earnings in the new occupation bears to the earnings in the original occupation. The state of disability must continue and periodically the level of benefit must be reviewed to take account of pay increases in the new job.

proposal form. A form completed by a party seeking insurance. The form is drafted by the insurer to elicit information that enables the insurer to assess the risk, prepare the policy, and set up the necessary administration. Certain questions are common to all proposal forms (eg identity of the party seeking insurance) but otherwise the questions will reflect matters material to the class of insurance concerned. The proposer does not necessarily satisfy the duty of disclosure (*see* UTMOST GOOD FAITH) by fully and accurately completing the form. If the form has been silent on a material fact affecting a particular proposer, the additional fact must be disclosed. It is customary for each form to contain a declaration whereby the proposer warrants the truth of the answers and agrees that the proposal form and declaration shall become the basis of the contract (representations are converted into warranties (qv)). The effect is that any inaccuracy in the form renders the policy voidable by the insurer regardless of materiality. However, under the statements of practice (qv) insurers agree that in regard to insurances effected by persons in their private capacity, the declaration will be completed according to the proposer's knowledge and belief. The statements of practice contain other safeguards for private policyholders. Proposal forms are not used in marine, aviation and large fire insurance. Also at

Lloyd's their use is mainly restricted to motor and life assurance cases.

proposer. The prospective insured, ie the party proposing to effect an insurance, often by the completion of a proposal form.

proprietary companies. Insurance companies constituted under the Companies Acts or by Royal Charter. The proprietors of a company are the shareholders who have supplied the capital.

pro rata method. 1. When two or more policies are called into contribution (qv), the insurers contribute rateably to the loss. The *pro rata* method distributes the loss in proportion to sums insured. For example, insurer A has a sum insured of £10 000 and insurer B a sum insured of £5000 on the same property; the loss is £3000. The loss is apportioned in the ratio of 2:1 with insurer A contributing £2000 and B £1000. If the independent liability method had been used then the insurers would have shared the loss equally but that is not equitable as company B will have earned double the premium. This method works best when the policies are concurrent and no average is applied. 2. *See* AVERAGE, PRO RATA.

pro rata temporis. In proportion to time.

prosecution clause. Fidelity guarantee policies (qv), ie commercial guarantees, include a clause that requires the employer to provide assistance to insurers to enable them to sue in the civil courts in the name of the insured employer for recovery of the loss. The use of the term 'prosecution clause' has been criticised as it relates to civil and not criminal action.

prosecution defence cover. The commercial form of legal expenses policy provides for representation of a firm and its employees in criminal prosecutions under such legislation as the Health & Safety at Work Act, Weights and Measures and the Trade Descriptions Act. It also includes the cost of appeal against improvement or prohibition notices under the Health and Safety laws. The insurance normally includes an allowance for witnesses' expenses but will not, of course, cover any fines (*see* PUBLIC POLICY). The cover can be combined with personal injury cover which covers the costs arising from the

pursuit of civil claims following death or injury through non-motor accidents arising from employment duties.

prospectus. A printed form or brochure describing in abridged form the services of the insurer or a particular type of insurance.

protected no claim discount. A no claim discount (qv) that is not automatically lost or reduced following a claim under a motor policy. A small extra premium is payable by the motorist for this benefit which usually means that the existing bonus or discount is retained provided that he does not make more than one claim in any two successive years. There are other approaches on the market. This benefit is normally confined to persons over 25 with at least two years no claim discount who have good recent claims and driving history.

protected rights. The benefits under a personal pension scheme or a money purchase contracted out scheme, deriving respectively from at least the minimum contributions or minimum payments, which are provided in a specified form as a necessary condition for contracting out.

protected risk. A risk which, as a result of the insurer's advice or insistence, is protected by the introduction of loss-prevention measures as in fire insurance (eg sprinkler leakage system installed) or theft insurance (eg intruder alarm installed).

protection. *See* LOSS PREVENTION and PROTECTION AND INDEMNITY CLUBS.

Protection and Indemnity Clubs. These mutual associations arose during the first half of the nineteenth century to meet the needs of shipowners for protection in respect of risks not usually covered in the marine insurance market. There are various clubs in operation and to participate the shipowner enters his vessel on a tonnage basis which determines his levy or call (qv) at the beginning of the financial year. If claims are heavy a further levy may be demanded. The most important classes are: (a) Protection. This protects the shipowner in respect of liability for loss of life or personal injury, damage to immobile objects, and one-quarter Running Down Clause (qv), and life salvage. (b) Indemnity. This reimburses shipowners who have indemnified cargo owners for damage caused by negligence of the crew. There are two other classes: war risks and freight war risks.

protest. A marine insurance claims document in the form of a statement sworn by a ship's master before a notary giving details of the casualty. He 'protests' innocence of blame for loss of, or damage to, the ship or cargo. If fuller information is required, a further statement, an extended protest, is made.

protracted default. A credit insurance term to describe a long overdue payment, eg failure by a debtor to pay the insured within 90 days of the due date. Protracted default is an insured event and, like non-payment due to insolvency, therefore entitles the insured to make a claim.

provision. 1. A term in a policy , contract or statute. 2. An accounting term often used to denote the amount set against an asset value for the purposes of depreciation or to indicate a reserve.

provisional damages. Section 6 of the Administration of Justice Act 1982 deals with personal injury claims where there is a chance that, in the future, an injured person will develop some serious disease or suffer some serious deterioration in his physical or mental condition. The court is empowered to issue a declaratory judgment which, in the event of such deterioration, enables the plaintiff to apply for a review of the original award. Where the declaration is made, the damages awarded are provisional.

provisional premium. The premium charged under a declaration policy (qv) at the inception. It is adjusted at the end of the year in the light of the actual exposure as revealed by periodic declarations of the actual values at risk. The practice in fire insurance is to make an initial charge of 75 per cent of the premium obtained by applying the rate of premium to the sum insured.

proviso clauses. An exclusion, limitation or special condition. As conditions in policies they must be complied with as a condition precedent to the insurer's liability or they simply limit the insurer's liability. For example, business interruption insurances carry a proviso relating to material damage (*see* MATERIAL DAMAGE WARRANTY). Under personal accident policies (qv) certain injuries may fall within more than one definition or might follow another (eg loss of limb followed by death). Proviso clauses may be used to stipulate that the sum for death is maximum liability of the insurer during the year of insurance.

proximate cause. The insurer is liable to indemnify the insured in respect of loss, damage or liability only when such loss, damage or liability is proximately caused by one of the perils specified in the policy. The legal maxim which expresses this principle is *causa proxima non remota spectatur*—the immediate not the remote cause is to be regarded. Immediate means closest in efficiency and not necessarily closest in time. The classic definition of proximate cause was given in *Pawsey* v *Scottish Union & National* (1907): 'the active, efficient cause that sets in motion a train of events which brings about a result, without the intervention of any force started and working actively from a new and independent source'. As an insured peril can operate concurrently with, or sequentially to, an excepted peril and/or uninsured perils, certain general rules can be set out to provide some guidance in establishing which of all the causes in a given situation is the proximate cause of the loss. (a) If the insured peril and uninsured perils (ie unmentioned perils) operate concurrently, the insured peril is the proximate cause. (b) If the insured peril operates concurrently with an excepted peril and the effects of the two cannot be separated the excepted peril is the proximate cause. (c) If the loss arises from a number of successive perils, the last peril is the proximate cause unless an earlier peril has set up a direct chain of causation in which the last peril is merely incidental and is the natural and probable outcome of the earlier cause. If the earlier cause is an excepted peril there will be no liability. If the earlier cause is an insured peril and there is no break in the chain of events the insurer will be liable as the insured peril will be 'nearest in efficiency' if not in time (*Leyland Shipping Co Ltd* v *Norwich Union* (1907)). Particular decisions on proximate cause include: *Marsden* v *City and County Insurance Co* (1866). Plate glass policy excluded loss by fire. Glass was broken by an unruly crowd watching a fire in neighbouring premises. Held: the exception did not operate as fire was not the proximate cause of the loss. The accident or event facilitating the loss (the fire) has to be distinguished from the accident or event which caused the loss (action of the mob). The fire was the remote cause (qv). *Winicofsky* v *Army & Navy General Assurance Co* (1919). Burglary policy excluded war risks and a burglary occurred during an air raid. Held: the excepted peril, war, did not start a direct chain of events or causation. Theft resulted from a new and independent peril (*see* INTERVENING CAUSE) so the excepted peril did not operate. *Coxe* v *Employers' Liability Assurance Corporation* (1916). A list of exceptions was prefaced by the words 'directly or indirectly'. Held: the words modified the ordinary rules of proximate cause so that even if the excepted peril is indirectly the cause (ie a remote cause) of the loss the insurer can avoid the loss notwithstanding the operation of the insured peril. A serviceman had been accidentally killed by a train while on duty during blackout restrictions and the policy excluded death 'directly or indirectly caused by, or arising from, or traceable to, war'. The train was the proximate cause of the death and war only the remote cause but the exception operated. *See also* QUALIFIED PERILS and CAUSES CLASSIFIED.

prudent insurer. A term used in the Marine Insurance Act 1906, s. 18(2). *See* PRUDENT UNDERWRITER.

prudent underwriter. An underwriter who underwrites risks on a reasonable basis and who is neither unduly apprehensive nor unduly incautious. The concept of the prudent underwriter is at the heart of the fundamental principle of utmost good faith (qv) as a fact will judged to be material (*see* MATERIAL FACT) if it is one that would have influenced the judgment of a prudent and experienced underwriter in his as-

sessment of the risk. The assertion that the particular underwriter would have been influenced by it does not make it a material fact and the fact that another would have ignored it does not prevent it from being material. The test is objective. In *Associated Oil Carriers Ltd* v *Union Insurance Society of Canton Ltd* (1917) Atkin J said 'There seems no reason to impute to the insurer a higher degree of knowledge and foresight than that reasonably possessed by the more experienced and intelligent insurers carrying on business in that market at that time'.

pseudonym. An abbreviation or set of letters used at Lloyd's for the purpose of identifying syndicates or brokers.

public access risks. A public liability term describing a situation where the premises risk provides a greater potential for claim than the work away (qv) risk. It is a situation where the public may come in large number to the premises, eg sports grounds, theatres, department stores etc. Premiums may be based on capacity, average attendance or similar indicator.

public authorities clause. Following a fire or allied peril causing material damage to premises, the cost of rebuilding may be increased because of local authority bye-laws which, for example, may call for an improvement in the interests of public safety. The clause brings the additional cost associated with the improvement within the scope of the policy provided that the sum insured is adequate and that the demand for the improvement was not made until after the occurrence of the insured event.

public conveyance accidents. An accident to a train, bus or other public conveyance. Some personal accident policies are written on the basis the benefits payable will be doubled or increased if the insured is injured following an accident to a public conveyance in which he was travelling as a passenger. Some policies also double the benefit if the accident occurs while the insured is in a burning building.

public hire vehicle. A hire car with passenger seating having not more than 12 seats which is used for the carriage of passengers for hire or reward and is licensed to ply the street for hire and from designated places, eg railway stations. Motor insurers consider them to have high exposure because of potential vehicle and driver fatigue. There is also a tendency for the employment of casual drivers in businesses running public hire vehicles. The market is more limited than it is for motor insurance generally. These vehicles are strictly controlled by the local authority.

public liability insurance. An insurance against legal liability to pay compensation to third parties for accidental bodily injury or accidental damage to property arising in connection with the insured's business. The insured's own costs are covered if incurred with the insurer's written consent. The indemnity limit is in respect of any one occurrence and is unlimited for the period of insurance. Cover applies within the UK and in connection within temporary visits abroad. Exclusions include: the employers' liability risk; damage to property in the insured's custody or control; liquidated damages and penalties; the products liability risk; advice or treatment for which a fee is normally payable; property being worked on; radioactive contamination risks; war risks; gradual pollution. Restrictive conditions may be added in respect of certain trade processes (eg processes involving the application of heat). Public liability policies can be extended to cover: pure financial loss; motor contingent liability; Defective Premises Act cover; indemnity to principal; legal defence costs (Health and Safety at Work Act); retrospective cover; accidental nuisance; cross liabilities. Where work away (qv) is the predominant feature, the premium is normally based on an annual wages and is adjustable to accommodate changes in the level of activity. Public liability insurance is not compulsory (but *see* RIDING ESTABLISHMENTS ACT 1970) but common prudence dictates that such an insurance is essential. The policy operates on a losses-occurring basis (qv).

public policy. The law will refuse to enforce or recognise an insurance which is against public policy, ie a policy with a mischievous tendency and therefore injurious to the state or the com-

munity. Insurance contracts without insurable interest are in effect wagering contracts and are therefore contrary to public policy and void.

'public warehouse'. The meaning of this term was under dispute in *Firmin & Collins Ltd.* v *Allied Shippers Ltd (Alder (Third Party)* (1967)). It was held to mean a business holding itself open to all comers and prepared to store goods for an indefinite period. It is a business selling accommodation for storage. A shipping and forwarding agent stored goods in uncovered premises belonging to a transport company. They were not a public warehouse.

punitive damages. These are damages awarded not as compensation but as punishment against the wrongdoer. They are also called exemplary damages and are rarely awarded in the UK. Libel cases in which the defendant has made a financial gain provide the main exception. In the USA punitive damages are awarded more readily to punish the offender and deter others. Liability insurers may exclude punitive damages from their policies especially where there is a USA exposure. Some insurers confine their indemnity to damages payable 'as compensation' and this wording has the effect removing punitive damages from the scope of the policy.

purchased life annuity. An annuity (qv) purchased from an authorised insurer under a contract approved by the Inland Revenue or by an individual out of his own capital. Unlike other annuities these are taxed as investments. As a result each instalment is in two parts—the capital content, which is tax free and the interest content which is treated as unearned income and taxed at source at the standard rate. The annuitant is responsible directly for any higher rate that may be payable. Exempted from these provisions are all annuities secured under approved pension schemes of any nature, including retirement annuities under the current legislation (Income and Corporation Taxes Act 1988). These continue to be taxed on the full amount of each instalment.

purchaser's interest clause. A clause in a fire insurance policy to protect the interest of the purchaser of property if, at the time of loss, the insured property is the subject of an uncompleted contract of sale. The policy covers the interests of the purchaser and vendor up to the completion date. The clause refers to buildings only and only to the extent that the property was not otherwise insured by the purchaser.

pure captive. A captive insurance company (qv) that confines its underwriting to the risks of its parent company.

pure endowment. A life insurance policy which pays the sum insured if the life insured survives the policy term but nothing in the event of earlier death. In the latter instance the premiums may or may not be returnable. This type of policy can be used on children's lives with the premiums payable during the parent's lifetime only. It can also be used in occupational pension schemes to provide that portion of the pension to be provided by the employee's contributions.

pure guarantee. A fidelity guarantee (qv) is a combination of an insurance guarantee and a pure guarantee. Under a commercial fidelity guarantee, for example, the relationship between the insurer and the employee is that of pure guarantee. In a pure guarantee it is not necessary to disclose facts which would be material to the validity of the insurance guarantee, unless and until a request is made by the surety (guarantor). This is subject to the proviso that there must be no fraudulent misrepresentation which will vitiate the contract. When an individual is the subject of a guarantee the insurer issues an applicant's form which must be answered honestly.

pure premium. *See* RISK PREMIUM.

pure reinsurer. An insurer whose authorisation to carry on business in the UK is restricted to reinsurance.

pure risk. Uncertainty as to whether a loss will occur. Under a pure risk situation there is no possibility of gain. The range of possible outcomes is from loss to no change. Such risks are static and inherent in the environment. Business efficiency is no safeguard against pure risks, eg fire and flood, which strike at random. Compare with SPECULATIVE RISK.

pure year figures. The figures relating to premiums, claims etc refer only to the particular year of account. Figures relating to business written in earlier years but transferred into that year are excluded.

Q

Qualified perils. Where the insurers use words to qualify an insured peril the insured must show that his loss was caused by the qualified peril and not the peril alone. Insurers may add an exception to an insured peril so qualifying it that the onus proof, which normally attaches to the insurer, is transferred to the insured. The standard fire policy contains qualified perils—fire, for example, is covered if not occasioned by or happening through, *inter alia*, riot and civil commotion. An insured must therefore show that not only did he suffer a fire but that the fire was not caused by riot or civil commotion. It will not be for the insurer to have to bring the fire within the scope of the terms 'riot and civil commotion' which would have been the case if those terms had appeared under the heading exceptions. *See* ONUS OF PROOF.

qualifying means. The minimum level of personal wealth (qv) each underwriting member of Lloyd's must prove to the Council of Lloyd's that he or she has before membership can be granted. *See also* MEANS TEST.

qualifying policies. Life insurance policies providing a capital sum on death are deemed to be qualifying policies if they satisfy certain conditions set out in the Taxes Act 1970, s.1 and the Finance Act 1976, s. 2. The main qualification requirements concern premiums which must be: (a) payable for a period of ten years or more (the ten year rule). (Where a term insurance exceeds ten years the premium must be payable for ten years or 75 per cent of the original term if that is shorter. Term insurances issued after April 1979 can be for as short as one year); (b) payable annually or more frequently (the premium spread rule); (c) evenly spread, ie premiums payable in any one year must not ex-

ceed twice the amount payable in any other year (the 'two times rule'), nor more than one-eighth of the total premiums payable over the first ten years (for whole life policies) or, for endowment policies, the term of the policy (the one eighth rule). There is also the 75 per cent rule (qv) which means that the sum insured on death must normally be at least 75 per cent (the percentage is reduced by 2 per cent for each year by which the life insured's age exceeds 55 at inception) of the total premiums payable if: (i) death were to occur at age 75 in whole life policies; and term insurances, issued after April 1976, expiring at age 75 or after; (ii) in the case of an endowment policy it ran its full term. Term insurances having no surrender value and not running beyond age 75 are exempt from the rule. The main tax advantages of a qualifying policy are: 1. Policies effected before 14 March 1984 attract Life assurance premium relief (LAPR) (qv) on the premiums. 2. The proceeds are free of tax provided the premiums are maintained for at least ten years or three-quarters of the term of the endowment if less. 3. Income and gains attributable to the policy while in force are taxed at rates applicable to the insurer who is responsible for any tax. Income tax at top-slicing (qv) rates may be payable if a non-qualifying policy is surrendered and in the event of early surrender there may be a 'clawback' (qv) of the LAPR.

quarter days. Four days in the year to which it was once customary to link certain transactions such as the renewal of annual policies. Fire and accident insurers extended the first period of annual insurances to the nearest quarter day: In England and Ireland—Ladyday (25 March); Midsummer (24 June); Michaelmas (29 September);

Christmas (25 December). In Scotland—Candlemas (2 February); Whitsun (15 May); Lammas (1 August); Martinmas (11 November).

quasi-managing agent. A members' agent which has entered into a contractual arrangement with a managing agent to delegate the day-to-day management of its members' underwriting to that managing agent but which has retained, in respect of one or more syndicates, the rights and duties regarding the investment of the premiums trust funds of such members.

Queen's Counsel Clause. A clause by which the insurer agrees to pay any claim without requiring the insured to contest it unless a Queen's counsel advises that it can probably be successfully defended. The clause commonly appears in professional indemnity (including directors' and officers' liability) policies to provide an arbitration mechanism in the cases where the insured prefers to settle the claim while the insurer wishes to dispute the third party claim against the insured in court.

Queen's enemies. 'Action of Queen's enemies' is specifically allowed as a defence to claims based on strict liability (qv) in innkeepers' liability (qv) and *Rylands* v *Fletcher* (qv). The onus is upon the defendant to prove that the loss was by act of Queen's enemies. The intention is to exempt the defendant from acts of war as such acts are clearly beyond his control. In marine insurance the term was said to mean 'the enemies of the carrier's Sovereign, whatever title he may enjoy— whether Queen, emperor, president, duke, doge or aristocratic assembly' (*Russell* v *Nieman* (1864)).

quotation slip. A slip used at Lloyd's which is accepted by the underwriter on the terms stated but without committing either party to an immediate transaction.

quota share reinsurance. This is a reinsurance by treaty or facultatively under which the insurer cedes and the reinsurer accepts a fixed proportion of the risk or, in the case of a treaty, risks within the agreed category. Quota share arrangements are proportional and expressed as percentages, eg 50 per cent quota share, 35 per cent quota share etc. Premiums and claims are shared in the agreed proportions. This can be a cheap, easily operated method of treaty reinsurance under which the insurer cannot select which risks he will or will not pass over to the reinsurer.

R

radiation risks. Since 1960 virtually all policies covering property and liabilities (other than marine and aviation) have excluded nuclear perils (qv). These risks attach to the operators of nuclear reactors (Nuclear Installations Act 1965 (qv)). However, other radiation risks can be covered by conventional policies. Radioisotopes, particle accelerators and similar applications are used in medicine, in biology, in pasteurisation of food, in industry, and in education. The UK Atomic Energy Authority lays down certain standards for the use of radioisotopes and provided these standards are rigidly observed the risk, depending on the type of policy, can be absorbed without difficulty. The radioisotopes used in industry are generally of low power with a short life and materials in contact with these isotopes do not themselves become radioactive. Underwriters study the risks involved and amend the basic rate where necessary.

radioactive contamination clause. *See* NUCLEAR PERILS.

railway accident. The meaning depends on the scope of cover intended by the insurer. Some personal accident policies, particularly coupon insurances (qv), may be so limited as to relate only to accidents in transit. In the context of such policies 'railway accident' may be defined as injury to the insured resulting from an accident to the train (or such other conveyance as may be defined). Other accidental injuries (eg caused by leaning out) are not 'railway accidents' for these purposes. Some policies, a little wider in scope, cover accidental injury attributable to the insured being a passenger on a train (or, in some cases, other vehicles) arising out of an act immediately connected with his being a passenger.

Railway Fires Acts 1905 and 1923. These Acts make the railway authority liable for damage to agricultural land or crops by sparks from a railway locomotive but with a maximum liability of £200 but British Rail has agreed to pay up to £400 without proof of negligence. There is no statutory liability for damage to moorlands, to buildings or to stacks.

rateable contribution. The basis upon which an insurer must contribute to a loss when contribution (qv) applies. *See* INDEPENDENT LIABILITY METHOD.

rate of gross profit. The rate of gross profit earned on the turnover during the financial year immediately before the date of damage. It is the ratio of gross profit to turnover. A business interruption policy pays an amount produced by applying the rate of gross profit to the reduction in turnover (qv). The method of defining gross profit when the policy, as is usual, is on the difference basis, is the amount by which: (a) the sum of the turnover and the amount of closing stock shall exceed (b) the sum of the opening stock and specified (uninsured) working expenses. The uninsured working expenses (eg packing materials, carriage outwards) are then listed and known as specified working expenses. *See also* STANDING CHARGES.

rate per cent. Premiums are frequently charged as a rate per cent, ie a rate per £100 of the sum insured. The premium for a building valued at £30 000 at 15p per cent is £45.

rate per mille. Premiums may be charged as a rate per mille, ie a rate per £1000 of the sum insured. The premium for property valued at £20 000 at £1.25 per thousand is £25.

ratification. The act of adopting a contract, or other transaction, by a person who was not bound by it originally, eg because it was entered into by an unauthorised agent. Ratification normally becomes effective from the date of the act which is ratified and may be made in various ways, formally or informally by parol or implied by conduct. An insurance contract can in certain circumstances be ratified by the principal after a loss has occurred (*Williams* v *North China Insurance Co.* (1876)).

ratio decidendi. The principle on which the case is decided. It makes the decision a precedent for the future development of the law.

ratios. The following ratios are important for monitoring activities or calculating premiums: 1. Burning ratio. Insurance claims as a percentage of total premiums for current policies. 2. Claims (or loss) ratio. Incurred losses in relation to earned premiums. 3. Expense ratio. Insurers' total expenses in relation to written premiums. 4. Combined or composite ratio. Sum of (2) and (3), a figure below 100 per cent indicating broadly that an underwriting profit has been achieved.

raw materials. A form of property exposed to the risk of loss and as a result usually included as an insured item under fire and additional perils policies and other material damage policies. The basis of value is the market value immediately prior to the loss or damage.

realised profits. The term is not entirely precise but is defined in the Companies Act 1985, Schedule 4, para. 91 as 'such profits of the company as fall to be treated as realised profits for the purpose of those accounts in accordance with the principles generally accepted with respect to the determination for accounting purposes of realised profits at the time when those accounts are prepared'. Broadly, they are profits which have already been converted into cash or could be so converted in a short time. Realised profits are significant mainly because the amount that a company can distribute is generally restricted to its net accumulated realised profits. In addition to the distribution of dividend, the company may have to

make repayments on debentures. The Companies Act 1985, s. 268 deals with the realised profits of long-term insurance business. They are defined as the amounts properly transferred to the profit and loss account from a surplus in the funds (ie an excess of assets over liabilities of the fund) as shown by an actuarial investigation carried out in accordance with Section 18 of the Insurance Companies Act 1982 and thus provide a link between the 'accounting Act' and the 'supervisory Act'.

reasonable care condition. Many policies require an insured to take reasonable care or reasonable precautions to prevent accidents (or for the safeguarding of goods and/or premises). Such clauses will not be construed as warranties (qv), breach of which will entitle the insurer to repudiate the liability, irrespective of a causal connection between the breach and the loss (*Lane* v *Spratt* (1970)). It would be repugnant to the commercial purpose of a policy indemnifying an insured against the consequences of his negligence or breach of statute to deny that indemnity for the very event that triggered the policy. This was the outcome in *Woolfall and Rimmer Ltd* v *Moyle* (1941) when lack of care resulted in inadequate scaffolding sending one man to his death and others to injury. The employers' liability insurer contended that the reasonable care condition imposed a condition on the insured that was co-terminous with his duty to his employees. The argument failed. Goddard LJ put it that the condition was there to protect the underwriters against the insured who regards himself, because he is insured, as free to carry on his business in a reckless manner. In short, the underwriter to prove a breach must prove recklessness, ie the insured neglected to take obvious precautions in reliance on the fact that if there was a loss he was insured against it in any event. The same outcome occurred in *Fraser* v *Furman* (1967) when it was held in regard to a liability policy that the precautions required by such a clause are not those which are reasonable as between the insured and third party—but those precautions which are reasonable as between the insured and his insurer. In the goods in transit case of *Lane* v *Spratt* (1970), the condition read 'the insured shall take all reasonable precautions for the protection and safeguarding of the goods'. The insureds employed a driver sent for an interview by the Labour Exchange (these days a job centre). He reported for work the next day and disappeared with a valuable lorry-load of bacon. Apart from one unsuccessful attempt to obtain a reference from a previous employer on the telephone, no steps were taken either to verify his identity or check that he was honest. The clause was held by the court to be limited to the taking of precautions for the physical protection and safeguarding of the goods and did not extend to the selection and vetting of staff. The insureds were entitled to an indemnity but had the clause been a warranty the outcome would have been different. Even if the clause had extended to cover selection of staff it is doubtful if the insureds' failure would have amounted to recklessness. It could more accurately be described as casual. A possible solution for the insurer is to impose a specific warranty that the insured will provide and put into effect certain precautions, eg an intruder alarm, so that any breach enables the insurer to refuse an indemnity under the policy. The reasonable care condition in a motor policy was also held in *Rendlesham* v *Dunne* (1964) to relate solely to the physical state of the car because it was associated in the clause with the term 'in an efficient condition' (qv). Allowing an unaccompanied provisional licence holder to drive his car did not cause the insured to break the condition. The motor insurer in *Conn* v *Westminster Motor Insurance Association* (1966) successfully invoked the condition on appeal against the trial judge's decision that their insured who breached the condition requiring him to take all reasonable steps to maintain his taxi in an efficient condition. After a crash the taxi was found to have two bald front tyres and a defective brake. It did not matter that the defects did not cause the accident which was thought to have been due to Mr Conn momentarily lapsing into sleep. It was clear that Mr Conn knew that at least one tyre had no tread and therefore he had not taken the reasonable steps required, although the trial judge was apparently satisfied with the insured's statement that the vehicle was to be overhauled two to three weeks later. The condition is one which is precedent to liability but it will not operate to defeat a claim by a third party or employee whose claim is for injury or damage covered by the compulsory insurance law. However, the insurer will have a right of recovery against the insured. *See also* 'IN AN EFFICIENT CONDITION'.

reasonable construction rule. A rule of construction (qv) to the effect that where there is ambiguity the reasonable construction is to be preferred.

reasonable despatch clause. Clause 18 in the Institute Cargo Clauses, called Avoidance of Delay, makes it a condition that the insured shall act with reasonable despatch in all circumstances under his control. The insurance operates while the goods are in the ordinary course of transit but if the insured chooses to interrupt the transit, the insurance terminates at the place of the interruption. The Marine Insurance Act 1906, s. 48 relieves the insurer of liability when there is unreasonable delay.

reasonable expectations. A standard laid down by the Insurance Companies Acts for judging life insurance bonus declarations.

reasonable man. The test in negligence (qv) is an objective one based on the acts or omissions of the reasonable man. He is well-known as the 'man on the Clapham omnibus'. He does 'not have to possess the wisdom of a Hebrew Prophet or the agility of an acrobat'. No person is an insurer of his fellow men—there has to be fault and in the context of negligence fault occurs when a person fails to live up to the standard of the reasonable man.

reasonableness. *See* TEST OF REASONABLENESS.

'reasonable precautions'. *See* REASONABLE CARE CONDITION.

'reasonably practicable'. The Factories Act 1961, s. 28(1) provides, *inter alia*, (*see* PROPERLY MAINTAINED for the other part of the obligation) that 'all floors, steps, stairs, passages, and gangways shall, so far as reasonably practicable, be kept free from any obstruction and from any substance likely to cause a person to slip'. This is the lowest of the duties (compare with properly maintained (qv) and all practicable steps (qv)). The occupier can weigh the cost against the risk and the expected efficacy of the measures. Reasonable practicability is considered stricter than negligence and it is for the employer to prove that compliance was impracticable.

reassurance pools. Pooling (qv) enables sub-standard lives to secure life assurance that otherwise would not be available to them. Pooling produces the advantage of averaging over a large number of similar lives. The specialist reassurance office accepts the risk and then shares it among the members of the pool on a quota share (qv) basis. Pools exist for persons suffering from such illnesses as diabetes and coronary disease.

rebellion. 'The taking up of arms traitorously against the government of the state. It is a graver form of insurrection (qv) for general purposes in which there is usurped power amounting to treason'. (F.H. Jones, *The Law of Accident and Contingency Insurance*, Pitman).

rebuilding cost. The basis on which the sum insured on private dwellings should be fixed. The Association of British Insurers publishes a guide (*How much would it cost to rebuild your home?*). The rebuilding cost should include an allowance for permanent fittings, such as central heating and additional charges such as demolition, professional fees and the requirements of local authorities. Additions should also be made for garages, fences, gates, and paths.

received for shipment bill. The bill of lading issued prior to shipment stating the particulars of goods and their apparent condition. Under the Carriage of Goods by Sea Act 1971 (qv) such a bill may be demanded by a shipper from the shipowner.

reciprocal duty. A duty which attaches to both parties in an agreement and not just one of them. The duty of utmost good faith (qv) is reciprocal in that it must be observed by both the proposer and the insured. While the duty affects the proposer to a marked extent because it is he who knows, or ought to know, all the material facts relating to a proposed risk for insurance, the insurers are bound to observe the duty of utmost good faith throughout the negotiations, as well as the general duty of good faith throughout the duration of the contract. Insurers must, for example, give accurate information regarding the proposed contract. They must not accept a premium on a property they know does not exist; they must not be parties to illegal contracts; and they must not issue a policy in terms which they know have not been mutually agreed.

reciprocal health agreements. The UK has reciprocal arrangements with other countries which entitle travellers from one country to another to obtain medical attention free or at reduced rates under the relevant national health provisions. As the insured under a travel insurance is responsible for the first portion of a medical expenses claim, possession of a certain form (Form E111) may enable the insured to receive a full indemnity in the event of injury or illness.

reciprocity. An arrangement for, and agreement to, share or exchange risks between insurers or reinsurers. A direct writing company may wish to redistribute its business and so widen its geographical spread. It may be willing to exchange a part of its own home business for an equivalent amount of foreign business from another direct insurer. This is 100 per cent reciprocity. If the two companies each retain their proportion of the total business and reinsure the balance with the other they will each end up with the same premium but the companies will each participate in the claims of the combined business. The result is the same as if the two companies had merged and produces a strong financial position. Reciprocity enables the two companies to write a higher combined capacity and, of course, the method can be extended to more than two companies. Professional reinsurers (qv) have no direct business to exchange and could not offer 100 per cent reciprocity for all of their business but they can offer their direct clients reciprocity. This means a share of other clients' incoming treaties often formed into a reciprocal pool. The outward reciprocal volume to the client is less than the inward volume as the professional reinsurer needs to keep some business for itself.

recital clause. The opening clause of the policy reciting names of the parties and stating that the insured has applied for the contract of insurance. The clause is also known as the 'Preamble'.

Recognised Professional Body (RPB). A recognised professional body such as the Law Society, the Institute of Chartered Accountants, and the Insurance Brokers Registration Council able to act under powers delegated by the Securities and Investments Board (SIB) (qv). These bodies are empowered to certificate those of their members seeking authorisation to act as independent financial advisers (qv). They issue rules and seek to control the investment activities of their members in order to protect the interests of investors.

rectification. This is the process of rectifying a policy document that fails to represent the terms agreed between the parties. Where one of the parties feels that a mistake has been made in the drafting of the policy they may ask for rectification. If the party requested, the insurer, refuses the insured can apply to the court for rectification. To succeed he will have to show that the policy does not represent the agreement between the parties and is not true evidence of the contract.

recurring clause. A clause in a permanent health insurance (qv) which sets a period of time that must elapse between a period of disability or a claim from a given cause and its recurrence before it will be treated as a new claim. This is important as many of the policies are subject to deferment periods (qv).

reducing extra risk. A life insurance term referring to an extra risk which is at its greatest at the inception (qv) and then decreases, eg tuberculosis after treatment.

refrigerator insurance. A policy issued by engineering insurers to cover breakdown and/or accidental damage to plant and the resultant damage to own surrounding property. A monetary excess applies. The policy is suitable for refrigerating machinery used with cold rooms or chamber for the storage of frozen or chilled goods or in connection with air-conditioning units for the control of temperature in offices and other buildings.

regional organisation (or regionalisation). *See* ZONAL ORGANISATION.

registered insurance broker. An insurance broker who has satisfied the registration requirements of the Insurance Brokers Registration Council upon whose register his name and address appears.

registration policies. Similar to declaration in arrears policies (qv) but enables the cover to be varied as the employer keeps a register of trips made and cover required which is then declared in arrears. Integrity and efficiency of the insured are important to the insurer.

rehabilitation benefit. A reduced benefit payable under a permanent health insurance (qv) after the insured returns to work in circumstances where his earnings have been reduced as a result of a disability. The reduction in earnings may be because the insured is limited to part-time working or is forced to work in a less well-paid job. The benefit starts only after 13 weeks of total incapacity and when a full claim has been admitted. The benefit normally terminates after 52 weeks or upon the insured attaining age 60, whichever is earlier. If, as a result of the disability, the reduced earning capacity is permanent, the rehabilitation benefit is payable until the policy completes its full period subject only to the insured keeping premiums up to date.

Rehabilitation of Offenders Act 1974. This, in effect, enacts that convictions that are 'spent' need not be disclosed to insurers as material facts (qv). The rehabilitation period is five years for non-custodial sentences; seven years for custodial sentences exceeding six but not exceeding 30 months. Sentences over 30 months do not become 'spent'. An agent or previous insurer who is aware of a spent conviction must not disclose it.

reinstatement. The restoration of the insured property to its former condition after a claim. The restoration can take the form of replacement, repair, or rebuilding. The liability of the insurer under a contract of indemnity to make good a loss is a liability to make a monetary payment. Generally, insurers insert a clause in material damage policies under which they acquire the option to settle either by a cash payment, replacement (qv), repair or reinstatement. Once an insurer elects to reinstate etc he cannot later withdraw. If an insured fails to co-operate in the reinstatement, the insurer is relieved of liability. Where the reinstatement puts the property into a superior condition the insured is called upon for betterment (qv). This obligation to contribute has resulted in the reinstatement clause (qv) with a view to shifting all costs to the insurer where a new item equivalent to the old one has to be purchased. *See also* AUTOMATIC REINSTATEMENT CLAUSE, SUCCESSIVE LOSSES, REINSTATEMENT AVERAGE, and the FIRE PREVENTION (METROPOLIS) ACT 1774.

reinstatement average. When an insurance is subject to the reinstatement clause (qv), it is provided that if the sum insured is 85 per cent or more of the value at risk at the time of reinstatement then no average applies. In fixing the sum insured the insured should allow for the period of insurance and the probable rebuilding or replacement time and this could mean projecting forwards for two or three years. Losses settled on an indemnity basis remain subject to the normal average (qv) clause.

reinstatement (reinsurance). A reinsurance clause which restores the amount of cover to the level existing prior to the occurrence of a loss under the treaty. The number of reinstatements to be allowed is usually negotiated when the treaty is placed. Reinstatements may be free, ie not subject to any additional premium, or charged at a percentage of the treaty premium. Depending on the circumstances the percentage could be in the range 50 per cent to 150 per cent. Reinstatement applies mainly to risk excess of loss treaties covering property, marine and aviation business, and all forms of catastrophe excess of loss treaties. There is a tendency towards limiting the number of reinstatements in respect of liability excess of loss treaties.

reinstatement basis of cover (or settlement). *See* REINSTATEMENT CLAUSE.

reinstatement by the insured. An insured may be obliged to reinstate by statute or by contract. Certain provisions in the Trustee Act 1925, s. 20 (4) (qv) may allow the trustee to reinstate the insured property. Under the Law of Property Act 1925, s. 108 (3) all money received under a fire insurance on mortgaged property or an insurance for which the mortgagor is liable under the deed shall, if the mortgagee so requires, be applied by the mortgagor for making good the loss or damage. In contract law the insured may be a tenant obliged by the terms of his lease to effect insurance on the property and use any insurance money on reinstatement.

reinstatement clause (otherwise called memorandum). A clause that obliges fire insurers to meet the cost of a new replacement of property of the same kind as the lost or damaged property up to the limit of the sum insured. No deduction is made for wear and tear but if the new property is superior, eg a more sophisticated machine, the insured makes a betterment (qv) contribution. The insurer will not pay on a new cost basis until the reinstatement has been carried out and this must be done within a reasonable period of time. The insured can elect a normal indemnity settlement and may do so if the property is no longer required. Where there is only partial damage average (qv) is applied by comparing the sum insured with the estimated cost of reinstating the whole of the property at the time of reinstatement. *See* REINSTATEMENT AVERAGE. The reinstatement clause can be used for insurances on buildings, contents, and machinery but not stock.

reinstatement memorandum. *See* REINSTATEMENT CLAUSE.

reinstatement of data. An optional section in a computer insurance. It indemnifies the insured in respect of the cost of reinstating data contained in the data-carrying material in consequence of: (a) accidental erasure resulting directly from loss or damage to the computer equipment from accidental cause including electrical and mechanical failure; (b) accidental failure of the public electricity supply when exceeding 30 minutes; (c) and the insured being denied access to the premises or use of the computer because of loss/damage to other property in the vicinity. Loss due to malicious erasure can be added to the policy subject to an additional premium. The policy normally carries an excess (qv) of £50. The sum insured is based on an aggregate of the cost of computer time, labour including cost of collating and inputting previously stored data and programs, and other additional costs.

reinstatement of life policy. During the period covered by the non-forfeiture condition (qv), it is normally possible to reinstate a life policy following the expiry of the days without payment of the premium. The policyholder must pay the overdue premiums with interest and a revival fee. This can normally be done without the policyholder having to provide evidence of health. *See also* REVIVAL CLAUSE.

reinstatement under statute. 1. *See* FIRE PREVENTION (METROPOLIS) ACT 1774. 2 (a) The proceeds of insurance on any property subject to a trust or settlement may be applied by the trustees in reinstatement subject to the terms of the Trustee Act 1925. (b) Where insurance is maintained by a mortgagor in accordance with a mortgage deed the mortgagor must apply policy proceeds in reinstatement if the mortgagee so requires (Law of Property Act 1925, s. 108(3)).

reinsurance. The insuring again by an insurer of the whole or part of a risk that he has already insured with another insurer called a reinsurer. Risk is transferred in exchange for premium payable to the reinsurer to enable the insurer (known as the ceding office) to reduce to acceptable levels the probability that a severe claim or accumulation of claims will ruin or threaten the financial stability of the insurer. There are two basic types of reinsurance and the contracts are written in two basic forms. In proportional reinsurance (quota share reinsurance (qv); surplus treaty (qv)) the reinsurer pays a proportion of the total claim. In non-proportional reinsurance (qv)—excess of loss or excess of loss ratio—the reinsurer pays a high proportion of a claim or claims above a fixed amount or percentage subject to upper limits agreed between the parties. The form of contract is either facultative (qv) or by treaty (qv).

reinsurance broker. A specialist intermediary involved in the placing of reinsurance (qv).

reinsurance clause. Marine reinsurances are effected in the same way as the original insurances and, except for this clause, there is usually nothing to distinguish the reinsurance from the underlying policy. The final seven words read 'to pay as may be paid thereon'. The meaning is more restrictive than it appears. The reinsurer is liable only for losses actually covered by his policy, regardless of claims paid on the original policy. Many reinsurances are more restricted than the original policy and the clause must then be qualified by terms such as 'but against total loss only'.

reinsurance commission. The commission paid by the reinsurer to a ceding office (qv) on premiums ceded. It takes account of the original commission paid to the broker or agent and the expenses incurred by the ceding office. The amount paid by the reinsurer to the reinsurance broker (qv), who linked the ceding office to the reinsurer, is called brokerage and should not be confused with the reinsurance commission. *See also* OVERRIDING COMMISSION, PROFIT COMMISSION (B), and MARINE REINSURANCE COMMISSION.

Reinsurance Offices Association. The main object of the Association was to bring together companies transacting reinsurance business. It encouraged co-operation between companies on technical matters of general interest and the study and development of reinsurance. The Association set up committees to investigate matters of common interest, eg the committee for education and training. On 1 January 1991, the ROA merged with the PSAC to form the London Insurance and Reinsurance Market Association (LIMRA) (qv).

reinsurance premium. The amount paid by an insurer in consideration of reinsurance (qv).

reinsurance to close. A reinsurance purchased by an active underwriter at Lloyd's at the end of a three-year accounting period. The Insurance Companies Act, s. 83 (2) requires that all premiums must be placed in a premium trust fund from which only claims, expenses and ascertained profits can be paid. The fund, in accordance with a Lloyd's rule, must be invested in secure short-dated investments. At the end of three years the underwriter forecasts possible future claims that will attach to the fund and calculates a closing reserve most of which is used to purchase a reinsurance to close policy. This policy indemnifies the fund against all future claims so that any balance in the fund is ascertained profit and can be withdrawn for the benefit of the Name (qv). The system defers the distribution of profit until better information is available on the pattern of claims. The estimated future claims figure, which determines the reinsurance to close, has to be 'true and fair' and consequently a set of explanatory notes was issued in December 1985 (Bye-Law No. 7 of 1984—Syndicate Accounting. Explanatory Notes—Reinsurance to Close, 9 December 1985).

reinsured/reassured. The party who is reinsured, ie the ceding office or cedant.

reinsurer. The party who accepts reinsurance (qv).

reinsuring clause. The clause in a reinsurance contract which sets out the terms under which a claim can made. It is the reinsurance equivalent of the operative clause (qv).

remote cause. A term used in the doctrine of proximate cause (qv) to distinguish a loss that has not been the dominant effective cause of a loss from the proximate cause but which was a part of the sequence of events. It may have been the event or accident that facilitated the loss as distinct from the event or accident which caused the loss. In *Marsden* v *City & County Assurance Co.* (1865) a fire broke out, a mob assembled and they broke the plate glass in neighouring premises with a view to looting. The plate glass insurance excluded the risk of fire and the insurer sought the protection of the exclusion but failed. The fire, the remote cause, facilitated the loss but the proximate cause was the action of the mob.

removal of debris. A clause that extends a fire policy to cover the costs of clearing away debris and dismantling, shoring up and propping up expenses following destruction or damage. Normally, sums insured are increased by 5–7.5 per cent to allow for these expenses. An insured with large risk values may find it more cost effective to insure this item on a first loss basis (qv)

removal or weakening of support accorded to land or buildings. A construction industry and civil engineering risk which will generally constitute a nuisance (*Bower* v *Peate* (1876)) making the creator or person who authorised it liable for the damage without proof of negligence. See JCT CLAUSE 21. 2. 1. and 'COLLAPSE' INSURANCE.

removers' insurance. An all-risks insurance arranged by furniture removers under the British Association of Removers' block policy for the benefit of their customers. See HOUSEHOLD REMOVAL INSURANCE.

renewal. The insurance contract normally expires on a due date. Most are issued annually and provide for renewal by mutual consent. The usual practice is for the insurer to invite renewal by renewal notice. With some exceptions (motor insurance and marine insurance) 15 days of grace are allowed for payment as a concession to the insured. The concession is not available if: (i) The insurers have declined to renew. (ii) The insured has intimated that he will not renew. (iii) The insured's conduct shows a clear intention of non-renewal. Any loss under the policy during the days of grace will be covered if the concession has not been forfeited and provided the premium is paid during the required period (*Simpson* v *Accidental Death Co.* (1857)). In motor insurance the policy is only valid for the purpose of the Road Traffic Act if a valid certificate has been delivered to the insured. As certificates cannot by law be backdated, it is customary to incorporate a 15-day Road Traffic Act certificate into the renewal notice. This obviates the need to issue revised renewal certificates to those who do not pay on or before the due date but pay within the 15-day period. In marine insurance payment is expected on or before the due date. No concession by way of days of grace is allowed.

renewal notice. The document issued by an insurer as a means of inviting renewal (qv). Some brokers issue their own renewal notices and in the case of Lloyd's the renewal notice will always come from the broker. In the case of motor insurance the insurer's renewal notice should always be used as it incorporates a temporary motor insurance certificate in order to comply with the Road Traffic Act.

rent-a-captive. A practice which enables a company to combine some of the benefits of internal funding with the benefits of forming a captive (qv) without subscribing capital or incurring formation costs. The company enters into an arrangement with an insurance company or existing captive which is prepared to single out the customer's account and treat it separately within its own business. The customer becomes, in effect, an insurance company within an insurance company while leaving the customer with a part of the risk. The premium paid includes a handling fee and is by way of deposit for later adjustment in line with actual experience. The investment income is credited to the customer's account.

replacement. 1. A possible method of indemnity by means of the reinstatement clause (qv). If insurers opt for reinstatement in the case of lost goods, replacement is the only means of carrying this into effect. The goods supplied as replacements must be equivalent to the lost goods, ie be of a similar nature and quality. If they are superior the insured may be called upon to make a contribution for betterment (qv). 2. In private car motor insurance some insurers agree to supply a new car in place of a car which sustains heavy damage within 12 months of the date it was first registered. The obligation to replace with an equivalent new car is triggered when the estimated cost of repair is equal to or greater than a given percentage (50 or 60 per cent) of the new price of the car. 3. *See* NEW FOR OLD POLICIES which modify the principle of indemnity.

replacement-as-new. *See* NEW FOR OLD and REINSTATEMENT CLAUSE.

replacement clause. Machinery in transit is susceptible to breakage or loss of small but integral parts rendering it unfit for the purpose intended. This could lead to a possible total loss claim. Consequently if the breakage risk is covered in a marine policy the Institute Replacement Clause is added. The clause provides that in the event of loss of or damage to any part of a machine the sum recoverable shall not exceed the cost of replacement or repair of such part plus charges for forwarding and refitting within the limits of the sum insured.

replacement value clause. A term occasionally used in place of the reinstatement clause (qv) in respect of the insurance of machinery.

reporting excess of loss treaty. A facultative obligatory treaty (qv) mainly used in marine cargo reinsurance calling for particulars of sums reinsured to be notified to the reinsurer.

representation. A statement made by the insured to the insurer before the contract is concluded. If the representation relates to a material fact (qv) it must be true. A representation may relate to a matter of fact or to a matter of expectation or belief. A representation as to fact is true, if it is substantially correct, ie, the difference between what is represented and what is actually correct would not be considered material by a prudent underwriter (qv). A representation as to a matter of expectation or belief is true if it is made in good faith. A representation may be withdrawn or corrected before the contract is concluded (Marine Insurance Act 1906, s. 20). Representations are often converted into warranties by a basis clause at the foot of the proposal form.

request note. A term used in facultative reinsurance (qv) describing a form of communications. A ceding office (qv) submits details of the policy to be reinsured and certifies the period and amount of the insurance. It includes a statement of the amount, if any, to be retained by the ceding office. If the reinsurer accepts a take note (qv) they accept the request stating the amount of reinsurance undertaken. In facultative reinsurance a policy is frequently dispensed with as reliance is based on the foregoing procedure.

reserve (retained) premium. The proportion of a premium payable under a contract of reinsurance that has been retained by the cedant under the contract to assist in financing the reinsurer's share of the cost of settling claims.

reserve value. The name given to the technical life insurance reserve that arises from the level annual premium system. In the early years the premium paid exceeds the amount needed to meet current claims and the excess, ie the reserve value, is accumulated to meet claims in later years. In those years the level annual premium is below the amount needed to meet current claims.

reserves. *See* FREE RESERVES AND TECHNICAL RESERVES.

res ipsa loquitur. 'The thing speaks for itself'. The maxim applies whenever it is improbable that such an accident would have occurred without negligence on the part of the defendant. The maxim places on the defendant the burden of disproving negligence.

respondentia. This is similar to bottomry (qv) but the loan is secured on the cargo only and is repayable only if the cargo is saved. The creditor has an insurable interest in the loan (Marine Insurance Act 1906, s. 10) and this extends to the interest payable.

restrictive covenant indemnities. These are generally granted to vendors or purchasers of land where there is an intention to develop or use land in a way that risks infringing a restriction, namely a restrictive covenant, governing the use of the land. The restrictions generally arise when a vendor places a negative burden on his purchaser and once the restrictive covenant attaches it generally 'runs with the land' in perpetuity. This means that the benefit of the covenant may be claimed by successors in title to the original contracting parties. Insurers issue restrictive covenant indemnities to indemnify a developer or other risk-

taker against the consequences of there being in existence someone able to claim the benefit of the restrictive covenant. Historically many restrictive covenants had their origin with great Victorian landowners who sought to preserve the character of their land and estates from the encroachments of the industrial revolution. The most commonly met with restrictive covenant imposed in connection with building is that restricting the density of housing land. Insurers may provide indemnities covering: (a) the insured's liability at law for damages in respect of the actual breach of the restrictive covenant; (b) the amount of the insured's ascertained net loss in the event of any action brought for the grant of an injunction (whether mandatory or interlocutory) on the grounds that the proposed user of the land will constitute a breach of covenant; (c) legal costs and expenses recovered by any claimant from the insured or incurred with the consent of the insurer; (d) (as an alternative basis of settlement in certain cases) all costs and expenses incurred by the insured with the consent of the insurer in making an application pursuant to s. 84 of the Law of Property Act 1925, for removal or modification of the restrictive covenants concerned. It is usual to grant restrictive covenant indemnities, without restrictions as to term, at a single premium payable at inception.

restrictive endorsements. 1. *Employers' liability insurance.* Endorsements limiting the cover otherwise provided under employers' liability policies. Generally the only exclusion in the printed policy form is one of limited application in respect of radio-active contamination. However, insurers use separate rates of premium for different categories of work (eg in the construction industries some firms work only on premises not more than two storeys in height and accept an endorsement restricting their activities to such work) within the same trade to distinguish between higher and lower risk activities. As a consequence endorsements are used to restrict the risk to one which is commensurate with the premium paid. In this way low risk categories do not subsidise higher categories by paying a premium for risks they do not run. Where a firm engages in a range of activities the insurer will use a restrictive endorsement, if any, pitched at the highest level so that only the categories of work not undertaken are excluded. Consequently the policy will cover a mix of high and low risk work and in these circumstances the insurer issues a dual or multi-rated policy and the insured gives breakdown of wages according to labour employed in the different types of work so that the relevant rate can be applied in each case. Restrictive endorsements introduce exclusions into the policies and they are not prohibited for the purpose of compulsory employers' liability insurance. 2. *Insurances generally.* Any endorsement (qv) which cuts down or restricts the scope of cover otherwise provided.

retained benefits. Retirement or death benefits to which an employee is entitled under the scheme of a previous employer.

retention. The proportion or amount of the risk that an insurer retains on his own account (qv). The retention is also known as the line. The amount of the basic retention will be influenced by the type of insurance, the degree of hazard present, the insurer's experience and financial strength, the insurer's capacity and the amount of business already written in the class concerned. The retention may vary within one class of insurance, eg a fire insurer will normally categorise risks according to type—shops, office, factories (further sub-divided according to trade—and apply different limits to each category or sub-division. Contrast retention with cession (qv). *Also see* EXCESS POINTS.

retention bond. A type of performance bond (qv) that enables a contractor to receive full payments as the work progresses. In the absence of the bond a percentage of the payments due to the contractor will be retained pending satisfactory performance of the work.

retroactive date. A date that may be introduced into policies written on a claims-made basis as a means of excluding losses occurring prior to that date that would otherwise be covered provided the claim is made during the period of insurance. If a retroactive date is not included in the policy the only requirement is that the claim should be made during the policy term (or any extended reporting period (qv) and the date of occurrence will not be material.

retroactive insurance. An insurance arranged after an event that constitutes a claim under the policy. This innovation is most likely to be practised on the occasion of a substantial liability claim the total cost of which is uncertain and which will take a number of years to settle. The insured is prepared to pay a high premium to substitute certainty for the uncertainty surrounding the uninsured losses. The insurer sees the advantage in obtaining a high premium for investment pending settlement of the claims. The investment income plus the premium itself and changes in value of money over time may create the mathematical possibility of making a profit particularly if the initial estimates of the claims later prove excessive. Insurance of this type is rare and in its early stages but is likened to cash flow underwriting (qv).

retrocession. This describes the transaction when a reinsurer himself reinsures.

retrospective cover. Liability policies may be extended to cover claims now made for losses occurring before the policy period. The intention is to close gaps that may exist because of the inability of the insured to trace previous insurers. The relatively high incidence of 'long tail' (qv) claims has created a demand for this extension.

retrospective legislation. This is sometimes termed retroactive legislation and means legislation which applies not just to the future. It applies also, often within limits, to events or actions antecedent to it.

retrospective ownership. Back-dated ownership which may be relevant to property insurance, particularly motor insurance. When an insurer pays a claim for the total loss of a car, ownership of the car transfers to the insurer retrospectively. The insurer then becomes responsible for the car in the interval between the accident and the date of the total loss settlement. If the insurer has undertaken to look after the wreck prior to settlement and the car is handled in a manner inconsistent with the rights of the car owner the insurer may be liable to pay damages for the tort of conversion (qv).

retrospective rating. A system when the rate to be charged for the insurance is finally determined at the expiry of the policy taking account of the experience during the policy period.

retrosurance. The reinsurance of reinsurance.

return premium. The amount refunded to the insured by law or by a provision in the contract. If the risk does not attach the insurer runs no risk and must return the premium. Once the risk has attached the insured is not entitled to any return. However, they may be payable under a provision in the contract relating to adjustable premiums, cancellation, laying up of vessels or vehicles, innocent double insurance, or in the event of the liquidation of the insurer.

revalued average band earnings. Band earning (qv) in line with national earning levels each year.

reverse liability. An item included in legal expenses insurance (or as an extension of a household or personal liability insurance) for individuals and families. If the insured is awarded damages in court for personal injury or damage to property and payment is not made within a given time (eg three months) then the insurer will pay in full up to £1m. When the insurance is an extension of an existing liability policy the insurer makes the payment only if the insured would have been entitled to an indemnity had the award been against him and not in his favour. *See also* UNRECOVERED DAMAGES and UNSATISFIED COURT JUDGMENTS.

reversionary annuity. An annuity (qv) providing that the annuity will become payable if the annuitant is living upon the death of the insured, such as the wife upon the death of her husband. If the annuitant dies first the premiums are forfeited. The insured's state of health is relevant to the insurer as it would be in the case of life insurance.

reversionary bonus. A sum added periodically during the currency of a with profits life insurance which becomes payable at the same time and in the same circumstances as the sum insured.

revival clause. This allows the holder of a life policy a period in which to apply for a revival of the contract, notwithstanding that the days of grace (qv) and the period of non-forfeiture (qv) have both expired. The period is one or two years from the days of grace. To revive the policy the policyholder must pay a revival fee, the overdue premiums plus interest and submit evidence of health as required by the office.

rider. A USA term meaning endorsement (qv), exclusion (qv), or extension (qv).

rider policy. *See* MOTOR CYCLE RIDER INSURANCE POLICY.

Riding Establishments Act 1970. Any person holding a licence to run a riding establishment must have public liability insurance. The insurance is to indemnify the licensee against legal liability for any injury sustained by any person who hires a horse or who is being instructed. The insurance must also apply to the liability of the hirer in connection with third party bodily injury. This is a compulsory insurance requirement under the Act.

riot. There are five necessary elements of a riot. (i) There must be at least twelve persons, (ii) all with a common purpose, (iii) where there has an inception or execution of that common purpose, (iv) with the intent of helping one another by force if necessary against any person who may oppose them in the execution of their common purpose, (v) using force or violence in such a manner to alarm at least one person of reasonable firmness and courage. This definition originated in *Field* v *Receiver of the Metropolitan Police* (1907) when the number was fixed at three but was increased to twelve by the Public Order Act 1986. The Field definition was approved in *Munday* v *Metropolitan Police District Receiver* (1949), in which the plaintiff's property was invaded by crowds turned away from a football ground.

riot, civil commotion. Riot (qv) has an exact legal meaning. It features with civil commotion (qv) and others in the operative clause (qv) of the standard fire policy as excluded perils. Cover can be obtained as an additional or special peril. *See* RIOT, CIVIL COMMOTION, STRIKES, LOCKED-OUT WORKERS etc.

riot, civil commotion , strikes, locked-out workers, labour disturbances, and malicious persons. These perils combine as one item to form an additional or special peril to be added to a fire policy (in a similar way they feature in household comprehensive policies). Damage caused in these various ways embraces fire damage and other forms of damage, eg wrecking and looting but losses caused by foreign enemy, civil war, rebellion, revolution, insurrection, military or usurped power, war, invasion, hostilities (whether war is declared or not), cessation of work or from confiscation or wilful destruction by a Government or similar authority or from ionising radiations or contamination by radioactivity are excluded. It is customary to require the insured to give notice of claim within seven days to assist insurers in pursuing their subrogation rights against the police authority under the Riot (Damages) Act 1886 (qv) which allows fourteen days for the particulars of the occurrence to be notified. The normal riot wording restricts damage caused maliciously to damage caused by malicious persons acting in connection with any political organisation although the restriction is by no means an invariable rule. *See* MALICIOUS DAMAGE.

Riot (Damages) Act 1886. Any person whose property is damaged by rioters can claim compensation from the police authority but if he has been recouped by way of insurance he can only claim to the extent that the compensation payable exceeds the insurance claim. Insurers who have paid a claim can exercise subrogation (qv) rights against the police in their own name.

risk. 1. The possibility of loss occurring. It has been defined as any situation arising out of an organisation's activities capable of giving rise to loss, injury, damage, liability or impairment of growth in social, moral and financial terms. This definition makes no distinction between speculative risks (qv) and pure risks (qv). A distinction

preferred by some is between manageable risks (qv) and entrepreneurial risks (qv). 2. The term risk is also used in connection with the particular insurance or its subject-matter eg business, premises etc. The word is used with great frequency. 3. The economist, Professor Frank Knight distinguished risk, which is insurable, from true uncertainty which is not. By this approach profit is the reward for true uncertainties such as changes in the level of demand for a product or service. Risks become insurable when past data makes it possible to predict or draw inferences about what may happen in the future. This division of risk approximates to the distinction that is made between speculative risks (qv) and pure risks (qv).

risk assumption (also called risk retention). This is where the individual or firm assumes the risk itself. Unplanned risk assumption results from ignorance or inertia, eg the risk of leaving an umbrella on a train may be uninsured and the individual assumes the loss having never contemplated the risk. Often these risks are of an inconsequential nature but it is serious if more costly risks are ignored including those of catastrophe potential because they have a low probability. Planned risk assumption is the result of a conscious decision. A national supermarket chain may decide to carry the risk of damage to its plate glass windows rather than insure as it already has a spread of risks and the maximum probable loss is relatively small. Larger firms have a greater potential for accurately assessing and spreading the risk. However, risk assumption is not exclusive to large firms. The owner of an old car may decide to insure on a third party basis as the value of the car is so low that its loss would not inflict serious financial consequences. *Also see* SELF-INSURANCE.

risk averter. A person who prefers a definite premium, even though it may exceed the loss expectancy, to unknown losses. If the loss expectancy has a monetary value of £50 he will pay more, say, £75 when the loss possibility range is 0–£10 000 given property valued at £10 000.

risk avoidance. This response to risk involves the removal of unacceptable levels of risk by selecting against high risk activities and in favour of those with the minimum amount of risk. For example, the risk of boiler explosion can be avoided by the selection of some other form of heating even though the latter may be more expensive. If risk avoidance means giving up certain activities (eg exporting products to the USA) the cost may be considered too high if more economic alternatives (eg insurance or risk reduction by safer products) are available.

risk combination. The combining of a number of individual risks into homogeneous groups in order that the losses of the few can be shared among the group as a whole. Two people combining to share each other's losses brings no substantial advantages. The large groupings that come together through insurance makes it possible to apply the law of large numbers. With a large number of similar exposure units the outcome of most pure risks can be predicted with an acceptable degree of accuracy for the group as a whole. The larger the number in the group the more reliable will be the outcome so reducing the degree of the residual uncertainty. The outcome for the individual remains uncertain. Risk combination is at the heart of virtually all insurance schemes and continues to bear out the statement made in the preamble to the Elizabethan Act 1601—'the loss lighteth rather easily upon many than heavily upon few'.

risk control. The part of the risk management (qv) process involving decisions and action on those decisions on the handling or controlling the risks after a review of the risk evaluation (qv) process. The insured may decide upon a combination of measures: risk avoidance (qv); risk prevention and pre-loss minimisation (qv); risk transfer (qv) including insurance (qv); risk assumption (qv) including self-insurance (qv). The measures take the form of physical control or financial control.

risk elimination. Means the same as risk avoidance (qv).

risk evaluation. Alternatively called risk measurement it is that part of the risk management (qv) process which involves (a) evaluating the probability and frequency of the risk event occurring; and (b) assessing the potential impact of such losses on the organisation and the potential variation in losses; ranking those losses in order of importance to the organisation.

risk excess. An excess of loss reinsurance contract which is limited to property risks. The reinsured is protected within his overall exposure on an individual risk basis, ie the limit and the deductible apply to 'each and every loss on each and every risk'.

risk financing. The part of the risk management (qv) process which involves making arrangements for the payment or funding of losses that are still likely to occur in an organisation after other measures have been taken. Insurance (qv), line of credit (qv), planned risk assumption (qv), self-insurance (qv), and captives (qv) are all examples of risk financing.

risk identification. The initial step in the risk management (qv) process to establish the risks to which the organisation is exposed. It is carried out by: reviewing all relevant data on business assets, activities and personnel; checking financial statements to identify potential sources of loss; checking all items in the balance sheet and profit and loss account to determine loss exposures. Other techniques include interviewing, observation and preparing flow charts to show all operations of the organisation and all loss-possibility situations at various points in the purchase-process-distribution sequence.

risk management. A concept which stresses the identification, evaluation and control of risks. Risk management has been defined as 'the protection of assets, earnings, liabilities and people of an enterprise with maximum efficiency and minimum cost'. It represents an attempt to reduce the likelihood and magnitude of losses through better understanding, management and the application of control procedures and, secondly, finding the most cost-effective way of financing the losses that still occur. The measures chosen then have to be monitored. Risk control (qv) and risk financing (qv) are at the heart of risk management. Large organisations appoint risk managers often with their own departments to focus upon the pure risks (qv) faced by the firm. *See also* RISK EVALUATION, RISK CONTROL and the RISK MANAGEMENT LOOP.

risk management loop. The risk management (qv) process is never complete. It starts with risk identification (qv), followed successively by risk evaluation (qv), risk control (qv), and monitoring of the risk situation and the effectiveness of the measures taken. The monitoring means that new risks may be identified and old ones may disappear necessitating a constant process of remeasurement, ie risk evaluation with adjustments in the risk control methods adopted. The situation is entirely dynamic.

risk manager. The person appointed to carry out risk management (qv) on behalf of an industrial or commercial organisation or any other organisation where the level or work is sufficient to require the services of a specialist. Risk managers may join the Association of Risk Managers in Industry and Commerce (AIRMIC) (qv).

risk measurement. *See* RISK EVALUATION.

risk (or pure) premium. The amount built into a premium to collect from each policyholder a sufficient amount to cover the present value of expected claims cost (qv) in respect of the class of business or type of risk (*see* EXPERIENCE PREMIUM RATING) concerned for the period of insurance. 'Present value' allows for the fact that premiums are payable in advance. The risk premium is derived from the unit (or measure) of exposure (qv) and the premium rate (qv). The other components in the calculation of the premium are: contingency loading (qv), expenses loading (qv), profit loading.

risk premium method reinsurance. A special form of reinsurance to protect life insurers against losses in excess of their accumulated reserves. The cedant retains all of the investment content of the premium. Cover is against the difference between the cedant's retention and the sum payable at death less accumulated reserves. The main risk is the occurrence of large individual claims by death. The reinsurer is not liable for claims by surrender value or maturity. The reinsurance premium is re-calculated each year as the amount of cover required reduces as the reserves increase. Premiums are heavily discounted in years 1 and 2 to reflect the underwriter's selection process as for these years their mortality experience should be above average. This method is used for permanent (endowment and whole life) policies but not term (or temporary) insurances. The risk premium method has the advantage over original terms reinsurance (qv) in that miscellaneous profits arising out of an excess of interest earned on life funds and profits from lapse and surrender will be available to the cedant.

risk reduction. Measures introduced into an insured organisation to mitigate the effects of risks that cannot realistically be avoided altogether. Specific measures vary according to the situation but the installation of burglar alarms, sprinkler leakage systems, implementation of quality control procedures are all examples. In some instances specific discounts are available from the insurer but in all cases they will have a favourable influence. The decision as to what measures to introduce will be the result of a cost-benefit analysis.

risk retention. *See* RISK ASSUMPTION.

risk retention groups. In the USA in the face of a 'hard market' (qv), a number of trade associations or groups of companies combined to form risk retention groups as allowed under the Liability Risk Retention Act 1986. The groups operate as insurance companies limited to writing liability covers for groups with a common interest. The companies are reliant on the input of capital from members which mean significant amounts. Many of the groups have geared their activities to pollution liability or product liability.

risks attaching. An excess of loss reinsurance of property may describe the period of cover as risks attaching. This means that cover will continue until the expiry of the original risks.

risk transfer. This is where one party transfers the financial effects of his loss to another party. In insurance the insured transfers the possibility of loss to the insurer in return for the premium.

The insured thereby converts the uncertainty of a relatively large loss into the certainty of smaller but fixed annual cost. Other forms of risk transfer can be found in contracts and leases which are used to transfer risk from one party to another to the extent permitted by law (*see* UNFAIR CONTRACT TERMS ACT 1977). Risk transfer of a different kind where an activity is transferred from one party to another, eg the sub-contracting of a process to another party but this could also be termed an example of risk avoidance. *See also* BOTTOMRY BONDS and RESPONDENTIA BONDS.

road. The Road Traffic Act 1988, s. 196 states that for the purpose of the Act road means 'any highway or other road to which the public may have access and includes any bridges over which roads may pass'. A road on a private estate has been held to be a road for Act purposes where the owners have failed to take steps keep the public out other than by erecting a sign saying 'no vehicular public right of way' (*Cox* v *White* (1976)).

Road and Highways Act bond. *See* STREET WORKS BOND.

Road Haulage Association Conditions of Carriage 1991. These standard conditions took effect from 1 June 1991 and have been submitted to the Office of Fair Trading and placed on the public register. They are widely used by RHA members. A number of the conditions are concerned with responsibility for loss of or damage to the goods. Condition 4 deals with loading and unloading and relieves the carrier of liability for damage, however caused, if the carrier is instructed to load or unload goods requiring special appliances which are not provided by the customer as required by the conditions. If the carrier is required to provide any service beyond the usual place of collection or delivery, this service is given at the sole risk of the customer. Condition 4(2) requires the customer to indemnify the carrier against all claims and demands whatever which could not have been made if the customer had not instructed the carrier to load or unload goods with special appliances that should have been provided by the customer. This indemnity also applies when the carrier is instructed to

provide a service beyond the usual place of collection or delivery. Condition 9 (2) provides that in respect of livestock and valuables (bullion, money, securities, stamps, precious metals and stones) the carrier will only be liable if (i) the customer agrees to pay the extra charges arising, and (ii) the loss, misdelivery or damage occurs during transit as a result of a negligent act or omission by the carrier. In respect of other goods the carrier will be liable for loss, misdelivery or carriage during transit unless within one of the stated exceptions and the carrier has used all reasonable care to minimise the effects of those exceptions which are: Act of God; war, invasion etc; seizure or forfeiture under legal process; error, act or omission by the customer or other owner of the goods; inherent waste, latent defect or inherent defect, vice or natural deterioration; insufficient packing etc; insufficient or improper labelling; riot, civil commotion, strike, lockout etc; consignee failing to take delivery of the goods within a reasonable period of time. The carrier is not liable in any circumstances for loss/damage arising after the transit (as defined in the conditions) has ended whether at fault or not. The conditions make provision for the carrier to contract out of the liability arising under Condition 9(2) including liability due to the carrier's acts, omissions or neglect. The carrier takes on a contractual liability that exceeds that which arises at common law and has to bring the loss within one of a number of exceptions to avoid liability. The exceptions relate to matters largely beyond the control of the carrier and do not appear unreasonable. The liability could be insured under a goods in transit (legal liability) policy provided it was not subject to a contractual liability exclusion that would strike out all cover save only the common law liability. Alternatively a goods in transit 'all risks' insurance could be effected. Condition 11 limits the liability of the carrier to the value of the consignment not exceeding £1300 per tonne on the gross weight of the consignment unless the customer has given seven days notice that he requires the carrier to increase his liability above that basic limit. A proportionate amount is paid for loss or damage to part of a consignment. The minimum limit of liability in respect of any one consignment is £10. The carrier does not accept liability for indirect or consequential loss or loss of market. Condition 12 obliges the carrier to insure his liabilities arising under the conditions.

road rescue cover. An insurance offered by some private car insurers to their own policyholders to supplement their car insurance. Typically a policy covers the cost of call-out and roadside repairs (subject to exceptions), vehicle recovery to a garage, hire car to continue a journey or return home, rail fare to cover cost of collecting the car after repair, transportation of the car and occupants to destination or home or overnight hotel accommodation up to specified limits. Home rescue is an extra which involves: (i) assisting the insured at his home or within one mile thereof in respect of call-out charges and up to one hour's labour; and (ii) the cost of transportation, if necessary, of the car and its occupants to the nearest suitable garage or home. A flat premium, which increases with the age of the car, is charged for insurances of this type.

road risks insurance. Most motor traders need a motor policy which permits them to drive their own vehicles and those belonging to customers. The road risks policy provides for insurance against accident, loss or damage while any vehicle (the property of the insured or in his custody or control) described in the policy, is on a road or temporarily garaged during the course of a journey elsewhere than in or on any premises owned in the occupation of the insured. There are alternative bases of rating enabling the proposer to select an appropriate rate to his own needs. Where the number of drivers is small and they are quite fully employed, or where hiring is not a prominent feature, the named driver or trade plate basis is appropriate. The most popular scheme is the points basis which has no restriction as to number plates or drivers. Several factors are taken into account in the rating, such as number of trade plates, number of vehicles owned or held for sale, private hire vehicles etc.

Road Traffic Act 1988 (Compulsory insurance requirements). In accordance with the requirements of the Road Traffic Act 1988 (ss. 143–158) and the Motor Vehicles (Compulsory Insurance) Regulations 1987 (SI 1987 No 2171) (qv) all users (*see* USE OF MOTOR VEHICLES) of motor vehicles on roads in the UK must be insured with an authorised insurer (qv) who is a member of the Motor Insurers Bureau (qv) against liability at law in respect of death or bodily injury to another person (including passengers) or damage to property and also the cost of any emergency treatment (qv) resulting from an accident. Liability for property damage may be limited under the insurance to £250 000 for any one accident. The user or owner is not permitted to exempt himself from liability in respect of injury to passengers. The policy is not required to insure liability in respect of: death or injury to employees arising out of the employment; contractual liability; loss/damage to property in the insured's custody or control; damage to the vehicle; damage to goods carried for hire or reward. By virtue of the Motor Vehicles (Compulsory Insurance) (No 2) Regulations 1973 all policies must include those liabilities which are compulsorily insurable in all other member states of the EEC and non-EC countries, Austria, Czechoslovakia, Finland, Hungary, Sweden and Switzerland. (It is in fact an offence to use a vehicle not so insured even though it may never leave the UK.) Sections 143-156 of the 1988 Act also cover, *inter alia*: motor insurance certificates (qv), duty to satisfy judgments (qv), avoidance of certain agreements as to liability towards passengers (see above), car sharing agreements for private vehicles (qv), bankruptcy of the insured not to affect claims by third parties. Section 143 does not apply to a vehicle owned by a person who has deposited and keeps deposited with the Accountant General of the Supreme Court the sum of £15 000. *See the* MOTOR VEHICLES (THIRD PARTY RISKS DEPOSITS) REGULATIONS 1967. Section 143 also allows a security against third party risks as an alternative to insurance.

robbery. Stealing by force (Theft Act 1968, s. 8).

rollers. A reinsurance system set up in the 1970s under which Lloyd's underwriters and a number of agents arranged reinsurance with companies in circumstances imposing no risk on the companies. Under most of these reinsurance schemes it was agreed that the claims under the scheme were not to exceed the premiums plus interest earned by the company on those premiums, less a commission to the reinsurers. The cedants (qv) could decide when a claim was due and call off the amount required from the reinsurance company subject only to the limits stated. Under most of the contracts any amount unclaimed could be 'rolled forward' as an addition to the indemnity for the ensuing year. This provision led to reinsurances of this type being called rollers. As there was no genuine risk in the first year on the part of the reinsurer, the payments described as reinsurances were in reality general reserves and tax deductions were obtained for these payments.

Rome Convention, 1952. This superseded the Rome Convention of 1933 and similarly deals with compensation to third parties on the ground as a result of death, injury or damage caused by foreign aircraft. It sought to provide a uniform system of compensation and laid down a requirement for the airlines to have compulsory insurance or a financial guarantee with compensation payable upon proof that the damage had been caused by aircraft or operator deemed to be liable for it. Liability was based on a figure related to the take-off weight of the aircraft with a limit of liability of 500 000 gold francs. The major powers have not ratified this Convention.

Room, The. The underwriting room at Lloyd's.

rovers. *See PIRATES.*

Royal Society for the Prevention of Accidents (Ro.SPA). Ro.SPA's accident prevention work is supported by the Association of British Insurers and individual insurance companies in financial, technical, and information terms. Ro.SPA encourages insurers to display and issue its posters and other literature. Insurers are generally represented on the Society's industrial safety committees which operate throughout the UK.

rugs, clothing and personal effects. A section in a comprehensive private policy indemnifying the insured (or the owner of such property at the insured's request) against loss or damage to rugs, clothing and personal effects while in or on the motor car by fire, theft or accidental means. Cover is generally limited to £100 per occurrence.

Rules for Construction of Policy. Twelve rules set out in the Schedule to the Marine Insurance Act 1906 for the purpose of interpreting the marine insurance policy where the context does not otherwise require. The rules relate to such phrases as lost or not lost; at and from; from; from the loading thereof; safely landed; touch and stay; perils of the sea; pirates; thieves; restraint of princes; barratry; all other perils; average unless general; stranded; ship; freight; and goods.

Rules of Practice. Rules established by the Association of Average Adjusters as a guide to average adjusters in their work in adjusting claims.

Running Down Clause (otherwise called the Three-quarters Running Down Clause or Collision Clause). The ordinary form of marine policy does not cover liability for collision damage (*De Vaux* v *Salvador* (1836)) but cover is added by the Running Down clause (Clause 8 of the Institute Time Clauses). The shipowner is thus insured for three-fourths of his liability for damage caused to other vessels up to a limit of three-fourths of the sum insured. Protection and Indemnity Clubs (qv) were formed to enable shipowners to insure the remaining one-fourth collision liability and other liabilities not insured by the hull policy on a mutual insurance basis. The Running Down Clause excludes claims for: loss of life or personal injury; removal of obstructions under statutory powers; cargo or engagements of the insured vessel; damage to stationary objects (eg harbours, piers).

running-off. A situation where an insurer is no longer underwriting new business but continues to meet its liabilities under existing contracts which are said to be running off. A running-off company can obtain a section 68 Order permitting an abridged DTI return to be filed. The running off may be in respect of all business or restricted to a class of business.

run-off. A term describing the settlement of a year of account (or part thereof) over a period of years. The pattern of settlements provides a statistical basis for insurers as a basis for the assessment of estimated liabilities on open years.

run-off account. A year of account of a Lloyd's syndicate which has been left open after the date at which that account would normally have been closed by reinsurance.

running-off company. An insurance company that has ceased to write new business but is still meeting its liabilities. Such a company may have to obtain a section 68 Order (qv) permitting an abridged DTI return to be filed.

run-off liability. The potential liability of an insurer that continues under policies that have terminated.

Rylands v Fletcher (1868). A case which gave its name to a rule of law creating strict liability for injury caused by the escape of a 'mischievous thing' from his land. The rule is 'a person who for his own purposes brings on his land and keeps there anything likely to do damage if it escapes, must keep it at his peril and . . . is answerable for all damage which is the natural consequence of the escape even if . . . guilty of no negligence'. A contractor filled a reservoir on the defendant's land and the water escaped into his neighbour's land. The thing must be brought and kept on the land, and the use of the land must be non-natural (qv). The defences are: default of the plaintiff; Act of God; Act of stranger; statutory authority.

S

sabotage. Wilfully doing illegal damage or other malicious acts to disrupt the insured. The term originates from the French word 'sabot' or wooden shoe, which disgruntled workers would use to damage property.

sacrifice. In marine insurance, certain things are done for the welfare of all interests. *See* GENERAL AVERAGE SACRIFICE.

safe place of work. The employer must take reasonable care to provide a safe place of work. It is not a duty to eliminate every foreseeable risk if the burden of doing so is too onerous (*Latimer* v *AEC Ltd* (1953, HL). 'The duty is not merely to warn against unusual dangers known to them, but also to make the place of employment . . . as safe as the exercise of reasonable skill and care would permit' (*Naismith* v *London Films Production Ltd* (1939)). The duty is higher than that owed to a visitor under the Occupiers' Liability Act 1957 (qv). The duty is not necessarily discharged by giving a warning and also applies to the means of access. Where premises are not under the control of the employer it may be necessary for him to visit them before the employees are put to work for there is a duty not to expose his employees to work on unsafe premises.

safe system of work. An employer has a common law duty to use reasonable care to provide his employees with a safe system of work. The term system of work includes, according to circumstances, such features as the physical layout of the work, the sequence in which the work is to be carried out, the provision where necessary of warnings and notices and the issue of special instructions. A system may have to be modified to meet particular circumstances as they arise. An employer must not only take reasonable care to prescribe a safe system but he must take reasonable care to see that it is followed. The duty applies most commonly where the work is of a uniform or regular nature but it can apply to single operations especially if complicated or unusual (*Winter* v *Cardiff RDC* (1950, HL).

'safeguarding vehicle from loss or damage'. This refers to the physical state of the vehicle and not the driving thereof even though a provisional licence holder as a driver may be in contravention of his licence by not being accompanied by a fully licensed driver (*Rendlesham* v *Dunne (Pennine Insurance Co (Third Party)* (1964)).

'safely landed'. The risk on goods and moveables continues until they are safely landed which must be in the customary manner and within a reasonable time after arrival at the port of discharge, otherwise the risk under the insurance ceases (Marine Insurance Act 1906, Schedule, Rules for Construction, rule 5).

safety certificate. A certificate to be issued by a local authority for each sports ground stand providing covered accommodation for 500 or more spectators. *See* FIRE SAFETY AND SAFETY OF PLACES OF SPORT ACT 1987.

safety loading. *See* LOADING.

sailing warranty. There is an implied warranty in a voyage policy on a ship that the voyage will proceed with reasonable despatch. Unreasonable delay may increase the hazards so permitting the insurer to avoid the policy.

salary sacrifice scheme. A pension arrangement under which the employee agrees, and the employer accepts, to forgo part of his earnings in return for a corresponding contribution by the employer to the scheme.

Sale of Goods Act 1979. An Act containing certain terms as to the quality, fitness, and description of the goods sold under contract in the course of business. The terms implied in contracts of sale have the effect of the seller promising the buyer that the goods are: (i) of merchantable quality (qv) s. 14 (2); (ii) reasonably fit for the purpose intended (qv) s. 14(3); as described (s. 13). If the goods are faulty the seller is likely to be in breach of contract and may be liable in damages including those that are to compensate for injury or damage caused by the faulty product. Liability arises under contract independently of negligence but a trader liable for any breach of duty may have a right of recovery against his own supplier especially if the goods are of a sort that normally get passed on in the form in which they are received by the end user.

salvage. 1. Property which is saved from a misfortune. 2. The remuneration payable under maritime law to third parties who voluntarily and independently of contract render services to maritime property at sea which are of material assistance in saving imperilled property. The third party concerned is the salvor and is entitled to retain possession of the property until the salvage is paid or an adequate security given. If he is not in possession he has a maritime lien which may be enforced in an Admiralty Court.

salvage agreement. If the parties involved in a maritime salvage operation enter into an express agreement the salvor forfeits his right to salvage charges (qv) as he no longer acts independently of contract. However, the parties usually subscribe to Lloyd's Standard Form of Salvage Agreement which, being on a 'no cure-no pay' basis, retains the essential condition of salvage. Under the agreement a successful salvor receives either the sum fixed in the agreement or, alternatively, the amount may have been left to the decision of an arbitrator to be appointed by the Committee of Lloyd's.

Salvage Association. The Committee of Lloyd's (qv), shipowners, merchants, and company underwriters set up the Association in 1856 to protect commercial interests in respect of wrecked and damaged property. The Association's committee now comprises marine insurers only but the Association will act for all interests if they arise in connection with a marine loss if instructed by an interested shipowner. The Association organises surveys, provides expert advice and supervises salvage operations. It has offices in important ports throughout the world which enables it to negotiate contracts for salvage.

salvage charges. Marine salvage charges are the award made to a salvor (qv), acting independently of any contract, who saves or helps to save property at sea. The party rendering the service can lawfully claim salvage in respect of the ship and/cargo actually saved. There can be no salvage award in respect of any property which is not eventually saved (compare SUE AND LABOUR CHARGES). The party whose property is saved can recover the sum payable as salvage charges from his insurer provided the charges were incurred in consequence of the operation of an insured peril. The measure of indemnity is exactly the same as for general average contributions (qv) but in England the salvage award is assessed on the value of the interests at the place where the services successfully terminate. General average contributions are assessed on the net arrived values at the place the voyage ends. *See also* SISTER SHIP CLAUSE.

Salvage Corps. The insurance industry sponsored Salvage Corps in the cities of Glasgow, Liverpool, and London to reduce the amount of a fire loss by attending fires, protecting buildings, salving property, and minimising water damage. The corps are now being phased out.

salvage loss. The loss incurred when goods damaged by a marine peril are sold at a port of refuge because it is reasonably considered they will be worthless by the time of reaching the original destination. The underwriter agrees to pay a total loss but sets against the insured value the net proceeds of the sale.

salvor. A person who saves property. In maritime law salvors have a lien on property saved. *See* SALVAGE.

Sasse affair. An instance of heavy overwriting of premiums (qv) which had serious repercussions for Lloyd's and in particular the 110 members of the syndicate headed by Frederick Sasse.

Excessive amounts were accepted on tenement blocks in New York and this, plus other issues, resulted in a loss of £21.5 m for the syndicate in 1976 and 1977. At one time it was estimated that each of the 110 syndicate members would lose £200 000 thus demonstrating the reality of unlimited liability (qv). Assistance from Lloyd's reduced this to about £60 000 per person. Events such as this prompted Lloyd's to set up a working party under Sir Henry Fisher to look at the Lloyd's regulatory structure and review all aspects of the market's operation. It culminated in the Lloyd's Act 1982 (qv).

satellite. Any manmade body, including spacecraft, launched by rocket into space and put into orbit around the earth. The use of satellites for communications has been greatly extended and and the aviation insurance industry has developed a range of policies to meet the resultant risks. *See* SATELLITE INSURANCE.

satellite consequential loss insurance. An insurance in respect of the consequential loss arising from the loss or partial loss of a satellite. Cover can be effected at any time during the lifespan of the satellite, from erection to the end of its life.

satellite insurance. This is otherwise called space insurance. The cover provided in respect of satellites is related to four phases of the satellite's lifespan. The erection period is covered under erection all risks (qv), the period from completion of assembly to launch is covered under pre-launch insurance (qv), the launch itself is insured under launch insurance (qv), during its working life it is covered under life insurance (qv). Other insurances available are consequential loss (qv) which can be effected during any phase, third party liabililty (qv), and extra expenses from delayed launch (*see* DELAYED LAUNCH).

satellite third party insurance. The re-entry into the atmosphere of two Russian Cosmos satellites has created a demand for third party insurance in connection with satellites in orbit.

satisfaction certificate. In motor insurance the insured must sign a satisfaction certificate before the insurer settles the repairer's account following an accident. Without the certificate the insurers could face complaints relating to the manner in which the work had been done.

schedule. The part of an insurance policy which sets out the detail which is specific to the individual contract. The insured is identified in the schedule by name and address. Other details common to nearly every case include the policy inception date (qv), the period of insurance, and the premium. The additional detail varies according to the nature of the insurance and type of insured, ie personal or business, which will determine whether it is the occupation, trade, business or profession that will be stated. Other details will relate to the property insured together with the sum insured and any special terms that have been agreed.

schedule policy. A policy form that has superseded the narrative form. All parts of the policy are clearly defined in sections and will be standardised for each type of insurance. The schedule (qv) itself carries the details peculiar to each individual insurance.

scheme administrator. The administrator of a pension scheme. In the terms of the Finance Act 1970, s. 26(1) he is 'the person(s) having management of the scheme'. The administrator has a general duty to ensure that the scheme is operated in accordance with the requirements of the authorities and its own trust deed and rules. He may have to give certain undertakings to the Superannuation Funds Office covering various matters including entry/exits of participating employees, transfer payments, general reporting requirements on refunds to employees, commutation in serious ill-health and triviality, and return of excess policy proceeds to the employer. The administrator is the key link between the scheme and the Inland Revenue.

school fees insurance. A life insurance effected for the purpose of providing cash at relevant times to assist the insured in the payment of school fees. A with profits endowment policy can be used with the sum insured payable in stages or against which loans can be taken out under the policy periodically after the policy has run for a planned number of years. The loans are then repaid out of policy proceeds when they become available on death or maturity. In the meantime the premiums and interest are paid by the policyholder. The insured who is able to pay school fees out of income may effect a decreasing term insurance to cover future fees in the event of his premature death before completion of the fee-paying period.

scienter. An allegation in a pleading that something has been done knowingly. At common law scienter referred to the knowledge that an owner had that his animal was wild or had dangerous propensities. When such knowledge could be imputed to the animal owner he was strictly liable for injuries caused by the animal whether wild by nature or known by its owner to be dangerous. Liability for animals is now governed by the Animals Act 1971.

scorching. Fire (qv) involves actual ignition. Scorching of materials placed too near to heat is therefore not fire damage within the meaning of fire as an insured peril. Scorching consequent upon a fire will be covered under the doctrine of proximate cause (qv) having been the natural and probable consequence of an insured peril.

seasonal increase clause. A clause to provide an automatic increase in the sum insured under policies where seasonal increases in stock values would render the existing sum insufficient. Clauses of this kind are typically but not exclusively used in connection with hotel, public house and similar establishments. The effect is to increase the sum insured on stock and other contents by a predetermined percentage, eg 50 per cent for stated periods of time during the year (eg Christmas period). The insured can negotiate an alteration in the periods stated in the clause if they are at variance with his own requirements. The clause helps the insured to avoid penalties for under-insurance while also avoiding the over-insurance that would occur if the maximum value at risk was fixed as the sum insured for the whole period of insurance.

seasonal risk. A risk or an increase in risk that attaches during only a part of the year.

seaworthiness. There is an implied warranty of seaworthiness in voyage policies (qv). To be seaworthy, the ship must be reasonably fit to encounter the ordinary perils of the sea of the voyage insured, ie competent in hull, and properly equipped with tackle and stores, etc. In the case of a steamship, it also means having an adequate fuel supply. There is no such warranty in a time policy (qv) but the insurer will not be liable for losses attributable to unseaworthiness of which the insured was aware when putting to sea in that state.

seaworthiness admitted. It is implied in cargo policies that the ship used for the carriage is seaworthy. As the cargo owners have no control over the condition of the ship, insurers introduce a Seaworthiness Admitted clause. The effect is that the insurer will not raise unseaworthiness as a defence to a claim under the policy by the cargo owner.

second loss insurance. A policy which is designed to contribute to a loss only when the loss exceeds the sum payable by a first loss policy (*see* AVERAGE for two conditions of average). A first loss policy contributes first to a loss which is covered in a less specific way under the second loss policy.

secondary exposure. The exposure to risk of a person not directly involved in the risk-producing process or activity but through an association with another person who was so exposed. For example, Mrs Gunn died of mesothelioma caused by inhaling asbestos dust from her husband's working clothes (*Gunn* v *Wallsend Slipway & Engineering Co. Ltd* (1989)).

second-hand bonds. A former tax avoidance device under which single premium life policies were sold by the original purchaser (eg a broker or agent) to the person really wishing to make the investment and hold the policy. This put the gains on non-qualifying policies out of reach of the income tax provision (*see* CHARGEABLE EVENTS) to become an asset subject to the lower rated capital gains tax. The Finance Act 1983, s. 18 closed this device by imposing income tax on gains arising from non-qualifying policies and annuities that are assigned for money or money's worth and not held by the original beneficial owner.

secret commission. A commission taken by an agent without the consent of his principal. In doing so the agent, who is required to exercise good faith in the performance of his duty, is in breach of that duty and forfeits his rights against the principal in regard to the relevant transaction. An employee, for example, must not accept an insurance commission on his employer's insurance without the employer's permission. Solicitors and assessors acting for third parties in liability claims are agents and payments to them by the insurers for their own benefit will be secret commission unless disclosed to, and agreed by, their principals. Insurers include a statement in their discharge forms on settlement referring to the payments of fees and costs. Secret commissions are forbidden by the Prevention of Corruption Act 1906 and any recipient is liable to criminal prosecution.

Section 68 Order. A Department of Trade and Industry concession to waive or modify certain requirements of insurance companies legislation for a particular insurance company.

Section 226 policy (s. 226 policy). A pension policy to which an employee not a member of a pension scheme or a self-employed person can contribute towards his pension. Since 1 July 1988, new s. 226 policies have to be personal pension plans (qv).

Section 32 buy-out. The option, on leaving a pension scheme, to transfer preserved benefits to an insurance company chosen by the individual. The option takes its name from the legislation, the Finance Act 1981, s. 32, that first facilitated this choice.

Section 49 Scheme. An occupational pension scheme which was formerly contracted out and which is still subject to supervision by the Occupational Pensions Board (qv) under the Social Security Pensions Act 1975, s. 49.

Securities and Investments Board (SIB). A special body with substantial regulatory powers under the Financial Services Act 1986 (qv). Its aim is to produce a consistent level of both investor protection and overall efficiency in the financial markets. A detailed rulebook puts the principles of investor protection into practice. The regulatory sanctions available to the Board range from reprimands, instigating criminal proceedings, through civil actions to obtain restitution of clients funds, where appropriate, and the withdrawal of authorisation from an investment business. It seeks to ensure that those providing any form of investment service are 'fit and proper to do so'. SIB can authorise investment businesses directly and does so in the case of very large concerns but in the main delegates its powers to Self-Regulatory Organisations (SROs) (qv) and Recognised Professional Bodies (RPBs) (qv). Excluded from the Board's responsibilities are some areas involving listing requirements for public issues, takeovers and mergers and insider dealing investigation and prosecution. Board members, including a full-time executive chairman, are appointed jointly by the Secretary of State for Trade and Industry and the Governor of the Bank of England. The SIB has established an independent procedure to investigate complaints and rules relative thereto are contained in the rules of the SROs. The SIB has also set up the investors' compensation fund under the operation of the Financial Services Compensation Manager Ltd. *See also* INVESTMENT BUSINESS and INDEPENDENT FINANCIAL ADVISER.

Security against third party risks. This may be provided as an alternative to insurance for the purpose of compliance with the Road Traffic Act's compulsory insurance requirements. Section 143 refers to a policy or insurance or a security . . . as complies with this part of the Act. This means that the security must be given by an authorised insurer or some other body carrying on the business of giving securities who has deposited £15 000 with the Accountant General of the Supreme Court in respect of that business. The security must consist of an undertaking to make good (subject to any conditions specified therein) any failure by the owner of the vehicle or such other persons or classes specified to discharge any 'Act' liability (s. 145 sets this out) required to be covered by a policy of insurance. The security must be for a sum of £25 000 in the case of public service vehicles and £50, 000 other vehicles. As a rule these securities are written by fidelity guarantee insurers. The security is of no effect for the purposes of the Act until a certificate in the prescribed form is issued to the person to whom the security is granted.

select mortality table. A mortality table based on selected lives only and not the general population, eg lives accepted for insurance.

selection. The process whereby an insurer decides how to categorise and rate risks (eg high, medium or low premiums according to the degree of risk), which categories should be excluded and how individual risks are to be treated. The aim is to produce a balanced portfolio, obtain a good spread of risk and secure premium contributions commensurate with the degree of hazard brought to the fund.

selection against the insurer. Insurance offered to insurers when the insured has a special motive for insuring, eg enquiries for insurance of property against subsidence and landslip mainly arise when a degree of hazard exists. There is also a tendency for the insured to insure only the hazardous aspects of a particular risk. *See also* ANTI-SELECTION.

selection of lives. The practice in life insurance of segregating 'lives' into categories of standard, sub-standard, and declined. The main object is to guard against anti-selection as the sub-standard lives are those with the greatest incentive to insure. This would disturb the mortality balance and the premiums charged would be inadequate. Standard lives are accepted on normal terms while sub-standard (ie impaired lives (qv)) are rated according to the nature of the impairment in the particular case. The main principles governing selection are: age, health (*also see* AIDS), occupation, place of residence, and hazardous pursuits.

select rate of mortality. This occurs when rates of mortality are differentiated by age and duration. Most mortality tables used in life assurance have two or three periods of select mortality.

self-administered pension schemes. Small self-employed pension schemes effectively enable the members and trustees of the scheme to control the investment policy. Such schemes are restricted to less than 12 members—in effect small companies and partnerships. This enables the company or partnership to borrow up to 50 per cent of the value of the scheme for the purpose of the business. The schemes are otherwise called privately administered schemes.

'self damage'. Actual damage to the insured item from internal rather than external causes. It is a feature of certain engineering insurance (qv) policies.

self-drive hire. The hiring out by a business in the motor trade or specialist company of a vehicle for a limited period on the understanding that the customer will be permitted to drive. Insurance can be arranged as a section of a motor traders' policy or by separate insurance. Most self-drive companies operate on a third party only basis (qv) as they have a sufficiently wide spread of risks to practise risk assumption (qv) in respect of accidental damage to their vehicles. The self-drive policy typically defines acceptable vehicles, eg saloons, vans and lorries up to 7.5 tons gross vehicle weight, motorised caravans, all not more than ten years old, and minibuses up to seven years old with seating for up to 15 including the driver. Acceptable drivers are experienced drivers between 21 and 70 years old, free of physical defect, and with a good history in terms of accidents and convictions, and not employed in certain 'excluded occupations', such as professional entertainment and sport, publicans and their staff, bookmakers, students, and itinerant merchants. The third party section protects the insured and the hirer and the policy contains excesses under the material damage section with the amounts being increased for young drivers (under 25s).

self-insurance. A risk financing (qv) method used by organisations which feel financially large enough to carry their own risks or at least some of them. At its simplest it means making deductions from the firm's revenue each year to create a reserve fund to cover future losses. Self-insurance is the result of a conscious decision as a result of the risk management (qv) process. The organisation sets aside funds to cover future losses. This does not preclude the purchase of insurance from commercial insurers who may provide cover in excess of the amount of risk retained and financed by way of self-insurance. The ultimate in self-insurance is the creation of a captive insurance company (qv).

self-investment. This means investment of part or all of the resources of a self-administered scheme in the business of the employer or that of an associated company in any of a range of investments, viz: shares and securities; mortgages on real property occupied by the company; freeholds and leaseholds owned by the fund's trustees but leased to the company but not freeholds and leaseholds let or leased to another organisation which sub-lets to the company; secured or unsecured loans to the company; unpaid interest, dividends, or rents on any of the investments in any of the foregoing.

Self-Regulatory Organisations (SROs). Organisations that are the chief means by which the requirements of the Securities and Investments Board (qv) are implemented at the level of the individual company or person. Each SRO has produced a rule book to which members must adhere and which must be agreed with the SIB in order for the SRO to be recognised. The rule book must offer protection to the investor in accordance with the requirements of the Financial Services Act 1986 and must be at least as stringent as the SIB's own rule book. They regulate the carrying on of investment business (qv) by their members, investigate problems reported to them, set up a complaints procedure and support the Investors' Compensation Scheme (qv). They are called 'self-regulatory' because their senior officers are, in the main, people from the industry to which the organisation applies. Each SRO has to be examined and approved as suitable for its duties by the SIB. The SRO for the marketing of life insurance and unit trusts (qv) is the Life Assurance and Unit Trust Regulatory Organisation (LAUTRO) (qv). For the other SROs *see* the ASSOCIATION OF FUTURES BROKERS AND DEALERS

(AFBD), the FINANCIAL INTERMEDIARIES, MANAGERS AND BROKERS REGULATORY ASSOCIATION (FIMBRA), the INVESTMENT MANAGEMENT REGULATORY ORGANISATION (IMRO), and THE SECURITIES ASSOCIATION (TSA). Members of SROs must appoint compliance officers to ensure that the rules imposed on them are observed.

senior captive. A captive insurer that has developed into a normal insurer taking risks from the market generally.

sentimental damage. A type of loss that cannot be recovered under a marine insurance policy. When cargo has been carried in a vessel that has suffered a casualty the fear of possible damage to the cargo causes it to be sold below normal price whereas the cargo proves to be sound. The resultant loss is sentimental damage and is uninsured.

sentimental value. The value that a person attaches to property or a person that is derived from feelings of emotion and affection and which is not related to monetary values. Such values cannot be insured as there is no way in which a loss could be quantified. Insurance is founded upon insurable interest (qv) which implies having a financial involvement with the subject-matter of insurance.

SERPS. *See* STATE EARNINGS RELATED PENSION SCHEME.

service risk. A life insurance/personal accident underwriting term in respect of the higher risk of accidental death in respect of a member of the armed forces. Life insurers may only require special terms when the proposer is about to proceed to a disturbed area or is engaged in inherently hazardous activities, eg bomb disposal. One approach is to charge an additional premium for a limited term, eg seven years.

services business. Overseas insurance or reinsurance business from overseas that is placed directly in the UK market. This is otherwise called cross frontier business and the underwriting profits make a substantial contribution to the UK's balance of payments as an invisible export. An insurer accepting business in this way is often termed a non-admitted insurer.

services clause. The name given to the clause in the fire policy on buildings in respect of the cover provided on items such as telephones, gas, waterpipes, and cabling which are partly outside the building. The cover is on an 'accidental damage' basis and applies to property belonging to the insured or that for which he is responsible.

services rendered insurance. A credit insurance (qv) in respect of the sums due in respect of services rendered as opposed to goods supplied.

set-off. A claim in a liquidated amount by the defendant who wishes to set it against the money claim made against him by the plaintiff. The amount may be included in the defence whether or not it is added as a counter-claim.

settled policy. A policy forming the subject of a trust (qv).

settlement. 1. An agreement to resolve a dispute. Many liability claims are resolved by out of court settlements. 2. A payment of an account or claim. 3. In respect of buildings it means movement in a lateral direction but in practice it is not so restricted. Every new property settles on its foundations and the stresses and strains of this movement cause cracks in the plaster and other minor damage. It is not easy to distinguish the damage caused by subsidence (qv) from the damage caused by settlement. 4. A document, such as a deed or will, defining the way of succession to land or other property or of enjoyment of the rents and profits thereof.

settling agent. *See* AGENT (11).

seven day clause. An hours clause (qv) that extends the period to 7 days. Some catastrophe occurrences may last for this period. The clause usually refers to 168 consecutive hours rather than 7 days.

seven year summary. A summary of the last seven closed (or run-off) accounts forming part of the annual report sent to Names (qv).

seventy-five (75)% rule. *See* QUALIFYING POLICIES.

severe inflation clause. A special form of the stability index clause (qv) which becomes operative only when the inflation rate exceeds a predetermined high level, eg 40 per cent. This means that the base index will be altered to 1.4 × Index at base date.

shadow director. A director with the same liabilities as formally appointed directors of a company. *See* DIRECTORS.

shareholders' funds. Insurance company funds that are not tied to liabilities to policyholders. They are also known as free reserves (qv).

shareholders' share purchase. *See* CROSS OPTION AGREEMENT.

ship. The First Schedule (rule 15) of the Marine Insurance Act 1906 states that the term 'includes the hull, materials and outfit, stores and provisions for the officers and crew, and in the case of vessels in a special trade, the ordinary fittings requisite for the trade, and also, in the case of a steamship, the machinery, boilers, and coals and engine stores, if owned by the assured'.

ship value. This is usually agreed each year between the shipowner and the leading underwriter.

shipowner's liability. The liability of a shipowner for loss, injury or damage to others or the property of others arising in tort, contract or under statute. *See* PROTECTION AND INDEMNITY CLUBS and RUNNING DOWN CLAUSE.

shipped bill. A bill of lading (qv) issued after the goods have actually been loaded. Under the Carriage of Goods by Sea Act 1971 (qv) a shipper may demand such a bill from the shipowner. Normally it is achieved by adding to the received for shipment bill (qv) the name of the vessel concerned and the date of shipment.

ships crew exclusion. A standard exclusion in a personal accident catastrophe excess of loss reinsurance. The accumulation of risk plus the exposure to regular danger are the reasons for the exclusion.

shop insurance. A business insurance for retailers who can acquire a package policy with standard cover or a tailor-made insurance covering a range of risks in one document as a result of the insured choosing from the alternatives available.

short closing. The practice by a broker in the marine market of overplacing the risk, ie securing acceptances that exceed the available cover with the result that, on closing, the line written by each underwriter is reduced proportionately. In this way the broker is able to spread the risk more widely in the market.

short period. An insurance for less than the normal period of insurance of twelve months. A higher premium may be charged than that calculated on a strict pro rata basis.

short tail. A term which describes insurance business where it is known that claims will generally be notified and settled quickly.

sickness benefit. A weekly or monthly benefit available as an add-on to the accident only (personal accident (qv)) policy or as the principal benefit under a permanent health insurance (qv). When the benefit is an add-on, the policy is known as a personal accident and sickness policy (qv) under which the selected benefits are payable for up to 52 weeks or 104 weeks depending on the insurer. *See also* INCOME BENEFIT.

signed lines/written lines. The written line is the one written on the slip when the risk is first offered to the underwriter. If the risk is overplaced there will be a short-closing (qv) meaning that all acceptances will be scaled down on a pro rata basis. The reduced line is known as the signed line.

signing down. The pro rata reduction of written lines where a slip (qv) has been more than 100 per cent subscribed.

silent risk. A risk or insurance in respect of premises where no activities are currently undertaken and no machinery used.

simple reversionary bonus. A bonus added to with profit life insurance policies which is expressed as a percentage of the sum insured only. Bonuses once declared are guaranteed and are paid with the sum insured when a claim is made at death or maturity.

simplified approval. A pension scheme approval procedure laid down in Joint Office Memorandum No. 94. *See* SIMPLIFIED PENSION SCHEMES.

simplified pension schemes. These are either simplified defined contribution schemes (qv) or simplified final salary schemes (qv) subject to the simplified approval procedure described in Joint Office Memorandum No. 94. These schemes may only be placed with authorised insurers. Membership of concurrent schemes other than those providing death in service and income benefits is not permitted. There are no restrictions in respect of benefits from other schemes for previous employment. A simplified final salary scheme does not allow membership/contributions for free-standing AVCs (qv); the basic pension must be in terms of 1/80th for each year of service (max. 40 years) but additional employer/employee contributions may boost this to 1/60th for each year (max. 40) with commutation rights at 3/120ths for each year for the basic pension and 3/80ths for each year if augmented (max. 40 years); no optional dependants' pension is allowed and lump-sum benefits cannot exceed twice final remuneration. Also no use of the uplifted tables for pension/cash is allowed. A simplified defined contribution scheme varies little from the normal. The main points are that contributions are limited to 17.5 per cent of which the employer may pay up to 15 per cent and the contributions limit of 17.5 per cent includes the national insurance rebates, incentive and any free-standing AVCs.

simultaneous payments clause. A clause in a reinsurance contract binding the reinsurer to pay a claim at the same time that the direct insurer makes a payment to the original insured.

single article limit. A limit as to the maximum amount an insurer will pay in respect of any one article. The limit is introduced into policies covering designated forms of property, eg personal effects or valuables (qv), on a collective basis under one sum insured, as a safeguard against under-insurance and unwittingly covering items of special value. The limit obliges the insured to specify any articles the value of which exceeds the limit.

single contract policy. A construction industry policy arranged for one particular contract.

single liability. As between shipowners whose ships have collided, in accordance with maritime law, where both ships are to blame, there are not two liabilities. There is single liability meaning the owner of the ship with the greater share of blame pays the other the difference between their respective liabilities. However, marine hull policies provide that claims shall be settled on the basis of cross liabilities (qv).

single premium. An insurance under which one premium only is payable for the duration of the insurance. In restrictive covenants (qv) and similar contingency policies one premium secures cover for an indefinite term. *See also* SINGLE PREMIUM BONDS.

single premium bonds. A policy issued by a life insurer in return for a single premium as opposed to regular premium payments. Since 1968 they have been non-qualifying policies so that the proceeds are subject to tax when received by the policyholder. After deductions for expenses and some limited life cover in respect of premature death the rest of the lump sum premium is invested usually in unitised funds (qv). The bond itself will provide guarantees in terms of income (*see* INCOME BONDS) or capital growth (*see* GROWTH BONDS. Life offices have fewer restrictions on their investments than unit trusts (qv) allowing unit-linked life insurers to offer a range of funds with bond switching (qv) facilities. Some insurers offer investment in unit trusts of which they are the managers. Insurance companies receive favourable treatment in respect of both corporation tax and capital gains tax and this enables them to secure investment advantages not available to the individual investor. Under some single premium bonds further premiums can be paid at any time. Under the Financial Services (Cancellation) Rules 1988 the policyholder has a right to cancel the agreement within 14 days of the receipt of the Notice of the Right to Cancel.

single premium method. A pensions method of determining the premiums payable under an insurance contract with the object of meeting within each year the cost of benefits relating to that year.

sinking fund policy. *See* CAPITAL REDEMPTION POLICY.

Sister Ship clause. This is Clause 9 of the Institute Time Clauses and follows the Running Down clause (qv). If two vessels in the same ownership or management collide or render salvage services to each other, there will be no right of recovery one against the other as a person cannot sue himself. The Sister Ship clause ensures that the insured's rights are not prejudiced by providing for the appointment of an arbitrator who will apportion liability as if the vessels had been in separate ownership. The insurer agrees to be bound accordingly.

sliding scale reinsurance commission. A system whereby the rate of reinsurance commission payable by the reinsurer is, within limits, directly related to the loss ratio of the treaty. Usually the reinsurer pays the minimum rate of commission on the premium received for one year at the end of which the loss ratio is calculated. This ratio is applied to a sliding scale to give the actual rate of commission to be paid. The lower the ratio the higher will be the commission payable to the ceding office.

sliding scale treaty. An excess of loss treaty under which the reinsurer's rate of premium is calculated on the burning cost method (qv) with minimum and maximum rates being agreed. *See* ESCAPE CLAUSE.

slip. The paper or electronic slip upon which the insurance broker sets out details of a risk proposed for insurance. If an underwriter accepts all or part of the risk, the underwriter initials the slip and marks down the proportion he is prepared to accept. The leading underwriter (qv) also inserts the rate to be charged and which will be followed by other underwriters. When the risk is fully written the contract is concluded. In practice the broker frequently overplaces the risk which then has to be written down proportionately for each underwriter (*see* SHORT CLOSING). The broker cannot increase any underwriter's share without specific agreement. Companies and Lloyd's underwriters may appear on the same slip.

slip agreement. An addition to the slip (qv) expressing the underwriter's agreement to an issue agreed by the underwriter after his initial acceptance.

slip policy. A slip (qv) which is signed and sealed by the relevant signing office in order to become the policy. The slip is used in this way for both marine hull and cargo risks. In the latter instance a certificate is issued and in all cases a formal policy will be issued on request.

small claims pool. Funds pooled by all Lloyd's syndicates out of which all small claims are paid.

smoke damage. 1. Damage done by smoke rather than an actual ignition. If the smoke has its origin in actual ignition the damage is fire damage for the purpose of the policy in accordance with the doctrine of proximate cause (qv). In the USA the extended cover endorsement includes, subject to restrictions, smoke damage even though there may be no ignition. 2. There may also be liability attaching to a person who pollutes the atmosphere by smoke originating from his premises or control. *See* POLLUTION.

social, domestic and pleasure use. A class of use (qv) in private car insurance. It means that cover under the policy is restricted to use of the car for private purposes including journeys between the insured's home and normal place of work provided no business calls are made on that journey. No element of business is allowed. This is the most restricted form as to use in which cover can be arranged and may or may not attract a discount from the rates for class 1 use.

Social Security Act 1986. An Act which, *inter alia*, makes important pension provisions: SERPS (qv) will reduce gradually from the year 2000 and will be reduced from 25 per cent of earnings to 20 per cent. The SERPS pension will be based on career average earnings and not just the best 20 years. Company schemes must provide 3 per cent annual increases on post April 1988 guaranteed minimum pensions (GMPs) (qv). GMPs will be reduced but are extended to widowers' benefits. The preserved pension requirements for early leavers now apply after two years' service instead of five. Contracting out has been simplified by the introduction of money-purchase tests and 'requisite benefits' have been abolished. Importantly, employees covered by occupational schemes can opt out of them and choose a personal pension or go into SERPS on an individual basis. There is an incentive to contract out as an extra 2 per cent of upper tier earnings will be paid until 1993 by the Government to new contracted-out schemes. The minimum contribution to personal pensions is equal to the 'contracting out' rebate. The Act authorises new pension providers (eg banks and building societies) but only insurance companies are permitted to sell annuities. Company schemes must offer the opportunity for members to pay additional voluntary contributions (AVCs) (qv).

Society of Fellows. A society created by the Chartered Insurance Institute to encourage continuing study by diploma-holders and stimulate research within the Institute. Membership is restricted to Fellows of the Chartered Insurance Institute. The objectives of the society are to: provide an environment in which Fellows can contribute to insurance education; encourage continuing professional development by providing an organisation and guidelines; sponsor research; organise seminars and discussion groups; maintain and develop educational links with universities and professional bodies in the UK and overseas; contribute to the maintenance and enhancement of the CII as a professional body and to its achievement of status of a learned society; engage in any other activities conducive to the achievements of the foregoing objectives and to enhance the status of Fellows generally.

'soft' disclosure of commission. *See* DISCLOSURE 2.

soft market. A market in which there is a ready supply of insurance for insureds. Competition among insurers drives premium rates down and terms and conditions ease as insureds find themselves able to negotiate better terms. The market for industrial and commercial risks is of a cyclical nature and when the premiums fall below an economic rate, suppliers leave the market which then begins to 'harden'. *See* HARD MARKET.

'solely and independently of any other cause'. This a key phrase the effect of which is to require that bodily injury shall be caused accidentally (as defined, *see* ACCIDENT) and that, in turn, the injury must directly and independently result in death or disablement. If any other event contributes to the outcome the insurer will not be liable notwithstanding that an accident within the meaning of the policy has occurred. An accident may activate a dormant disease which may or may not contribute to the result. It may prolong or cause the disablement and the effect of the accident is merely to lead to an earlier diagnosis than would otherwise have been the case. The sufferer may have a hernia or be in the first stages of tuberculosis. If the insured merely has a predisposition to hernia, then the injury is due to the accident and not the insured's condition because it did not previously exist (*Claxton* v *Travellers Insurance Co of Hartford* (1917)). Alternatively an existing disease may have no affect at all and any death or disablement may remain wholly attributable to the accident. If it is not possible to separate the effects the insurer will not be liable. In *Cawley* v *National Employers Assurance Association* (1885) a man suffering from gallstones suffered an accidental blow and died. He would not have died from gallstones and the blow by itself would not have killed him. In the absence of the phrase solely and independently etc or a specific exclusion, the insurer would have been liable but the policy did not operate as the accident was not the sole cause of the death. Neither is there any cover for death when the insured in hospital with a broken leg contracts an infectious disease with fatal results. There will be no liability for the death but there will be liability for any disablement entirely attributable to the accident prior to the death.

Solicitors Act (Amendment) 1974. This obliges solicitors to carry professional indemnity insurance (qv) with a limit of at least £50 000 or £30 000 for each partner in a partnership. Insurance must be arranged through the Law Society Scheme.

solvency. As insurers sell promises of financial security their own solvency is sufficiently important to be defined in special terms (*see* TECHNICAL INSOLVENCY). It is not enough that a company's assets should be sufficient to cover its liabilities. Assets and liabilities have to be valued and it is a fundamental principle of insurance company supervision that assets must exceed liabilities by a minimum amount. A company which fails to maintain this minimum faces winding-up on the grounds of insolvency. The Insurance Companies Act 1982 lays down margins of solvency (qv) for new and existing companies in the UK. *See also* FREE RESERVES and TECHNICAL RESERVES.

solvency margin. *See* MARGIN OF SOLVENCY.

sonic bangs clause. A sonic bang is the result of pressure waves caused by aircraft travelling at sonic or supersonic speeds. A clause excluding damage caused in this way is incorporated into all policies other than those covering solely employers' liability, public liability, personal accident, theft, fidelity guarantee, or contract guarantee. In motor insurance, the exclusion appears only in respect of any 'own damage' cover that may be included.

space insurance. *See* SATELLITE INSURANCE.

special circumstances clause. A clause in a business interruption policy (qv) under which, when a claim is assessed, adjustments can be made to allow for the trend of the business and for variations in or special circumstances affecting the business. The aim is to produce a figure that as nearly as possible represents the results that would have been achieved by the business but for the interruption caused by the damage. The clause is otherwise called the 'exceptional circumstances clause' or 'bracket provisions'.

special condition of average. *See* AVERAGE.

special drawing rights (SDRs). An international reserve asset. This means that, in transactions between central banks in different countries, SDRs are treated as money and are an acceptable way of settling international debts. They are issued by the International Monetary Fund with the value of an SDR now being expressed daily by reference to a basket of 16 currencies. The SDR is used in the Warsaw Convention (qv) as a monetary unit on which limits of liability are based.

special peril. Any risk added to a policy not originally written to cover that risk (eg storm and tempest cover added to a fire policy). Special perils is the term used for insurance consisting of a collection of the following perils: dry perils (qv), wet perils, and miscellaneous perils added to a fire policy and included with fire cover in household comprehensive policies. Additional perils (qv) is an alternative term.

'special purpose' captive. A captive insurance company formed to finance a particular exposure. It provides an in-house facility for totally or partially financing risks where conventional insurance may be considered expensive or difficult to obtain. Such exposure may include professional indemnity, credit or insolvency risks, product guarantee, warranty or other 'special situations'.

'special relationship'. *See* NEGLIGENT STATEMENT.

special reserve fund scheme. A scheme approved by the Inland Revenue under which Names (qv) at Lloyd's are allowed to set aside a small tax-deductible amount of their underwriting income. The reserve is available to meet underwriting losses if the need arises.

special types. A generic term used by motor insurers to describe vehicles or mobile plant designed for special purposes. They may be insured under motor, engineering or public liability policies. Some insurers take the view that, apart from the compulsory Road Traffic Act cover, that these are essentially risks for the engineering and public liability departments. The special types category includes: mobile cranes, self-propelled contractors' plant, mobile shops, dust carts, road sweepers, tower wagons, and watercarts. They may be used on the road but are most often used on sites as a tool of trade (qv).

special waiver clause. A clause in certain professional indemnity policies under which the insurer agrees not to exercise their right to avoid the policy where there is an allegation of non-disclosure or misrepresentation of facts or untrue statements at inception or any subsequent renewal. The insured has to establish that the non-disclosure, misrepresentation, or untrue statement was entirely innocent. Where the non-disclosure prejudices any claim, the insurer is able to reduce the amount payable to the sum that would have been payable in the absence of such prejudice.

special settlement. A transaction through Lloyd's Central Accounting when a premium or claim is paid outside the normal monthly settlement. It occurs where the brokers or underwriters require settlement quickly, normally within seven days.

specification. Usually it amplifies the schedule (qv) and gives details of the breakdown of the total sum insured shown in the schedule. Additional clauses may also appear in the specification.

specified motor cycle insurance policy. A motor cycle policy under which the cover operates only in respect of a specified motor cycle as notified to the insurer. *See* MOTOR CYCLE RIDER POLICY for an alternative way of arranging cover.

specified (or named) perils. The events listed in an insurance policy which, if their happening causes a loss or damage to the subject-matter insured, will constitute a valid claim. This differs from all risks insurance (qv) which covers all risks of loss or damage that are not excluded.

specified vehicle insurance. A goods in transit insurance (qv) covering the goods whilst in, on or unloaded from, specific vehicles or trailers for an agreed sum for each vehicle and trailer. It is usual to make each sum insured subject to pro rata average (*See* AVERAGE.) This is an alternative to a declaration policy which covers the goods while in, on or being unloaded from any road vehicle (or railway train) and whilst temporarily housed in the course of transit.

specified working expenses. A business interruption term describing business expenses that are not at the risk of the insured perils as they vary according to the level of production. For example, carriage and packing expenses cease to be payable when a business is not operating and should not therefore be insured as a part of the gross profit (qv).

specifics. Items which are specific to a particular insurance and not generally applicable. There may be specific exclusions or additions endorsed or written into the policy.

speculative risk. A risk where the outcome may range from loss to gain. The prospect of gain induces businessmen to take risks. They may or may not sell their goods or services at a profit. They may be eased out by competitors or they may be adversely affected by a downturn in the economy. Firms often succeed at the expense of others. Businesses seek to control their speculative risks by means of sound business practices such as market research, cost control, stock control etc and they can form limited liability companies. Insurance is not available to protect firms against business failure as such an insurance would remove much of the incentive for efficiency. Moreover, no insurance fund would be sustainable as profit-making firms would not be prepared to contribute some of their profits to create a fund from which inefficient firms would be compensated. Unlike pure risks (qv), losses having their origin in speculative risks do not strike at random.

spent convictions. *See* REHABILITATION OF OFFENDERS ACT 1974.

spontaneous combustion. This means overheating by oxidation without the application of external heat. Some substances heat spontaneously more readily than others. The risk can be minimised by careful attention to storage and use. The standard fire policy excludes damage to property happening through its own spontaneous fermentation or heating but the actual fire damage communicated therefrom to other property is covered. In marine insurance when insuring commodities (eg bituminous coal) which are liable to spontaneous combustion, it is customary to specifically include fire or heating damage to the property from this cause. As with the fire policy, the fire damage communicated to other property (eg ship and other cargo) is covered in any event.

spread loss reinsurance. A form of excess of loss reinsurance cover. A ceding office may limit the amount it retains in respect of any one loss but over a period, usually five years, it pays premiums to the reinsurer for all of the loss it has recovered under the treaty plus a loading to cover the reinsurer's expenses and profit. The ceding office 'spreads' its losses over a five year period. Similarly a stop loss reinsurance can be spread so that it covers a period in excess of one accounting year.

spreader clause. A clause in an aviation policy providing that if the declared number of passengers is exceeded, the insurer's limit of liability per passenger will be automatically reduced.

sprinkler leakage insurance. Fire insurers reduce premiums for insureds who protect their premises by installing sprinkler leakage systems which automatically distribute water in the event of fire. However, the accidental discharge of water constitutes a risk (eg damage to installation by fork-lift truck, or freezing of water) which can be covered by sprinkler leakage insurance.

spurious selection. This occurs when the results of an investigation appear to indicate an unexpected variation in mortality due to selection. It may be due to statistical faults in the data, or abnormal experience.

stability clause. This features in many excess of loss reinsurance treaties (especially those protecting liability portfolios) to give the reinsurer some protection against an unfair share of the effects of inflation. Inflation pushes some claims above the excess point and so increases the claims frequency for the reinsurer. Moreover, claims previously above excess point will now become more costly with the entire extra cost falling on the reinsurer. The intention of the clause is to maintain a stable relationship between the ceding office's retention and the limit of liability of the reinsurer by reference to a stated index (eg a specific wages index). For example, a cedant's retention might be £100 000 with excess of loss above that figure up to £500 000. A claim may be notified in year 1 but settled in year 6 for £240 000. If the clause applies and the stated index has increased by 40 per cent then the retention for adjustment purposes becomes:

$$\frac{140 \times £100\ 000}{100} = £140\ 000$$

The upper limit of the treaty becomes:

$$\frac{140 \times £500\ 000}{100} = £700\ 000$$

The relationship between the retention and the limit of liability has remained at a ratio 1:5. The cedant now bears £140 000 of the loss with the reinsurer covering the excess of that figure, £100 000. Without the clause, the reinsurer would have to pay £140 000 and so carry an undue share of the effects of inflation. *Also see the* CLAIMS CONTROL CLAUSE which deals with the effects of inflation on reinsurance.

stacking of limits. The adding together of indemnity limits under liability policies for two or more years to produce the overall indemnity limit to be applied to a given claim. This is likely to occur with long-tail cases where the disease is of a gradually operating nature. For example, the insurer who fixes a limit of £1m any one year might end up paying £5m where on risk for five of the critical years of the progress of the disease. This is almost certainly not what the insurers intended as under many of the policies the insurers will have imposed a limit for any one accident or occurrence and an overall limit for all claims in the year. The problem has caused some insurers to favour a claims-made policy (qv) wording.

staff engineer. A motor vehicle specialist employed by a motor insurer to inspect vehicles that have sustained significant damage and to check the estimate of the repairer. He may then arrange for that repairer (or another) to carry out the repairs if the claim is in order. Where the cost of repairs is uneconomic in relation to the value of the car the engineer may recommend that the vehicle is written off as a total and will make recommendations as to the value of the wreck. The engineer will also consider the pre-accident condition of the vehicle to check that the insured has complied with the condition requiring him to take reasonable care to safeguard the vehicle from loss or damage and maintain it in an efficient condition. The term motor vehicle assessor is sometimes used as an alternative to staff engineer but is more commonly applied to independent specialists.

staff insurance schemes. Insurance schemes agreed between employers and insurers to enable the former to offer insurance as a staff benefit. The schemes are optional unless the employer is meeting the whole cost but are attractive as the scheme usually attracts preferential terms. The most obvious scheme is an occupational pension scheme but private car insurance, legal expenses insurance and other personal line covers can be arranged in this way. Some employers may be prepared to pay the premium and then deduct it from salary over a period of time.

stamp duty. A tax on documents such as insurance policies. Stamp duty is now chargeable only on life insurance policies.

standard construction. A term used by fire insurers to refer to buildings constructed of brick, stone or concrete and roofed with slates, tiles, metal, asbestos or concrete. The term itself does not appear in the policy but the description of the construction given in these terms is generally stated.

standard excess. An excess that is written into the standard or basic policy such as the young and inexperienced drivers excess (qv). Other excesses are either of a voluntary nature or added by the insurer as an underwriting measure in regard to the particular risk.

standard policy. A policy form in general use.

standard lives. Proposers acceptable for life insurance on normal terms because there is no evidence to show serious ill-health. *See* SELECTION OF LIVES.

standard turnover. In ascertaining the liability of the insurer under a business interruption insurance (qv) it is necessary to apply the rate of gross profit (qv) to the fall in turnover after adjustments. *See* SPECIAL CIRCUMSTANCES CLAUSE. The fall in turnover is the difference between the standard turnover and the turnover achieved in the indemnity period (qv). The standard turnover is the turnover (qv) achieved during the twelve months before the date of the material damage corresponding to the indemnity period.

standing charges. A business interruption term describing expenses that continue despite the interruption of the business by material damage. Such expenses, eg rent, are at the risk of the insured perils, eg fire. When the 'difference' basis is used to calculate the sum insured, ie the gross profit, cover is secured by deducting the specified working expenses (qv) from the turnover. This leaves a margin to cover standing charges and net profit. Under an earlier method the standing charges were identified and insured by being added to the net profit.

starter discount. A discount allowed by

private car motor insurers for new proposers with satisfactory driving records but with no recent or previous insurance history in their own name and therefore unable to claim a no claim discount (qv).

state of the art defence. Defendants may argue that at the time the plaintiff was exposed to the risk of injury or disease the state of the art, ie scientific and technical knowledge, was such that at the time of manufacture, sale or distribution their actions were proper and they could not have been expected to have discovered the defects or other causative factors leading to the injury or disease. The defendant may also claim that warnings at the time in the light of contemporary knowledge were unnecessary or given as appropriate. Where the claim against the defendant is based on negligence and the corollaries of foreseeability and reasonableness, this defence will be accepted. In *Gunn* v *Wallsend Slipway & Engineering Co. Ltd* (1989) the defendants were not liable for Mrs Gunn's death from mesothelioma caused by inhaling asbestos dust from her husband's working clothes. In 1965 no duty regarding this secondary exposure (qv) was owed as no one in the industrial world realised the risk to another person from an asbestos worker's person or clothes. The Consumer Protection Act 1987 (qv) specifically allows such a defence. *See* DEVELOPMENT RISKS DEFENCE.

State Earnings Related Pension Scheme (SERPS). A Government scheme which provides a pension in addition to the basic stated pension based on pay in band earnings (qv). The Social Security Act 1986 provided, *inter alia*, that: SERPS will reduce gradually from the year 2000 and will be cut from 25 per cent of earnings to 20 per cent of earnings; the pension will be based on career average earnings and not the best 20 years; employees covered by occupational schemes can opt out of them, and either choose a personal pension or go into SERPS on an individual basis. Also the Act provided a positive incentive to contract out (qv) as an extra 2 per cent of upper tier earnings will be paid until 1993 by the Government to new contracted-out schemes.

Statement of Long-term Insurance Practice. Similar to Statement of Non-Life Insurance Practice (qv) it is issued by the Association of British Insurers and Lloyd's to protect private policyholders only. The Statement applies to long-term business, ie mainly life insurance and includes industrial life insurances even though they continue to enjoy the protection afforded under the Industrial Assurances Acts 1923 to 1969.

Statement of Non-Life Insurance Practice. A statement issued by the Association of British Insurers and Lloyd's underwriters to protect policyholders from any unfair treatment brought by the terms of insurance contracts. The statement was issued as insurance contracts are not regulated by the Unfair Contract Terms Act 1977 (qv). By adopting the Statement the insurers of private policyholders (not business policyholders) agree not to unreasonably repudiate liability on grounds of non-disclosure or breach of warranty. In particular the insurers will not take advantage of mere technical breaches, ie non-disclosure or misrepresentation that would not have materially affected the insurer's judgment of the risk or breach of warranty or condition unconnected with the loss. Also insurers will accept statements made by a proposer to his best knowledge and belief. The Statement is not binding in law. Account is taken of arbitration (qv) and other referral arrangements (eg Insurance Ombudsman Bureau (qv).

statement of particulars. The annual return submitted by a practising insurance broker or enrolled body corporate (qv), together with audited accounts, to the Insurance Brokers Registration Council. The statement must be supplied within six months of the year end.

statute barred. A civil claim not brought within the time allowed by statute is 'statute barred'. If a writ is issued after the stated period has run its course the defendant may plead that the claim is statute barred. The chief Act is the Limitation Act 1980 (qv), but the Latent Damages Act 1986 (qv) is also relevant.

Statute of Frauds 1677. Passed for the

prevention of frauds and perjuries it has now largely been replaced by later enactments but s. 4 remains. It provides that no action shall be brought upon a guarantee unless the agreement is in writing and signed by the party to be charged, or his agent. *See* UNENFORCEABLE CONTRACTS for the effect on contracts of fidelity guarantee (qv).

statutory absolution. *See* REHABILITATION OF OFFENDERS ACT 1974.

statutory declaration. A written statement of facts where the person making it signs and solemnly declares it as being true before a commissioner or magisterial officer. The Statutory Declarations Act 1835 substitutes declarations for oaths in some cases. Statutory declaration means a declaration under that Act. In the claims condition of insurance policies the insurer calls for proofs of loss (qv) and may demand statutory declarations to verify the truth of an insured's claim and the particulars thereof. When a motor insurance policy is cancelled the Road Traffic Act requires the insured to surrender his certificate of insurance within seven days. If the certificate has been lost or destroyed the insured must make a statutory declaration to that effect.

statutory duty. A duty or liability imposed by some statute.

statutory examinations. The Factories Act 1961 lays down compulsory examinations for specified items of plant and machinery used in a factory. The maximum statutory periods under the Act are: steam boilers—fourteen months; steam and air receivers—26 months; solid drawn air receivers must have an hydraulic test not exceeding four years; hoists and lifts, power six months; manual twelve months; chains, ropes and miscellaneous lifting tackle, eg hooks, shackles, eye-bolts, etc, six months; cranes and other lifting machines, eg hook hoists, pulley blocks, gin wheels, etc, fourteen months; water-sealed gasholders not less than 5000 c.f., two years.

statutory exclusions. The Marine Insurance Act 1906, s. 55 lists several losses for which underwriters are not liable unless the policy otherwise provides. The insurer is not liable under the Act for: wilful misconduct; delay; wear and tear, ordinary leakage and breakage, inherent vice, or loss caused by rats or vermin; injury to machinery not caused by maritime perils.

statutory notice. The notice of cancellation which must be issued under the Financial Services Act 1986 to most investors in life and pensions products. Two forms of cancellation notice are prescribed—one for 'linked policies' and one for other policies. In all cases the notice will contain essential details of the contract and the person who recommended it. The notice informs the proposer that he may withdraw from the contract within fourteen days without loss.

statutory returns. Under the Insurance Companies Act 1974, authorised insurers must make statutory returns to the Department of Trade and Industry. The statistical and accounting returns enable the DTI to monitor the activities of insurers and their solvency position in particular.

statutory solvency margin. Lloyd's as a whole completes a solvency margin statement as part of its statutory return to the Department of Trade and Industry. The return at 31 December 1989 showed the assets available as being equal to 11 times the required margin of solvency.

statutory solvency test. *See* ANNUAL SOLVENCY TEST.

steam boiler insurance. *See* BOILER AND PRESSURE PLANT INSURANCE, a type of insurance that covers loss or damage caused by explosion and collapse. Explosions of domestic boilers (qv) are insured within the terms of fire policies. Engineering insurers insure boilers used for other purposes.

stipulation. A policy condition that does not go to the root of the contract. Consequently breach does not give the insurer the right of avoidance or affect liability, but the stipulation may be enforced against the insured. The insurer's remedy is the right to sue for damages. The requirement that an insured should submit a wages or some other declaration under adjustable policies (qv) illustrates a stipulation.

stock deterioration insurance. An insurance designed for the owners of refrigerators or cold stores used for the temporary storage of foodstuffs. The policy covers loss of or damage to the stock in the cold chamber of the refrigerator by deterioration or putrefaction caused by rise or fall of temperature within such a chamber. Cover is wide enough to include breakdown and wear and tear. The only exclusions are fire, lightning, explosion, flood, earthquake, aircraft and leakage from a sprinkler installation, a deliberate act of the supply authority and consequential loss. The policy is issued by the engineering department which also offers an inspection service.

stock endorsement. An endorsement used in fidelity guarantee insurance (qv) to extend the policy to cover loss resulting from a person guaranteed, eg an employee, misappropriating or improperly dealing with stock-in-trade.

stop loss treaty. *See* EXCESS OF LOSS RATIO TREATY.

storage risk. A term used in fire insurance in respect of warehouses and the like where property is stored in bulk. The extent of the risk is not only related to the nature of the goods as the fire insurer will take account of the increase in risk due to the storage aspects. Even goods of a non-hazardous nature may be rated up when stored in bulk.

storage tanks. An engineering insurance is available to cover damage to the tanks and cover is also available in respect of loss of contents. Cover includes a periodic inspection for tanks of 2000 gallons capacity and over and: sudden and unforeseeable physical damage to the tank; physical damage to surrounding property (other than the contents) directly caused by accidental escape of the contents or by damage to the tank. Cleaning costs resulting from an insured loss are included; loss of contents by accidental leakage, discharge or overflow or contamination. Where the capacity is below 2000 gallons and the tank is for fuel oil storage, the insurance can be provided without an inspection service. Most industrial firms have storage facilities for liquids at their premises and the value of the stored contents of a tank can be very high. There is no cover for seepage, evaporation, overflowing, inherent vice, contamination, lack of heat, or normal trade loss.

Other exclusions: consequential loss; heaters, pumps or supporting structures; wear and tear; theft; subsidence or ground movement; fire, lightning, earthquake, aircraft etc.

'stored or kept'. The meaning of this term was the focal point in *Thompson* v *Equity Fire Insurance Co.* (1910), 103 L.T. 153. A small amount of gasoline in a cooking stove did not mean 'stored and kept' for the purpose of an exclusion in a fire policy. The exclusion did not operate as the term implied a considerable amount of gasoline or at least keeping it in stock for trading purposes.

storm. Defined by Veale J in *Oddy* v *Phoenix Assurance Co* (1966) as 'some sort of violent wind usually accompanied by rain or hail or snow. Storm does not mean persistent bad weather, nor does it mean heavy rain or persistent rain by itself'. Equally eloquent was Thesiger J 'Storm must be something more prolonged and widespread than a gust of wind. One swallow does not make a summer and one may have a gust of wind without a storm although during a storm there will almost certainly be gusts' (*S & M Hotels Ltd* v *Legal & General Assurance Society* (1972)). The *Shorter Oxford Dictionary* defines it as 'a violent disturbance of the atmosphere, manifested by high winds, often accompanied by heavy falls of rain, hail or snow, by thunder and lightning and (at sea) by turbulence of the waves. Hence sometimes applied to a heavy fall of rain, hail, or snow, or to a violent outbreak of thunder and lightning, unaccompanied by strong wind'.

storm and tempest. Risks insured as additional perils under fire insurance and household policies subject to an excess. The underwriter concerns himself with the age and state of the buildings and their exposure to violent winds often accompanied by rain, snow or hail. There has to be a violent commotion of the atmosphere. Winds of ordinary or normal velocity do not amount to storm and tempest. It is usual to exclude damage caused by frost, subsidence and landslip, and to fences and gates and property in the open.

stranding. This occurs where a vessel

takes the ground in an unusual manner and remains hard and fast for an appreciable length of time owing to some extraneous and accidental cause and not in the ordinary course of navigation.

straying, liability for. The Animals Act 1971 (qv) s. 8 (1) removed the immunity farmers once enjoyed from liability for accidents caused by animals straying on the roadway. Liability is now determined by the ordinary rules of negligence so that a farmer or other person will be liable for any failure to take proper fencing precautions to contain his animals. Section 8(2) provides that there is no breach of duty for placing an animal on common land and in *Davies* v *Davies* (1974) the defendant was not liable when his sheep strayed on to the highway from registered common land. *See* CATTLE TRESPASS.

street works (or Road and Highways Act) bond. A type of performance bond (qv) that guarantees to a highway authority that a building developer will fulfil his obligation to construct roads on the estate or area of his development. The bond is usually set at 100 per cent of the construction costs involved.

strict liability. Liability without fault. It occurs where a person acts at his peril and is responsible for accidental harm independently of the existence of wrongful intent or negligence. Liability for the escape of dangerous things (*Rylands* v *Fletcher* (1868)) is strict and is based on the rationale that the person who created the risk should be responsible for the consequences. Strict liability is also imposed by statute, eg Consumer Protection Act 1987 (qv). In all of these cases a limited number of defences is available to the defendant and hence this term has superseded the term 'absolute liability'.

strike. Withdrawal or cessation of labour by employees.

strikes clauses. The Institute Strikes Clauses (Cargo) (1/1/82) cover loss or damage to the subject-matter by (a) strikers, locked-out workmen, or persons taking part in labour disturbances, riots or civil commotions; (b) any terrorist or any person acting from a political motive. Under the Institute War and Strikes Clauses (Hulls— Time) similar cover is included with the addition of damage by 'any person acting maliciously'.

sub-agency agreements. Agreements between underwriting agents at Lloyd's that give access to the syndicates of one for the Names of another. *See* ONE AGENT/ONE CLASS RULE.

subject approval no risk (SAPNR). A phrase used by an underwriter when he feels that the proposer may not accept the terms indicated on the slip. The effect is that the proposer's confirmation of acceptance is required without delay before the risk can attach.

subject-matter of the insurance. This is the object, property or potential liability that is described in the policy and to which the insured must be so legally related as to have an insurable interest (qv). For example, the subject-matter of marine insurance is the actual vessel or cargo, in fire insurance it is the insured building or stock. Compare with subject-matter of the insurance contract (qv).

subject-matter of the insurance contract. This is the insured's interest in the subject-matter of the insurance (qv). The insurer cannot guarantee to restore the goods or cancel a liability but they can protect the insured's interest against financial loss.

subject to average. A phrase against an item or sum insured to indicate that in the event of under-insurance average (qv) will apply.

subject to survey. A phrase to indicate that the insurer's acceptance of a risk is provisional only pending completion of a survey by the office's fire surveyor.

subrogation. This is a corollary of the principle of indemnity and literally means to ask 'in someone else's name'. After payment of a claim the insurer becomes entitled to any right the insured may have whereby his loss may be extinguished or diminished from other sources (eg a car owner who has claimed against his insurer subrogates to the insurer his right of claim against the negligent third party who caused the damage—he cannot take with both hands as to do so would create a profit). A subrogation condition in the policy enables the insurer to take action against third parties in the insured's name before the indemnity payment has been made. Subrogation can arise by (i) tort (see negligence above); (ii) contract (eg tenancy agreement may give the owner a right against the tenant for fire damage); (iii) statute (Riot (Damages) Act 1886 (qv)) gives certain rights against the police; (iv) subject-matter of insurance (qv) (if the insured has been indemnified for total loss on property, the insurer is subrogated to the salvage).

subrogation condition. *See* SUBROGATION.

subsidence. Damage to buildings due to a movement of land on which the property is situated. Cover is available as an additional (special) peril added to a fire policy and within the perils listed in household policies. The cover excludes normal land settlement, coastal erosion and damage to walls, gates and fences unless the buildings are damaged at the same time. Normally a substantial excess will apply.

substance hazardous to health. Any substance that has by law to be labelled as 'very toxic', 'toxic', 'harmful', 'irritant', or 'corrosive'. Substances for which a maximum exposure limit (MEL) has been set or an occupational standard has been set. Harmful micro-organisms, substantial quantities of airborne dust or other substances which create comparable health hazards. Such substances include: dusts, fumes/gases, solvents, resins, pesticides, acids, alkalis, mineral oil, contaminants such as arsenic and phenols. *See the* CONTROL OF SUBSTANCES HAZARDOUS TO HEALTH REGULATIONS 1988.

substituted expenses. In the interests of economy a course of action alternative to the normal one may be adopted when a casualty has occurred. The expenses arising from the alternative course of action (eg towing a ship to its destination) may not qualify as general average expenditure (qv) but they can substitute for expenses that do so qualify (eg discharge, warehouse and reload cargo at a port of refuge following damage to the ship). If the substitution shows a saving, the substituted expenses are allowed in general average.

subterranean fire. This is bracketed with earthquake and excluded from the standard fire policy. It refers to a fire of volcanic origin but would embrace a fire in a coal field or oil well. The risk, however, is insurable as an additional (special) peril. Underwriters experience no difficulty with risks within the UK but some overseas risks have to be approached with caution and the possibility of catastrophe borne in mind.

successive causes. A loss may be the result of a number of separate causes occurring sequentially. Wherever there is a succession of causes (ie chain or sequence of events) which must have existed to produce the loss, or may have contributed to produce it, the doctrine of proximate cause (qv) is applied to ascertain which of the successive causes is the cause to which the loss is to be attributed within the intention of the policy. This is important as often an insured peril competes with an excepted peril in a sequence of events in the determination of which is the proximate cause, the *causa causans* (qv) and which is the remote cause, or *causa sine qua non*, which only indirectly causes the loss, ie it may facilitate the loss rather than cause it.

successive losses. Two or more losses occurring in the same period of insurance. Recovery in respect of a loss does not prevent the insured from recovering for a second loss and any number of subsequent losses during the policy term. The policy may, however, fix a maximum sum (the sum insured) beyond which the insurer's liability does not extend so the policy is exhausted once the claims reach that figure. Usually the insured can pay an additional premium to reinstate the sum insured after a claim. Some policies provide for the automatic reinstatement (qv) of the full sum insured or limit of indemnity after a claim. *See* UNREPAIRED DAMAGE.

'sudden and accidental' pollution. Insurers have to decide on their approach to pollution and the extent of cover they are prepared to provide, if any. One approach is to exclude all liability arising out of pollution but then override the exclusion in regard to pollution caused either by an immediate discharge consequent upon an accident or a similar wording such as the exclusion does not apply if such discharge, dispersal, release, release or escape is sudden or accidental. This latter wording received a surprising interpretation in the New Jersey case of *Summit Associates Inc.* v *Liberty Mutual Fire Insurance Co* (1988). The plaintiff, a real estate developer, bought land previously used by a township as a sewerage treatment facility but at the time of purchase it was overgrown with trees and undergrowth. The plaintiff did not know of the sludge and the other hazardous substances buried on the site. In July 1983 workmen discovered a hole from which a blue liquid was seeping and this led to the discovery that the liquid contained several hazardous substances. The plaintiff was ordered by a government agency to remove these toxic substances and this involved 150 tons of sludge and 50 000 gallons of liquid at a cost of $438 599. The plaintiff's claim under the policy was refused as the occurrence was not sudden or accidental. The court took a different view holding that the pollution was neither expected nor intended from the insured's standpoint so the words failed to protect the insurer. The judge took the view that the words sudden and accidental, not being defined, should be given their ordinary meaning. He argued that the discovery of toxic waste was sudden and accidental and therefore not within the exclusion. The insurers can be considered unfortunate in that their argument that the occurrence took place long before the policy was issued was not accepted. It might seem to many, possibly including a British court, that the plaintiff had simply bought a piece of land from which certain expenses arose. The bargain was not quite as good as they had expected but they might well have been on enquiry in view of the known previous use of the land. The American courts appear to be prepared to work hard to produce interpretations that will deny the insurers the benefit of such exclusions. The New Jersey judge held that the occurrence took place in July 1983 when the discovery was made and that the damage occurred when the clean up was enforced. Finally, the judge referred to

public policy saying that the 'health, safety and welfare of the people of the state must outweigh the exception provision of the insurance policy'. It appears that the words were interpreted not in accordance with their real meaning but as a matter of expediency to place the loss where it could most conveniently be accommodated. This has been described as an example of the deep pocket theory (qv).

sudden and unforeseen physical damage. The widest form of material damage cover under engineering insurance policies. It includes breakdown risks (qv), including electrical and mechanical breakdown, and accidental damage. In short the damage can be from internal or external causes.

sudden death clause. An immediate termination provision in the inception and termination clause of a reinsurance treaty to facilitate cancellation of the treaty if certain events occur, eg one party going into liquidation; outbreak of war involving the companies' countries of domicile. Special provisions may be made for termination of obligations in such circumstances.

sue and labour clause. A clause (incorporated in no. 19—Duty of Assured Clause in the Institute Cargo Clauses and in number 13 of the Institute Time Clauses—Duty of Assured (Sue and Labour)) to remind the insured to act at all times as though he was uninsured. Sue and labour charges are expenses incurred deliberately by the insured or his agents for preservation of the property when threatened by an insured peril and would include payments under prearranged salvage contracts (*see* SALVAGE CHARGES). The clause is a supplementary agreement enabling the insured to recover these charges from the marine insurer in addition to any claim (Marine Insurance Act 1906, s. 78).

Suicide Act 1961. The Act abolished the rule that suicide by a person of sound mind was a crime. *See* SUICIDE CLAUSE.

suicide clause. This is a clause in a life insurance policy enabling the insurer to avoid the contract if death occurs by suicide within a specified time (one or two years of inception). Some offices omit this suicide exclusion altogether.

sum insured. The limit of the insurer's

liability under the policy. Except in the case of first loss policies (qv) it should represent the maximum value at risk on property otherwise there will be penalties for under-insurance. *See* AVERAGE.

sum insured basis. A method of fixing the sum insured for business interruption insurance (qv). Under the sum insured basis (qv) the proposer estimates his gross profit during the maximum indemnity period (qv) beyond the year of insurance. No additional premium will be payable when the actual gross profit for the year is known but claims are subject to the under-insurance condition. When applied to a property owners' combined policy the sum insured should represent not less than the gross rentals expected throughout the whole length of the maximum indemnity period. Full allowance should be made for rent reviews during both the insurance period and the maximum indemnity so that the sum insured represents not less than the gross rentals expected during the maximum indemnity period from a date commencing at the very end of the financial year. The insurer's liability is limited to the sum insured and if that proves inadequate these claims too become subject to proportional reduction.

summary jurisdiction. *See* SUMMARY PROCEEDINGS.

summary proceedings. Proceedings in respect of criminal offences that are tried summarily, ie by magistrates. Under an employers' liability insurance the insurer agrees to pay the solicitor's fee for representing the insured in a court of summary jurisdictions , provided the circumstances include an injury to an employee. Under a motor policy the insurer undertakes to pay the solicitor's fee for defending the insured in any proceedings relating to an event which may be the subject of indemnity under the policy, eg as a result of third party injury the insured may face prosecution for driving without due care and attention.

summons. Strictly, a citation to appear in answer to a complaint or representation made according to law. More popularly, the first stage of proceedings in an Inferior Court (magistrates

court or county court). A liability or legal expenses policyholder covered for legal defence costs (legal expenses insurance) must inform the insurer and pass on the details of any summons received in the time scale laid down in the policy conditions—this may be immediate (qv).

sums assured (insured) in force. The total face value of life policies currently in force.

sunk. This means the vessel must be fully submerged.

sunshine deficiency insurance. *See* PLUVIUS INSURANCE.

Superannuation Funds Office. A part of the Inland Revenue with the responsibility for the approval of occupational pension schemes under the Finance Act 1970. The SFO ensures that the tax relief given to approved pension schemes is not abused.

supplier default cover. A credit insurance term to describe an insurance against loss due to the insolvency of a supplier.

suppliers' extension. A business interruption policy can be extended to apply to loss of gross profit and increased cost of working following interruption caused by loss or damage at the premises of a supplier of raw materials or component parts. Cover is expressed as a percentage of the gross profit, which is deemed to take account of the degree of significance of that particular supplier to the business of the insured. The extension can be applied to the premises of specified or unspecified suppliers.

Supply of Services (Exclusion of Implied Terms) Order 1982. The Supply of Goods and Services (Exclusion of Implied Terms) Act 1982, s.13 provides that any supplier of a service is acting in the course of business. It is implied in his contract that he will use reasonable skill and care. Section 12 (4) enables the Secretary of State to exclude certain services from this implied term and by this Order he has provided that services supplied by a company director to that company are outside s. 13. The Order also preserves the traditional immunity of advocates not only when acting professionally in court but also before any tribunal, enquiry or arbitrator, or carrying out certain other work.

surplus. 1. An accounting expression to

describe the excess of income over expenditure of mutual companies. The term profit is inappropriate. 2. The amount ceded by way of reinsurance after the direct office has decided upon his retention (qv). 3. In life insurance, the difference between assets and liabilities as revealed at the annual valuation, out of which bonuses are paid to with profits policyholders.

surplus treaty reinsurance. This is a proportional reinsurance working on the basis of lines. A line is the amount retained by an insurer (ceding office) for its net account and will vary according to the quality of the risk (eg a fire account might have a minimum line of £12 000 and a maximum of £120 000. It might retain the minimum for a plastics works and the maximum for an office block). A treaty is expressed in a multiple of lines to indicate the reinsurance capacity, eg a four line treaty based on a retention (line) of £50 000 will enable the ceding office to accept risks up to £250 000 automatically. If the risk is £50 000 or less it is wholly retained by the ceding office, a risk of £100 000 will be shared equally between the office and the treaty reinsurers, whereas a risk of £250 000 is shared 20 per cent ceding office and 80 per cent reinsurers. For risks exceeding £250 000, the ceding office could seek facultative reinsurance for the excess, retain the unaccommodated balance, or negotiate a higher retention with the reinsurers. Alternatively second or third treaties may exist. The arrangement described above is a first surplus treaty. The second and third treaties pick up proportions of the risk after the first treaty has been filled. In proportional treaties premiums are passed to reinsurers in proportion to the amount of risk they have accepted. The treaty works on the basis of a percentage of all claims, barring for those risks below the retention level, being recovered under the treaty. In addition, the ceding office can arrange non-proportional treaties (qv).

surrender. 1. The act of terminating an existing life insurance (whole life or endowment) and receiving the current surrender value (qv) in cash. 2. A pensions term to describe allocation (the giving up of part of a pension in return for a pension payable to the member's spouse or dependants) or commutation (qv).

surrender value. The amount of cash due when a life insured terminates his policy before maturity. The existence of a reserve makes payment of the sum possible but due allowance is made for expenses incurred by the office, claims to other policyholders and the cover granted under the policy. Insurers include a surrender value clause in the policy and some even give guaranteed surrender values. Often no surrender value is payable in the first two years.

suspension of cover. Any period during a contract when the insurer agrees to come off risk pending notice from the insured to reinstate the cover. In motor insurance, if the car is off the road it is common practice for the insured to return the certificate of insurance and so secure a return premium to be set against the next renewal premium. During the period of suspension it is usual for the fire and theft risks to continue so the return premium is not wholly pro rata.

suretyship insurance. *See* FIDELITY GUARANTEE INSURANCE.

switching facility. *See* SWITCHING INVESTMENTS.

switching investments. Most insurance companies issuing investment bonds and unitised funds (qv) offer a variety of investments linked to property, equity, a managed and a fixed-interest fund, and sometimes a cash or gilt fund. In return for a fee (approximately 0.5 per cent of value) most companies will permit the holder to switch his investment from one fund to the other. As the money remains invested in the same life policy liability to tax does not arise as is normally the case when shares are sold. The holder who makes shrewd use of this switching facility can improve the result that would have been achieved by remaining in the same fund for the duration of the contract.

sympathetic damage. Where damaged cargo taints other cargo, the resultant loss is known as sympathetic damage. If the original damage was occasioned by an insured peril without any intervening cause then the sympathetic damage is covered by the policy. Goods liable to cause this type of damage include: hides and skins, certain cheeses, guano and carbon disulphide.

syndicate. A grouping of Lloyd's underwriters. *See* LLOYD'S SYNDICATES.

syndicate allocated capacity. The maximum amount of business that can be written by a Lloyd's syndicate, based on the capacity of all the Names of the syndicate.

syndicate solvency. A part of the Lloyd's solvency test is to determine the position of a syndicate on each year of account after provision has been made for: (a) estimated future liabilities; (b) disallowed assets, and to divide the result among the participating Names (qv).

syndicate stamp. A document setting out the names of, and share taken by, the members of a Lloyd's syndicate. It defines the constitution of the syndicate for each year of account and must be registered at Lloyd's.

synopsis sheet. A Lloyd's term referring to a document presented in a non-marine claims settlement.

system of check. The system that is used by an employer to check the work of an employee(s) who are subject of fidelity guarantee insurance. The insurer will seek details on the employer's form and may well make further enquiries. The insurer will be concerned to know about cash handling and banking procedures, and details of the arrangements for checking the books of account, financial statements, customers' accounts, checking stock, supervision, and the balancing and auditing of books. In a positions policy where the individual is not identified as such the system of check and methods of appointing staff to those positions is the principal underwriting information needed.

system of work. *See* SAFE SYSTEM OF WORK.

Take note. A document used in facultative reinsurance (qv) to indicate an acceptance by a reinsurer of a risk offered in a request note submitted by a ceding office. The note indicates the amount accepted by the reinsurer.

'tail'. A colloquial term for an extended reporting period (qv) or discovery period (qv). The term also describes the run-off risk associated with policies operating on a losses-occurring basis (qv). The policy may have completed its term but latent diseases or damage may be gradually operating for many years prior to their discovery. Such policies are triggered by the time of damage and not time of discovery and the interval between the two is the 'tail'. The elapse of long periods of time will not extinguish the plaintiff's right of claim in such cases as under the Limitation Act and the Latent Damages Act time runs not from the date of injury or damage but from the date of knowledge of it.

tail series. In the event of cargo arriving damaged, for the purpose of applying the now discarded franchise (3 or 5 per cent) (qv) most commodities were divided into 'customary averages' (eg tea—10 chests) as application of the franchise to the total value insured resulted in uninsured amounts of a sum greater than the cargo owner could bear. The use of 'series' did not preclude the insured from applying the franchise to the whole of the shipment where he could claim an amount in excess of the sum produced by applying it to each 'series' separately. Where the number of packages in a shipment did not divide into a complete series, the few remaining packages formed a 'tail series' and if the claim amounted to the required percentage the claim would be recoverable from the insurer.

taint damage. See SYMPATHETIC DAMAGE.

taking down. The presentation by a broker of details of an insurance transaction to Lloyd's Policy Signing Office for recording and processing.

target risk. A very large risk which because of its size attracts the attention of brokers and insurers and is offered widely in the market-place. The term is also used to describe a risk that is offered to almost every insurer because of its undesirable, hazardous features.

tariff association. An association of independent insurers who enter into a collective agreement on various matters, particularly not to charge premiums below the minimum level set in the agreement. They also agree to standard policy wordings, standard commission rates, and free exchange of statistical information. The formation of tariffs has generally been prompted by highly competitive markets and the risk of driving premiums down to below an economic level. The tariff movement in the UK was represented by the Fire Offices Committee (qv), which ceased on 30 June 1985 and set minimum premiums and standards in fire insurance, and the Accident Offices Association which started on 11 June 1906 and whose rating and policy form functions ended on 1 January 1969. Tariffs under the AOA existed in motor insurance and employers' liability. The tariffs broke down for a number of reasons—insurers large enough to use own statistics for rating purposes; competition from reputable non-tariff offices (qv); tighter supervision of insurers by the Government rendered some aspects of the tariff unnecessary.

tariff company. A company that belongs to a tariff association (qv).

tax havens. A term generally applied to low tax areas offshore. Most captives (qv) are set up in such places and in particular this means Bermuda (the most popular), the Cayman Islands, Guernsey, Gibraltar, and the Isle of Man. A key attraction appears to be the deferment of tax on profits until they are repatriated. Also the formalities of formation are more straightforward and, given that captives will have one main or only customer, this is not entirely inappropriate as the procedures generally applicable in the developed countries are necessarily stringent as the aim is to protect the general public. The more favourable tax treatment is a stimulus to growth and enables the captive to increase its capacity for the benefit of its parent. Another advantage of tax havens is the development in these locations of the expertise needed to set up and run captive insurance companies. *See* CONTROLLED FOREIGN COMPANIES.

tax holiday. The period for which weekly/monthly disablement benefits under accident, sickness and health insurances can be received before income tax is levied on them. No tax is payable on weekly benefits until they have been paid for a full tax year (ie 5 April to 5 April) so that the actual 'holiday' could be much longer than a year.

technical insolvency. Impairment of an insurance company's assets to the point where it no longer maintains the required margin of solvency (qv) but which would not make a non-insurance company insolvent. As a result the company would be required to stop taking any new business and could ultimately be wound up.

technical reserves (Lloyd's). The technical reserves of a syndicate consist of the underwriting balances in respect of the two open years of account, the oldest of which has received the premiums for the reinsurance to close (qv) earlier years of account. The assets supporting the technical reserves must be held in a trust fund in accordance with the provisions of a trust deed approved by the Secretary of State.

technical reserves. Funds against possible claims. Insurance companies as a matter of law and prudence need to maintain sufficient reserves to meet their outstanding liabilities at any one time. The composition of technical reserves in the UK is governed by law and, except in the case of certain marine business, must include (a) to (d) below. As a matter of prudence, companies may also create the technical reserves described in (e) and (f) which may not be held specifically being represented instead in the shareholders' equity or excess of assets over liabilities for mutuals (qv): (a) Unexpired premium reserve (qv). The reserve for that proportion of the premium income attributable to the period of risk running beyond the end of the year, ie the valuation date. (b) Unexpired risk reserve (qv). An additional reserve which is required if an estimate of the total liabilities (ie including expenses) up to the valuation date exceeds the unexpired premium reserve. (c) Outstanding claim reserve. The amount reserved to meet outstanding claims, ie those reported before the end of the year but not yet settled. (d) I.B.N.R. reserve. At any one time there will be a number of claims incidents that will have occurred but not yet been reported to the insurer. A reserve is required to meet future liability arising from these incidents. (e) Catastrophe reserve. Claims of huge dimensions of an unpredictable nature can arise. Reserves (a to c above) are built on normal claims experience and would not be adequate to cover occurrences such as earthquakes. Consequently it is sound management to set up this additional reserve especially if providing cover on a world-wide basis. (f) Claims equalisation reserve. A reserve to enable the insurer to smooth out any large year-to-year fluctuations in claims experience. N.B. The Committee of Lloyd's prescribes minimum technical reserves for its syndicates.

technical words meaning rule. A rule of construction to the effect that where technical legal words are used in a policy they are to be given their strict technical legal meaning unless the policy shows a different intention. In *London and Lancashire Fire Insurance Co. Ltd v Bolands* (1924) All E.R. Rep. 642 four men held up the insured's employees with revolvers and stole cash. There was no other disturbance in the neighbourhood and the burglary policy excluded 'riot'. An essential part of the then-definition of riot was that there should be at least three persons (it is now twelve) with a common purpose threatening violence. The exception applied as there had technically been a riot.

tempest. A severe storm (qv) (*Oddy* v *Phoenix Assurance Co Ltd* (1966)). The *Shorter Oxford Dictionary* states 'a violent storm of wind, usually accompanied by a downfall or rain, hail, or snow or by thunder'. *See* STORM AND TEMPEST.

temporary annuity. An annuity (qv) under which the payments to the annuitant will cease at the end of a given period or at death whichever shall occur the first.

temporary disablement. Inability following sickness or accident to attend to one's occupation. The policy usually offers a weekly disablement benefit for total and partial disablement.

temporary insurance/assurance. *See* TERM INSURANCE.

temporary removal clause. The clause added to a fire policy to cover items, other than stock, while temporarily removed for cleaning, renovating, repair, or similar purposes to any situation in the UK or Republic of Ireland subject, normally, to a 10 per cent limit of the sum insured.

temporary repairs. Where, in marine insurance, temporary repairs to a ship are effected with a view to economy, or because no other repairs are possible, insurers accept liability for both the temporary and subsequent permanent repairs, but limited in all to the insured value. Temporary repairs for the convenience of shipowners are not allowed except for liners running to advertised sailing schedules.

tenancy in common. Where two or more persons are entitled to property if one dies his interest passes to his estate and he can make provision in his will for his share to pass to another.

tenant's liability. The liability of a tenant for loss or damage to the premises leased to him. The liability may arise under contract or in tort. The custody exclusion (qv) in a public liability policy is usually overridden in connection with property leased to the insured so that he acquires cover on a legal liability but not first party (qv) basis. The household contents policy includes a tenant's liability section. This indemnifies the insured as tenant but not owner of his home following: (a) damage caused by the perils named in a typical buildings policy, ie fire and additional perils to the house or interior decorations; (b) accidental damage to underground service pipes and cables; (c) accidental breakage of fixed glass and sanitary fixtures. This section does not operate if the house is left insufficiently furnished for full habitation; in respect of wear and tear or normal maintenance and redecoration costs; and the exceptions normally applicable to the named perils (fire etc).

tender bond. *See* BID (OR TENDER) BOND.

tender clause. This Institute Time Clause (No. 10) calls for the immediate notification of accident so that the insurers can appoint their own surveyor. The insurer can also decide at which port repairs will be effected and have a right of veto concerning a place of repair or ship-repairing firm. Failure to comply with the provisions of the clause involves a penalty deduction of 15 per cent of the amount of the claim.

ten plus policy. A term used to describe a ten-year endowment or whole life policy under which premiums must be paid for a minimum of ten years otherwise it will not rank as a qualifying policy (qv).

term insurance/assurance. A life policy that pays the sum insured only if death occurs within the term of the policy. If the life insured survives the term cover ends and no survival benefit is payable to the insured. This type of policy is also called temporary insurance (or assurance). *See also* DECREASING TERM INSURANCE and CONVERTIBLE TERM INSURANCE.

terminal bonus. An additional bonus added to existing life assurance benefits when a 'with profits' policy becomes a claim by death of survival of the policy term. *See* BONUSES.

terminal funding. A pensions arrangement, not common in the UK except for discretionary pension increases, whereby a payment to meet the present value of a benefit is made only when the benefit is due to commence.

termination of adventure clause. In certain circumstances, eg war, the shipowner is able to terminate the contract of affreightment at a place other than the original destination. Provided notice is given to the cargo insurer and any additional premium paid, the goods are held covered until sold and delivered at such place or during forwarding of delivering to the policy destination subject always to a limit of sixty days after discharge at the final port.

termination of risk. Under a voyage policy this is when the ship has moored at anchor 24 hours in good safety at the stated port of destination. To prevent overlap with the succeeding policy which normally runs 'at and from' (qv), that policy is claused 'no risk to attach until expiry of the previous policy'. Under the ordinary form of policy on cargo the risk terminates upon the goods being safely landed at the port of destination but account has to be taken of the clauses which normally extend the cover.

terms of business/engagement letter. Under FIMBRA rules this means a short form of agreement issued by certain members (categories A(1) and A(2)) as opposed to a full client agreement required by members of higher categories. For the contents of such a letter *see* CLIENT AGREEMENT.

'terms to be agreed' (t.b.a.). An indication on a slip (qv) that certain of the terms of the contract have to be finally agreed. It is common practice for marine underwriters to accept the risk at a rate to be agreed although other aspects of the risks, eg commencement date, can be covered by the term. It may be necessary to refer to the context in which the agreement was made to discover whether a binding contract has been made pending the agreement on the terms to be agreed. An alternative to t.b.a. is t.b.a. l/u meaning 'to be agreed with the leading underwriter (qv)'.

'terms to be agreed with the leading underwriter (t.b.a. l/u). *See* TERMS TO BE AGREED (T.B.A.).

territorial limits. The territorial (geographical) limits stated in the policy within which the insured event must occur. For example, a public liability policy (qv) often operates only in connection with occurrences within the limits of Great Britain, Northern Ireland, the Channel Islands, or the Isle

of Man. The employers' liability policy (qv) operates only whilst the employee is (a) employed in Great Britain, Northern Ireland, the Isle of Man, or the Channel Islands (including off-shore installations in territorial waters around Great Britain and its Continental Shelf), or (b) temporarily employed anywhere else in the world provided the employee is normally resident in the territories stated. The latter clause, (b), is a safeguard for the insurer against having to defend their insured in a foreign court; otherwise a jurisdiction clause (qv) may be used to ensure that any court action may be before a UK court. In products liability the policy operates on a world-wide basis provided the product was supplied from the UK. Other policies that may have territorial limits: 'all risks'; personal accident and sickness; motor (*see* FOREIGN USE).

terrorism. *See* UNLAWFUL ASSOCIATION.

test of reasonableness. A test laid down in the Unfair Contract Terms Act 1977 (qv) for the purpose of establishing the validity of exclusion clauses (qv) used in business. A trader who imposes an exclusion clause has to show that it is 'fair and reasonable'. In deciding whether a clause meets the test the court is required to have regard to the circumstances that were (or ought reasonably to have been) known to the parties when the contract was made and pay particular attention to such matters as the bargaining strength of the parties, whether the customer received any inducement to accept the exclusion clause (such as a special discount), whether the goods or suitable alternatives could be obtained from another source without the exclusion clause, whether the customer knew or ought reasonably to have known of the existence of the clause, and whether the goods were made to the customer's specification. Where a trader seeks to limit his liability under an exclusion clause to a specified sum of money the courts are required to have regard for the resources which he could expect to be available to him to meet such liability and how far it was open to him to cover himself by insurance. Also the 'test of reasonableness' requires the trader to prove that the clause was reasonable; the customer is not required to prove that it was unreasonable.

Thatcham (Motor Insurance Repair Research Centre). A centre where research is conducted with a view to obtaining a knowledge of repair costs and repair techniques and to further their research. The centre is jointly financed by the Association of British Insurers (qv) and Lloyd's. 'Write-offs' are bought in and repaired under research conditions before being sold. The findings of the centre are made available to motor manufacturers, equipment manufacturers, and vehicle repairers.

theft. Defined in the Theft Act 1968 (qv) s. 1 as 'dishonestly appropriating property belonging to another with the intention of permanently depriving the other of it'. The term is too wide for most insurance purposes as it would include pilferage (qv) and shoplifting. Insurers therefore define the cover provided on business risks. For example, the wording may be 'theft involving entry to or exit from the premises by force' or 'theft following violent and forcible entry into or exits from the premises'.

Theft Act 1968. An Act that changed the legal definitions that had been used since the Larceny Act 1916. Insurers until then had generally been able to introduce the legal terms into the policies as the insured perils but the new definitions obliged insurers to adopt their own definitions to give effect to the cover they intended to offer. *See* AGGRAVATED BURGLARY, BURGLARY, THEFT and VIOLENT AND FORCIBLE MEANS.

theft insurance. Insurance on property to indemnify the insured against loss or damage occasioned by theft as defined in the policy. Policies issued to commercial and industrial concerns limit cover to theft following forcible and violent entry into or exit from the premises (qv). The term theft (qv) as defined in the Theft Act 1968 is too wide in scope for business premises theft policies. Wider cover is available under householders' policies.

theft, or any attempted theft. This is a specified peril insured under household comprehensive policies on buildings and contents. In the latter instance there is an exclusion of theft of money and stamps or theft while the dwelling is lent, let or sub-let. The term itself embraces anything covered by the Theft Act 1968 (qv). The cover is suspended while the dwelling is unoccupied, ie a period of 30 days or more or is insufficiently furnished for full habitation or normal residential purposes, or furnished but not lived in.

'thieves'. According to the Marine Insurance Act 1906, Rule of Construction number 9, the term 'thieves' does not cover clandestine theft or a theft committed by any one of the ship's company, whether crew or passengers. The peril in a marine policy appears to cover loss or damage by assailing and violent thieves. Institute Cargo Clauses B and C do not cover any form of theft. The Institute Time Clauses 1/10/83 cover in clause 6.1.3. 'violent theft from persons outside the vessel and in clause 6.1.5. there is cover for 'piracy'.

The Securities Association. A Self-Regulatory Organisation (qv) created by the merger between the Stock Exchange and the International Securities Regulatory Organisation. Member firms carry on business in connection with such activities as dealing and arranging deals in shares, debentures, Government and other public securities, warrants, certificates representing securities, rights and interests in securities, and financial futures and options on securities and their derivatives and on foreign currency; and in connection with advising corporate finance customers and arranging deals for them. Member firms may also be concerned, but not as their main activities, with advising on investment deals in the foregoing investments, with managing such investments or with arranging and advising on transactions in life insurance and collective investment schemes.

3/4 Collisions Liability Clause. An Institute Time Clause Hulls (1/10/83). Insurers pay 3/4ths of any amount the insured becomes legally liable to pay and does pay in consequence of a collision with another vessel resulting in damage to that vessel and property thereon; delay or loss of one or other vessel or property thereon; general average or salvage charges incurred by the other vessel or property thereon. Legal costs are payable in addition up to 3/4ths thereof. Settlements are usually on a cross-liabilities basis (qv) unless one or other of the vessels has limited liability by law (with a minimum for insurers of 3/4ths of the insured value of the vessel). The clause excludes claims for: removal of wreck; any property not on board the other vessel; cargo or property on the insured vessel; loss of life, person; except of the other vessel or property thereon.

Three-quarters Running Down Clause. *See* RUNNING DOWN CLAUSE.

Third Parties (Rights Against Insurers) Act 1930. This enacts that the rights in his policy, so far as it covers the insured's liability to third parties, vest in the third party in the event of the insured becoming insolvent after incurring liability but before payment is made. The third party's claim against the insurer is no better than the claim of the insured so that the insurer may be able to plead a breach of utmost good faith or policy conditions precedent to liability. *See Bradley* v *Eagle Star.*

third party. The person or organisation who becomes a claimant against the insured by alleging a breach of legal duty by the insured. The alleged breach may be linked to injury or damage within the scope of a liability policy, eg a road accident victim is a third party who may allege negligence against the insured, who will seek an indemnity for this legal liability under a motor insurance contract.

third party fire and theft. *See* MOTOR INSURANCE.

third party insurance. When a policy insures a person against his legal liability for injury or damage to others (ie third parties other than employees), it is a third party insurance. If the policy is confined to legal liability for injury to employees it is an employers' liability insurance. The term is also used in connection with the insurance business by a captive company in the open market for a party other than its parent company. Marine third party liability is the primary business of

Protection and Indemnity Clubs (qv).

third party notice. *See* THIRD PARTY PROCEEDINGS.

third party only policy. *See* MOTOR INSURANCE.

third party proceedings. Where a defendant in a civil action feels that he has a right of indemnity or contribution from a third party he can join the third party in the action by the issue of a third party notice. This will contain particulars of the nature of the claim and include a statement of the claim. No leave is required to issue a third party notice where the action is begun by writ and the notice is issued before the defence is served. The notice puts the defendant and third party into the same relationship that exists between plaintiff and defendant. The third party may counterclaim against the defendant but not the plaintiff. The use of third party proceedings avoids the cost of a separate action.

third party sharing agreement. A market agreement between participating motor insurers. Where two motorists are involved in an incident and third parties are injured, the insurers agree not to apportion blame but share third party claims equally. Any injury to the driver of either vehicle or any injury to any employee of the insured is excluded by the agreement. The same criteria of similar portfolios apply for the agreement to operate effectively as exists for knock-for-knock agreements (qv).

three-year accounting system. Lloyd's syndicates run a three-year accounting system so an underwriter who opened an account on 1 January 1988 will have kept it open until 31 December 1990. He will have opened new accounts on 1 January 1989 and 1 January 1990. This means that the underwriter will have 'earned' all the premium credited to the 1988 before it is closed and will have dealt with all the major claims. Hence there is no need to estimate 'unearned premium' and the number of outstanding claims is manageable, although as most of these are liability claims, they are hardest to estimate. A reserve for this outstanding liability, which is carried forward by the actual signing of a reinsurance policy into an 'open year' which 'open year' is responsible for the settlement of claims until it, too, is closed. Insurance companies generally use 'annual accounting'.

tied agent. *See* APPOINTED COMPANY REPRESENTATIVE.

tied annuity option. The option to use the proceeds of a pension plan to buy an annuity from the insurer concerned at its current market rate as an alternative to taking the guaranteed annuity option (qv). *See also* OPEN-MARKET OPTION.

time. *See* TIME POLICIES and TIME LOSS INSURANCE.

time and distance policies. Policies by which an insurer can reinsure a claim the amount of which is known but the date of settlement uncertain. Such policies are helpful to insurers with long-tail liability business (qv) by making it possible to pay out a smaller sum now by way of premium while receiving a larger sum later when settlement takes place. This simplifies an assessment of the insurer's solvency position at the time of effecting the policy by avoiding the complications of 'discounting of reserves'. Lloyd's Bye-Law 7 of 1984 now precludes discounting for solvency purposes. Discounting allowed an insurer to discount the expected settlement figure by a suitable rate of interest in recognition of the earnings accruing to the fund pending settlement.

time excess. An excess (qv) or deductible (qv) expressed in terms of hours or days as opposed to a monetary amount. Under an engineering consequential loss policy it is customary to exclude the first 24 hours (or some other period) of any period of interruption following damage to or breakdown of plant or machinery. The object is to exclude small claims as minor breakdowns may be relatively frequent with no serious consequences in terms of the period of interruption.

time loss insurance. An early form of business interruption insurance (qv). The insurer paid an amount (sum insured divided by the number of working days in the year) for each day's stoppage of the business. The system is still used on occasions in engineering consequential loss in respect of the time lost following the breakdown of a machine.

time on risk. A period during which the insurer has been on risk for an insurance that has been discontinued. A 'time on risk' premium is charged.

time penalty clause. This clause was introduced to prevent insurers being held liable under freight policies for loss resulting from detention caused by insured perils. In an earlier case a ship ran ashore while sailing to the port of departure and the subsequent delay caused the charterers to throw up the charter and engage another vessel (*Jackson* v *Union Marine Insurance Co.* (1874)).

time policy. A policy which insures the subject-matter, normally a hull (qv) for a stated period of time (Marine Insurance Act 1906, s. 25(1)) as opposed to a specific voyage. Hull risks are usually insured in this way. *See also* INSTITUTE TIME CLAUSES.

tinnitus. This is noise in the ears which sometimes accompanies loss of hearing. The presence of tinnitus may have a significant effect on the damages awarded in claims based on occupational deafness (qv).

'to any vehicle'. The risk insured under the own damage section of a motor policy continues to cover the vehicle as a whole even though part of the vehicle is detached from the main body. Any vehicle therefore means all of the component parts of the vehicle. In *Seaton* v *London General Insurance Co Ltd* (1932) the engine had been removed from the vehicle to a workshop 150 yards away where it was damaged by fire.

'to pay as cargo'. As cargo may change hands when in transit, if the buyer has insufficient information regarding the insurance, he may arrange a supplementary insurance with different insurers worded 'to pay as cargo' for an increased value. The amount fixed under the cargo policy by the seller may be inadequate for the buyer's interest. The phrase means that any claim met by the primary cargo insurer will be met proportionately by the supplementary insurer.

'to pay as may be paid'. A clause in a reinsurance contract (*see* REINSURANCE CLAUSE) under which the reinsurer agrees to pay when the reinsureds are themselves legally liable to make a payment to the original insured. The provision does not bind the reinsurer to pay such amount as the reinsureds may choose to pay (*Martin* v *Steamship Owners' Underwriting Association* (1902)). The liability of the reinsurer arises as soon as the reinsureds have taken proper steps to ascertain the amount payable under the original policy.

tonner reinsurance. 1. A form of total loss only reinsurance of (i) vessels over or between specified tonnages, or (ii) aircraft over or between specified hull values and/or seating capacities. The policies are normally effected on a policy proof of interest (qv) basis and without the benefit of salvage to the insurer. In 1981 Lloyd's introduced rules to prohibit its underwriters from placing or accepting tonner policies which it regarded as purely gambling policies with no legitimate commercial interest. 2. An aviation reinsurance under which the reinsurer agrees to pay a fixed amount if an air crash results in a stated number of deaths.

Tontine Bonus Method. A method of distributing bonuses to 'with profits' life assurance policyholders which has been used in the USA but not in the UK. There are many variations but the general principle is that declared surpluses are retained in the funds and distributed only to those policyholders who survive a certain fixed period.

tool of trade risk. The risk arising out of the use of a special type (qv) (mobile plant) as a tool of trade as distinct from its use on the road in the manner of a motor vehicle. When used in circumstances to which the Road Traffic Act compulsory insurance requirements apply a motor insurance certificate must be issued and this risk must therefore be covered under a motor policy. The Road Traffic Act risk is therefore excluded from public liability policies. Special types (excavators, dumpers etc) are primarily used on premises that are not subject to the Road Traffic Act and the third party risks arising in these circumstances, ie tool of trade risk, can therefore be insured under a commercial vehicle motor insurance or a public liability policy. It is important that the insur-

ance is arranged in such a way that there is no gap in the cover that must be granted by a motor insurer and the additional insurance effected.

Tooley Street fire. London's second largest fire, which occurred in June 1861, is a landmark in the development of fire insurance. It highlighted inadequacies in both the method of pricing (rating) fire insurance and fire-fighting arrangements. Differential rates of charges were introduced to penalise unsatisfactory features and reward favourable ones to encourage better standards of loss prevention. The previous system had lacked that kind of sophistication. A new committee, the London Wharf and Warehouse Committee was set up to deal with charges for wharfs and warehouses. The Metropolitan Fire Brigade Act 1865 established the first municipal fire brigade in London and set the pattern for local authority fire brigades in place of the inadequate fire-fighting forces run jointly by fire insurers.

top hat scheme. A pension scheme for selected directors or high-earning employees normally provided by means of endowment policies. It is also called an executive scheme.

top slicing. A method of calculating income tax liability on life insurance benefits. Income tax may be payable on: (i) 'Qualifying policies' (qv) surrendered or cashed-in within 10 years (or 75 per cent of the maturity term if that is shorter) or becoming paid-up (qv). Tax is levied on the chargeable gain, ie the difference between total benefits and premiums paid. (ii) The proceeds of non-qualifying policies. In the event of the death of a non-qualifying policyholder, the total benefits are taken as the surrender value immediately before death. When a 'gain' occurs, it will not be liable to income tax at the basic rate or capital gains. The only liability is to higher rate income tax, if applicable, to the taxpayer. When the proceeds are paid, the chargeable gain is divided by the number of complete years the policy has run to produce an 'average gain' or 'slice'. The slice is added to the taxpayer's income in the relevant year and is treated as the top slice of his taxable income to determine whether the 'slice' is subject to higher rate tax and the rate thereof. The rate applicable to the slice is then applied to the whole of the gain on the basis of the difference between the higher marginal rate of tax and the basic rate of income tax, eg the policyholder whose 'average gain' places him in the 40 per cent tax band pays a top-slicing rate of 15 per cent (40 - 25, given a basic rate of 25 per cent) on the whole of the gain.

top-up cover. An additional insurance for private car policyholders to cover the difference between their total loss indemnity payments and the price of a replacement car. The insurance is offered only by a very small number of insurers.

tornado. A storm of wind of extreme violence. It originates in a funnel-shaped cloud which rotates. The barometric pressure may drop so severely and rapidly that buildings may actually explode from within. Tornado insurance is required in some territories.

tort. A civil wrong the remedy for which is an action for unliquidated damages and which is not exclusively the breach of contract or breach of a trust. Negligence and nuisance (qv) are examples of torts of relevance to liability insurers.

tortfeasor. The party who commits a tort (qv).

Torrey Canyon Disaster. A major disaster that alerted all countries to the risks and dangers of oil pollution. On 18 March 1967 the *Torrey Canyon* (a Liberian oil tanker) went aground 24 kilometres north-east of the Scilly Isles liberating her cargo of crude oil. On 24 March 1967 there was a 64-kilometre long oil slick with an average width of 16 kilometres off Land's End. A detergent was sprayed on the floating oil to emulsify and 'sink' it, then the ship was bombed, some of the oil being burned while the remainder was swept away by the sea. The burning consumed about one-third of the total cargo. A great deal of oil landed on the Cornish beaches to produce further costly cleaning up activities. Some drifted across the English Channel causing the French Government to take prompt action to safeguard the beaches and oyster fisheries of Brittany. The Merchant Shipping (Oil Pollution) Act 1971 was passed in order to make oil pollution insurance compulsory for certain tankers.

total assets. *See* ASSET.

total declared resources of members. *See* LLOYD'S MEMBERS' MEANS.

total loss. *See* ACTUAL TOTAL LOSS and CONSTRUCTIVE TOTAL LOSS.

'total loss of sight'. This does not occur if the eye can distinguish daylight from darkness (*MacDonald* v *Mutual Life and Citizens Assurance Co* (1910)). This will be so even though the eyesight is so poor that it prevents the insured under a personal accident policy from following his occupation (*Copeland* v *Locomotive Engineers' Insurance Association* (1910)).

total loss only. Marine insurances, particularly hull facultative reinsurances, are sometimes arranged on the basis that the insurer or reinsurer, as the case may be, is liable only in the event of a total loss.

'touch and stay at any port or place whatsoever'. A marine clause which only permits the vessel to call at the customary ports on the voyage and for purposes connected with the voyage. Such calls do not amount to deviation (qv).

tow and assist clause. A clause in the Institute Time Clauses stating that the vessel will not be towed except where towing is customary or the ship is in need of assistance to the first place of safety. It is also provided that the ship shall not undertake towage or salvage services under a previously arranged contract.

toxic. Anything of a toxic nature is of major concern to liability insurers and insureds knowingly handling toxics or disposing of toxic waste must disclose the facts to the insurers. Toxics are capable, through chemical action, of killing, injuring, or impairing an organism.

trade association clauses. The Institute of London Underwriters (qv) has drafted and agreed standard clauses with a number of trade associations to give them the comprehensive cover they require. The trades affected include: rubber, timber, coal, sugar and flour.

trade contents. This term often appears as an insured item under the combined policies effected by small businesses. It may bring together in one sum stock, trade fixtures, fittings, and machinery. An alternative is to cover stock separately while combining other forms of trade property into a single figure under the title trade contents. When insured in this way trade contents are sometimes covered on a new for old basis (qv).

trade endorsements. Endorsements to vary the policy terms to reflect the requirements of a trade or category of risk within a particular trade. They are especially used in employers' liability insurance. *See* RESTRICTIVE ENDORSEMENTS.

trade plate basis. A method of rating motor traders' road risks policies under which the insurer charges a flat rate for each set of trade plates. Cover is limited to vehicles carrying a set of specified trade plates. For alternative methods of rating *see* NAMED DRIVER BASIS and POINTS BASIS.

trade wastes. Wastes of organic and inorganic origin discharged by industrial and commercial concerns. Organic wastes are discharged on a considerable scale by the food industries: canneries, dairies, breweries, abbatoirs and fish-meat factories. Other significant contributors of waste include paper-mills, tanneries, petro-chemical works, textile manufacturers and laundries. Inorganic wastes include acids, alkalis, cyanides, sulphides and the salts of arsenic, lead, copper, chromium and zinc. Underwriters concern themselves with the methods of waste disposal used by firms as considerable pollution damage and cleaning up costs can arise. Care is exercised in the underwriting of pollution risks. Any discharge of waste into the air, soil or water can create major problems not least for liability insurers.

trailer. This is defined in the Road Traffic Act and the Road Traffic Act regulations as a vehicle drawn by a motor vehicle. There is no requirement that the vehicle has to be mechanically propelled and that type of vehicle is not excluded. In *Garner* v *Burn* (1951) a towed empty poultry shed was held to be a trailer. According to the Act a broken down articulated vehicle (unit and unladen trailer) is treated as a single trailer. The usual form of goods-carrying vehicle policy contains a general exception to strike out all cover when the vehicle is towing a trailer except any one disabled mechanically-propelled vehicle. This is important as 'trailer', for the purpose of the exception, does not refer to a lorry being towed (*Jenkins* v *Deane* (1933)). Goddard J. regarded a trailer as something increasing the space available for the carriage of goods and he could not regard a broken down lorry in this light. Insurers are prepared to cover trailers while attached or detached on either a comprehensive or third party basis. The private car policy does not exclude the towing of trailer and the policy will operate in the normal way but any insurance on the trailer itself will have to be specially arranged. Agricultural policies provide third party cover while trailers are attached and cover as many trailers as the law permits to be attached at any one time. Some policies provide own damage cover automatically to trailers while attached although there may be a value limit. Where it is not a part of the standard cover, damage cover to trailers while attached can usually be purchased for an additional premium, as can third party and damage cover while trailers are detached.

transshipment. The transfer of goods from one vessel to another. It is often contracted for in 'through' bills of lading. Transshipment during an insured voyage is only covered when necessitated by an insured peril, but the Transit Clause (qv) provides transshipment without additional premium. Transshipments increase the insurers' risk but where it is usual or expected the insurer can take account of it when fixing the rate.

transfer of business. A procedure whereby an insurance company can, subject to supervision by the Department of Trade and Industry, transfer its rights and obligations under policies issued to another insurer without obtaining the formal consent of the policyholders concerned.

transfer premiums. A type of state scheme premium which can be paid when accrued benefits in excess of guaranteed minimum pensions (qv) have been transferred to an occupational pension scheme that is not contracted out.

transfer value. The value of a pension in a previous employment when transferred to a new employer's pension scheme.

Transit Clause. An Institute Cargo clause (1/1/82) under which cover begins when the goods leave the warehouse etc at the place named for the commencement of transit. Cover continues during the ordinary course of transit and ceases: on arrival at final warehouse; on arrival at any other warehouse used for storage or allocation/distribution; on expiry of 60 days after whichever of the foregoing first occurs. If the intended destination is altered after discharge, cover ceases on commencement of transit to new destination, unless it has already ceased under the above conditions. Cover continues (subject to the foregoing and to the Termination of Contract of Carriage clause) during delay beyond the control of the assured and during any delay, forced discharge etc or any variation of the adventure out of a liberty granted to the shipowner/charterer under the contract of affreightment.

transit insurance. See GOODS IN TRANSIT INSURANCE.

travel insurance. This is for anyone going on holiday abroad (not often effected for UK holidays) or non-manual workers on business trips (prior declaration policies (qv)). It pays the cost of most disasters or misfortunes—medical expenses; loss/theft of luggage and personal possessions; loss of money; cost of cancelling or curtailing the holiday. Lump sums for accidental death or serious disablement (eg loss of limb) and 'disablement from working' benefits. It is also possible to insure against the insolvency of the tour operator or airline. Policies, sometimes referred to as holiday insurance, are sold on a 'package deal' or 'selected benefits' basis.

treaty. The term that describes the contract made between a ceding office and a reinsurer to provide automatic reinsurance facilities. See TREATY REINSURANCE.

treaty reinsurance. Under treaty arrangements the reinsurers agree to accept the risks offered by the ceding office (qv) without the option of declining.

This enables the ceding office to grant immediate cover for large amounts without first seeking the consent of the reinsurers. See also QUOTA SHARE, SURPLUS LINE, EXCESS OF LOSS, and FACULTATIVE-OBLIGATORY TREATIES.

trespass. A tort (qv) committed with 'force and violence' on the person, property or rights of another. All three types are actionable per se without proof of damage. (a) Trespass to land is 'the direct interference with the land of another'. It can even occur innocently and the violence may only be implied. (b) Trespass to the person can take one of three forms: battery (the actual application of force); assault (a threat that puts someone in fear of battery); false imprisonment (total restraint of a person's freedom of movement). (c) Trespass to goods is the direct act of interference with goods in the possession of another. The interference must be intentional or negligent. The law relating to wrongful interference with goods is now contained in the Torts (Interference with Goods) Act 1977. Also see CONVERSION. As liability policies do not cover intentional injury or damage and as negligence is a prerequisite of liability for injury to persons or goods few insurance types claims are likely to be based on trespass. Also trespass, eg just wrongfully entering someone's land, may occur without causing the injury or damage needed to trigger a liability policy. However, the operative clause (qv) of a public liability can be widened to include legal liability arising from trespass, false arrest, invasion of the right of privacy, detention, false imprisonment, false eviction, and, amongst other things, false arrest. Note (i) that some cover exists for trespass under the Loss of Documents (qv) extension in a professional indemnity policy; (ii) some cover may be available under legal expenses insurance (qv) where an allegation of trespass has given rise to a dispute.

tribunalisation. A process of scrutiny by the Committee of Lloyd's (qv) of the financial standing of agencies and other organisations proposing to produce business as coverholders (qv) through binding authorities (qv). All cover holders have to be approved by the tribunal staff. The binding authority bye-law (No. 4 of 1985) provides that every binding authority must be evidenced in writing and presented to the Lloyd's Policy Signing Office by the relevant Lloyd's broker. Only an approved cover holder can receive such authority. The tribunal staff operate within a regulatory framework laid down by the Council of Lloyd's (qv).

'trigger'. The event that 'triggers' the policy is specified in the policy as being an essential event that must occur before the insurer can be held liable for any loss. In liability insurances, for example, the policy may be triggered by the time of occurrence of the damage (*see* LOSSES-OCCURRING POLICIES) or by the time of the claim (*see* CLAIMS-MADE POLICIES). *See also* TRIPLE TRIGGER THEORY.

triple trigger theory. The term 'any one event (or occurrence)' (qv) applies in respect of the insurer's limit of liability under both liability policies and excess of loss treaties. The burning down of a house by a negligent builder can take place in a short time scale but latent diseases occur slowly over time, pollution can also occur slowly over time, while the effects of unsafe pharmaceutical products may not be apparent for years. As most liability policies are on a losses-occurring basis it has to be decided when the 'event' as required to trigger the policy has occurred and how the limit of indemnity will be applied. In terms of the triple trigger theory, the event could be the exposure to the injury, the manifestation of the symptoms, or the discovery of the loss, damage or disease. These problems caused a shift at one time towards claims-made policies (qv). To deal with the problem of limits of indemnity insurers or reinsurers can define how the limits are to be applied, eg a products liability reinsurer could use an aggregate extension clause to define how a series of claims is to be covered. *Also see* BATCH CLAUSE.

true monthly premiums. A life insurance premium which is paid monthly and is not an instalment of an annual premium. Consequently when death occurs there is no deduction from the claim payment in respect of the premiums that would have been payable

had the policy run its full term in the year when death occurs. The monthly premium incorporates a loading to compensate the insurer in respect of the loss of interest due to the premium not being paid in advance and for the risk of loss of premium on death.

trust. A relation or association between one person(s) on one hand and another person(s) on the other based on confidence, by which property is vested in or held by one person, on behalf of and for the benefit of another. The holder of the property is the trustee and the other party, the beneficiary (*cestui que trust*), is the beneficial owner. The beneficiary not only has the right to have the property administered by the trustee but has an interest in the specific trust property and assets themselves. The terms of the trust are normally set down in a trust deed the terms of which bind the trustees. Trusts were originally devised as a means of transferring wealth from one generation to another. Trusts are now used for a variety reasons including: the enabling property to be held for persons (eg minors) currently unable to enjoy or administer that property; the preservation of property for persons in succession; the protection of property from family creditors; the making of investments through unit trusts (qv); the provision of pensions for retired employees and their dependants; and the minimisation of the incidence of tax. *See* PARTNERSHIP ASSURANCE, MARRIED WOMEN'S PROPERTY ACT 1882, and TRUST POLICIES.

Trustee Act 1925, s. 20 (4). Money recovered under an insurance on property held in trust may be applied by the trustee (or by the court) in reinstating the property, but the consent of any person whose consent is necessary under the trust instrument must be obtained.

trustees. The person or persons appointed to carry out the terms of a trust (qv). A trustee has an insurable interest in respect of the legal right or interest in the trust property vested in him if permitted or directed by the trust deed.

trust deed. The legal document setting out the responsibilities of the trustees, ie holders of property, and the rights of the beneficiaries. In the case of unit trusts (qv) the trust deed concerns the trustees and the fund managers and lays down the framework within which managers must operate.

Trust policies. A policy which forms the property to be held in trust for the beneficiary. *See* INDIVIDUAL TRUST POLICIES FOR PARTNERS. People whose capital is used in their business or profession often effect whole life insurances on trust under the Married Women's Property Act 1882 (qv) for the protection of dependants and cannot normally be claimed by creditors in the event of bankruptcy. A child's deferred insurance could also be arranged in trust for a child under the same Act.

turnover. The monetary value of work done or goods sold in a period of time. The figure reflects the level of activity in a firm or organisation and may be used as a unit of exposure (qv). This is the case, for example, with products liability. *See* ADJUSTABLE POLICIES. *See also* STANDARD TURNOVER in regard to business interruption insurance.

twenty-fourths method. A method of computing the unearned premium reserve (qv). It is assumed that, on average, policies run from the middle of the month of inception. The appropriate number of twenty-fourths of premiums relating to the policies commencing in each month is then carried forward as unearned.

twins insurance. A policy which pays an agreed sum upon the occasion of the birth of twins to the mother named in the insurance. The object is to provide a benefit that helps the insured meet the additional expenses that arise following this event, eg extra clothes, domestic help etc. If more than two children are born the benefit is usually doubled. In calculating the premium the insurer takes account of: the mother's age, any history of multiple births in the families concerned going back three generations, and number of children already born to the insured mother. The insured selects a benefit required from the range offered by the insurer, eg £500 to £2000. The cover does not operate if the multiple birth follows the use of any fertility treatment or if only one child survives for more than 24 hours. There may also be restrictions in respect of premature births, eg cover not to apply if the birth is more than six weeks premature.

two-risk warranty. A warranty used in catastrophe excess of loss reinsurance (qv) to ensure that the reinsurance is not invoked unless at least two distinct risks are involved. Involvement in single losses means that it is effectively operating as a working cover excess of loss treaty (qv). The warranty is used in life, personal accident, catastrophe property and reinsurance in the London excess market (LMX).

two-tier bonus system. A life assurance bonus system that awards 'with profits' policyholders one rate of bonus on the sum assured and a different rate of bonus on the declared bonuses.

two times rule. *See* QUALIFYING POLICIES.

U

uberrimae fidei. A Latin phrase meaning 'of the fullest confidence'. *See* UTMOST GOOD FAITH.

UK Equities. Usually it means ordinary shares issued by a UK incorporated company, not being an investment trust, and which are quoted in the official list of a recognised stock exchange in the UK, or dealt in on the Unlisted Securities Market.

ullage. The loss of liquid, otherwise called trade loss, when shipped in bulk or in casks, and occurring during a voyage as a result of shrinkage or evaporation. The insurer pays only for leakage losses in excess of a stated figure in order to make some allowance for this situation.

ultimate net loss clause. In excess of loss reinsurance, the reinsurer assumes liability for the excess of the ceding office's 'ultimate net loss'. This means the sum or sums paid by the ceding office in settlement of all losses arising out of one event, including any litigation or other expenses connected therewith, but excluding: the salaries of the employees of the ceding office who were involved with the investigation of claims; recoveries by way of salvage and otherwise; sums recoverable under other reinsurances.

umbrella arrangements. This is defined in the Umbrella Arrangement bye-law (no. 6 of 1988) as 'an arrangement between a Lloyd's broker and a non-Lloyd's broker whereby the Lloyd's broker permits the non-Lloyd's broker to use the name, Lloyd's Policy Signing Office number and pseudonym of the Lloyd's broker for the purpose of placing insurance business with or on behalf of underwriting members'. The non-Lloyd's broker must intend becoming a Lloyd's registered broker within three years, must be registered with the Insurance Brokers Registration Council and may not have entered into such an arrangement with more than one Lloyd's broker. The non-Lloyd's broker must undertake to submit to all Lloyd's bye-laws and regulations. The Lloyd's broker is responsible for premiums due to the underwriting members, a fact which must, with the name of the non-Lloyd's broker, be entered on the slip.

umbrella brokers. A broker operating in the Room (qv) at Lloyd's under the name of a Lloyd's broker. *See* UMBRELLA ARRANGEMENTS.

umbrella liability policy. A policy providing high limits of indemnity in excess of the primary and excess liability insurances and giving additional excess cover for perils not covered by the primary policies. The term umbrella is derived from the fact that it is a separate policy and above the insured's other liability policies.

unauthorised passengers. A passenger in or on a conveyance without the permission of the person responsible for the management and control of the conveyance. Such a person, eg a hitchhiker, might be permitted to ride in a motor vehicle by a driver in contravention of the express instructions of the owner of the vehicle. The display of a notice, eg 'no liabililty to passengers' or 'passengers travel at their own risk' will be of no effect as the 'unauthorised passenger' will have a right of claim under a provision in the Road Traffic Act and the liability will be covered by a policy issued in pursuance of the compulsory insurance requirements of that Act.

unborn persons. *See* CONGENITAL DISABILITIES (CIVIL LIABILITY) ACT 1976.

uncalled capital. A concept employed by Lloyd's underwriters who do not call upon their Names (qv) to contribute capital until there is a loss on a particular year of account and capital is needed. They then have the right to call for as much capital as the circumstances demand.

under-insurance. Insurance where the sum insured is less than the full value at risk and would not be adequate to meet a total loss. The amount of under-insurance is an unknown quantity so the rate of premium bears no definite relationship to the risk run. Partial losses are very frequent compared with total losses and this produces a greater loss ratio where under-insurance exists. Consequently, under-insurance is penalised by average clauses (qv).

underwriter. A synonym for insurer.

underwriter. The term originated in the very early days of marine insurance when merchants (not insurers) combined to share risks as a part of their normal trading activities. They indicated their acceptance of a share of a risk by signing their names at the foot of a document (later to be called a policy). The term is now used in various ways: 1. At Lloyd's it refers to an underwriting member or Name (qv). 2. Insurers in general. The term underwriter is a synonym for insurer. 3. An employee of an insurer, ie Lloyd's syndicate, insurance company, insurance pool, or other organisation with the power to accept, reject or fix the terms of the insurance on behalf of his employer or principal. In effect any person who makes decisions of this kind. 4. It is a shortened version of underwriting agent (qv) or underwriting manager. 5. In the USA a life insurance company's full-time commission earning sales agent is called an underwriter. 6. Active underwriter who is a full-time professional working for a Lloyd's syndicate. 7. The head underwriter is the principal active member of a Lloyd's syndicate. 8. The lead or leader (qv).

underwriting. This is the process undertaken by the insurer (or underwriter (qv)) in deciding whether or not to accept a proposed risk and, if so, on what terms. The term is also used to describe the act of insuring risks for one's own account and the activities of an underwriting agent, broker or insurer with authority from an insurer to accept risks on its behalf.

underwriting agency. A firm managing and carrying out underwriting for an insurance company, group of companies, or Lloyd's Names. The agency is appointed under the terms of an underwriting agency agreeement (qv). At Lloyd's there is a distinction between a managing agent (who manages one or more syndicates) and a members' agent (who acts for Names in other capacities and may place them on syndicates run by managing agents), although the majority of agents carry out both functions. An underwriting agent must have satisfied the requirements of the Council of Lloyd's for carrying out an underwriting agency at Lloyd's.

underwriting agency agreement. A contract made between a Lloyd's underwriter or company and an underwriting agent. It sets out the duties, powers and remuneration of the agent. The Lloyd's Agency Agreement Byelaw (no. 1 of 1985) laid down that from 1st January 1987 only the standard agency agreement would be permitted.

underwriting by occupation. In a number of personal lines insurances (qv) the occupation of the insured may be significant in determining the extent of the risk. This may be due to the occupation itself or even to the life-style commonly associated with given occupations. In personal accident insurances the occupation above all distinguishes one proposer from another as the risk of accidental bodily injury will be reflected by the type of work undertaken (sedentary or hazardous), the usual working conditions and the machinery used. Also in some occupations (eg pianist) even a minor injury can cause disablement from working. Some motor insurers offer special schemes to attract people in given occupations, eg civil servants, members of the police force. This may reflect the (limited) extent of the motoring undertaken and/or life-styles, attitudes or other characteristics that will influence the risk. In life insurance the occupation is relevant when it presents a special hazard, eg pilots and members of the armed forces. In some trades and business insurance rates and terms of insurance are based on the trade or work undertaken. *See* RESTRICTIVE ENDORSEMENTS.

underwriting excess of loss reinsurance. An alternative term for working cover excess of loss (qv).

underwriting factors. Factors that will influence an underwriter in his assessment of the risk. Underwriting factors will embrace all material facts (qv) but will often embrace other issues. For example, a proposer (qv) is not required by the duty of utmost good faith (qv) to disclose facts of law and matters of common knowledge. Consequently, in assessing an employers' liability risk it will not be necessary for the proposer to point out that liability may arise through breach of certain statutory duties but they will be considered by the underwriter. Also a proposer for household insurance in Belfast will not have to be told that the political unrest may increase the risk of damage.

underwriting profit. Money earned by an insurer in its underwriting (qv) activities as distinguished from money earned in the investment of assets. This is sometimes called a technical profit.

underwriting reserves. An alternative term for technical reserves (qv). Funds reserved against claims.

underwriter's guarantee. In lieu of general average deposits (qv) shipowners may accept an underwriter's guarantee to pay the finally assessed general average contribution assessed against the particular interest insured by the underwriters. If the shipowner insists on an unlimited guarantee underwriters seek a counter guarantee from the insured to safeguard themselves against the consequences of under-insurance.

underwriting and claims control clause. A clause in a reinsurance treaty which reserves the right of control of underwriting and claims negotiations to the reinsurer.

unearned premium. This is the proportion of the premium on a policy which refers to the time that the policy still has to run (eg £50 if a twelve months policy costing £100 has six months still to run). The insurer earns the premium as the policy term proceeds. *See* UNEARNED PREMIUM RESERVE.

unearned premium insurance. This can be added to an aviation hull policy. If a total loss occurs before the policy has run its full term, the insured has paid an 'unearned premium' (qv) for the time after the loss. This insurance reimburses the insured for the loss of the unearned premium.

unearned premium reserve. As all insurances do not expire at the close of the insurer's financial year, provision has to be made for proportions of risk still to run when preparing the annual accounts. In non-life insurance it was common, on a rule of thumb basis, to reserve 40 per cent of premium income but today more exact methods are used whereby 1/365 of each premium can be reserved for each day the policy has to run. Consequently the unearned premium reserve is the sum of all the unearned premiums of unexpired policies at the relevant accounting date. *See also* TWENTY-FOURTHS METHOD.

unenforceable contracts. A contract that is unenforceable is defective only in the sense that it cannot be enforced by direct legal action. The effect is that as the contract, though unenforceable, is valid and subsisting, a transferee of property gains a good title, and a deposit paid may be retained. A contract that fails to satisfy the requirements of the Statute of Frauds 1677 (qv) is unenforceable. A contract of fidelity guarantee (qv) not in writing would be unenforceable because of non-compliance with the provisions of the Statute of Frauds.

unexpired risk reserve. A fund created to cover any deficiency in the unearned premium reserve (qv). This usually occurs where the insurer feels that its premiums on existing policy have been inadequate to meet the claims likely to arise on current policies as yet unexpired.

Unfair Contract Terms Act 1977. An Act which restricts the ability of a business or trader to limit liability. A business cannot exclude or limit its liability for death or personal injury arising from negligence. It can exclude or restrict liability for other loss or damage (eg damage to property) resulting from negligence only if the exclusion clause (qv) meets the test of reasonableness (qv). A business dealing with a consumer or dealing on its own written standard form of contract cannot exclude or restrict its liability for breach of contract or allow the provision of an inadequate service unless it can show that the clause satisfies the test of reasonableness. Nor can a business require a consumer to indemnify it against any loss incurred through negligence or breach of contract unless it can show that the clause satisfies the same test. In the context of these provisions, 'negligence' includes breach of any contractual or common law duty to take reasonable care or exercise reasonable skill. These provisions generally extend to contracts for the supply of services as well as goods, but in certain cases, eg innkeepers (qv) and carriers (qv), the right to limit liability is given by statute. Certain types of contract, notably insurance contracts, are exempt from the provisions of the Act. Exemption led to insurers entering voluntarily into Statements of Practice (qv) for the benefit of private policyholders.

unified claims system. See LIMNET.

uniform bonus system. A method of allocating a part of a life office's surplus to its with profits policyholders. The bonus is uniform, ie the same for all policyholders, and is usually expressed as a sum assured and existing bonuses. See UNIFORM COMPOUND REVERSIONARY BONUS (a) and uniform simple reversionary bonus (b) under bonus. See also CONTRIBUTION SYSTEM.

uniform accrual. The method of determining benefits for early leavers under the terms of the 'preservation' conditions of the Social Security Act 1973/1985. Retirement benefits are treated as being earned equally over the period of potential pensionable service to normal pension date.

uninsurable risk. A risk which cannot be insured. It is a risk which fails to meet the essential requirements of an insurable risk (qv). It may be because of: (a) sentimental value; (b) lack of insurable interest; (c) the inability to employ the law of large numbers making the risk unquantifiable; (d) public policy; (e) widespread losses (eg war damage to property on land, unemployment); (f) excessive cost; (g) entrepreneurial or speculative risks (qv); (h) certainty as to loss as op-

posed to uncertainty. The presence of any one of these features is generally sufficient to make a risk uninsurable.

uninsured losses. Losses not covered by a first party insurance (qv). For example, a motorist who insured his car against loss or damage under a comprehensive private car policy may pay the first part of the own damage (qv) claim under an excess (qv) and have to hire a car while his own is being repaired. The amount of the excess and the hire charges are his uninsured losses. If a third party can be held liable for those losses he may be able to recover from that third party who in turn may be indemnified by his insurer. Motor legal expenses insurance includes uninsured loss recovery (qv). Other uninsured losses may include out-of-pocket expenses, treatment or transport for injury, compensation for personal injury, and loss of earnings.

uninsured loss recovery. A legal expenses insurance (qv) available as an extension of an existing policy or section of a legal expenses insurance policy offering full cover to businesses (commercial legal expenses insurance) or families. The victim of an uninsured loss (qv), eg a vehicle owner, is covered for his legal expenses in pursuing his claim (qv) against a third party such as a negligent motorist.

uninsured motorist. A driver who is not covered by third party insurance as required by the Road Traffic Act. See MOTOR INSURERS BUREAU.

uninsured working expenses. Business expenses that are not at risk of loss by fire as they vary directly with the level of turnover. They are deducted as specified expenses (qv) from the turnover for the purpose of ascertaining the gross profit to be insured under business interruption insurance (qv).

unit allocation. In a unit-linked insurance contract, the percentage of the premium which is used to buy units. It varies according to the charging structure of the policy and the age of the policyholder.

United Kingdom Society of Average Adjusters. Formed in 1981 between a number of firms of average adjusters,

in fear. Buildings insurance on properties in Northern Ireland exclude loss or damage arising from unlawful, wanton or malicious acts by persons acting on behalf of or in connection with any unlawful association.

unlimited liability. This is the distinguishing feature of Lloyd's which separates it from all other insurers. Names (qv) at Lloyd's, who group into syndicates, can be held personally liable to the full extent of their personal wealth for their share of underwriting losses. As a result applicants for membership have to be sponsored, undergo a means test, and, if successful in the application, make a monetary deposit or deposit in trust with the Committee of Lloyd's securities against underwriting commitments.

unliquidated damages. Damages which are assessed by the court. They are not worked out in advance and stated in a contract as is the case with liquidated damages (qv). Unliquidated damages are usually the main component of the claims settled by liability insurers.

unoccupancy. Sometimes a theft insurer may require that the premises never be left without an inhabitant and introduces a definition into the policy to give effect to his requirements. One version is to state that the 'Premises within described are never left without some person acting on behalf of the insured actually in occupation'.

unoccupied, becoming. The words 'becoming unoccupied' mean actual as distinct from constructive occupation. In *Marzouca* v *Atlantic and British Commercial Insurance Co Ltd* (1971) a fire policy provided that cover ceased to apply if the building 'becomes unoccupied' and this meant a daily regular presence of someone on the premises. Cover was stated, in the policy, to cease if the premises, a hotel, 'become unoccupied for a period of more than 30 days'. The premises were vacated on 30 September 1963 and remained empty until 20 November 1963 when conversion work began. A policeman was employed as a nightwatchman but he never entered the building and from his hut his view was restricted. The hotel was burnt down on 19/20 May 1964. Occupation does not necessarily involve using the premises as a dwelling but there should be a daily presence of a regular nature.

unplanned risk assumption. *See* RISK ASSUMPTION.

unrecovered damages. Damages awarded by the court against a defendant who has failed to pay the damages. *See* REVERSE LIABILITY and UNSATISFIED COURT JUDGMENTS for insurance solutions to this problem.

'unrepaired damage'. If, for some reason, a damaged ship is not repaired and has not been sold in her damaged state during the policy term, then on expiry the insured can claim the reasonable amount of depreciation resulting from the unrepaired damage not exceeding the cost of repairing that damage (Marine Insurance Act 1906, s. 69(3)). If the vessel is not repaired and later becomes a total loss by an insured peril during the same policy term, the insurer is liable for the total loss only (s. 77(2)). If the total loss occurs in a subsequent period of the policy, the insured is able to recover both the unrepaired damage and the total loss if they are both caused by insured perils.

unreported claims. *See* IBNR for claims incurred but not yet reported.

'unroadworthy'. This means not fit for the road. In the case of *Clarke* v *National Insurance & Guarantee Corporation Ltd* (1963) the insurer used a general exception excluding liability while the car 'is being driven in an unsafe or unroadworthy condition'. C. packed eight people into his Ford Anglia and the car proceeded down a steep hill, swerving from side to side in the process until it hit an oncoming car killing the driver and injuring one of C's own passengers. NIG relied on the exception. The Court of Appeal found that the gross overloading of the car made it unroadworthy and they were helped by marine insurance precedents. The term therefore is not confined to the soundness of the vehicle but the circumstances in which it is used.

'unsafe'. The word appears in some motor insurance policies (*see* UNROADWORTHY) exceptions or conditions to safeguard the insurers from claims arising when the vehicle is used in an unsafe condition. It is a question of fact in each case as to whether a breach has occurred. Driving an un-lighted vehicle at night has been held sufficient to make a vehicle 'unsafe' (*Trickett* v *Queensland Insurance Co Ltd* (1936)). However, it has to be the ve-hicle that is in that condition and not equipment such as a tow rope (*Jenkins* v *Deane* (1933)).

unsatisfied court judgments. An exten-sion in an employers' liability under which the insurer agrees, at the re-quest of the insured, to pay unsatisfied court judgments obtained by the in-sured's employees against third par-ties. The extension operates in respect of bodily injury to the insured's em-ployees caused during the period of insurance and arising out of employ-ment by the insured in the business. In other words the extension operates if a valid claim would have arisen under the policy had the judgment been against the insured instead of a third party. The insurer will pay the dam-ages if they are wholly or partly unsatis-fied six months after the judgment provided no appeal is outstanding. It is a condition of the payment that the employee concerned or his legal rep-resentatives will assign the judgment to the insurers. For similar insurances *see* REVERSE LIABILITY.

unspecified personal effects. *See* PER-SONAL EFFECTS.

unspecified working expenses. Expenses that are insured as a part of the gross profit item under a business interrup-tion insurance. They relate to expen-ses that will continue despite the interruption in the business, eg rent and interest payments. Wages can be insured in this way as only specified working expenses (qv) are removed from the insurance.

untraced drivers. A driver who fails to stop after an accident in the hope of not being identified or traced or who is unaware that he has been involved in an accident. The lack of identity of a potential defendant deprives the plaintiff of the prospects of a judg-ment and the recovery of damages paid by the driver's insurers. Where the injury is caused in circumstances to which the Road Traffic Act's com-pulsory insurance requirements apply the Motor Insurers' Bureau (qv) com-pensate the victims provided that, on balance of probabilities, the untraced person would have been liable to pay damages for the injury. Deliberate run-ning down of the victims is not within the scheme but victims may be able to secure compensation from the Crimi-nal Injuries Board (qv). The agree-ment covering untraced drivers is the 'MIB (Compensation of Victims of Un-traced Drivers) Agreement' which goes back to an agreement with the Minister of Transport in 1969.

unvalued policy. A property insurance under which the sum insured repre-sents the insurer's maximum liability in the event of a loss that will otherwise be settled on a normal indemnity basis subject to any deductions for excesses (qv) or under-insurance (qv). In marine insurance s. 16 of the Marine Insurance Act provides a basis of valu-ation for the insurance of hulls, car-goes and freight etc, which, in the absence of any agreed value, must be used for the purpose of indemnifying the insured. Hulls and cargoes are in-variably insured under valued policies (qv) but freight is generally insured under unvalued policies.

'use' of motor vehicles (statutory duty). A person has use of a vehicle on a road if he has an element of controlling, man-aging or operating the vehicle at the relevant time (*Elliott* v *Gray* (1960)). It is not lawful for any person to use, or cause or permit any other person to use a motor vehicle on a road unless there is in force in relation to the user a policy that complies with the com-pulsory requirements of the Road Traf-fic Act 1988. 'Use' is not synonymous with 'drive'. An employee driving an employer's vehicle is using it but so to is his employer when the journey is car-ried out in the course of his business. It would be within the law to have a policy restricting driving to the employee as long as both he and the employer are indemnified, the latter as user, the for-mer as driver-user. Where the em-ployee is driving and using his own car on the employer's business, the em-ployer 'causes' the driver to use it (*Ellis* v *Hinds* (1947)) but is still a user and must be indemnified so the employer's indemnity under the third party sec-tion of the private car policy assumes a special significance. An employee who drives an uninsured vehicle belonging to his employer will not be convicted if he proves that the vehicle did not belong to him, that he was using it in the course of employment and that he neither knew nor had reason to know that the requisite insurance was in force. A policy which indemnifies the user but not the driver-user is sufficient for the purposes of the Act as there will be in force a policy in relation to the user (*Ellis* v *Hinds* (see above)). Similarly, if quite out of keeping with long established practice, an employee-user's own insurance did not give an indemnity to his employer, also a user, the law would not be contravened. A passenger is not necessarily the user of a vehicle (*Brown* v *Roberts* (1963)). An owner, who permits his car to be used by a person who is not insured against third party risks as required by the Act, is liable in damages to the third party injured by the negligent driving of the uninsured person (s. 201) (*Monk* v *Warbey* (1935)).

usurped power. This is '(a) invasion by foreign enemies to give laws and usurp the government, or (b) internal armed force in rebellion assuming the power of government by making laws and punishing for not obeying those laws. Usurped power involves organised tumult or open warfare, and must be something more than action by a mere unorganised rabble; it implies a more or less organised body with more or less authorative leaders'. (F.H. Jones, *The Law of Accident and Contingency Insurance,* Pitman.)

utmost good faith (*uberrimae fidei*). A contract is *'uberrimae fidei'* when the promisee is bound to disclose to the promisor every fact or circumstance which may influence him in deciding to enter into the contract or not. The duty to disclose material facts exists whether such information is requested or not. All contracts of insurance are subject to the duty of utmost good faith while ordinary commercial contracts are subject to the doctrine of *caveat emptor* (qv). Insurance is different from ordinary contracts as the parties are not on an equal footing and one, particularly the proposer, could draw the other, the insurer, into a contract in ignorance of material facts and believing the contrary. It may not be possible for an insurer to acquaint himself with the defects of the proposer's case other than by way of the disclosure by the proposer. In other commercial contracts the buyer may acquaint himself with defects in the goods he is purchasing by carrying out an inspection. The duty of utmost good faith is reciprocal but in practice weighs more heavily on the proposer than the insurer who is rarely in a position to withhold facts to the detriment of the proposer. A material fact is any fact that will influence the judgment of a prudent underwriter in his assessment of the risk. The duty extends to cover all material facts that the proposer ought to know as well as those actually known to him. Any breach of the duty makes the contract voidable *ab initio* (qv) at the option of the aggrieved party. Breaches may arise through: (a) Concealment—deliberate suppression of a material fact(s). (b) Non-disclosure—unintentional failure to disclose material fact(s). (c) Fraudulent misrepresentation—deliberate supply of misleading information relating to a material fact. (d) Innocent misrepresentation—unintentional supply of misleading information relating to a material fact. Where the right of avoidance is exercised by the insurer on account of (b) or (d) above, the insurer must give a full return of premium having given no consideration for it. Fraudulent proposers cannot demand a return of premium. Where fraud is involved the insurer is entitled to sue for the tort of deceit and claim damages accordingly. The right is rarely exercised. The duty of disclosure is pre-contractual and continues until negotiations are complete and the risk attaches. Material facts arising during the contract do not have to be disclosed unless such disclosure is required by policy conditions. Under annual renewable contracts the duty revives at renewal as this is tantamount to a new contract. At common law the proposer fulfils his duty by making representations (qv) (written or verbal) as to material facts that are substantially true (ie true to his best knowledge and belief). Honest representations regarding expectations or intentions do not have to be realised. The insurer often extends the inherent duty of utmost good faith to a contractual duty by requiring the proposer to complete and sign a proposal form (qv) containing a declaration which shall become the basis of the contract. In this way all representations (whether material or not) are converted into warranties (qv) and have to be literally true. Any inaccuracy, material or otherwise, entitles the insurer to avoid the policy. Statements of Practice (qv) issued by the Association of British Insurers and the Life Offices Association to which member offices adhere are consumer protection measures applicable to private insurances and life assurances in connection with which insurers agree, inter alia, not to take advantage of breaches of a merely technical nature. *See also* REHABILITATION OF OFFENDERS ACT 1974.

V

valuables. Items of property of above average value (or considerable worth) the loss of which would be regarded as a serious financial loss by their owner. The household contents policy covers valuables within the term 'personal effects'. The single article limit (qv) of this policy is applied to curios, works of art, articles of gold etc and causes many valuables to be specified separately either under the policy itself or insured separately. Many valuables are portable and their high value in relation to bulk causes many insureds to arrange a separate insurance on an 'all risks' basis. An 'all risks' policy may cover unspecified valuables or the valuables may be specified. Unspecified valuables may comprise cameras, binoculars and the like, furs, gold and silver articles. The single article limit for unspecified valuables is normally £500. Valuables exceeding the stated limit should be specified separately. Specified valuables comprise various types of property but typically might include jewellery, small curios, stamp or coin collections, pictures, expensive cameras and the like. Besides the single article limit many household contents policies contain a proviso to the effect that the total value of articles of gold, silver and other precious metal, jewellery, or fur shall not exceed one-third of the declared value of the contents unless specially agreed.

valuation. 1. A statement or certificate confirming the value of items of insured property, usually prepared by an independent professional. 2. In life insurance this is the annual assessment of the insurer's assets and liabilities in the manner required by law (*see* VALUATION REGULATIONS.

valuation linked scheme. A fire insurance scheme under which the insured chooses an inflation rate for the policy year and for each year the work of reinstatement may be necessary.

valuation regulations. Rules, found in the Insurance Companies Regulations 1981, stating how assets and liabilities should be valued for the purpose of the DTI return.

value. In insurance this generally means the estimated worth of something in money terms. It does not include sentimental value (qv). The standard fire policy offers to pay the insured the 'value of the property' and the average clause (qv) refers to the 'value of the property at the time of fire'. Following the rules of construction the term will be given its ordinary meaning and the word will be given the same meaning wherever it appears in the policy unless a contrary intention is shown by express words or definitions contained in the policy. Under unvalued policies (qv) value generally means market value unless the policy is written on a reinstatement basis (qv). In marine insurance policies are generally issued on a valued policy (qv) basis.

value added tax (VAT). A well-known indirect tax. The settlement of a claim is affected by the VAT position of the claimant. If the claimant is VAT-registered the payment is made net of VAT as it can be recovered through normal VAT accounting procedures operated with the Customs and Excise Department. The insurer makes no such deduction in the case of claims from private policyholders, non-VAT registered businesses or exempt rated businesses. In the case of zero-rated commodities the trader will still be able to claim VAT on input.

valued policy. Also known as 'agreed value policy'. This is a policy in which the amount to be paid in the event of a total loss is agreed at the inception and not at the time of the claim. In effect, the insurer agrees that, in the event of a total loss, the actual value of the insured property shall not be a matter of negotiation between them as the agreed value will be paid. If the value changes after the inception then the amount paid may be more or less than an indemnity (qv). The contract is not a perfect indemnity, but indemnity in the 'manner agreed'. Insurers confine the issue of such policies to articles of stable or increasing value (eg jewellery, works of art) and insist upon an independent valuation at the outset. Non-marine insurers normally state in the policy that the agreed value relates only to total losses. Consequently partial losses are settled on a normal indemnity basis by reference to the actual amount of the loss. Marine insurers issue agreed value policies on hull and cargo risks. The indemnity is to be 'in the manner and to the extent agreed'. The intention is to provide a commercial indemnity rather than a strict common law indemnity. For example, in cargo insurances the anticipated profit is included in the agreed value so that, where cargo is lost or damaged, the insured is placed in the same position as if the voyage and transaction had been successfully completed. In partial loss cargo claims the insurer is liable in such proportion of the agreed value as the insurable value of the part lost bears to the insured value of the whole. In partial loss hull claims the insurer pays the reasonable cost of repairs so the agreed value applies to total losses only. Where a marine insurer does not issue a valued policy, the insurable value is computed in accordance with s. 16, Marine Insurance Act 1906.

variable annuities. An annuity (qv) contract under which the payments to the annuitant will vary with the results of an investment portfolio or will be linked to a cost of living index.

vehicle laid up clause. A clause appearing in both private car and goods-carrying vehicle policy forms to allow a rebate when the insured vehicle is off the road out of use. The minimum 'laying up' period is four weeks for cars and six for goods-carrying vehicles. The laid-up rebate is conditional upon the insurance being renewed and is allowed as a deduction against the renewal premium.

vendor. A seller of property or goods. The vendor of property can be held liable for work done on premises before disposing of them by sale or lease (Defective Premises Act 1972 (qv)).

vendor's indemnity. An extension to a products liability policy (qv) to indemnify any vendor of the insured's product (other than a subsidiary company) but only with respect to the sale and distribution of the insured's products. The indemnity does not apply where the injury or damage to third parties arises out of: intentionally changing the physical or chemical make up of the product; demonstration, installation, servicing or repair of products; labelling, packing or repacking of products by the vendor other than repacking into the original packing; the fault or negligence of the vendor. The vendor must observe the terms and conditions of the policy in so far as they can apply.

vested rights. A pensions term meaning (a) benefits to which active members would be unconditionally entitled on leaving service; (b) the preserved pension benefits for deferred pensioners; (c) pensions representing the entitlement of current pensioners; including where appropriate the related benefits for spouses or other dependants.

vesting bonus. Bonus declared in respect of, and allotted to with profits life policies. Once declared it is said to 'vest' and is added to the life insurance benefit and the existing bonuses. All vested bonuses become payable under the same conditions as the with profits benefits and once added cannot be taken away.

violent entry. See FORCIBLE AND VIOLENT ENTRY.

violent means. The word violence read in the context of the whole of the personal accident policy definition of accident (see ACCIDENT) emphasises the insurer's intention to avoid liability for gradually operating causes of an internal nature. The degree of violence is not of any consequence as the smallest degree will suffice.

visible means. The word visible (qv) emphasises the importance to the insurer of restricting personal accident cover to bodily harm caused by accidental external means. Anything which is external is also visible. Exceptions to this strict meaning arise in connection with the taking of poison or the inhaling of gas provided they are not deliberate acts. If a person consumes poison when they intend to take a prescribed medicine, the act is at least visible and there is undoubtedly a fortuitous element involved.

vocational Names. Working members of Lloyd's who are allowed to become Names (qv) on preferential terms. Often their deposits are financed by their employers.

void contract. A contract that has no legal effect; legally it does not exist. All fraudulent contracts are void. The Gaming Act 1845 rendered all gaming contracts null and void. If an insurance policy is arranged against fire, theft or another peril where it is known by the proposer that the property does not exist but he intends to stage a loss, the contract is void. The same is true where a grossly inflated sum insured is fixed by the proposer. Certain contracts entered into by minors are void but contracts for necessaries (things suitable for their condition in life and actual requirements at the time of sale and delivery) are among those which are binding. Insurance contracts will often fall within the term 'necessaries'.

voidable contracts. A contract is voidable if it is open to one of the parties to treat it as void, should he choose to do so. If this is done, then it is void for all purposes. On the other hand if election is made to treat it is as binding, then it is binding on both parties thereto. Certain contracts by minors are voidable. Insurance contracts secured by the insured's misrepresentation or non-disclosure are voidable at the insurer's option. Where a declaration and basis clause (qv) are used then any inaccuracy renders the contract voidable. Otherwise a policy may become voidable because of breach of warranty during the term of the policy. Any right of avoidance should be exercised in a reasonable period of time.

Volenti non fit injuria. 'To him who is willing there can be no injury.' No act is actionable as a tort by a person who has expressly or impliedly assented to it; no one can enforce a right he has voluntarily waived or abandoned. The maxim applies to (a) intentional acts that would otherwise be tortious, eg taking part in a boxing match; (b) running the risk of accidental harm which would otherwise be actionable as negligence. For '*volenti*' to succeed as a defence the consent of the plaintiff must be real and given without force, fear or fraud. There is no consent when a man acts under a moral or legal constraint. For example, a person injured when attempting to rescue a third party endangered by the defendant's negligence does not consent to the risk and by acting under a moral constraint has been denied the freedom of choice essential to *volenti*. Equally knowledge of a risk is not equivalent to consenting to it, especially where the plaintiff is under economic constraints such as being an employee (*Smith* v *Baker* (1891)). Where a term in a contract or notice purports to exclude or restrict liability for negligence a person's agreement to or awareness of such term is not of itself an indication that he voluntarily accepts any risk—Unfair Contract Terms Act 1977, s. 2 (3) (qv).

voluntary excess. An excess (qv) for which the insured volunteers in order to get the benefit of a reduced premium. It is quite common in motor insurance.

voyage policy. A marine insurance policy that covers the subject-matter from the port of departure to destination irrespective of any time element. In practice when cargo is insured on this basis, the Transit Clause (Institute Cargo Clause No. 1) extends the cover to include a time element. Cover then operates from the time of leaving the warehouse at the place named until delivered to the consignee's or other warehouse stated in the policy provided always cover does not go beyond 60 days after discharge from the oversea vessel.

W

wager. A promise to give money or money's worth upon the determination of an uncertain event. The essence of wagering is that one party is to win and the other party to lose on a future event. Wagers were rendered void by s. 18, Gaming Act 1845. *See also* WAGERING POLICY.

wages. Wages may be insured under a business interruption policy as an unspecified working expense (qv) or left uninsured by its removal from the gross profit figure as a specified working expense (qv). *See also* PAYROLL COVER and DUAL WAGES BASIS.

wagering policy. A policy effected without insurable interest (qv) is a wager but *see* POLICY PROOF OF INTEREST (PPI).

wagering policies. Policies declared illegal by the Life Assurance Act 1774 which enacts that all policies shall be null and void if the insured has no interest (*see* INSURABLE INTEREST) in the event insured against or if they are made by way of wagering or gambling. The Act (known as the Gambling Act) also states that no greater sum shall be recovered from the insurer than the value of the insured's interest in the event (*see* INSURABLE FOR 'TIME OF INTEREST' which may be at inception or time of loss). The Act despite its name is not confined to life assurance. Under the Marine Insurance Act 1906 wagering policies are void and the person effecting such a policy is liable to criminal prosecution.

wages declaration. A declaration at the end of the period of insurance when the insured makes a return of the wages paid during that period, normally one year. The declared figure is compared with an estimated figure upon which the premium has been paid. The policy provides for adjustment of the premium. The insurer calls for an additional premium if the wages paid exceed the estimate. Con-

versely, a return is allowed if the level of activity, as evidenced by the declaration, has been less than the estimated level. *See* ADJUSTABLE PREMIUMS. The insured is obliged by policy to maintain records to facilitate the declaration.

'waiters'. The uniformed staff of the Corporation of Lloyd's, who perform general duties, wear red gowns and are known as 'waiters' much as in the times of the original coffee house from which Lloyd's originated.

waiting period. Some policies exclude claims that arise within a certain period, ie the waiting period, of the attachment of the risk. For example, a legal expenses insurance generally excludes any claim arising from a contract where the cause of action arises within the first three months of the first period of insurance. Under a personal accident and sickness insurance, the insurer may exclude liability for sickness claims arising within the first three or four weeks of inception. The waiting period protects insurers against claims by persons who either take out the insurance aware of the impending claim or who are unwittingly approaching a claims situation.

Waiver Clause. 1. When an insured gives a marine insurer 'notice of abandonment' (qv), the insurer declines to accept the notice until in full possession of the facts. Thereafter neither party will make any move which may prejudice his position—for example, attempts by the insured to save the property might be construed as a waiver of abandonment. Similar attempts by the insurer may be taken as acceptance of the abandonment. In the meantime the property may perish. The Waiver Clause, which follows the Sue and Labour Clause (qv) in the policy, makes it clear that no act by the insured or the insurer in attempting to recover or preserve the property shall be considered as a waiver or acceptance of the abandonment. *See also* CONSTRUCTIVE TOTAL LOSS 2. A provision in a life or permanent health insurance which relieves the insured of the obligation to pay the premium during periods of disability.

war. Defined by F. H. Jones (*Law of Accident and Contingency Insurance*, Pitman) as: 'Armed conflict of states in which each seeks to impose its will upon the other by force. It is not a blind struggle between mobs of individuals without guidance or coherence, but a conflict of organised masses moving with a view to co-operation, acting under the impulse of a single will and directed against a definite objective'.

warranted free from particular average. A marine insurance term applied when the policy does not cover partial loss other than a general average loss. Since the introduction the new Institute Cargo Clauses (1/1/82) the term 'particular average' no longer appears but in practice the old terms will be used in marine insurance circles where the meaning is well known.

warranties. Warranties in insurance contracts are equivalent to conditions in other contracts and so a breach enables the aggrieved party to repudiate the contract. Warranties are used by insurers to contain the risk, eg good housekeeping and to reinforce their rating assumptions (no storage of hazardous materials warranted in a fire policy). Warranties may be undertakings that certain things shall be done (waste removed from premises daily), shall not be done (see above), or whereby the insured affirms or negates a certain state of affairs. The statements in a proposal form are normally converted into warranties by means of a declaration.

warranty insurance (boats). The insurance provides cover against structural failure of the hull and spares and mechanical failure of the engine and steering gear for 12 months from the date of purchase in the case of second-hand boats. The boats must be less than six years old and cover is granted following a survey. Defects noted are excluded until they are remedied and passed by the surveyor. *See* EXTENDED WARRANTY INSURANCE.

war and civil war agreement. *See* WAR RISKS 2.

war perils (marine clauses). The cover given by the Institute War Clauses (Cargo) is in respect of: capture (being taken by an enemy); seizure (every forcible act of possession); arrests, restraints or detainment, all resulting from war, civil war, revolution, rebellion, insurrection, or civil strife arising therefrom, or any hostile act by or against a belligerent power or caused by war, civil war etc. It also covers loss/damage caused by derelict mines, torpedoes, bombs, or other derelict weapons of war. The Institute War and Strikes Clauses (Hulls-Time) provided similar cover but extends to strikes, terrorists, confiscation and expropriation.

war risks policies (aviation). War, hi-jacking and similar risks are underwritten in a specialist market and in the marine and aviation market. Cover for liabilities is underwritten in the aviation market only.

war risks. 1. *Marine insurance.* War risks are excluded from both the Institute Cargo Clauses and Institute Time Clauses and reinstated to a limited extent in the Institute War Clauses (Cargo) and the Institute War and Strikes Clauses (Hulls-Time) respectively. In effect, these clauses cover the cargo only while in the oversea vessel, except that damage caused by derelict mines or torpedoes is covered while the cargo is in craft. Separate policies are effected for the insurance of hulls against war risks. This, following the Waterborne Agreement (qv), brings marine insurance into line, as far as possible, with non-marine insurances on property which in effect exclude war risks on land. 2. *Non-marine.* In 1937 insurance companies and Lloyd's underwriters made the war and civil war agreement to exclude liability for the consequences of war, invasion, act of foreign enemy, hostilities (whether war be declared or not), civil war, rebellion, revolution, insurrection or military or usurped power. This attitude has been accepted by the government which introduced its own scheme to cover loss by war risks during the 1939–45 war. Consequently war risks, uninsurable in the commercial insurance market, feature as a standard exclusion in property and liability insurances but the risks (see 1. above) are insurable in the marine and aviation markets. Life insurance does not exclude war risks but personal accident policies have the exclusion.

war risks. A grouping of perils that generally have their origin in political and similar matters capable of causing widespread damage beyond the scope of private enterprise insurers. These risks are in effect fundamental risks (qv). War risks are excluded from material damage policies covering property on land and as such are more properly covered under central government schemes. The perils that are grouped in this way include: war (qv), civil war (qv), rebellion (qv), insurrection (qv), usurped power (qv), military or usurped power (qv), civil commotion (qv), martial law (qv).

Warsaw Convention. An agreement reached in 1929 and updated by the Hague Protocol 1955 between a number of countries to establish uniform legislation affecting the legal responsibility of international air carriers for passengers and goods. The plaintiff does not have to prove negligence but the convention (or laws acted in conformity) limits the liability of air carriers of signatory countries to specific amounts for each passenger claim for bodily injury and also provides limits for damage to luggage and other cargo. The agreement only relates to international flights. It is now governed in the UK by the Carriage by Air Act 1961.

Waterborne Agreement. Insurers generally reached an agreement (*see* WAR RISKS 2) in 1937 that protection of property against war risks was beyond their scope. However, in marine insurance it has been considered essential to give cover against war risks in peace as well as in war to facilitate overseas trade. Consequently, the Institute War Clauses provide the cover but on a more restricted basis (*see* WAR RISKS 1) than the period provided by the normal marine policy with the Institute Cargo Clauses attached.

water mains bonds. A type of performance bond (qv) relating to the laying of water mains.

WBS (without benefit of salvage). A marine policy written on the terms that the insurer is not to get the benefit of the salvage. Such a policy is not legally enforceable but voiding the insurance is obviated when salvage is clearly impossible. As a result tonner reinsurance (qv) contracts are written both WBS and PPI (qv).

wear and tear. Wear and tear arises out of the normal use of property and is excluded from property insurances. However, there is now a tendency for household contents insurers to offer 'new for old' policies, ie a replacement rather than an indemnity insurance. *See also* REINSTATEMENT POLICIES.

weather insurance. A special version of the abandonment of events (qv) which pays if heavy rain causes cancellation or restricts attendance at outdoor events. There is a standard version called Pluvius which requires no proof of financial loss The insured collects if the rainfall reaches specified levels at stated times. It departs from the fundamental principles of insurance. It is sometimes effected by holidaymakers and cricketers for their benefit matches.

wedding insurance. A recent innovation to give financial protection against various losses and risks arising in connection with a wedding. It is a hybrid policy covering cancellation expenses, material loss or damage, and public liability risks. The cancellation cover operates up to the amount selected by the insured (eg £2000) in connection with expenses incurred due to necessary cancellation of the wedding or the reception as a result of any fortuitous cause (eg death, injury or unemployment of the bride, bridegroom or any of their relatives). If the wedding photographs have to be retaken due to non-appearance of the photographer, or loss of, damage to, or non-development of the negatives a claim arises up to the agreed amount. Loss or damage cover is available in respect of bridal attire and wedding presents. Public liability cover operates in respect of organisation of the wedding and reception and extends to liability for damage to hired premises other than tents or marquees. The food and drink risk is also covered.

Wellington Agreement. An agreement concluded in Washington, DC to facilitate the joint settlement of asbestos claims in an Asbestos Claims Facility (qv). The agreement was made on 19 June 1985 and involved 34 US manufacturers of asbestos, 16 US liability insurers, Lloyd's and a number of companies based in the London market (qv). The agreement was named after its 'architect', Harry Wellington (dean of Yale Law School). Following internal dissension the Facility was dissolved in October 1988 but has been succeeded by the Centre for Claims Resolution (CCR) (qv). The agreement set rules to be applied by the Facility in examining over 30 000 claims by asbestos victims and allocating the cost to liability policies effected by manufacturers with individual insurers. The basic rule of the agreement specifying the scope of cover so provided was based largely on the interests of the manufacturers. Cover was provided under all liability policies in force at the time when the claimant's physical state was continuously impaired. First call was made against all policies covering asbestos products effected by the mid-1970s which cover asbestos products before any call was made against subsequent policies which excluded the asbestos risk to an increasing extent or imposed large deductibles on the manufacturers. Subsequent policies held by manufacturers, or the manufacturer himself, did not attract any liability until all policies in the Initial Coverage Block providing effective cover of asbestos claims had been exhausted. Not all manufacturers or insurers participated in the agreement and they dealt with the liabilities by normal legal processes. The agreement as a voluntary action succeeded in cutting the overhead costs of resolving asbestos claims. It eliminated duplicate fact-finding, established uniformity unlikely to be achieved in the US courts, and avoided protracted litigation on issues such as liability, policy interpretations for which the insurer was liable. The need for a successor, the CCR, is important as the latency and long-tail (10 to 20 years after exposure) means that a number of insurers may be involved in any one case. Also it may not be easy for the plaintiff to identify which manufacturer's product caused the injurious exposure and in a number of US asbestos cases market share liability (qv) has been considered.

wet risk. A Lloyd's term for non-marine risks, ie it is not connected with hulls, marine cargoes or maritime liability, but has a maritime association. Examples include the insurance of dock and port structures, offshore oil and gas structures, bridges, wharves and dams.

whole policy rule. A rule of construction to the effect that the whole of the policy must be looked at and not merely a particular clause. An exception against 'loss by freezing' was held to mean 'loss immediately caused by freezing'. The policy covered 'immediate' loss by leakage, etc, and it was held that damage caused by the escape of water from a pipe which had burst through water freezing in it did not fall within the exception, but was covered by the policy. The same words bear the same meaning wherever they appear in the policy but the object of particular clauses must still be considered and the same words may bear different meanings in different clauses. Also where a proposal is expressly incorporated in a policy by the terms of the policy the two should be read together.

winding up of an insurance company. The operation of putting to an end the carrying on of the business of an insurance company, realising its assets and discharging its liabilities, settling any question of account or contribution between the members, and dividing the surplus assets (if any) among the members. Companies generally can be wound up compulsorily by the court or voluntarily. In the case of an insurance company, the Secretary of State may petition for a winding up on the ground that: the company is unable to pay its debts; the company has failed to satisfy an obligation imposed by one of the Insurance Companies Acts; the company has failed to keep or to produce proper accounting records and he is unable to ascertain their financial position; it is expedient in the public interest that the company should be wound up.

windscreen breakage. Under private comprehensive car policies, insurers agree that, if a claim for damage consists solely of damage to the windscreen or windows, payment will be made without prejudice to the insured's entitlement to no claim discount. The term 'windscreen cover', which is commonly used, is really a misnomer as the cover on the windscreen already exists but the insurer provides a concession in the policy to protect the insured's no claim discount. The type of claim is one over which the insured usually has no control.

windstorm (including tornado and cyclone) insurance. Insurance against damage done to property by unusually high winds or cyclone or hurricane. The risks are usually insured as additional perils but it is possible to insure against these perils alone.

wilful blindness. The ignorance which occurs when a person deliberately and wilfully refrains from inquiring into a situation or deliberately disregards a situation in the hope of profiting from it. It applies to assignees for value who seek to gain advantage by this 'acquired' ignorance by giving notice of an assignment under the Policies of Assurances Act 1867 (qv) ahead of previous assignees they know or suspect to exist who have not yet given notification. These assignees are not permitted to use this conduct as a means of gaining priority.

with privity of the assured. In a time policy (qv) there is no implied warranty of seaworthiness but where, with 'privity of the assured' the ship is sent to sea in an unseaworthy state, the insurer will not be liable for any loss due to unseaworthiness (Marine Insurance Act 1906, s. 39(5)). In this context 'privity of the assured' means with his 'knowledge and consent'. The shipowner needs to have knowledge of the facts and must also need to know that those facts will make the vessel unseaworthy. The shipowner, however, is not entitled to turn a 'blind eye' to the facts.

with profits policies. Whole life policies and endowment policies (qv) which attract bonuses representing a share in the profits (*see* DIVISIBLE SURPLUS). The bonuses are declared periodically (every year) and once declared, the bonus becomes a guaranteed addition to the sum assured with which it ultimately becomes payable unless taken as a cash bonus. Unlike without profits policies they provide some protection against inflation but each pound spent buys less initial cover by way of sum insured.

with proportion. A term to indicate that if an annuitant (qv) dies before the next annuity payment is due, a pro rata payment will be made in respect of the period from the last payment to the date of death.

without prejudice. A phrase normally used during the negotiations of third party claims settlements indicating that liability is not admitted. Statements made 'without prejudice' cannot subsequently be used in evidence at court proceedings.

without (or non-profit) profits policies. Life insurance policies that guarantee a fixed sum on death or survival (according to whether whole life or endowment (qv) without any addition to represent a share in the profits of the insurer. The real value of the sum insured is eroded as inflation proceeds but at the same time the real cost reduces as the premium is fixed in money terms at the outset. At the outset each pound spent buys more cover than under an equivalent with profits policy (qv).

work away risk. A term used to describe a public liability risk where the main hazard stems from the work undertaken by the insured on the premises of third parties. Electricians, plumbers and other tradesmen are mainly engaged in installation, repair or maintenance work on the premises of others. Visits to the insured's premises by customers is not a major feature of the risk.

working cover. The first layer of an excess of loss treaty under which the ceding office and reinsurer accept that losses will be frequent. The treaty thus protects the normal daily exposure of the ceding office. The excess points are relatively low and claims almost routinely come within the layer arranged in this way. The reinsurer is exposed to claims arising from any one event or any one risk. Compare with catastrophe cover (qv).

working layer. *See* WORKING COVERS.

working member. A Lloyd's underwriter principally occupied with the conduct of business at Lloyd's by working for a Lloyd's broker or underwriting agent.

working partners. *See* INJURY TO WORKING PARTNERS CLAUSE.

work in progress. A property item exposed to the risk of loss or damage by fire and various additional perils (qv). An item together with sum insured should be included in the policy schedule. Its value is based on the cost of raw materials plus the cost of labour and other resources used in creating it up to the time of loss.

works damage insurance. *See* GENERAL WORKS DAMAGE INSURANCE.

wrap-up cover. *See* PRINCIPAL'S COVER.

writ. A document issued in the Queen's name by which an action is commenced in the Superior Courts of Law as distinguished from a plaint or summons in a county or other inferior court.

write business. To provide the insurance cover.

write-off. A piece of property, eg a car, is said to be a 'write-off' when it is damaged beyond economical repair or is the subject of a constructive total loss (qv).

written lines. *See* SIGNED LINES/WRITTEN LINES. It is otherwise called a closed line.

written premium. Premium income in respect of business written during the financial year regardless of the portions earned.

written words prevail over printed word rule. A rule of construction (qv) to the effect that where there are both written and printed words in a policy, the policy is to be construed as a whole, but the written words are more specific than the printed word and will therefore prevail in the event of any inconsistency. The written or typewritten words are specially inserted to show the intention of the parties.

wrongful act. Loss arising from any wrongful act is the insured-event under a directors' and officers' liability insurance (qv). It is defined within the policy in these terms: 'any actual or alleged breach of duty, breach of trust, neglect, error, misstatement, omission, breach of warranty of authority, or other act done wrongfully attempted by any Director (qv) or Officer (qv).'

wrongful conversion. *See* CONVERSION (qv). The wrongful conversion section of the motor trader's policy covers the insured for (a) the loss which occurs when a vehicle, purchased from a person who is not the true owner, is reclaimed by the true owner or to whom compensation has to be paid; and (b) loss following the sale of a vehicle in circumstances where the trader is unable to pass a valid title to the purchaser who may claim damages against the trader. The insurance is conditional upon the trader carrying out a check on possible hire purchase agreements that may be in force before parting with his cheque. The trader generally carries the first 20 per cent of any loss.

wrongful trading. The Insolvency Act 1986, s. 214 provides a civil remedy for wrongful trading. Consequently a director may, by Court Order, be made personally liable for a company's debts if he allows a company to continue trading at any time when he knew or ought to have known that there was no reasonable prospect that the company would avoid going into liquidation unable to pay its debts and the expenses of winding up. He will not be liable if, once he knew or ought to have concluded that there was no reasonable prospect of avoiding insolvency, he took every step which he ought to have taken to minimise the loss to creditors. The standard to be applied as regards what he ought to have concluded or done is that of a reasonably diligent person having (i) the knowledge, skill and experience that may reasonably be expected of a person carrying out his functions; and (ii) the knowledge, skill and experience that he actually has. The directors' and officers' liability insurance (qv) covers liability arising from any wrongful act (qv) unless excluded.

yacht insurance. Insurance of a vessel that is generally used for pleasure purposes as distinguished from a commercial vessel. The policy covers accidental loss or damage to the yacht, salvage charges, sue and labour charges and liability to third parties including passengers.

year of account. The transactions relating to policies signed at Lloyd's Policy Signing Office in a calendar year in which members of the syndicate on the stamp for that year participate. A year of account is generally closed by reinsurance at the end of 36 months.

York–Antwerp Rules 1974. A voluntary code governing the adjustment of general average (qv) incorporated in most contracts of affreightment in view of the many divergences in national laws. They are binding as between the shipper and the shipowner but have no effect on the contract of marine insurance unless specially agreed. Also where cargo owners are members of the Maritime Law Association they bind themselves as members to the York–Antwerp Rules. They consist of two sets of rules, lettered rules (A, B, C etc) and numbered rules (I, II, III etc). The lettered rules define general average and the circumstances in which a loss, damage or expense is a general average loss. The numbered rules deal with most situations leading to a 'general average' situation. These include rules about jettison, sacrifice of part of the ship, extinguishing of fires on ship, voluntary stranding, salvage remuneration, expenses of lightening a ship, using ship's material as fuel, port of refuge expenses etc. When claims are settled it may be possible to set-off against the claims made by one party a counter-claim made by another based on negligence. It is the duty of average adjusters (qv) to ensure a fair apportionment of the general average loss.

young/inexperienced driver's excess. A standard excess (qv) which imposes an own damage excess (qv) in respect of certain drivers of cars, commercial vehicles and motor cycles. A young driver is generally someone under the age of 25 in the case of cars, motor cycles, and commercial vehicles. An inexperienced driver is someone over 25 with a provisional UK licence or who has had a full UK licence for less than 12 months. The excess is usually overridden in respect of fire and theft claims which are paid in full regardless of the age and experience of the driver or person in charge of the vehicle.

Z

zillmerisation. A process whereby an adjustment is made in the actuarial valuation of long-term business to take credit for the future recovery of the costs of acquiring new business.

zonal organisation. A system whereby an insurance company divides the country into say six or seven regions each under the control of a regional or zonal office. The regional office is vested with considerable power and decision-making authority and administers a number of branches within its region. Head office lays down broad policies and provides some central services.

APPENDICES

APPENDICES

APPENDIX 1
COMMON ABBREVIATIONS AND SHORT FORMS

ABI	Association of British Insurers	**CPA**	Claims paid abroad
ACII	Associate of the Chartered Insurance Institute	**CTL**	Constructive total loss
		CV or CMV	Commercial (motor) vehicle
ACT	Road Traffic Act or policy to cover Road Traffic Act liability only	**Dis**	Discount
		D/N	Debit note
		DOC	Driving other cars
AD	Accidental damage	**DOM/C**	Driving other motor cycles
AIOA	Aviation Insurance Offices' Association	**DTI**	Department of Trade and Industry
AIRMIC	Association of Insurance & Risk Managers in Industry and Commerce	**EAS**	European accident statement
		EC	European Community
AIT	Association of Insurance Teachers	**ECU**	European currency unit
		EFL	Estimated future liability
ALM	Association of Lloyd's Members	**EIL**	Environmental impairment liability
AOA	Any one accident	**EL**	Employers' liability
AOE	Any one event	**EML**	Estimated maximum loss
AOL	Any one loss	**EPI**	Estimated premium income or earned premium income
AP	Additional premium		
AR	All risks		
AS	All sections	**Exd**	Examined
ASLO	Associated Scottish Life Offices		
		FCII	Fellow of the Chartered Insurance Institute
BDI	Both days inclusive	**FDO**	For declaration only
BI	Business Interruption	**FEA**	Fire Extinguishing Appliances
BIEC	British Insurers European Committee		
BIIBA	British Insurance and Investments Brokers' Association	**FFA**	Fellow of the Faculty of Actuaries
		FIA	Fellow of the Institute of Actuaries
Bsst	Brick or stone built and tiled or slated	**FIMBRA**	Financial Intermediaries Managers & Brokers Association
CA	Court of Appeal		
Canc	Cancelled	**FPA**	Fire Protection Association
CAR	Contractors' all risks	**Fpf**	Fireproof
cc	Cubic capacity	**FTA**	Freight Transport Association and Agents
CEA	Comite Eurpeen Des Assurances		
CII	Chartered Insurance Institute	**Gd flr**	Ground floor
		Gds	Goods
C/N	Cover note; credit note	**GIC**	General Insurance Committee
Comp	Comprehensive		

HG	Household goods	**LUC**	London Underwriting Centre
HG & PE	Household goods and personal effects	**LUCRO**	Lloyd's Underwriters Claims Records Office
HL	House of Lords	**LUNCO**	Lloyd's Underwriters' Non-marine Claims Office
Htg	Heating	**LUNMA**	Lloyd's Underwriters' Non-marine Association
IBA	Insurance Broking Account		
IBNR	Incurred but not reported	**MAT**	Marine, aviation and transport
IBRA	Insurance Brokers (Registration) Act 1977	**M/C**	Motor cycle
IBRC	Insurance Brokers Registration Council	**M&D**	Minimum and deposit
IIB	Institute of Insurance Brokers	**Mgee**	Mortgagee
		Mgor	Mortgagor
IIC	Institute of Insurance Consultants	**MIRAS**	Mortgage interest relief at source
IITC	Insurance Institute Training Council	**MIRRC**	Motor Insurance Repair Research Centre (Thatcham)
IMRO	Investment Management Regulatory Organisation		
IOB	Insurance Ombudsman Bureau	**NAIC**	National Association of Insurance Commissioners
		NCB	No claims bonus
JCT	Joint Contracts Tribunal	**NCD**	No claim discount
		NM	Non-marine
LACC	Lloyd's Aviation Claims Centre	**NPI**	Net premium income
LAPR	Life assurance premium relief	**OCA**	Outstanding claims advance
		Occ	Occupation
LATF	Lloyd's American Trust Fund	**Occd**	Occupied
LAUA	Lloyd's Aviation Underwri-ters' Association	**OOD**	Owner only driving
LAUTRO	Life Assurance & Unit Trust Regulatory Organisation	**OPB**	Occupational Pensions Board
LCA	Lloyd's Central Accounting	**O/R**	Overriding commission
LCTF	Lloyd's Canadian Trust Fund	**PA**	Personal accident
LIA	Life Insurance Association	**PAN**	Premium advice note
LIBC	Lloyd's Insurance Brokers Committee	**P/C**	Private car
		PD	Property damage
LIC	Life Insurance Council	**PE**	Personal effects
LIRMA	London Insurance & Reinsurance Market Association	**P&I**	Protection and Indemnity
		PHI	Permanent health insurance
		PI	Premium income
LLAG	Linked Life Assurance Group	**PI**	Professional indemnity
LMUA	Lloyd's Motor Underwriters' Association	**PIAS**	Personal Insurance Arbitration Service
		PL	Public liability
LMX	London market excess	**PML**	Probable maximum loss
LPC	Loss Prevention Council	**P/N**	Promissory note
LPSO	Lloyd's Policy Signing Office	**PPI**	Policy proof of interest
LTA	Long term agreement	**Ppl**	Proposal
L/U	Leading underwriter	**Ppr**	Proposer
LUA	Lloyd's Underwriters' Association	**PR**	Pro rata
		PRF	Personal reserve fund
LUAA	Lloyd's Underwriting Agents Association	**Prov**	Provisional
		Pte	Private

PTF	Premiums trust fund	**Sty**	Storey
PW	Party wall	**SV**	Subject to valuation; stop valve
QBD	Queen's Bench Division		
Q/S	Quota share	**TAR**	Time all risks
		TBA	To be agreed (advised)
RDC	Running down clause	**Tbr**	Timber
Renl	Renewal	**Thd**	Thatched
RHA	Road Haulage Association Ltd	**TLO**	Total loss only
		TOR	Time on risk
R/I	Reinsurance	**TP**	Third party
RP	Return premium	**TPFT**	Third party fire and theft
RPB	Recognised Professional Body	**TPO**	Third party only
		TPPD	Third party property damage
RTA	Road Traffic Act		
		UKIBEC	United Kingdom Insurance Brokers' European Committee
Sched	Schedule		
SD & P	Social, domestic and pleasure	**UNL**	Ultimate net loss
		UTA	Unit Trust Association
SFO	Superannuation Funds Office		
SG	Ships and goods	**Vald**	Valued
SI	Statutory instrument		
SIB	Securities and Investments Board	**Wtd**	Warranted
		Wty	Warranty
Spklr	Sprinkler		
SRF	Special reserve fund	**X/L**	Excess of loss
SRO	Self Regulatory Organisation		
S to A	Subject to average	**YOA**	Year of account

APPENDIX 2
COMMON ABBREVIATIONS AND SHORT FORMS
– MARINE INSURANCE

A1	First-class
aa	After arrival
A and CP	Anchors and chains proved
ABS	American Bureau of Shipping (Classification Society)
ACV	Air Cushion Vehicle (hovercraft)
AGWI	Atlantic/Gulf/West Indies
AHF	American Hull Form
aoa	any one accident
aob	any one bottom
aol	any one loss
aoo	any one occurrence
aos	any one shipment
AP	Additional Premium
APL	As per list
Apps	Apparatus
Appvd or h/c	Approved or held covered at a premium to be agreed
AR	All risks
Arr	Arrive; arrival
Assd	Assured
Atl	Atlantic
Aux	Auxiliary; fitted with auxiliary engine
bdi	both days inclusive
bdx	bordereaux
B/E	Bill of Exchange
Bg	Bag; brig
B/H	Bordeaux/Hamburg
B/L	Bill of Lading
Bl	Bale; barrel
BOP	Blow out Preventer (used in drilling)
B/S	Bill of Sale
B/s	Bags; bales
BV	Basis of Valuation or Bureau Veritas (Classification Society)
Ca	Cases
CC	Cancellation clause; continuation clause
C & F	Cost and Freight
CFR	Cost and Freight (formerly C & F)
cgfrec	Credit given for recovery
CIF	Cost Insurance and Freight
CIM	International Convention on Carriage of Goods by Rail
CIP	Freight carriage and insurance paid to . . .
Ck	Cask
cl	Craft loss
CMR	International Convention on Carriage of Goods by Road
C/N	Cover Note or Credit Note
Cons	Conveyances
COW	Control of Well or Crude Oil Washing
C/P	Charter Party; custom of ports
CPA	Claims Payable Abroad
Cpd	Charterer pays dues
CRO	Cancelling Returns Only
C/s	Cases
CT	Combined Transport
CTL	Constructive Total Loss
CTO	Combined Transport Operator
D/C	Deviation Clause
DCOP	During currency of policy
DCP	Freight or carriage paid to . . .
Dd	Delivered
DD	Damage done
DDP	Delivered duty paid
Dis or Disbts	Disbursements
Dk	Dock
dpr	daily pro rata
DRC	Damage received in collision
D/V	Dual Valuation
D/W	Dock Warrant
DWT	Deadweight Tonnage

Ea	Each
e & ea	Each and every accident
e & el	each and every loss
e & oe	Errors and Omissions excepted
ERV	Each round voyage
EXQ	Ex Quay
EXS	Ex Ship
EXW	Ex Works
FAA	Free of all average
FAS	Free alongside
FCAR	free of claim already reported
FCL	Full container load
FC & S	Free of capture and seizure
FCV	Full contract value (building risks)
FDO	For declaration purposes only (a nominal premium paid when policy signed and adjusted subsequently)
FEU	Forty foot equivalent unit (size of container)
FFO	Fixed and floating objects
FGA	Foreign General Average
FIA	Full interest admitted
FOB	Free on board
FOD Abs	Free of Damage Absolutely
FOR/FOT	Free on rail/Free on truck
FOW	First open water (chartering); free on wharf
FPA Abs	Free of Particular Average Absolutely
FPIL	Full premium if lost
FRO	Fire Risk Only
FWD	Fresh water damage
GA	General Average
GAD	General Average Deposit
GCA	Gold Clause Agreement
GMT	Greenwich Mean Time
GNPI	Gross Net Premium Income
Grs	Grains; gross
GRT	Gross Register Tonnage
GS	Good safety
H/C	Held covered at premium to be agreed
H & M	Hull and Machinery
h & o	Hooks and oil damage
HW	High water
HWD	Heavy Weather Damage
ICC	Institute Cargo Clauses
if	in full
IGS	Inert Gas System

ILU	Institute of London Underwriters
IMO	International Maritime Organisation
In trans	In transitu (in transit)
i/o	in and/or over
iop	irrespective of percentage
iro	in respect of
ISO	International Standards Organisation
ITC	Institute Time Clauses
IV	Increased Value
IVC	Institute Voyage Clauses
IW	Institute Warranties
JHU	Joint Hull Understandings
j & lo	jettison and loss overboard
j & wo	jettison and washing overboard
Kt	Knot
L/C	Letter of Credit
LCL	Less than container load
Ldg and dly	Landing and delivery
L and DS	Live and dead stock
L/I	Letter of Indemnity
LNG	Liquid Natural Gas
LNYD	Liability not yet determined (used in collision cases)
LOH	Loss of Hire
LPG	Liquid petroleum gas
LPSO	Lloyd's Policy Signing Office
LR	Lloyd's Register
LSA	London Salvage Association
LSDBF	London Standard Drilling Barge Form
Ltg	Lighterage
Ltr	Lighter
L/U	Leading Underwriter or Laid Up
LUA	Lloyd's Underwriters' Association
LUCRO	Lloyd's Underwriters' Claims and Recoveries Office
Machy	Machinery
MD	Malicious damage
MIA	Marine Insurance Act
M/R	Mate's receipt
MSA	Merchant Shipping Act
MSC	Manchester Ship Canal
MV	Motor Vessel
NA	Net absolutely; North America
NAR	Net absolutely rate
N/C	New charter

NCAD	Notice of cancellation at anniversary date (used on "always open" contracts)	**RTBA**	Rate to be agreed
		Ry or rly	Railway
ND	Non delivery/No discount	**S**	Salvage
N/E	Not entered	**SA**	Salvage Association [might refer to London or United States Salvage Association (see LSA)]
NKK	Nippon Kaiji Kyokai (Classification Society)		
NPI	Net premium income		
NRAD	No risk after discharge	**S & FA**	Shipping and Forwarding Agent
NRAL	No risk after landing		
NRAS	No risk after shipment	**S and L**	Sue and labour
NRTOR	No risk till on rail	**SANR**	Subject to approval, no risk till confirmed
NRTWB	No risk till waterborne		
NUR	Not under repair	**SBT**	segregated ballast tanks
NV	Norske Veritas (Classification Society)	**S/C**	Salvage charges
		SD	Sea Damage; small damage
		SDR	Special Drawing Rights
o/b	On or before	**SG Policy**	Ship and Goods Policy Form
OBO	Ore/Bulk/Oil carrier	**Shpt**	Shipment
OC	Open Cover; off cover	**Sk**	Sack
O/c	Open charter	**S/L**	Sue and Labour or Short landed
O/D	On deck		
OGR	Original gross rate	**S/L Cl**	Sue and Labour Clause
ONR	Original net rate	**Sld**	Sailed
OR	Original Rate; owner's risk	**S/o**	shipowner
ORB	Owner's risk of breakage	**SOL**	Shipowner's liability
ORL	Owner's risk of leakage	**s & p**	seepage and pollution
O/S	Open Slip	**SR & CC**	Strikes, riots and civil commotions
pa	per annum	**SRL**	Ship Repairer's Liability
PA	Particular Average	**SS or str**	Steamer
PC	Profit Commission	**SSO**	Struck submerged object
P Chgs	Particular charges	**sv**	sailing vessel
PD	Property Damage; port dues	**SWD**	Sea water damage
PI	Personal Injury		
P & I	Protecting and Indemnity	**T/A**	Transatlantic
PIA	Peril Insured Against	**t and s**	touch and stay
Pkg	Package	**TCATLVO**	Total and/or Constructive and/or Arranged Total Loss of Vessel Only
po	part of		
poc	Port of call		
por	Port of refuge	**TCH**	Time Charter Hire
PP	Parcel Post	**TEU**	Twenty foot equivalent unit (size or container)
PPI	Policy proof of interest		
pr	pro rata	**Thro' B/L**	Through bill of lading
PT	Premium Transfer	**TL**	Total Loss
		TLO	Total Loss Only
RDC	Three-fourths Running Down Clause	**Tonn**	Tonnage
		TPL	Third Party Liability
regs	Registered tonnage	**TP & ND**	Theft pilferage and non-delivery
RHA	Road Haulage Association		
RI	Registro Italiana (Classification Society)	**t/s**	transshipment
R/I	Reinsurance	**u/c**	under construction
ROD	Rust, oxidisation and discolouration	**ucb**	unless caused by
		U/D	Under deck
Ro/Ro	Roll on/Roll off carrier	**UKC**	United Kingdom/Continent
ROW	Removal of Wreck	**ULCC**	Ultra large crude carrier
RP	Return of Premium		

UNCITRAL	United Nations Commission on International Trade and Law
UNCTAD	United Nations Conference on Trade and Development
UNL	Ultimate net loss
U/R	Under repair
vd	valued
VLCC	Very large crude carrier
vop	value on policy
WA	With average

wb	Water ballast
WBS	Without benefit of salvage
Whf	Wharf
WOB	Washing overboard
WP	Without prejudice
WRO	War Risk Only
Wtd	Warranted
WW	world-wide
Xs	Excess
YAR	York-Antwerp Rules

APPENDIX 3
ABBREVIATIONS AND SHORT FORMS – PENSIONS

ACA	Association of Consulting Actuaries	**CT**	Corporation Tax
ACT	Association of Corporation Tax	**CTT**	Capital Transfer Tax
AGM	Annual General Meeting	**DBPS**	Defined Benefit Pension Scheme
APC	Auditing Practices Committee	**DSS**	Department of Social Security
APL	Association of Pension Lawyers	**DTD**	Definitive Trust Deed
APPS	Appropriate Personal Pension Scheme	**ECON**	Employer's Contracting Out Number
APT	Association of Pensioner Trustees	**ED**	Exposure Draft
ARP	Accrued Rights Premium	**EF**	Earnings Factor
ASC	Accounting Standards Committee of the CCAB	**EGM**	Extraordinary General Meeting
AVC	Additional Voluntary Contribution	**EOC**	Equal Opportunities Commission
		EPB	Equivalent Pension Benefit
BE	Band Earnings	**FA**	Finance Act
		FIMBRA	Financial Intermediaries Managers and Brokers Regulatory Association
CA	Certified Amount		
CA	Companies Act	**FSAVC**	Free Standing Additional Voluntary Contribution
CCA	Current Cost Accounting		
CCAB	Consultative Committee of Accounting Bodies	**GAD**	Government Actuary's Department
CEP	Contributions Equivalent Premium	**GDP**	Gross Domestic Product
CGT	Capital Gains Tax	**GMP**	Guaranteed Minimum Pension
CIMPS	Contracted-in Money Purchase Scheme	**GN**	Guidance Notes
CIPS	Contracted-in Pension Scheme	**GPPP**	Group Personal Pension Plan
CIR	Commissioners of Inland Revenue	**HC**	Historical Cost
COE	Contracted Out Employment	**ICTA**	Income and Corporation Taxes Act
COMPS	Contracted Out Money Purchase Scheme	**IHT**	Inheritance Tax
COPRP	Contracted Out Protected Rights Premium	**IMRO**	Investment Management Regulatory Organisation
COSRS	Contracted Out Salary Related Scheme	**IPA**	Individual Pension Arrangement
CPIC	Company Pensions Information Centre	**ITD**	Interim Trust Deed

JOM	Joint Office Memorandum	**SDCS**	Simplified Defined Contribution Scheme
LAUTRO	Life Assurance and Unit Trust Regulatory Organisation	**SERPS**	State Earnings Related Pension Scheme
LEL	Lower Earnings Limit	**SFO**	Superannuation Funds Office of the Inland Revenue
LIC	Life Insurance Council of the ABI	**SFSS**	Simplified Final Salary Scheme
LRP	Limited Revaluation Premium	**SI**	Statutory Instrument
		SIB	Securities and Investments Board
MLI	Market Level Indicator	**SOI**	Statement of Intent
NAPF	National Association of Pension Funds	**SORP**	Statement of Recommended Practice
NPA	Normal Pension Age	**SPA**	State Pensionable Age
NPD	Normal Pension Date	**SPC**	Society of Pension Consultants
NRA	Normal Retirement Age		
NRD	Normal Retirement Date	**SR**	Statutory Regulations
		SR&O	Statutory Regulations & Orders
OPAS	Occupation Pensions Advisory Service	**SRO**	Self Regulating Organisation
OPB	Occupational Pensions Board	**SSA**	Social Security Act
		SSAP	Statement of Standard Accounting Practice
PAYE	Pay as You Earn	**SSAPS**	Small Self Administered Pension Scheme
PAYG	Pay as You Go		
PHI	Permanent Health Insurance	**SSAS**	Small Self Administered Scheme
PIL	Payment In Lieu		
PMI	The Pensions Management Institute	**SSB**	Short Service Benefit
PN	Practice Notes	**SSP**	State Scheme Premium; Statutory Sick Pay
PPPRP	Personal Pension Protected Rights Premium		
		SSPA	Social Security Pensions Act
PPS	Personal Pension Scheme	**TCN**	Third Country National
PRAG	Pensions Research Accountants Group	**TPI**	Tax and Prices Index
		TSA	The Securities Association
PRP	Pensioners Rights Premium		
PUP	Paid Up Pension	**UEL**	Upper Earnings Limit
RPB	Recognised Professional Body	**VAT**	Value Added Tax
RPI	Retail Prices Index	**WGMP**	Widow's/Widower's Guaranteed Minimum Pension
SCON	Scheme Contracted Out Number		

APPENDIX 4
GLOSSARY OF SPECIAL TERMS

A fortiori	much more; with stronger reason
Ab initio	from the beginning
Actio personalis moritur cum persona	a personal action dies with the person (an old Common Law rule that has now been largely superseded by Statute Law)
Actus Dei nemini facit injuriam	the Act of God prejudices no one
Ad hoc	for a special purpose
Ad idem	of the same mind; agreed
Ad litem	for the suit (a guardian *ad litem* is a person appointed to defend an action for a minor or other person under a disability)
Ad valorem	according to the value
Aliunde	from elsewhere (eg, indemnification *aliunde*)
Assecuratus non quaerit lucrum sed agit ne in damno sit	the Insured does not seek to make a profit, but takes steps to secure himself against loss
Ats. (ad sectam)	at the suit of
Bona fide	in good faith
Causa proxima non remota spectatur	the immediate, not the remote, cause is to be considered
Caveat emptor	let the buyer beware
Cestui que trust (pl. cestuis que trust)	the beneficiary under a trust
Ceteris paribus	other things being equal
Chose in action	a personal right of property, which can be enforced only by action, eg, a debt
Consensus ad idem	in perfect agreement
Cum testamento annexo	with the will annexed
Damnum	loss or damage
Damnum absque injuria	loss without wrong
Damnum sine injuria esse potest	there may be damage or loss inflicted without any act being done which law deems an injury
De die in diem	from day to day
De facto	as a matter of fact
De jure	as a matter of law
De minimis non curat lex	the law does not concern itself with trifles
De novo	anew
Delegatus non potest delegare	a delegate cannot delegate (an agent may not delegate his authority)
Duress	actual or threatened violence, or imprisonment
Ejusdem generis	of the same kind
Ex contractu	arising out of contract
Ex delicto	arising out of wrongs
Ex gratia	as of favour
Ex hypothesi	from the hypothesis
Ex nudo pacto non oritur actio	out of a bare promise no action can arise
Ex parte	on the one side; an action by one party in the absence of another
Ex turpi causa non oritur actio	an action does not arise from a base cause
Exempli gratia (eg)	for example

Factum est	it is done	**Passim**	in various places; here and there
Feme covert	a married woman	**Pendente lite**	while litigation is pending
Feme sole	an unmarried woman	**Per capita**	by heads; by the number of individuals
Force majeure	superior power		
Habeas corpus	(lit.) you have the body – a writ to a jailer to produce the body of one detained in prison and to state the reasons for such detention	**Per se**	by itself
		Per stripes	by the number of families
		Pro hac vice	for this occasion
		Pro tanto	for so much
		Qua	in the capacity of
		Quantum	amount
Ibidem (ibid.)	in the same place	**Quantum meruit**	as much as he has earned
Id est (i.e.)	that is		
Ignorantia juris quod quisque scire tenetur non excusat	ignorance of the law which everybody is supposed to know does not afford excuse	**Qui facit per alium facit per se**	he who acts through another is deemed to act in person
In camera	not in the open court	**Quid pro quo**	something in return for something (lit. 'what for what'); a mutual consideration
In esse	in actual being		
In extenso	at full length		
In re	in the matter of		
In statu quo	in the former position	**Ratio decidendi**	the reason or ground of a judicial decision
In transitu	on the way; in passing		
Infra	below	**Res ipsa loquitur**	the thing speaks for itself
Inter alia	among other matters		
Inter vivos	during life; between living persons	**Res judicata pro veritate accipitur**	a thing adjudicated is received as the truth
Intra vires	within the powers of		
		Respondeat superior	let the principal answer
Lex loci	the law of the place		
Lex mercatoria	mercantile law		
Lex non scripta	the unwritten, or Common Law	**Scienter**	knowingly (eg, that the owner of an animal knows of its dangerous propensities)
Lex scripta	the written law, ie, Statute Law		
Locus in quo	the place in which	**Sine die**	without fixing a day
		Sub judice	under consideration
Mala fide	in bad faith	**Sui generis**	of its own kind
Mutatis mutandis	the necessary changes being made	**Sui juris**	without disability
		Supra	above
Nemine contradicente (nem. con.)	without opposition	**Uberrima fides**	utmost good faith
		Uberrimae fidei	of the utmost good faith
Nemo dat quod non habet	no one can give what is not his	**Ultra vires**	beyond the legal power
Novus actus interveniens	a new act intervening	**Versus (v)**	against
		Videlicet (viz)	namely; that is to say
Obiter	by the way	**Vis major**	irresistible force (Act of God)
Obiter dictum	a saying by the way (as in a judgment without creating a precedent)	**Viva voce**	by word of mouth (oral testimony)
		Volenti non fit injuria	that to which a man consents cannot be considered an injury
Pari passu	with equal step, ie, ranking equally		

APPENDIX 5
USEFUL ADDRESSES

Associated Scottish Life Officers (ASLO)
23 St Andrew Square
Edinburgh EH2 1AQ

Tel: 031 556 7171

Association of British Insurers (ABI)
Aldermary House
10-15 Queen Street
London EC4N 1TT

Tel: 071 248 4477

Association of Burglary Insurance Surveyors (ABIS)
Aldermary House
10–15 Queen Street
London EC4N 1TT

Association of Consulting Actuaries, The (ACA)
Watson House
London Road
Reigate
Surrey RH2 9PQ

Tel: 081 668 8040

Association of Insurance and Risk Managers in Industry and Commerce (AIRMIC)
The Secretary General
6 Lloyds Avenue
London EC3N

Tel: 071 480 7610
Fax: 071 7022 3752

Association of Insurance Teachers (AIT)
Secretariat:
Department of Business Studies
Basingstoke College of Technology
Worthing Road
Basingstoke, RG21 TN

Tel: 0256 54141

Association of Pension Lawyers (APL)
Ian Pittaway, Hon Secretary
c/o Nicholson, Graham & Jones
19-21 Moorgate
London EC2R 6AU

Tel: 071 628 9151

Association of Underwriters & Insurance Brokers in Glasgow
Ingram House
227 Ingram Street
Glasgow G1 1DA

Tel: 041 221 9521

Assurance Medical Society (AMS)
Dr C R W Gill MCRP, Hon Secretary
Blossoms 1
23 Lawrence Lane
London EC2 V8D

or

C Trew
Trew Mercantile & General
Reinsurance Co PLC
Moorfields House
Moorfields
London EC2Y 9AL

Tel: 07372 41144

Aviation Insurance Offices' Association (AIOA)
London Aviation Insurance Group
110-112 Fenchurch Street
London EC3M 5JJ

Tel: 071 628 1266

British Fire Services Association (BFSA)
86 London Road
Leicester LE2 0QR

British Insurance and Investment Brokers' Association, The (BIIBA)
BIIBA House
14 Bevis Marks
London EC3A 7NT

Tel: 071 623 9043

British Insurance Law Association (BILA)
90 Bedford Court Mansions
Bedford Avenue
London WC1B 3AE

Tel: 071 375 0471

British Insurers' International Committee
Aldermary House
10–15 Queen Street
London EC4N 1TT

Tel: 071 248 4477

Building Societies Commission
15 Great Marlborough Street
London W1V 2AX

Tel: 071 437 9992

Chartered Institute of Loss Adjusters, The (CILA)
Manfield House
376 Strand
London WC2R LOR

Tel: 071 240 1496

Chartered Insurance Institute, The (CII)
20 Aldermanbury
London EC2V 7HY

Tel: 071 606 3835

CII College of Insurance
Churchill Court
90 Kippington Road
Sevenoaks
Kent TN13 2LL

Tel: 0732 450 888

CII Tuition Services
31 Hillcrest Road
South Woodford
London E18 2JP

Tel: 081 989 8464

Corporation of Insurance and Financial Advisers
6-7 Leapole Road
Guildford
Surrey GU1 4JX

Tel: 0483 39121

Criminal Injuries Compensation Board
Blythswood House
200 West Regent Street
Glasgow G2 4SW

Tel: 041 221 0945

Department of Trade and Industry (Insurance Division)
10-18 Victoria Street
London SW1H 0NN

Tel: 071 215 5000
Fax: 071 222 9280

Fire Protection Association (FPA)
140 Aldersgate Street
London EC1A 4HX

Tel: 071 606 3757

Home Services Insurers Group
Aldermary House
10–15 Queen Street
London EC4N 1TT

Tel: 071 248 4477

Incorporated Association of Architects & Surveyors (Fire Surveyors' Section) (IAAS)
Jubilee House
Billing Brook Road
Weston Favell
Northampton NN3 4NW

Tel: 0604 404121

Industrial Assurance Commissioner
15 Great Marlborough Street
London W1V 2AX

Tel: 071 437 9992
Fax: 071 437 1612

Institute of Actuaries
Napier House
4 Worcester Street
Oxford OX1 2AW

Tel: 0865 794144

Institute of Automotive Engineer Assessors (IAEA)
1 Love Lane
London EC2V 7JJ

Tel: 071 606 8744

Institute of Insurance Brokers (IIB)
Higham Business Centre
Midland Road
Higham Ferrers
Northants NN9 8DW

Tel: 0933 410003

Institute of Insurance Consultants (IIC)
PO Box 381
121a Queensway
Bletchley
Bucks MK1 1XZ

Tel: 0908 643364

Institute of London Underwriters (ILU)
49 Leadenhall Street
London EC3A 2BE

Tel: 071 488 2424

Institute of Risk Management, The
140 Aldersgate Street
London EC1A 4HY

Tel: 071 796 2119
Fax: 071 796 2120

Institution of Fire Engineers (IFE)
148 New Walk
Leicester LE1 7QB

Tel: 0533 553654

Insurance Brokers Registration Council (IBRC)
15 St Helen's Place
London EC3A 6DS

Tel: 071 588 4387

Insurance Industry Training Council
Churchill Court
90 Kippington Road
Sevenoaks
Kent TN13 2LL

Tel: 0732 450801

Insurance Ombudsman
31 Southampton Row
London WC1B 5HJ

Tel: 071 242 8613
Fax: 071 242 7516

International Association for the Study of Insurance Economics
Association Internationale pour L'Etude de l'Economie de l'Assurance
18 Chemin Rieu
1208 Geneva
Switzerland

Tel: (022) 47 09 38
Fax: (022) 47 02 78

International Credit Insurance Association
PO Box 16
7018 Films-Waldhaus
Switzerland

International Union of Aviation Insurers
6 Lovat Lane
London EC3R 8DT

Tel: 071 626 5314

International Union of Investment and Credit Insurers (Berne Union)
17-18 Dover Street
London W1X 3PB

Life Assurance Legal Society
D F Gallaher, Hon Secretary
Equity & Law Life Assurance Society plc
Equity & Law House
Amersham Road
High Wycombe
Bucks HP13 5AI

Tel: 0494 33377

Life Insurance Association, The (LIA)
Citadel House
Station Approach, Chorleywood
Rickmansworth
Herts WD3 5PF

Tel: 0923 285333

Linked Life Assurance Group (LLAG)
12-16 Watling Street
London EC4M 9BB

Tel: 071 236 0861

Liverpool & Glasgow Salvage Association
179 Sefton House
Exchange Buildings
Liverpool L2 3QR

Tel: 051 236 3821

Liverpool Underwriters Association
179 Sefton House
Exchange Buildings
Liverpool L2 3QR

Tel: 051 236 3821

London Insurance & Reinsurance
  Market Association
41/43 Mincing Lane
London EC4N 5BH
(For ex-Reinsurance Office Association
  Members)

Dexter House
Royal Mint Court
London EC3 NQN
(Policy Department)

Tel: 071 480 5999
Fax: 071 283 6726

Loss Prevention Certification Board, The
Melrose Avenue
Borehamwood
Herts WD6 2BJ

Tel: 081 207 2345

Loss Prevention Council, The
140 Aldersgate Street
London EC1A 4HY

Tel: 071 606 1050

Loss Prevention Council Technical
  Centre
Melrose Avenue
Borehamwood
Herts WD6 2BJ

Tel: 081 207 2345

Manchester Marine Insurance
  Association
Maritime Insurance Co Ltd.
Brook House
64/72 Spring Gardens
Manchester M2 2BQ

Manufacturing Science and Finance
  (MSF)
79 Camden Road
London NW1 9ES

Tel: 081 871 2100

Motor Insurers' Bureau
152 Silbury Boulevard
Central Milton Keynes
MK9 1NB

Tel: 0908 240000

Mutual Insurance Companies Association
NFU Mutual
Tiddington Road
Stratford-upon-Avon
Warwickshire
CV37 7BJ

Tel: 0789 204211

The National Association of Pension
  Funds Limited (NAPF)
12-18 Grosvenor Gardens
London SW1W 0DH

Tel: 071 730 0585/0734

National Federation of Independent
  Financial Advisers
Mike Owen, Chairman
GMM Life
Goodison House
57 Wolborough Street
Newton Abbot TQ12 1JQ

National Supervisory Council for
  Intruder Alarms (NSCIA)
Queensgate House
14 Cookham Road
Maidenhead
Berks SL6 8AJ

Tel: 0628 37512

Occupational Pensions Board
Thames Ditton
Surrey KT7 0DP

Tel: 081 398 4242

One-Fifty Association
CURM, Latham House
16 Minories
London EC3N 1DQ

Tel: 071 283 7500

Pensions Management Institution, The
PMI House
124 Middlesex Street
London E1 7HY

Tel: 071 247 1452
Fax: 071 375 0603

Personal Insurance Arbitration (PIAS)
Aldermary House
10–15 Queen Street
London EC4N ITT

Tel: 071 236 8761

Policyholders' Protection Board
Aldermary House
10–15 Queen Street
London EC 4N 1TT

Tel: 071 248 4477

**Registry of Friendly Societies, Central
   Office**
15 Great Marlborough Street
London W1V 2AX

Tel: 071 437 9992

Securities and Investments Board (SIB)
3 Royal Exchange Buildings
London EC3V 3NL

Tel: 071 283 2474

**Thatcham (The Motor Insurance Repair
   Research Centre)**
Colthrop Lane
Thatcham
Berks RG13 4NP

Tel: 0635 68855

Unit Trust Association (UTA)
Park House
16 Finsbury Circus
London EC2M 7JP

Tel: 071 628 0871

APPENDIX 6
SPECIMEN POLICIES

Specimen Liability Policy
Source: Royal Insurance

DEFINITIONS

1. The "Insured" means any person or any company registered in Great Britain Northern Ireland the Isle of Man or the Channel Islands and described in the Schedule

2. "Injury" means bodily injury and includes death and disease and "Damage" includes loss of

3. "Property" means material property

4. "Financial Loss" means a pecuniary loss cost or expense incurred by any person other than the Insured resulting from

   a escape or discharge of any substance or gas from any premises the property of or in the occupation of the Insured

   b stoppage of or interference with pedestrian vehicular rail air or waterborne traffic

   not caused by Products

5. "Business" for the purpose of this insurance is only as described in the Schedule but it shall include the provision of catering social sports and welfare facilities for Employees fire first-aid and ambulance services and private work undertaken with the consent of the Insured by an Employee for a director partner or Employee of the Insured

6. "Employee" means

   a any person under a contract of service or apprenticeship with the Insured or

   b any person supplied to or hired or borrowed by the Insured

   while engaged in the course of the Business

7. "Territorial Limits" means

   a Great Britain Northern Ireland the Isle of Man or the Channel Islands

   b elsewhere in the world in respect of

   i any act or ommission occurring within the territories specified in 7a above

   ii Injury to or the acts or omissions of persons normally resident in the territories specified in 7a above but temporarily engaged in the Business outside such territories

   iii Injury or Damage caused by Products

8. "Products" means goods (including containers and packaging) not in the custody or control of the Insured sold or supplied by the Insured in connection with the Business from any premises within the territories specified in 7a above and any error in connection with the sale supply or presentation of such goods is deemed to be included in this Definition

9. "Principal" means any party (other than a director partner or Employee of the Insured) on whose behalf the Insured in the course of the Business is undertaking work excluding the sale or supply of Products

10. "Pollution or Contamination" means

    a all pollution or contamination of buildings or other structures or of water or land or the atmosphere and

    b all Injury Damage or Financial Loss directly or indirectly caused by such pollution or contamination.

Section 1: COVER PROVIDED AND PERSONS INDEMNIFIED

A — Indemnity to Insured

1. In the event of

   a Injury to any person

   b Damage to Property other than

   i Property belonging to the Insured or in his custody or control or

   ii Property in the custody or control of any Employee

   happening during the Period of Insurance in the Territorial Limits and caused either in connection with the Business or by Products the Insurers will subject to the Limits of Liability indemnify the Insured against legal liability for damages and claimant's costs and expenses incurred in respect of such Injury or Damage

   In Paragraph 1b the expression "custody or control" shall not apply to

   i any building (including its fixtures fittings and contents) provided that in respect of any building which is leased hired or rented to the Insured the Insurers shall not be liable in respect of

   a Damage to its contents

   b the first $100 of each and every claim for Damage caused other than by fire or explosion

   c liability arising solely because of a contract

   ii visitors' directors' partners' and Employees' personal effects including motor vehicles and their contents

2 If the Insured comprises more than one party (which term in the case of a partnership includes each individual partner) the Insurers will indemnify each in the terms of this Policy against liability incurred to the other as if such other was not included as an Insured

3 The Insurers will in addition pay

   a solicitors' fees for representation at any Coroner's Inquest or fatal inquiry or Court of Summary Jurisdiction in respect of any event which may be the subject of indemnity under Paragraph A1

   b costs and expenses incurred with their written consent

Limits of Liability

claims for Injury to Employees	As specified in Schedule (EMPLOYERS' LIABILITY)
any other claim or number of claims arising out of one cause	As specified in Schedule LIMIT A

Provided that the Insurers' liability in any one Period of Insurance in respect of

i Injury Damage or Financial Loss arising directly or indirectly from Pollution or Contamination which is deemed to have occurred during any such Period shall not exceed	As specified in Schedule LIMIT B
ii Injury or Damage happening during any such Period and caused by Products shall not exceed	As specified in Schedule LIMIT C

B — Indemnity to Other Persons

The Insurers will indemnify in the terms of this Policy

a if the Insured so requests

i any director or Employee in respect of liability for which the Insured would have been entitled to indemnity if the claim had been made against him

ii any officer or member of the Insured's canteen social sports or welfare organisations and fire first-aid and ambulance services

b any Principal to the extent that the contract between the Insured and such Principal so requires in respect of liability arising from the performance of work on behalf of such Principal

c the legal personal representatives of any person entitled to indemnity under this Policy in respect of liability incurred by that person

If the Insurers are liable to indemnify more than one party the total amount of indemnity to all such parties including the Insured shall not exceed the Limits of Liability

C — Financial Loss

The Insurers will indemnify the Insured against legal liability incurred by the Insured during the Period of Insurance in respect of Financial Loss

Subject otherwise to the terms of this Policy

D — Liability for Motor Accidents

Notwithstanding Exception E and provided the Insured is not more specifically insured under any other policy the Insurers will indemnify the Insured in the terms of this Policy in respect of Injury Damage or Financial Loss

a caused by any motor vehicle owned by or in the possession of or being used by or on behalf of the Insured which is

i not licensed for road use and which is being used in circumstances which do not require insurance or security under any road traffic legislation

ii designed or adapted primarily for use as a tool but this indemnity shall not apply to liability in respect of which any road traffic legislation requires insurance or security

b arising during the act of loading or unloading a motor vehicle or the bringing to or taking away of a load from such vehicle

E — Insured's Motor Contingent Liability

Notwithstanding Exception E the Insurers will indemnify the Insured and no other person in the terms of this Policy in respect of Injury Damage or Financial Loss arising out of the use of any motor vehicle not the property of or provided by the Insured and being used in the course of the Business

The Insurers shall not be liable in respect of

a Damage to any such vehicle

b Injury Damage or Financial Loss arising while such vehicle is being driven by the Insured

Provided that the Insurers shall not be liable under this sub-Section if the Insured is entitled to indemnity under any other insurance

Section 2 — EXCEPTIONS

Exception A — Radioactive Contamination

The Insurers shall not be liable in respect of any legal liability of whatsoever nature directly or indirectly caused by or contributed to by or arising from

a ionising radiations or contamination by radioactivity from any nuclear fuel or from any nuclear waste from the combustion of nuclear fuel

b the radioactive toxic explosive or other hazardous properties of any explosive nuclear assembly or nuclear component thereof

but the liability of Injury to any Employee shall apply only when the Insured under a contract has either undertaken to indemnity or to assume the liability of another party in respect of such Injury

THE FOLLOWING EXCEPTIONS B TO I (inclusive) DO NOT APPLY TO LIABILITY IN RESPECT OF INJURY TO EMPLOYEES

Exception B — War

The Insurers shall not be liable in respect of

any consequence of war invasion act of foreign enemy hostilities (whether war be declared or not) civil war rebellion revolution insurrection or military or usurped power

Exception C — Contractual Liability

any liability for

a any amount in respect of liquidated damages fines or penalties

b Injury or Damage caused by Products

c Financial Loss

which attaches solely because of a contract

Exception D — Defective Work and Damage to Products

a the cost of rectifying defective work

b Damage to or the cost of recalling removing repairing or replacing Products arising from a defect in or an error in connection with the sale supply or presentation of such Products and all consequential losses flowing therefrom

Exception E — Vehicles and Craft

Injury Damage or Financial Loss arising out of the use of or caused by any craft designed to travel in on or through water air or space (other than hand propelled craft) or any motor vehicle which is owned by or in the possession of or being used by or on behalf of the Insured

Exception F — Deliberate Act or Omission

Injury Damage or Financial Loss which results from any deliberate act or omission of the Insured his partners directors or managerial Employees and which could reasonably have been expected having regard to the nature and circumstances of such act or omission

This Exception shall also apply in respect of any deliberate act or omission of any other person claiming indemnity but only so far as indemnity to such person is concerned

Exception G — Principal's Professional Risk

any liability for Injury Damage or Financial Loss which attaches solely because of a contract and arises out of or in connection with the exercise by any Principal or any person acting for him or on his behalf having professional qualifications of professional skill associated with such qualifications

F — Health & Safety at Work Act

Provided Endorsement 2 is not operative the Insurers will indemnify the Insured and at the request of the Insured any Employee or director of the Insured against legal costs and expenses incurred in the defence of any criminal proceedings brought for a breach of the Health and Safety at Work Act 1974 or the Health and Safety at Work Act (Northern Ireland) Order 1978 committed or alleged to have been committed during the Period of Insurance including costs of prosecution awarded against the Insured and legal costs and expenses incurred with the consent of the Insurers in an appeal against conviction arising from such proceedings

Provided that the Insurers shall not be liable for the payment of fines or penalties

G — Defective Premises Act

The Insurers will indemnify the Insured in the terms of this Policy against legal liability incurred by the Insured under Section 3 of the Defective Premises Act 1972 or Section 5 of the Defective Premises (Northern Ireland) Order 1975 in respect of Injury or Damage occurring within a period of seven years from the expiry or cancellation of this Policy

Provided that the Insurers shall not be liable under this sub-Section if the Insured is entitled to indemnity under any other insurance

H — Right of Recovery

The indemnity granted by this Policy is deemed to be in accordance with the provisions of any law enacted in Great Britain Northern Ireland the Isle of Man or the Channel Islands relating to the compulsory insurance of liability to employees

But the Insured shall repay to the Insurers all sums paid by the Insurers which the Insurers would not have been liable to pay but for the provisions of such law

I — Consumer Protection Act

Provided Endorsement 3 is not operative the Insurers will indemnify the Insured and at the request of the Insured any Employee or director of the Insured against legal costs and expenses incurred with the Insurers' written consent in the defence of any criminal proceedings brought for a breach of Part II of the Consumer Protection Act 1987 committed or alleged to have been committed during the Period of Insurance including costs of prosecution awarded against the Insured and legal costs and expenses incurred with the consent of the Insurers in an appeal against conviction arising from such proceedings

Provided that the Insurers shall not be liable for the payment of fines or penalties

Exception H – Aircraft Products

Injury or Damage caused by Products incorporated in a craft designed to travel through air or space which have been specifically supplied by the Insured for that purpose and are directly connected with the safety of such craft

Exception I – Pollution or Contamination

Injury Damage or Financial Loss arising directly or indirectly from Pollution or Contamination other than caused by a sudden identifiable unintended and unexpected incident which takes place in its entirety at a specific time and place during the Period of Insurance

For the purposes of this Exception all Pollution or Contamination which arises out of one incident shall be deemed to have occurred at the time such incident takes place

Section 3 - CONDITIONS

Condition 1 – Compliance with Policy Terms

The liability of the Insurers will be conditional on the Insured complying and as appropriate any other person entitled to indemnity complying as though he were the Insured with the terms of this Policy

Condition 2 – Reasonable Precautions

The Insured shall take and cause to be taken reasonable precautions to prevent Injury Damage or Financial Loss

Condition 3 – Claims Procedure and Requirements

a The Insured must report all accidents claims and civil proceedings to the Insurers in writing as soon as possible

b Every letter claim writ or other document relating to any accident claim or civil proceedings must be sent to the Insurers immediately and unacknowledged

c No admission of liability or promise of payment may be made without the Insurers' written consent

d The Insured will give all information and assistance as required

Condition 4 – Insurers' Rights

a The Insurers are entitled to take over and conduct the defence or settlement of any claim at their discretion

b The Insurers may at any time pay the Limit of Liability after deduction of any sum or sums already paid or any less amount for which any claim or claims can be settled and shall then relinquish the conduct and control thereof and be under no further liability in respect thereof except for the payment of costs and expenses incurred prior to the date of such payment

Condition 5 – Adjustment of Premium

The premium has been calculated on estimates supplied by the Insured and he shall keep an accurate record of information on matters for which estimates have been given which shall be available to the Insurers for inspection Within one month of expiry of each Period of Insurance the Insured shall supply the Insurers with a true statement of the particulars necessary for assessment of premium and should these particulars differ from the estimates upon which premium has been paid the difference in premium shall be met by a further proportionate payment or refund as the case may be Failure to supply such particulars shall entitle the Insurers to estimate if they so wish such particulars and to assess the further premium due calculated on such estimated particulars

Condition 6 – Non-Contribution

If the liability which is the subject of a claim under this Policy is or would but for the existence of this Policy be insured under any other insurance the Insurers shall not be liable under this Policy except to the extent of any excess beyond the amount payable under such other insurance had this Policy not been effected

Section 4 — ENDORSEMENTS

THESE ENDORSEMENTS ARE OPERATIVE ONLY IF THE NUMBER SET AGAINST THEM APPEARS IN THE SCHEDULE AND ARE EACH SUBJECT OTHERWISE TO THE TERMS EXCEPTIONS AND CONDITIONS OF THIS POLICY

Endorsement 1 - This Policy shall apply only in respect of Injury to an Employee
Employers'
Liability Only

Endorsement 2 - This Policy shall not apply in respect of Injury to an Employee
Public Liability
Only

Endorsement 3 - This Policy shall not apply in respect of
Excluding
Products
    a Injury to any person not being an Employee

    b Damage

    caused by Products other than

    i food and drink sold or supplied through any facility or service mentioned in Definition 5

    ii goods in the custody or control of the Insured

Endorsement 4 - This Policy shall not apply in respect of Injury or Damage arising from design
Products
Liability
Excluding Design
or Formula
    of or formula for Products

Condition 7 — This Policy may be cancelled
Cancellation

    a by the Insurers sending thirty days notice by recorded delivery letter to the last known address of the Insured who shall be entitled to a pro rata return of premium

    b by the Insured who shall be entitled to a return of premium after deduction of premium at the Insurers' short period rates for the period the Policy has been in force calculated if Endorsement 2 is not operative up to the date of the return of the Certificate of Employers' Liability Insurance

    c where the Policy is issued or renewed on the basis of monthly premiums by the Insurers sending seven days notice by letter to the last known address of the Insured in the event of non-payment of any monthly premium on its due date

Specimen Life Insurance Policy

Source: Eagle Star

FIRST SCHEDULE

LIFE 2

1. PROPOSAL

The Proposal(s) mentioned in the Second Schedule hereto shall be deemed to include any other written statement(s) made by the Grantee(s) and/or Life/Lives Assured to the Company disclosing facts regarded by the Company as relevant in assessing the risk.

2. GOVERNING LAW

This Policy shall be governed by and construed under the law of England unless otherwise stated herein.

3. GENDER

In this Policy words importing the masculine gender shall include the feminine and vice versa.

4. CURRENCY

All payments which fall due under this Policy shall be made in £ Sterling unless otherwise stated herein.

5. LIFE/LIVES ASSURED

If more than one life assured is mentioned in any schedule hereto then references to the death and survival of the Life Assured shall mean in the case of

(a) Joint Lives Assured the death of the first to die and survival of any or all of them.

(b) Last Survivor Lives Assured the death of the last to die and survival of any or all of them.

6. AGE

Inadvertent mis-statement of age will not invalidate this Policy but if it be found that age has been mis-stated an equitable adjustment will be made to the premium(s) and/or Sum(s) Assured under this Policy.

7. LOAN VALUE

Should this Policy contain a benefit under which a surrender value accrues the Company will subject to obtaining a First Charge on the Policy advance upon its security an amount not exceeding 90 per cent of the net surrender value (after deducting any amounts due to the Company) without any cost beyond the amount of stamp duty (if any) on the Loan Agreement and the legal charges (if any) at such rate of interest as may be mutually agreed.

8. PREMIUM PAYMENT

(a) Each premium shall be payable as stated in the Second Schedule hereto or until the earlier death of the Life Assured.

(b) Premiums must normally be paid by such Standing Order and to such account as the Company may from time to time designate. All premiums payable at monthly intervals must be paid in this way. Other premiums may be payable by

(i) Standing Order; or

(ii) any other method approved by the Company if the amount of each premium (being the total premium as shown herein) is not less than the amount below which the Company may from time to time stipulate that payment must be made by Standing Order.

(c) Thirty days of grace are allowed for payment of each renewal premium due at yearly, 6 monthly or 3 monthly intervals unless premiums are payable by Standing Order in which event a period of grace at the discretion of the Company will be allowed only if any premium remains unpaid by reason of accidental omission by the Company or the remitting bankers.

If the death of the Life Assured occurs during any period of grace any unpaid premium(s) will be deducted from the Sum(s) Assured payable under this Policy.

(d) A receipt for any premium or part thereof shall not be valid unless on the Company's printed form.

(continued)

FIRST SCHEDULE (continued)

9. OVERDUE PREMIUM

If any premium remains unpaid after the days of grace (if any) this Policy will lapse unless the Policy contains a benefit which has acquired a surrender value in which case the net surrender value (after deducting any amounts due to the Company) will be utilised to maintain the entire Policy in force. If the net surrender value is sufficient the total of the unpaid premium will be advanced therefrom to keep the Policy in force until the next premium due date; otherwise the surrender value will be applied to keep the Policy in force for such a period as the Company shall determine after which the Policy will lapse without value. Compound interest will be added to all advances at a rate that from time to time shall be decided upon by the Directors of the Company. All advances under this clause and the accumulated interest thereon shall constitute a First Charge on the Policy in favour of the Company taking precedence of claims of third parties and may be repaid at any time during the currency of this Policy either in one sum or by not more than four instalments.

10. PAYMENT OF BENEFIT

Unless otherwise stated herein any sum(s) payable by the Company will be payable at the Head Office of the Company to the Grantee(s) or the Successor(s) in Title of the Grantee(s) upon proof satisfactory to the Directors of the Company of

(a) the age of the Life Assured (or ages of the Lives Assured if more than one)

(b) the happening of the relevant event(s)

(c) the title thereto.

11. SUICIDE

Should the death of the Life Assured occur within thirteen calendar months of the commencement date of this Policy (or during the term of this Policy if less than thirteen calendar months) by his or her own hands (whether at the time sane or insane) or by the hands of justice this Policy shall be void (and all premiums paid shall be forfeited) except by way of indemnity to any third party in respect of any bona fide interest therein which shall have been previously notified in writing to the Company and shall be proved to the satisfaction of the Company to have been acquired for pecuniary consideration and to be subsisting and not recoverable in any other way at the time of death.

12. ALTERATIONS

This Policy may not be varied nor may any constituent part be discontinued without the consent of the Company provided always that any such consent shall be limited to such changes as are compatible with the requirements for a qualifying policy of Schedule 1 to the Income and Corporation Taxes Act 1970 or any amendment modification or re-enactment thereof.

13. NOTICE

The Company shall not be affected by notice of any fact in any way relating to this Policy unless and until express notice in writing of such fact shall have been received by the Company at its Head Office and no variation in the terms of this Policy shall bind the Company unless reduced into writing and signed by a duly authorised Official of the Company.

SCHEDULE WL1

WHOLE LIFE ASSURANCE SCHEDULE

1. The Sum Assured shall be payable on the death of the Life Assured.

2. After three full years' premiums have been paid:

   (A) this Benefit will have a cash surrender value which is guaranteed to be at least one third of the premiums paid (excluding the standing charge and any other premium(s) paid for other benefit(s) or for occupation, travel, foreign residence or other special risk).

   (B) if application be made while this Benefit is still in force it may be converted into a paid-up Benefit payable on the death of the Life Assured provided that the amount of such paid-up Benefit is at least one hundred pounds. Should the premium cease to be payable after a specified term or on the earlier death of the Life Assured then the amount of the paid-up Benefit (subject to payment of any amounts due to the Company) shall be in addition to all then existing reversionary bonuses (if any) attaching to this Benefit an amount bearing the same or a greater proportion to the sum assured as the total amount of premiums paid bears to the total amount of premiums payable throughout the term of the Benefit (excluding in each case the standing charge and other premium(s) as aforesaid). The eligibility (if any) of the paid-up Benefit for continued participation in profits, and the basis of such participation, shall be determined by the appointed Actuary of the Company.

Specimen Fire Policy
Source: Eagle Star

EAGLE STAR
GENERAL INSURANCE DIVISION

FIRE POLICY

In Consideration of the Insured named in the Schedule hereto paying to Eagle Star Insurance Company Limited (hereinafter called "the Insurers") the first premium

The Insurers agree (subject to the conditions contained herein or endorsed or otherwise expressed hereon which conditions shall, so far as the nature of them respectively permit, be deemed to be conditions precedent to the right of the Insured to recover hereunder) that if after payment of the premium the property described in the said Schedule, or any part of such property, be destroyed or damaged by

- (1) **FIRE** (*whether resulting from explosion or otherwise*) *not occasioned by or happening through*
  - (a) *Its own spontaneous fermentation or heating or its undergoing any process involving the application of heat;*
  - (b) *Earthquake, Subterranean Fire, Riot, Civil Commotion, War, Invasion, Act of Foreign Enemy, Hostilities (whether War be declared or not), Civil War, Rebellion, Revolution, Insurrection or Military or Usurped Power;*
- (2) **LIGHTNING;**
- (3) **EXPLOSION,** *not occasioned by or happening through any of the perils specified in 1 (b) above,*
  - (i) *Of boilers used for domestic purposes only;*
  - (ii) *In a building not being part of any Gas Works, of Gas used for domestic purposes or used for lighting or heating the building;*

at any time before Four o'clock in the afternoon of the last day of the period of insurance named in the said Schedule or of any subsequent period in respect of which the Insured shall have paid and the Insurers shall have accepted the premium required for the renewal of this Policy, the Insurers will pay to the Insured the value of the property at the time of the happening of its destruction or the amount of such damage or at their option reinstate or replace such property or any part thereof.

Provided that the liability of the Insurers shall in no case exceed in respect of each item the sum expressed in the said Schedule to be insured thereon or in the whole the total sum insured hereby, or such other sum or sums as may be substituted therefor by a memorandum hereon or attached hereto signed by or on behalf of the Insurers.

For and on behalf of the Company

L. A. Agius
Executive Director

Home Standard Fire

For your own protection you are recommended to read your Policy and all its Conditions to ensure that it is in accordance with your intentions.

EAGLE STAR INSURANCE COMPANY LIMITED
REGISTERED IN LONDON NO 82051   REGISTERED OFFICE 60 ST MARY AXE LONDON EC3A 8JQ

SCHEDULE

POLICY No........................

THE INSURED	
AGENCY	BRANCH

PERIOD OF INSURANCE, from the

To Four o'clock in the afternoon of the

FIRST PREMIUM	RENEWAL PREMIUM
	DUE

THE PROPERTY INSURED	Sum Insured thereon.

TOTAL SUM INSURED £

POLICY SIGNED ON THE	EXAMINED	ENTERED

COMPLAINTS PROCEDURE

Any enquiry or complaint you may have regarding your policy, or a claim notified under your policy, may be addressed to the Agent or Broker acting for you or to the branch of Eagle Star which issued the policy. Please have details of the policy, including your policy number, available to enable the enquiry to be dealt with speedily.

If you are not satisfied with the handling of a complaint you should write to the Manager of the branch which issued your policy. If you are then still not satisfied with the action taken by the Company, write to the Chief Executive of Eagle Star at 60, St Mary Axe, London EC3A 8JQ.

Should you remain dissatisfied, short of court action, you may approach the Consumer Information Department of the Association of British Insurers for assistance. The address and telephone number of the London HQ of the Association are as follows:

> **Association of British Insurers**
> **Aldermary House**
> **Queen Street**
> **London**
> **EC4N 1TT**
>
> **Telephone 01-248 4477**

The Association can also be contacted at one of its Regional Offices for which addresses and telephone numbers can be found in local telephone directories.

THE CONDITIONS REFERRED TO IN THIS POLICY

1. This Policy shall be voidable in the event of misrepresentation, misdescription or non-disclosure in any material particular.

2. This Policy shall be avoided with respect to any item thereof in regard to which there be any alteration after the commencement of this insurance

(a) by removal

or (b) whereby the risk of destruction or damage is increased

or (c) whereby the Insured's interest ceases except by will or operation of law,

unless such alteration be admitted by memorandum signed by or on behalf of the Insurers.

3. This Policy does not cover

(a) Destruction or damage by explosion (whether the explosion be occasioned by fire or otherwise), except as stated on the face of this Policy,

(b) Loss or destruction of or damage to any property whatsoever or any loss or expense whatsoever resulting or arising therefrom or any consequential loss directly or indirectly caused by or contributed to by or arising from

(i) ionising radiations or contamination by radioactivity from any nuclear fuel or from any nuclear waste from the combustion of nuclear fuel,

(ii) the radioactive, toxic, explosive or other hazardous properties of any explosive nuclear assembly or nuclear component thereof,

(c) Goods held in trust or on commission, money, securities, stamps, documents, manuscripts, business books, computer systems records, patterns, models, moulds, plans, designs, explosives, unless specially mentioned as insured by this Policy,

(d) Destruction of or damage to property which, at the time of the happening of such destruction or damage, is insured by, or would, but for the existence of this Policy, be insured by any Marine Policy or Policies, except in respect of any excess beyond the amount which would have been payable under the Marine Policy or Policies had this insurance not been effected.

(e) Loss or destruction of or damage to any property in NORTHERN IRELAND or loss resulting therefrom caused by or happening through or in consequence of—

(i) civil commotion

(ii) any unlawful, wanton or malicious act committed maliciously by a person or persons acting on behalf of or in connection with any unlawful association.

For the purpose of this condition:—

"Unlawful Association" means any organisation which is engaged in terrorism and includes any organisation which at any relevant time is a proscribed organisation within the meaning of the Northern Ireland (Emergency Provisions) Act, 1973.

"Terrorism" means the use of violence for political ends and includes any use of violence for the purpose of putting the public or any section of the public in fear.

In any action, suit or other proceedings where the Insurers allege that by reason of the provisions of this condition any loss, destruction or damage is not covered by this policy the burden of proving that such loss, destruction or damage is covered shall be upon the Insured.

(f) Loss or destruction or damage caused by pollution or contamination except (unless otherwise excluded) destruction of or damage to the property insured caused by

(i) pollution or contamination which itself results from a peril hereby insured against,

(ii) any peril hereby insured against which itself results from pollution or contamination.

4. On the happening of any destruction or damage the Insured shall forthwith give notice thereof in writing to the Insurers and shall within 30 days after such destruction or damage, or such further time as the Insurers may in writing allow, at their own expense deliver to the Insurers a claim in writing containing as particular an account as may be reasonably practicable of the several articles or portions of property destroyed or damaged and of the amount of destruction or damage thereto respectively having regard to their value at the time of the destruction or damage together with details of any other insurances on any property hereby insured. The Insured shall also give to the Insurers all such proofs and information with respect to the claim as may reasonably be required together with (if demanded) a statutory declaration of the truth of the claim and of any matters connected therewith. No claim under this Policy shall be payable unless the terms of this condition have been complied with.

5. If the claim be in any respect fraudulent or if any fraudulent means or devices be used by the Insured or anyone acting on their behalf to obtain any benefit under this Policy or if any destruction or damage be occasioned by the wilful act or with the connivance of the Insured all benefit under this Policy shall be forfeited.

6. If the Insurers elect or become bound to reinstate or replace any property the Insured shall at their own expense produce and give to the Insurers all such plans, documents, books and information as the Insurers may reasonably require. The Insurers shall not be bound to reinstate exactly or completely, but only as circumstances permit and in reasonably sufficient manner and shall not in any case be bound to expend in respect of any one of the items insured more than the sum insured thereon.

7. On the happening of any destruction or damage in respect of which a claim is or may be made under this Policy the Insurers and every person authorised by the Insurers may, without thereby incurring any liability, and without diminishing the right of the Insurers to rely upon any conditions of this Policy, enter, take or keep possession of the building or premises where the destruction or damage has happened, and may take possession of or require to be delivered to them any of the property hereby insured and may keep possession of and deal with such property for all reasonable purposes and in any reasonable manner. This condition shall be evidence of the leave and licence of the Insured to the Insurers so to do. If the Insured or anyone acting on their behalf shall not comply with the requirements of the Insurers or shall hinder or obstruct the Insurers in doing any of the above-mentioned acts, then all benefit under this Policy shall be forfeited. The Insured shall not in any case be entitled to abandon any property to the Insurers whether taken possession of by the Insurers or not.

8. (a) If at the time of any destruction of or damage to any property hereby insured there be any other insurance effected by or on behalf of the Insured covering any of the property destroyed or damaged, the liability of the Insurers hereunder shall be limited to their ratable proportion of such destruction or damage.

(b) If any such other insurance shall be subject to any Condition of Average this Policy, if not already subject to any Condition of Average, shall be subject to Average in like manner.

(c) If any other insurance effected by or on behalf of the Insured is expressed to cover any of the property hereby insured, but is subject to any provision whereby it is excluded from ranking concurrently with this Policy either in whole or in part or from contributing ratably to the destruction or damage, the liability of the Insurers hereunder shall be limited to such proportion of the destruction or damage as the sum hereby insured bears to the value of the property.

9. Any claimant under this Policy shall at the request and at the expense of the Insurers do and concur in doing and permit to be done all such acts and things as may be necessary or reasonably required by the Insurers for the purpose of enforcing any rights and remedies or of obtaining relief or indemnity from other parties to which the Insurers shall be or would become entitled or subrogated upon their paying for or making good any destruction or damage under this Policy, whether such acts and things shall be or become necessary or required before or after their indemnification by the Insurers.

10. Every Warranty to which the property insured or any item thereof is, or may be, made subject, shall from the time the Warranty attaches apply and continue to be in force during the whole currency of this Policy, and non-compliance with any such Warranty, whether it increases the risk or not shall be a bar to any claim in respect of such property or item; provided that whenever this Policy is renewed a claim in respect of destruction or damage occurring during the renewal period shall not be barred by reason of a Warranty not having been complied with at any time before the commencement of such period.

11. If any difference shall arise as to the amount to be paid under this Policy (liability being otherwise admitted) such difference shall be referred to an Arbitrator to be appointed by the parties in accordance with the Statutory provisions in that behalf for the time being in force. Where any difference is by this Condition to be referred to arbitration the making of an award shall be a condition precedent to any right of action against the Insurers.

12. If at the time of destruction of or damage to any building hereby insured the Insured shall have contracted to sell their interest in such building and the purchase shall not have been but shall be thereafter completed, the purchaser on completion of the purchase, if and so far as the property is not otherwise insured by or on behalf of the purchaser against such destruction or damage, shall be entitled to the benefit of this Policy so far as it relates to such destruction or damage, without prejudice to the rights and liabilities of the Insured or the Insurers under this Policy up to the date of completion.

13. Reference to the payment of premium includes payment by monthly instalments. If the Insured pays by this method the policy remains an annual contract and the date of payment and the amount of instalments are governed by the terms of the credit agreement. If an instalment is not received by the due date then subject to the Consumer Credit Act 1974 (if applicable) the credit agreement and the policy will be cancelled immediately.